RAYBURN

A Biography

RAYBURN
—A Biography—

By D. B. Hardeman & Donald C. Bacon

TexasMonthlyPress

MR

Texas Monthly Press, Inc.
P.O. Box 1569
Austin, Texas 78767

A   B   C   D   E   F   G   H

Library of Congress Cataloging-in-Publication Data

Hardeman, D. B., 1914–
  Rayburn.

  Includes index.
  1. Rayburn, Sam, 1882–1961. 2. Legislators—United States—
Biography. 3. United States. Congress. House—Biography. 4. Texas—
Politics and government—1865–1950. I. Bacon, Donald C. II. Title.
E748.R24H37 1987   328.73'092'4 [B]   86-30061
ISBN 0-932012-03-5

Text design by David Timmons

*For Barbara
with love*

Contents

———

Acknowledgments   *ix*

Introduction   *1*

1. Growing Up   *11*

2. Ambition Kindled   *23*

3. State Legislator   *35*

4. Young Congressman   *59*

5. Wilson Days   *91*

6. Republican Years   *105*

7. Metze   *121*

8. Kingmaker   *133*

9. "The Fight for Economic Justice"   *145*

10. "The Greatest Congressional Battle in History"   *167*

11. Up the Ladder   *201*

12. Majority Leader   *215*

13. Ambition Fulfilled—and War   *243*

14. Wartime Speaker   *279*

15. Gains and Losses   *303*

16. Minority Leader   *323*

17. Mr. Sam   *343*
18. Rayburn for President   *357*
19. The Peak of Power   *375*
20. Rayburn and Johnson   *389*
21. The Golden Years   *409*
22. Johnson for President   *427*
23. "The Worst Fight of My Life"   *447*
24. Willow Wild   *467*
Sources and Notes   *475*
Index   *523*
Photography Credits   *555*

Acknowledgments

————

A book that takes so long to write is bound to involve a lot of people. How can I thank them all, including some I never met? If D. B. Hardeman were here, he would do it right. He would smile and lift a glass to all who helped him get the project off the ground in the late 1950s and who over the years kept faith in it—and in him. He would thank former colleagues on Rayburn's staff and on House Democratic Whip Hale Boggs's staff, where Hardeman worked after Rayburn's death. Poring over Hardeman's voluminous notes and manuscript fragments, I am struck by the hundreds of pages typed with professional care by people whose identities are unknown to me. Most were congressional secretaries working, I assume on their own time, solely for the satisfaction of helping a friend. As only another author with no financial backing can fully appreciate, Hardeman was deeply indebted to them, as I am.

I can single out only a handful of the dozens of people who gave generously of their time, skills, and insights in support of this biography: John Holton, Bernice Frazier, Martha Freeman, Alla Delphia Clary, Jane Bartley and Lorraine "Rene" Kimbrough from Rayburn's staff; Hale and Lindy Boggs; Margaret Tucker Culhane and Argyll Campbell from Boggs's staff; Speakers John McCormack and Carl Albert; House Parliamentarian

William Holmes Brown and Assistant Parliamentarian Charles Johnson; Professor Robert Peabody of Johns Hopkins University; Neil MacNeil of *Time*; Robert Odle and Eileen Timlin.

I am particularly beholden to H. G. Dulaney, director of the Sam Rayburn Library, not only for his care and feeding of me during periods of fruitful research in Bonham but also for his patience in waiting for the completion of this book. Eventually, some thirty linear feet of interview transcripts, notes, clippings, and other research items used in the preparation of this biography will be turned over to the Rayburn Library to enhance its already impressive collection on the history of Congress and the Speaker. Hopefully, this material will help bring the library a little closer to fulfilling Rayburn's dream of becoming a nationally recognized center for scholars studying Congress and the congressional process. Today, far off the beaten path, it remains one of the best-kept secrets of academia. Dulaney and his assistant, Jerri Williams, maintain the library almost precisely as Rayburn left it, even to the point of having only one telephone line. (Rayburn thought two phones were an extravagance.) A visitor cannot help but sense the pervading presence of the Speaker throughout that marvelous marble mausoleum.

The Rayburn Library's value to scholars has been bolstered in recent years by the oral-history interviews of political scientist Anthony Champagne of the University of Texas at Dallas. A good detective as well as a scholar, Professor Champagne tracked down a number of Rayburn contemporaries, mostly Texans, still living in the early 1980s. I am grateful to him for helping me, a north Floridian, get a better understanding of Rayburn's north Texas and round out a picture of the Speaker's life and problems at home in his later years.

A special bow is also due to Director Harry Middleton, Oral History Projects Director Michael Gillette, and the able research staff of the Lyndon B. Johnson Library in Austin. Their warm hospitality during our stays in Austin and their encouragement of this project over many years meant much to Hardeman and me.

Finally, I owe an unrepayable debt to my wife, Barbara Bacon, the person most responsible for keeping this book alive through long periods when neither Hardeman nor I wanted anything more to do with it. To justify her faith in us was, in the end, the main reason I returned to the long-neglected job of finishing the manuscript after Hardeman's death in 1981.

D. C. B.

Introduction

On a crisp December day in 1956, House Speaker Sam Rayburn was reminiscing. He was at the wheel of his old Chevrolet, squinting at the road, gesturing with both hands, explaining to a visitor what it was like to grow up at the turn of the century on a tiny north Texas cotton farm. "We were always so poor at home and everybody worked like the devil," he said. "That's what made me determined to try to help the average man get a break."

The Speaker, then 75, had invited a friend to the big, white-columned family home on Highway 82, about a mile west of Bonham, for a midday meal—"dinner," he called it—and an afternoon of talk about the Rayburn family. The two living Rayburn sisters, Medibel Rayburn Bartley and Katherine Rayburn Thomas, fixed a typical north Texas lunch—fried pork shoulder, pork sausage, buttered hominy, asparagus, grapefruit salad, applesauce, hot biscuits, apple pie, and coffee. Later, Rayburn suggested a drive out to nearby Flag Springs to see the site of the original Rayburn home in Texas and the old schoolhouse where the eleven Rayburn children received their early education. "A man ought to live in the very best house he can afford," he said as they drove. "If a man doesn't get his chief pleasure in life after he goes home and closes the door behind him, he doesn't get much pleasure."

At Dodd City, the old man pointed out the spot where the house of his uncle, Monroe Waller, once stood—"where I spent my first night in Texas"—and the nearby pond "where the baptizing was done." At Windom, he identified the houses that were standing when he, a boy of 5, and his family first arrived from east Tennessee in 1887. He turned down a narrow road and stopped by a furrowed field, now grass-covered, with a few grazing cows. He stepped out of the car, ducked under a single electrified wire, and stood in the field. "This is all that's left of the old home place, not a rock or board or anything left," he said. "It nearly kills me." Spotting an old well, covered with a big stone, he got his bearings. "Here's where the chimney stood. The well was right near the back porch, and near the well was the old hackberry tree." The tree had special meaning for all the Rayburn children. "We could play anywhere within sight of that tree," he recalled. "But when the tree got out of sight, we hightailed it home." The house had seven rooms, two upstairs filled with Rayburn boys. Shortly after the family moved to Bonham, it burned down. Except for the well and the hackberry tree, there remained no trace of this part of Rayburn's childhood.

Later, in the car, Rayburn continued to reminisce. "I resent that people say I came from a poverty-stricken family," he said. "That's not so. My father and mother raised eleven children. We were short of money, but we had a comfortable home, plenty to eat. My father couldn't put us all through college, but most of us went anyway."

He drove on to Flag Springs to look at the old schoolhouse that his father had helped to build. Little had changed. Even the potbellied stove he stoked as a boy and some of the tiny desks once occupied by Rayburn children remained in service. He rubbed his fingers across the initials "W. C. R." carved on a desk top. Could that have been a Rayburn? he was asked. The old man snorted his displeasure at the question. "You won't find any Rayburn initials on any desks," he snapped. "No Rayburn ever cut a desk. If any of us did that, our little mother would have worn out our asses with a rod. Mother often spanked us—

too much, I thought at the time. My father sometimes tried it, but if you started crying, he'd let you go."

Sam Rayburn's extraordinary life was rooted firmly in the rich black dirt of north Texas. In a sense, although he served in the United States House of Representatives for forty-nine years, he never left home. His uncluttered rural values, founded on honesty and common sense, his compassion, and his dedication to service never wavered, even when he reached the second-highest seat of power in American politics. Speaker of the House for almost twenty years—twice as long as any predecessor—he died on November 16, 1961, seven weeks short of his eightieth birthday. In his last decade, he was "Mr. Speaker," "Mr. Democrat," and, to those who knew him and millions of others who felt that they knew him, simply "Mr. Sam."

He had a large, round head, as hairless as a billiard ball, with hot brown eyes that flashed when he was angry. Five foot six inches tall, he grumpily reminded friends that Napoleon was only five foot four. His carefully cultivated scowl worn like a protective shield broke easily into a broad smile at the slightest provocation. In Washington, he was often depressed by loneliness that closed in each day after he left Capitol Hill for his "shabbily genteel" bachelor's apartment at 1900 Q Street Northwest. Strongly attractive to women, the young Rayburn never lacked female companionship; in old age, his companions were mostly male. One of his most deeply admired and trusted friends was his chauffeur, a gentle, discreet Irishman named George Donovan.

More than a benign figure of congressional authority, Rayburn was a master in the use of power. "I like power, and I like to use it," he said frankly. Patience, reason, and compromise were his major tools. He led by rewarding loyalty, and occasionally punishing disloyalty. He was stern, never mean. Beneath his fabled gruffness was a deeply sentimental man. Two of his mentors, Senator Joseph Weldon Bailey of Texas and Vice-President John Nance Garner, questioned his ability to rise to the top in politics because he lacked a zest for destroying his enemies. "Now, I don't hate anybody," Rayburn used to say with a grin.

"But there are a few shitasses that I loathe."

There were two Sam Rayburns: the stern, no-nonsense master of the House of Representatives and the unadorned, warm, often lonely human being who liked nothing better than to sit with friends, sip good whiskey, and swap great yarns. Although he avoided injecting levity into his speeches—"I tried telling a joke once, and before I finished, I was the joke"—he was a humorous, chuckling man. He liked funny stories. Above all, he knew how and when to relax. Bonham was his favorite spot on earth. A man of strong ties to his family, especially his mother, he returned home as often as he could. Foreign shores held no attraction for him. "I'd rather see north Texas than any European capital," he would say. He left the United States only twice: on a pre–World War I junket to the Panama Canal, during which he endured sharp pangs of homesickness, and on a short excursion into Mexico.

He loved the House of Representatives and understood its workings perhaps better than any member before or since. He marveled at Congress's intricate machinery, much as a watchmaker admires a fine timepiece. On the House floor, in committee meetings, and in the back rooms of the Capitol, he fought dozens of historic battles—winning most, losing some, but never hesitating to spill political blood to achieve a goal he believed in.

Rayburn never thought of himself as anything special, and in a sense he was right. "I am just an average man; no better, I know, no worse, I hope, than other average Americans," he often said. He was masterful at passing laws, analyzing politics, and manipulating power—no American before or since has done it better—but beyond those spheres of specialization, he was severely limited. He ran a horse-and-buggy shop in the jet age, and even his friends questioned his leadership style. Unconcerned with schedules and efficient management of his time, he was probably the most accessible public official in Washington. Anyone with a problem who was willing to wait his or her turn could see Sam Rayburn. "He's a piss-poor administrator," said Lyndon Johnson, Rayburn's devoted pupil. "He doesn't anticipate problems, and he runs the House out of his back-ass pocket." Others were even harsher in assessing his methods—or seeming lack of them—but they seldom could fault the results.

He led the House the way he led his own life: simply, tire-lessly, unhurriedly. His role was seldom easy. There was constant criticism from within his own party, the White House, and the press—criticism that intensified as he grew older and as a better-educated, more skeptical breed of lawmakers began to arrive in the 1950s. He sought unity between diverse elements within his party and within the country as a whole, and he pursued that goal almost as a religion. Liberals, restless for action, often blamed him for failing to expedite their initiatives, for yielding too willingly to the policies of a Republican President, particularly in foreign affairs, and for refusing to impose strict discipline on House Democrats. But the awe, love, and respect accorded him by the majority muted the critics. And, despite his limitations, his prestige grew with the years.

He worked best behind the scenes and never sought the lime-light. "Damn the fellow who's always seeking publicity," he used to say. As a result, today he is arguably the most underrated public official in twentieth-century American politics. "He is the one man who has never really had his place defined enough," noted former Texas Congressman Frank Ikard in 1980. "There are many things that he should have a good deal of credit for, though they are not attributed to him. He was a rare man." Even in Rayburn's day, few outside the Democratic leadership could tell you that he had been a major architect of New Deal legislation in the 1930s; that Presidents from Woodrow Wilson to John Kennedy had sought his counsel; that he had managed two strong contenders for his party's presidential nomination (John Garner and Lyndon Johnson)—both of them wound up as Vice-Presidents and one as President; that he had been the "the vital cement" that held together the bipartisan foreign policy crucial to America's global supremacy in the tumultuous years after World War II; or that he had reshaped the House Speakership, adding power and prestige to Congress's highest office and strengthening the House's ability to handle problems of an increasingly complex society.

He postponed hard decisions as long as possible; most problems, he believed, disappeared in time. Open conflict was his last resort. He had learned that once an angry battle is joined, scars and bitterness inevitably remain whether you win or lose. He believed every public official had a responsibility "to be fair, to be just, to be reasonable." For years, he put off a showdown with conservatives over control of the House Committee on Rules. Only after a coalition of Republicans and southern Democrats on the committee threatened openly and defiantly to thwart the programs of a new Democratic President, John F. Kennedy, did Rayburn throw down the gauntlet. The resultant clash between two wily, septuagenarian legislators—Rayburn and Rules Committee Chairman Howard W. Smith of Virginia—produced a historic, tensely dramatic confrontation that was to be Rayburn's hardest-won, sweetest, and last victory.

Shoulders squared, chest out, his small, powerful frame erect as Napoleon, Rayburn would stride into the House Chamber exactly at noon, mount the Speaker's rostrum, bang the gavel vigorously, and announce: "The House will be in order." Old, wise, kind, tough, honest, he symbolized the House of Representatives at its best. To some he *was* the House—the embodiment of its history, traditions, simplicity, and closeness to the people.

Whatever history ultimately may say of Sam Rayburn, he was to contemporaries a legend unto himself. He linked the beloved past with the space age, and he was adequate for both. By act and word, he demonstrated a love of country, never chauvinistic but always sincerely believing that this was the best government ever devised. He strove to make the system work—to advance the poor, restrain the greedy, reach toward that day when none would have too little or too much. His lifelong conviction was that the rich and powerful are entitled to justice but that the less fortunate are entitled to a helping hand from their government. He had the rare capacity to grow more progressive as he grew older, always to believe that tomorrow would be better than today if everyone did his and her own part in the national effort. "What Sam wanted," said Medibel Bartley, "was that every human being be happy and comfortable. If Sam could have brought happiness and comfort for every person on earth, he would have done so."

The long span of his eighty years covered almost half of the whole history of the nation. His interest in politics first was born when Grover Cleveland was President. It lasted through the Presidency of John F. Kennedy—from the twenty-first President to the thirty-fourth. From his service as a Texas state legislator to his death as Speaker of the U.S. House, he helped to make laws regulating the daily lives of Americans for fifty-five years—longer than anyone else in American history. He had a significant part in guiding the nation through the depressions of 1920–1921 and 1929–1933, two world wars, and the Korean War.

A Democrat "without prefix or suffix," he was the last of his kind in American politics—an anachronism, born in the nineteenth century, imbued with all the unstinting patriotism and loyalty that is associated with the men and women who pioneered the nation and lived close to the soil. As a national leader, he came to epitomize honesty and integrity in public service. To many he represented patriotism at its best—proud of his country, confident of its future, aware of its shortcomings, conscious of its need to help and to lead others less fortunate.

This biography is the result of research begun thirty years ago by the late D. B. Hardeman, a former state representative, teacher, and journalist with deep Texas roots, who first got to know Sam Rayburn when the two worked together in a futile attempt to rally Texas Democrats for the Stevenson-Sparkman ticket in 1952. In 1956, Hardeman, having published articles in *Harper's* and other magazines, came to Washington with the intention of writing a short profile of the Speaker. He informed Rayburn of his plans, got his approval, and immersed himself in the project, poring over records, interviewing Rayburn's colleagues, friends, and adversaries. He accumulated notes, documents, and transcripts that one day would fill a small room.

In the spring of 1957, his interest in Rayburn expanding and his research far from finished, Hardeman's savings ran out. A Guggenheim grant fell through, as did a promised staff position on the House Oversight Subcommittee. It was in this setting

that Rayburn one day in June summoned Hardeman to his office
and offered him a job. "I can use somebody with your background," the Speaker said, not having the slightest idea, Hardeman was convinced, what really to do with him. Reluctant at
first, Hardeman ultimately agreed with friends who advised
him to accept. "You'll get to know him in a way you never
would otherwise," they counseled.

Rayburn never had "employees" on his staff; they were all
"my co-workers." John Holton, who was like a son to Rayburn,
was his administrative assistant for nearly twenty years. Alla
Clary, who guarded Rayburn's door like a sentinel, served as his
personal secretary for forty-two years. In that unusual office no
one gave—or had authority to give—orders to others. They all
worked for Rayburn himself, and everyone was expected to
pitch in and do whatever needed to be done. After a period of
waiting for assignments that did not come, Hardeman edged ex-
perimentally into a role he carved out for himself in an effort to
be useful: trying to be an extension of Rayburn's eyes and ears.

Like all politicians, Rayburn passionately wanted to know
what was going on, and to know it first. He delighted in being
able to say, "Oh, I heard about that yesterday"—a form of
oneupmanship common in politics. Hardeman began scanning
newspapers, reports, books, and periodicals and talking to reporters, other Capitol Hill staffers, and members of Congress.
Every day he placed a news summary and piles of clippings on
Rayburn's desk. The Speaker, who earlier had been a voracious
reader but in later years had little time to read, found this a
useful service. They began spending more time together.

One day he told Hardeman: "Come over to the apartment
Sunday morning. We'll have some breakfast and read the Sunday
papers." That was the first of many Sundays the two bachelors
spent together, Rayburn leaning back in an old reclining chair in
the corner of the living room, while Hardeman selected and
read aloud interesting items from the *Sunday Star*, *Washington
Post*, and *New York Times*. A faithful employee at the Anchorage
Apartments, where Rayburn lived for more than thirty years,
brought their breakfast from a restaurant across the street. Rayburn let Hardeman talk until the meal was finished. Then, over

coffee, the Speaker reminisced about his family, childhood, political experiences, friends, acquaintances, and personal philosophy. When the visits stretched into afternoon, he occasionally suggested an automobile ride or a long walk.

Hardeman, becoming more and more engrossed in his research, eventually suggested a regular series of interviews with the Speaker and a few minutes with him daily to go over specific current questions. It was a bold request; he had no idea how the old man would react. Finally, Rayburn said: "If George Stimpson had lived, I would have commissioned him to do my life story. You know, to do a man's life story, the writer should spend a lot of time with him. I wouldn't spend that much time studying anybody. But if you want to, I'll cooperate with you on it." (Stimpson, a kindly bachelor, had been a correspondent for the *Houston Post* in the 1930s, a beloved member of the Washington press corps, and an intimate friend of Rayburn's.) Having given his blessing, the Speaker then suggested interviews with his family in Texas. He made available, without restriction, his congressional papers and personal correspondence. Finally, he allowed Hardeman to use, with scant reserve, his own reminiscences.

That was all a long time ago. Challenging new interests and a series of personal blows, climaxed by Rayburn's sudden decline and death in 1961, caused Hardeman gradually to put aside the unfinished biography. His research and revealing interviews with key figures of the 1950s, many now dead, lay fallow for nearly twenty years. Eventually, Hardeman invited me as a writer-friend to join him in completing the research and writing the final manuscript. The work, regrettably, was still incomplete when Hardeman died in 1981. Thus, any errors of fact, interpretation, or omission in this volume obviously rest solely with the surviving partner.

Here, then, is our story of Sam Rayburn—too long delayed but perhaps more useful because time has sharpened Rayburn's place in history and because the recent availability of important new interviews and personal papers has added insight to one of the most intriguing and least-known leaders this nation has produced. It is also largely Rayburn's own story, as he saw it during the last decade of his life. It is not an authorized biography in any sense. Nothing that, in the opinion of the surviving member of the Hardeman–Bacon partnership, illuminates Rayburn's personality, motives, and methods has been omitted. Rayburn, an intensely private person, perhaps would not have approved of all that is included here. Certainly he would have found uncomfortable any public discussion of his brief, tragic marriage. But it's all important, we think, in filling out the mosaic of a life so simple that it was infinitely complex.

Donald C. Bacon
Washington, D.C., January 1987

I

Growing Up

In his twilight years, when he had met and observed most of the prominent men and women of the world, Sam Rayburn still remembered his gaunt, bearded father and his busy, black-eyed mother as the most remarkable people he had ever known. His feelings were far more than the love of a child, however strong, for his parents. In his mind, they had not only been kind, loving parents to whom he owed an everlasting debt, but had possessed an inner strength and nobility of purpose that made them outstanding human beings completely separate from their parental role. A need to prove himself worthy of them drove him relentlessly—sometimes painfully—throughout his life.[1]

Rayburn perhaps regarded his father with greater awe than did his older brothers and sisters, for Will Rayburn was 41 years old when Sam was born. It was Will Rayburn who instilled in young Sam a lifelong interest in politics. Rayburn remembered his father as "the intensest Democrat you ever saw," a "good citizen who never missed an election." Will Rayburn stood just under six feet. He was thin, bearded, and quiet. A taciturn, often melancholy man, he frequently sat off to himself, whittling aimlessly by the hour. He craved the outdoors and had an unusual interest in animals, especially horses. He was known for his four great loves: his family, the Primitive Baptist Church, the Democratic party, and horses. It was said that he could drive a team of horses faster than any man in north Texas.

Many limbs of the Rayburn family tree are obscured by the mists of history. The best evidence is that the Rayburns were Ulster Scots who came to America from Northern Ireland about 1750.[2] One family tradition is that two Rayburn brothers came first to Pennsylvania, then moved south to Virginia. About the middle of the eighteenth century, Rayburns—or Reburns, as the name appeared in one of its many early spellings[3]—began showing up in the Shenandoah Valley of Virginia as part of a heavy influx of Scotch-Irish immigrants who poured down the "Great Wagon Road." The dour settlers, now twice removed from their Scottish origins, brought with them fervent Presbyterianism, democratic views, love of education, and a passion for hard work.[4]

Sometime after 1820, John Rayburn, an orphan, was brought out of the Shenandoah Valley to live with an uncle, John McNatt, in Roane County in east Tennessee. In 1829, he married Lucinda Amos, the South Carolina-born daughter of a Roane County farmer. The marriage produced five children, including, in 1840, William Marion Rayburn, whose son 100 years later, almost to the day, took over the second most powerful position in the United States—the Speakership of the House of Representatives.

Will's father died six months after he was born. His widowed mother and her five children were forced to move in with her aging parents. Hard, poverty-stricken years lay ahead of them. Lucinda Rayburn's father, William Amos, was more than 60 years old and now had to make a living for a combined household of ten. By 1850, his net worth in real estate was a mere $200.

The Rayburns—young Will especially—found their dependence on the charity of the Amos family hard to bear. When he was 14, Will convinced his mother that he was old enough to provide for the family and that it was time for them to get a place of their own. They soon built themselves a little cabin and, with all the children pitching in, began carving out a precarious living on a rocky hillside in east Tennessee.

The burning issue of the day was slavery. The practice was generally supported in much of the state but was widely condemned in the eastern region, where slaves were few. Even before New England abolitionists began their crusade, east Tennessee crackled with antislavery sentiment. It naturally followed that most east Tennesseans were strongly opposed to the secession movement that ignited most of the South.[5]

When the question of leaving the Union came before the voters of Tennessee, Roane County voted nearly four to one against separation. The state as a whole, however, voted to secede and to send representatives to the Confederate Congress. The war that erupted in 1860 cut deeply and painfully in Tennessee, splitting families, neighbors, churches, and lodges. The tragic years that followed saw brothers killing brothers, cousins warring on the field of battle, and feuds that lasted for generations arising between families and neighbors.

The Rayburns opposed secession; but when Tennessee joined the Confederacy, they accepted the verdict and gave their loyalty to the South. In August 1861, 20-year-old Will Rayburn joined the 1st Tennessee Cavalry Regiment. Later, after Colonel Henry M. Ashby, a dashing young officer of high promise, took command of the unit, Will Rayburn became part of Ashby's 2nd Tennessee Cavalry. In August 1862, he went into action against the Yankees and for three years was almost constantly on the move—raiding Kentucky again and again, skirmishing with Union forces, destroying supplies, seeking beef cattle for hungry Confederates. Ashby's men rode south to fight at Chickamauga, Missionary Ridge, Dalton, Ringgold, and a score of other places. In October 1862, the unit reported to a new commander under whom it was to serve for the remainder of the war—Brigadier General Joe Wheeler, then 26 years old and destined to become one of the great Confederate cavalry leaders.

A muster roll of Rayburn's company in March of 1864 showed that out of 134 officers and men listed, only 23 were present and ready for duty, Rayburn being one. All the unit's officers were dead, wounded, or AWOL. A sergeant was in command. Rayburn's superiors urged him to become an officer and lead the unit himself, but he declined, arguing that the job required someone who could read and write, and he could do neither. He had attended school only three weeks in his life.[6]

After the war, Will Rayburn returned home to find a land ravaged, looted, and embittered by the back-and-forth marching of Federals, Confederates, Lincolnites, bushwhackers, and common robbers.[7] The young ex-cavalryman set two goals: to provide a living for his mother and himself and then to find a wife and raise a family. Though living itself was hard, it was a struggle shared by all. The war played no favorites in east Tennessee. Its wrath and destructiveness fell with fine impartiality on Union and Confederate sympathizers alike.

Eventually, Will's determination paid off. He began showing some financial progress, and on May 14, 1868, at age 27, he married 21-year-old, strong-willed Martha Clementine Waller at Union Crossroads in Roane County. Will had married into a respected, well-to-do family—far above the Rayburns from almost any perspective. The Wallers not only were Roane County pioneers—they were, by community standards, aristocratic. Martha's father, John Barksdale Waller, was a proud, dignified man given to wearing white shirts and a silk hat. Moreover, he could read and write and served for thirty-two years as a county official. In the family, dating back to twelfth-century England, there had been a long line of doctors, lawyers, and public officials. Owner of a big, two-story log house, considered splendid in those times, John Waller was a man of high standing in the community.[8]

The Will Rayburn family grew quickly. First there was a son, John Franklin, then Charles, then Katic, followed by Lucinda. Next came "those wild twins," Will and Jim, and another girl, Medibel. After twelve years of married life, the Rayburns had seven children.

Martha "Mat" Rayburn was close to all of her own family, particularly her younger sister, Eliza. As girls the two spent much time together, and when Eliza married a Roane County neighbor, Samuel Taliaferro, and moved west to the Indian Territory (Oklahoma today), Mat missed her continually. On January 6, 1882, a few years after Eliza moved away, Martha's eighth child was born—a healthy boy with his mother's deep, dark eyes.[9] Thinking of sister Eliza and her husband in the far-away Indian Territory, Mat named the child Samuel Taliaferro Rayburn. Three more Rayburn children followed—Dick, then Tom, and, finally, after the family moved to Texas, Abner.

Young Sam and his family did not live long in the log cabin where he was born. Soon thereafter Grandfather John Barksdale Waller, growing old, persuaded the Rayburns to move in with him to keep him company. The Waller house was a two-story frontier mansion, built of split logs with rock chimneys and a rock foundation. It had four rooms downstairs, three upstairs, and a long front porch supported by eight logs that held up the roof. The home, on a hill several hundred yards from the swift-flowing Clinch River, had been built by William, the first Waller to occupy the land, in 1804. The house faced west, into a cone-shaped, timber-covered ridge. In summer, the women of the family liked to wait for the sun to go behind the ridge before they undertook their outdoor chores, for then they still had several hours of bright but shaded daylight. On a twenty-foot pole on the north of the house, near the front porch, was a big bell that was rung for two purposes: a call to meals and a call for help.

The Clinch River was a deep, navigable stream, and Kingston, eleven miles west of the Waller home, was a thriving ship-building center and river port. Steamboats churned up and down the Tennessee, Clinch, and Holston rivers. Chattanooga, Kingston, and Knoxville were the principal ports between Muscle Shoals in Alabama and the headwaters. As a small boy, Sam watched the riverboats with awe and fascination. The blowing of their whistles sent a shiver up his spine—a thrill he could recall with intensity all his life.

Although life for the Rayburns improved after the family moved in with Grandpa Waller, Will Rayburn was restless. As a cavalryman in the Civil War, he had fought side by side with a hard-riding band of Texans—the 8th Texas Cavalry, famous in history as Terry's Texas Rangers. At camp horse races, which Will often organized and usually won, and around campfires he heard wonderful tales of the opportunities, the climate, the soil, and the size of Texas. He was seized with a fierce longing to pull up stakes and go there, and would have done so immediately after the war had it not been for the obligations he felt to his widowed mother in Tennessee. When he married and began raising a family, the dream of going to Texas slipped further away but never left him.

Others had the fever, too. So many people in Kentucky, Tennessee, and Missouri sold their farms and businesses and moved to Texas after the war that postmasters began marking undeliverable mail with the letters "G.T.T."—Gone to Texas.[10] Among the migrants was Martha's brother, Monroe Waller, who married and took his bride to Fannin County in northeast Texas. Then Will's sister, Elizabeth, married Abner Dickey, and they, too, moved to the same blackland.

Life was still financially hard for the Will Rayburns. Their sixty-acre farm produced little, no matter how hard they worked. The soil, after producing corn and tobacco crops for generations, had lost much of its fertility. The farm, and its potential, seemed all the poorer when the Wallers and the Dickeys in distant Texas sent enticing word of an abundance of sticky, deep black, unbelievably rich soil that would grow almost anything. In 1886, 83-year-old Grandpa Waller died, freeing Will and Martha Rayburn from their last family ties to Tennessee. They discussed the future, talking of Texas and the dream that had possessed Will for twenty years. A move would entail great risks, but it held great opportunities, too, they concluded.

In the autumn of 1887, when Sam was 5 years old, the Rayburns made their decision. They sold their farm, livestock, furniture—everything but their bedclothes. They packed their few belongings and dressed their ten children for traveling. In an open wagon, loaded to the tailgate with suitcases, boxes, and children, they rode to Lenoir City, there to board a train for the four-day trip to Dodd City, Texas, where they would begin a new life.

The Rayburns' first night in Texas was spent with their relatives, the Dickeys and the Wallers. The family had to be split

into two groups because neither host could accommodate all
twelve of them. Young Sam went with "Uncle Roe" Waller, who
lived on the road to Bonham, the county seat of Fannin County,
four miles to the west.

Eager to get his family settled in a place of their own, Will
Rayburn set out on horseback early the next morning to find a
farm. Eventually, three and one-half miles south of Windom, he
found for sale forty acres of land on which a Dr. Eaton had built
a sturdy, two-story frame house. The land was gently undulat-
ing, rising to a low ridge in the west. It was rich black dirt such
as Will had dreamed of. And the price was right; $1,362 for
everything, including a good barn. With $600 down and a prom-
ise to pay the balance within three years, the Rayburns moved
into their new home. Soon the eleventh and last Rayburn child—
Abner—was born.

Most of the years on the farm, there were fourteen in the family—Will and Martha, the children, and, finally, Jim Rayburn,
Will's bachelor brother, who came from Tennessee to live with
them. Mary McFarland Jennings, a Rayburn family friend, recalled: "Sam's brother Jim was the Rayburn I 'went with,' but
those closely knit early families knew each other very well and it
was a special day for us when the Rayburns passed going into
town, on horseback or in buggies. Then, as we would pass their
house on our way to Bonham in our surrey, we would see those
cute Rayburn boys sitting on the fence, little dreaming that
young Sam one day would become famous."[11]

Despite his big family, Sam Rayburn remembered himself
as "a quiet and lonely child," who often spent hours leaning
against the fence of his father's farm, "gazing down those long,
muddy lanes over which cotton was hauled to market and pray-
ing that just one buggy might pass." In conversations with close
friends, he often brought up these feelings. "I have known the
loneliness that breaks men's hearts," he told Roger D. Greene of
the Associated Press in 1954. To author David Cohn, he once
observed: "Loneliness consumes people. It kills them eventually.
God help the lonely."[12] Recalling his childhood, he told one of
his staff members in later life, "I do not know how anybody
could get any lonelier and not die."[13] His brothers and sisters

scoffed at the idea that the young boy could have been lonely in
the midst of such a large and energetic family.

As a family, the Rayburns were particularly close. On winter
nights, the parents would gather the children in a semicircle before the big fireplace at the west end of their living room for
hours of reading, talking, and storytelling before bedtime. As
adults, the brothers and sisters retained their clannishness, always staying in close touch and assembling without prearrange-
ment each Sunday at Sam's house in Bonham when he was
there.

It was around the family fireplace, first in Tennessee, later
in Texas, that Martha taught the illiterate Will Rayburn to read.
He became, as Sam Rayburn later recalled, "a ravenous reader,"
devouring books, newspapers, any printed material available.
Cash was scarce, but when itinerant booksellers came through
the farmlands peddling their volumes, Will seldom failed to buy
some new books. Sixty years later, the Rayburns remembered
with particular vividness a beautifully bound *Life of Queen Vic-
toria*, purchased from a peddler, which was read and reread until
its covers were threadbare. The family also had biographies of
Presidents and other political figures—mostly Democrats—as
well as a gigantic, well-thumbed Holy Bible.

Twice a week the entire family looked forward to the arrival
by mail of the semiweekly edition of the *Louisville Courier-
Journal*. The *Courier-Journal* was edited by "Marse Henry" Watterson, a talented and colorful figure of the day, who became
one of the most influential and articulate spokesmen of the
"New South." The elder Rayburn had a special feeling for Watterson, who, as a youngster, had been chief of scouts for General Joe Wheeler's cavalry in the fateful Atlanta campaign. Though
they never met, Rayburn felt a kinship to the famous editor.
Watterson's *Courier-Journal* was the Rayburn "family paper" back
in Tennessee and continued to be their staple reading for many
years.

While the father found a deep satisfaction in his own Primitive Baptist faith, he did not try to force his religion on other
members of the family. Most of them attended the regular Baptist church in Windom, while Will often went alone to the Oak

Grove Baptist Church. He avoided moralizing or preaching to others, but his children always believed that his own church gave him, as Sam Rayburn put it, "a belief in God without reservation," a hidden source of strength for life's struggles. Nor did Will Rayburn attempt to influence his children in choosing a life's work. His advice always was that it mattered little what calling a person undertook, "but do something and do it hard." On the other hand, he was very positive as to what he considered the most important thing in life—to live honorably. That was what he wanted most for his children. Time and again, he reminded them that one day they would be on their own. "All I have to give you is character," he told them.

The center of the household was the big kitchen, under the command of Martha, a tiny, white-haired dynamo who brooked no backtalk from her children or, for that matter, from her husband. She ran her household with an iron hand, was justly proud of her cooking, and, with the Rayburn girls, worked long hours preparing meals for the healthy brood. It was at her table that young Sam acquired a lifelong habit of bolting down his food. Even in later years, when he dined at the finest tables in Washington, he assaulted his food with a ferocity that astonished and amused other guests. "When you eat at a table with fourteen hungry people, you learn to eat fast or you don't get fed," he would explain.

Relatives and friends remembered Martha—"Aunt Mat"— Rayburn as an industrious, determined, constantly busy woman. Weighing just over ninety pounds, she reminded friends of a Dresden doll. Her dark brown hair turned white years before her death, while her eyebrows stayed jet black. Her face was dominated by a pair of deep, inscrutable, dark brown eyes— eyes that looked straight and level at a person without revealing the thoughts behind them. Sometimes, in repose, the corners of her mouth would turn down slightly, and her face would assume an almost melancholy cast. All her children had that sad look at times, especially her son Sam.

Outwardly contented and reflective, Martha never complained, not even when Will's brother Jim came from Tennessee to live, swelling the family to fourteen. She was, at the same time, frank and forthright—too frank, some thought. "She would always tell you just what she thought, even if it hurt," relatives recalled. "She indulged no pretense or double-talk. She believed in plain speaking."

As a homemaker, she kept everything and everyone strictly in line, particularly the children. An order was meant to be obeyed, and disobedience brought a sure and swift penalty, usually a well-administered spanking. The children learned that on the rare occasions when Will Rayburn tried to spank them, he would stop if they cried loud and long enough. "Easy Boss," they called him. Mat Rayburn was immune to such tactics; she simply whacked them all the harder.

To rear eleven children on the proceeds of a forty-acre cotton field, the household director had to be thrifty, a role for which Mat Rayburn was well qualified. The months of hardship during and after the Civil War in Tennessee were good training. Never waste anything—including time—was the rule she followed and relentlessly pressed upon her children. Another rule: she demanded punctuality, in herself and her family. If one of the children was late for school, the punishment was swift and sure—a whipping when he or she got home. As a result, the Rayburn children were seldom late. Punctuality later became a trademark of Sam Rayburn. As a young congressman, he was almost always the first member to show up for a meeting or hearing. In later years, he became intolerant of others who kept him waiting.

When Sam was 7, he joined the other children to walk to the two-teacher Burnett School two miles away. Years later, his first teacher, Ivan Moreland, recalled him as "a wiry little fellow who wouldn't stay still in the classroom or on the playground."[14] The first year, Moreland often had to hold the squirming little boy on his lap to keep him still long enough to receive instruction.

The next year Will Rayburn and his neighbors, George Wigley and "Prairie Sam" Payne, chipped in $75 apiece, together with lesser amounts from other neighbors, and built a new school at Flag Springs, about a mile and a half southeast of the

Rayburn home. The new school became the center of social and educational life for the surrounding farming region. It was there that Sam Rayburn attended grammar and high school.

Martha insisted that all the children study hard in school, which, with occasional lapses, they did. A failing grade was certain to be followed by a sound whipping. It was a nightly ritual for the boys and girls to sit around the dinner table, studying by the flickering light of a kerosene lamp until the lessons were done. Sam did well in school despite an energetic mischievousness that kept him from long periods of concentrated study. He was often at the center of classroom disruptions, for which he would be sentenced by the teacher to hours of incarceration in a special chair reserved for "bad boys."

He exhibited early a marked love of books, a taste acquired from his mother and later reinforced by his father. He found history and civics particularly exciting and easy, much to the amazement of his brothers and sisters who struggled with such subjects. Medibel Rayburn remembered her brother as "always a manly little boy":

> He used to embarrass my father by staying with some grownup and discussing politics so seriously and at great length. When he was with grown people he was very manly and acted older than his years, but with the kids he was his age, always wanting to be in the middle of everything. He was a natural leader—always pretty good at telling the others what to do. He always liked the girls and liked to go to social things. He didn't dance until he got to Washington, and then he learned to dance a little.[15]

As Sam grew toward manhood, his reading became more intense. Political figures became his heroes. He read every political biography he could find and eagerly pored over each issue of the *Louisville Courier-Journal* with its skilled and detailed reporting of political affairs. "My father and I used to almost scrap over the paper to see who could get to read it first," remembered Rayburn. At night, he would lie awake thinking about the prominent political figures he knew only from reading "bee-ographies," as he always pronounced the word, and newspapers.

"I wondered how they looked. Were they tall or short, fat or lean, and whether they were whiskered or clean-shaven. It all appealed to me very much." He imagined their voices as they poured forth torrents of political boasting and invective. Years later, Rayburn recalled the influence on his life of one figure in particular: fellow Tennessean James K. Polk, who went to Congress and became Speaker of the House, later was governor of Tennessee, and, finally, was President of the United States.

Out in the field, as he pulled the heavy cotton sack up and down the endless rows, the young Rayburn made hundreds of political speeches to imaginary throngs, often throwing in passages memorized from the moving orations of the times. Seventy years later, he would recall that it was in those fields, when he was 8 or 9 years old, that he decided on a career of law and politics. "After I made that decision, it was settled. I never worried a minute after that about what I ought to do or was going to do. I kept that ambition strictly to myself. I didn't tell my parents or my brothers and sisters or anyone. They would have laughed me out of the county."

2

Ambition Kindled

Sam Rayburn grew to manhood in the golden age of Texas politics—when political giants debated and decided the burning issues of the hour. The 1890s was one of those unpredictably recurring periods in American history when politics becomes the serious concern, as well as the pleasant pastime, of almost every citizen. Political speakers often held huge crowds in rapt attention for two, three, even four hours of fervent oratory. Public debates, in the style of Lincoln-Douglas, were once more in vogue, and weighty as well as trivial issues, ranging from prohibition and tobacco's evils to America's "manifest destiny," were subjected to passionate consideration in hamlets and cities across the land.

Newspapers of the era gave a generous share of their editorial columns to political reporting. In 1892, the *Galveston News* carried practically word-by-word reports of the epic debates between Governor James Stephen Hogg and his corporation-backed opponent, George Clark. On a single day, the newspaper devoted twenty-five solid columns to such reporting on just one Hogg-Clark debate.

Across the breakfast table, in the country stores, over plow-handles, and from the hurricane decks of countless cowponies, every move and motive of the politicians was analyzed and argued with eagerness and intelligence. Parents were gratified when their sons showed an inclination toward politics, and many of the ablest, most ambitious young Texans of that generation chose public service as a noble calling of the highest prestige.

When Rayburn was 8 years old, big-bodied, strong-minded James Hogg became Texas's first native-born governor, sweeping into office on a platform of curbing the abuses of the railroads, alien landowners, corporations, and other economic freewheelers. In four embattled years as the state's chief executive, Hogg so firmly established himself as "the champion of the people" that he won common acceptance as the Lone Star State's greatest governor—a rating in history not seriously challenged to this day by any Texas governor. Emerging from the frontier phase of its colorful history, Texas had acquired sufficient wealth and population to insist upon an influential role in national affairs and had an able, dedicated coterie of legislators pleading its case in Washington.

Texas then, as now, had a unique status in American politics. The overwhelming majority of those who colonized and developed the state came from the Old South. Even so, the state's economic and political interests had as much in common with the West as with the South. From the end of the Civil War until the Hoover Rebellion of 1928, Texas voted overwhelmingly Democratic along with the rest of the Old South. Yet, through the period of Rayburn's boyhood, Texas's political thinking was strongly colored by the agrarian radicalism most colorfully exemplified in the populist movement. The campaigns for strict regulation of railroads, lower tariffs, cheap freight rates for farm and ranch products, the breaking up of trusts and monopolies, and tight control of "Wall Street" found vociferous acceptance from a majority of Texas voters.

When the Democrats were in control of Congress, the Lone Star State held positions of great power in the federal government's legislative branch. Congressman (later Senator) John Reagan, who had been postmaster general in the Confederate cabinet, was perhaps the man most instrumental in creating the Interstate Commerce Commission to regulate railroad rates—a historic step in establishing the doctrine that the federal government should regulate mighty economic forces in the public interest. A fellow Texan, David Culberson, was chairman of the important House Judiciary Committee, while his son, Charles, was embarking on a distinguished 32-year career that included service as state attorney general, governor, and finally U.S. senator for twenty-four years.

The House Ways and Means Committee, which controlled taxes, tariffs, and other revenue matters, was headed by a nationally respected tariff expert, Roger Q. Mills, who narrowly missed being Texas's first Speaker of the national House of Representatives because he would not embrace William Jennings Bryan's "free-silver" theories. And holding a careful rein on the nation's spending as chairman of the House Appropriations Committee was conservative old Joseph D. Sayers, who resigned his powerful post to become governor of Texas when Rayburn was 17 years old. In the opinion of many, Texas political life in the closing years of the nineteenth century boasted more shining stars than at any time in its history, and in the galaxy of leadership no star shone more brilliantly than that of Joseph Weldon Bailey.

To Joe Bailey, life was to be acted in the grand manner.[1] Whether one loved or hated him, all agreed that Bailey walked, talked, gestured, and dressed with an air of bewitching grandeur. He never dropped his lordly mantle, either in ecstatic victory or in anguished defeat. From birth to death, he acted out his role with scornful majesty. Almost every facet of his personality and his career was outlined in terms of the extravagant and the grandiose. His enormous capacity for friendship won him a fanatical following for whom Joe Bailey could never do a wrong. Yet equally extravagant was his capacity for hatred. To him, a man was either friend or enemy, and Bailey neither forgot nor forgave his enemies—his goal was the absolute ruin of his foes. They responded with a personal hatred for Bailey that persisted long after he was dead.

Tall, commanding, handsome, and big-headed, he was a man of consummate power and virility. When he walked into a room, all eyes turned to see "what manner of man is this?" Smooth-shaven, with a ruddy, boyish complexion, distinguished features, and dark, flashing eyes of great force and beauty, his countenance was striking. "Indeed he looks a good deal like a big, healthy happy boy, and when he smiles he is positively captivating," one contemporary wrote. "He is graceful in his gestures, apt and precise in diction; he expresses himself, no matter how fatuous his arguments may be, in clear and rounded sentences, and always with an air of the utmost sincerity, with an implied idea that he is saying the last word—that nothing he enunciates can be open to question."[2]

Bailey's greatest asset was his voice, which many thought more beautiful than the golden tones of his fellow congressman, William Jennings Bryan. Soft and melodious, with a timbre often recalling an organ's deep tones, his voice was used with the skill of a great musician. From the days of his youth in Mississippi, Bailey concentrated on the study of oratory as well as politics and law, and by maturity he was familiar with—and often had fully memorized—many of the great orations of history. His vocabulary—legal, descriptive, and vituperative—was one of the most extensive of his times. A Joe Bailey speech, no matter how trivial the subject, was a grandiose performance that, while it might anger or inspire listeners, never left them indifferent.

His dress was unconventional and spectacular. In college he wore a long, dull black frock coat, flowing white tie, stiff collar, and broad black felt hat, and he clung to this attire even when he was almost the last to wear it.

At 22, Bailey moved from Mississippi to Gainesville in north Texas, where he married and began the practice of law. His capacity for making friends and his resplendent oratory quickly spread his fame throughout the region. Three years later, he was nearly selected for Congress, but he sonorously informed the convention that, if chosen, he would not be old enough to take his seat. He waited two years to become constitutionally eligible and, although he had lived in Texas less than five years, was sent to Congress by an overwhelming vote.

In Washington, his colorful dress, his grand manner, and the fact that he was the youngest member of the U.S. House of Representatives quickly brought him the attention he craved. Less than two months after reaching Washington, he spoke to the House, condemning the leadership of his own Democratic party in a speech so brilliant that a veteran newspaperman wrote, "It is said that never in years has any young man and a new member made such a fine impression and been treated with such consideration." After only three terms in Congress—when he was 34—the Democrats nominated him as their candidate for Speaker. He was not elected, but he became the party's dramatic leader in the House. Years later, Rayburn asked Speaker Champ Clark whom he considered the ablest member he had ever served with. "If I had to pick one, it would be Joe Bailey," Clark replied. Asked the same question by another congressman, noted Republican Speaker Joseph G. "Uncle Joe" Cannon answered without hesitation: "Joe Bailey."

Early in his career, Bailey was a flaming champion of the plain people, carrying the banner of the masses against the big interests in fierce congressional battles for railroad regulation, federal income tax, and the free coinage of silver. This reputation as a progressive has been all but lost in history as a result of Bailey's later activities as the embodiment of extreme conservatism and the staunch defender of the privileged rich. To teenaged Rayburn, eagerly absorbing everything he could read and hear about politics and politicians, Joe Bailey was a dazzling, heroic figure. Moreover, he was Rayburn's own congressman.

When Rayburn was 15, he saw his congressman and heard him speak for the first time. From that day forward, his political goal—going to Congress—was fixed. Bailey had come to speak at an old settlers' reunion at the fairgrounds in Bonham. Sam, having gotten his father's permission to attend, was full of anticipation. Out of bed at daybreak, he saddled his horse and rode twelve miles to the county seat.

In the fairgrounds pavilion, a buzzing throng had assembled to hear the dynamic young congressman. The timid young Rayburn was ill at ease in the presence of the well-dressed townspeople. He lingered on the edge of the crowd, under the pavilion's eaves, too shy to move in closer. But he could watch the tall, eagle-eyed congressman and every sweeping gesture and

could hear every word rolling forth in a mighty, sonorous bari-
tone that held the crowd spellbound. After the speech, Bailey
walked to the Bonham public square, surrounded by a crowd
of friends. Rayburn followed at a distance, watching his every
move and gesture. "I was dying to shake hands with him," he
once admitted. "But he was with a finely dressed lady and her
husband, and I was just too shy. I just didn't have the guts to go
up and shake his hand."[3] Rayburn never forgot that day. Sixty
years later, he told a friend: "I have never met a man who
impressed me like Joe Bailey did. He had the finest physique
and bearing, the noblest head, one of the biggest brains and
probably the most irresistible personality I ever came in contact with."[4]

After the Bailey speech, Rayburn's youthful ambitions were no
longer a secret. To anyone who inquired about his future, Rayburn would briskly reply: "I'm going to study law and go into
politics and be a congressman." Just how he could fulfill those
ambitions, he was not sure. College cost money, and his parents
were finding it difficult to support their large family on the income from a forty-acre farm, much less save enough to provide
college educations for their children. Still, Rayburn's mind was
made up. Somehow, he would find a way.

About twenty miles south of the Rayburn farm, in Commerce, Texas, a fiery-eyed, ceaselessly energetic, ideal-filled
professor burned with a passion to educate young people. All
his life, Kentucky-born William Leonidas Mayo was possessed
by an unquenchable longing to help people learn. Moreover, he
had an unshakable faith that any boy or girl who really wanted
an education could find a way to get one.

After teaching school a few years, Mayo started a private
"normal college" where he was president, janitor, librarian, gar-
dener, religious instructor, and finance chairman all at once.
With the aid of his wife and his own unflagging zeal, he built
East Texas Normal to his own specifications.[5] Texas colleges
then were few, far apart, and too expensive for most young
people. But at "the Professor's" school, an ambitious boy or girl
always seemed to find some way to enroll and remain until he or

she got a diploma.

As his student body grew, Mayo sent solicitors through the cotton fields of north and east Texas, armed with pamphlets and enthusiasm, telling young men and women of the opportunities offered by East Texas Normal School. To Rayburn, pondering his options as he dragged a cotton sack across the black, steaming earth, the Commerce school seemed his best—his only—hope for a college education. Farm boys and girls like himself made up its student body, and there was a chance to find enough work to pay his way through school. In the autumn, when he was 18 and the cotton crop was picked, Rayburn talked over his hopes with his father, who pointed out that he had no money to help him. "I didn't ask you to send me," Rayburn replied. "I just asked you to let me go."

Sam was almost grown now. His thick body was strong and sturdy, but he was the shortest Rayburn boy. At maturity he would be only five foot six inches tall. His large, round head was well covered with silky, dark brown hair that had a reddish cast. His fair complexion was prone to freckles. Dominating his well-chiseled, almost handsome face were deep, dark brown eyes like his mother's.

There were two distinct sides to his personality—serious and mischievous. He was more bookish, serious-minded, and sturdily self-reliant than his brothers and sisters. He was quiet but doggedly determined whenever there was a chore or a challenge to be undertaken. Then, when the serious business was completed, he once again was a gregarious, even prankish, youngster. He seemed instinctively to separate "the time to work" from "the time to play." Sam "wasn't cocky but never lacked for self confidence," his sister Medibel Rayburn Bartley recalled. "He always thought he could do whatever he set out to do and in his mind there was never any question about it."[6]

To see him off to college, the entire family drove to the train depot at Ladonia, where he was to begin an eighteen-mile trip to Commerce by way of Wolfe City. The boy's emotions were welling within him. All his life he was a keenly emotional man, one whose eyes were quick to moisten at mention of a loved one or a poignant recollection. When the train puffed into Ladonia,

Sam climbed aboard, suitcase in hand. His father followed, while the rest of the family waved their good-byes from the platform.

The older Rayburn fumbled for words but was unable to express his feelings. Instead, he grabbed his son's hand, pressed something into it, and stumbled down the steps of the coach. As the train pulled out, Sam looked at his gift—$25 in bills—a year's savings and a veritable fortune to a family of fourteen squeezing out a living from blackland farming. The lonely boy, leaving the warmth of an affectionate home life for an unknown destiny, allowed tears to break through the dam of self-restraint. He was still crying softly when the train pulled into Wolfe City.

He went straight to see the Professor. A small, well-built man, Mayo had a strong face usually softened by a winsome smile. The dominant feature of his large head was a pair of dark, deep-set eyes. These flashing eyes together with his nervous energetic movements conveyed the feeling of a tense, restless man of action. Mayo put the young Rayburn at ease, as he listened to his story of a burning youthful ambition faced with great financial hardship. It was a story Mayo had heard before from countless boys and girls. Yes, the Professor thought some way could be worked out for Rayburn to enter East Texas Normal, that is, if he was really serious about wanting an education.

To begin with, Rayburn could have his room and board on credit for the first year. If paid in advance, this would have amounted to approximately $100. To pay the $3 a month tuition fee, Mayo had just the right job for Sam. The assembly and dismissal of each class during the day was signaled by the ringing of an 850-pound bell. Ringing this bell for each class and making the classroom fires on winter mornings would take care of his tuition. Eventually, Sam found an additional job—sweeping out the local public school each day—that took care of his laundry and other incidental expenses. He also earned occasional extra money by milking farmer W. A. O'Neal's cows.

In the autumn of 1900, East Texas Normal had 324 students. Mayo had started the college with 35 students. Before he died, enrollment had grown to more than 3,000, and during his stewardship he made possible an education for more than 30,000 boys and girls. Since the school was Mayo's personal property, he operated it according to his own ideas of how a college should be run. To him, a good teacher was a person dedicated to helping young people discover themselves. And a college should be designed to meet the differing needs and capabilities of its students.

The college operated eleven months out of twelve. Students could enter or drop out at any time. They got credit for whatever they accomplished. This made it easier for the boy or girl who could go to school only when it did not interfere with duties on the farm back home. D. E. Denney of Wolfe City was a Rayburn classmate:

> I first knew him in the spring of 1902 when he and an old friend, B. J. Alexander, roomed together in a one room shack just North of the main building at school. These boys were poor like the rest of us and did their own laundry and pressed their pants between the mattresses. Each boy had to bring his pillows, bed linens and cover from home. We studied by coal-oil lamps for the most part, had our own axe and chopped our own wood for the little sheet-iron stoves that one could make red hot with a newspaper, and freeze the next moment. Sam used to be the first one to enter a room for the next class and poke fun at the girls when they came in. They all liked that.[7]

Another former student recalled: "We were a bunch of poor boys and girls, mostly from farms, mostly in need of polish, social grace, self-confidence and leadership attributes. For this reason Professor Mayo encouraged all of us to be active in the literary societies, debates and oratorical sprees that he loved so well."[8] Whether Mayo shrewdly devised the Saturday night literary society meetings as his own plan for combating juvenile delinquency is not known, but these meetings were the scene of great rivalries, being filled with lively debates, recitations, reports, and parliamentary discussions. The students once did their version of Shakespeare's *Julius Caesar*, with Rayburn taking the part of Brutus.[9]

Every member of the senior class was required to write,

memorize, and deliver publicly an original production, for Mayo thought it was imperative that they all be able to speak and express their thoughts. "Sam was a noisy debater," remembered Gladys Mayo, the Professor's daughter and Rayburn's lifelong friend. "You should have heard his orations as well! Eloquent and passionate as if he were a modern Herodotus reviving oratory before the Athenian assembly, or enjoying verbal bouts with Demosthenes!"[10]

The highlight of each day was the chapel session. Attendance was voluntary, but few students missed these exciting, inspiring assemblies. The thirty-minute chapel period usually opened with the singing of a well-known hymn, after which the student body repeated the Lord's Prayer in unison. Mayo himself usually presided over these gatherings. The students never knew what to expect on the program. Perhaps a local political leader would deliver a sermonizing address or, quite unexpectedly, some famous person passing through the region had been prevailed upon by the Professor to give the address of the day. Less serious items frequently were offered—sleight-of-hand performances, demonstrations of ventriloquism, musical recitals, or art exhibitions. In planning the potpourri of entertainment, Mayo seemed to be guided by the philosopher's rule: "Let nothing human be wholly alien to you." At most convocations, a chapter from the Bible and a famous poem or two were read, mail was distributed, and official announcements were made. The students were happiest, however, when the Professor himself was the speaker, as he often was. On these mornings, he spoke with vividness of the thing closest to the hearts of his students—what life held for them. In an emotion-packed voice, he poured forth his philosophy of how to make the most of life. When he began, "Young ladies and young gentlemen," an ex-student recalled, "every student in the audience would feel an inch taller."

A thorough student of the Bible, Mayo frequently quoted from the Book of Proverbs to underscore his pronouncements on the virtues of hard work, perseverance, honesty, and self-sacrifice. "It is study," he emphasized, "long-continued, intense mental action that enables one to scale the lofty peaks of honor or to engrave his name upon the pyramids of fame."[11] Such golden promises set ablaze the youthful ambitions of Rayburn and his fellow students. One of them remembered that "many a time I filed out of the Chapel Hall, after listening to Mayo, boiling over with enthusiasm and determination, and often with tears streaming down my cheeks, with a feeling there was nothing impossible for me to attempt and accomplish, and no high or honorable position beyond my power or merit to obtain." Coupled with his own dogged determination, such faith imparted by Professor Mayo made Rayburn certain that he would someday achieve the summit of his ambition. One who worked hard enough, and long enough, could not fail.

Rayburn enrolled in the pedagogic department, where one could earn a bachelor of science degree in two years. In his first year, he took courses in arithmetic, geometry, geography, rhetoric, civic government, physiology, United States history, Texas history, penmanship, parliamentary law, vocal music, and debating.

After his first year, still completely without funds and in debt to Mayo for an entire year's room and board, the 19-year-old Rayburn decided to drop out of school until he could earn enough money to pay off his indebtedness. He despised owing money to anyone. One of the inflexible rules he later required his employees to follow was that they must pay their bills. "I won't have a man working for me who won't pay his honest debts," he declared. Armed with a smattering of information and a temporary teacher's certificate, he got a job teaching at the one-room rural school at Greenwood in Hopkins County, about thirty miles southeast of his home. From that year's total income of $330, he saved enough to pay the money he owed Professor Mayo.

In the autumn of 1902, he returned to college for his second— and final—year. His courses, none of which ran very deep, included Latin, bookkeeping, literature, moral science, school management, general history, and chemistry. With an eye on his future career, each term Rayburn signed up for courses in debating or orations. Eventually, as his confidence and voice developed, his abilities at the podium began to be recognized by fellow students and others who attended campus debates in which he participated. He remembered the first person—aside from himself—to suggest he might someday wind up in Congress: E. K. Frieze, a barber in Commerce, who made the remark casually while trimming the young man's thick brown mop.

His ambition burning more brightly than ever, Rayburn finished his second year, got his diploma in July 1903, and set out to find a job. He still clutched the dream of "making a lawyer" and getting into politics, but that would have to wait. First of all, he had no money. Nor did he have any idea how to go about becoming a lawyer. Studying in some law office was ruled out, because he knew no lawyers. He might go to the University of Texas Law School in Austin, but that was far too expensive to be considered. He decided to get a job teaching school again, save his money, and wait.

For the next two years, Rayburn taught school in Dial, a tiny rural community in his home county. It proved to be an ideal place to start. Not only did he enjoy teaching—he always liked children—but he found it gave him an opportunity to read and study. Above all, as the community's only schoolteacher, the job gave him prestige, and a chance to meet a lot of people. Later, when he got into politics, these people would be voting for or against him, and he intended that they should vote for him. He attended every gathering and made as many new friends as he could. In the fall of 1905, he got a better, higher-paying job at the three-teacher school in Lannius, another small Fannin County community. His eye on the future, he continued to make friends—and wait.

3

State Legislator

Rayburn soon found his opening into politics. In 1905, the Texas Legislature, joining the "progressive movement" then sweeping the country, adopted the Terrell Election Law. Candidates for public office no longer would be chosen by party conventions, long dominated by powerful, often corrupt party bosses. Instead, starting in 1906, they would be nominated by the vote of all party members in direct primary elections. Rayburn saw this as a lucky break for him. In a convention he would have little chance of getting a nomination, for he knew none of the influential political leaders in the county. But in a primary—that was another story.

His mind was quickly set: he would run in the next Democratic primary as a candidate for the Texas House of Representatives. Winning the nomination would be tantamount to election in the overwhelmingly Democratic state. The office seemed a natural stepping stone—a perfect place to train for his ultimate goal, the United States House of Representatives. Moreover, members of the legislature were paid $5 a day for the first sixty days of each biennial session and $2 for each day of session thereafter. After two years of teaching school, Rayburn saw that as a munificent sum. With that income, he could enroll in the University of Texas Law School and perhaps "make a lawyer."

Over in Honey Grove, another determined young man had reached a similar decision. Sam H. Gardner, locally popular and ten years older than Rayburn, threw his hat into the ring. For the next five months, the two candidates waged a sincere if amateurish and uninspiring campaign throughout the county. Rayburn, sometimes on horseback, sometimes in a buggy, rode from farm to farm introducing himself, passing out campaign cards, and—whenever he found a farmer willing to pause long enough to listen—discussing burning local issues, such as prohibition and the falling price of cotton. Women, who along with blacks and Hispanics were disfranchised in Texas, got a courteous tip of the candidate's hat but little of his time.

Henry A. Cunningham was running for county judge in the same election. Occasionally, he and Rayburn shared a buggy, partly to hold down costs, partly to break the boredom of the long rides between towns. "Rayburn was quiet, unobtrusive, but certain to see and shake hands with everybody at meetings," Judge Cunningham recalled. "We didn't get to speak very often. There wasn't much speaking then, mostly handshaking and passing out cards."[1]

Rayburn and opponent Gardner also made the rounds together, sharing a one-horse buggy. As Medibel Bartley remembered it, "They'd ride into a small town, gather a crowd together, and one, then the other, would stand at the back of the buggy and talk."[2] At that time, neither had a firm political philosophy, much less a definite platform. Rayburn, not yet 25, spent much of his time trying to convince voters that he was dry behind the ears. In an effort to appear more mature, he bought himself a black wool suit, string tie, and black broad-brim hat and, despite the blazing Texas heat, wore the outfit to every public gathering. The costume, combined with his naturally somber countenance, gave him the appearance of an apprentice undertaker, but it served his purpose.

The campaign proved to be unusually free of bitterness, especially as the novice candidates became better acquainted. Their instant liking for each other blossomed into genuine friendship. They began praising each other in such lavish terms that voters often were puzzled as to why such good friends were competing for the same job.[3]

Saturday was election day, but the votes were not all counted until the following Tuesday. The Rayburns, all of whom had joined the fray with enthusiasm, waited tensely in the family living room for the returns. The race was neck and neck— Rayburn winning by wide margins in Bonham, Windom, and surrounding areas, Gardner scoring big in his part of the county. When, finally, the last returns trickled in, the clan broke into whoops of joy. Rayburn had won—by a scant 163 votes.

On January 8, 1907, two days after his 25th birthday, the stocky, restless youth raised his hand in the historic old Texas House of Representatives in Austin to take the oath of office as a legislator for the first time—the beginning of the longest law-making career in American history.

Never one to dream small, Rayburn had already set his mind on becoming Speaker of the Texas House, a presumptuous thought indeed in light of his age, inexperience, and lack of powerful friends. But, still overflowing with the lofty proverbs implanted by Professor Mayo, he sincerely believed that with hard work any goal was achievable. "I made up my mind that I had to be Speaker," Rayburn later recalled. "I don't know why, but I just had to."[4]

Rayburn's leadership potential was not immediately apparent to R. Bonna Ridgway, an eager young politician from west Texas who roomed with the future Speaker that year. "I remember him as being quiet, modest and attentive to what others said," Ridgway recalled in 1957. "Had I an idea then that he would later be one of the nation's greats, I would have kept notes."[5] Judge Cunningham of Bonham said:

> Sam built slowly. He led a good life, not afflicted by drink or chasing women. He had integrity and was never caught in any kind of shady deal. He was diligent to take care of his district and always got along with everybody. But we didn't know he was anything exceptional until just before he was elected Speaker of the U.S. House of Representatives. Then folks at home began to take notice of him. It was hard for some to see his real strength and picture him

as a great man because they knew him as a neighbor dressed in work clothes like themselves.[6]

For $30 a month, the two young state legislators—Ridgway was only 23—got a room at a boarding house on Lavaca Street. They had two single beds, three good meals a day, and not much else. Rayburn, planning to enroll in the University of Texas Law School as soon as his finances permitted, put aside as much of his $5-a-day legislative salary as he could afford. His frugality was legendary among his colleagues. One night, as Rayburn lay in bed, he broke out in laughter so loud that he awakened his roommate. "If it's that funny," growled Ridgway, "why don't you tell me?"

"Well," Rayburn chuckled, "I was out walking a while ago and ran into old Pharr.[7] I told him I'd buy him a cold drink if he'd walk to the drug store with me. We got there, and he ordered a Coca-Cola. Just about then, I ran my hand in my pocket and found I only had a nickel. So I told him I wasn't feeling too good and didn't believe I'd drink anything. I don't know what I'd done if he'd ordered a dime drink."

To achieve his dream of someday becoming Speaker, Rayburn set out to make friends with as many of his colleagues as possible. He worked diligently at the task, so much so that some of the old-timers began eyeing the eager newcomer suspiciously. Most of the legislators, however, found him genuinely likable, if a bit stiff and moralistic. What Read Granberry, then a Texas House page, later to become the body's parliamentarian, remembered most about the Windom freshman was that he was "so well liked by everyone."

His friendships outside his family all centered around his work. Strict upbringing set him apart. He liked women but was shy and dated little. He seldom went out with "the boys" and never joined in their after-hours carousing with the ever-available, free-spending lobbyists. Unless the House was working late, he was in bed by ten. Sometimes, during the dreaded night sessions when the governor was battling to keep a quorum for some important vote, Ridgway and a few of his rambunctious friends would sneak out a back window of the House chamber, edge across a narrow, slanting ledge, and escape. Rayburn would serve as lookout and wish them well, but always stayed behind.[8] His colleagues admired his diligence. But he was soon to reveal a trait they admired even more—his fierce and dogged loyalty to friends.

The budding lawmaker arrived in Austin to find his dazzling hero—Joseph Weldon Bailey—in serious trouble. Bailey's political life was in jeopardy. Soon Rayburn was plunged into his first battle, defending the man who had inspired his own entry into politics, a man he inexplicably idolized though they had little in common and, in fact, barely knew one another.

In 1907, Bailey was a U.S. senator, having been elected at the age of 36 after four spectacular years as the Democratic leader of the U.S. House of Representatives. As a senator, Bailey's gestures became grander, his always-abundant arrogance increased, and his dramatic performances drew more and more attention. This meteoric career left its mark on the young senator. As his pride and arrogance grew, he made even more enemies, and he reveled in their hatred, returning hate for hate.

Bailey always had expensive, even lavish tastes. He was a prodigal spender, and his appetite for living on a grand scale required more and more money. One of his more resplendent hobbies was a $250,000 string of trotting horses and horse farms in Kentucky and Texas. To finance these undertakings, he actively engaged in the practice of law, receiving a number of huge fees, particularly in the years after he went to the Senate. One hard-fisted Texas lumberman alone, John Henry Kirby, paid him nearly $150,000 in legal fees in a four-year period. Bailey stoutly defended a senator's right to build a nest egg for his old age through the practice of law, arrogantly sneering at charges that employment by rich clients, usually corporations, could influence his voting in the Senate. Shortly before he moved to the Senate, Bailey began an association that in time was to prove his undoing.

A shadowy concern known as the Waters-Pierce Oil Company operated in Texas in the late 1800s and early 1900s. Many Texans, including the state's attorney general, believed Waters-

Pierce was secretly controlled by the notorious Standard Oil Company, the corporate mechanism through which John D. Rockefeller exercised his impenetrable monopoly over the most widely used fuel of the period, kerosene. Eventually a state suit against Waters-Pierce resulted in the company's conviction for violating the antitrust laws, although no ruling was made on the alleged connection with Standard Oil. Banned from operating in Texas, the president of Waters-Pierce turned to Joe Bailey for help.

Bailey later said that Henry Clay Pierce approached him about employment with the company to help it obtain reinstatement in Texas and that he had refused. He did, however, secretly borrow $3,300 from Pierce and sign a demand note for that amount. Bailey also later accompanied Pierce to Austin, where the two held a series of conferences with state officials and worked out a plan to keep the company alive in the Lone Star State. Under the plan, the old Waters-Pierce Company was dissolved, then reorganized as a new corporation. After filing an affidavit with Texas authorities stating that it was not controlled by Standard Oil, the company was permitted to resume operations.

Rumors of Bailey's role in the maneuver spread, and the 1901 Legislature decided to investigate them just before he was due to be elected to the Senate for the first time. "Coal Oil Joe," as he was then known far and wide, stoutly denied ever taking a fee from Waters-Pierce. Exonerated by the investigating committee, he was chosen overwhelmingly by the Legislature to be the state's next United States senator. He did not then or later mention the $3,300 loan from Pierce. Henry Pierce, meanwhile, charged off that and later loans to Bailey as an expense to the company, which listed them as "legal fees."

For several years, the affair was largely forgotten. Bailey continued his arrogant ways, allowing his extravagant style of living to inflate in direct proportion to his ever-increasing legal fees. Shortly before he had to stand for re-election in 1907, two events occurred almost simultaneously to burst his bubble.

First, a suit brought by the state of Missouri forced Standard Oil officials reluctantly to confess that they had secretly controlled Waters-Pierce since 1884. That being true, the affidavit Waters-Pierce had filed in Texas was false, and Bailey unknowingly had been assisting Standard Oil, then the *bête noire* of the trusts.

The atmosphere for such a revelation could not have been worse for Bailey. The nation, inspired by aggressive young President Theodore Roosevelt, was in a period of frenzied trust-busting. "Muckrakers" Lincoln Steffens, Ida Tarbell, and others were exposing the horrors and tragedies of monopolized oil, steel, meat-packing, tobacco, and other industries. The tide of progressives, bent upon public control of the economic giants, was rising swiftly. An irate citizenry was ready to pounce on any public official who appeared allied with one of the trusts.

In Texas, a disgruntled former employee of Waters-Pierce, one J. P. Gruett, Sr., was threatening to blow the lid off the whole Bailey-Pierce affair. Gruett, the company's longtime secretary, had been fired by Pierce after a bitter episode. Before leaving, he rifled the office files, taking with him Bailey's correspondence with Pierce, his signed notes, and other damaging documents. When Gruett's clumsy attempt to blackmail Bailey was met with scorn, word of the documents' existence spread like a prairie blaze to the senator's enemies, among them the attorney general of Texas.

In September 1906, the attorney general filed suit against the Waters-Pierce Company, seeking to cancel its charter and to collect millions of dollars in penalties for violation of the antitrust laws. Among documents that the attorney general requested be produced in court were: "various vouchers of specified number and date purporting to show payments to Joseph Weldon Bailey." Faced with direct challenge to his repeated denials of having received a fee from Waters-Pierce, Bailey for the first time admitted that he had signed two notes to Pierce—one for $3,300, another for $1,700. These, he said, were personal loans, nothing more. "Certainly the most stupid man must know that if I had felt even a sense of impropriety . . . I could and would have conducted my transactions without reducing them to paper," Bailey argued. Public sentiment was sharply and angrily divided. Bailey's friends rallied feverishly to his defense. His

enemies rejoiced in believing that they at last had proof of dis-
reputable, even dishonorable conduct. In this angry atmosphere, the 30th Legislature convened on January 8, 1907.

"Baileyism" and prohibition—new legislators were forced to
choose quickly on which side of those two overriding issues
they stood.[9] For some freshmen, the Bailey question was an especially painful introduction to hardball politics. For Rayburn,
the choice was easy. He was totally committed to defending his
childhood hero. The prohibition question also was resolved as
far as Rayburn was concerned. As the representative of one of
Texas's driest counties, his position was a foregone conclusion,
although he approached the obligation without enthusiasm.

The Legislature faced two problems regarding Bailey. First,
there was mounting demand that his financial activities be thoroughly investigated. There also was the question of re-electing
Bailey, who already had been nominated by the Democratic
party for another six-year term. By law the Legislature, which
until 1913 chose United States senators, was directed to hold its
election on January 22—before a full investigation of the charges
against Bailey could be completed. Bailey's enemies vocifer-
ously argued against re-electing him before the charges against
him could be investigated, but most legislators felt the law was
mandatory. The election proceeded on schedule.

Rayburn, representing the senator's young supporters, made
his first legislative speech as he seconded Bailey's nomination.
"No man in the Southland ever wielded a mightier influence in
standing in the face of opposition and pleading the cause of the
plain, common people," the neophyte legislator intoned, his
voice reaching out in vain hope of matching the eloquence of his
tarnished hero. "He is the peer of John Marshall in constitutional law, the equal of Daniel Webster in eloquent argument,
and the unchallenged leader of the Democrats in the United
States Senate."[10]

The House voted overwhelmingly to re-elect Bailey. One of
the handful opposing the action was a lanky young loner from
the Texas Hill Country named Sam Johnson, whose yet-to-be-
born son one day would become Rayburn's protégé in Congress.[11] The following day, in a joint session, the result was an-

nounced. Outside of Texas, the vote seemed to confirm what people already believed about the Texas Legislature. As the *Washington Post* put it: "Bailey's election was due to the debauchery and corruption of the Legislature. . . . Money was spent like water, and wine, women and song were the integral parts of the campaign."[12] In fact, Bailey's victory margin mostly reflected the fact that even his staunchest enemies felt morally obligated as Democrats to support the party's official nominee.

Bailey still faced a thorough airing of his tangled finances by the Legislature. The investigation would be conducted by a House committee and monitored by the Senate, which was determined to render its own separate verdict. Bailey's powerful friends—Rayburn siding with them on each test vote—tried every trick to kill the investigation. But public indignation was so aroused that, in the end, they also voted for it.

From January 18 to February 26, the tense and colorful hearings continued while the entire state—and politicians all over the nation—read every morsel of news about the flamboyant senator and the charges against him. A flood of witnesses came forward. Rules of evidence were flagrantly disregarded, and truth and fiction vied with each other in the lengthy testimony. Bailey, allowed to attend the hearings, spent most of this time glowering at the brilliant freshman legislator from San Antonio, William A. Cooke, who had been chosen to serve as his adversary. From the lowest to the highest walks of life, witnesses came to support or deny the allegations. Gruett, who had stolen the Bailey papers from the Waters-Pierce files, testified, as did many of the company's officials. Bailey himself took the stand with unrestrained arrogance. Before the probe ended, the Texas Senate, believing that the presiding officer had overloaded the Senate's investigating body with Bailey enemies, voted a full exoneration for Bailey. This further enraged the anti-Bailey faction, and tempers flared higher than ever.

The House committee split four to three in its findings, the majority voting for Bailey's exoneration on every count. The minority, while noting that "the evidence fails to establish any act of corruption . . . or malfeasance in office," found the senator's dealings "inconsistent with sound public policy and indiscreet." Rayburn, a background player throughout most of the episode, busily helped line up support for the crucial vote ahead. He did not participate in the angry House debate that dragged on past supper time and ended in a 70–41 vote to adopt the report completely exonerating the senator. He was quick, however, to join in a wild and noisy victory demonstration staged by the Bailey men. Amid the cheers, punctuated by the occasional blast of a hunting horn with which one crochety old member tried to restore order, a committee was sent to bring their hero in for a speech of celebration. Frustrated anti-Bailey legislators, bitter at what they viewed as a grievous miscarriage of justice, filed out of the chamber.

The speech—and the lesson it carried—was to remain deeply etched in Rayburn's memory. As the committee escorting Bailey neared the House chamber, the Windom freshman and his colleagues rushed out of the hall and hoisted the tall senator to their shoulders. Through the cheering throng, they carried him triumphantly to the Speaker's rostrum. There, pale, his voice husky, his commanding eyes narrowed and flashing fire, Bailey began: "My countrymen . . . they have drawn the line. These infidels who have waged war on me . . . have made their own graves. We are going to lay them gently away in those newly made graves. We are going to bury them face down so that the harder they scratch to get out, the deeper they will go towards their eternal resting place."

Bailey's anger and resentment—all the repressed bitterness of the long fight—rolled forth in a torrent of hate. The hour-and-fifteen-minute speech was so venomous that even his friends were shocked and sickened. Several members motioned for him to shift the direction of his speech. But he could not be quieted:

> My friends say this is a bitter speech. I intend it to be bitter. . . . I sometimes wish I might possess words of pure hate, words that would writhe and hiss like snakes, for only then could I express my opinion of the men who organized and conducted this conspiracy . . . I will not forgive them this side of the grave . . . I owe no grudges that I have not tried to pay to my enemies, and I owe no obligation that I have not tried to pay my friends. . . .

In my home I intend to put the photograph of this Legislature. Two pictures will embrace that photograph. Over
the one I am going to write, "The Roll of Honor" . . .
over the other, "The Rogue's Gallery". . . . I am going to
swear my children never to forget the one or forgive the
other . . .[13]

Joe Bailey had won his last race. Although none could have
known it then, his political star was setting. With his own words,
he had thrown away victory.[14] Throughout his long career in
politics, Rayburn never heard another speech that compared
with Bailey's tirade. That night, Rayburn's old hero left him
heartsick.

Rayburn's active role in the Bailey fight marked him as a
comer in the Legislature. House members on both sides of
the Bailey question noted their solemn-faced young colleague's
sense of loyalty to friends, his dogged determination, and his
willingness to be a team player. House leaders, rewarding his
enthusiasm and ignoring his inexperience, gave him good assignments on the committees on constitutional amendments,
state asylums, education, and common carriers.

He had particularly wanted a place on the Common Carriers
Committee, which handled all railroad legislation. The Texas
and Pacific Railroad, a part of the Jay Gould system, served his
county. Gould, far more interested in pirating the railroads than
in providing service, had allowed the property to run down. Ac-
cidents on the line were frequent; service was bad and rates exorbitant. Rayburn thought the railroads' attitude toward the
public was inexcusable. He believed the state should require
better rail service and curb the political and economic power of
the railroad trust.

The Committee on Common Carriers in 1907 had a heavy
workload. It held lengthy hearings on practically every phase of
railroad business, which Rayburn religiously attended—remembering his mother's admonitions, he made a special effort to arrive on time. He asked few questions. He felt his ignorance on
the subject, but he wanted to learn. The railroad question was
involved and intricate—one in which Texas, with more miles of

railroads within its borders than any other state, had an unusual stake. From expert witnesses, such as Texas Railroad Commissioner O. B. Colquitt, Rayburn received an education in the practices of the New York rail barons whose power reached across the continent and who, in Colquitt's words, "buy up Texas railroads as you buy your beefsteak for breakfast every morning." The impressionable freshman soon was convinced that Texas's railroad problems stemmed from the carriers' absolute domination by the big, out-of-state railways and the mysterious eastern holding companies.

The 30th Texas Legislature, moved by the progressive philosophy then stirring the nation, proved one of the most constructive in years, establishing far-reaching new regulation of the insurance and banking industries, enacting a pure food law, and creating an office to aid farmers. Not for generations would Texas see another Legislature as friendly to labor. Among its actions: a maximum fourteen-hour workday for railroad employees and an eight-hour workday for telephone operators and railroad telegraphers. Rayburn voted for each of these measures. The heart of the progressive program enacted that year consisted of statutes banning railroads from issuing free passes to public officials and reporters, curbing "special-interest lobbyists," and drastically revising the state's antitrust laws to make them the most stringent in the nation. The young Fannin County legislator heartily supported each measure.

Ranking next to the "Bailey question" as the period's most controversial issue was the "prohibition question." During the preceding fifteen years, county after county had voted to ban the sale of alcoholic beverages on a local option basis, but the prohibition forces, spearheaded by the Anti-Saloon League, Women's Christian Temperance Union, and Protestant Church, were determined to make the ban statewide. In defense of their property rights, the brewers and saloon keepers marshaled their forces. With his county favoring prohibition by a two-to-one margin, Rayburn was an announced "dry" in his views. Although a moderate on the subject, compared with some of his colleagues, he supported every piece of "dry" legislation to come before the Legislature and tried unsuccessfully to build support for a proposal of his own—a measure making it a penitentiary offense to sell intoxicating liquors in dry areas.

Racial segregation, practiced in Texas as throughout the South, was an issue only in that the moderates—including Rayburn—constantly battled the radicals to prevent them from coming down even harder on blacks. Segregation was an accepted way of life; Rayburn never questioned it. It was seldom mentioned in campaigns, but the issue was always like a time bomb.

Aside from his activities in behalf of Senator Bailey, Rayburn as a freshman legislator did not try to assert strong leadership. He introduced only four bills, none of which passed. One was notable as his first—and last—bill designed to regulate people's personal habits. At the urging of church groups and others fighting the new fad of cigarette smoking, he introduced House Bill 315, "An act to prohibit the sale, giving away or other disposal of cigarette papers in the State of Texas." The bill had a short life. Two weeks later, a House committee voted the proposal down "for the reason there is no demand for any such law in this state."

With the adjournment of the 30th Legislature, Rayburn turned to the next phase of his ambition: the study of law. In September 1907, he entered the University of Texas law school, remaining there for seven months. For once he did not immerse himself in the task at hand. He made only average grades. Already he knew that politics, not the practice of law, would be his life's work. But he regarded the knowledge of law and a license to practice it as an excellent asset in getting votes, for example, in a race for Congress.

Cutting short his stay at the university because he "ran out of money," Rayburn returned home to finish his legal training in the office of two experienced lawyers—Tom P. Steger and Preston C. Thurmond, both a generation older than himself. The following summer he went before a committee of lawyers, demonstrated enough knowledge of the law to win the panel's hesitant approval, and was licensed by the district court. Now a full-fledged lawyer, he joined with his new partners in the firm of

Steger, Thurmond, and Rayburn. Business was slow. In seven months, he brought the firm a total of $70, of which his share was less than $12. His ineptness as a practicing lawyer eventually became something of a local joke. At least one political opponent used it as a point of ridicule. The Legislature was his consuming interest, not the life of a small-town lawyer. In all the years Rayburn practiced, he never earned a fee larger than $700.

Not that Steger and Thurmond were doing badly. They managed some large accounts, among them the Santa Fe Railroad, which paid the pair a monthly retainer fee for representing the road's interests in Fannin County. As a partner, Rayburn was entitled to share those fees, and, at the end of his first month in the firm, Steger brought him a check for one-sixth of the Santa Fe payment. Rayburn declined to accept it, pointing out that as a member of the Legislature he had been called upon, and probably would be again, to vote on bills regulating the railroads. With the unhappy episode of Joe Bailey still fresh in his mind, he told Steger: "Men who represent the people should be as far removed as possible from concerns whose interests he is liable to be called to legislate on."[15]

After three years with Steger and Thurmond, Rayburn decided to break away from the firm and hang out his own shingle. His intention was to practice alone. Soon, however, he was sharing his office with another lawyer, A. P. Bolling, like himself a former schoolteacher and ex-student of Professor Mayo's East Texas Normal. Rayburn had bumped into Bolling on the street shortly after the former classmate had passed his bar exam and moved to Bonham to launch his career. Bolling had not reckoned on there being so many lawyers already trying to make a living in Fannin County. He was having trouble getting started. "I understand your situation," Rayburn told him. "Go up to my office and start practicing law." Overwhelmed by Rayburn's spur-of-the-moment offer, Bolling stammered, "I'll make any deal you want."

"No deal is necessary," said Rayburn. "You just start practicing law."[16] They shared the office until 1914, when Rayburn gave up the practice of law entirely.[17]

As the youngest man ever elected to the Legislature from Fannin County, Rayburn felt that he received a solid vote of confidence when he was elected to a second term without opposition. His own confidence was growing. With the opening of the 31st Legislature in January 1909, he began quietly concentrating on his goal of becoming Speaker of the Texas House. He continued his effort to make friends and carefully avoided, as much by nature as by design, harsh and acrimonious clashes with other members or the injection of personalities into heated debates over issues.

In the 1909 race for Speaker, Rayburn actively supported A. M. Kennedy of Waco, a staunch comrade-in-arms in the Bailey fight two years earlier. As a reward, the 27-year-old Windom legislator was made chairman of the important Committee on Banks and Banking, which would handle one of the year's important pieces of legislation—the bank deposit insurance bill. He also was allowed to remain on the Common Carriers Committee, where he could keep his hand in railroad regulation.

The banking bill gave Rayburn a chance to delve into another subject about which he knew little. The panic of 1907 had created a keen interest in proposals for a fund to insure bank deposits, and William Jennings Bryan, who had just lost his third presidential race, was championing the idea. The Texas bill failed at the regular session that year, but finally became law in a special session, thus antedating by twenty-four years the Federal Deposit Insurance program enacted in the early days of the New Deal.

The young lawmaker was getting the feel of the Legislature. He was much more active than he had been two years earlier. He had acquired a good knowledge of parliamentary procedure, was more mature, and, most important of all, was well acquainted with most of the members. He was beginning to build a reputation for persuasion and legislative skill. Writing thumbnail sketches of each House member for the *Houston Post*, the House chaplain observed: "S. T. Rayburn, Windom, has a thinking machine of his own; listens to advice and suggestions, then forgets and does as he pleases." In a lengthy article praising

Rayburn, the *Fort Worth Record* concluded: "He never has to seek a dark spot to hold a conference."[18]

Other House members were beginning to seek out Rayburn for advice and help. When Bonna Ridgway, chairman of the Committee on Education, introduced a compulsory school attendance bill, requiring children between 7 and 17 to attend school, he turned to Rayburn to manage it. The measure, pushed by progressives of the day, was highly controversial. Farmers fiercely opposed the idea, arguing that it imposed an economic hardship on them. If anybody could get it through the House, Ridgway reasoned, the former Fannin County rural school-teacher could. He was right. Rayburn ultimately maneuvered the bill through the House[19]—after persuading Ridgway to lower the maximum age limit to 14—but it died a quiet death in the Senate.

Rayburn's sense of personal loyalty, already proven in the Bailey episode, was to be tested again in the 31st Legislature as he found himself embroiled in another bitter fight in defense of a colleague. This time the dispute centered on the ethical conduct of Speaker Kennedy, his close ally in the Bailey matter. Kennedy, following a not uncommon practice of members of legislative bodies, then and now, had kept a former personal secretary on the public payroll while she was, in fact, visiting relatives in Kansas City. When Kennedy's enemies got wind of his indiscretion, they leaked it to the newspapers.

Kennedy himself was forced to lead the call for a House investigation. He insisted that he had done nothing wrong. Before the investigating committee, however, he was evasive and handled his case ineptly. Always controversial, Kennedy had won the Speakership after a bitter fight. He found, when the chips were down, that he had many determined enemies and precious few friends. The committee voted to condemn the Speaker for paying the woman $120 in state funds (he was also accused of splitting the money with her, a charge never substantiated) without requiring her to perform any services.[20] Subsequently, a resolution calling for his resignation was introduced.

Outraged that his friend had been singled out, Rayburn spoke out angrily during the nine-hour debate that raged over the demand for the Speaker's resignation. "There is not one scintilla of evidence that Kennedy is corrupt," Rayburn declared. Kennedy may have been indiscreet and unwise, but "he has not been guilty of intentional wrongdoing." His error was "in following a custom which should never have been inaugurated and should no longer be tolerated." Rayburn proposed that, instead of asking Kennedy to step down as Speaker, the House should change its rules to prevent similar incidents in the future and should demand repayment of the money.[21] The House would have none of it. "A whitewash. . . . milk and cider," yelled the anti-Kennedy forces. After burying Rayburn's proposal in an avalanche of "nays," the House then demanded Kennedy's resignation, by a vote of 70–48.

Although bitter and humiliated by his inability to help Kennedy, Rayburn again found that his courage and loyalty in standing up for a discredited friend had sent his own reputation soaring. His colleagues, even in disagreement with him, saw in him qualities of courage and character they admired. That same night, Ridgway launched a movement to elect Rayburn as Kennedy's successor. In a short time, 67 members—a bare majority—had signed a petition promising to vote for Rayburn. The *Galveston News* predicted that Rayburn would be named Speaker, the youngest in Texas history.

But it was not to be. As soon as he heard of the Rayburn boom, former Speaker Thomas B. Love, a strong prohibitionist and bitter Kennedy foe, went into action. Late into the night he cajoled and threatened legislators who had signed the endorsement. Voting for a man who sought to whitewash Kennedy would be like signing their own political death warrant, he told them. Their constituents, he insisted, would not tolerate the elevation of a man who tried to "cover up" for a disgraced colleague. The argument was effective. Several legislators told Ridgway they were frightened and wanted their names removed from the petition. The boom collapsed as quickly as it rose. Soon it was clear that Rayburn could not win. Reluctantly, he withdrew from consideration. His dogged ambition to be Speaker would have to wait.[22]

Patience, even then, was evident in Rayburn's character. He

had learned early that haste usually leads to disappointment and that, especially in politics, a young man in too much of a hurry arouses needless jealousies and resentments that often frustrate his ambition. "Wait a minute—that's just about the smartest thing anybody ever said" was one of Rayburn's favorite statements throughout his life.

Meanwhile, Rayburn's popularity at home was building. The *Bonham Daily Favorite* reprinted the laudatory article that had appeared earlier in the *Fort Worth Record*,[23] causing more local folk to begin thinking that maybe the young man from Windom might amount to something. News that he might become Fannin County's first candidate for House Speaker boosted his standing at home even more.

In 1910, Rayburn was elected without opposition to a third term, upsetting a local precedent limiting members of the Legislature to no more than two terms. He was, by this time, an accomplished politician, whose skill in his chosen life's work was beginning to match his ambition. To Rayburn, a third term meant one thing: he would have another chance to be chosen as Speaker. After moving his residence to Bonham—a better place all around for a budding political career to grow and prosper— he began contacting other representatives almost immediately to seek their support for the House Speakership. Arriving in Austin the following January, he rented two rooms in the Avenue Hotel for a campaign headquarters. In a step so far ahead of its time that it impressed his colleagues, he even installed a private telephone.

Also mounting a strong drive for the Speakership was Clarence Gilmore of Wills Point, a popular young man of considerable ability. Both candidates were prohibitionists—the burning issue around which the selection of a Speaker would turn. The antiprohibitionists, while formidable, lacked the votes to elect a Speaker who shared their view on the sale of alcoholic beverages. They had to choose between two prohibitionists; for most, Rayburn was the lesser of two evils because he was considered a moderate on the issue, while Gilmore was a rabid "dry." Rayburn also had the ardent support of Bailey's friends, both because of his staunch fight for Bailey in 1907 and because Gilmore had been lukewarm toward the senator and had on occasion voted with the anti-Bailey forces.

When the House met on January 10, 1911, to choose its Speaker, neither Rayburn nor Gilmore was confident of victory. The body had 133 members; 67 votes were needed to win. A handful of undecided members held the key. The race was excruciatingly close as the clerk read the ballots, one by one. As the balloting neared the end, the two candidates were tied, 64–64. Rayburn and Gilmore split the next two votes. Then the next vote went to Rayburn—so did the next, and the next. It appeared that Rayburn had won. The House broke into pandemonium. "Sam jumped up and gave a cotton-patch yell and then sat down real quick like he was ashamed of himself," remembered former State Representative J. Lee Aston of Sherman County.[24]

But something was wrong. The tellers counted 136 ballots—3 more than there were members eligible to vote. The tension became almost unbearable. The House voted again, each member this time walking down to the front of the hall to drop his vote in the ballot box. A collective sigh of relief echoed through the chamber when, on the second balloting, Rayburn emerged an easy winner, 70–63.[25]

Brought to the well of the House to receive the oath, the young Speaker-Elect was introduced with a oratorical flourish by Secretary of State Townsend ("a Caesar without his ambition, a Frederick without his tyranny, a Napoleon without his selfishness and a Washington without his reward").[26] In the gallery, a contingent of University of Texas students, there to cheer a former law school colleague, erupted with cheers of "Hullaballoo, Hooray, Hooray" and other old Texas yells. When the students had finished and marched triumphantly out of the hall, Rayburn delivered a short, sentimental speech. He spoke movingly of his white-haired old father and his "sainted little mother up there in Fannin County who will be so proud to receive this news of their boy." After thanking his friends for their support and forgiving his enemies, he settled in, eight days after turning 29, as the youngest Speaker in the history of the Texas House.

Rayburn's special talent as a presiding officer was quickly apparent. Quietly but firmly, he took command over the often raucous House, where haughty lobbyists roamed freely, members chatted in groups or slept in drunken stupors at their desks, and arguments often were settled with fists.[27] State Representative J. C. Hunt of Canyon wrote his constituents: "We have never had a Speaker superior to Rayburn. He is quick to rule, accurate, honest and sincere. He is fair to every member and is universally popular. You always know where to find him." His fairness and impartial approach to sensitive issues such as prohibition gained him respect from the press as well as from his colleagues. He is "a man not only of ability but of rare command of mind," said the *San Antonio Express*.

Rayburn was not only well suited for the job, but found that he thrived on the responsibility it carried. "My time as Speaker of the Texas Legislature was one of the most enjoyable experiences I ever had," he said years later. "The job had real power—that's what a man wants—but power's no good unless you have the guts to use it."[28]

Rayburn surprised many of his older colleagues by refusing to be coerced or pressured against his will. One incident—his refusal to rehire one of the stenographers involved in the Kennedy investigation two years earlier—underscored his toughness. Under House rules, the Speaker hired all employees of the body. Although employed by Kennedy, the woman had been disloyal to him, Rayburn thought, and he rejected her application for employment in the 1911 session.

As it turned out, the woman had friends among the members, and they urged Rayburn to reconsider. He was adamant. The requests soon turned to threats. "If you don't hire her now," one member told him, "I'm going to lay on your desk a petition signed by more than a majority of the House members telling you to hire her." His face a fiery red, his eyes blazing, Rayburn snapped: "You can bring me a petition signed by every member of this House, but I'm telling you that woman will not be on the payroll as long as I'm Speaker." That ended the matter.

Such incidents did not seem to dim Rayburn's standing among the members. When the regular session ended, he was warmly praised for his performance as the presiding officer and given the customary presents—a handsome Gladstone bag from the black porters, a matching suitcase from the pages, gold cuff buttons from the clerks and stenographers, and a gold pocket watch from the legislators. Rayburn was to carry the watch for the next forty years.

The watch was presented by Rayburn's old friend, ex-Speaker Kennedy, who recalled how Rayburn had stood beside him in his time of adversity. "He spoke to me words of encouragement that have been an inspiration to me from and since that very hour," Kennedy said. "His name is a synonym for the epigram 'a public office is a trust and not a private snap.'" He expressed hope that Rayburn would one day serve in the United States Congress.

Throughout the session Rayburn had watched for an opening that would permit him to run for Congress in 1912. On the last day of the regular session, the opportunity arrived. His district's incumbent congressman, Choice B. Randell, announced that he was vacating his seat in order to challenge Joe Bailey for the U.S. Senate.[29] Hoping to foreclose others from entering the race, Rayburn announced his candidacy for the U.S. House of Representatives the next day.

Rayburn's attempt to intimidate would-be opponents failed. The race soon attracted a host of challengers. From Rayburn's standpoint, the most formidable were Tom Perkins of McKinney, a popular newspaper publisher and state senator, and B. L. Jones of Sherman, a highly respected judge.

Under Texas law at the time, political nominations were settled in a single contest, with the person receiving the greatest number of votes winning the primary. The runoff primary had not yet been instituted. Five counties, all blackland farming areas similar in economic interests and almost totally white Anglo-Saxon in population, made up the Fourth Congressional District.

Rayburn was well known only in his home county. In order to win, he would have to wage a long, intensive campaign in the other counties. This called for a modern, streamlined campaign, requiring more rapid means of transportation than the horse and buggy he had used in his race for the Texas House. Splurging with most of his savings, he bought an open Model T Ford, a revolutionary vehicle just introduced by Henry Ford only three years earlier and still a rarity in north Texas.

Rayburn was not without support. "He has a habit of getting anything he goes after," noted the *Trenton Times*. Added the *Mineola Monitor*, "In the National Congress, if the voters have the wisdom to elect him, Rayburn would soon be numbered among the leaders of that distinguished body." State Representative W. T. Bagby of Hallettsville, a leader of the antiprohibitionists in the Legislature, told reporters that "while Rayburn is a prohibitionist, he should be supported by every antiprohibitionist in Texas. He is a man of judicial temperament and of analytical mind . . . without prejudices. No man has any right to question the honesty of any of his rulings." How much this antiprohibitionist endorsement helped Rayburn in the bone-dry Fourth District was open to debate, but Bagby was trying to help.

On October 29, 1911, Rayburn stated his platform, beginning with the words "I am a Democrat." He favored a tariff for revenue only, advocating "as near complete free trade as possible." He promised to support a federal income inheritance tax, recalling that, as a state legislator, he helped to pass the Texas inheritance tax law. He favored the direct election of United States senators and the abolition of the electoral college in order to elect the President and Vice-President by popular vote, but he was adamantly against the initiative and referendum, declaring that they were "too untried." He also was for the right of labor to organize, "state's rights," and better pay for rural mail carriers. He sharply condemned public officials who received "retainer fees" from corporations, and he promised legislative action against gambling in farm product "futures." "Any species of gambling is a moral wrong as well as an economic wrong," he asserted, adding: "If the people think I am the proper man to send to this high station, I will be mighty glad." [30]

Early in March, the grueling five-month campaign began. Rayburn devoted every waking hour to vote-seeking. His photograph—a serious-looking young man with high collar and dark hair beginning to recede on the left—became a familiar sight on the front pages of newspapers throughout the district.

Bonham and Fannin County, which in previous years had paid only passing notice to the ambitious young legislator, rallied proudly to his candidacy. Automobile caravans from Bonham—sometimes as many as five cars to a caravan—toured the district, with the occupants contacting their friends in other towns, handing out literature, and touting Rayburn to all they met. Bursting with local pride, the *Bonham Daily Favorite* noted: "Fannin County has never had the honor of having one of her own chosen" for Congress.

One of the less formidable contenders, Ivan B. Erwin, apparently believed Rayburn was the leading candidate, singling him out for personal attack. He condemned Rayburn for "trying to whitewash" former Speaker Kennedy. An antiprohibitionist himself, Erwin charged that Rayburn was trying to straddle the issue. He noted that in Rayburn's election as Speaker, he had received more antiprohibitionist than prohibitionist votes and later had appointed many antis to committee chairmanships— all the while pretending to be a prohibitionist. Snidely, Erwin reminded voters that Rayburn had lived in Texas only twenty-five years. Erwin's final charge—the one that nettled Rayburn the most—was that the young Speaker was a poor lawyer. "He has had no more court cases than he has had new suits of clothes," Erwin declared. "He was vaccinated as a lawyer but it didn't take."

One charge Rayburn felt he could not ignore: that as Speaker he had slighted the prohibitionists. Speaking at a gala rally at the Bonham courthouse, he explained: "My opponents charge that I named committees to suit the antiprohibitionists. . . . One thing I did do—I saw that my friends got the good appointments and those who voted against me got none. The man in politics who is not faithful to his friends is not worthy to be the scavenger of the smallest town in Texas."

Through the burning summer days the race became more and more exciting. Large sums of money—by 1912 standards— were being spent, and the eight candidates were becoming more and more aggressive. Detached observers predicted a close race, a toss-up among Rayburn, Perkins, and Jones.

Predictions of a breathtakingly close race proved true. Several times the lead shifted among Rayburn, Jones, and Perkins as election returns poured in on the night of July 27, 1912. Trickling in more slowly were the results from the many small, isolated voting boxes in the predominantly rural Fourth District. The race obviously was so tight that the winner would not be apparent for hours, perhaps days. Remembering Sam's first race for the State Legislature, the Rayburn clan braced for another long siege of tense waiting. Still, no one expected the suspense to last as long as it did. For five days, the results remained inconclusive as votes were counted. On July 31, the *Dallas Morning News* reported that Rayburn had a lead of 31 votes and predicted that it would increase. The next day, as his lead indeed expanded, Rayburn claimed victory. The official count later showed that he had been elected by a margin of 2 percent, 490 votes, over Senator Tom Perkins.[31] The once outrageously optimistic dreams of a Texas farmboy had come true. At the age of 30, he was on his way to Washington.

4

Young Congressman

Carrying the Gladstone bag and suitcase given him by his leg-islative friends, Sam Rayburn boarded the train in Bonham on February 27, 1913, bound for Washington. Always intensely close to his family, the stocky young congressman–elect was deeply moved as he waved farewell to his mother, his father, and his brothers and sisters. Traveling with Rayburn was Hal Hor-ton, a college friend who had campaigned actively for him the previous summer and had accepted an offer to be his secretary. At Bells, they were joined by another young congressman–elect, Hatton Sumners, who had made a brilliant record as prosecut-ing attorney in Dallas.

A highlight of the two-day trip, according to Horton, was his own first lesson in the difference between a congressman and a secretary. When the group went into the dining car for dinner the first night, Horton had to be seated at another table—across from an attractive young girl who, as it turned out, was a stu-dent at National Park Seminary in Washington. He soon had her telephone number and other basic information for a 26-year-old single man. "It was practically love at first sight. I thought Washington was going to be wonderful," Horton recalled.

Then I made my mistake. I took her back in the Pullman

car and introduced her to Sam and Hatton Sumners. She
was all smiles for this young congressman, and Sam waded
in and took over in a big way. She simply neglected me, and
I do not believe she ever saw me from that minute until we
reached Washington. I heard her giving Sam the same wonderful greeting she had just given me, and did he take it in
and under. She invited him to the school and I saw him
take out his little note book and write down her name and
address. I never saw her again, but I learned a new word
that day: Protocol.[1]

The slow journey gave Rayburn time to review the past and
plan the future. At 31, he felt well satisfied with the progress he
had made. Five goals, which seemed so difficult and forbidding
in the cotton patch at Flag Springs, had already been reached.
He had obtained a college education, he had "made a lawyer,"
he had been elected to the Texas Legislature, he had served as
Speaker of the Texas House—and now he was on his way to
Congress. He realized there would be a long, long period of
hard work, careful planning, and continual friend-making before he would be eligible for the final goal: to serve as Speaker of
the U.S. House of Representatives.

Rayburn was confident he could master the job of congressman. He considered his three terms as a state legislator the finest
possible background for serving in the national legislative body.
Moreover, his term as presiding officer of the Texas House gave
him a background in parliamentary law that few freshman congressmen could match and many never acquired. Joe Bailey had
told him, "You are a man of splendid ability, and if you will apply yourself with diligence to the study of public questions, you
will soon become one of the foremost men in Congress."[2]
Rayburn had already read all the books on government and politics that he could find in north Texas, including Woodrow Wilson's five-volume *History of the American People*, which he rushed
out to buy soon after he learned that the former Princeton professor would be the new President.[3]

He was determined to succeed. It was to be more than a career, it was to be his whole life. Nothing and nobody would

come between him and what he most sought in life: fame. He hoped to achieve it by staying in the good graces of the voters of the Fourth Congressional District of Texas and devoting the rest of his years to the House of Representatives, one day becoming its presiding officer. He had no thought of using his election to Congress as a stepping stone to a legal or business career, or as an interlude on his way to the governorship of Texas, the U.S. Senate, or any other office.

The young congressman's confident mood quickly vanished as he stepped off the train in icy Washington on March 1, 1913, and got his first glimpse of the magnificent Capitol dome towering over Union Station. At that moment, he felt very small and insignificant. Rayburn never forgot that initial if transitory feeling of inadequacy. A cartoon by the *Washington Evening Star*'s Cliff Barryman best captured the mood, he used to say. One panel depicted a newly elected congressman speaking to a farewell banquet in his honor. Forcefully, defiantly, he was telling his friends how he would make his views felt when he got to Washington. The other panel showed the same congressman in Washington, looking frightened, embarrassed, and small indeed beside the massive pillars of the U.S Capitol. "A new congressman always feels so unalterably lonely and useless," Rayburn often said.

Together with Texas colleague Hatton Sumners, Rayburn found lodging at the Driscoll Hotel near the Capitol, where many lawmakers made their home. One was House Democratic Whip Claude Kitchin of North Carolina, whose passion to become Speaker rivaled Rayburn's own and whom Rayburn came to regard as perhaps the most able person in debate he ever served with.[4]

The Constitution in 1913 provided that new members of Congress did not meet until the first Tuesday of December of the year in which their term began. For Rayburn, that meant an excruciatingly long delay from the time he won the Democratic nomination—tantamount to election in Texas—in July 1912. Legally, he was elected to the 63rd Congress in the general election that November. However, the new Congress was not sched-

uled to convene until December 4, 1913—thirteen months after
he was elected and sixteen months after he won the Democratic
nomination. There were, however, strong indications that the
new President, Woodrow Wilson, would call a special session of
the 63rd Congress to enact his beautifully enunciated "New
Freedom" program. In any event, the new members were to
take their oath of office on March 4, as the 62nd Congress ex-
pired, and the Democratic Speaker-Elect, James Beauchamp
"Champ" Clark of Missouri, had summoned all his party's congressmen to a caucus on March 5, the day following Wilson's
inauguration.

The installation of Woodrow Wilson as President of the United
States had made a profound emotional and political impact on
the nation. His incisive mind, his mastery of language, his flair
for the dramatic, his call to America's noblest instincts caught
the imagination of the people and moved their minds to expect
great events in days ahead. Not until decades later, under President John F. Kennedy, was a national mood evoked that approached the spirit of confidence and potential greatness summoned by Wilson. Out of the angry turmoil of the preceding
years, when the forces of government struggled to tame the ava-
rice of unbridled capitalism, the national government, under
Wilson's guidance, now promised strength and leadership as the
protector of all the people, liberator of a vigorous people's energies, and vibrant voice of a rising new nation in the world.

To southerners, Wilson's election was particularly meaningful.
For the first time since the era of James K. Polk, ending in 1849,
a true southerner would sit in the White House. The long nightmare of Reconstruction was followed by two generations of
economic oppression by northern and eastern "trusts," as the
southerners saw it; while they had supported Grover Cleveland
as the first Democrat to be elected President since the Civil War,
his hard-money policies ran counter to southern economic welfare. In Wilson, the South had a President born and educated in
Virginia, reared in Georgia, South Carolina, and North Carolina—a man who would understand and appreciate southern
ideals and aspirations.[5] To freshman Congressman Rayburn,
Wilson's inauguration seemed almost a day of deliverance, a har-

binger of great things to come for the nation, the people of the Fourth Congressional District of Texas, and himself.

March 4, 1913, was raw and crisp as Rayburn and Sumners joined other members of Congress and notables on the east steps of the Capitol to await the inaugural ceremonies.[6] The spreading throng of onlookers cheered as the lean, smiling Wilson, accompanied by huge, jovial President William Howard Taft, emerged from the Capitol's rotunda and walked slowly toward the rostrum. When he reached the rostrum, Wilson quickly saw that the police were keeping the crowd far back, leaving a wide open space in front of the speakers' stand. To the police he called: "Let the people come in." A mighty roar went up as the people surged to the foot of the rostrum.[7]

To millions of Americans, this simple, unplanned incident seemed symbolic of the promise of the "New Freedom" that "Professor" Wilson had outlined as America's way forward. In a strong, clear voice, calm and dignified, Wilson delivered one of the most moving inaugural speeches in history, speaking of his "vision of a new day":

> This is not a day of triumph; it is a day of dedication. Here muster, not the forces of party, but the forces of humanity. Men's hearts wait upon us; men's lives hang in the balance; men's hopes call upon us to say what we will do. . . . Who shall live up to the great trust? Who dares fail to try? I summon all honest men, all patriotic, all forward-looking men, to my side. God helping me, I will not fail them, if they will but counsel and sustain me.

Deeply moved, caught up in the inspiration of the moment, Rayburn felt that this was a leader he could follow with intense devotion. Yes, he could happily "counsel and sustain" such a man. Again and again, a phrase from the inaugural address ran through his mind—"justice, and only justice, shall always be our motto." That was about perfect as a rule of conduct, for freshmen congressmen and new Presidents alike, Rayburn thought.

The next day, Rayburn and his colleagues got down to serious business. Rayburn and Sumners, together with forty-three others, were temporarily assigned offices in the Maltby Building north of the Capitol until space could be made available in the House Office Building.[8] It was the least desirable home for a new congressman. "When a roll call was ordered in the House, he literally had to run to get there in time to answer his name," recalled Jack Cochran, then an aide to Congressman William L. Igoe of Missouri.[9] The regular House Office Building, vastly overcrowded, was being expanded with the addition of another floor: the size of the House of Representatives had been increased from 391 to 435 because of the nation's growth in population.

The most important problem facing the new representatives was getting assigned to at least one major committee. House committee work was particularly important, inasmuch as there normally was not time to perfect and polish a bill during debate before the full House membership. On sensitive legislation, moreover, members often were barred by procedural restrictions from even offering amendments.

Winning an assignment to a major, active committee was a crucial first step for any new member of Congress out to make a name and to be noticed by colleagues, the public, and the press. There a representative who could continue being re-elected by home constituents was certain to rise to a position of power and authority, perhaps even becoming chairman, a position of high prestige in the congressional world. The seniority system, under which the House and Senate then operated in strict obedience, would see to it that every member who hung around long enough would be rewarded. To Rayburn, the matter of an important committee assignment was particularly pressing. It was his route to the Speakership. The House leadership, almost without exception, was drawn from those who became chairmen of important committees where they proved their ability and repeatedly won the attention and approval of their colleagues.

The most powerful committee for Democrats was Ways and Means, which, in addition to having jurisdiction over all tax, tariff, and other revenue measures, served as the "committee on committees." With the advice and suggestions of party leaders, it made the actual assignments of Democrats to committee vacancies.

When Speaker Champ Clark called the caucus to order on March 5, the Democrats were in a jubilant mood. They had a whopping majority—270 Democrats to 127 Republicans and 18 members of minor parties. The new Democratic President had captured the imagination of the country, and he had summoned the 63rd Congress into special session on April 7 to carry out the party's pledge to reduce tariffs—a highly popular measure in most Democratic districts.

After hours of speech-making, the caucus filled the vacancies on the Ways and Means Committee. Over the opposition of the House leadership, which planned for him to take another important assignment, a tough-talking, hard-hitting southwest Texan named John Nance Garner was overwhelmingly elected to fill one of the vacancies. This was a real break for Rayburn. Garner, as Texas's only member on the committee, would have the decisive voice in the assignment of the six new congressmen from the Lone Star State. Rayburn was not well acquainted with Garner, who was beginning his eleventh year in the House, but they had met several times and had a multitude of mutual friends. Moreover, the fact that both had served in the Texas House and Garner had been born in northeast Texas not far from Rayburn's home provided something of a bond between them. Garner, like Rayburn a decade later, had used his influence in the State Legislature to carve out his own House district during congressional reapportionment.[10]

Rayburn, after thoroughly and cautiously canvassing all the committee possibilities, had picked the one he most wanted: Interstate and Foreign Commerce. As usual, events were working in his favor. In an effort to give all members assignments more equal in stature, the House Democratic Caucus had voted that members who held posts on any of the eleven most important committees could serve on no other committees. In the past, members with considerable seniority held a place on several important committees, thus leaving little for the new members.

Here was another instance of the "Rayburn luck" about which his brothers often teased him. They believed that he had a charmed political life and that he got all the breaks. For instance, if Texas had not passed a primary-nomination law in 1905, Rayburn in all probability could not have gone to the Legislature in 1906. It is doubtful that he could have won the nomination at the county convention, since he was not well known to the political leaders. And many believed that if Texas had used the two-primary system, where the top two candidates in the first primary meet in a runoff election, Rayburn might not have been elected in 1912, because he came from one of the smaller counties in his district.[11] Rayburn himself was a strong believer in luck. During all his years in Congress, he carried not one but two lucky pieces—a 1798 Spanish silver dollar and a St. Christopher's medal.

As a result of the caucus action, William R. Smith of Texas gave up his seat on the Committee on Interstate and Foreign Commerce to retain the chairmanship of the Committee on Arid and Irrigated Lands, which was particularly important to his district. Rayburn was determined to take Smith's place on Interstate and Foreign Commerce.

The committee was one of the most important and respected in the House. Its jurisdiction was vast, taking in all legislation concerned with commerce and trade, railroads, pipelines, dams and navigable streams, food and drug regulation, exports, the merchant marine, the Interstate Commerce Commission, light houses, the Panama Canal (then under construction), and public health. In political circles, it was considered the fourth most powerful committee in the House behind Rules, Ways and Means, and Appropriations. In 1913, the committee enjoyed unusual prestige. Its members had earned a high reputation for doing outstanding legislative work. Members worked with a minimum of partisanship, cooperating regardless of party affiliation to handle a tremendous volume of legislation with efficiency, caution, and sincerity. To serve on the committee in that era was a distinct honor.

Rayburn felt particularly well equipped for the assignment. In the Texas House, he had served on the Common Carriers Committee for four years—a committee on the state level closely equivalent in jurisdiction to the House Interstate and Foreign

Commerce Committee on the national level. He had a thorough, although not expert, knowledge of the enormous, vexing railroad problem, and he had some specific ideas as to how the railroads should be revamped and reformed.

It was fairly certain that one of the six new congressmen from Texas would fill the vacancy on Interstate and Foreign Commerce, because the state, with about one-fifth of the nation's total railway mileage, was entitled to a seat by common agreement and tradition. Fresh from having served as Speaker of the Texas House, Rayburn had the greatest prestige among the six Texas newcomers. He was confident and determined as he stated his case to Garner, citing his reasons for wanting the committee slot and his qualifications for it. Readily agreeing that Rayburn should have the assignment, Garner promised to help. On June 3, Rayburn's assignment was announced.

Named just ahead of Rayburn to the same committee—and outranking him—was a loquacious, fun-loving freshman from Kentucky, Alben Barkley. Barkley went on the committee before Rayburn because Kentucky was admitted to the Union before Texas and because his name began with a *B* instead of an *R*. He retained his seniority over the Texan until he moved to the Senate in 1926. In later years Barkley frequently claimed that he was the best friend Rayburn ever had. "If I hadn't decided to go to the Senate, Sam never would have been committee chairman and could never have been elected Speaker," he asserted. Both were popular members of the committee. "Although Barkley stood a notch above Sam in committee seniority, we Democrats considered them rivals," former Congressman, later Senator, Tom Connally of Texas recalled. "Each was looking for promotion in committee influence, but the odds were stacked against Barkley because William C. Adamson, the ranking Democrat there, installed Rayburn as his favorite and pushed him ahead."[12]

Plunging eagerly into his new assignment, Rayburn made a special effort to befriend Chairman Adamson, a kindly, conscientious veteran legislator from Georgia, for whom the committee and its work were the glory of his life. Adamson, an intelligent but unpolished country lawyer, liked Rayburn immediately. He found the freshman well ordered, well groomed, ambitious, and confident without being bumptious.[13] Rayburn made it clear to his chairman that he had come to work and that he would take any and all assignments. He intended to be a work horse, and any chore that other members might not want, he would welcome. Adamson was delighted.[14]

Adhering firmly to his rule of punctuality, Rayburn always appeared at the committee meetings on time. "I figured it was just like going to school at Flag Springs," he later explained. "You were supposed to be there at 8 o'clock or you got a licking."[15] Often he and the chairman were the only ones present, and they had to wait for other members to straggle in. Deeply impressed, the upright Georgian began to take a fatherly interest in the enthusiastic Texan. Adamson decided that this was somebody going a long way, somebody worthy of his time and help. The two legislators spent many hours together, the elder teaching the younger the ins and outs of committee work.

Relations between Congress and the White House were relaxed in those first months of the new administration. President Wilson had the time and desire to keep up with the most minute details of the legislative operation. Garner, then serving informally as House Democratic whip, was the highest-ranking House leader on good terms with the President and visited him secretly every week.[16] Adamson, as chairman of a major committee and an ardent Wilsonian, was particularly welcome in the Oval Office. Often he would call on Wilson informally at night to talk about legislation and political problems. Sometimes he asked his new young friend from Texas to accompany him. Rayburn remembered those visits half a century later: "Wilson was a cold snake. No, snake's not the word—cold fish. He'd look at you cold and steady through those thick glasses. From his eye to his jaw he had the longest face I ever saw. He was horse faced. He loved people in the mass, but I don't think he gave a damn about them as individuals."[17]

The work of every committee includes much drudgery, particularly the preparation of formal reports on a mass of non-controversial measures. From the first, Rayburn was given more than his share of this type of work. Recognizing his knowledge of the railroad problem, Adamson appointed Rayburn to sub-committees investigating railroad safety and the handling of freight. When a subcommittee was created to investigate the entire cotton industry—which was the major livelihood of Rayburn's district—Adamson named him to its membership. Years later, Rayburn invariably advised new members of Congress, "Get to know your committee chairman, let him know you want to work and help him to do a good job of running the committee so it can make a record, and he'll help you with your problems."

In committee hearings, Rayburn asked few questions during the early years. In contrast, Alben Barkley was from the start an eager interrogator of committee witnesses. When he did speak, Rayburn's questions or statements were terse and incisive, designed to illuminate an obscure point. "I didn't know enough to talk much," he explained years later.

In the Texas Legislature his attendance record had been almost perfect, and in Congress and on the committee he maintained the same habit of never missing a meeting unless it was absolutely unavoidable. Advising new members through the years, one of his stock phrases came to be: "When Congress is in session, your place is here; when Congress is not in session, your place is in your district." He assiduously followed that advice himself throughout his career. His behavior on the committee did not miss the eagle eye of John Garner. The highly popular, rugged, tough-minded Garner intended to be Speaker of the House himself, and he worked at politics with a care and constancy seldom seen even in Congress. He made a particular effort to seek out, encourage, and help young men who appeared to him to show promise of leadership. If he helped them to develop, they probably would back him as trusted lieutenants in the fights ahead.

Fellow Texan Tom Connally once tried to pinpoint the source of Garner's popularity. In later years, Garner often appeared disheveled, coarse, and out of place in an increasingly sophisticated America. But in his prime, Connally remembered, the wiry, frontier lawyer from Uvalde "had a sort of dash about him." He "walked rapidly, had manly gestures and boasted a reputation as a good businessman and a sure-winner poker player. Although some members complained that he fought their logrolling, others liked to quote his remark, 'Every time one of those Yankees gets a ham, I'm going to do my best to get a hog.'"[18]

Garner, with a critical eye, quickly sized up Rayburn as someone who acted "kind of timid"—perhaps too reserved to get ahead in the rough-and-tumble world of national politics.[19] Still, they instinctively liked each other and began to spend more and more time together. They shared many traits: both were painfully truthful, even blunt; equally ambitious, they understood and respected each other's desire to advance; both found a genuine satisfaction in grappling with the problems of a great nation. The credo of the southwestern frontier was their code—tell the truth, let your word be your bond, love your country, stand by your friends. Both were dogged and relentless fighters when engaged in a contest. Garner, with his pet phrase "you've got to bloody your knuckles," was the rougher of the two. And he was more colorful and outspoken than Rayburn, whose method was more one of everlasting persistence and determination that finally prevailed. A Texas colleague remembered: "Sam was a close friend of Garner's, but Garner held Rayburn and everyone else at a distance. He was anxious not to appear to have favorites or pets. Garner loved to test the mettle of men, usually by jumping on them. He tried to make them mad to see how they would react, but he always went to bat for Texans and others he believed in."[20] At first, Rayburn was in awe of Garner. He had never known anyone quite like him. "Most radical man I ever met in Congress," he would tell friends. Then, rapidly clinching his fist, he would add: "He's got a steel-trap mind that can grab a fact."[21]

"Jack" Garner was a master of the art of politics; while Rayburn in 1913 was far from an amateur, there was much the older man could teach, and the young congressman was eager to learn. Garner summed up his views of how to be a successful congressman in three inflexible rules: 1. Always take care of the needs of your home district; 2. Keep quiet until you know what you're talking about; and 3. Become the foremost authority in the House, through work and study, in one particular field of legislation.[22] "You can't know everything well. Learn one subject thoroughly and find out as much as you can about the others. Get useful information for the members of this House when you are going to speak," Garner insisted. "You can't spend your time better. It's finer recreation than fishing. There is nothing more useful or more thrilling than facts. Your colleagues here want information and will listen to a man who has knowledge of his subject. They ought not to have to give ear time to anyone else."[23]

Judging Garner to be "a man of rare intelligence and industry,"[24] Rayburn listened, agreed, and followed the counsel of his rough-and-ready colleague. The two became fast friends, a friendship bolstered by the warm sentimental affection Garner's dedicated wife, Ettie, and the young man felt for each other. Once Garner, then Vice-President, told an audience in Rayburn's district: "If I was jealous of my wife, I'd have shot Sam years ago."[25] The warm devotion between Ettie Garner and her husband's ambitious protégé lasted until her death.

Rayburn's first months in Congress were tremendously satisfying to him. He was in his element, living the life for which he had been preparing all these years. One old-timer recalled that in the early years he often saw the eager freshman bounding up the Capitol steps three at a time.

There was only one disagreeable aspect to the job. In 1913, the Democratic party had been out of power for sixteen years. Now Democrats were hungry and greedy for federal jobs —as postmasters, rural mail carriers, clerks, executives, and the rest. By the tens of thousands, applicants beleaguered Democratic members of Congress to get on the government payroll. Most adamantly insisted that jobs were available, if only their representative would help them. The bureaucracy then was relatively small, and most appointments were made strictly on the basis of politics. A system for hiring most federal workers on the basis of nonpartisan examinations was still in the future. The representatives had to choose among the vehement, insistent applicants, and while they might receive some political gratitude from the one selected, the dozen or so frustrated losers often became furious and dedicated political enemies. In Rayburn's case, some of the scars inflicted in the patronage scramble of 1913 lasted for more than forty years.

Seven weeks after arriving in Washington, Rayburn felt largely at home while awaiting his committee assignment. His self-confidence was soaring. He always was realistic in his self-appraisal; when he thought he had the capacity to do a certain thing, he never pretended otherwise, either to himself or to others. His ambition to be Speaker, for example, was never concealed from his colleagues. "From the beginning, Sam let everyone know he intended to be Speaker," recalled former Congressman Marvin Jones. "This rubbed some people wrong, but the fact that he worked very hard and did not ask special favors helped him. His personality clashed with people like Tom Connally, but not his ambition."[26] Connally and others in the Texas delegation often joked about their colleague's practice of "wearing his ambition on his sleeve,"[27] mainly because they thought he nurtured a dream far beyond his reach.

Rayburn's sense of awe on arriving in the nation's capital had vanished by April when he made his first speech to members of the Texas Society of Washington. He was not overly impressed with what he had seen so far, he told fellow Texans. Congress was not as efficient as the Texas Legislature. Why, "Texas alone could supply enough able men to fill all the important posts in this government and make an improvement over what we have now," he brashly declared.[28]

When Congress assembled in special session on April 8, its first order of business was a subject in which Rayburn had a passionate interest and on which he had firm views that remained unaltered throughout his life—the tariff.

Wilson electrified the Congress by appearing in person to address a joint session, the first President to do so since John Adams's final appearance on November 22, 1800. The following day, Wilson went to the Senate cloakroom to confer informally with the Senate Finance Committee, which no President since Abraham Lincoln had done.

The House Ways and Means Committee quickly reported the Underwood tariff bill, carrying out the Democratic party platform pledge by making the first general tariff reduction since 1857. To replace the revenues lost through tariff reductions, the Democrats proposed to levy the first constitutional income tax in the nation's history. The 15th Amendment, authorizing such a tax, had just been added to the Constitution. Tall, sagacious Congressman Cordell Hull of Tennessee offered the income tax proposal, which would levy a graduated income tax on individuals and corporations. It was designed to yield $70 million the first year. Rates, by standards of later years, were remarkably low, beginning for individuals at 1 percent on income above $4,000. A person with a net income of $10,000 would pay a tax of $60.

Shortly after 8 o'clock on the night of May 6, the stocky, balding freshman congressman from north Texas rose to make his maiden speech, a fervent plea in behalf of the graduated income tax. With great care he had written the speech in longhand, then had it typed and retyped as he struggled for the precise words that would express his views while striking just the right tone. Half-heartedly he recognized the House custom that a new member should remain silent for many months:

> I should have regard to some extent for the long-established custom of this House . . . that discussions of questions shall be left in the main to the more mature members from the standpoint of service. On the other hand I feel that as a representative and commissioned spokesman of more than 200,000 citizens of the Fourth Congressional District of Texas, I should be allowed to break . . . whatever of this custom remains and speak my sentiments on this floor and refuse to be relegated to that lockjawed ostracism to some extent typical of the dead past.

Scornfully, he attacked the tariff policies of the Republican party: "This country has carried the prohibitive tariff of Republicanism until the American consumer is stooped and weary of his all-too-heavy load. They have turned them out of the high places of power and called the party of Jefferson and Jackson again to power." He contrasted the Republican tariff policy with that now proposed by the Democratic leadership, pointing out the exact effect it would have upon those dwelling on farms. With fervor in his voice, he labeled the Republican tariff "the most indefensible system the world has ever known, a tariff levied not for revenue but for protection. . . . This eternal Republican solicitation for the American manufacturer makes me tired . . ."

After outlining his own free-trade views, he began closing the twenty-minute oration—designed, some suspected, more for the voters back in Texas than for his listeners. "I came to this body a few weeks ago with childlike enthusiasm and confidence. It has always been my ambition since childhood to live such a life that one day my fellow citizens would call me to membership in this . . . greatest lawmaking body in the world. They have done this." His voice rising, he moved toward the finale:

> It is now my sole purpose here to enact such wise and just laws that our common country will . . . be a happier and a more prosperous country.
>
> I have always dreamed of a country which I believe this should and will be . . . one in which the citizenship is an educated and patriotic people, not swayed by passion and prejudice, and a country that shall know no East, no West, no South, no North, but inhabited by a people liberty-loving, patriotic, happy and prosperous, with its lawmakers having no other purpose than to write such just laws as shall in the years to come be of service to humankind yet unborn.[29]

Perhaps few in the House chamber that night paid more than courteous attention to the earnest first effort. One close listener was Cordell Hull, the zealous advocate of lower tariffs all his life, who one day was to father the policy of reciprocal trade treaties. Hull saw in the serious newcomer a staunch new ally. A friendship that was to become a deep bond and last for more than a third of a century began that night. Rayburn became, in Raymond Moley's words, "a darling of Cordell Hull."[30]

Woodrow Wilson's first year as President saw two major planks in the 1912 Democratic platform written into law—the Underwood tariff and the creation of the Federal Reserve System to provide a more flexible financial structure for the nation. Rayburn enthusiastically supported both measures.

On January 20, 1914, the dynamic President appeared before Congress to ask enactment of his antitrust program to bring under governmental control those corporations whose conduct he considered injurious to the national welfare. As governor of New Jersey, he had pushed through a similar program of seven laws called "the Seven Sisters." After much discussion between the President and congressional leaders, three bills were outlined to carry out the administration's wishes. The first, historically known as the Clayton Antitrust Act, was designed to close loopholes and strengthen the Sherman Antitrust Act of 1890. The other two bills came within the jurisdiction of the House Interstate and Foreign Commerce Committee. One involved the creation of a federal regulatory agency to police unethical business practices. As finally written, this law created the Federal Trade Commission. Chairman Adamson named Rayburn to the subcommittee that would work out the exact form of this commission. It was the freshman legislator's first major assignment and, in his eyes, his first mark of recognition. The other bill—"the capstone of Wilson's program," according to Ray Stannard Baker, Wilson's official biographer—gave the Interstate Commerce Commission the power to review and approve all stocks and bonds of railroads and other common carriers before they were issued.[31]

Rayburn took an exceptional interest in this proposal. Now he was on familiar ground. In 1893, Texas had passed such a law, the most rigid in the nation, to keep railroads from issuing worthless or overvalued securities. While the railroads and many experts considered the law too harsh and insisted that it hampered railway expansion and improvements, all agreed that it achieved its primary purpose—the prevention of overcapitalization of railroads.

The financing of American railroads from their beginning had been a notorious scandal out of which many great fortunes

were built. Free from restraining laws, speculators and financiers
manipulated railroads like toys, selling billions upon billions of
dollars' worth of overvalued stocks and bonds to the investing
public. Bankruptcy followed bankruptcy, scandal piled on top
of scandal, as the manipulations continued in railroad after railroad. Public fury rose to its peak with the exposure of the New
Haven and Hartford Railroad manipulations, in which J. P. Morgan was a leading figure. Some authorities estimated that fully a
fourth of railway securities—worth about $4 billion—in the
public's hands were "watered." Because more than half of these
securities were owned by banks, savings institutions, insurance
companies, and educational institutions, the effects were felt
across the land. Investors and railroad customers joined public
officials in demanding action.

The idea of having the ICC pass upon all new securities prior
to issuance struck many as too radical. Conservatives argued
that a government agency should not be entrusted with such
power, while many progressives feared that ICC approval of
railroad securities would amount to a government guarantee of
their validity and value.[32] The House Interstate and Foreign
Commerce Committee held exhaustive hearings. The railroads,
represented by their lobbyist—skillful Alfred P. Thom—dared
not openly oppose the measure, but sought by indirection to
delay or stop its passage. Rayburn followed the proceedings
with keen interest, although he let others do the questioning of
witnesses. Sensitive to his deficiencies in education and congressional experience, he was reluctant to risk embarrassment in
trying to match wits with the articulate, often brilliant witnesses
who paraded before the committee. He showed no hesitancy,
however, to speak up in informal, after-hours discussions with
Chairman Adamson and other senior members of the committee. Behind closed doors, he impressed colleagues with his
grasp of the issue, drawn from Texas's experience in drafting
similar legislation at the state level.

When the hearings were completed, the committee decided
to propose a new bill embodying its views. Adamson, uncertain
about the measure's effect on states' rights, was unwilling to
have his name attached to it. Instead, he invited Rayburn to be

the author. The freshman eagerly accepted. Rarely in the history of Congress had a first-termer had his name put on a major piece of legislation. Now, one year after arriving in Washington, the "capstone" of the Wilson antitrust program was to be called the "Rayburn bill."

Burning with enthusiasm, working day and night, Rayburn sought to marshal every conceivable argument for his bill. In substance, it had two main provisions: 1. the Interstate Commerce Commission must approve all issues of railroad stocks and bonds before they were offered for sale to the public; and 2. no individual would be allowed to serve as an officer or director of more than one railroad—an attack on the evil of interlocking directorates.

Cordell Hull was presiding over the House the night of June 2, 1914, when Chairman Adamson introduced Rayburn as the bill's manager during debate. Although a young member, Adamson declared, "the author of the bill . . . is old in wisdom and accomplishment."[33] For an hour and ten minutes, the young Texan explained and argued for his bill. His quick, surefooted answers to a barrage of technical questions from House members demonstrated that he had learned his subject thoroughly. He was heeding John Garner's advice: keep quiet until you know what you're talking about, study your subject, give the members information they can use.[34]

"What we are driving at in this bill," Rayburn emphasized, "is to have a house-cleaning among the railroads of this country that they may not overload themselves with unnecessary and spurious securities." In detail he discussed the railway scandals that had shocked the public. "Bad management on the part of the railway officials" was to blame, he said. "I believe that guilt is personal, and I believe that punishment should be personal." Simply fining a corporation and allowing malefactors to go free was not enough. Under his bill, he pointed out, individual violators could be singled out for fine and imprisonment. He denied charges then widespread that the Wilson administration and the Democratic party were hostile to business, but he concluded: "We intend to do simple justice to business, and we are determined that business shall deal justly with the people. No honest man will ask more, and no man, be he honest or otherwise, may expect less." Democrats applauded thunderously. His speech, firm and resolute, had been interrupted by applause five times. Members agreed it was a notable performance, particularly for a freshman. Garner—though personally opposed to the bill—nodded approvingly. The young congressman had won his spurs.

After ten hours of debate, stretching over three days, the House on June 5 passed the Rayburn bill by an overwhelming margin, 325–12. Only 4 Democrats voted against the bill, including Garner, who thought the measure would undercut Texas's own stronger railroad securities law. The easy House victory was misleading, however. Across the Capitol in the Senate Committee on Interstate Commerce, the bill was being subjected to scorching opposition.[35] Thoroughly alarmed, some railroad executives exchanged their covert opposition for bristling warnings of ruin if the bill became law. Union Pacific President Robert S. Lovett predicted bankruptcy for "many now solvent railroads" if the bill passed. Another executive declared that the ban on interlocking directorates would "have the effect of removing practically every railroad president in the United States." Edward S. Jouett, general counsel of the Louisville and Nashville Railroad, rumbled that "not even in the palmiest days of Venice, nor in Russia, was such unrestricted authority given as it is proposed to give the [Interstate Commerce] Commission and its agents in this bill."

Far more serious to the bill's future, however, was a shift in the views of Louis Dembitz Brandeis, the brilliant Boston lawyer whose dogged probing of the New Haven's affairs eventually unearthed that fantastic scandal. Brandeis at the time was Wilson's most influential adviser on economic policy. A political scientist rather than an economist, the President listened with unusual attentiveness to the persuasive "people's lawyer" on all economic proposals. When he appeared before the House committee, Brandeis favored the principles of the Rayburn bill, but with more thought he came to share the fear of many fellow progressives that ICC approval of the securities would amount to a government guarantee of their soundness. The ICC already had more work than it could handle, and adding the burden of reviewing approximately 1,000 securities issues a year might well bog down its work hopelessly.[36]

Working with Pennsylvania Railroad President Daniel Willard and others, Brandeis proposed as a substitute that the law simply prescribe and limit the purposes for which new securities could be issued. The Senate committee disregarded Brandeis's views and approved the Rayburn bill in slightly amended form. Brandeis carried his argument to the President in person. Still buoyed by his first major success, Rayburn did not sense the trouble his bill was in. His mood soared even more with the arrival of this personal note of thanks from the President himself:

My Dear Mr. Rayburn:

We have all looked on with admiration and genuine appreciation as your stock and bond bill has been put through the House. It seems to me you deserve a great deal of praise for your part in the matter, and I want to make my humble contribution to the congratulations which I am sure you must be receiving.

Cordially and sincerely yours,
Woodrow Wilson

Rayburn was exceedingly proud of the Wilson note and, in his campaign for re-election in 1914, reminded voters at every opportunity that it was extremely rare, if not unprecedented, for a freshman House member to be honored with a personal letter of thanks from the President of the United States. The letter—the centerpiece of his campaign—was reprinted in full on the back of the wallet-size campaign cards that his supporters handed out by the thousands.[37]

Engrossed in the battle over his bill, Rayburn had intended to remain in Washington as long as possible while his friends and family campaigned in his behalf. For a while he thought he would have no opponent in the Democratic primary; but, ultimately, State Senator Tom Perkins, who had come within 500 votes of victory against Rayburn two years earlier, decided to try again.

In June, Rayburn abruptly put aside his work on the railway stock and bond bill and rushed home to Bonham—but not
to campaign. His brother Abner, youngest of the Rayburn
children, born four years after the family moved to Texas, was
gravely ill.

Sam always took special delight in his youngest brother and
through the years grew increasingly attached to the boy. As a
young man, "Ab" was one of the handsomest youths in north
Texas. His fine, wavy brown hair, chiseled features, and strong
physique were set off by "the most beautiful eyes I ever saw,"
Rayburn would recall years later. The Rayburns all agreed that
friendly, outgoing Ab was by far the "best politician in the family." He was Sam's special joy. The youthful lawmaker remembered the hours spent with his youngest brother as among the
happiest of his life. As a state legislator, Sam had gotten Ab a
one-year job as a House page and lately had looked forward to
having Ab one day live and work with him in Washington.
When his secretary, Hal Horton, announced he was taking a
higher-paying job in the executive branch, Rayburn immediately thought of his youngest brother as a replacement.

Early in the summer of 1914, Ab was suddenly stricken with
typhoid fever, a disease that doctors of the day were almost
powerless to treat. As the weeks passed, the young man grew
weaker and weaker until, in July, he died. To Sam, at Ab's bedside almost constantly in his final weeks, "it was the greatest
personal blow I have ever had, or ever expect." In a letter to
sister Kate, he poured out his grief: "I loved him almost too
well, and the awfulness of his death bears harder on me each
day. . . . His commanding personality . . . when ripened into
the all-commanding personality that settled manhood, would
have made him irresistible anywhere. He could have made my
speeches for me on the stump, his judgment on matters political
and otherwise I would have taken without question, and in my
absence, he could have been my other self."[38] The death two
years later of his father, who never recovered from the shock of
Ab's death, affected him far less profoundly.

Meanwhile, the election drew nearer and meaner. Perkins was
giving Rayburn no quarter as he pelted the freshman lawmaker

with a string of blistering charges, the most serious of which was that Rayburn had opposed prohibition efforts. Perkins also told Gordonville voters that, while Rayburn had suspended all campaign activity to be at Ab's bedside, his brothers were busy campaigning throughout the district, which was untrue.[39] On the day Ab was buried, phony circulars were passed around the Fourth District, signed by a group calling itself the "Anti-Submission Club of Texas." The leaflets urged voters to support a list of candidates, including Rayburn, who were, by implication, against prohibition legislation. Rayburn felt such potentially damaging material could not be ignored and issued a terse response: "Today as I returned from his [Ab's] grave, this base circular was handed to me . . . I appeal to the fair-minded voters of the Fourth Congressional District in the name of truth, clean politics and common decency to repudiate such villainous campaign methods."[40] Two days later, Rayburn won his crucial first re-election bid, sweeping all five counties to defeat the pesky Perkins by a comfortable 10,000 votes.

Still grieving over Ab, Rayburn returned to Washington soon after the election and plunged feverishly back into his work. Try as he might, he could not dispel the dark mood that enveloped him. Such moods, marked by severe loneliness, were to return from time to time.[41] In the weeks following, he spent many hours alone in thought as he tried to sort out—maybe for the first time—life's meaning and his own truest values. His family, always important to him, now loomed even more vital. He thought constantly of his aging mother and father and, though he was already building a comfortable new home for them on Bonham's outskirts with money saved from his first year's salary, wondered how he could do more.[42] Earlier, he had penned a long, gushing letter to his mother in which he described his "tender love of you and dear old daddy" and confessed that "the burning desire to be worthy to be your son have [sic] been the main factor in making whatever I am and has kept me from straying many times." Now, in a long, rambling outpouring of grief over the loss of Abner, he bared more of his innermost thoughts to his mother and father: "I knew he once loved me better than anybody on earth save you two but you know I am of

such a nature that I cannot believe many folks have a very tender
devotion for me and when I find one who I know has, they can
have my all."[43] Such weighty matters as love, life, and death still
flooded his thoughts in late August as he wrote to Lucinda and
Medibel:

> My dear sweet sisters,
> I have been intending to write you both ever since I came
> back here and express to you both the fullness of my love
> for you and the thankfulness I feel each day that I have been
> blest with such sisters. Your devotion to your family is the
> most beautiful thing in the world. Your ministry to our
> baby in his fatal sickness was sublime and showed to me
> what I had to live for—such loved ones.
> Now, you have another and that is our dear old father and
> mother. They are getting very old and need all the warmth
> of love and affection that can possibly be given. I know you
> will care for them tenderly and my great regret is that I
> cannot be there with them and you, but my life has been
> thrown in a path that leads away for the present . . . [44]

The atmosphere in Washington—and the world—had changed
dramatically in the few weeks Rayburn had been away. A severe
decline in the economy had begun during the summer and was
being eyed with increasing alarm at 1600 Pennsylvania Avenue.
In retrospect, this unfavorable trend was part of a worldwide
economic recession brought on by threats of war arising from
the turbulent Balkan states. Opponents of the Wilson administration blamed it, however, on the Underwood tariff law, the
new income tax, and the antitrust program. Whistling in the
dark, Wilson on June 25 told a group of Virginia editors that
the United States was on the verge of the "greatest boom in history when the antitrust program was complete." That very day
the H. B. Claflin Company, the largest wholesale dry goods concern in the nation, went into receivership.

Wilson, his eyes on the November congressional elections, decided the time had come to court big business.[45] In a series of
conciliatory gestures, he sought to reverse the antagonistic trend

against his administration. The *Nation* commented acidly: "Big business might be excused for falling into the hackneyed 'This is so sudden' in the presence of the amorous advances which President Wilson made to it . . . it is so long since anybody thought of it as a beloved object. And now the very master of ceremonies comes up to make proposals of marriage."[46]

At ten minutes to eleven on June 28, an 18-year-old Serbian student in far-off Sarajevo fired three shots at Austria-Hungary's heir-apparent, Archduke Franz Ferdinand, killing him and his wife. The day the Senate committee favorably reported the Rayburn bill, aging Emperor Franz Joseph in Vienna sent a humiliating ultimatum to little Serbia, Russia moved to Serbia's support, and, as Earl Grey, Britain's foreign minister, noted, "lights started going down" all over Europe.

American financial circles reacted quickly. European investors had furnished much of the capital for the nation's expansion in preceding decades and held billions of dollars' worth of American stocks and bonds. If war came, most of these securities would be dumped on the market to obtain money with which to finance the European war. In the case of American railroads, between $3 billion and $5 billion in railroad securities was held by Europeans. A sudden sale of these investments would throw the already troubled railroads into financial panic.

On July 28, Austria-Hungary declared war on Serbia. Two days later, the New York Stock Exchange, along with nearly every other exchange and curb market in the United States, was closed. During the first few days of August, all of Europe was engulfed in what was to become the greatest war then known to history. The spreading conflict left the American economy profoundly shocked. Foreign trade came to a standstill; the markets for farm products, particularly cotton, dwindled; railroad freight traffic fell off sharply. The railroads faced bankruptcy. On August 1, 1914, more than half a billion dollars' worth of railway securities were already in default, and another half billion were to come due before the end of the year. With the drying up of the European investment markets, the drop in freight traffic, and general economic uncertainties, the outlook for the sale of railroad securities was dismal.

Opponents of the Rayburn bill, making the most of their opportunity, intensified their lobbying efforts. By August 28, the President had decided not to press for its enactment at that session of Congress. "It was the first casualty, due to the war, in Wilson's comprehensive programme of domestic reforms," wrote Ray Stannard Baker.[47] With great reluctance Rayburn agreed to a temporary postponement, but he let it be known that he had not abandoned the cause and, as soon as world conditions eased, he would resume the fight for his bill.

When the 64th Congress convened on December 6, 1915, Rayburn again introduced his measure. This time he had been outsmarted by the bill's enemies. To stall further railroad regulatory legislation, lobbyist Thom and the railroad executives conceived a plan to have an extended, thorough inquiry into all phases of the transportation problem, ostensibly to determine what needed to be done to make the transport system ready for any war emergency. President Wilson, in his message to the new Congress, threw his weight behind the inquiry. In the Senate, Francis G. Newlands, chairman of the Interstate Commerce Committee, introduced a resolution creating such a committee, and it quickly passed.[48]

Rayburn, seeing the tactic as a clever plot to block all remedial railway legislation, went to work. He enlisted the support of his own committee, which, after a brief hearing and in defiance of the White House, reported the Rayburn bill favorably. Wilson countered by persuading the Rules Committee to keep the bill from reaching the House floor for debate. This obstacle Rayburn could not overcome. He tried a longshot—to go around the Rules Committee and take up the bill by unanimous consent of the House. Again and again he tried this stratagem, to no avail. Thwarted at every turn by the unseen hand of the White House, he decided on direct action.

His only hope, he decided, was to face Wilson directly: perhaps the President could be persuaded that the bill was necessary after all. Rayburn asked Chairman Adamson to intervene for him in arranging an appointment, which was granted.[49] Late in the afternoon of May 1, 1916, Rayburn walked nervously into the Oval Office. Wilson, seeming "as tall as a telephone pole," listened to his arguments, then coldly declared that the bill would have to wait until after the war. "There will be a lot of loose money floating around then," Rayburn argued. "That's when you need a law like this."

"You may be right, Mr. Rayburn," said the President, his irritation rising, "but we're already accused of being antibusiness. Your bill will have to wait. You must remember that we have an election we must win." He said it again: "We have an election to win." When he repeated the line a third time, Rayburn stood up. "I'm sorry I can't agree with you, Mr. President, but I'm going to keep on trying to get my bill passed," he said. "It's getting on toward your supper time, and I've kept you too long." Wilson's eyes flashed angrily as he rose from his chair and hastily escorted the young congressman to the door.

The session, lasting barely five minutes, was over. What the Scotch-Irish congressman didn't understand at the time was that the Scotch-Irish President did not take kindly to such insolence. Others, closer to the enigmatic President, knew that, as historian Arthur S. Link put it, "Wilson's mind could not work under opposition, for he felt all opposition to be merely irritation."[50] It was to be the last face-to-face meeting between the two men— although Wilson was not content to let it go at that. He would remember this brash upstart as someone he would just as soon not have nipping at his heels. "It makes me quiver to think how impudent I was to the President," Rayburn later recalled. "I should have laid the bill aside as he requested."[51]

Rayburn would have reason to remember his last face-to-face meeting with President Wilson when, in June, he returned to Bonham to campaign for re-election. With war clouds gathering and Congress planning to remain in session through the summer, he postponed leaving Washington as long as possible. He continued to resist even when friends wrote in alarm over political developments in northeast Texas and urged him to "come home as soon as you can." The Democrats have only a 22-vote majority, he reminded them. "If you think for a moment, you will know that it will be absolutely suicidal for me to leave here now, or any time soon."[52] Actually, he was hearing

conflicting advice. "It is my judgment that it will not be necessary for you to come home at all," wrote his brother-in-law,
W. A. Thomas, whose faulty advice on such matters Rayburn
soon came to recognize and ignore.[53]

He faced two challengers—Dr. T. W. Wiley, a political novice,
and Andrew Randell, a formidable opponent indeed. Randell, a
recent Princeton graduate, was the son of former six-term Congressman Choice B. Randell, whose decision four years earlier
to vacate his House seat in order to run for the Senate had given
Rayburn his route to Congress. Unsuccessful in his Senate bid
(he was defeated by Morris Sheppard), Choice Randell returned
to his legal practice in Sherman, where he waited impatiently
to reclaim the House seat he thought was rightfully his. Ultimately, it was decided that the son—smart, handsome, closer to
Rayburn's age—should be the one to return the Randell name to
Congress. To Rayburn, the challenge came almost as a relief. "I
think it had just as well come now as any time, for the reason
that I have known ever since I was elected to Congress that I was
going to have to fight the Randells sooner or later," he wrote.[54]

Andrew Randell's aggressive campaign had been going strong
for months before Rayburn finally heeded the urgings of his
advisers to launch his own. Returning home, he was for the first
time on the defensive. With time only to make one whirlwind
tour of the district, he found himself at every stop answering
an array of Randell charges, among them that Rayburn opposed child-labor laws and was therefore antilabor,[55] that he secretly supported the antiprohibitionists, and, worst of all, that
he had flagrantly misrepresented his relationship with President
Wilson.

Rayburn, as in his re-election campaign two years earlier, intended to make his closeness to the highly popular President the
focus of his campaign. His speeches invariably dealt with (and
no doubt embellished) his role in helping the administration enact its program. The June 1914 letter from Wilson praising him
for his handling of the railroad stock and bond bill again was
widely circulated—until, shortly before the election, Randell
played his ace.

Ridiculing Rayburn's "famous congratulatory letter," Randell said he, too, had had correspondence with the President. A family friend and former student of Wilson's, Randell had written Wilson to complain of Rayburn's implied claim of a presidential endorsement. Wilson promptly responded. Disavowing any real interest in the impertinent congressman who had threatened to defy him a few weeks earlier, Wilson deftly declared his neutrality in the race while leaving little doubt which of the two candidates he preferred:

> My Dear Mr. Randell:
>
> I learn that certain things I have said from time to time in praise of the work of Mr. Rayburn in the House have been interpreted to mean that I was opposed to your nomination. It is hardly necessary to assure you that this is an unjustifiable construction. I do not feel at liberty to express a preference in any congressional fight and would certainly take no such position when a friend like yourself was involved.
>
> Cordially and sincerely yours,
Woodrow Wilson[56]

Randell, waving his letter before audiences across the district, taunted his opponent. Wilson's disavowal embarrassed Rayburn but knocked him off stride only briefly. Ever the resourceful campaigner, he soon saw a way to turn the issue to his advantage. He began pointing out that Wilson's response to Randell had included the phrase "things I have said from time to time." "What that means," Rayburn told voters, "is that the President has praised me more than once."[57] He also successfully handled Randell's charge that he had harmed the rights and health of America's children by opposing a federal child-labor law. Rayburn's main objections were based on his belief that such laws were a state, not federal, responsibility. "I can see no reason for the federal government to force its hand into our local affairs," he wrote.[58] To his north Texas constituents, however, he stressed another, and to him highly valid, reason to oppose the measure: not only would it impose economic hardship on farm families, whose members of all ages worked the fields—it also would deprive young boys of the healthful benefits of hard outdoor work. His sermon on the benefits of hard work, especially for

young people, would not be complete until he had again reminded voters of his own childhood and those long days in the
hot sun, dragging cotton sacks down the rows. As for Randell,
he concluded, "Not an hour of toil ever soiled his silken palms,
so that he doesn't know the necessity of labor, nor realize the
good effects of keeping boys employed."[59]

He won his third term by a comfortable 4,500 votes. His
skillful handling of the Randell challenge and his final acceptance by the agrarian majority as one of their own gave him the
breathing room he had hoped for: a few years with no serious
political opposition, precious time in which to pursue with un-
divided attention his dream of becoming a famous national legislator. Rayburn always looked back on the 1916 campaign
as one of his most difficult, but he could never bring himself
to admit that what made the election memorable was that his
onetime political idol—Woodrow Wilson—had turned against
him and tried to have him defeated.

Returning to Washington to resume his lonely fight for the
Rayburn stock and bond bill, the congressman was furious to
find that his adversaries' tactics of delay and divide were succeeding all too well. On January 4, 1917, the Newlands Committee asked for a one-year extension in which to complete its
work. Even when Adamson, his friend and committee chairman, asked for House approval of the extension by unanimous
consent, the Texan rose stoutly but alone in opposition.

On January 9, Rayburn made the only speech of his congressional career in which his anger showed through his usually
calm demeanor. Aroused and frustrated, he heatedly spoke
against continuance of the Newlands Committee. "I do not like
to fight and I never do unless I have to or unless I am performing
a public service," he began. "I dislike very much to disagree
with the majority or with the members of the committee of
which I am a member." Denouncing the Newlands Committee
as a plot masterminded by the Southern Railway's general counsel, he declared: "its object is to destroy the rights of the states to
control transportation. . . . its purpose is to kill all House legislation which would be remedial. . . . They will not complete

this investigation in seven years. . . . In seven months they have examined one witness fully and three partially." Soon he was shouting: "We are always told, 'Wait for the report of the New-lands Committee'. . . . Everybody has to wait, wait, wait. . . . I say the Newlands Committee is chloroform." Scanning the chamber for support, he found none. Instead, Republican John J. Esch of Wisconsin rose to tweak his nose one more time.

The young congressman "should not be disappointed," Esch chided. "The longer he serves in this House the more of such disappointments he will have. Why, I remember bringing legis-lative children into this House for adoption only to find they were soon absolutely kidnapped and appeared under the name of a foster parent in a subsequent Congress." The represen-tatives roared with laughter. Rayburn was not amused.

In April 1917, the United States entered World War I, and in December of that year the government took complete control of the railroads. When the war ended, a Republican Congress had been elected, and Rayburn's chance to sponsor his bill was lost. In November 1919, the House passed the Esch-Cummins Act, which broadly revised the nation's transportation laws. Rayburn was not on the committee that drafted the law, but it included, practically word-for-word, the language of the Rayburn bill of 1914.

Sitting quietly in his seat on the House floor, the once-angry Texan heard Chairman Esch admit: "If the 1914 bill had been enacted, in my opinion, we would not have had the shameful financial record of the Frisco, the Rock Island, the Pere Mar-quette and the New Haven . . ." Moreover, Esch pointed out, sentiment in favor of the principles of this regulation had be-come so unanimous since 1914 that every regulatory plan sub-mitted to the House committee in 1919 included its provisions. Although it was a Republican-sponsored law, Rayburn saw vic-tory crown his long fight for the regulation of railway securities when the Transportation Act of 1920 became effective.

The most important phase of Rayburn's first four years in Congress lay not in his voting on the House floor, nor in his dogged fight for the regulation of railway securities. He was shaped in these years mostly by the friendships he formed—with Chairman Adamson, John Garner, and others—and by his apprenticeship on the highly important, overworked Interstate and Foreign Commerce Committee, which gave him a broad perspective on the federal government's activities that would be invaluable through the rest of his career.

At the end of his second term in Congress, Rayburn was 35 years old, a veteran of ten years as a lawmaker. Thus far, the timetable of his ambitions had been met with amazing accuracy. The achievement of his greatest ambition—to become Speaker of the House—was still years in the offing. To reach that goal, he must first become chairman of the Interstate and Foreign Commerce Committee; that depended upon, first, the Democrats retaining a majority in the House, and, second, his own seniority. One must be patient, very patient.

5

Wilson Days

Amid brilliant lightning flashes and ear-splitting thunder, a stinging rain swept the illuminated dome of the Capitol in the early morning hours of April 6, 1917. It was Good Friday. Inside the enormous building another storm raged—a storm of passions excited by Woodrow Wilson's call for America to go to war. The House of Representatives had been in session continuously for almost seventeen hours when the roll call began on the declaration of war. Many members of Congress were on the verge of tears brought on by weariness and their anguished consciences.

Handsome, dynamic Claude Kitchin of North Carolina, the Democratic floor leader, his voice quavering and his eyes brimming with tears, had broken with the Wilson administration, telling his colleagues that he would vote against the declaration. "Appreciating to the fullest the penalties which a war-mad moment will impose, my conscience and judgment, after mature thought and fervent prayer for right guidance, have marked clearly the path of my duty," he declared.[1]

When the roll call reached the *R*s, the entire membership stopped to watch Jeannette Rankin of Montana, the first woman ever to sit in Congress. This was her first vote. She had been distressed for days as to what course to follow. When the clerk first called her name, she did not answer. He called it again. Unconsciously twisting and twisting a handkerchief in her hands, Rankin haltingly rose in her seat, gripped the chair in front with her right hand, and, with tears rolling down her cheeks, said: "I want to stand by my country, but I cannot vote for war." She still had not cast her vote.

Someone shouted: "You're in a man's game now. Play it." The clerk came to her seat, asked how she was to be recorded. She whispered: "No."[2]

Also casting his first vote that night was another new House member—Marvin Jones of Amarillo, whose career was destined to be intertwined with Rayburn's for more than a quarter century. Forty years after that Good Friday vote, he mused: "That was the hardest vote I ever cast. I'm still not sure we did the right thing."[3]

Neither Sam Rayburn nor anyone who watched the House proceedings that night ever forgot the tension, the deeply stirred emotion, the anguish of conscience that beset both friends and foes of the war declaration. "That was the most serious hour of my life, and the vote I cast upon that occasion gave me more pause than any other vote I have cast," Rayburn told his colleagues two decades later.[4] For a time during the debate, he became physically ill and worried that he might have to leave the floor to vomit. But, as he later remembered it, his doubt faded and his stomach settled as the vote approached. "Of course, any man hates like the devil to vote for war," he recalled. "But it was something we had to do. We had no choice."[5]

In May, Congress passed the Selective Service Act, requiring all men between the ages of 21 and 31 to register for the draft. For Rayburn, as for many other young representatives, the declaration of war posed a painful decision. Although he was, at 35, four years over the maximum draft age, he felt like many of his colleagues that those who vote to send others to war should offer to go themselves. Yet the work of Congress was also vital to the war effort. Several members did rush to volunteer for service on the day they voted for the declaration of war. John Garner, too old for the military himself, ordered his son Tully to sign up for the army. Congressman Carter Glass of Virginia halted his efforts to enlist only after the President personally asked him not to do so. "I beg that you will not think of enlisting," Wilson wrote. "Surely you are just as much serving the colors there as you could be in the ranks of the Army." To all members of Congress who inquired, Wilson made the same request.[6]

If his involvement in the war was going to be confined to the halls of Congress, Rayburn decided, he would make the most of it by participating as actively as possible in war-related legislation. His first opportunity was soon at hand.

Beginning in 1776, the United States had provided pensions for veterans of every war. After the Civil War, the pension rolls grew to enormous proportions, until, by 1917, there were 673,000 names on the list.[7] "The existing system of pensions was as unscientific as the distribution of prizes from a Christmas tree," Treasury Secretary William Gibbs McAdoo wrote. "It included thousands of men who had never seen a battle and thousands whose entire service [consisted] of a month or two spent in a training camp, a period of frolic and boyish escapades. For this they were on the pension list for life."[8]

McAdoo and others conceived the idea that the pension system in the future should be replaced by a system of compensation for death or disability incurred in military service. This would be modeled after the workman's compensation laws, providing government payments in proportion to the veteran's disability or, in case of death, payments to his survivors. McAdoo's ideas went further. He knew that men could not get life insurance from private firms once in uniform, so he proposed that the government should offer such insurance at rates the soldiers could afford. After a series of conferences, the War Risk Insurance Act—dubbed the Soldiers and Sailors Insurance Act by the press—was drafted. Joshua W. Alexander of Missouri introduced the bill in the House, and it was referred to the Interstate and Foreign Commerce Committee.

It was the type of war legislation Rayburn had been waiting for. He was determined to grab the bill and run with it as his own. At the committee hearings, he showed up so well prepared and was so uncharacteristically aggressive that other members stood aside and let him lead the questioning of McAdoo and other witnesses. When he volunteered to write the committee report, the panel's new chairman, Thetus W. Sims,[9] was happy to oblige; and when he asked to handle the bill on the floor, Sims bowed to that request, too.

A war-frenzied nation, eager to show the soldiers its appreciation, enthusiastically followed each step of the bill's progress. Opposition was reduced to a relative handful of ardent pension advocates who called it unfair, inequitable, and excessively stringent and insurance company executives who complained it would put the federal government in competition with them. House debate on the bill lasted four days.[10] Rayburn was on his feet most of the time, explaining, answering questions, clarifying, settling disputes, and, always, keeping the debate moving forward. This was a more experienced Sam Rayburn, one that members had not seen before —confident, expansive, scholarly, even humorous. (When a congressman spoke of the "War of the Rebellion," Rayburn gently corrected him: "Call it the Civil War.") On September 13, the measure passed unanimously. Still a junior congressman, he had performed masterfully as manager of the bill that President Wilson called "one of the most admirable pieces of legislation" of the war. Forty years later, Marvin Jones would rank it as Rayburn's best legislative performance.[11]

In February, Rayburn began another crusade involving an old adversary, the railroad interests, which was to last many months. At the time, the railroads were America's most important industry—weak, mismanaged, repeatedly the victim of financial buccaneers who robbed and pillaged investors and the public—but still the nation's most vital single business. With the coming of the war and the almost exclusive reliance on railroads to move goods and troops to ports of embarkation, the industry assumed staggering new burdens and tremendously enhanced importance.

The railroads were in no shape to take on such responsibility. Stung by such financial scandals as the New Haven, Frisco, and Rock Island debaucheries, American investors turned a cold shoulder to offers of new railway stocks and bonds issued to raise the money urgently needed for new and replacement equipment and for improvements in the operating systems. From 1913 on, the railroads steadily deteriorated, in terms of physical plant as well as personnel. When America entered the war, railroad workers were drafted indiscriminately, and their replacements were either ill-trained or simply not available.[12]

To maximize profits, the railroads would carry freight to the eastern seaboard, then hold the cars until there was a return load westward. As a result, badly needed cars piled up in eastern yards, often for weeks or months, while urgently needed war material languished at inland points awaiting shipment to the fighting fronts. In August 1917, Congress passed a priorities law giving the President the power to expedite movement of such traffic as he deemed vital to national defense. Rayburn handled the bill in the House. The legislation fell far short of its authors' hopes. By the end of 1917, the Pennsylvania Railroad found that 85 percent of the freight in its Pittsburgh division was moving under a priority. By giving all shipments priority, those carrying out the law simply created a worse tangle. The transportation system had reached a crisis. Ships bound for Europe could not sail for lack of coal; the severe car shortage grew worse as loaded cars—180,000 above normal—jammed eastern tracks. The condition of the railroads disturbed President Wilson more than any other war problem at that time.[13]

Two days after Christmas, the President used his war powers to take complete control of the nation's rail system, placing Treasury Secretary McAdoo in charge as director-general. Rayburn foresaw grave danger for democratic institutions if the government remained too long in the railroad business. The young congressman feared the taxpayers might one day have to compensate the rail owners—a $20 billion burden that would double the national debt. Even more troubling were the ramifications of possibly having to add 1,700,000 railroad employees to the federal civil service rolls. "With the power and influence that they and their connections would have," he warned, "it would ultimately destroy our form of government." An unscrupulous President with that much property and that many employees "in the hollow of his hand . . . could perpetuate himself in office."[14]

In speech after speech, Rayburn exhorted his colleagues to prepare for the return of the railroads to their owners at the earliest
possible moment after the war and to turn a deaf ear to all proposals for government ownership.

Shortly after the armistice, Rayburn took the House floor for
his last major drive to get Uncle Sam out of railroading. He confessed concern at what he thought was a growing trend: "Instead
of legislating to cure evils that grow up in industry, from many
quarters the only suggestion that comes is for the government to
take over and operate the industry—and every time some sick
and tottering makeshift of an industry gets into the deep waters
of real affairs, it comes running to the government, crying,
'Take me ere I perish'. . . . It is the province of government to
govern business, where there is need, not go into business."
Government ownership would mean "more political logrolling
by members of Congress and influential organizations to get
new roads built, existing lines extended and ornate depots built
in ambitious towns than there has ever been with rivers and harbors or with public buildings, with all the stench of pork-
barrel. . . . The politicians would be torn between the public
demanding better service and the 2,000,000 employees demanding increased wages."[15]

Rayburn's views were sharply disputed by powerful groups,
among them organized labor, which embraced a controversial
panacea known as the Plumb Plan. Named for Glenn E. Plumb,
the brilliant general counsel of the four railway brotherhoods,
the plan called for the government to buy the railroads from private owners and set up a board of directors consisting of five
members named by the President, five by the employees, and
five by the operating managers or executives. Profits would be
divided between the employees and the government. Conservative forces everywhere considered the Plumb Plan the beginning of socialism on a grand scale. The *New York Times* called it
"a very long step toward the principles of Lenin, Trotsky and
the Soviet government."

When Plumb appeared before the Interstate and Foreign Commerce Committee to explain his brainchild, Rayburn went on
the attack. He accused the brotherhoods of misrepresenting the

plan's sweeping impact on union members and said he alone had received some 200 letters from railroad workers in Denison, a leading town in his district, "all in the same language, starting with 'Sam Rayburn, Esq.'" These workers, he inferred, did not know what the Plumb Plan actually was and therefore could not be said to favor it.[16]

Rayburn's unbending attack on government ownership soon had organized labor fully aroused, not only in Denison but around the country. One labor spokesman threatened "a revolution" if the Plumb Plan was not adopted. Such threats only served to stiffen opposition in Congress and around the nation.[17] Ultimately, the plan was rejected by the House Interstate and Foreign Commerce Committee. President Wilson's subsequent announcement that he would return the railroads to their private owners on March 1, 1920, triggered a race in Congress to enact a bill governing the return before the deadline.

Weary of war and the shortages it created, frightened by the looming specter of world socialism, the voters in November 1918 decisively rejected President Wilson's partisan plea for election of a Democratic Congress. Republicans took control of both the House and Senate. Rayburn, in his first congressional race without a serious opponent, already had been re-elected in his state's Democratic primary. Republican John J. Esch of Wisconsin became chairman of the House Interstate and Foreign Commerce Committee. The Progressive Era—and life in Washington as Rayburn and other Democrats had known it—was coming to an abrupt end.[18]

Ironically, it was a Republican Congress that passed the most sweeping regulatory law enacted to that time—the Esch-Cummins Transportation Act of 1920, covering practically every phase of railway operation rates, finance, and labor. Calling the bill a "conscious betrayal of the public interest," organized labor opposed it violently and threatened to defeat all who supported it.[19] Rayburn, whose ill-fated plan for railroad stock and bond controls was resurrected for inclusion in the bill, was one of the measure's most adamant supporters, in defiance of his party's position and sound political logic. Already anathema to labor, the Texas congressman exacerbated the situation by insulting union leaders when they complained of not being consulted on the bill. "Men who say labor was not consulted place themselves in the category of common scolds and common slanderers," he told the House. Back in Denison, his remarks stirred indignation and widespread determination among union members to retire him from Congress at the earliest opportunity.

The battle over Esch–Cummins was hard fought, with Rayburn taking an active role in the final floor debate.[20] He aimed much of his fire at the American Federation of Labor, headed by tough old Samuel Gompers, and at the railroad brotherhoods. "Has it come to pass in this country that the free representatives of a free people can be scared by the threat of Mr. Gompers or anyone else who represents less than 5 percent of the people of this land?" he asked. He recalled that "a few years ago when we had up the antistrike provision before our committee, I heard Mr. Gompers make the defiant declaration that if Congress adopted it, he served notice in advance that he would violate the law. Surely after making such a declaration . . . he cannot be considered a wise and a sane leader." The overenthusiastic Texan had, by then, hopelessly alienated an important voting bloc in his district. He also put himself at odds with the overwhelming majority of House Democrats and, more importantly, with his colleagues from Texas.[21] On the crucial vote, 205 Republicans and only 45 Democrats supported the measure. Only 3 members of the Texas delegation joined with Rayburn in voting for the bill. Even John Garner opposed it. Although Rayburn did not realize it, it was his last major legislative role for more than a decade.

During his first years in Congress, as through most of his career, Rayburn defied classification as either a liberal or a conservative. He intensely disliked such labels, believing that each legislative measure should be judged on its reasonableness, justice, and fairness, rather than on whether it was "liberal" or "conservative."

Like most of his colleagues, he felt the painful dilemma of the times—the sharpening conflict between the old Jeffersonian doctrine of "states' rights" and the newfound necessity for using the power of a strong central government to curb the excesses of economic forces, which for the first time had become nationwide in their impact and which the states found it increasingly difficult, often impossible, to control in the public interest. Few felt this dilemma more than President Wilson himself.

The issue of nationwide prohibition of the sale of intoxicating beverages illustrates Rayburn's philosophical quandary. Politically, he was a prohibitionist, yet he believed the sale of alcoholic beverages was an issue best settled by the states, not Washington. When the first nationwide prohibition amendment came before the House in 1914, he voted against it on the basis of states' rights. On all succeeding votes, however, he backed national action. On the same basis, he consistently opposed the woman suffrage amendment, insisting that the right to determine who should vote was deliberately and specifically reserved to the states by the authors of the Constitution.

On the other hand, he approved of the new governmental technique of "grants-in-aid" to states that first became popular during the Wilson administration. Under the grants-in-aid system, the federal and state governments share the cost of building public projects, such as highways, which can be used for postal routes and for military purposes. Ordinarily, in such programs, the federal government puts up 50 percent of the money, to be matched by the state. Rayburn in 1914 voted enthusiastically for the first federal highway grants-in-aid program, which gave impetus to the construction of all-weather roads throughout the nation. In the Wilson years, similar grants were used to create the county agent and home demonstration programs, which helped farmers and their wives with farm problems, provided training for vocational education teachers, and created maternity and child welfare services on a local level. Rayburn supported each of these programs.

With few exceptions, the young congressman loyally supported Wilson's major legislative goals. The Underwood tariff reduction, Federal Reserve System, Federal Trade Commission, and Clayton Antitrust Act had his enthusiastic backing. However, he opposed as "socialistic" the President's proposal to construct a government-owned railroad in Alaska.[22] He consistently voted for legislation to assist the farm population and showed a particular interest in proposals to make credit easier for farmers, although he had no part in shaping such measures. He opposed a federal child-labor law, contending it was unconstitutional, a view shared by President Wilson.

His sharpest difference with Wilson concerned the restriction of immigration. In 1915, Congress passed a bill subjecting all immigrants to a literacy test as a means of slowing the flood of newcomers from foreign lands. In a sharply worded message, Wilson vetoed the bill, and the veto was sustained. Rayburn, for the first time, voted to override the President's veto. In 1917, Wilson again vetoed an almost identical bill, but this time Congress overrode the veto. Again Rayburn broke with the President to favor the restriction of immigration.[23] Immigration legislation is a good example of the shifting of opinions on public questions that Rayburn was to witness during a long legislative career. In 1915 and 1917, most "progressives" or "liberals," including social workers and leaders of organized labor, strongly favored the restriction of immigration. But by the 1940s, the situation had changed: a relaxation of immigration barriers was a cardinal plank in most so-called liberal programs.

After the outbreak of war in Europe and the almost imperceptible drift of the United States toward it, Rayburn staunchly followed Wilson's leadership in preparedness. In college, he had read and reread the views of the learned Princeton Professor Wilson, expressed in his popular treatise *Congressional Government*: "When foreign affairs play a prominent part in the politics and policy of a nation, its Executive must of necessity be its guide; must utter every initial judgment, take every first step of action, supply the information upon which it is to act, suggest and in large measure control its conduct."[24]

Those views Rayburn adopted as his own. Throughout his career, the Texan held fast to one of his deepest convictions: in time of crisis, follow the President, whether he be Democrat or Republican.[25] "When the nation is in danger, you have to follow your leader," he often said. "The man in the White House is the only leader this nation has; if he doesn't lead or can't lead, then the country has no leader. Although we may disagree with him, we must follow our President in times of peril, regardless of which party he belongs to."[26]

Although he had traveled little and had scant knowledge of the world beyond America's shores, Rayburn was always an internationalist, convinced that America's fate was linked irrevocably with that of other free nations. He watched with grave concern as the isolationist Senate smashed Wilson's dream of the League of Nations. Years later, he speculated: "I always thought Wilson made a mistake in not taking some Republican to Paris with him to help draft the League of Nations covenant. . . . He probably would have gotten his League of Nations ratified by the Senate."[27]

In the fall of 1913, after he had been a congressman for just a few months, Rayburn took his only trip out of the United States at government expense. His committee had charge of all legislation in the House concerning the Panama Canal, then nearing completion. After the session adjourned, several committee members were delegated to go to Panama by ship to "inspect" the canal and report on the construction progress. Rayburn found the gigantic project interesting, but he did not enjoy the trip. The entire time, he was miserably homesick for his family and for Bonham.[28] That was his first—and last—overseas "junket." Years later, at his own expense, he visited Mexico City for a few days.

In his position as a shaper of national policies, foreign as well as domestic, Rayburn acquired a good basic knowledge of the problems and potentialities of foreign nations; and over a period of nearly a quarter century, he had conferences and private visits with many of the foreign leaders who came to this country. His interest in foreign affairs was always keen and his information generally sound, yet except for those two instances he never crossed the borders of the United States. "Hell, I haven't seen nearly all of this country yet," he once told a friend who was curious as to his lack of interest in foreign travel. In 1935, he signed up to accompany a party of representatives and senators who had been invited as guests of the Philippine government to the inauguration of that country's first president, Manuel Quazon. After the inauguration, the delegation was to tour the Orient. Rayburn abruptly canceled his plans when he discovered that the group would be abroad three months. "I wouldn't give three months of my life to see all the countries of the world," he grumbled.

When he became an elder statesman, he often counseled younger members against overseas travel at taxpayer expense. The voters don't like it, he warned, and until you get firmly established, you had best spend all your spare time at home with your constituents. Many of the more than 3,000 congressmen and congresswomen with whom he served had, in his opinion, been defeated because they "went traipsing around the world" instead of paying close attention to their districts.

"When Congress is in session, your place is in Washington; when it is not in session, your place is home in your district." That advice, which he gave to hundreds of young members, Rayburn religiously followed himself. As soon as Congress adjourned, he caught the first train back to Bonham. The weeks or months of adjournment he spent going from community to community in his district, greeting old friends, making new ones, answering any question that a citizen wanted to ask, and, above all, asking a lot of questions of his own. He always kept his political fences up at home by probing the minds of his constituents to discover their worries, needs, and opinions.

This hard work paid off. In 1914, 1916, and 1918, he was re-elected by substantial majorities. For a young member, these first re-election campaigns are particularly dangerous. Survival of these races usually clears the way for a long congressional career; after six or eight years in office, an incumbent has acquired such seniority and political power that even some voters who do not subscribe to the same views will support him "because he can do so much for our district."

As the 1920s dawned, Rayburn for the first time in his political career found himself a member of the minority. A different group of political leaders was calling the signals, implementing politics that Rayburn thought would seriously injure the nation's welfare, particularly the well-being of "the little man." The

Texan, now almost 40 years old, looked to the years ahead with considerable concern, for both his own and the country's welfare. He would have a lot of re-adjusting to do.

6

Republican Years

When he had finished half a century of lawmaking, Rayburn looked back upon "the Republican years" between 1919 and 1931 as the most frustrating, least productive, and unhappiest of his entire career. The Democratic party was out of power—forever, some thought. Republican policies, in both international and domestic fields, seemed destined, as the scrappy Texan put it, "to run the country into the ditch." But in the moral and economic madness that marked the Roaring Twenties, few Americans were listening.

For Rayburn, it also was a time of personal trial. Although he continued making progress—in 1920, he was named chairman of the Democratic Caucus, a distinct honor for so junior a member—his ambition of becoming Speaker began to look hopeless. In 1922, after ten years in Congress, he narrowly escaped defeat at the polls. And, tragically, in the middle 1920s, his mother died, followed by his oldest brother, John Franklin, and his brief marriage ended in failure, smashing his dream of having a large family of his own. The twelve Republican years under Presidents Harding, Coolidge, and Hoover were for Sam Rayburn "a time of troubles." He would later recall: "There wasn't any use trying to do anything constructive. If you had a bill everybody was for, before it got out of committee, they'd hand it over to a

Republican, and that was that. You just had to wait for a Democratic Congress. I kept a book in my office and one at my apartment, and I averaged reading two books a week during those
years. There wasn't much mail then."[1]

The Republicans made quick use of their newly won power to
reverse most of the national policies espoused by the Democrats
during the Wilson era. Isolationism—embodied in the rejection
of the League of Nations—replaced Wilson's vision of American
leadership in the world. Low-tariff policies were junked in favor
of higher and higher tariff walls against foreign manufacturers.
Sweeping tax revisions were made, primarily for the benefit of
the wealthy taxpayer, both individual and corporate. An orgy of
speculation in stocks and bonds such as the nation had never experienced found encouragement rather than restraint from the
nation's rulers in Washington. Agriculture, stricken by a postwar
depression, lay in the economic ditch throughout the Republican years. As the decade opened with the Harding administration, Washington was honeycombed by corruption whose trail
led almost to the White House itself.

"All we could do in those days was to vote against the Republicans and cuss 'em," remembered former Texas Congressman,
later U.S. District Judge, Luther Johnson of Corsicana. At one
particular party caucus "we were at our lowest ebb," he recalled.
"We were awfully blue. Some felt we would never be back in
power. Hatton Sumners and Sam Rayburn made speeches, saying we would come back and that time would prove us right.
That perked us up some."[2]

Not only was there little mail—about five letters a day in
Rayburn's case—for Democrats there were also no jobs to dis-
pense, no postmasters to name, no government programs to announce. As he approached his 40th birthday, the north Texas
congressman for once in his life had time for leisure. From his
days in the cotton fields at Flag Springs to his hectic baptism by
fire as a young member of Congress, he had seldom before
found time for anything save the promotion of his career.

He decided to use this first real lull in his life to speed up his
education. He read constantly. Upon finishing one book, he got
another from the Library of Congress. He also acquired a mod-

est library of his own—"I never bought a book that I didn't read"—and began a lifelong habit of scrawling "SR" on page 99 of each volume he read. He read mostly American history or political science. "The best way to learn history," he believed, "is to study the biographies of famous men. Don't bother with straight history books. Read how those who made history lived and thought and acted. That way you'll remember history."

His reading was drawn largely from a list of books compiled for him earlier by Speaker Champ Clark, who took a shine to the young congressman. Rayburn had potential but needed more seasoning and a great deal more education, Clark thought. During a train ride from St. Louis to Washington shortly after the farm-reared Texan's election to Congress, Clark—a man of limited education himself—presumptuously wrote out a study program. He suggested that Rayburn read *Union, Disunion, and Reunion* by S. S. Cox; *Thirty Years in Congress* by Thomas Hart Benton, and biographies of Washington, Jefferson, John Quincy Adams, Jackson, Lincoln, and others. Rayburn carried Clark's list in his wallet for thirty years and, eventually, read every book on it.[3]

Aside from reading, walking, and an occasional round of golf, few outside activities competed for his leisure hours in Washington. He was not a man of varied tastes in the style of Jefferson. His three great interests were people, public affairs, and agriculture. He had absolutely no interest in art or music. "I don't want to know anything about them. I'd just as soon hear somebody beat on a wash tub as play the piano," he once commented.[4] Painting, sculpture, poetry, ballet, fiction—these branches of the arts were completely outside the scope of his interests. He liked sports, although he got most of his exercise from his ritual two-mile walk each day between his 16th Street apartment and the Capitol. As occasional pitcher for the House Democratic softball team, he demonstrated good fielding and a strong right arm. He tried golf in the twenties and showed promise of becoming an excellent player, but he eventually decided it was too time-consuming and gave it up.

His friend Jack Garner was an inveterate, highly successful poker player. Legend had it that the crusty Texan financed his

first campaign for Congress from poker winnings. Garner denied it. What he couldn't deny was that, almost every night, he
could be found dealing pasteboards at the no-limit table of the
downtown Boar's Head Club, a private gambling and drinking
hangout for lawmakers and lobbyists, operated by Uncle Joe
Cannon, the dethroned but still popular former Republican
Speaker from Illinois.[5]

In its heyday, the Boar's Head on K Street was Washington's
most important place for making political contacts, and Garner
took full advantage of it. He enjoyed luring freshmen into a
friendly game so he "could size 'em up." But Rayburn would
not be enticed. He drank very little in those days, limiting himself to one or two highballs after work, and he never gambled.
Garner made a virtue of his bad habits, often reminding voters
of his weakness for alcohol and cards. Such tactics would have
proved disastrous in the Bible Belt of northeast Texas. To have
been exposed as a drinker, gambler, or womanizer would have
meant the end of Rayburn's career—a risk he was not about
to take.

The idea of running for statewide office never appealed
greatly to Rayburn, even though he felt qualified and entitled to
be governor or U.S. senator. Although he rarely admitted it, he
also envied the broader recognition and respect commanded by
holders of those offices. Many Democrats in northeast Texas
had been talking of running Rayburn for the Senate for years. In
1922, with the old and ailing Senator Charles A. Culberson
likely to win a fifth six-year term by default unless a worthy
challenger appeared, Rayburn's credentials began looking better
and better to party leaders. As pressure on him mounted,
the congressman's dilemma—to run or not to run—became
more and more painful, as he described in a telling letter to sister Kate:

Do you know I have several times since I was home seriously considered entering the race for the Senate? Some
pretty strong people have put it up to me very flatteringly. I
really believe that a clear majority of the people of Texas do

not want anybody who is now running. . . . If the campaign could be properly financed what would all think of the chances—that is, in case the pressure gets pretty hard on me to enter the race. I have discouraged the movement all along.

I have never had any consuming ambition to go to the Senate. My ambition rather has been to rise in the House. But nobody can tell when the Democrats will come into power, and a race every two years gets pretty irksome. Once in the Senate means a lifetime if a fellow wants it and will behave. Of course, I have a good position in the House—none better—but they will finally get a fellow in a district. I feel that in all probability this is my call—my last call—to the Senate.[6]

But less than three weeks later, W. A. Thomas received a letter from his brother-in-law, informing him: "I have definitely determined that I will not make the race for the Senate. I feel better now since I have made a definite and unalterable decision."[7] Instead, he would rededicate himself, once and for all, to a career in the House:

I have all my life worked toward the position that I now hold. Every move since I have been old enough to think has been a part of the dream that I am now realizing in part. Probably I have got as high here as I will ever get but I hope not. . . . I have sacrificed every thing, and many that would have been very sweet and dear, to live this life. I have not let anything come between me and the darling of my dreams, and that is fame. I would rather link my name indelibly with the living pulsing history of my country and not be forgotten entirely after while [sic] than to have anything else on earth.[8]

Since writing to Kate, Rayburn had weighed more seriously his prospects in a statewide contest. The unsurmountable problem, looming like an unwelcome ghost from the past, was old "Coal Oil" Joe Bailey. Though his reputation was shattered, Bailey still worked the backwaters of Texas politics. Two years

earlier, he had run for governor and lost badly. To a new generation of voters, Bailey personified the overbearing and corrupt
politics of the past, and they wanted no part of him—or anyone
associated with him. Now, in 1922, Rayburn's onetime idol was
making political noises again and dredging up memories that
could not possibly benefit his former supporters. As he explained to Thomas:

> Just as long as Bailey is everlastingly coming to the front
> as a candidate that long it will be practically impossible for
> me to become the state figure that I have reason to expect to
> become. You probably do not know that of all the men in
> Texas who followed his flag in his black hour that I am the
> only one who today holds an office. I am truly the last of
> the Mohicans. . . . The press in Texas is ninety-five per-
> cent anti-Bailey and every time he bobs up they are re-
> minded that I am the last of the old crowd, and I am pun-
> ished. As an example, when I was elected chairman of the
> Democratic Caucus here, the second highest honor that the
> Democrats of Congress can bestow, the nomination for
> Speaker being the only one higher, there was not a paper in
> Texas outside of my district that commented editorially on
> the fact. There must be a reason . . .[9]

There was another reason for Rayburn's unwillingness to
gamble on a statewide campaign: voters in Texas, as throughout
the South and Southwest, were in an unpredictable, disturbed
frame of mind. Farmers were angry because a depression had
sent their prices plummeting; small-town merchants and trades-
people were upset because the farmers no longer could afford
their goods and services; and organized labor was furious because its members' wartime gains were slipping away. Society itself was in the throes of historic change. Religious fanatics were
fighting passionately against the inroads of scientific theories
such as evolution. Young people were embracing the Jazz Age
with relaxed standards of conduct that horrified their elders.
With the collapse of Wilsonian idealism, the whole nation grew
by the day more cynical toward almost all moral values.[10] The
white South was deeply troubled by what it imagined was a new

"biggety" attitude among blacks, many of whom had worn the American uniform "to make the world safe for democracy" and now coveted additional freedoms. It was all made to order for the race-and-religion hatred of the Ku Klux Klan, dormant since Reconstruction but now reborn more violent than ever and spreading across parts of the nation like a prairie fire.[11]

When Rayburn went home to face his constituents in the summer of 1922, he found he was in serious trouble. The district was heavy with discontent—economic, racial, and religious. Farmers were suffering a sharp drop in income that began in 1920 and was to continue until the New Deal days. Organized railroad workers, who still listed him among "members of Congress whose records are so objectionable that they should not be supported for re-election," welcomed a new and powerful anti-Rayburn ally in the radical Farm Labor Union, which, without any basis in fact, was accusing him of helping the Republicans keep farm prices low and labeling him "the enemy of the farmer."[12]

The congressman knew he was in for a rough battle when Ed Westbrook of Hunt County announced against him in the Democratic primary. Westbrook, a seasoned campaigner, had opposed Rayburn in 1920. Now he was back with impressive new support from labor, restive farmers, and the notorious but powerful Klan, of which he was a member. In a way, Rayburn was eager to take on Westbrook again. "If, after all the noise that they have made, I can beat them badly this time, it will make any man who has respect for himself ponder long before he will announce in the future," Rayburn determined.[13] What's more, he had no love for Hunt County, which had consistently snubbed him at the polls, and he especially despised "the old haters" of Greenville, whose motto, on a huge banner spanning the main street, boasted: "The Whitest People, the Blackest Soil."

Shortly after Rayburn began campaigning, he got more bad news. The Railway Labor Board announced wage cuts that sent 400,000 shopworkers nationwide streaming off their jobs in protest. The strike had immediate repercussions in the Fourth Congressional District, especially in Denison. Cecil Dickson was then telegraph editor of the *Denison Herald*: "The strike was so bad. They were bringing strike breakers in from Cleveland, and places like that. We were having a lot of people hurt. There were burnings and fires and a lot of destruction. They brought in the Texas Rangers . . . with their saddles and bridles on their backs, but they didn't have their horses. They quieted things down some, but every time a new load of strike breakers came in, why all hell would break loose."[14]

Dickson had a brainstorm: why not invite Rayburn over to Denison to address the nervous community? With dubious logic, he reasoned that Rayburn, a key figure in drafting the legislation responsible for much of the workers' discontent, might help quell some of the fears. It was risky, but if he succeeded, he might also defuse some of the strikers' animosity toward himself. Dickson's editor bought the scheme; Rayburn was more skeptical. "Well, it might be a tough thing," he protested. But, when assured that "everything is all right as far as protection is concerned," he finally agreed. Dickson remembered: "I arranged for the theater, the biggest there. I told Tom Hickman [commander of the Texas Rangers] and I went to the sheriff, deputies, and constables. I said, 'If anything happens to this man, I'll kill all of you'—I was pretty tough talking to them—'and I'll blast hell out of you in the paper, too.' So Rayburn came over and made his speech. There was a crowd that could have filled a half-dozen theaters. I remember a quietude came over them."[15]

The appearance may have been good politics on Rayburn's part, but it is debatable how many strikers heard his message. Certainly, few union members would have found comfort in what he said. His feelings about the violent strike were widely known. As he later told the House of Representatives: "If I were responsible for this government, I would not allow the right of any man to work to be interfered with, and if men wanted to go into these shops to repair those trains, I would protect them in the right to work if it took every man in the standing army of the United States."

Rayburn was less forthright in stating his position on the resurgent Klan. Although he refused to join the hooded order, he made no open issue with the Klan in the 1922 campaign. "I didn't go around cussing the Klan because, God Almighty, everybody in this county was a Klansman," he later explained.[16] Nor did Rayburn deviate from the standard pro-segregation rhetoric of the day. "I do not make this a threat, but the Negroes of Fannin County are not going to vote in this coming primary," he said in one rabble-rousing campaign speech. "By the Eternal God, my ancestors' blood has been spilled on nearly every hill in this land, that this should be a white man's country . . ."[17]

As the campaign entered its final days, Rayburn was convinced that the combined opposition of the Klan, the railway strikers, the Farm Labor Union, and old enemies had beaten him. He proved to be overly pessimistic. Union members voted solidly against him, but the voters in Greenville failed to give Westbrook the boost he needed. Finally, Fannin County voters turned out in heavy numbers. The winner by 1,284 votes, Rayburn would long remember the 1922 campaign as "my closest race."[18]

Despite the discouragement and frustration of the Republican years, Rayburn was a better-trained, more skillful, and more self-reliant lawmaker at the end of the period than he was at its beginning. The broad field of the Committee on Interstate and Foreign Commerce offered an education in itself, and the Texan, who became the senior Democrat on the committee in 1925, worked diligently at his job. He continued to attend hearings— on time and without fail—and listened seriously and carefully to the parade of witnesses who came to testify. Usually he asked few questions, but he filed away in his retentive memory a storehouse of information on a wide variety of national problems. Marvin Jones, who roomed with Rayburn for two of the Republican years, remembered: "Sam never seemed to tire of talking politics. He got most of his information that way. He always had a tendency to select companions from people who had substance and could teach him things. He always had a stream of visitors, usually other members of Congress, at our apartment where we'd talk politics for hours. Sam never cared much for the foppery and make-believe of Washington social life. He'd much rather talk politics with a bunch of men than go to some party."[19]

Rayburn especially enjoyed being part of a small band of House cronies, led by John Garner and his Republican pal, Speaker Nicholas Longworth of Ohio, that gathered after the close of business each day in a secluded room of the Capitol. Among the "regulars" were Bert Snell of New York, John Tilson of Connecticut, John McDuffie of Alabama, Edward Pou of North Carolina, Tuck Milligan of Missouri, and Rayburn. Known to outsiders as the Board of Education—Garner and Longworth called it the *Bureau* of Education—these informal sessions gave friends a chance to unwind, talk over the day's issues, and, as Garner colorfully put it, "strike a blow for liberty."[20] Garner had two kinds of whiskey—good whiskey, which he drank himself, and rotgut, which he offered to new congressmen in huge cafe-type tumblers to test their character.[21] "He always judged them on whether or not they took it well," Rayburn recalled, adding, "Garner was so tight he never had ice. He'd just go to the sink and draw branch water."

Notable for its high ceilings and ornate chandelier, the hideaway was reached by way of a long, narrow corridor that opened just off the Rotunda to the left of the statue of Stephen F. Austin. The room was directly across the hall from a suite that later was to become Rayburn's district office for nearly two decades. Bookcases shielded with green cloth lined the windowless walls. Each regular attendee had his own case for storing liquor.[22] After an hour or so of drinking and talking, the group would begin breaking up. Garner and Longworth would pile into the latter's electric runabout and head downtown to dinner or to continue their drinking at a club or saloon.[23] Rayburn often would hitch a ride with them back to his 16th Street apartment.

Around this pair of unlikely friends—"I was the heathen and Nick was the aristocrat," Garner used to say—clustered most of the outstanding members of the House, Democrats and Republicans alike. It was almost a ritual that shortly after 4 o'clock Garner would appear behind the brass rail at the rear of the House and, with a crook of his finger, signal to Longworth, who was presiding as Speaker. As quickly as possible, Longworth would adjourn the House, and the band of cronies would repair to the secret room.[24]

Longworth, a wealthy Ohioan married to Alice Roosevelt, vivacious daughter of President Theodore Roosevelt, was a striking contrast to Garner in every way. Possessed of Old World charm and courtliness, impeccable in speech and dress, he was a strange companion for the hard-drinking, rough-talking, "use-your-bloody-knuckles" Garner. Yet Rayburn, surveying his personal memories of nearly half a century in Washington, could recall no friendship between congressmen that matched theirs for warmth and mutual devotion.

Garner and Longworth were staunch partisans, poles apart in their economic and political beliefs. According to Lewis Deschler, House Parliamentarian from 1925 to 1976, "Garner's ambition always was to drive Longworth out of the chair to debate, but he never succeeded."[25] The verbal clashes between the two men, both on the House floor and in the secret room, were full of fury and passion. But when the battle was over, they would walk away from the arena arm in arm.

In the Bureau of Education, the issues of the day were vigorously debated, personalities dissected, and legislative deals struck between the Republican and Democratic House leaders. Rayburn, now firmly installed as Garner's chief lieutenant, was in constant attendance at these meetings, which gave him unparalleled opportunity to learn all phases of the legislative trade as well as to pick up inside gossip on the personalities and events of the times. Occasionally, Republicans would be excluded as Garner assembled his Democratic lieutenants to plan strategy for harassing, delaying, or derailing the GOP majority. "I was Garner's lieutenant for fifteen years, and God, what a chore it was at times," recalled Rayburn. "But when the time came for him to throw his feet out for you, he went all the way."[26]

Garner was the undisputed master of the seventeen-member Democratic delegation from Texas, and he ruled with an iron fist. Most of the time he persuaded—sometimes he browbeat—the Texans into voting as a bloc. "If we all vote together, then no one of us can be criticized too much at home because we can point out that every other Texas congressman voted the same way," he argued.[27] Since the Texas delegation usually constituted approximately one-tenth of the total Democratic strength in the

House during the Republican era, Garner and the Texans had a powerful voice in party councils.

During the twenties, Rayburn began to doubt, for the first time, that he would achieve his ambition of becoming Speaker. Even if the Democrats regained control of the House, Garner and several other qualified Democrats had a stronger claim on the leadership positions. "There were lots of blue moments," said Rayburn in 1956. "John was ten years ahead of me. He was able and he was entitled to it. There just wasn't any way around it. If anybody had offered me a job, I probably would have taken it."[28]

On his own committee, his advancement was blocked by Alben Barkley of Kentucky, who was appointed to the committee in 1913, just ahead of Rayburn. Barkley was youthful, vigorous, popular, and able. If the Democrats came back to power, he—not Rayburn—would become chairman. But again, as it had so many times throughout his life, fortune smiled on the Texan. In 1926, Barkley ran for the Senate and was elected. His departure from the House cleared the way for Rayburn to become the committee's senior Democrat. Suddenly, the chairmanship seemed just a matter of time.

The problem of Garner's blocking his path to the Speakership was more serious, because it brought into conflict Rayburn's burning ambition and his strong personal loyalty to the one who had helped him most to get ahead in Congress. Garner's professed ambition also was to be Speaker. He was in magnificent health. He had no desire whatsoever to serve in the Senate. One of the most gifted legislative technicians in American history, a man of remarkable mental powers and leadership—"a terrible, table-thumping Democrat," as Rayburn once called him— Garner clearly was entitled to be Speaker when the Democrats returned to power. Rayburn resigned himself to it. As Garner's chief lieutenant, he even looked forward to it, although he knew what it meant to his own ambitions. There would be considerable House prejudice against having two Texans in the Speaker's chair in the same era, particularly with Texans, because of their seniority, holding several important committee chairmanships. Though discouraged, Rayburn never despaired about his chances of becoming Speaker and continued to work earnestly at his job.

To the public, Rayburn was scarcely known in the 1920s. Even to fellow House members, he was inconspicuous. But he was well known to the Democratic leaders in and out of Congress. To the "insiders" of both parties who gathered daily with him at the Bureau of Education, he was exceptionally well known, and his talents were respected. Now and then, his real stature in the House was glimpsed by some acute observer. Marvin Jones recalled that, by 1920, when Rayburn had been in Congress only seven years, he had become the third most senior member of the Texas delegation and was "already one of the uncrowned leaders of the House."[29] In 1922, the *Saturday Evening Post* named him one of eight Democrats—and one of nineteen congressmen of all parties—who were the "leaders of the House."[30] Despite such occasional instances of encouragement and recognition, Rayburn felt that precious years were slipping away while he made no perceptible progress toward the summit of his ambition.

When the Republicans took control of the House in 1919, Rayburn was 37 years old; before the Democrats came back to power, he would be 49. These were usually the critical years in a career, the time when a person should approach his or her goal if that goal is ever to be achieved. Yet to the stocky Texan during this period, it often seemed that the Speakership was becoming more and more remote.

Toward the end of his career, Rayburn looked back upon Calvin Coolidge as the most capable of the three Republican Presidents who followed Woodrow Wilson. He had low regard for Warren Harding, whom he never met personally, but even during the height of the Teapot Dome scandals, he limited his criticism to Harding's policies and refrained from assailing the man.[31] Coolidge, Harding's successor, appealed to Rayburn very much. "I liked Coolidge, and he came out all right," he used to say.[32] The quizzical New Englander and stocky southwesterner got along well because, in many respects, they were alike. Both were taciturn in public but often garrulous in private. They were men of simple tastes and habits, lacking in pomposity and pretense, who believed in telling the plain truth in all circumstances. Both came from rural, late Victorian backgrounds. And, for all their experience in the cities, both remained men of the soil.

Coolidge's famous comment on the virtues of silence—"A man never has to explain something he didn't say"—strongly appealed to the Texas congressman. "That's about the wisest thing I ever heard outside the Bible," he used to say. A favorite Rayburn anecdote told of Coolidge's reply to a senator who rushed into his office one day, breathlessly demanding action on a certain problem. Coolidge, feet on his desk, droned lazily: "Don't you know that four-fifths of all our troubles in this life would disappear if we would only sit down and keep still?" A quarter century later, Senator Lyndon Johnson had much the same experience with Rayburn. Upset about some minor political crisis, Johnson frenetically told his colleague, "Sam, we've got to move. We've got to get off our fannies and do something." Rayburn, his dark eyes flashing, replied: "Well, Lyndon, in forty years I've seen damned few of these things that I couldn't sit out."[33]

Rayburn had more official dealings with Herbert Hoover than with any other Republican President except Eisenhower. As secretary of commerce from 1921 to 1929, Hoover was an unusually active and imaginative Cabinet officer, who made frequent appearances as a witness before the Committee on Interstate and Foreign Commerce. Rayburn watched the personable, Iowa-born administrator carefully and concluded that, while he was an effective Cabinet member, he probably would be a poor President. As he later recalled: "I thought Hoover was a fine member of the team but would make a hell of a poor captain. He was an engineer and didn't know a thing about politics. A lot of those fellows are taught to hate politicians, and they just can't get the feel of politics. They just can't grasp it, so they can't make a success in politics."[34]

While Rayburn held his tongue in public, he was severe in his private assessments of the unfortunate President Hoover. To a Texas friend in 1932, he wrote that Hoover was "a toadying master engineer who has proven to be the poorest excuse of a President that we have had in the history of the Republic." Moreover, Rayburn was in sulphurous disagreement with Hoover's views on foreign policy, especially his advocacy of a "Fortress America" free from foreign entanglements. "Hell, I'd rather fight in Budapest than in Bonham," the Texan once declared.

From the days of his youth, Rayburn fervently believed that Republicans, wedded to their Hamiltonian economic theories, simply did not know how to run the country. The stock market crash of 1929, he was convinced, was the direct result of fatal flaws in the Hoover administration's "trickle-down" economic politics. He believed the nation's best hope—perhaps only hope in those darkest peacetime hours—lay in a return of the Democrats to the White House in 1932.

Meanwhile, Rayburn was approaching a milestone in his career. In the 1930 congressional elections, the Republicans retained their majority in both houses by a breathtakingly thin margin. Aroused by the deepening depression and the ineffectiveness of the Hoover antidepression program, voters were swinging back toward the Democrats.

The new Congress, under prevailing election procedures, did not meet until December 1931—thirteen months after the election. In the interval, twelve representatives-elect died, Speaker Longworth among them, shifting control of the House to the Democrats. For the first time in twelve years, the Democrats were back in command. John Garner was elected Speaker, while other senior party members took charge of the committees. Sam Rayburn, passing a major way station in his own quest for the Speakership, became chairman of the Committee on Interstate and Foreign Commerce.

7

Metze

Rayburn never spoke of his failure in marriage, not even with his own family. That was most unusual, because there were few secrets within the close-knit clan. Whatever lay behind the breakup seemed too painful for him to discuss. The brief marriage itself quickly faded from public memory. In Washington and in the Fourth Congressional District of Texas, a generation grew up believing that Rayburn was a lifelong bachelor. The story of this long-forgotten episode in his life resurfaced in the mid-1950s when an alert reporter, assigned to cover the demolition of the famous old Sedberry Hotel in McMinnville, Tennessee, came across this entry in a dusty guest register: "Congressman & Mrs. Sam Rayburn."

Questioned about the entry, Rayburn confirmed that he had indeed been married in a Texas ceremony in October 1927. Immediately afterward, he and his bride caught a train bound for Tennessee, where they visited relatives and took delivery on a new car that they drove on to Washington. Then, with a faraway look in his eyes, he added: "It was so long ago, it doesn't seem as though I was ever married."

Members of his staff cautiously tried through the years to draw Rayburn into a discussion of the marriage. It was a subject that intruded into the most sensitive area of his psyche, so inquiries had to be carefully worded to elicit a response other than anger. One day in the late 1950s, during a particularly cordial discussion, one of his aides asked Rayburn: "What is the hardest blow you ever had?"[1] Rayburn cut his eyes around, alert as a deer. "You mean politically or personally?"

"Both."

The old man looked daggers, thought a minute, and said with a finality that ended the conversation: "None—that I didn't get over."[2]

Another time, an aide came across a long, favorable newspaper article about the Speaker that contained a brief mention of the marriage. Rayburn later read the piece and liked it. "Cut out that part about that marriage and then it can go in the scrapbook," he told the aide.[3]

Rayburn's marriage to 27-year-old Metze Jones of Valley View, Texas, on October 15, 1927, shocked their friends in Washington and northeast Texas. Few had known of their virtually secret, mostly long-distance courtship, and fewer still would have predicted that Rayburn, everybody's favorite example of the confirmed Washington bachelor, could have been lured into matrimony with any woman. Beautiful, vivacious, strong-willed Metze (pronounced "Meets") was the youngest sister of Rayburn's close friend and onetime roommate, Congressman Marvin Jones of Amarillo. Rayburn had known and sometimes courted Metze for at least eight years before the marriage. She was a stunningly attractive woman with delicate facial features, fair complexion, and lovely, silky, red-tinged hair. When Alla Clary joined his staff as secretary in 1919, Rayburn advised her that he would be receiving occasional letters from a Miss Jones in Valley View. These were personal and were to be delivered to him unopened. From time to time, Metze also mailed Rayburn boxes of homemade cookies.[4] In the intervening years, she made infrequent visits to Washington, ostensibly to see her brother. On these occasions, she invariably would drop by Rayburn's office, and often she and the congressman would leave together.

Throughout his life, Rayburn put his ambition and his family first, his personal desires second. Therefore, the taking of a bride years younger than himself, when he was in middle age, was a risk—personally, politically, and in family terms—of the sort the cautious man seldom took. He could have not overlooked the inherent difficulties of changing his bachelor's habits in middle age and of having the independent Metze fit amicably into the Rayburn clan.

Politically, Rayburn knew that a wife could either greatly advance or gravely injure his career. She could help or hurt in a major way, not just in the Washington world, but, more importantly, with the voters of the Fourth Congressional District of Texas. To Rayburn, his career was the focus of his existence. Why, then, did he do it? Rayburn never doubted that, one day, he would find just the right woman to love and marry. Although he found close attachments to anyone outside his family extremely difficult—"I am of such a nature that I cannot believe many folks have a very tender devotion for me"[5]—he was comforted by the idea, abstract though it was, that he would have someone to share his life and ease the painful loneliness that often consumed him. He loved children and dreamed of having lots of them. What he lacked most in life, he would say plaintively as he grew older, was "not having a little towheaded boy to teach how to fish."

His reasons for not marrying as a young man were as complex as Rayburn himself. Inherently shy, trained to conform to a strict moral code, and brought up on a farm with few opportunities to meet young women, he had had little contact with the opposite sex as a youth. Moreover, Rayburn had powerful psychological ties to this mother. He idealized her and compared all women individually to that ideal. As a result, the women he met, almost without exception, were measured carefully and found wanting.

Rayburn did not marry while his mother lived. Their closeness was extraordinary. Many felt that Sam had inherited more noticeable Waller traits—strong will, penetrating mind, ravenous desire for learning, and those deep, dark eyes—than any of the other Rayburn children. Mat Rayburn seemed as instinctively drawn to her middle son as he was to her. He wrote to her every Sunday—long, descriptive, idolizing letters. Her affectionate correspondence is filled with maternal pleadings for him to return as often as his responsibilities permitted and with her thinly disguised deep disappointment when he chose to stay in Washington during a congressional recess.

Sam worshipped his mother, leaned on her, and undoubtedly drew strength from her. While she lived, he decided, marriage—even in the unlikely event he found the "right" woman—was out of the question. "Two women under the same roof can't be in charge of a house," he said. He also repeated often: "As long as a man has his mother, he is a rich man. When she dies, he is forever poor." On February 21, 1927, six months before her eighty-first birthday, Mat Rayburn died. In October, Sam and Metze were married.

Metze, who had a talent for decorating, planned the wedding details. For the ring ceremony, the church altar was transformed into an old English garden. As the *Dallas Morning News* described the setting: "From the trellised walls smilax trailed. Stately palms screened the seats. Ferns and tall baskets of plume chrysanthemums and gilt cages in which sang golden-throated canaries added to the beauty of the scene. Frank Jones sang, 'I Love You Truly' and 'Because.'" William Rayburn was best man; Marvin Jones gave the bride away.

The bridal chorus from *Lohengrin* boomed from the pipe organ as Metze, dressed from veil to slippers in black, came slowly down the aisle. Her unusual attire, against the backdrop of airy trellises and white chrysanthemums, provided a spectacular contrast. She wore, as the *Dallas Morning News* society reporter described it, "an imported afternoon frock of black transparent velvet, heavily adorned with cut stones and dewdrop pearls. Her hat was a French creation of black velvet and blue suede. She carried a colonial bouquet of sweetheart roses and valley lilies."[6] Some of the couple's friends had misgivings: "You know what they say: when the bride wears black, the marriage is doomed."

Congress, after a brief recess, was due to reconvene soon, so Rayburn and his bride decided to go straight to Washington without stopping in Bonham. As a result, the pair never spent a night as man and wife in his congressional district—another reason why his constituents knew little or nothing of the brief union. The trip by train and car was to be their honeymoon. The first leg by train took them to Memphis, where brother Will was waiting with a new Buick he had picked up for Sam at the factory in Michigan. Then followed a leisurely, though strenuous, drive to Washington. Paved roads were a rarity, and travel through the eastern mountain states was slow and tiring. In east Tennessee, Rayburn stopped to introduce his new bride to cousin Mose Waller and his family. Metze, despite her beauty and charm, did not hit it off with Mose Waller: "I took her up to see the old log house where Sam was born. On the way back, Metze got some cockleburs in her stockings. She really pitched a scene. It made me mad; I was really disgusted. When we got back to the house, I told my wife: 'Honey, Sam's married a damn fool.'"[7]

Details of the decay of the marriage are hidden, probably for all time. One can make guesses, but there is no proof. Spouses of members of Congress often have great difficulty adjusting to Washington life. Uncertain working hours, the attention that members receive from admirers of both sexes, an erratic home life, the demands of entertaining constituents, associates, and friends—most of whom are scant acquaintances of the spouse—all contribute to a high rate of separation and divorce among senators, representatives, and their staffs. The Rayburn marriage began with still another, perhaps fatal, impediment: the eighteen-year disparity in the couple's ages. Rayburn had been a confirmed bachelor whose intimate relationships with women were few and ephemeral. Although far from careless in his personal habits, he was accustomed to a casual atmosphere and, at 45, "mighty 'sot' in my ways."

Some who knew Metze felt that she was disgusted with the moral tone of Washington, particularly the free flow of bootleg liquor. It was the middle of the prohibition period; while the sale of all alcoholic beverages was banned under the Constitution and the law, the Jazz Age was in full swing. Bootleggers—including one immortal character known simply as "the man in the green hat," who made regular deliveries in the halls of the

Capitol itself—flourished. Rayburn, a true protégé of John Garner, consumed his share of the green-hatted man's products.

Metze freely expressed her strong feelings about drinking to one and all. Witnesses remembered a Christmas party, given by the chairman of the House Interstate and Foreign Commerce Committee, at which Metze "made a public scene" when she saw her husband imbibing an alcoholic drink. Sensing that her behavior might well hurt his reputation among his colleagues, perhaps jeopardize his career, Rayburn was enraged. The couple quarreled heatedly.[8]

Metze also took an immediate dislike to the modest upper 16th Street apartment that Rayburn found and rented on his own and where he expected Metze to spend her days—and evenings, too, when he was working late or detained at the Bureau of Education. Mrs. Schuyler Otis Bland, then wife of a Virginia congressman, recalled:

> I had known both Metze and Sam for several years before they were married, so when they got to town, I gave the only party ever given in Washington for Mrs. Rayburn.
>
> I also know about the first fuss they ever had in their married life. Sam had taken this new apartment for his bride. One of the few things he moved over from his previous place was an old daybed that he liked to relax on. When Metze saw that old bed, she pointed to it and said it was the most disreputable thing she ever saw.
>
> Sam bristled, "That's the most comfortable bed I ever relaxed on."
>
> Metze said, "I don't care. It's a disgrace and it's got to go."
>
> Sam was good and mad, and he snapped back, "We don't put on airs in my family."
>
> It was a first-class fuss, and, as I remember it, the bed stayed.[9]

On January 7, 1928—after two months and twenty-five days of living together—Metze left her husband and returned to Texas, claiming a sinus attack. She never came back. She settled in Dallas, took a job at the Neiman-Marcus department store, and told her friends: "I am going to spend the rest of my life here." She never spoke disparagingly of Rayburn or explained the breakup.[10] Later that year, Rayburn asked his Bonham attorney and close friend Fenner Leslie to file suit for divorce. Metze, represented by her brother Marvin Jones, did not contest the suit. In October, the divorce was granted. Rayburn undoubtedly was relieved that the divorce was granted quietly—as Leslie later put it, "without publicity or talk about it." A few months later, the divorce papers disappeared from the Fannin County courthouse—stolen, most likely, by one of Rayburn's lawyer friends—and with them went all official trace of the brief episode that he would remember as his biggest disappointment.

No details of the divorce ever surfaced. There were rumors—never substantiated—that Metze was in love with another man back in Texas and that Sam advised her to go home and marry him.[11] She eventually remarried (Jeff Neely of Amarillo) and raised a family. "I don't know myself what happened," said Marvin Jones years later. "My own feeling is that it was a case of two people too set in their ways before they were married and just not flexible enough to work it out."[12] Fenner Leslie said in 1965, "I know what it was supposed to be, but I don't want to comment on it."[13] Jones's theory is a logical one. Why, then, did the principals, by their absolute silence, perpetuate the mystery and speculation?

Rayburn's silence may have been bolstered by the example of one of his heroes, Sam Houston. Shortly after the divorce, the congressman read a popular recent biography of Houston— *The Raven* by Marquis James. In compelling detail, James explored the mysterious and still-unfathomed failure of Houston's first marriage when he was governor of Tennessee, a personal tragedy that drove the great frontier statesman into years of drunkenness and, eventually, to glory in the Texas Revolution. Stories about the breakup were legion, but Houston never confirmed or denied any of them. Perhaps he simply was following the southern gentleman's custom of never speaking ill of a lady; perhaps there were other motivations. For whatever reason, Rayburn chose a similar course.

Once, in 1956, during a relaxed evening at the home of Congressman Hale Boggs of Louisiana and his wife, Lindy, Rayburn seemed to drop his guard just a little. Conversation had turned to the subject of Adlai Stevenson's divorce. "The divorce is cutting us a lot deeper than people realize," commented one guest, a member of the Democratic presidential nominee's staff. "It is really hurting the campaign."

"God Almighty," Rayburn burst out, "what the hell is a man supposed to do when his wife picks up her panties and goes home to mama? Why should the man be blamed for it? Hell, death and divorce are two of the greatest deliverances known to man." He caught himself, stiffened. The conversation ended.

Without question, Rayburn liked women. "If they were good-looking, they had some influence on him," remembered Buster Cole, a longtime friend.[14] He enjoyed their company, and in his youth and middle years he had a relatively active sex life. Now and then, he bragged a little about his prowess with the opposite sex, but he was always a model of discretion. His ambition to succeed was the central fact of his life, and any indiscretion, sexual or otherwise, that might hinder that ambition was unthinkable. His decision in middle age to marry a younger woman was an aberration.

Well into old age, he was a rather handsome, virile ("vi-rile," he pronounced it) man, considered a prize catch. A few women chased him at times. With some he had sexual relationships, but if the situation showed signs of getting serious, or if the gossip columnists mentioned the relationship, he abruptly ended it. He escorted Alben Barkley's widow to parties for a while, but when the press began writing about the couple, he broke off the friendship. Mrs. Barkley issued a public statement denying any romantic involvement. One of Rayburn's former women friends recalled in 1958: "He used to take me to parties all the time. Then Drew Pearson mentioned it in his column, and he never took me out again. If he sees me at a party alone, he'll take me home. But he is not about to have any romance gossiped about."

A male friend who had been close to Rayburn for many years said:

Sam was one of those men who was very naive about

women. For years, he thought women were either black or white, that there were no grays. He thought they were either pure, chaste, and wonderful, or they were shameless whores. He had no idea that there are many women of character who, with no thought of marriage, still like sex. I don't think Sam could quite realize that sex, the physical union, is a part of a successful marriage. It didn't coincide with his dream of the beautiful chaste flower.

He always put women—the good women—on a pedestal. He put his mother there, and he put his sister there. I'm sure he put his wife there. He had sex with various women but not ever with one he had on a pedestal. I am convinced that Sam's marriage to Metze was never consummated. He had her on such a pedestal that he could not ever quite get around to the physical union.

Rayburn maintained off-and-on intimate relationships with several women over the years. He and they grew old together. At least two widows of very prominent men were interested in him, causing him to squirm and dodge for a while. He'd joke about his great appeal to women, but he was determined, after Metze, to remain free and unencumbered. In later years, he abandoned sex in the belief that such activity in old age had led to heart attacks and death for some of his friends. He had an eye for beautiful, stylish, well-dressed women who were at ease in the Washington political atmosphere and who could talk knowledgeably about public affairs. He had no tolerance for chitchat, wouldn't take part in it, and didn't care to be around those who did. He preferred women whose interests were attuned to his; he once said of a woman friend: "Don't you like her? She thinks just like a man."

In describing Rayburn, women he dated seldom failed to mention his extraordinary gestures of kindness. A former girlfriend said in 1959:

He came by one night to pick me up. Just as I was leaving, I noticed in the mirror that I was dripping with perspiration. I had to go back and powder my back. Sam hated to wait for anyone. When I got to the car, he was grumbling,

"What the hell took you so long?" So I explained.

"You mean you don't have air conditioning?"

"Sam," I said, "you know good and well I can't afford it."
A week later I walked into my apartment and found that a
new air conditioner had been installed. Sam did that. He
never said a word about it until I confronted him with it.

At social gatherings, especially in later years, Rayburn would
be surrounded by admiring women. He grew accustomed to
being kissed, hugged, and patted. He enjoyed the attention, but
he understood that sexual attraction goes hand in hand with
power, and so he never took it too seriously. Supreme Court
Justice Tom Clark, a Rayburn contemporary, once said to him:
"Sam, you and I go to lots of the same parties. The ladies always
shake hands with me and are very polite. But when you come
in, they swarm all over you. What's your secret?" Rayburn replied with a smile: "Well, Tom, when it comes to women, a
man's either got it or he ain't got it. And I got it." [15]

In the third of a century that Rayburn lived after his marriage
was ended, there never appeared to be any trace of bitterness between the families involved. Marvin Jones and Rayburn continued their close, admiring friendship until Rayburn's death.
When any members of the large Jones family came to Washington after Rayburn became Speaker, he put his chauffeured car at
their disposal. His former mother-in-law, who lived past 100,
got a birthday greeting from him every year without fail. Not
long before he died, Rayburn asked Marvin Jones if Metze ever
came to Washington. "Not often," Jones answered.

"Well, next time she comes," Rayburn said, "I wish you'd
bring her by the apartment. I'd love to have a good long talk
with her."

The marriage occupied only a small part of Rayburn's long
life, but it left an indelible scar. Outwardly, he quickly recovered, his confidence and ambition intact. Inwardly, the divorce was a cruel blow to his pride. It represented the one thing
he could not stand in himself or others: failure. "The saddest
word in the English language," he used to say.

Some months after Metze left him, Rayburn and Hatton Sumners were driving to Texas. They stopped to have lunch with Mose Waller and his family in east Tennessee. Waller, unaware of the breakup, waited for Rayburn to mention Metze. Finally, he asked, "Sam, how's your wife?" Rayburn put down his knife and fork, looked straight at his cousin. "Mose," he said, "my marriage was a failure." Without another word, he resumed eating. The subject was closed.[16]

Metze died in 1984, maintaining her silence until the end.

8

Kingmaker

Although in his twentieth year as a congressman, Rayburn in 1932 had little experience in national politics. He had never campaigned for himself or others outside his own little corner of north Texas and was scarcely known beyond his home state and Capitol Hill. That was soon to change. As manager of a bizarre bid by John Garner for the Democratic presidential nomination, Rayburn wound up a key participant in the selection of an historic ticket.

Garner had barely settled into his new job as Speaker when his name began appearing in the press as a possible choice for higher office. The idea took root in Texas and blossomed in California, where millionaire publisher William Randolph Hearst decided Garner was the one person who could stop Franklin D. Roosevelt's seemingly inexorable march to the Democratic presidential nomination.[1] The movement to Garner, then the highest-ranking elected Democrat in the land, was hardly a ground swell. But in Texas, which had had no serious contender for the Presidency since Sam Houston in the 1850s, there was enthusiasm. And, with Hearst throwing his vast newspaper empire behind Garner, there was hope. Supporters organized, staged a festive rally in San Antonio, and named Sam Rayburn as chairman of a national Garner for President campaign drive.

The main problem was Garner himself. He refused to discuss his availability with anyone, including Rayburn. He did not order his supporters to cease what they were doing; he simply would not discuss it. "I do not know whether Mr. Garner takes very seriously the movement to make him a candidate or not," Rayburn told a friend.[2] Equally baffled was another long-time Garner confidant, John McDuffie of Alabama, who complained to Rayburn that every time the candidacy is mentioned, "John growls like an old bear."[3]

Rayburn could only guess that Garner, by his silence, approved of the efforts then underway in his behalf. When he became Speaker, Garner had made clear that his chief concern would be fighting the depression and, in so doing, establishing a Democratic record for the November elections. He said the economic situation was too serious for partisanship and threw his full weight behind the Hoover antidepression program. Ruling with an iron fist, despite his wafer-thin Democratic majority, Garner by spring had pushed through the House almost all of Hoover's proposals to stimulate the flow of capital, expand credit, and put more money in circulation. To create jobs in a hurry, Garner wrote his own massive public-works program, which he got through the House, over Hoover's objections, after taking the Democrats into a binding caucus and forcing them to vote unanimously for the measure on the floor.[4] A fanatic on balancing the budget, he allowed the House to pass no new spending measure without a corresponding tax increase.

The feisty Texan served, in effect, as both Speaker and majority leader. Ignoring the elected party leader— the inept Henry T. Rainey of Illinois—the new Speaker plunged actively into the horse-trading and cajoling that inevitably surrounds any controversial measure. His biggest task often was to keep his own party in line. The Democrats had been out of power for so long, they had forgotten how to work as a team. Some had a habit, acquired during the long Republican reign, of failing to show up for crucial votes. As Garner remembered:

As Speaker I had a tender majority of three. It was always

very close whenever we had an important vote. I'd never let
the press or lobbyists know what would come up until Pou
[Congressman Edward W. Pou of North Carolina] got up
and said, "I offer this resolution . . ."

My relief came from Fiorello H. LaGuardia [Republican
of New York]. I could never pronounce his first name, so I
just called him "Frijole"— he liked that. He came to see me
one afternoon and said, "Mr. Speaker, you need help and I
can help you. I've got about fifteen votes that I can deliver
on important bills. You stay with me on some things I
want, and I'll stay with you." He always did.[5]

Although he wanted to be President, Garner rightfully felt
that, given the precarious political balance in the House, he
could not voice any such aspirations, much less involve himself
in any effort to win him the nomination. It would, he thought,
only stir up jealousies, cast doubt on his motives and decisions
as Speaker, and endanger the slim majority upon which his
leadership was based.

Moreover, he believed Roosevelt was the party's strongest
candidate and ought to be nominated. The New York governor
was far ahead of other contenders in terms of delegate support.
Barring a convention deadlock, his nomination seemed assured.
Above all, Garner wanted no part of any "Stop Roosevelt"
movement. If a deadlock developed, and Roosevelt was unable
to put together the two-thirds majority required for nomination, then and only then was Garner available. All his friends
knew, or thought they knew, that he had no interest in the Vice-
Presidency. Over the years, Garner had repeatedly and vividly
told his friends how puny and insignificant that office was, especially when compared to the Speakership.

As the Garner boom was beginning in January 1932, Rayburn
wrote former Congressman Oscar Callaway:

I have been of the opinion that Roosevelt was our best bet,
but if Roosevelt is stopped, it appears to me that Garner will
be the best. I think the best thing for Garner's friends to do
is to adopt a little bit of watchful waiting for the next two

months. . . . Garner is a little bit embarrassed right now
by the talk as he desired to become reasonably well seated
in the Speakership before small jealousies are created by his
being talked about for a higher position.[6]

Garner's refusal to confide in Rayburn was not surprising.
Theirs was not always an easy relationship. Rayburn admired
the Speaker's common sense, courage, and fierce loyalty to his
friends. He was grateful for the older man's tutelage when he
first came to Congress. He believed that Garner was one of the
most astute students of American government of his generation.

But there was another side of Garner's nature that kept Rayburn at a distance. The Speaker had a hard, sometimes cruel
facet to his personality. He kept everyone at arm's length. He
took great delight in testing the mettle of his associates by "giving them hell" in a ferocious, personal way. Sometimes, in the
Bureau of Education, Garner would direct his acid tongue at
Rayburn, dressing him down for some minor infraction or failure to act in a crisis. "I don't think I could have taken it," Tom
Connally once remarked. From Garner's standpoint, it was nothing personal—just his way of dealing with people—from Presidents on down. Rayburn was gruff, short-spoken, often hard,
but basically, he was kind and gentle in his personal relationships—a world apart from Garner's "bloody-your-knuckles"
methods.

Furthermore, Garner had his own stalwart band of supporters
in the House, and those who did not belong to it he considered
genuine adversaries. He resented the fact that Rayburn did not
share his attitude. For years, there had been a keen personal
rivalry, even hatred, between Garner and Congressman Finis
Garrett of Tennessee, Democratic leader in the 1920s. Rayburn
and Garrett, on the other hand, were devoted friends and spent
much time together. Garner once considered standing against
Garrett as a candidate for House Democratic leader. Rayburn
counseled against it: "You can't win, John." Garner refrained,
but he was not happy with Rayburn's friendship with the Tennessean. During all those years, however, Garner continued to
include the man from Bonham in the little circle of lieutenants

who went with him regularly to the Bureau of Education. The two Texans were confederates, not bosom companions.

Rayburn got along better with Mrs. Garner, who served as her husband's secretary, always calling him "Mr. Garner" and treating him with slavish devotion. Between Rayburn and the gentle, kindly Ettie Garner there was deep affection and admiration. One day, Rayburn walked past a table in the House restaurant, where Ettie Garner was dining alone. "Sam," she said, "Mr. Garner tells everybody that he's not a bit interested in the Vice-Presidency. I happen to know better. But don't let him know I told you."[7]

Now Rayburn knew better how to proceed. He personally would be happy to see Garner become Vice-President, not only because it was what the Speaker wanted, but also because of the effect the move might have on Rayburn's own career. As long as Garner remained Speaker—and Garner was predicting that he would hold the job longer than any predecessor—Rayburn had no chance of ever achieving his own highest ambition. Rayburn saw this as a compelling personal reason to win a place on the Democratic ticket for his colleague. "I just had to get him the Presidency or Vice-Presidency," confided Rayburn years later.[8]

Garner continued his policy of silence until the very day Rayburn was to leave for the Democratic convention in Chicago. Garner himself had decided to remain in Washington. On his way to Union Station, Rayburn paused in the doorway of the Speaker's Rooms. "If John has anything to say to me," he told Garner aide Harry Sexton, "he'd better say it damn quick because my train leaves in thirty minutes."

Sexton scurried into the Speaker's private office. Soon Garner was in the doorway, beckoning Rayburn to come in. They sat down on a wide windowsill, where Garner, for the first time, confided in his campaign manager his innermost thoughts about his candidacy. These were the older man's words, as Rayburn remembered them:

There is one thing we've got to make sure that we don't do, Sam. We are going to win the election this fall unless we make damn fools of ourselves as we did in 1924. If we deadlock that convention and pick a compromise candidate, we will lose the election, and I want to live long enough to see a Democrat in the White House again. So we must make certain that we don't have a deadlock in Chicago. Sam, you and I both know that I am not going to be nominated for President. But a lot of these people who have been pushing me are loyal friends, and they think they are doing me a big favor so I couldn't very well say no to them. As you know, I have been wanting to quit politics for several terms [Rayburn knew no such thing], but my people won't let me. There might be a chance for me to be nominated for Vice-President, and it might be a nice way for me to taper off my career by spending four years presiding over the Senate.[9]

With those meager instructions, Rayburn headed for Chicago to do his best to win the presidential or vice-presidential nomination for his colleague.

A wild, raucous scene confronted Rayburn in the convention city. Supremely confident that this was to be a Democratic year, joyous delegates from the forty-eight states jammed the lobbies of the hot, stuffy hotels. When Rayburn got his first glimpse of his own Texas delegation, he shuddered. Earlier he had urged Texas Democrats to send only "serious and earnest" delegates who would leave their "broad-brimmed hats and Tom Mix boots" at home and devote their energies to "trying to find the answer to the grave question of who should be the candidate . . . to lead us out of the terrible situation into which we have been led by [Hoover] who has proven to be the poorest excuse of a President that we have had in the history of the Republic."[10]

Rayburn's advice went unheeded. The Texas entourage, with no fewer than 368 delegates and alternates, was the largest, noisiest, and most unruly at the convention. The Old Gray Mare Band, which accompanied the delegation on a special train, played incessantly in the lobby of the Sherman Hotel, the Texas headquarters. Bootleg whiskey flowed abundantly within the Texas contingent, and not only among the "wets," who argued and fought continuously with the "drys" over repeal of the 18th Amendment.[11] Vowing to back Garner's candidacy to the bitter end, rambunctious Texans stormed the other hotels daily, passing out Garner literature and praising the "Andrew Jackson–like" virtues of the enigmatic Speaker of the House.

At his state's first caucus on Sunday, June 26, Rayburn saw the hopelessness of effectively advancing Garner's candidacy through the delegation. Texas's 46 convention votes were divided among 184 delegates, each with one-fourth of a vote. Splitting the vote into quarters gave the state the largest delegation, but it also ensured confusion and dissension. At one particularly wild caucus, delegate Amon Carter of Fort Worth implored his fellow Texans "not to make a spectacle of yourselves by acting like you're crazy."

Including Texas's 46, Rayburn counted 90 votes for Garner. All of Garner's strength outside of Texas was in California, where his name had been entered without his consent in the state Democratic primary the previous month; with no effort on his part, he had beaten Roosevelt and Al Smith of New York in a three-way race. Under California law, delegates were committed to vote for the primary winner until released by him.

To win the Democratic presidential nomination at that time, a candidate needed a two-thirds majority, or 780 delegate votes. Roosevelt came to the convention with a clear majority of the delegates behind him, but he was short of the required two-thirds by perhaps 100 to 120 votes. The avowed strategy of all the other candidates, except Garner, was to hold fast to their own support for as long as possible—four ballots, at least—and hope for Roosevelt's support to fade. In Rayburn's account:

> A lot of people wanted to stop Roosevelt, but if they did, they were probably going to get Al Smith, and they didn't want that.
>
> I was sent by our people to this penthouse, owned by a fine Democrat, where all the "Stop Roosevelt" people were having a meeting. I listened and listened to them talk about how they were going to stop Roosevelt and put over Al

Smith. I decided there's nothing in this for John Garner, so I left. Later, Al Smith called me and said, "Are our lines holding?" I said, "No, I don't think they are," and he slammed the phone down.

Silliman Evans [in charge of the Garner headquarters at the Sherman Hotel] was running around. One night he came up and got me out of bed—or, more like it, out of my shirttail with some woman—a prominent Democratic woman, too—and told me I had to come talk to Jim Farley [Roosevelt's campaign manager].

We went over. Silliman, myself, and Farley talked. No mention was ever made then or later about the Vice-Presidency for Garner. But I just knew if we switched to Roosevelt, they'd be sure to nominate Garner for Vice-President.

Farley said, "Can you switch on the first ballot?"

I said, "Hell, no, we've got a lot of people up here who've never been to a convention before, and they've got to vote for Garner a few times." No pledges were made, no agreement. We just talked.[12]

Farley had a slightly different remembrance of the meeting. He later said he told Rayburn that "we would positively give Garner the second-place nomination" if Texas would switch to Roosevelt immediately after the first ballot. "Sam said he had to vote for Garner for two or three ballots at least and asked how long I could keep our forces intact," Farley recalled. "Quite frankly, I told him certainly for three ballots, very likely for four, and possibly for five. Sam's answer was, 'We just must let the convention go for a while even if we are interested in the Vice-Presidency, and I'm not saying we are.'"[13]

What Rayburn did not know was that Farley, shopping frantically for votes to put Roosevelt over the top, was also dangling the Vice-Presidency before other candidates. Still, convention rumor had it that a Roosevelt-Garner deal was set. In Washington, the Speaker scoffed at the reports, telling reporters he had no interest whatever in the Vice-Presidency. Rayburn, the only Democrat in Chicago able to get through to Garner on the telephone, also denounced the rumors, reminding fellow Texas delegates in a rousing caucus speech that they had come to Chicago to nominate Garner for President and that this was still possible, if Texas would show as much enthusiasm for the candidate as California did.

On Thursday, June 30, the voting for President began. The first roll call gave Roosevelt 666¼ votes, Smith 201¾, Garner 90¼. On the second, Roosevelt gained 11½ votes, Smith lost ground, Garner held steady. After an all-night session, Roosevelt supporters forced still a third ballot before agreeing to a fourteen-hour recess that would allow the dead-tired delegates some time to rest and caucus. As weary Democrats headed back to their hotels, FDR's strength stood at 682½ votes, Smith's at 190¼, and Garner's at 101¼. On the third ballot, Garner picked up 11 votes from Oklahoma. Rayburn recollected:

> On the night they took three ballots, I was under the platform with Arthur Mullen, Burt Wheeler, and Cordell Hull and some others. It was 6 o'clock in the morning, and everybody was hot and sweaty. Nobody had shaved and a lot of people were drunk. I told them, "If you want to nominate Roosevelt, you'd better recess this convention and let people have some conferences and so forth." Finally, I persuaded them to recess it.
>
> At 3 that afternoon, I talked to Garner. He said, "Sam, we don't want to deadlock that convention. Roosevelt has a clear majority on every ballot. He is the choice of the convention and ought to be nominated."
>
> I told Garner, "All right."
>
> Garner wouldn't talk to anybody in Chicago but me. He was one man that could do that. Hearst supported him, but do you think he called or wired or wrote Hearst his thanks? He did not. He was that way.
>
> We were to have a Texas caucus at 6 o'clock that evening. Amon Carter and the bunch were raising hell. Amon was attending his first convention and running around, saying he had talked to this one and that one. He was going to nominate Garner whether he had the votes or not. I turned

the gavel over to Silliman Evans and went to call Garner.
I got him right away. I knew somebody would challenge
my releasing the delegation, so I asked him two questions:
"Do I have permission to release the Texas delegation now?"
He said, "Yes."
I said, "Do you release the Texas delegation now?"
He said, "Yes."

I started back to the caucus and ran into McAdoo [William
Gibbs McAdoo, head of the California delegation and a key
Garner supporter]. He asked me what was happening. I told
him Garner had just released the Texas delegation, and in
my opinion we were going for Roosevelt. Earlier, McAdoo
had told me that California would stay with Garner to
the end. He rushed off, got his people together, and they
switched to Roosevelt. While we were still caucusing, he
got a motorcycle escort to the convention hall. I went back
in the caucus and told Silliman: "You get to the convention
hall right now and get word to Farley that Garner has released the Texas delegation." [14]

Then I told the delegation what had happened. Amon
Carter had to make another speech. The women were crying. [So was Rayburn, according to witnesses. J. E. Kilday,
a Houston delegate, observed in his notes: "Sam Rayburn,
tired and drawn and wearing an emaciated look from loss of
sleep, announced with a breaking voice and tears in his eyes
that Garner had released us."]

Everybody was saying they wouldn't desert Mr. Garner,
and I said, "You're not deserting him. He doesn't want your
votes. He wants you to be released." Finally, by a vote of 54
to 51, they decided to go for Roosevelt.

I knew there were three delegations about to leave Roosevelt—Iowa, Mississippi, and Wisconsin. I don't know
where they were going, but they had been turned against
Roosevelt.

On his way out, Silliman ran into Pat Harrison [senator
from Mississippi], who had just come from the Mississippi caucus. Pat said Mississippi had just voted to leave
Roosevelt. Silliman told him that Garner had released Texas.

Pat started running back to the Mississippi caucus, turned around, and came back and said, "Say that again." Silliman told him again. Pat rounded up the Mississippi delegates and told them there was no use switching.

When the Texas delegation finally got to the hall, McAdoo was on the podium announcing that Garner had released his delegates.[15]

Believing that Rayburn and Garner had quit prematurely, many Texas delegates were furious. At the time of the climactic Texas caucus, the convention was alive with rumors of deals— Smith was throwing his support to Garner on the next ballot, the South was deserting Roosevelt for Garner, Tammany Hall was ready to support Garner. Rayburn discounted them all, deciding instead to telephone Garner for permission to release the Texas delegation. Most agreed that Rayburn had acted wisely and at the right time, not only to assure Garner second place on the ticket but also for the greater glory of avoiding a bloody deadlock and enhancing the Democrats' chances in the fall election. Rayburn never had second thoughts. Still, some Garner stalwarts—Amon Carter among them—argued: "We quit too soon."

"We realized that Garner's only chance for the presidential nomination lay in a deadlock," Carter said upon his return to Texas. "I felt we had a horse all saddled up for a two-mile race, but one of the jockeys pulled him up at the quarter-mile post. We had a chance of a lifetime to nominate a President from Texas, but a few of our friends were just a little weak-kneed."

In Washington, Garner's colleagues and friends gathered around a radio in the Speaker's reception room of the Capitol to hear the nominating speeches and the unanimous acclamation of Garner as the party's vice-presidential nominee. Jubilant, anxious to congratulate the Speaker, they waited for him to emerge from his private office. He never appeared. While they clustered around the radio, Garner slipped quietly out a side door, rode unnoticed to his apartment, and took a nap.

9

"The Fight for Economic Justice"

Rayburn and Roosevelt both turned 50 the year the Democrats were swept back to power. For Rayburn, twenty-four days older than the new President, his remaining years were to be the most productive, satisfying, and exciting period of his life. "All of us hate to see the twenties, thirties, or forties slipping away," he used to say. "But every stage of life has its compensations. Some men apparently ripen earlier than others and burn out early. I know that the period after age 50 was the best for me."[1]

At 50, he was in full vigor both mentally and physically. In superb health, he had a voracious appetite, walked a lot, golfed occasionally, slept well. He weighed 176 pounds, a level he maintained without fluctuation until fatal illness struck twenty-nine years later. His full, firm face lacked the deep lines that gave it marvelous expressiveness in old age. His premature baldness was nearly complete, save for a thick fringe of dark brown hair around his ears and the base of his skull. His personal life was singularly free of troubles. The poignant sense of loss resulting from his mother's death had eased. Reconciled to the painful failure of his marriage, he had no interest in marrying again. He now knew his dream of fathering a large family could not be.

In the big, white-columned house in Bonham, his unmarried sister Lucinda began to fill the void left by his mother's death.

Tall, stately, "Miss Lou" was regal and aloof, but her warm humanity and her abundant common sense were widely acknowledged. Until she died in 1956, Lou Rayburn gave her younger brother great devotion, wise counsel, and a bolstering confidence that greatly compensated for his lack of wife and family.

At 50, Rayburn was as ambitious as ever. The pessimism that tortured him during his forties had been replaced by renewed hopes that he might yet reach his goal of becoming Speaker. His future had never looked brighter: Democrats were back in power, in both Congress and the White House. He was chairman of a great committee, and his fellow Texan, John Nance Garner, had become Vice-President, leaving Rayburn the senior member of the powerful Texas delegation. What's more, Texas had more influence in the House than any other state. Five Texans headed important committees—Appropriations, Judiciary, Interstate and Foreign Commerce, Rivers and Harbors, and Public Buildings and Grounds. Garner, although moved to the Senate end of the Capitol, still had extraordinary influence in the House. This collective Texas power, Rayburn knew, might be decisive if and when he got a chance to move up the leadership ladder.[2]

Still largely unknown to the general public, Rayburn enjoyed unusual personal prestige in Congress. His painstaking fairness—almost a nonpartisan approach—as chairman of the Interstate and Foreign Commerce Committee was well known. His ability to think clearly plus his obvious common sense inspired confidence among his colleagues. During twenty years of congressional service, he had grown intellectually through continuous study, observing and questioning of experts in many fields, and scrupulous attendance at committee and House sessions.

The election of 73-year-old Henry T. Rainey of Illinois as Speaker, replacing Garner, came as no surprise to Rayburn, although he and Garner had backed the candidacy of Bureau of Education regular John McDuffie of Alabama. Politicking for the vacant Speakership began soon after Garner's nomination for Vice-President. Several Democrats openly solicited support. Rayburn briefly considered jumping in, but ultimately agreed with Garner that the House might resent another Texan trying to succeed a Texan.[3] Besides, he still needed to build a record for himself as chairman of a major committee.

Rainey's victory was assured when another candidate for the post, Joe Byrns of Tennessee, dropped out and threw his support to the white-maned Illinois liberal. In turn, Rainey backed Byrns for majority leader. Although the Garner clique was frozen out of the leadership, Rainey's ascension had its compensation for Rayburn: unlike McDuffie, six years Rayburn's junior, Rainey was old and could not look forward to a long tenure. Rayburn could afford to wait.

The worst days of the Great Depression were at hand on the frigid March 4 afternoon that Franklin Roosevelt was sworn in as the nation's thirty-second President. The speculative binge of the 1920s had produced a national nightmare: 14 million unemployed, 5,000 banks closed, 100,000 businesses bankrupt, the lifelong savings of millions of individuals wiped out. In the air was a feeling of panic and doubt whether this nation, or any nation, could survive as a democracy. Seated on the east portico of the Capitol in the biting, misty chill, Rayburn listened attentively as the new President—a Democratic President, at last— outlined his program of hope and determination, his "New Deal" for America. It was a program Rayburn, a lifelong believer in affirmative government action, could enthusiastically support.

Facing a cold, discouraged, undemonstrative crowd, the new President, tossing his large, handsome head from side to side and speaking in a confident voice that soon would become known the world over, analyzed the economic paralysis that afflicted the United States: "Plenty is at our doorstep, generous use of it languishes in the very sight of the supply. . . . Rulers of the exchange of mankind's goods have failed, through stubbornness and their own incompetence, have admitted their failure and have abdicated. Practices of the unscrupulous money changers stand indicted in the court of public opinion. . . . The money changers have fled from their high seats in the temple of our civilization."[4] The quiet, impassive crowd broke into loud applause for the first time.[5]

Roosevelt's speech gave only the barest hint of the key role

Rayburn was destined to play in the new administration. "There must be an end to a conduct in banking and in business which too often has given to a sacred trust the likeness of callous and selfish wrongdoing," said the President. "There must be strict supervision of all banking and credits and investments; there must be an end to speculation with other people's money." [6] Well before the Democratic convention in 1932, Roosevelt and his brain trust knew that, if they were elected, a cleanup of Wall Street would be one of their first orders of business. The Democratic platform—like the party's standard bearer in his campaign—demanded congressional action to protect unwary investors from the Street's unscrupulous financiers.

Three and a half weeks after his inaugural, the new President sent Congress his proposal—a far-reaching plan for strict federal supervision of investment securities sold in interstate commerce. Rayburn introduced the draft bill, labeled the Securities Act of 1933, for the administration. [7] It was referred to the Interstate and Foreign Commerce Committee, beginning a bitter, three-year series of battles that ultimately would encompass six of the New Deal's most sweeping proposals and pit the down-to-earth, farm-reared Texan against the ablest lawyers, accountants, publicists, and lobbyists that Wall Street could enlist. One key New Deal figure remembered:

> The first time Roosevelt really waked up to the big financial people was with the Securities Act of 1933. The first people to stand up against Wall Street were the Texans— Garner and Rayburn. You couldn't find any of the northern liberals who would stand up to them, but Garner and Rayburn were not a bit afraid. The Wall Street crowd was so afraid that any legislation would cut their throat that they didn't even read what was proposed. Sam stood up to them, and I think that's why he always liked Roosevelt—because the President stood up against Wall Street pretty well, too. [8]

In the wake of the stock market crash, the need for better public protection in the sale of marketable securities was clear. A Senate Banking and Currency subcommittee, headed by its brilliant, dedicated counsel, Ferdinand Pecora, developed a picture of sordid speculation in high financial circles that shocked and angered an already shaken public. The high priests of American finance, accustomed to operating in secrecy, had the veils surrounding their financial temples ripped asunder in the investigation. The public watched with grim fascination as such Wall Street giants as J. P. Morgan and his partners—Otto H. Kuhn of Kuhn, Loeb and Co. and Charles E. Mitchell of National City Bank—were forced to reveal to the world their most carefully concealed financial devices. The inquiry, one observer summarized, "laid bare financial practices which were generally legally permissible but were morally wrong, not to say abhorrent to a people caught in the backwash of depression. Juggling of capital gains and losses by the enormously wealthy so as to avoid all income taxes, netting huge profits from the marketing of securities that later lost most of their value, granting favors to the powerful while the poor were fleeced—proof of these tricks made Wall Street a fair mark for public attack."[9]

Rayburn's committee had been preoccupied since 1931 with its own major investigation of railroad holding companies— increasingly widespread paper corporations through which the chieftains of high finance circumvented regulatory laws to manipulate and siphon off profits of railroad operating companies. The study of railroad finances began under the chairmanship of New York Republican James Parker and continued under Rayburn when the Democrats came to power. Heading the probe was a brilliant Texas scholar who had been hired by Parker at Rayburn's urging—Dr. Walter M. W. Splawn, former professor of economics and onetime president of the University of Texas.[10] His methodical, low-key approach soon won him wide respect. Under his direction, the investigation focused almost entirely on the railroad companies' books, which were subjected to endless scrutiny and analysis. The professor's painstakingly detailed report ultimately led to the Emergency Railroad Transportation Act of 1933, bringing railroad holding companies under the authority of the Interstate Commerce Commission for the first time. As Splawn recalled in 1957: "The railroad holding company probe was helpful on many bills that came up later. From it, Rayburn learned to understand financial relationships. He worked hard on the bill—harder than any one man in either House, and the Senate went along with him. After the bill passed, everybody knew it was inevitable that he would become Speaker. He showed that what he wants, he wants."[11] Splawn subsequently led the committee through similar investigations of privately held gas and electric utilities. In 1934, at Rayburn's insistence,[12] President Roosevelt named Splawn to the Interstate Commerce Commission.[13]

As the House Interstate and Foreign Commerce Committee began its examination of the administration's plan to regulate the sale of stocks and bonds, the reputation of Wall Street for financial wisdom, care of other people's money, and common honesty was never lower.

The Securities Act of 1933, as proposed, was a catchall, hastily drafted by Washington attorney Huston Thompson, formerly of the Federal Trade Commission.[14] It contained about every scheme ever conceived for regulating securities. Its basic aim was to require the FTC's approval before securities could be sold to the public. All securities would have to be registered with the FTC, which would have sweeping power to deny or revoke issuance of a security on almost any grounds from fraud or misrepresentation to vaguely described abuses of "sound principles" or "the public interest." The commission, in effect, would become the czar of American business, for, without its approval, a company could raise no capital in the open market.[15]

Although he had introduced the measure for the administration, Rayburn decided he wanted no part of it, as written. "We have passed a lot of laws since we met here on the fifth of March, but I do not think we have given anybody that much power yet," he told the committee.

Rayburn was unrelenting in his questioning of administration experts who appeared before his committee to defend the measure. "Do you believe that an administrative officer of the government ought to be given that much power . . . to pass upon whether or not a man's business is based on sound principles?" he asked Ollie Butler of the Commerce Department. "If you want to delegate absolute authority, you can write that in a very short statute. But the question this committee has got to determine is whether or not they want to give anybody that kind of authority."[16] Four days of expert testimony exposed the bill to be even more vague and poorly drafted than Rayburn originally suspected. He was deeply disturbed.

The Texas legislator's own knowledge of the stock market in 1933 was so scant as to be almost nonexistent. He had never seen Wall Street, did not study newspaper financial pages, had no personal interest in stocks and bonds. He once invested $1,000 in Kirby Petroleum stock, but he worried over potential conflict of interest—even though his district then produced no oil or gas—and soon sold it. Concerned that one day he might have to judge legislation that could affect such securities, he never again owned a corporate stock or bond. Instead, all his modest savings went into U.S. government bonds, land, and cattle.

He instinctively felt that the Thompson plan was unworkable and unfair. Yet, knowing next to nothing about securities himself, he could offer no counterproposal. To Raymond S. Moley, then at the height of his influence as head of Roosevelt's so-called brain trust, Rayburn said, "I need help on this thing. I need somebody who knows something."

Moley turned to Harvard Law School professor Felix Frankfurter, who kept close touch with outstanding young lawyers across the nation and who had been invaluable to the New Deal in recruiting able, dedicated young people for positions at many of the new agencies. The job of rewriting the securities bill could be done in a weekend, Frankfurter said. He told Moley he knew just the right person to help—short, wiry, hawk-faced James M. Landis, a 33-year-old Harvard professor whose study of state "blue sky" laws had given him an intimacy with the field of securities regulation. In addition to Landis, he suggested young New York lawyer Benjamin Cohen, an expert on the English Companies Act, under which securities sales were regulated in Great Britain.[17]

Within days, the three lawyers, joined by another Frankfurter protégé—scintillating, cocky Thomas G. Corcoran, counsel for the Reconstruction Finance Corporation—met with Rayburn in Washington to go over their assignment. As Cohen remembered it:

> Rayburn wanted to be sure that it was in the right form and written right. He said he had been told that we could give him the right advice and that he hoped we could give him a bill he could fight for without reservation.
>
> The bankers were claiming the bill was too extreme, but they were so discredited in the public eye that Congress was ready to pass anything. Rayburn was concerned; he did not want to be hoodwinked by the bankers, but on the other hand, he did not want the law to be too extreme. Sometimes I have to laugh—the financial interests were so discredited then that anything would have passed. So it may just be that the dangerous Harvard boys in those days, by writing reasonable bills, actually saved the bankers and other financiers from something much worse.[18]

Landis and Cohen, assisted by Corcoran, began working on a new plan. Within thirty-six hours, a hurried draft was completed. The new approach relied on the theory of the English Companies Act by requiring full and fair disclosure of the nature of the security being offered. It contained no authority for the Federal Trade Commission to pass upon the investment quality of the security, but if the commission found that the registration statement contained misrepresentations or withheld full information, then the registration might be suspended.

Rayburn called a special meeting of the Interstate and Foreign Commerce Committee to consider the new proposal. There he watched Landis and his two assistants—Cohen and Corcoran—in action for the first time, the beginning of a long, fruitful, and historic association. In twenty years in Washington, the Texas congressman had encountered nothing quite like the dazzlingly brilliant young duo of Corcoran and Cohen. Corcoran was ebullient, talkative, at ease in any setting. Cohen was his opposite—reserved, moody, almost shy. "Taken together those two fellows made the most brilliant man I ever saw," recalled Rayburn. "But during all those days, they never bossed me around. I always told them what I wanted, and by God, when you told them, they'd give you what you wanted."[19] Their proposed bill, while still in rough form, was logical and fair; their explanations of its provisions were clear and concise. Rayburn wanted to know if they would stay as consultants to the committee. They agreed to remain, believing the job would require only a few more days. In fact, it took nearly two months. Recalled Landis:

I was impressed with Rayburn's sincerity, his inquiring mind. He was not out to hurt anybody. . . . We did about nine or ten drafts of the bill. Wall Street tried desperately to find out what was in the drafts, but not a thing leaked. Finally, Moley got scared and insisted that Rayburn and the committee go over the draft with some selected representatives of Wall Street. Rayburn balked at first but finally agreed.

The meeting took place on a Saturday morning. John Foster Dulles, Arthur Dean, and Alexander Henderson—some of the top men on Wall Street—came. I was 33 years old, new to politics, and I was worried that Rayburn couldn't stand the pressure, that he would cave in to this high-finance group.

Dulles started the attack, arguing that the legislation would undermine the American financial system. That irritated Rayburn, who insisted that all that was being demanded was that the system should live up to its pretensions. Then Dulles, who was not well prepared, said something completely wrong. Being young and unable to control myself, I blurted out, "That's not in the bill."

Rayburn, by now plainly irked by Dulles's attitude and garrulity, said, "Will you point out that section, Mr. Dulles?" Dulles couldn't find it; he was caught out in left field and never did get back on track. Sam was an expert in human behavior.

Later, I was down in my basement office when the telephone rang. It was Rayburn. "Landis, come up here," he said. I knew that this was it, that he was going to tell me he had decided to soften the bill.

I remember how he glared at me from behind his desk. He ordered me to sit down. Then he sort of smiled and said, "I've never seen such shitasses in my life." That's when I knew that we were on the right track.[20]

The Landis-Cohen-Corcoran draft won the committee's approval with only minor changes.[21] On May 5, Rayburn walked to the well of the House to open the debate on HR 5480—the Securities Act of 1933—the first of a series of historic battles for New Deal legislation that were to win him respect and fame inside and outside of Congress.

He apologized for reading his remarks, something he rarely did during his congressional career. "I have been with this matter for three weeks, day and night, and frankly I am just a little tired," he explained. It was a tremendous grind, Cohen later recalled. "He had hearings all morning, was on the floor all afternoon. There was a constant stream of people wanting to see him, and he had to see most of them. Then he conferred with Tom and me, often at night, sometimes at breakfast. People would present him with a new argument, and he'd ask if there was anything to it."[22]

Bluntly, Rayburn told the House: "With this bill we are embarking upon a practically new and untried sea. This is the most technical matter with which I have ever been called upon to deal." The bill was more a response to the reticence of financiers than to the frauds of criminals, he continued:

> Today we are forced to recognize that the hired managers of great corporations are not as wise, not as conservative, and sometimes not as trustworthy as millions of Americans have been persuaded to believe. . . . The people expect the government of the United States to be clean. They expect the men who run it to be clean. . . . Their representatives have the right to demand that the men who run the business of the country shall conduct a clean business, to be fair and honorable with the other people of the country. In this bill we demand not only a new deal, we also demand a square deal. Less than this no honest man expects nor a dishonest man should have.

With Cohen at his side to advise on technical questions, Rayburn was in full command. The House, after perfunctory debate, passed the bill without a record vote.

The Senate Banking and Currency Committee, busy with its own investigation of Wall Street, was unable to assign to the securities bill experts comparable to Cohen, Landis, and Corcoran. As a result, the measure that ultimately passed the Senate closely resembled the original Thompson draft discarded by the House committee. In the House-Senate conference committee, assembled to reconcile differences between the two measures, Rayburn successfully maneuvered to have the more carefully drawn House version adopted as the basis of a final bill. The few changes made in conference mostly strengthened the original bill. In final form, the Truth-in-Securities Act sailed easily through both houses and was signed by President on May 27.[23]

When the Truth-in-Securities Act passed without a dissenting vote in 1933, the captains of high finance were so discredited that they dared not make a public fight against it. Even their behind-the-scenes efforts to dilute its regulatory features were timid and ineffective. The situation was far different when Congress met in 1934. Wall Street had revived a bit, at least in terms of its willingness to fight, and some leaders were convinced that survival of the capitalistic system was at stake. Moreover, Wall Street lawyers, who had never before had difficulty finding loopholes in legislation affecting business, had discovered that the Truth-in-Securities Act was, as Bernard Flexner wrote, "substantially lawyer-proof."[24] The only effective way to deal with the problem, they decided, was to defeat or dilute further regulatory legislation before it became law.

Roosevelt already had signaled his next move in controlling Wall Street: a statute to regulate the stock exchanges themselves. In February, the President's message requesting such legislation went to Capitol Hill. Sponsoring the bill—a product of close collaboration among Ben Cohen, Tommy Corcoran, Jim Landis, and two young assistants, Telford Taylor and Isaac (Ike) Newton Phelps Stokes II—would be Rayburn in the House and Duncan U. Fletcher of Florida in the Senate. The bill had three goals: 1. the control of inside manipulations in the exchanges, which had often resulted in the fleecing of investors; 2. the strict control of "margins"—the buying of stock on credit; and 3. the registration of all securities, old as well as new, to protect investors against misrepresentations.[25] Once again, the Texan was dealing with a subject of which he had scant personal knowledge.

Introduction of the bill set off an angry storm on Wall Street. The captains of finance understood clearly that if this bill, or any similar bill, was passed, the old ways of high finance were dead. It was outrageous enough to threaten the profits of speculation; it was even more unthinkable that government should presume to invade the sacred precincts of "The Street," which was—in the eyes of most members of the New York Stock Exchange—a strictly private club. Some of the mightiest names of high finance, flanked by their legal and financial experts, came swarming into Washington for public hearings before Rayburn's committee. Leading them was one of the most imperious men in America—swelled with intense and burning pride in his class, his family, himself, and the New York Stock Exchange, which he headed—muscular, six-foot-two Richard Whitney.[26]

Whitney regarded the Securities Act of 1933 as offensive, punitive, and unnecessary. The proposal to regulate the stock exchanges was absolutely unthinkable to the man who considered the New York Stock Exchange "a perfect institution." He was ready for a war to the finish with the New Deal, and he brought to the battle unlimited financial resources, the ablest talent that money could hire, and unflagging determination. Moving his whole general staff to Washington, Whitney set about the task of convincing members of Congress that regulation of the exchanges was best left to the exchanges themselves—a proposition that most lawmakers found preposterous in light of Wall Street's past performances.[27]

Hearings before Rayburn's committee began on February 14 and ran for five and a half weeks as witnesses debated the merits of government regulation versus self-regulation of the stock markets. Leading off for the administration was Landis, who had just been appointed by FDR to the Federal Trade Commission, the agency that would regulate the exchanges under the proposed legislation. There was widespread agreement that the exchanges needed regulating to prevent a recurrence of past abuses, Landis testified. He also pointed out that self-regulation had been tried—and had failed disastrously.

Chief spokesman for the bill's opponents was Whitney, openly showing his disdain for the "politicians" on the Rayburn committee. The bill, he asserted, vested in the FTC not only the power to regulate "but actually also to supervise and manage all stock exchanges." The measure, he added, was "unworkable" and would "have destructive effects not only upon stock exchanges but also upon the value of securities and the business of the country." Snapped Rayburn: "Your statement is rather broad. We have got to take the risk that the law will be administered by reasonable and fairly wise men."

Whitney proposed a long list of amendments. "With the changes, would you support the bill?" Rayburn asked. Whitney hedged. Repeatedly the chairman and the unyielding witness crossed swords, with Whitney contending the bill as written was "unworkable" and Rayburn pressing him for specific proposals for a "workable" bill. Though inconclusive, the intellectual duel between the aristocratic financier and the rural legislator helped lay the foundation for Rayburn's later argument on the House floor that what Wall Street really wanted was no regulation at all.

As witness after witness came before the committee with general criticism of the unfairness and unworkability of the bill, Rayburn pressed time and again for suggestions as to what legislation would be advisable and necessary. All he got as the weeks rolled by was hedging and evasion.

Midway in the hearings, he asked Landis, Cohen, and Corcoran to draft still another version of the bill, taking into account some of Wall Street's criticisms. But that failed to pacify the opposition, which—led by Whitney and others—continued a vicious campaign to block any regulatory legislation. Forged letters, purporting to be from irate citizens protesting this "Communistic" proposal, flooded Capitol Hill and the White House. A massive propaganda drive distorting the proposal's purpose and effect rallied many local bankers and business leaders to the opposition.[28] "The amount of money which was spent to defeat this measure has never been estimated, but it was obviously a staggering sum," wrote an observer. "The newspaper and radio propaganda against the bill alone was tremendous. Every known method of exerting pressure on Congress was used. The longer the battle raged the more apparent it was that the [opposition] lobby was gaining success in its drive to intimidate Congress."[29] Roosevelt, returning from a fishing trip in southern waters, remarked that to get the bill through Congress, he obviously would have to use the same "tough guy" tactics that he had used in fighting "the barracuda and the shark."[30] Finally, tired and exasperated, Rayburn warned the Wall Streeters: "There is going to be a bill of some kind, and we might as well make up our minds to that."

On April 30, the Rayburn bill reached the House floor for debate. It proved to be a genuinely nonpartisan measure, having won the endorsement of every member of the committee save one—Republican Schuyler Merritt of Connecticut. "Few bills have ever had such thorough consideration," said Rayburn, opening the debate. "We have worked out the terms of this bill under the pressure of the most vicious and persistent lobby that any of us have ever known in Washington, a lobby that has relentlessly opposed the bill, not only in the original form, but in the present form and which would, I am convinced, protest against it in any form so long as there was a tooth left in it."[31]

Rayburn's attack focused on the Wall Street propaganda campaign: "There is not one of us who has not recognized how subtly and how cleverly the sources of pressure against us have been chosen, how there have been sent against each of us the most carefully chosen delegations of our personal and political friends, nor how bluntly there has been drummed into us the fact that this is an election year, when we need friends."[32]

It was clear from the start of the debate that the bill had strong bipartisan support despite the financial community's determined opposition. The public was demanding that the stock markets be brought under government supervision, and only a handful of House members were willing to risk their own political future by taking Wall Street's side. A few, however, denounced the measure as a bureaucratic nightmare and, worse, charged that it was "Communist-inspired." "It is not the Fletcher-Rayburn bill; it is the Corcoran-Cohen bill," complained Republican Harold McGugin of Kansas. "These gentlemen are a couple of self-styled intellectuals, a couple of Felix Frankfurter's proteges, a couple of men who do not have and could not obtain the support of any congressional constituency in the United States, yet they can write the bill, sit in the galleries and watch Congress move while they crack the whip."[33]

Fred Britten, Republican of Illinois, chimed in with a claim that the bill was "conceived in the little red house in Georgetown," where Cohen, Corcoran, and several other young government workers lived. "The popular demand for stock exchange regulation has given the Professor Felix Frankfurter cheerleaders a vehicle to control all credit and corporate practices such as not even Russia can boast of today."[34]

Angrily, Rayburn jumped to his feet in defense of his young advisers and his own dependence on them:

> I thought on yesterday we had enough of this "little-red-house" stuff—and it is stuff. We are laymen, not experts. If we were as able as some people in this country think they are, and as some members of this House think they are, we would feel so self-sufficient that we would have to call in no experts. Special privilege always has counsel in the committees of this House. Now, because we call in Mr. Cohen and Mr. Corcoran, two of the ablest young men that it has ever been my privilege to know . . . they are held up—by men who are really opposed to this bill but who are not going to have the guts to vote against it when the roll is called—as being somebody from Russia or being tainted with socialism or communism.[35]

Later, after beating back several weakening amendments with the indispensable help of the committee's senior Republican, Carl Mapes of Michigan, Rayburn called for the yeas and nays. The bill passed by a wide margin, 281–84. A similar bill, introduced by Senator Fletcher, sailed through the Senate a few weeks later.

In the House-Senate conference committee, Rayburn made
one key concession to the bill's opponents, who had argued
strongly against placing stock exchange regulation under the
Federal Trade Commission. He agreed, after talking to
Roosevelt, to a proposal advanced by Senator Carter Glass of
Virginia and others for the creation of a new agency, the Securities and Exchange Commission, whose sole responsibility
would be to oversee the securities markets. This represented a
reversal of mind for the Texan, who had first opposed the idea
when it was suggested by Cohen and Corcoran. Fearful that
Wall Street would dictate the SEC appointments, Rayburn
sought and got FDR's assurance that that would not happen.
Cohen later commented:

> The stock exchange people were strong for a new com-
> mission rather than putting regulation under the FTC. Part
> of it was that they were afraid of Jim Landis, who was head
> of the FTC securities section, but also they were afraid of
> being in an agency where many other things were being
> done instead of concentrating on stock market affairs. So
> we made that concession in conference, and it was a good
> one. Later, FDR just moved Landis over to the SEC.[36]

Before Congress adjourned in June, Rayburn successfully
brought before the House another important New Deal measure—to unify and regulate the growing broadcast and wire
communications industries. Again the wrath of conservative
business interests fell upon Rayburn as he fought in committee
and on the House floor for the administration's plan to create a
Federal Communications Commission.[37] Working against the
pressure of adjournment, the Texan pressed the Senate to accept
his version rather than a more stringent and, some thought,
more punitive measure written by Senator Clarence Dill of
Washington, who authored the Radio Act of 1927. Among its
provisions, the Dill bill provided machinery for government
censorship in war or other emergency, which Rayburn firmly
opposed. Now an experienced legislative negotiator, Rayburn
prevailed in the House-Senate conference committee that drafted
the final bill.[38]

The bill as finally passed included a ban on wiretapping, which became the basis of an enduring controversy on the subject. Who proposed the provision remains a mystery. Rayburn, who considered wiretapping "a dirty business," strongly favored the ban, but he never claimed to have originated the idea. Years later, he added: "When we wrote that bill, we made a mistake in not forbidding ownership of radio stations by newspapers. We could have done it then with no trouble; now it is so entrenched we probably could never break it up."[39]

Coming to grips with the leaders of high finance was a disillusioning experience for Rayburn. From the days of his political indoctrination by Senator Bailey, he had considered himself a solid conservative. That, coupled with his lifelong, almost naive faith in the fundamental honesty of people in general, made Rayburn poorly prepared for his experience with Wall Street. He made a fetish of telling the truth himself; he did not think that any worthy person would lie. Plainly honest in his own financial dealings, he found it hard to believe that people of substance would deliberately try to steal "other people's money." His experience in the running battle with Wall Street was to teach him otherwise. "Hell, I'm a conservative, but even a conservative can smell garbage in his front yard," Rayburn exploded during the fight. He found the lack of vision of many of the nation's financial leaders discouraging. On December 4, 1933, he wrote an old friend, W. P. Hobby of Houston:

> Some of our people want everything static and always preach that any movement that goes forward is socialistic and destructive. The movement at this time seems to be led by the U.S. Chamber of Commerce and the large city bankers. The large bankers . . . have been of little help, have shown as little statesmanship and as little patriotism in the last four years as any group in the land. I do not know whether they should be called Tories, but I do know that their environment and their selfish interests do not quite fit in with the interests of the average man.

In later years, his disgust with the smug and uncaring attitude of some organizations had an effect on his social life. He gave

orders that all invitations to attend banquets or social events
sponsored by the U.S. Chamber of Commerce and the National
Association of Manufacturers were to be automatically turned
down. "I don't have to go and listen to their guff," he snorted.[40]
In his view, two other organizations rivaled the Chamber of
Commerce and the NAM for lack of constructiveness—the
American Medical Association and the American Farm Bureau
Federation. He always insisted there was a hidden political link,
perhaps financial ties as well, between those two organizations.

Rayburn could feel in mid-1934 that he was at a new high
point in his career. As chairman of a highly competent, universally respected committee, he had won praise for the calm, judi-
cious, scrupulously fair manner in which he presided. Even the
irate leaders of Wall Street, who loathed the committee's actions,
admitted that they had received their day in court.

Moreover, the battle with Wall Street had shown the public
for the first time what House members long had known—the
stocky Texan was a fighter. Writing in *Collier's*, Ray Tucker referred to his "don't-give-up-the-bill doggedness": "His rough-
hewn manner and appearance suggest latent force. Unspec-
tacular and undemonstrative, even unimpressive, he has always
had a definite and serious aim. . . . He knew what he wanted
when he came to Congress and though it took almost 20 years,
he got it. . . . Rayburn never budges or gives an inch on the floor
or in committee. He prefers to outfight and outargue the other
fellow. Since he had to resist powerful pressure from radio,
railroad and financial organizations his successes have been
surprising."[41]

The combative side of Sam Rayburn surfaced again in 1934 as
he fought against a bill, supported by the administration and the
major oil companies, to impose federal controls over the production of oil, which had been glutting the market since discovery in 1933 of the East Texas Field, a vast pool of petroleum
forty miles long and five miles wide. Rayburn, who favored
state controls, worked with Texas independent producers to
keep the bill from coming to a vote. He managed to have the
measure sent to his committee, where it sat for months. Interior

Secretary Harold Ickes, who under the legislation would have emerged as federal oil "czar," could not pry it loose.[42] Neither could Roosevelt. "We have to do *something!*" the President wrote Rayburn in frustration.[43] Although uncomfortable in the obstructionist's role, the Texan would not be budged. He nearly attacked Tom Blanton of Abilene, who accused him of killing the bill. "You chloroformed this bill, and you know it," Blanton chided during a heated exchange on the House floor. Rayburn, "his face livid, arose and started toward Mr. Blanton," reported the *New York Times.* Only the intervention of six-foot Martin Dies "prevented a brawl between the two."[44] The bill did not pass the House. Later, a weaker bill, not calling for federal controls, passed with Rayburn's support.

At the height of his newly won fame, Rayburn got his first chance at the Speakership. On August 19, Speaker Henry Rainey died suddenly of a heart attack, touching off a wide-open race to succeed him. Rayburn, resting in Bonham after another grueling re-election battle, acted quickly by announcing his candidacy four days after Rainey's death. Because the Texan was known as a careful man, always sure of what he was doing, his confident entry into the race brought knowing nods in Washington, where it was widely assumed that he had the support of the White House. The *New York Times* pointed out on August 23, "That Mr. Rayburn is well liked by Mr. Roosevelt is well known in many quarters." Observed one pundit knowingly: "The President calls him Sam." The 74-year-old Rainey had been an amiable but weak Speaker. Many members said they wanted a presiding officer of more decisiveness and drive—a man, they said, such as Rayburn.

The next day, Majority Leader Joe Byrns threw his hat into the ring. Generally considered the front-runner, the genial Tennessean had a fistful of trump cards to play. He was good-natured, easygoing, anxious not to offend. As chairman of the Committee on Appropriations, he had been in a position to advance pet projects of many Democrats. Also, as chairman of the Democratic Congressional Campaign Committee in 1934, he dispensed funds and other favors that might mean victory or defeat for members seeking re-election. Finally, Byrns had the tradition of seniority going for him. He was majority leader, and in this century the Democrats had never failed to promote their majority leader to Speaker when a vacancy occurred. The day after Byrns became a candidate, a third powerful entry appeared—William B. Bankhead of Alabama. Chairman of the Committee on Rules, scion of one of Alabama's most distinguished political families, almost universally popular, a great compromiser of differences, Bankhead was the choice of the southerners.

Trouble developed almost immediately for Rayburn. His former roommate and ex-brother-in-law, Marvin Jones, popular chairman of the Committee on Agriculture, got in the race, splitting the Texas delegation. Then two Texans, James P. Buchanan and Thomas L. Blanton, revealed their support for Byrns. The big Texas delegation was divided three ways. Even the White House support for which Rayburn had hoped never developed. Roosevelt apparently decided that it would be too risky to involve himself in an internal House battle.

As summer turned to autumn and autumn turned to winter, the canvassing for support became fierce. By letter and long-distance telephone and in person, the candidates sought support, member by member. With Congress out of session, Rayburn remained in Bonham—and even made a short visit to Mexico, his second and last trip outside the United States—while other candidates, especially Byrns, actively solicited votes. Throughout the period, Rayburn's key contact in Washington was longtime journalist and Rayburn confidant Cecil Dickson, who sent periodic notes detailing Byrns's activities. Dickson recalled: "Byrns was a worming sort of guy . . . a devious man of great determination. In the race against Rayburn he created as majority leader the idea of assistant leaderships and regional whips, and passed out these jobs to key state delegations in return for their support for Speaker."[45]

Returning to Washington in early December, Rayburn found that Byrns had all but sewed up the election. Marvin Jones had quit the race a few weeks earlier, asking his supporters to vote for Rayburn, but that was of small help. A landslide Democratic victory in the November elections—bringing scores of new party members to the House—had turned the tide strongly toward Byrns. Byrns claimed the support of most newly elected members, whom he had helped as chairman of the Democratic Congressional Campaign Committee.

Even Garner, working quietly behind the scene, was having scant success persuading Democrats that Rayburn was more qualified and deserving than Byrns. The notion of Texans holding both the Vice-Presidency and Speakership bothered some. Also, Garner had left a long trail of enemies during his House years, and many of them now saw an opportunity to settle an old score by striking back at Garner's most trusted supporter. Early in December, the Vice-President announced after a conference with Roosevelt that the President was taking no part, thus publicly abandoning Rayburn. When the Pennsylvania delegation caucused a few days later and decided to cast its entire twenty-three votes for Byrns, the Speakership was settled.

Byrns, meanwhile, put out feelers to both Bankhead and Rayburn, hinting that the majority leadership would go to the first man to drop out and back him. That proposition held no appeal for Rayburn. He disliked Byrns intensely and had no desire to be part of his leadership team. Byrns and Garner had been open enemies when both were in the House, and Rayburn, as a former Garner lieutenant, felt that he could not work successfully with Byrns. Rayburn and Bankhead discussed the situation. "We just don't have the votes to win, Bill," said Rayburn. "He'll make a trade with either one of us for the majority leadership, but I'm not a bit interested. I'm going to Texas."[46] Cecil Dickson saw Rayburn a short while later:

> When he decided to withdraw, he was catching the train home and gave me a statement to release an hour after he left. He would not listen to the idea that he try for majority leader. . . . After he left, I went to Bankhead and urged him to announce that night for the majority leadership. He didn't want to. The House wouldn't elect two men from adjoining states, he said. But I said, "You underestimate your own popularity." He finally agreed to let me that night announce his candidacy for majority leader, which he won.[47]

Rayburn's withdrawal statement was typically terse: "I am no longer a candidate for Speaker. There are no alibis. Under the circumstances I cannot be elected." The two-day train ride gave him time to take stock of the situation. He had made a fool of himself, reaching for the brass ring too quickly—at least in the eyes of his colleagues—and compounding the mistake by waging an amateurish, halfhearted campaign. He wondered if his successes as a legislative leader during the last two years and the widespread acclaim he had received in the press had blinded him to his weaknesses. He had let his burning ambition override his normal common sense, impelling him into a rash act that might have ended all hopes of reaching his goal. It was a long, unhappy ride back to Bonham.

"The Greatest Congressional Battle in History"

Rayburn had little time to brood over the setback to his ambition. The 1934 elections produced an even larger Democratic majority, adding momentum to the New Deal. Traditionally, the President's party loses seats in the House in off-year elections. Thus, the addition of nineteen Democrats was viewed as a great vote of confidence in Roosevelt's programs. The White House reacted with increased pressure on the Texas congressman to proceed with the third—the most uncertain and fierce—battle to reform and regulate the giants of high finance.

At issue in this third titanic clash between the New Deal and Wall Street were the investor-owned public utility holding companies, many of which had been gouging consumers with exorbitant rates and bilking investors with worthless or watered-down stock for years. The major holding company interests fought ferociously against the New Deal efforts to establish public safeguards and regulations. An unyielding opponent of holding company abuses since his days in the Texas legislature, Rayburn was cast as a central figure in this crucial showdown, remembered by participants and bystanders alike as "the greatest congressional battle in history."[1]

Holding companies, which began gaining recognition as legal entities by state legislatures in the late 1800s, grew and prospered in the rapidly developing gas and electric power industry. It was perhaps natural that this burgeoning industry—the "glamour industry" of the first third of the twentieth century—should attract speculators and dishonest financial manipulators to prey on the operating utilities and their unwary customers.[2]

The holding companies, by and large, were mere financial devices—parasitic corporations, which allowed bankers and other investors and speculators of the era to control the stock of an operating utility and extract profits from the arrangement. Often holding company was piled on holding company, sometime to the seventh or eighth degree, with each layer squeezing a profit from the company or companies below. At the bottom of the heap were the service-providing utility operators, which generated and distributed gas and electric power. They also were expected to generate the handsome profits by which all those above prospered. Besides turning over their profits from service revenues, the operating companies were frequently compelled to buy construction, engineering, and management services at outrageous rates from the parent holding companies.[3]

All of this meant that users of electricity had to pay higher rates than would otherwise be necessary. Moreover, through skillful manipulation of holding-company stock, a speculator could gain control of a huge utility empire for a relatively small financial outlay. In the hands of an unscrupulous management, a holding company could sell stock at inflated prices to a gullible public, which grabbed up utility certificates as fast as they came off the presses in the decade preceding the Great Depression. Stocks and bonds of the twenty-five top electric utility holding companies had a market value of $19.2 billion in 1929; four years later, they were worth less than $3 billion.[4]

The abuses of utility holding companies were documented in two lengthy investigations. One was conducted between 1928 and 1935 by the Federal Trade Commission under the supervision of its general counsel—a dour, somber-faced, honest Vermonter named Robert E. Healy. The other investigation was led by the enormously capable special counsel of Rayburn's own committee, W. M. W. Splawn, who worked quietly and meticulously, outside the glare of publicity, gathering information on the techniques and operations of the industry. Splawn, who had won Rayburn's respect with his earlier investigation of railroad holding companies, compiled a massive final report totaling 8,927 pages. Supplementing Healy's exposés, it formed the basis for congressional action to break up the paper pyramids that were strangling honest investors and utility customers alike.

Incisive, fastidiously thorough, Splawn never resorted to a subpoena to get holding-company records, a feat of which both he and Rayburn were proud. With quiet persuasion, tact, and patience, Splawn convinced utility executives to give his staff investigators full access to their files. The meticulous investigator and his able staff worked in near obscurity, as demanded by Rayburn, who always had an intense dislike of noisy, sensational, headline-catching investigations. Legislation should be based on facts, not emotion, he insisted, and facts could only be arrived at with calmness, patience, and hard work. The skill with which Splawn and his staff conducted their new investigation and presented the results won high praise. Splawn had an unusual ability to analyze and organize a highly complex set of facts so lucidly that they could be easily understood by the non-expert. Rayburn's personal admiration for his chief investigator was unbounded. Years later, he recalled Splawn as "a big-brained man—the greatest braintruster of them all."

Convinced that immediate action was necessary to correct the utility holding company abuses, New Dealers argued whether to attempt to regulate the companies or abolish them. Roosevelt seemed undecided. The President's State of the Union message in January 1935 called for the "abolition of the evil features of holding companies"—in other words, regulation—but when he delivered the message to Congress, his tongue slipped and he said, "abolition of the evil of holding companies."[5]

Finally, Roosevelt referred the question of regulation versus abolition to a committee of government officials, which included Rayburn, Splawn, Healy, and the administration's twin masters of the art of legislative drafting—Ben Cohen and Tommy Corcoran—among others. Cohen and Corcoran had drafted a bill that stopped short of abolition. The committee consensus, however, plainly favored a law ridding the nation of all utility holding companies that could not prove they served a useful purpose.[6]

This was drastic medicine, bordering on the type of "punitive legislation" that Rayburn had avoided throughout his career. But he could see no satisfactory alternative that would assure the purge of the financial "bloodsuckers," as he called the parasitic elements in the industry, and bring about the other extensive protective reforms he knew were necessary. Still withholding his own public endorsement of the extreme legislation, Roosevelt privately gave Corcoran and Cohen the go-ahead to draft a bill calling for the abolition of holding companies. As Ben Cohen remembered:

> I really had to scratch because I didn't think it really was possible legally to abolish them. What I did was to change some language in the bill to make it seem more militant and severe than it really was. For political reasons, they wanted to be able to say they were abolishing holding companies. It's amusing that before the fight was over that year, some who had been at that conference were not willing to go even as far as the original bill which we were ordered to revise.[7]

Roosevelt asked Rayburn to introduce the bill in the House. Rayburn agreed. Only then did Roosevelt call in Burton K. Wheeler of Montana, the capable, outspoken chairman of the Senate Commerce Committee. Roosevelt told Senator Wheeler that Rayburn already had been asked to carry the fight for the administration's bill—news that surprised and irritated Wheeler, who had planned to push his own less-sweeping bill. Roosevelt "was deliberately turning the job over to Sam and ignoring me," the short-fused Montanan complained later. "I forget why, but I was not in too good graces with FDR at the time."[8]

Wheeler told Roosevelt of his own bill and left. Corcoran and Cohen were not far behind, urging the senator to lay aside his bill and support the administration's. "They said I wouldn't have to do anything until after the bill passed the House," he later recalled. "I agreed to go along; their bill was more carefully drafted than mine." Soon Wheeler would be up to his elbows in the holding-company fight. He became a relentless advocate, keeping the legislation alive during the darkest moments of a long struggle.

Rayburn laid out the results of the Splawn investigation in a House speech in January. A well-documented, detailed, 45-minute presentation, it was one of the longest speeches he ever made. This was Rayburn at his best, denouncing sin and evil in a righteous tone that had the Wall Street moguls cowering in anticipation of divine wrath. Utility holding companies, he said, had become "a master" of the American people. "This master is soulless, impersonal, intangible, immortal and well-nigh all-powerful," he added scornfully.[9]

Congress had only two choices—regulate or abolish these companies—he declared. "We must discourage this cancerous growth on our body politic and remove it. If left alone it will jeopardize our financial institutions and perhaps destroy the Republic. The abuses of holding companies are indeed a major influence that brought on the Great Depression." The stage was set for round 3 in the escalating battle between the New Deal and Wall Street. On February 6, Rayburn and Wheeler introduced the administration's bill, calling for the abolition of unjustifiable utility holding companies.

The utility industry was astounded. It had expected a drive to regulate holding companies, not abolish them. Reaction was swift and powerful. Using its enormous economic and political resources, the industry immediately mobilized from coast to coast. Banks, insurance companies, wealthy investors, and industrialists were summoned into the fight "to save free enterprise." The Rayburn-Wheeler bill was aimed at breaking the traditional American corporate structure, the nation was warned, but its main victims would be the millions of ordinary holders of utility stocks and bonds, who were invariably described in the industry propaganda as "widows and orphans" dependent on their dividends.

Some unnamed person in the utility industry, whose genius should not have gone unrecognized, described the bill as being tantamount to a "death sentence" for holding companies.[10] The

description cut through the bill's complexities and caught the
public's imagination. From then on, the blood-chilling words
were applied whenever the bill was mentioned. Years later,
Rayburn still bristled at the term. "It was no such thing," he
would snort. "The utilities succeeded in tricking the investors
that they had been defrauding into fighting the utilities' battle." [11]

Through newspaper, magazine, and radio advertising and
through zealous, fear-inducing letter-writing campaigns, the
utilities sought to marshal public opinion. Millions of stockholders were misled into believing that the bill threatened their
entire investment. Lists of stockholders were compiled by congressional district and distributed to each member of Congress
to emphasize the bill's adverse effect on constituents. As Ben
Cohen recalled: "In 1934 we thought we had seen the ultimate in
propaganda, but in 1935, we saw the worst yet. The great flood
of telegrams . . . was foolish and harmful, but they did an excellent job of having the right calls made to congressmen from
bankers, for example, who told them: 'You don't realize what an
effect this bill will have on the estate I'm planning.' They really
alarmed many honest congressmen." [12]

In a radio interview, Rayburn counterattacked. The nation's
2,000 utility operating companies, worth $20 billion, were con-
trolled by about 50 holding companies, Rayburn said. In turn,
banks controlled the holding companies. One banking house
thus controlled more than one-fourth of the nation's electric
companies. [13] One of Rayburn's greatest legislative assets was an
ability to reduce complex issues to simple, everyday terms.
"The holding device is so clever," he explained to the radio audience, "that a schoolgirl cannot use her curling iron, a house-
wife cannot clean her rug with a vacuum cleaner or preserve her
food in an electric refrigerator, a schoolboy cannot turn on a
light to read his lesson, a cook cannot light the gas in her stove
without paying tribute to a holding company. It is included in
the rate paid for the lights and the gas."

Replying to charges that his bill was punitive, Rayburn said it
had never been his purpose "to pass laws to punish any but the
guilty." Rather, he added, his goal had been "to bring about
simple justice for all people. All sorts of attempts will be made

to frighten people. . . . You have to trust someone. Why don't you trust your government rather than the people who sold you securities at 100 that are now selling for about 10?"

For two months, the House Committee on Interstate and Foreign Commerce listened patiently as witness after witness threaded through one of the most complex bills ever to come before Congress. The testimony of thirty-four opponents consumed sixty-five hours, ten minutes. Eleven proponents took forty-nine hours, fifty-five minutes.[14] Rayburn sought to hear all points of view. One weary witness suggested the committee might be terribly tired of the discussion. "That may be," Rayburn replied, "but we have got to take it." Early on, Rayburn made it clear that he favored abolition, not regulation, of most holding companies. Finally, in March, Roosevelt ended his own vacillation on the issue. On March 12, in a message to Congress, the President declared: "The utility-holding company with its present powers must go."

Lead-off witness for the utilities before the Rayburn committee was the brilliant, tousle-haired president of Commonwealth and Southern Corporation, Wendell L. Willkie. His outstanding record as a utility executive, gift with words, and power of personality made him a natural leader for a discredited industry trying to make its best case before Congress and a skeptical public. Willkie avoided the mistake of New York Stock Exchange President Richard Whitney in the earlier fight against Rayburn's securities exchange bill. Whitney had refused to admit anything was amiss in the stock market. Yes, Willkie conceded, there had been abuses—grave abuses—in the utility industry. But, he argued, that was no reason to destroy the holding companies, which were necessary to provide financing for the operating companies. Effective regulation would prevent the recurrence of such abuses, he said. It was a dramatic and impressive performance. "He did not sit at a table reading a prepared statement," noted one reporter, "but strode up and down before the committee seated on a dais before him. At times his voice was angry as he turned to answer some allegation against holding companies. Again, it was soft and trembling as he told of the years of work, vision and dreams on the part of men who had brought holding companies into existence to make the power industry more efficient."[15] The rakishly handsome Willkie had most of this audience spellbound, but not the committee chairman, who interrupted the witness five times to challenge his assertions.

"Before conviction, I would like to have a trial," Willkie complained.

"Well," snapped Rayburn, "we are giving you one now." Although Willkie made a favorable impression on the committee, the press, and the country, Rayburn never warmed to him. "I always thought he was kind of a smart-ass," he said years later.

Following Willkie came a succession of other industry witnesses, who resorted to worn-out shibboleths and negativism. Preston Arkwright, president of the Georgia Power Company, warned that abolition of holding companies "would paralyze the nation." S. R. Inch, president of Electric Bond and Share Company, asserted the bill would bring about nationalization of the power industry. Into the record went a letter from A. J. Duncan, president of Texas Electric Service Company, declaring "the Rayburn-Wheeler bill would take from Texas rights for which Texas has shed blood; it would destroy the investments of literally thousands of people who have attempted to provide for old age by investing in the securities of this and other companies; it would . . . largely destroy the fundamental principles of states' rights."

To Rayburn, Wall Street once again was performing as it had on the 1933 Securities Act and the 1934 Securities and Exchange Act. Flagrant abuses were freely confessed, yet the high financiers were not willing to recommend effective reforms to prevent the repetition of such abuses. That, to Rayburn, was not acting in good faith.

After two months of exhaustive hearings, the painstaking job of redrafting the original bill began. A six-member subcommittee, headed by Rayburn, scrutinized all of the important sections line by line. When they reached section 11—the so-called death-sentence section—strong differences of opinion emerged. The Republicans and some Democrats were adamantly opposed. This troubled Rayburn, who had long been proud of the committee's reputation as the least partisan committee of Congress. Now the cleavage was wide and bitter. The subcommittee, and the full committee as well, was hopelessly deadlocked over the question of abolishing holding companies. Reluctantly concluding they did not have the votes in either the subcommittee or the full committee to save the crucial death-sentence provision, Rayburn, Corcoran, Cohen, and Senator Wheeler worked out a new strategy. Rayburn would slow down, allowing the Senate, which was more amenable to the death-sentence section, to act first.[16] Favorable Senate action, Rayburn concluded, might strengthen some backbones in the House.

Fighting and winning his own battles with the well-armed utilities lobby, Wheeler brought his bill to the Senate floor in late May. As expected, most of the debate focused on section 11, which called for abolition or reorganization within three years of all utility holding companies that were not parts of geographically or economically integrated systems. After Wheeler read a "Dear Burt" letter from Roosevelt unequivocally endorsing section 11, the Senate voted 45–44 to retain the controversial provision. The bill itself then passed easily, 56–32. Now the ball was back in Rayburn's court.

Rayburn was tired, worried, grim. Never had he been in such a struggle before. From February to June, he had been under incessant pressure from utility lobbyists, New Dealers, the President, House members, and constituents. He faced political trouble at home. In June, columnists Drew Pearson and Robert S. Allen reported: "Because of his hard-hitting efforts in behalf of the President's holding-corporation bill, Texas utilities have already started a movement to defeat Rayburn. . . . His district is being flooded with 'literature' attacking him and urging his replacement."[17] Twice Rayburn reported to Roosevelt on his problems. The President cheered him up, but it did not last. Finally, the subcommittee voted to eliminate the death-sentence provision. After seventy-one days of deliberation, the logjam was broken. The bill was quickly approved by the full committee and sent to the Committee on Rules, where the conditions for its debate by the full House would be determined.

Although Rayburn appeared beaten, he saw one slim chance to save the death-sentence section when the bill came before the full House. If the Rules Committee gave Rayburn a chance to have a roll-call vote on his proposal, he might win. Give the people a chance to see where their representatives stood, he urged. But the committee, rebuffing Rayburn and the White House, sent the bill to the House floor under a rule that prevented a roll call on the controversial section 11. The decision was to prove expensive to Rules chairman John J. O'Connor's political future.

A secret poll of House members showed Rayburn about forty votes short on the death-sentence provision. Faced with the worst legislative defeat of his career, the Texan decided to press for the strongest bill he could get and hope that the Senate language, particularly section 11, would prevail when House and Senate conferees met to iron out differences in the two versions.

As the struggle moved onto the House floor, both sides stepped up their pressure. Utility propagandists flooded Washington with tons of telegrams and letters. By one count, more than 600 utility lobbyists were operating in the nation's capital— one for each of the 531 members of House and Senate, and then some. The utilities openly boasted that they had the most powerful force ever mustered to bring pressure on Congress.

The President's lieutenants roamed the halls of the House office buildings and the Capitol, pleading, threatening, offering to trade work-relief projects, jobs, and juicy appointments for a vote. Corcoran set up headquarters in a vacant office next to the Rayburn committee's hearing room. His job was to keep tabs on Democrats who said they would stand with the administration and see to it that nobody strayed off the reservation.

With brilliant thoroughness, the utility magnates mobilized excruciating pressure against the bill. Utility employees in one state after another were told their jobs were in jeopardy and were asked—in many cases ordered—to write their senators and representatives. Stockholders, warned by letter, advertisements, and in person that their investments were about to be lost, were enlisted in the fight. So were customers of savings banks and insurance companies, which held large blocks of utility stock. Bankers, businesspeople, suppliers, newspaper editors, lawyers—all those who had any connection with the utility industry—were called upon to apply maximum pressure on elected officials in Washington. Mail to individual offices came not in bundles but by the sackful. Congressional staff members had a hard time sifting their important correspondence from the "pressure" mail.

Eventually, in their frenzy, some utility companies resorted to forgery of signatures on letters and telegrams. In June, Rayburn received more than 100 letters from the small town of Denison, Texas, opposing the bill. When he acknowledged them, 52 of his letters came back undelivered. There were no such persons at the addresses. Many were dead, some had moved away, others were children under voting age. Obviously, an old city directory had been used for the names and addresses, and the signatures had been forged.[18] One Texas utility company furnished stationery and stamped envelopes to its employees and ordered them to write their congressman a letter opposing the bill. Many employees put the blank paper in the envelope and mailed it.

From congressional districts throughout the country, the utilities brought scores of prominent citizens to Washington to lobby their representatives and senators. Campaign managers, big contributors, lifelong friends, influential political leaders came at utility company expense. Some stayed for weeks. Special pressure was applied on Rayburn by such diverse individuals as Joe Tumulty, former secretary to President Wilson, now in the employ of the utilities, and Winthrop Aldrich, head of Chase National Bank.

A Miami bank president drew attention with a five-foot-long placard, which he mailed to Congress as a postcard. "Let's look at the facts," the banker wrote. "Who are against the bill?" His list was impressive: "A majority of newspapers, hundreds of thousands of investors, investor organizations, practically all businesses, commercial banks, trust companies, savings banks with 14 million depositors, insurance companies," and so on through twenty major categories. "Who," the banker asked, "are for the bill?" That list seemed pitifully short: "President

Roosevelt, Senator Wheeler, Congressman Rayburn, Tom Corcoran, Ben Cohen and a few who have long had a prejudice against the public utilities and are advocates of government ownership."[19]

In his book *Pyramids of Power*, Marion L. Ramsey labeled his chapter on the holding-company fight "Five against the Gods." These five, he wrote, "dared the putative wrath of 14 million savings-bank depositors, more millions of insurance-policy holders, the regiments of investment bankers and the army of American citizens generally to say nothing of the wrath of all the mighty utility-holding-company supermanagements."[20]

Thursday, June 27, found Washington sweltering in 95-degree heat. It was the hottest day of the year so far—and the humidity was suffocating. In such weather, midsummer madness often grips the nation's capital, which squats and swelters, always disconsolate in the hot months, along the breezeless mud flats of the Potomac. "Congressmen scream at each other and tell on each other," observed the *New York World-Telegram*. "Tempers explode. Men say things they later delete from the record. Nerves are raw and frayed."

The *World-Telegram* continued, seeking to explain the congressional mood on opening day of House debate on the holding-company bill: "But more than the heat, the humidity and the physical weariness and brain fatigue counts for the tenseness. For one thing, the barons of big business, really hit for the first time in a vital spot by the public-utility bill, are striking back with a vengeful fury not heretofore witnessed in the Roosevelt administration." The arrogant utility lobby, openly threatening to defeat any member who voted for the death-sentence section, was matched by an equally arrogant administration lobby, which made it clear that those who voted against it would be marked men in the New Dealers' books.

Rayburn was sorely tired. Bone-weary from the unrelenting pressure and overwork, he had lost control of his committee for the first time. Moreover, relations had worsened between Speaker Joe Byrns and himself. The two had detested each other for years; now Byrns was telling friends that Rayburn had miserably mishandled the holding-company bill in committee. For the first time in his life, Rayburn could not sleep. Worry over the bill—and the gloomy prospect that he might fail in this, his greatest legislative effort—caused him to toss and turn all night long, night after night. "I knew that if I ever was going to be Speaker, I just had to succeed," he later recalled, "and by God, I would rather have died than to have failed."

In mid-afternoon, the stocky, well-groomed Texan stood in the well of the House to open debate on the utility bill. Perspiration gleamed on his bald head as the blazing sun beat through the leaded-glass roof of the House chamber. There never had been a bill before Congress, he began, that had any longer, more conscientious study than this bill—or one that had been more misrepresented. To dramatize his case, he had set up two large charts showing the incredibly complicated organizations of two of the most severely criticized holding companies— Associated Gas and Electric and Cities Service—which showed company piled on top of company in a maze of intercorporate relationships almost impossible to untangle.

First, he catalogued a long list of evils that had arisen from the holding-company setup: evasion of income taxes, secret and exorbitant salaries and bonuses, fictitious stock subscriptions, extravagant writeups of assets, manipulation of securities, absentee management of operating companies, and so on. This sort of thing, he said sarcastically, is "just as necessary to the public welfare as piracy on the high seas or as robbery on the land. . . . These companies that have fattened off the investors of this country . . . are the companies that are fighting this legislation. They are the ones that do not want to die. . . . do not want to be crippled. . . . do not even want to be regulated." Applause broke out on the House floor.

Rayburn's voice rose: "What I want to do is to take from the backs of the clean, honestly-operating operating companies of this country these leeches and blood-sucking holding companies." Citing specific abuse after abuse, he named companies, quoted figures, explained how the bill would correct the shortcomings. Angrily, he pointed his finger at a group of utility representatives sitting in the jam-packed gallery, including John W.

Carpenter, president of Texas Power and Light Company. These men, he shouted, are the ones who for years have defeated all effective utility regulations by the Texas Legislature. Texas Power and Light was among many companies owned by one of the largest holding companies, Electric Bond and Share. Carpenter and his associates, Rayburn declared, were "little more in this great setup, this powerful group, than glorified office boys." "Instead of taking power, authority and management away from the local communities, I want to take it away from New York, from the Insulls in Chicago, and give it back to the communities of this country where it belongs," he insisted.[21]

Rayburn was the sole speaker on the bill at Thursday's session. It had been an erudite, impassioned speech, a logical, lucid statement of the case for the death-sentence provision. While it heartened his supporters, it is doubtful that it made any new converts to his cause. The lines were already hardened. Throughout his remaining years, Rayburn said he regretted his personal attack on Carpenter. It is always a mistake to become personal in legislative matters, he believed. Legislation should be considered on the basis of facts, of merit, not of personalities. It was, in Rayburn's view, unfair to attack Carpenter when he could not reply. His emotions had overcome his judgment. It was a mistake he vowed never to repeat.

Rayburn's chief adversary—the leader of the House forces opposed to the death-sentence provision—was a small, fiery, red-headed Alabamian, George Huddleston, Sr., of Birmingham, a congressman noted for his flaming oratory and keen intelligence. A veteran of twenty years in the House, Huddleston was outranked on the committee only by Chairman Rayburn. For many years they had sat side by side at the committee table and had generally worked together harmoniously.

During his early years in the House, Huddleston was considered one of its most radical members, a fearless champion of the "common man," organized labor, and small business, and the archenemy of public utilities, "big money," and the "big interests." But, in time, both Huddleston and Rayburn changed in their political and economic philosophy. Huddleston moved steadily to the right, becoming an archconservative, while

1. Martha Waller Rayburn

2. William Marion Rayburn

3. *Will and Mat Rayburn, Uncle Jim Rayburn, Abner, Dick, Sam and Lucinda at old family home near Flag Springs, Texas*

4. Family members on porch of old family home near Flag Springs, Texas

5. Rayburn clan, about 1908. Back row: *Frank, Sam, Dick, Tom, Jim.* Front row: *Will Jr., Abner, Mr. and Mrs. Rayburn, Lucinda, Katherine, Medibel*

6. *1903 graduating class, East Texas Normal College; Rayburn is second from right.*

7. *Rayburn at his desk in Texas House of Representatives, 1907*

8. *Rayburn at 21*

9. Among the first in Texas to campaign by car, Rayburn poses with prospective voters in his maiden race for Congress in 1912.

10. Congressman-elect Rayburn at 30

11. *John Nance Garner, 1913. "Cactus Jack" was a mentor and lifelong friend of Rayburn's.*

12. *John O'Connor, beaten for House majority leader by archrival Rayburn, manages a smile.*

13. *Rayburn, 1936*

Bride of Today

NEA

14. *Rayburn's marriage to beautiful Metze Jones shocked many North Texans.*

15. *Sam and Metze on honeymoon*

16. *Rayburn and Speaker William Bankhead in a light-hearted moment*

17. *The Speaker in his official chair, 1942*

18. Lyndon Johnson in Navy uniform at General McArthur's headquarters during World War II. The photograph is affectionately inscribed to Rayburn's sister.

19. Rayburn, on his 61st birthday, shows off a gift from FDR.

20. *Speaker,* center, *escorts FDR and Barkley to 1944 Inaugural.*

21. *Alben Barkley, Sam Rayburn, John McCormack, and Scott Lucas, 1944*

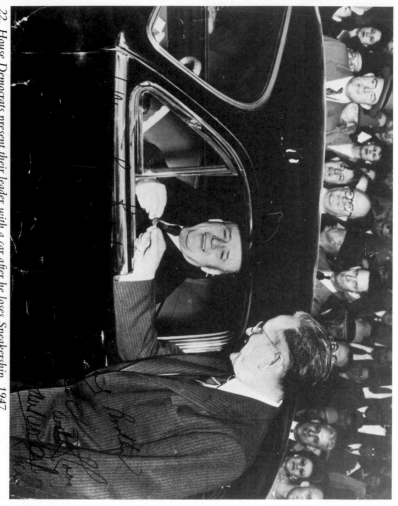

22. House Democrats present their leader with a car after he loses Speakership, 1947.

23. *Rayburn joins Truman's 1948 whistlestop campaign in Texas.*

24. *Friendly adversaries Martin and Rayburn*

25. Truman and Rayburn confer in Key West after 1948 election.

Rayburn, once proud of his designation as "the most conservative man in the House," moved gradually toward a more progressive position. The two were worthy adversaries. Small in stature, they both were exceptionally effective speakers. Huddleston, quick-thinking, very well-informed, was a master of ridicule, sarcasm, and invective, whose speeches flashed with fire. Rayburn was a more reserved speaker. He relied on simplicity of expression—Anglo-Saxon words and clear logic—but when he was aroused, anger and toughness sometimes crept into his rich, deep voice.

After Rayburn's impassioned plea opening debate on the holding-company bill, it was Huddleston's turn to state the case for the milder House bill that omitted the death-sentence provision. On the second day of debate, as Washington still sweltered in oppressive heat, Huddleston, a feisty little bantam-cock, rose to face a crowded House chamber. Utility and administration lobbyists jammed the galleries. "A meek looking fellow," as one observer saw him, Huddleston began with a sarcastic attack on Chairman Rayburn. He feigned amazement that Rayburn, while introducing the committee bill, had said nothing to indicate his endorsement of it as written.[22] Indeed, he had indicated a preference for provisions of the Senate bill. Rayburn was in an awkward position, and Huddleston knew it. A committee chairman normally defends the product of his committee; this Rayburn could not do conscientiously.

With withering ridicule, Huddleston chided Rayburn for abandoning the committee bill. "So, unworthy as is this abandoned child of my friend from Texas, ugly as it may be, out of a spirit of chivalry I am impelled to come to its rescue and to take the hapless waif into my slender bosom," the Alabamian declared. Laughter and applause from the House floor and the galleries rocked the chamber. "What is the issue?" he shouted. "The issue is whether we will regulate or whether we will destroy." Huddleston read the 1932 Democratic platform calling for "regulation" rather than abolition. "Upon that plank I stand," he asserted. Again thunderous applause, as he drew blood once more.

He turned to the plight of holding-company investors. Their

only crime was that they were too credulous. "For what they paid $100 for, the average price is now between $20 and $30," he said. "Now they look up and see their great government, led by the gentleman from Texas, trying to take away from them the last few remaining pennies left of what they had invested." The death-sentence provision was bad for the country, Huddleston argued. It was highly deflationary; it would discourage enterprise; it retarded recovery. It might cost many jobs.

"The bill is a mystic maze," written by Cohen and Corcoran, "two bright young men brought down from New York to teach Congress 'how to shoot,'" he went on. "I pay them a tribute for the exceeding skill which they have shown in weaving in and weaving out, piling words upon words, phrase upon phrase, clause upon clause, until a Philadelphia lawyer would get down on his knees and pray to be delivered from the task of interpretation." Laughter and applause interrupted him.

Savagely, Huddleston attacked the Federal Trade Commission's utility probe. "It was like writing the story of a man's life in which you tell every unworthy thought that ever entered his mind and ignoring altogether all the good things that might have been said in his behalf," he said. "And which among you gentlemen could stand up with that kind of biography? They whipped the country into a rage. . . . demagogues grasped their opportunity. . . . like vultures riding the storm, they mounted on this wave of ill will and opinion against the utilities. . . . This is the finest demagogue bait ever spread."

Shouting at the top of his voice over the almost continuous cheers and applause of both Republicans and Democrats, the Alabamian pressed his remorseless attack, denouncing with equal fervor the pressure from utilities and the White House, which "has tended to prevent fair and just decisions. . . . Both sides are guilty. Both have interfered with a fair and just decision upon the part of Congress." His voice trembling with emotion, Huddleston brought his case to a close: "I will support 'regulation' and not 'destruction'—correction and not vengeance. I will do justice without fear or favor, and neither the imps of darkness nor those who have seen a new light shall move me the breadth of a hair. Upon this rock I take my stand. And the gates of hell shall not prevail against it."

The House chamber was pandemonium. Most members were on their feet, cheering, applauding lustily. The redheaded congressman was swarmed by members who wanted to shake his hand, pat his back, hug his shoulders. In defiance of House rules, spectators in the galleries shouted and clapped their hands. Minute after minute the demonstration continued, one of the most thunderous ovations in the history of the House. Friend and foe alike sensed that Huddleston had made a historic speech.[23] Observers instinctively knew what this meant—the House was overwhelmingly opposed to the death-sentence provision. Moreover, for the first time since Roosevelt took office, the House was in full rebellion against him. Three years of accumulated grievances over White House pressure, emergency legislation, and patronage snubs had culminated in this moment of noisy revolt.

Rayburn knew the House had set its face against him. There would still be hour after hour of angry, loud debate, much of it more emotional than enlightening, but it would have a negligible effect upon the outcome. The House was against the death-sentence provision, and that was that. Yet Rayburn had to continue, as he later told it, "the hardest task a man can choose—to fight to win when he knows that he must lose."

Convening an hour or two early each day as the blistering weather continued, the House met Friday, even Saturday, and again on Monday, debating the bill hour after hour. President Roosevelt, at a press conference, raised the political temperature by damning the utility propaganda as the most dangerous and most powerful in history. Compared with the utility lobby, he said, the labor lobby was a child and the veterans' lobby an infant. He backed the death-sentence provision to the finish. The debate ran for five days. An extraordinary total of sixty-six House members either spoke or asked questions. The House spent a total of twenty-two and a half hours considering the bill—one of the longest debates in modern times for a parliamentary body where debate is strictly regulated.

Monday, July 1, was the day of decision. The House was in a

state of high emotion. It was in a rebellious, tense mood. "The
floor was filled with meditative members silently determined to
break with their President on an issue that might cost their political careers," reporter Robert C. Albright wrote in the next
day's *Washington Post*. The halls swarmed with lobbyists, both
for and against the death-sentence provision, applying last-
minute pressure to members as they made their way into the
chamber.

As always when great issues are to be resolved, there was confusion in the chamber. Members huddled in small groups to
trade gossip or to argue. There was a hubbub in the galleries.
Speaker Byrns repeatedly pounded his gavel for order, demanding that members clear the crowded aisles. "We can't hear a thing
for the noise being made in the galleries," shouted an angry
member.

About 2 p.m., Rayburn rose to close debate. He began quietly,
"This is the day we long have sought and mourned because we
found it not." The congressmen laughed and applauded.

This, he pointed out, had been a long and bitter struggle for
the members of his committee. "For some of us—I know it will
be for me"—next year's election would be "a long and bitter
struggle," he said. "I know I am one of those marked for dis-
favor." Rayburn's voice rose: "I know the power, political and financial, of the people with whom we deal. But I want to say to
them in closing this debate that for the propaganda, for the misrepresentations, for the falsehoods that have been circulated in
my section of the country, I despise their methods and defy
them." The chamber burst into applause. The choice was clear,
he said: "Will you stand by the chosen leader of the American
people, the President, or will you follow the man who has
fleeced the American people?"[24]

Rayburn shouted angrily: "When these people came to talk to
me, I said, 'I am not an enemy of your business, but I want to
get the desperadoes out of it who are disgracing it.' What I want
to do with this great, this fine, this growing business is to take
from its back these leeches, these bloodsuckers, these milkers,
and let it stand alone, free from these influences that have made
the very name of utility an anathema in the minds of many

American people." As he concluded, the House exploded in a wild demonstration for the embattled Texan. Cheers and standing applause continued minute after minute. The demonstration was so prolonged that some observers wondered whether the death-sentence provision might not be approved after all.

The Committee on Rules had turned down Rayburn's plea for a record vote on the death-sentence amendment. The vote would be by "tellers," a method that assured a precise count without requiring the individual members to announce their position. A teller vote required a leading proponent and a leading opponent of the issue to take a position in the center aisle of the House and, as the members marched single file up the aisle, to count first those voting for, then those voting against the question. After every voting member had filed through the tellers, the totals would be announced, but there was no official record of how any individual voted.

For weeks the Scripps-Howard newspaper chain had vigorously supported the death-sentence provision. It conducted its own investigation into utility holding company practices and was an energetic follower of the legislation as it proceeded through Congress. Ruth Finney of the Scripps-Howard bureau in Washington, through her daily coverage of the fight, made a substantial contribution to public awareness and understanding of the issues involved.

Outraged by the House's attempt to avoid a record vote on the controversial bill's most controversial question, the Scripps-Howard bureau decided to piece together a "roll call" of its own. When the House met on the day of decision, twenty-six Scripps-Howard reporters filed into the House press gallery. To assure getting good seats, they arrived four hours early. Each was responsible for identifying certain representatives as they marched between the tellers. Reporter Charter Heslep, who knew all of the members, knelt on a front-row stool and called the name and state of each. The next day, in a classic example of journalistic enterprise, Scripps-Howard newspapers across the country printed the unofficial tally. Members were furious. As reporter Raymond Clapper viewed the scene from the press gallery: "The ruthless intensity of the fight was such that no matter

which way a member voted, he was tagged as either bought by
the administration or bought by the utilities. The hapless members, as they seethed into the well of the House to go down the
line like nameless sheep, wore the hunted look of fugitives
at bay."

The presiding officer announced the result: the death-sentence
amendment had been rejected, 216–146. Roosevelt and Rayburn
had suffered a devastating defeat, far worse than even the pessi-
mists had predicted. It was the New Deal's sharpest blow to
date. The House was in full rebellion.[25] The Democratic leadership had largely deserted Roosevelt. The acting Democratic
majority leader, the chairman of the Democratic Steering Committee, and the chairmen of the Rules and Appropriations committees ducked the vote. The Democratic whip voted against
the death-sentence provision. The "machine" Democrats from
New York City and Chicago voted in droves with the utilities.
To Rayburn this was worse than defeat—it was disaster. His
only consolation was that his conduct as committee chairman
won repeated praise in the debate from both friends and foes of
the death-sentence section.[26]

But Rayburn found scant comfort in such praise. He was engulfed in a sea of legislative and political troubles, and he knew
it. More than most politicians, he was consistently a realist
about himself. He always sought to face facts squarely and
scorned the luxury of self-deception, a disease to politicians.
His situation was harsh and disturbing. For the first time as
chairman of a great committee, he had lost control; he had been
voted down both in subcommittee and in the full committee. As
leader of New Deal forces in the House, engaged in the fiercest
legislative battle since Roosevelt took office, he had suffered a
severe defeat in spite of the do-or-die pressure the administration had thrown behind him.

Rayburn often said, "A leader has to have his head bloodied to
become a leader, but he can damn well have his head bloodied
too often." Three times Rayburn had been bloodied. He well
understood that confidence in his leadership, both at the White
House and among House Democrats, was dangerously shaken. If
that confidence was lost, his prospects for achieving the Speaker-

ship would come to nil. His career, in his eyes, would end in failure. Moreover, he was in political trouble at home. The utilities and other special interests, abundantly financed, were grimly determined to defeat him in 1936.

But over and above the dangers to his career and to his leadership, Rayburn was deeply involved emotionally in this fight. The years of investigation, the months of testimony before his committee, and the disclosures all across the nation had revealed such corruption, wanton theft of other people's money, and financial recklessness by utility holding companies that, in his opinion, "this cancer" had to be abolished.

Another aspect of the struggle reinforced Rayburn's determination to fight through to victory. The integrity of the House of Representatives itself had been called into question. After the teller vote, the highly respected *St. Louis Post-Dispatch* editorialized, "The power industry was too strong for Congress."[27] Columnist Heywood Broun in the *New York World-Telegram* was more plainspoken: "The story of the defeat . . . is simple enough. The House can be had."[28] From Rayburn's perspective, the death-sentence provision simply had to be enacted into law. But how? After defeating the death-sentence amendment, the House passed the bill, 323–81. The next round would be fought in the House-Senate conference committee.

A few minutes after the bill cleared the House, the battle took an unexpected turn. Republican Owen Brewster of Maine rose on the House floor to charge that he had been threatened by Tommy Corcoran, one the most active and forceful of the White House lobbyists, who had been assisting Rayburn behind the scenes. Brewster alleged that Corcoran came to him "in the lobby of this Capitol and stated . . . with brutal frankness" that if Brewster voted against the death-sentence provision, the White House would stop construction on the mammoth, multimillion-dollar Passamaquoddy Dam in Brewster's district. The House sat in stunned silence. Then someone whistled. Angry charges and countercharges flew back and forth—accusations and denials. In short order, the House voted to have its Committee on Rules investigate all charges of improper influence on members in connection with the bill, by proponents and opponents alike.[29]

Earlier that day, Alabama's lean, aggressive Senator Hugo Black, fresh from a headline-making investigation of favoritism in the award of ocean and airmail contracts under the Hoover administration, called for a special committee of five senators to investigate propaganda and lobbying on the holding-company bill. The Senate voted to give Black's committee $50,000 for its investigation.[30] Congress now had two investigations aimed at exposing the tactics of both the utilities and the White House during the holding-company struggle. For the next six weeks, as the two committees competed over witnesses and headlines, the attention of the nation was riveted on the sensational disclosures revealed by these investigations.

The House Committee on Rules, chaired by John J. O'Connor of New York, made the first headlines as Brewster and Tommy Corcoran angrily disputed as to whether Corcoran had threatened Brewster.[31] Rayburn, seated with the spectators, leaned forward to catch every word. In the first hearing, Brewster shouted, "You are a liar," when Corcoran testified that the Maine congressman suggested that he might duck the vote on the death-sentence amendment. The crowded hearing room was thrown into confusion.

Rayburn staunchly defended Corcoran's behavior during the holding-company fight. "If you ever have to handle a bill like the Securities Act of 1933, the Stock Exchange Act of 1934 or the holding-company bill of 1935," Rayburn reminded the committee, "you will want all of the expert advice and help you can get. I met Mr. Corcoran in the latter part of 1933 or 1934. He impressed me. . . . If he ever made a move that was important without coming to me first and asking my consent or what I thought about it, I do not remember it." The hearing shifted away from the Brewster-Corcoran quarrel to the potentially more important question raised by the intensive lobbying on both sides.

Rayburn and the White House had little confidence that the conservative-dominated Rules Committee would produce any disclosures that would be helpful in changing enough votes to revive the controversial amendment. On the crucial vote, four of the committee's ten Democrats sided against Rayburn, four stayed away, and only two voted for the death-sentence amendment. Chairman O'Connor himself had ducked the vote.

In the Senate, meanwhile, the Black committee performed with ruthless efficiency. The morning after the committee was created, two investigators entered the Mayflower Hotel offices of the chief of the utility lobby, Philip H. Gadsden, and hustled him off to the Capitol, where Black and other committee members were waiting. Five minutes later, committee room doors were flung open as Black delightedly announced: "Tell the boys of the press to come in. The show is about to begin." [32] On the witness stand, the spry, silver-haired Gadsden, chairman of the Committee of Public Utility Executives, freely testified that his committee had already spent $301,866 in an effort to defeat the Rayburn-Wheeler bill. More headline news was made when Gadsden returned to the hotel to find that in his absence a committee investigator had rifled both his official and personal files. "He actually went through my personal checkbook," Gadsden cried.

For days, Black's investigation dominated the front pages of newspapers from Maine to California. These headlines from the *St. Louis Post-Dispatch* were typical:

Tells of Faking Wired Protests on Utility Bill

Witness Declares Utility Man Said He Was Ordered to Destroy Lobby Records

127,000 Telegrams on Subject Received in Washington in 15 Days—Associated Gas Spent $700,000 to Beat Measure

Dead Men's Names Signed to Utilities' Telegrams of Protest to Congress

Signatures Borrowed from Tombstones and Payroll Lists as Well as City Directories for Flood of Messages

While one sensation after another came from Black's committee room, Senator Wheeler, chairman of the conference committee, deliberately delayed calling the conference into session,

waiting for the revelations to arouse public opinion. When the
conference finally convened, members found that Rayburn and
Wheeler had brought along Ben Cohen, who had drafted much
of the bill, and Dozier Devane, Federal Power Commission
counsel. Huddleston demanded that they be excluded. When
Rayburn and Wheeler refused, Huddleston and two House Republican conferees angrily stalked from the room. The conference broke up. A few days later, the committee convened again.
Rayburn and Wheeler still insisted on Cohen's being present as a
technical adviser. Once again, Huddleston and the House Republicans broke up the meeting, after Huddleston and Wheeler
engaged in a heated shouting match.

Meanwhile, day after day, Black pursued his relentless un-
masking of the frantic and questionable lobbying activities of
the utility companies. He was tough, merciless, brilliant in his
cross-examination of witnesses. "The severity with which witnesses are being handled . . . is unprecedented in recent Senate
history," one press dispatch noted.

The grimness of the inquiry had one day of comic relief. Paul
Elmer Danielson, 19-year-old Western Union messenger from
Warren, Pennsylvania, was called to the stand. Wearing his Sunday best, the pink-cheeked, wide-eyed young man told of receiving three cents from Associated Gas and Electric for every
signature he could get for telegrams to congressmen protesting
the Rayburn-Wheeler bill. He got signatures for six telegrams—
from his mother, a friend, a neighbor, and three others—he
said. "I just asked them if they wanted to sign a telegram." The
committee was fascinated by the young witness's story.[33]

Did you tell them what they were signing?" asked Black.
"I explained the Wheeler-Rayburn bill," Elmer grinned. The
hearing room burst into uproarious laughter. When the laughter subsided, Black asked the young man how he stood on the
bill. The lad opened his mouth, shut it, finally smiled: "I'm
neutral now." The Christian Science Monitor observed: "The
laughter that shook the committee room boded no good for the
power interests."

Rayburn decided it was time to test House sentiment again by
asking the House to instruct its conferees to accept the Senate's

death-sentence provision. Such a move could not be made until twenty days after the conferees had been appointed. On the twentieth day, Rayburn acted.[34] Under the bill, he told the House, many holding companies could continue to live, but the revelations of the Senate investigations demonstrate "to every man, I believe, who loves justice and fair play and who stands for the preservation of the best that is in our social, our economic and our political lives that of these companies, many of them must die if the Republic is to live."[35] The House chamber rang with applause.

Rayburn played his trump card. That morning the Black investigators had called to the stand a New Jersey public-relations man, E. P. Cramer, who admitted advising Electric Bond and Share Company to initiate a whispering campaign that New Dealers and especially "the New Dealer-in-Chief" were either incompetent or insane.[36] Rayburn had the clerk read a press dispatch, just minutes old, that cited Senator Black's question: "Did you have any basis for attempting to create an impression in the minds of the people of this country that their President was insane?"

"None whatsoever," Cramer replied.

Curtly Rayburn said, "Mr. Speaker, I submit that without any comment."

Opponents of the death-sentence amendment were on their feet to reply. John G. Cooper, Republican of Ohio, recalled that during the debate on the floor Rayburn exhibited organization charts of just two utility companies—Associated Gas and Electric ("the black sheep of all the utility companies in this country," Cooper said) and Electric Bond and Share. "Was he afraid to exhibit the charts of the good companies?" Cooper asked. "It was not fair."

Fiery George Huddleston jumped into the attack. Referring to Rayburn's reading of the press release, he demanded, "Why did the gentleman from Texas have that statement read at this time? Is it the purpose of the gentleman from Texas to still further inflame public sentiment? Is it his purpose to further intimidate those who honestly disagree with him?" Furthermore, Rayburn had misstated the differences between the House and

Senate bills, Huddleston contended. "The distinction is between a trial in court and a lynching bee. The gentleman from Texas champions the lynching bee." He shouted: "The gentleman from Texas moves that we surrender to the Senate on Section 11. I am not surprised. He surrendered to Mr. Cohen when the latter handed him the bill and he introduced it in the House." Rayburn himself, said Huddleston, prepared the toothless House bill, then "abandoned his new-born child and walked away with this Senate jade." He taunted: "The gentleman from Texas hitherto established with me great confidence in him as a fighting man. Now he has come to be just about the best little surrenderer that ever was seen." The House broke into laughter and applause.

Stung by the attack, Rayburn replied, "I do not surrender when I act like I want to act. I do not change my position. I have stood for the elimination of the holding companies from the beginning. I have not surrendered one iota from the time this bill was introduced until this moment." Applause swept the chamber. His voice hardened. "I want to take these giants off the little operating companies," he declared. "I want the management, the control and the fixing of the policies in my state moved from New York to Texas." He continued: "I am not an enemy of business—clean business. What I want to do here is to take from this field the desperadoes in the utility business who in the past by their action and their deeds have brought the whole utility business into disrepute. I want to take the Insulls and the Hopsons and the Dohertys out of this business so it will stand before the American people as it deserves to stand—clean, honest, with the people having full faith and confidence in it." Once again, members burst into applause.

When the House voted, Rayburn's motion met a stunning defeat. The vote was 209–155. Weeks of sensational testimony before the Senate investigators had gained only 9 votes for the death-sentence provision. Huddleston moved quickly to get House authorization to exclude Ben Cohen and other outsiders from the conference. The House backed him, 183–172.

Rayburn was dejected. The revelations of the investigation had been less effective than he had thought. Perhaps he had erred in timing. "If the impetuous Rayburn had delayed one or two days," editorialized the *St. Louis Post-Dispatch*, "he would have had the newspaper accounts working for the administration's side. Nothing is less impressive than a hastily prepared speech on the floor of the House where the members usually do not pay much attention to what is being said even if they can hear over the din." Whatever the reason, Rayburn had failed badly. Now odds were against passage of any bill. It had been galling to Rayburn when his committee turned against him on the death-sentence amendment; now that the entire House had overwhelmingly repudiated his stand, it was bitter medicine indeed. It was one of the lowest ebbs of a long career.

While Rayburn was gloomy over his chances of pushing the bill through to final passage, Senator Black was not dismayed. He believed that, with added time, his committee could dig up instances of "illegitimate lobbying" that would shock the nation and eventually change enough votes in the House to pass the bill. All along, Black had his eye on the sprawling Associated Gas and Electric empire, such a black sheep in utility circles that it was deliberately excluded from joining the Committee of Public Utility Executives that was set up to lobby against the bill. Black had already produced evidence that AG and E employees had faked thousands of telegrams; that it spent more than $800,000 fighting the bill; that AG and E's president, Howard C. Hopson, had milked the company of nearly $3 million during the depression while stockholders went without dividends; and that, by controlling a small amount of voting stock in the top holding company, he controlled $900 million worth of subsidiaries. Both the Senate and House committees wanted to question Hopson, but he was in hiding, avoiding a congressional subpoena. A nationwide search for him began.

For two weeks, sweltering Washingtonians had their minds diverted from the heat by accounts of the committee's mad search for the elusive tycoon. When a witness testified that Hopson spent the previous night at the Shoreham Hotel, investigators for both committees piled into cars, roared through Washington traffic at breakneck speed, swarmed through the

Shoreham, rapped at doors, questioned employees. It was a false alarm.

The House investigators heard a rumor that Hopson might be hiding out at the Virginia estate of Patrick J. Hurley, Hoover's secretary of war and one of Hopson's lawyers. When they arrived at the Hurley home, reporters were already there. Hurley was outraged at this invasion of his privacy. Hopson was not there. "This whole lobby investigation," Hurley roared, "reminds me of the firm Baloney, Baloney, Horsefeathers, and Baloney." While U.S. marshals and forty-two committee investigators scoured the country for Hopson, he suddenly surrendered himself to Chairman O'Connor of the House Rules Committee, from whom he correctly expected to receive much gentler treatment than from Senator Black.

The lofty and commodious caucus room of the House office building was jammed when Hopson, jauntily swinging a cane, made his first appearance. A bald, roly-poly little man, with a mouth that seemed to stretch from ear to ear, he reminded one reporter of a bulldog. On the witness stand Hopson was hostile, contemptuous of the committee. Asked about his income, his face grew crimson. "I don't think this committee has any right to pry into my private affairs," he replied.[37]

"If gas and electric rates are too high," Hopson snapped, "get a Diesel engine." When he told committee member Eugene Cox of Georgia that he was no gentleman, the quick-tempered Georgian threatened to kick him bodily out of the room unless he retracted. Hopson withdrew the statement.[38] As Hopson was leaving the committee room, a Senate committee investigator tried to serve him with a summons to appear before Black's inquiry. Hopson's guards bodily shoved him aside and whisked the arrogant financier away in a waiting automobile.

Enraged, Black got the Senate to cite Hopson and his attorney for contempt. Denouncing Chairman O'Connor and the House committee for shielding the utility magnate, Black called Hopson "a dodging, hiding, running witness." After the two committee chairmen exchanged angry words in the press, Black revealed that O'Connor's brother Basil, former law partner of President Roosevelt, had received $25,000 in attorney fees from the Hopson empire. With this revelation, O'Connor lost control of the House investigation. Suddenly the House committee overrode its chairman, deciding it would question Hopson in the mornings and let Black have him for afternoon questioning.

When Hopson appeared before Black's committee, he tried the arrogant, contemptuous tactics that had succeeded before the House committee. Black cut him short: "Just state the facts. We don't want speeches here. . . . We don't want philosophy." Time after time Hopson and Black heatedly clashed. Finally, Black, with the backing of his entire committee, read Hopson a statement reminding him that contempt proceedings, with a possible jail sentence, were still hanging over his head. "The committee," intoned Black, "has unanimously reached the conclusion that it will no longer tolerate the conduct previously indulged in by the witness."

"Hopson's truculence melted magically as Black concluded the statement," reporter Paul Y. Anderson noted in the *Post-Dispatch* on August 20. "His fountain of speech, which had spouted indefatigably for weeks, dried up, and his manner became strangely subdued." Hopson answered in low-toned monosyllables. He seemed thoroughly whipped.

Day after day, Black extracted from the rotund witness the story of his financial high jinks. While the 350,000 investors in AG and E had received no dividends for years, Hopson and his sisters had been paid $3,187,000 between 1929 and 1933 through his control of the company. He had invented the "widows and orphans" propaganda gimmick to drum up support against the Rayburn-Wheeler bill. He had spent nearly a million dollars fighting the bill, all of which had been borrowed from banks. Threatening to withdraw his advertising, Hopson had brought pressure to bear on unfriendly newspapers such as the *New York Times.* As disclosure piled on disclosure, and sensational headlines hit the nation's front pages day after day, public indignation mounted. Congress sensed the change in public opinion. From the beginning, utility leaders knew that Hopson and AG and E were the most fearsome skeleton in their closet. They were right. Once Hopson's activities were publicly aired, the battle was lost.

While Black was making his sensational disclosures, the dead-lock over the bill itself continued unabated in the conference committee. Senate conferees stood firmly for the death-sentence amendment; among the House conferees, Rayburn insisted on it, but he was outnumbered by Huddleston and the Republicans. Finally, Roosevelt decided it was time to seek a compromise—new language that would still eliminate the holding companies but at the same time allow House members to save face. White House and congressional leaders, minus Rayburn and Wheeler, worked together to hammer out a new section 11, keeping the essence while avoiding some of the harshness of the original bill. Rayburn and Wheeler accepted the change.

The compromise was offered to the conferees by Senator Alben Barkley of Kentucky and became known as the Barkley Compromise. Among the conferees, Huddleston and the House Republicans turned it down flat. The stalemate continued. Now Rayburn's only alternative was to get the weary, embattled House to instruct its conferees to accept the compromise. It was risky business, but he saw no other way.

On August 22, Rayburn told the House that the conferees had reached an impasse. Then he asked the clerk to read a letter from Roosevelt. "I have seen the proposed compromise," the President wrote Rayburn. "From the point of view of the House, this proposal certainly constitutes a most generous concession on the part of the Senate conferees." He urged the House to accept it. Rayburn carefully explained that the compromise was more lenient than the original Senate death-sentence language, which would have eliminated all holding companies beyond the first degree by 1942. Under the compromise, the Securities and Exchange Commission could make exceptions to this ban. The bill would be "effective, workable and fair," Rayburn insisted.[39]

Opponents of the compromise leaped to their feet. "Messrs. Corcoran and Cohen, the authors of the original decree to eliminate holding companies, have rewritten that decree in new language, but the sentence of death remains," shouted Ohio Republican John G. Cooper. "Do not think anyone will be deceived by this different shroud of language in which death has been newly wrapped." George Huddleston opened a stinging attack on Rayburn. "The gentleman from Texas again invites the House to surrender to the Senate," he barked. "This motion is an affront to the dignity and the independence of the House. Four times has the gentleman from Texas placed the members of this House in this stultifying position; four times has he asked us to sacrifice our convictions in the interest of saving someone's face." He shouted: "The Rayburn proposal is merely the death sentence in a different form of words. This new version means the same as the original death sentence. The only purpose of this juggling is to afford any weak-kneed brethren an opportunity to recant."[40] Laughter and applause resounded in the chamber.

But the House had had enough. The Hopson episode, faked telegrams, and other sordid disclosures of high-pressure, extravagant lobbying by the utilities had turned the tide. By a vote of 219–142, the House reversed itself, instructing its conferees to accept the compromise. On August 24, exactly two hundred days after Rayburn first introduced the bill, the most fiercely contested legislative battle in the history of Congress came to an end, not with a bang but with a whimper. The House then gave final approval to the public utility holding company bill by a vote of 222–112. Senate approval was a foregone conclusion. Later, at a White House ceremony, as Rayburn, Wheeler, Barkley, Cohen, Corcoran, and others stood behind him, Roosevelt signed the bill into law. "This is the fattest bill I ever signed," said the President, patting the 297-page document.[41] It was also the most controversial and hardest won.

As the first session of the 74th Congress came to its close, syndicated columnists Pearson and Allen listed as one of the year's memorable scenes: "Representative Sam Rayburn, floor leader for the holding-company bill, being thunderously applauded by Republicans as well as Democrats for his fairness and patience in the utility fight."[42] Rayburn's stature among his colleagues, already high, grew tremendously as a result of the holding-company battle. He had demonstrated technical mastery of one of the most complicated pieces of legislation that Congress had ever considered. His parliamentary skill in keeping the death-sentence amendment alive through many dis-

couraging months was of the highest order. His doggedness in
the fight, week after week, in the face of personal abuse, cruel
political pressures, and seemingly overwhelming odds impressed
friend and foe alike.

Watching the struggle from the House gallery was SEC Commissioner William O. Douglas, whose agency would administer
the act if it was passed. In 1956, after he became an associate justice of the Supreme Court, Douglas recalled his impressions as
he watched the floor fight:

> Rayburn's management of the bill was superb; the as-
> tuteness and skill with which he worked behind the scene
> lining up votes was brilliant. At times he seemed to stand
> almost alone. Without him I don't think the bill could have
> been passed.
>
> He has the kind of mind that can master details, but he
> doesn't let himself be sidetracked by details. In the death-
> sentence fight, he trusted Tommy and Ben on the details,
> and he stuck to the central theme. I think that fight demon-
> strated what might be called the Main Street point of view
> which he represents—the average man's doubts of the deal-
> ings of the financial wizards.[43]

Said the late Congressman John J. Dempsey of New Mexico:
"In that fight, Rayburn had the correct answer all the time. He
had a technical mastery of the bill no one else possessed."[44]
Rayburn knew that his handling of the bill had enhanced his
standing among his colleagues. Equally important, the success
with which he carried the Roosevelt banner in the struggle made
him one of the White House favorites, which was to be a powerful asset when the time came to make his bid for a House leadership position.

But if Rayburn's prestige on Capitol Hill and at the White
House had risen, he knew that he faced serious political trouble
in his own district. The utilities had targeted him for defeat, and
their agents already were preparing to finance serious opposition for him in the 1936 election. Tired and worn though he was
in the late summer of 1935, he had to go home to cover his district, seeking to convince his constituents that his attack on the

utilities had been in their best interests.

Strange are the ways of politics—a man who owned neither stocks nor bonds, who for the first fifty years of his life neither understood nor cared about the intricacies of Wall Street, was called upon to lead the fight for the laws that sought to regulate the activities of high finance as never before in American history. It had been a battle of unprecedented intensity between big money and big government. Years later, Rayburn reduced the struggle to stark simplicity: "Just call it the fight for economic justice."

I I

Up the Ladder

With passage of the Public Utility Holding Company Act, Rayburn could at last afford to relax. The back-breaking pressure of the New Deal's first three years, which had brought him the only insomnia of his life and carried him to the brink of exhaustion, had been highly productive. He had co-authored five major pieces of legislation: the Emergency Railroad Transportation Act, the Truth-in-Securities Act, the Stock Exchange Act, the Federal Communications Act, and, most important, the Public Utility Holding Company Act.

He was to sponsor one more important bill: the Rural Electrification Act of 1936. That law together with legislation creating farm-to-market roads he remembered as his proudest achievements because they helped "the real people"—those who lived close to the soil and who to him constituted the strength and backbone of the nation. For such people, living quietly on farms and ranches and in small towns of America, he felt a strong responsibility. "Rayburn," observed his friend Cecil Dickson, "is always watching out for what he calls 'the real people'—those who come into life without many advantages and try to make a living and raise their families. The other people, well-born and with advantages, can get just about everything they want without government help, but 'the real people' need the protection of the government."[1]

Rayburn did not originate the concept of a national program
to electrify the farms, although he eagerly embraced the idea.
The beginnings of such a program were provided nearly a year
earlier in the Emergency Relief Act of 1935.[2] That plan, creating
the first Rural Electrification Administration, was implemented
by executive order of the President mainly to provide work for
the jobless. It made little progress, however. As a relief measure,
it was impractical. Its goal was to spend large sums of money
quickly in order to put many people, most of them unskilled, to
work without delay. Such aims simply were incompatible with
planning and building rural electric lines. Moreover, the original plan was to use private utility companies to construct the
lines. They showed almost no interest in doing so, even if the
federal government provided grants and subsidies. They were
convinced the whole idea of rural electrification was impractical. Rayburn once told the House of Representatives:

> I remember that in my county in the early 1930s there
> was not a mile of rural electrification in that great rich
> county of 45,000 square miles. Finally there was one mile
> built. That farm on which I live is a mile from the city lim-
> its. We finally got rural electrification out to that farm, and
> it was the only mile in that county until after rural elec-
> trification came about. The rates were such that we could
> not operate an electric stove on that farm. We could not as
> farmers pay the bill.[3]

During the autumn of 1935, the entire thrust of the program
was radically revised. Instead of relying on private companies or
cities to build the lines into the country, a plan—brilliant in
retrospect—was devised whereby farmers would band together
into nonprofit cooperatives, borrow the money from the REA,
and build and own the lines, repaying the federal loan through
profits from the sales of electricity to farmers. In addition, individual farmers could borrow money to wire their houses, install
electrically powered water systems, and buy stoves, refrigera-
tors, washing machines, irons, and other electric appliances.

That proposal was the basis of the bill that Rayburn and Senator George Norris of Nebraska, the father of the Tennessee Valley Authority, introduced on January 6, 1936—the Texan's 54th birthday. No major opposition emerged. The utility companies, battle-scarred and financially poorer from the raging "death-sentence" battle of the year before, had little stomach for another contest with the New Dealers. Moreover, they were still convinced the program would fail. "They said it would never work," recalled Rayburn. "But they had never seen a mother and sister over a washtub as I had; they had never seen them heating irons in a fireplace; they had never stuck their hands in dirty coal-oil chimney lamps."[4] The measure sailed through the House without the formality of a record vote. Shortly thereafter, the Senate passed its own version. Minor differences between the two versions were quickly resolved, and a final bill was sent to the President for his signature on May 20.

An unexpected dividend of Rayburn's sponsorship of the REA bill was the beginning of a firm friendship with Senator Norris, one of the most constructive legislators in American history. Congress, with more than 500 members, each beset with a multitude of time-consuming problems, affords little leisure for the formation of close friendships. Besides, the House of Representatives and the Senate are physically separated—the Senate chamber at the north end of the Capitol, the House at the south end. Each body has its own office buildings, separated by hundreds of yards. Close and intimate contact between senators and House members is rare, except for the leaders.

Rayburn and Norris had served in Congress together for nearly twenty-four years, yet scarcely had more than a nodding acquaintance when they first faced each other as members of the House-Senate conference committee on the REA measure. It was the start of a long, mutually admiring friendship. The Texan always contended that Norris was the most practical progressive with whom he ever served—a rare individual who not only aroused the citizenry with a new idea but one who developed the skill to write a bill and pilot it through hazardous legislative shoals to become the law of the land.

If 1936 gave Rayburn some respite from congressional battles,

it was not a year of restful activity. The widely admired but controversial FDR was standing for re-election for the first time.
And, in his own district, the public utility companies, still
vengefully angry over the "death-sentence" bill, were determined to defeat the tenacious legislator they held most responsible for its passage. In his own campaign, Rayburn was taking
no chances. Although his principal opponent—Jess Morris—
was the man he had defeated in both 1932 and 1934, there was
no reason for overoptimism. Morris had run well in both previous races, and this time he would have a bountiful financial
backing he had not had before. Moreover, in his second race,
Morris had received a substantially larger vote than in his first.
The utility companies, making no secret of their determination
to punish Rayburn, opened their purses to his opponent.[5]

Faithful attendance in the House of Representatives was a cardinal tenet in Rayburn's book. "When Congress is in session,
your place is here, and when Congress is not in session, your
place is in your district," he often counseled fellow congressmen.
But during the spring and summer of 1936, he ignored his own
advice, missing many House sessions as he campaigned inten-
sively across the length and breadth of his district.

His campaign strategy was to run as a fierce champion of
Franklin Roosevelt, praising the New Deal and apologizing for
nothing. In addition, he would talk much about a $40 million
federal project—the Denison Dam and reservoir—that he hoped
to get approved for his district before the election. Building the
Denison Dam had been a dream of many community leaders in
the northern end of Rayburn's district for years. The congressman
had devoted interminable labor over a decade or more to its
fulfillment. But one obstacle after another—including high
cost, questionable economic justification, opposition of farmers
whose land would be condemned, and the determination of the
power companies to prevent the inclusion of hydroelectric gen-
erating capacity—appeared to frustrate his efforts.

Arguments for the dam were numerous. The Red River,
which serves as the border between Texas and Oklahoma for
several hundred miles, frequently produced devastating floods—
inundating millions of acres of productive farmland, destroying

livestock, washing away buildings, and raising the floodwaters of the lower Mississippi River—as it coursed through Texas, Oklahoma, Arkansas, and Louisiana. Construction of the dam near Denison would harness approximately half the waters of the Red River, protecting some 1,600,000 acres of land downstream. Farms in the lower valley would benefit from a dependable water supply. Its hydroelectric generators could head off a potential power shortage in the region. And it would provide 17,000 new jobs the first year, a major plus at a time when unemployment in the area was widespread.[6]

For Rayburn personally, the political situation was pressing. He had been in Congress for twenty-four years; he claimed to be a great influence in New Deal circles; he had been promising the dam for years—and still the dam had not been approved. Wasn't it time, said his critics, for the Fourth District to elect a new congressman—a doer, not just a promiser? It was all a political hoax perpetrated on the voters, they insisted.

In late 1935, Roosevelt personally promised Rayburn that funds for a detailed survey for the dam would be in the Public Works Administration's budget for 1936—a bit of happy news that the congressman quickly announced to the Texas press. However, when the list of approved PWA projects came out, the Red River dam was not among them. Angry and humiliated, Rayburn wired Interior Secretary Harold Ickes: "Opposition papers are saying that this is Roosevelt-Rayburn ballyhoo and nothing will be done and it is becoming rather embarrassing Stop I am wondering if you cannot get authorization to make this allotment at once."[7]

Ickes, meanwhile, had his own problems; ever since FDR had decided to administer PWA allotments himself, the President had made promises of money right and left to almost anybody who could get to him. It was Ickes's job to tell them later that there was no money. All he could do was offer sympathy. "I realize embarrassing position in which you find yourself Stop . . ." he wired in response to Rayburn's appeal for help.[8]

Rayburn was under pressure even from his own brother. "I am just wondering how you feel about your R. R. Dam?" Dick Rayburn wrote. "Lots of people are asking me and I am at a loss to tell them other than it wasn't in the President's program as yet. I feel you should put it over if possible in some way. It will give your opposition lots of bull to strow [sic] if you don't."[9] The dam's approval before the 1936 primary had become a political necessity for the Texas congressman. From the President on down, the New Dealers understood his predicament. Shortly before the election came yet another FDR promise that something would be done.

Campaigning as a fierce champion of the New Deal, Rayburn rode the crest of FDR's unsurpassed popularity. His renomination was virtually assured when, a few weeks before the state primary, the President capped a whistle-stop tour of the Southwest with a visit to Denison to embrace Rayburn and personally announce his approval of funds to begin the Denison Dam survey. That was followed by another boost—this from Democratic National Chairman Jim Farley, who named the Texan as chairman of the Democratic National Campaign Speakers Bureau, a meaningful post and a clear sign to voters of the Fourth Congressional District that their representative was an important figure in the New Deal "establishment." When the votes were counted, Rayburn had won easy renomination despite the utility companies' lavish expenditures to defeat him. He snorted: "The utilities can make more noise and produce less votes than any outfit I know of."[10]

While campaigning in Texas, Rayburn slipped away for a short fishing trip. There he got word of an unexpected event that was to spark the most important personal fight of his life: Speaker Joseph W. Byrns had died suddenly; for the third time in as many years, the job Rayburn coveted was vacant. By the time Rayburn learned of Byrns's death, an official delegation led by President Roosevelt and including Vice-President Garner and most members of the House was already en route to the funeral in Nashville. Rayburn hurried to join them there.

Returning with them on the train to Washington, he finally was able to size up the situation: because Byrns had died while the House was in session—the first Speaker to do so—the House could conduct no further business until a new Speaker was chosen. Within hours, the Democrats had nominated and elected Majority Leader William Bankhead of Alabama without opposition. Adjournment for the year being only days away, the Democrats then decided to postpone naming a new majority leader until the new Congress convened in January. Newly elected members, it was argued, should have a chance to vote.

The choice of a majority leader to succeed Bankhead took on extraordinary importance, both for President Roosevelt and for Rayburn. Through custom, both the Democratic and Republican parties in the House had been advancing their majority leaders to the Speakership when a vacancy occurred,[11] and Bankhead was in precarious health. A few days before he was elected majority leader in 1935, he suffered a massive heart attack and was not present at the Democratic caucus at which he was elected. The caucus was told simply that he had a bad cold. During 1935, he was unable to attend a single session of the House. His duties during that period unofficially fell to the chairman of the Committee on Rules, John J. O'Connor of New York. Bankhead's sudden elevation to Speaker with only two weeks remaining in the session again thrust O'Connor into the role of acting majority leader. O'Connor immediately announced his desire to hold the post permanently and began campaigning for the job on the way to Byrns's funeral. For Roosevelt, this was a delicate and dangerous political situation. If he was re-elected—and the odds seemed to favor it—he would need a thoroughly loyal majority leader to steer the program of his second administration through the House.

Roosevelt was deeply indebted to Rayburn for his successful handling of a major part of the administration's program. Yet the President and his lieutenants were not completely satisfied with him. They often complained privately that he was too cautious, too slow to move, did not have enough spirit of "sock 'em in the jaw," and at times was too independent of White House suggestions and demands. In this fight, however, Roosevelt felt he had no choice. The alternative was worse.

On the record, O'Connor seemed a loyal New Dealer. But Roosevelt knew better. It was O'Connor, as chairman of the Rules Committee, who had refused to allow a record vote in the House on the crucial "death-sentence" section of the holding-company bill, despite White House pleading. Although O'Connor's brother Basil was FDR's former law partner and close friend, the hostility between the President and John O'Connor, while publicly disguised, was well known to Washington insiders. As majority leader, O'Connor certainly would be a source of trouble and, even more, a major threat to New Deal legislation.

The situation posed unexpected problems for Rayburn. In spite of his abortive efforts to win the Speakership in 1934, his ambition for the office still burned feverishly. Challenging O'Connor, who seemed poised to take the majority leader's post by default, would not be easy. Remembering his humiliating loss to Byrns two years earlier, Rayburn vacillated, telling friends on the train that he had not made up his mind. He knew well that a second failure in a leadership contest would probably permanently wreck his chances for the Speakership.

One who had no doubt about the ultimate decision was his friend Cecil Dickson, chief of the Associated Press staff in the House. Even before Rayburn learned of Byrns's death, Dickson filed a story for the AP declaring flatly that Rayburn would be a candidate for majority leader. Rayburn was livid when he saw the article. He immediately phoned the reporter. "Dick, what the hell are you doing to me?" he snapped.

"Sam, I've just elected you majority leader," Dickson said happily. "You have to be that before you can be Speaker."

"I guess you're right," said Rayburn.[12] Still, he made no formal announcement of his candidacy, although news stories in succeeding months consistently listed him as a probable contender.

The Democrats, meanwhile, had a national election to think about. In mid-August, Rayburn went to New York City to take charge of the party's national speakers' bureau for the presidential campaign. He would be responsible for furnishing speakers not only on behalf of the Roosevelt-Garner ticket but also for Democratic candidates for the House, Senate, and, in some cases, governor. For two and a half months, he made his headquarters at the Biltmore Hotel. Looking back years later, he considered that autumn one of the most miserable periods of his life. He despised living in the big city. "The place depressed me," he recalled. "There wasn't anybody to eat dinner with." He could not remember ever being more lonesome. Much of the time he had influenza, although he kept going—directing the assignment of speakers and making many speeches himself.

The whole experience reinforced his lifelong conviction that people should live in the country or in small towns if they could. "I think our land would be better and happier if no city ever reached a population of more than 500,000," he once said. "So many diversified interests are affected by each move that it is sometimes unpleasant to live in a big city."[13] Close to the soil, people were closer to each other, he believed. He felt sorry for those who had to live in fast-moving and impersonal cities where, he concluded, there was no time to know and care about relatives and neighbors, to think, and to watch the changing seasons and growing plants.[14]

That November, Roosevelt and Garner were re-elected by the greatest landslide the nation had known. As Jim Farley had predicted, the ticket carried every state save Maine and Vermont. Republicans in Congress were crushed by the Democratic sweep. When the dust had cleared, Democrats had won 333, Republicans 89, and minor parties 13 of the 435 House races.[15] As soon as the election returns were in, Rayburn told his family he was leaving for Washington to campaign for majority leader. "I want that job," he declared.

He clearly understood the critical nature of the contest he was entering. In 1934, he had reached for the Speakership and failed. A second failure in a leadership contest would probably permanently ruin his chances of ever becoming Speaker. If he waited, O'Connor, only 51 years old and in good health, almost certainly would succeed Bankhead and serve for many years. For Rayburn, it was now or never.

There were serious obstacles in his path. Foremost was O'Connor himself. An able, affable, tough-minded New Yorker, he was personally perhaps more popular with his colleagues than Rayburn. He was a Catholic in a House where Catholics were numerous. As chairman of the powerful Rules Committee, he had collected many political IOUs from members by helping get floor action on their pet measures. Furthermore, there was a feeling among some members that a Rules Committee chairman was, more or less, "next in line" in the leadership hierarchy. O'Connor began exploiting this feeling as soon as Byrns was buried.

In a large sense, the fight shaped up as another holding-company battle. Rayburn was anathema to the utilities and their financial allies; Wall Street had many old scores to settle with him. On the other hand, the utilities were beholden—and grateful—to O'Connor for his covert support in the "death-sentence" fight. Shocked by the magnitude of the Democratic landslide, business conservatives looked to O'Connor as a "brake" on New Deal liberalism that might otherwise run rampant.

The fact that Rayburn was from Texas—a John Garner protégé at that—was another handicap that O'Connor supporters exploited. The rough, sometimes cruel Garner left behind many scars and hatreds in the House. More damaging to Rayburn, however, was his own "southern" label.[16] The South already held too much power in Congress, many felt. The Vice-Presidency, the Speakership, twenty-four of forty-seven House committee chairmanships all belonged to southern and border South states. Six House chairmanships were held by Texans.

Most of the newly elected Democrats were from the North and West. To them, the O'Connor forces argued that if the Democratic party was to be a national party, its high offices must be divided among the various regions of the country. The election of a Texan as majority leader, they noted, would give the entire House leadership to the South. Rayburn's supporters replied rather feebly (as Lyndon Johnson's supporters were to do when he sought the Presidency in 1960) that Texas was a western not a southern state. While basically accurate, the argument was hard to sell politically.

Two important factors bolstered Rayburn's chances: the widespread assumption that Roosevelt preferred Rayburn and the fact that serious defections were occurring inside O'Connor's own delegation.

The Rayburn managers, led by Fred Vinson of Kentucky,[17]

flatly asserted to their colleagues that FDR wanted the Texan elected, although Roosevelt himself said not a word. The President faced a painful problem: he did want Rayburn as leader—felt that he must have him if his program was not to be in jeopardy—but was reluctant to involve himself actively lest he offend O'Connor and cause an angry Democratic split in the House. If O'Connor was defeated for leader, he still would be chairman of the Committee on Rules, a position of great influence to help or hinder future New Deal legislation. Roosevelt's vaunted political finesse seldom was put to a more crucial test.

In mid-November, a carefully contrived White House plan to bolster Rayburn's candidacy began unfolding. The President left by navy cruiser to attend the Inter-American Peace Conference in Buenos Aires, not to return for a month. He would be safely out of the leadership contest. His departure was followed by John Garner's surprise announcement from Uvalde that he was returning to Washington to help Rayburn win his fight. "I am for Sam Rayburn 200 percent for the House leadership," declared the Vice-President. "My guess is he will win and I will contribute all I can for that purpose." Although the two men had worked side by side in Congress for twenty years, the Vice-President's open endorsement was out of character and caught Rayburn by surprise. Years later, Garner explained: "I was always for Texas and Sam was a much better man than O'Connor. O'Connor would have had to ask Tammany if he could take a shit in the morning. We didn't want that."[18]

Did Garner speak for the President, the press wanted to know. "Ask him," replied Rayburn. Roosevelt, by then well out to sea, could not be reached. The stunned O'Connor forces conferred for several hours, then came out swinging against Garner for his "gratuitous intrusion" into affairs "with which the Vice President has nothing to do" and which "will be resented by members of the House." His intervention, they claimed hopefully, would serve only to cinch O'Connor's victory.[19] That afternoon the New Yorker got another jolt. His high hopes of getting Louisiana's eight votes were dashed when the state's delegation, after a stormy caucus presided over by Governor Richard Leche, voted to support Rayburn unanimously.[20]

Crucial was the 27-member Pennsylvania delegation, controlled by state Democratic chairman Joseph F. Guffey, then a U.S. senator and close ally of the President. Guffey's refusal to back Rayburn against Byrns in the 1934 race for Speaker had doomed the Texan's chances. This year, the delegation's decision would be weighed carefully by other House members. Its endorsement of Rayburn would be correctly interpreted as representing the President's wishes. Guffey's own interest in the race was more than casual. He wanted insurance that Pat Boland of Pennsylvania would continue as House Democratic whip. Rayburn was agreeable. Also, Guffey had hopes that he might secure the Democratic presidential nomination for Governor George Earle in 1940. It would not be harmful to have Rayburn, as majority leader and a southwesterner, on his side in such a fight. At an acrimonious, Guffey-led caucus on December 3, Pennsylvania voted, 18–6, to support Rayburn. It then voted to apply the unit rule, pledging the Texan all 27 of the delegation's votes.[21]

The bandwagon was rolling. In Massachusetts, Congressman John McCormack of Boston became the first New Englander to declare for Rayburn, a decision that was to help his career tremendously. Congressman Tom O'Brien of Chicago persuaded his city's twin bosses, Ed Nash and Ed Kelly, to put their nine representatives in the Texan's camp. Other big-city bosses followed. Perhaps most important of all, Rayburn picked up the quiet support of two powerful figures in O'Connor's backyard: Bronx boss Ed Flynn and Tammany leader Tom Cullen. Much of the credit went to Tommy Corcoran, Roosevelt's covert agent in the leadership fight, whose job it was to see that Rayburn got at least some support from the big New York delegation. As Corcoran later remembered it:

The big task was to block off Jim Farley from helping O'Connor. Farley was coming back from Europe on one of the 'Queens,' and all the Tammany bunch was waiting for him on the dock to see what he was going to tell them about this [House] leadership business. I got a friend connected with the Coast Guard to give me a launch and went out to meet Farley's ship. I climbed a ladder up the side of the ship and found Farley. "Rayburn's our man," I told him. Then I beat it back to the dock. When Farley met the Tammany bunch, he knew what to say.[22]

House Democrats caucused on the afternoon of January 4, 1937. Rayburn appeared to have a commanding lead, but O'Connor's supporters had waged a last-minute blitz—and in politics nothing is certain until the votes are counted. Tension ran high. O'Connor was faintly hopeful.

The hope was short-lived. When Tammany boss Tom Cullen, a longtime O'Connor enemy, rose to second Rayburn's nomination and it became evident that seven other New Yorkers were abandoning O'Connor, the die was cast. If a contender fails to hold his own delegation in such a contest, the psychological effect is devastating. Rayburn was elected, 184–127. O'Connor's motion made the vote unanimous. Later, the pair posed smiling for pictures. Returning to his office, the new House majority leader told Alla Clary, "I'm glad it was close. That will make for a better feeling all around."[23]

12

Majority Leader

Looking back on a long life in public service, Rayburn remembered his elevation to majority leader as his "most thrilling moment in politics." It meant the anguish and nagging fear of failure that had plagued him since childhood were, at last, over. He knew that, in due time, the Speakership would be his. Mentally and physically, he was in his prime. He had been an elected official for thirty years, more than half his life. He was one of the senior members of the House—only three had served longer—and his career was still on the ascent.

His health at age 55 was robust. His face was full and unlined, except for crow's-feet about his eyes. His weight constant at 176 pounds, he was variously described by reporters as "bulky," "heavy-set," or "slightly corpulent." He walked and stood with ramrod erectness, getting the maximum height out of his five foot six inches. Emotionally he was serene and relaxed.

In Washington, he had settled into a pattern of living that was to change little for the rest of his life. He lived quietly and alone in a tiny, two-room rented suite at the Anchorage Apartments at 1900 Q Street Northwest—a block north of Dupont Circle. His second-floor, northwest-corner flat overlooking Q Street and Connecticut Avenue was indifferently furnished and had no cooking facilities, save for an electric hot plate on which he

heated an occasional can of Gebhardt's chili. Usually, he either
dined out or, more often, ordered meals sent over from the
Pierre Restaurant across the street. In good weather, he continued his routine daily exercise—walking the two and a half
miles to work each morning. But now, upon reaching the foot
of Capitol Hill, he often took a taxi or streetcar the rest of
the way.

He worked long hours and looked forward to a relaxing drink
or two with a few political friends at day's end. He drank either
Scotch or bourbon, depending on his mood and on which
bottle he happened to grab first from his liquor cabinet, which
was never without ample reserves, thanks to gifts from friends
and other well-wishers. Rayburn began drinking bourbon late
in life but still preferred Scotch. "I never want it to show on
me and I can gauge Scotch better," he told newsman George
Dixon.[1] While brand names were not important to him, quality
was. Cheap liquor ladened with poisonous fusel oil had wrecked
the health of many a man, he insisted. A lifelong smoker, he
consumed daily one, sometimes two, packs of Camel cigarettes,
the strongest he could readily buy.

Off duty, he lived quietly, largely ignoring the pomp and protocol of Washington's social life. He much preferred to dine
quietly at his apartment or at a restaurant with old friends.
A good evening's entertainment for him was watching the news-
reels that played continuously at the nearby Trans-Lux. He
owned a tuxedo but joked that "the moths have eaten more
meals in it than I have," a line he picked up from a long-ago
opponent, who had used it to ridicule Rayburn's sparse ward-
robe. He dressed conservatively but well, disdaining colorful
ties or suits. Urged by his staff to purchase a bright topcoat to
replace his drab one, he refused: "Nope, when a man my age
starts wearing gay clothes, you can put him down as getting
light in the head." He arranged to be at home early three or four
nights a week. "A fellow's got to get his rest if he's going to do
his job here," he would say. Retiring early, he followed his own
firm rule: stay in bed at least nine hours, whether asleep or
awake. "Lying flat on your back is good for your innards," he
believed.

Others in high positions were at first amused then captivated by his total lack of pretense. "Sam Rayburn is one of the few men I know who still wears the same size hat as the day he arrived here," quipped Roosevelt. Supreme Court Justice William O. Douglas, a close friend for thirty years, believed Rayburn's secret of success was his insistence on "always just being himself." In 1956, Douglas said:

> He never tries to play some role other than himself. He's honest with himself. He's no pretender. He possesses great common sense. He's just plain Sam Rayburn, all the time, with everybody. I've seen him with Roosevelt and others, and he's always the same. When he didn't like something, or it seemed a little off color, he'd say so. I think the most memorable times I've had with him were at Billy Martin's Restaurant in Georgetown, in the back room eating steaks. Then the real Sam Rayburn comes out. I've never seen him being unkind, but sometimes he can be severe in his criticism of others. I remember especially that about 1940 when Corcoran and Cohen were tossed aside by FDR. It wasn't popular to say anything good about them. Rayburn stood by them in their darkest moments. He always defended them, publicly and privately.[2]

As certain as the seasons, Congress's adjournment every summer would be followed by Rayburn's hasty departure by rail for northeast Texas. As he told colleagues in 1939: "I want to go back with my own blood for a while and with my friends of a lifetime." Reporters eager to know when the House would finish its work usually could get an accurate clue by learning the date of his train reservation. Two nights and a day in a Pullman compartment (which he often shared with Wright Patman or another congressman) he found to be good medicine. He read pulp detective and western novels, and "by the time I got to Texas, I was unwound." One or more of his brothers would meet the train at Denison, twenty-eight miles from Bonham. Often a delegation of local political or business leaders was also there to report the latest news from their communities. On the drive to Bonham, the brothers reviewed the political situation in the district and, he later recalled, "by the time I got to Bonham, I pretty well knew what my people were thinking about."

Bonham was his Mecca, the source of his strength, the place he would rather be than any other. In the handsome Mount Vernon–style house, surrounded by relatives and friends, Rayburn spent his happiest days. And a few miles away was his cherished farm, with its rustic bunkhouse, thirty head of registered Jersey cows, crops in the field. He found life in Bonham—"where people are close to each other and care when you die"—satisfying, warming, reinvigorating. To him, there was no other place on earth so wonderful.

Tall, stately "Miss Lou" was always at home to greet her younger brother. Rayburn adored her and trusted implicitly her judgment about people and politics. As he did not coddle others, she did not coddle him. She allowed no liquor in her house, producing an involuntary abstinence he would have tolerated from no one else. She regularly rebuked him for expressing harsh judgments—"Now, Sam, that's enough of that," she would say—and he would desist. The big white house usually was overrun with the clannish Rayburn relatives, delighting in each other's company. Through the years, he watched each pregnancy in the family, hoping the new arrival would be a boy named Sam. He never arrived.

Restless by nature, he stayed busy, even at home. He enjoyed mending fences and working his cows. At home, he wore old khaki pants and a beat-up hat and always seemed to have a chaw of tobacco in his mouth.[3] Sometimes he would don overalls and chop wood—good exercise and a useful chore, he thought. It also was good politics. He made sure to do much of his work in the open, so that neighbors could drive by and see him sweating in the fields, just as they did. He could still split a six-inch log with three blows of a double-bitted axe when he was 75. If there was no wood to chop, he would wash the car or go horseback riding. "He can never sit still," observed Medibel Rayburn Bartley in 1957. "He always wants to do things now. If you say to him, 'Later on, I want to talk to you about so-and-so,' he'll say, 'Let's talk about it now.' Our Mother was that way."[4]

Rayburn's prestige at home soared following his election as majority leader. Until that time, relatively few voters in the Fourth Congressional District of Texas paid him much attention. When they thought of him at all, it usually was in terms of his being diligent, able, dependable, honest, down-to-earth—not much different from the way they viewed themselves.

In Washington, he was known as a congressman's congressman—highly respected for his skill and integrity by his colleagues and other followers of Congress. To the general public, however, he remained almost unknown. Inwardly, it offended him that some men of lesser ability than himself were hogging the limelight while he toiled in the shadows. Outwardly, he pretended not to care. Although he did not shun recognition, he would not seek it either. When friends urged him to hire a press agent, he proudly refused. "Damn the fellow who's always trying to get credit," he would bluster. "I've found that in life a fellow gets all the credit he's entitled to, and usually a damn sight more." He once told a friend: "I used to want to be a big, tall fellow, but I found I can dart in and out and between 'em and get things done before they see me."[5]

John Garner, who badgered Rayburn for years about his excessive modesty, once told Cecil Dickson, "Sam has more ability than any Republican or most any Democrat, but he sits over there in that committee, hunches his shoulders, and won't move. His modesty is so vast that it almost overshadows his ability. You tell him that." Dickson sheepishly relayed the message, then had to listen as the stocky Texan exploded in a scorching burst of invective. "You tell John to mind his own damn business," he said. Later, in a cooler moment, Rayburn told Dickson: "John Garner doesn't realize that we are two different people and that I've got to do things that are within my ability to accomplish. I can't be something I'm not."[6]

Shortly before Rayburn became majority leader, columnist Paul Mallon accurately described him as "one of the outstanding obscure statesmen of the House."[7] On the House floor, Rayburn did not speak unless he felt there an urgent reason to do so: some argument overlooked, some pertinent information not brought out, some appeal that no other member had made. When he spoke, his resonant bass voice could be strong and compelling. He confined himself to short, powerful, Anglo-Saxon words—"one-cylinder words"—incapable of being misunderstood. He was particularly effective in his use of emotion-weighted words such as "honor," "duty," "my country," "our people."

In debate, he carefully avoided singling out or vilifying his opponents. That was not only decent but also wise, he believed. "You say something mean or sarcastic about some member—humiliate him in public—and he'll never forget it," he advised new members. "You probably will, but he won't. He'll lay back of that log for twenty years if he has to, and some day he'll pay you back with compound interest."[8]

If a visitor to the House galleries happened to recognize Rayburn—which was unlikely in the 1930s—he was likely to be found standing behind the high brass rail along the rear of the chamber. His arms draped across the rail, his right hand clutching a cigarette, he would watch eagle-eyed the quiet maneuvering that invariably takes place during a House debate—a group from a certain state talking in whispers, a debate leader circulating among the members, the Republican leadership conferring. Often such movements have political meaning, and Rayburn would make it his business to find out what, if anything, was going on.[9]

He had one regret arising from his promotion to floor leader: having to surrender his chairmanship of the Committee on Interstate and Foreign Commerce. The committee was a source of great pride to him. It had been a workhorse of the New Deal, keeping intact its century-old reputation for diligence and bipartisan harmony among its high-caliber membership. In his six years as chairman, the committee had rebelled against him only once—in 1935 on the bitterly contested "death-sentence" provision. Rayburn was particularly pleased that he had surrendered none of the panel's jurisdiction but had broadened it. His successor, said Robert LaFollette's *Progressive*, was inheriting a committe now "even more looked up to than the House Ways and Means Committee."

Rayburn quickly learned that he was not well suited for the role of a House floor leader. The job required a strong partisan attitude and a combative spirit that he lacked. It required a certain amount of wheeling and dealing, which he found vaguely distasteful, and a zest for partisan repartee on the House floor, which never appealed to him either. Worst of all, it required him to submerge his own opinions and fight for all the proposals and whims—even those he personally disapproved—of the Democratic President. When former Congressman John McDuffie complained to his old colleague about some trends in the Roosevelt administration, Rayburn replied: "Frankly, I am not far from you in your views, although you know we have to go along with the program whether it is argued out with us before it is advanced or not." [10]

Such were his misgivings when Roosevelt revealed his plan to enlarge the Supreme Court, whose conservative majority had thwarted much of his New Deal program and had been an issue in the 1936 elections. By "packing" the Court with up to six new members, whom he would appoint, the President would have a pro–New Deal majority for the next round of liberal programs he had planned in his second term. Ostensibly aimed at helping to ease the work load on the Court's older members, the bill allowed Roosevelt to appoint one new "co-justice" for each Court member who had served ten years or more and was past age 70. Six current justices, all conservatives, qualified. If nobody retired, the bill would enlarge the Court to fifteen members and ensure a pro–New Deal majority on almost any issue.

Breathtakingly daring in premise, the scheme had been concocted by FDR himself, working in secret with Attorney General Homer S. Cummings. Years later, John Garner vividly remembered the Cabinet meeting at which FDR and Cummings first disclosed their intentions:

> I sat at one end of the table, Roosevelt at the other. . . . Cummings gave the law. Everybody sat silent for a moment, then I said, "Mr. Attorney General, before that law comes back up here for the Boss's signature, many, many moons will pass."

Roosevelt smiled and said, "Aw, John, you get out of here". . . . . Roosevelt had control of the executive branch, he dominated the legislative branch, and he wanted to stack the judiciary. If he had succeeded, he could have been king or czar.

He never really got mad at me over the Supreme Court plan. It was the hardest thing I ever had to try to put through for him.[11]

After the chilly reception from his own Cabinet, Roosevelt decided not to discuss his plan with House and Senate leaders. They remained in the dark until summoned to the White House for a briefing just two hours before the plan was to be sent to Capitol Hill. In glum silence, Bankhead, Rayburn, Senate Majority Leader Joseph T. Robinson, Senate Judiciary Chairman Henry F. Ashurst, and House Judiciary Chairman Hatton Sumners listened as Cummings explained the proposal.

Rayburn agreed that the Court was endangering much of the New Deal's good works and felt that something should be done to "liberalize" it. Expansion was strong medicine, he thought, but if that was what Roosevelt wanted, he would go along. "Frankly, I do not see how an addition in number to the Supreme Court would affect the fundamentals of the Court or of the Government," he told a constituent. He was a friend of all the courts "from highest to lowest," he said. "I do think, however, that the Supreme Court as presently constituted has gone just a little far into policy, which, of course, is a matter for the Legislative and Executive Branches."[12]

As for Sumners, never comfortable with the New Deal anyway, FDR's Court scheme was the last straw. "Boys, this is where I cash in," Sumners said when the group arrived back at the Capitol.[13] His adamancy in refusing to cooperate further with the administration would only make Rayburn's job harder. The two had been close friends when they first came up from Texas in 1913. But over the years, they had drifted apart. Their interests—and their whole outlook on life—were vastly different. Once a brilliant prosecutor, Sumners by the 1930s had soured on people in general and had little use for old friendships. "He was not young in spirit," seen through the forgiving eyes of a young Lady Bird Johnson. When Rayburn decided to help Roosevelt, it was the end of their relationship. Later, when Rayburn sought a seat on the Judiciary Committee for leftist Vito Marcantonio of New York, Sumners took it as a personal affront. "I think he made a deal with the Commies in New York City," said Sumners years later. "I don't understand my old friend doing that to me." [14]

Roosevelt's strategy called for House action first, but when only a hundred supporters for the measure could be found and when Judiciary Committee Chairman Sumners refused to endorse it, Rayburn convinced the White House to shift its attention to the Senate. [15] However, in that body as well, the bill quickly bogged down. Even the best efforts of Majority Leader Robinson and Judiciary Chairman Ashurst could not overcome the resistance of Senators Burton K. Wheeler of Montana, Carter Glass of Virginia, Tom Connally of Texas, and others who broke with the administration. When the Judiciary Committee voted to send the bill to the full Senate with an unfavorable recommendation and when, the same day, 78-year-old Justice Willis Van Devanter announced his retirement, paving the way for the first FDR appointment, the scheme seemed dead for certain. Reacting to the President's assault, the Court had already begun moderating its anti–New Deal rulings. Van Devanter's retirement meant that Roosevelt had won; the New Deal could look forward to a relatively comfortable 6–3 majority on most future decisions pitting liberals against conservatives.

But Roosevelt persisted. With so much of his own prestige on the line, the President felt he had to have some kind of Court-expansion bill. Finally convinced he lacked the votes to pass the original bill, he offered a modified version that raised the age limit to 75 and limited his expansion appointments to one year. Senate Majority Leader Robinson promised to do his best to sell it.

Roosevelt had depended on Garner to direct the Senate fight, but Garner was disgusted with the course the New Deal was taking, particularly FDR's apparent lack of concern for a balanced budget, his soft attitude toward the sit-down strikes that were sweeping the country, and his insistence on pursuing the party-splitting Court fight. At the height of the session, he packed up and went home to Uvalde for the summer. The Vice-President's rare vacation during a congressional session underscored his general dissatisfaction. Roosevelt, then Rayburn, sought unsuccessfully to entice him back to Washington.

To Robinson fell the task of lining up Senate support for the revised plan. Unfortunately for Roosevelt, the 65-year-old majority leader, driven to exhaustion by the lure of FDR's promise of a seat on the expanded Court, collapsed and died of a heart attack before he could bring the measure to a vote. Whatever sympathy remained for the Court plan faded with him. Interrupting his hiatus to attend Robinson's burial in Little Rock, Garner rode the funeral train back to Washington. His conversations with senators on the train convinced him that the bill was dead. He decided it was time to give "the Boss" the bad news. This time, Roosevelt listened. He instructed the Vice-President to take any compromise he could get.

A week later the Senate voted 70–21 to send the bill back to the Judiciary Committee with instructions to remove the portions dealing with Court expansion. For Roosevelt, it was a fiasco that transcended the bill at hand, undermining his vaunted popularity and prestige and, more important, destroying the fragile unity of the Democratic party. On Capitol Hill, the fight had spawned a new coalition of Republicans and southern conservatives that would rise again and again to battle liberal programs. Congress would never be the same.

Rayburn's troubles as majority leader were just beginning. A sudden new recession late in the year plunged the nation back into despair. Even among the most ardent New Deal supporters, there was doubt whether Roosevelt had the answers to the nation's problems. Having tasted blood in the Court plan fight, the newly formed bipartisan conservative coalition stood ready to attack almost any measure of the slightest controversy that the White House submitted. Even the overwhelming Democratic majority in Congress proved more a bane than a blessing, virtually impossible to organize and manage. In terms of legislative accomplishment, the years 1937 and 1938 would be remembered by Rayburn as "my worst two years in Congress."[16]

The passage of all meaningful legislation was complicated by a tide of fear that swept much of the nation in the late 1930s. Horrified by the ominous rise of fascism in Europe, Americans looked askance at any new proposal that seemed to enhance the President's powers. Charges that Roosevelt sought "dictatorial power," first raised in the Court fight, reached feverish levels when the wage and hour bill, setting minimum standards for workers, came before the House in December of 1937. Such fears rose to new highs when FDR submitted his bill for reorganizing the executive branch. To an alarmed constituent, Rayburn wrote: "I think it will be a long time in this Government before there is a dictator as the people have the right every four years to change the Executive and every two years to change the popular branch of the legislative end of the Government. I don't believe Mr. Roosevelt has any desire to be a dictator as I believe he is too democratic a man."[17]

Although Rayburn strongly supported wage and hour legislation—in the face of strong Texas opposition—he failed miserably to produce the necessary votes for it in the House; 108 Democrats defected, handing Roosevelt his worst House defeat.[18] After it was rejected again in 1938, a modified version finally passed in 1939. The Executive Reorganization Act took a similar course—stinging defeat, followed by compromise, followed by hard-won narrow victory. Rayburn was instrumental in structuring a bill the House would support. "Just now I have a thoroughly discombobulated Congress," Roosevelt complained to Felix Frankfurter.[19]

Increasingly short of congressional friends and hurt by Congress's rebellious attitude, the President turned more and more to the House majority leader for legislative and political advice. Rayburn's visits to the White House became more frequent. But even as Roosevelt drew him closer, the loyal Texan was being pulled in the opposite direction by the disillusioned Garner, who had had his fill of Roosevelt and the New Deal.

The 1938 congressional elections took a heavy toll of Democrats. The Republicans gained seventy-five seats in the House, seven in the Senate. In a way, the results were a relief to Rayburn and other leaders, after the ordeal of trying to manage a top-heavy, uncontrollable majority. But not to Roosevelt, who had sought in the election to "purge" a number of errant Democrats. The President traveled the country, lending support to Democratic primary opponents of House and Senate members he judged disloyal to his programs. The purge flopped. Of those targeted, only Representative John O'Connor of New York, whose Rules Committee had bottled up much New Deal legislation, failed to win re-election.

Rayburn, for a change, had no opposition in the 1938 Democratic primary. It was an unexpected though welcome break for the Texan, who deplored campaigning. During his half century in Congress, Rayburn seldom had an easy opponent, almost never a free ride, a fact that both irritated and puzzled him. "It does seem that since I have been elected leader of the Party in the House that my standing would be such that no one would talk about running," he once complained. "But it seems that I am one of those unfortunates that it matters not what position I occupy nor what I do, I cannot escape the constant opposition of some people." [20] Rayburn's own re-election headaches convinced him for a while that the House would function more efficiently if elections came every four instead of two years. Ultimately, however, he concluded that two-year terms were best because they kept members closer to the people.

Speaker Bankhead's health continued to deteriorate, his frequent illnesses placing an extra burden on Rayburn. Increasingly, in Bankhead's absence, the Texan had to preside over the House. It was arduous duty, dividing his attention between the responsibilities of a Speaker *pro tempore* and the more mundane partisan and legislative activities of the majority leader. [21] But the months he spent filling in for the ailing Bankhead would make him uniquely prepared for this own tenure as Speaker, when and if that day arrived. Two national magazines conducted separate polls to find the "most useful" and "most influential" House member. Rayburn led both.

His influence extended into the White House, where the chastened, apparently lame-duck President respected his candor and advice, even if he did not always heed it. Roosevelt, at Rayburn's insistence, made one major concession: there would be no more surprises like the 1937 Court-packing plan. The Texan also demanded that overzealous White House lobbying be curbed, that the number of White House agents assigned to Congress be reduced, and that all White House business with the House be conducted through his office. FDR simply ordered his congressional liaison staff not to send so many agents up to the Hill at one time.

As majority leader, Rayburn was particularly embarrassed by the lack of adequate communication between the President and the House leadership. One day he told Tommy Corcoran, then a premier lobbyist for the White House: "The President ought to be having a meeting every week with his House and Senate leaders so we could tell him what we're planning, and he could tell us his plans. It could eliminate a lot of confusion. See what you can do—but don't you dare let him know I suggested it 'cause he thinks he 'borned' every idea that ever was."

Corcoran handled the task skillfully. On Rayburn's next visit to the White House, Roosevelt said, "Sam, I've been thinking. Maybe it would be a good idea if I had a meeting with Bill [Bankhead] and you and Jack [Garner] and Alben [Barkley] about once a week to talk over what all of us are planning."

"Mr. President," replied Rayburn, "that's one of the smartest ideas I ever heard." [22] So were born the periodic meetings with congressional leaders that all subsequent Presidents have used to varying degrees.

For years, Roosevelt and Congress failed to see—or, at least, to act on—the darkening situation in Europe. An isolationist himself during the first part of his administration, FDR subordinated foreign policy to his strenuous efforts to bring about domestic economic recovery and reform. In a nation still deeply disillusioned by its experiences in the aftermath of the world war, discussion of military rearmament was anathema. Roosevelt felt growing concern over the march of the dictatorships, but when he suggested in his famous "quarantine" speech in late

1937 that an international quarantine of aggressors was the only means of preserving peace, he raised a firestorm of criticism that made him back away. Even his proposal for a modest increase in military expenditures in 1938, after Hitler's armies overran Austria, raised a hostile chorus of criticism in Congress and on editorial pages across the country. Some FDR critics said he was trying to draw attention from his domestic policy failures.

In 1935, Congress passed the Neutrality Act, intended to keep the United States out of war by embargoing the export of war implements and ammunition to any belligerents in wartime. In 1938, Roosevelt sought to have the embargo repealed and the act amended in such a way that the United States might help Great Britain, France, and Poland against Germany without going to war itself. The President's appeal was received coldly in the House, where isolationists and internationalists were about evenly divided. Always an internationalist, Rayburn argued that Congress must give the President the latitude and the tools he needed to conduct foreign policy, or else America would have no effective foreign policy: "Foreign affairs are so definitely an Executive function, that we in the Legislative Branch are loath to make any moves without full consultation with the President and the State Department, as those moves, however well intentioned, may cause embarrassment to those responsible for the foreign policy and its execution."[23]

Crippling amendments made FDR's proposal to repeal the Neutrality Act worthless by the time it cleared the House in July. A Rayburn-led fight to defeat the amendments failed by two votes. In the Senate, the Foreign Relations Committee tabled the bill until the following year. Not until Hitler invaded Poland on September 1 did Congress awaken to the urgency of the international crisis. The neutrality repeal bill was quickly resurrected and passed by both Houses. Other measures bolstering support of the European allies and increasing America's own preparedness, including a peacetime conscription law, also were enacted—over the objections of a determined isolationist minority.

Casting a long shadow over all of Roosevelt's second term was the 1940 election. Everyone was asking: would FDR run again? Although no President ever had challenged the two-term tradition established by George Washington, there was support, beginning as early as 1937, for a third Roosevelt term. FDR, while publicly refusing to take himself out of consideration, privately told friends he looked forward to returning to Hyde Park after 1940. But his continued ambivalence caused no little confusion and consternation inside the Democratic party.

Rayburn assumed the President would retire. He began early in FDR's second term subtly nudging Garner into a run for the 1940 nomination. As in 1932, Garner refused to discuss his own thoughts on the matter, but Rayburn nonetheless persisted in passing along to Mrs. Garner favorable press notices, letters, and comments about the Vice-President. When a political acquaintance, pollster Emil Hurja, sent Rayburn a long, glowing analysis of Garner's potential strengths as the Democratic nominee, he immediately fired it on to the Garners in Uvalde and penned a separate note to Hurja, thanking him for a "very, very interesting" letter.[24]

Despite his open break with Roosevelt over the President's Court plan, softness toward the sit-down strikers, and apparent blindness to dangers of budget deficits, Garner's personal popularity was undiminished. To most New Dealers, Garner was a prairie politician lacking in breeding as well as fresh ideas. Harold Ickes found him "almost a disgusting sight." But most Americans saw more in him than appeared on the surface—a wizened old hayseed in an increasingly sophisticated society. What many saw was a shrewd, engaging patriot who behaved with a refreshing air of independence not usually found in politicians, particularly Vice-Presidents. The press accorded him much attention, and the whole nation got a chuckle when industrial labor organizer John L. Lewis called him a "labor-baiting, poker-playing, whiskey-drinking, evil old man."

Not everyone was amused by Lewis's comment, however. Within hours, a quickly drawn resolution extolling Garner and denying all of Lewis's allegations was circulating among the Texas delegation. It was an innocuous expression of confidence in a colleague under fire, a worthless piece of paper without

the delegation's unanimous support. The petition was probably
Rayburn's idea. At any rate, everyone went along except for one
holdout—30-year-old Congressman Lyndon Johnson, first elected to the House in 1937 as an ardent New Dealer, refused to
sign. His first, perhaps only, loyalty at that time was to Roosevelt.
He had no devotion to the tough-talking senior Texan and, in
fact, shared the disgust of many New Dealers for him. Garner's
feelings toward organized labor were well known, and to deny
he had a fondness for poker and whiskey was so ridiculous that
to declare otherwise would make the delegation look foolish,
Johnson argued.

Johnson was right, of course, although Rayburn could not see
it. To Rayburn, the issue went to the core of his own sense of
loyalty. Twice he tried to persuade the young congressman to
sign the petition; twice Johnson refused. According to Johnson,
Rayburn at one point warned the upstart, "Lyndon, I'm looking
you right in the eye." Johnson said he replied: "And I am looking you right back in the eye."[25] A watered-down resolution—
one that the stubborn young man would sign—eventually was
drafted. Afterward, Johnson delighted in describing the incident, adding self-serving embellishments at each retelling, to his
friends at the White House. Wrote Harold Ickes: "Johnson says
that he kept his temper and that after it was all over, Rayburn
apologized to him."[26]

An apology of any kind from Rayburn was highly unlikely.
Such defiance by a junior congressman—especially if handled as
arrogantly as Johnson claimed—undoubtedly would have infuriated the short-tempered Rayburn and prompted at least a
threat of retribution. The fact that he quickly forgot the matter
and that his growing affection for the ambitious young man continued to flourish casts strong doubt on the accuracy of the
Johnson-Ickes version.

By 1939, as Roosevelt's ability to cope with a rebellious
Congress sank to a new low, Garner's power and popularity
increased. He still had influence over Congress and was courted
shamelessly by politicians and lobbyists with an interest in legislation. Garner was a political phenomenon. As Vice-President

he seldom commented publicly on controversial issues, preferring to make his influence felt behind the scenes. When Roosevelt's Court plan was read to the Senate, Garner stood at the door of the Senate cloakroom, holding his nose and pointing his thumb toward the carpet.

Roosevelt neither sought nor received much direct advice from Garner. Shortly after the 1936 election, the President and Vice-President fell into a discussion of Roosevelt's unwillingness to intervene in the sit-down strikes, which to Garner amounted to unlawful seizure of private property by the strikers. Soon both were shouting and pounding the table. That was an exception. Garner seldom pressed his personal views on the President. He recalled an incident early in their relationship which convinced him that Roosevelt wanted advice only when he asked for it:

> Sometime in 1933, Roosevelt, myself, and a few others went to the President's camp in the Maryland mountains— his "Shangri-La," he called it. It was like a king taking his court along to entertain him. We played 50-cent-limit poker all night. FDR was not a good player; he just talked all night. Sometime during the evening, or the next morning, I said, "Cap'n, you ought to recognize Red Russia."
>
> He looked at me, kind of half smiled, and said, "John, you tend to your business and I will tend to mine." That was the last time I ever offered him any advice on my own.[27]

When Garner moved from the House to preside over the Senate in 1933, he took his liquor supply with him. Throughout his Vice-Presidency, he continued his after-hours "Bureau of Education," which became known to many senators more appropriately as "The Doghouse." The little drinking room off the old Supreme Court Chamber was Garner's center of influence, where he held court, chastised errant Democrats, and did much of his business. Tommy Corcoran was a frequent visitor:

> I'll never forget the first time I met John Garner. Frankie saw a disagreeable conversation coming up with Garner, and he didn't want it to happen. So he sent me down to try

to head him off. Rayburn introduced me to him. Garner knew damn well the President sent me there because he was trying to weasel out of some commitment to Garner. "Have you had a drink?" Garner said.

"No," I said.

He urged me to have one. I tried to beg off. He kept insisting, and finally said, "When I'm going to have an intellectual discussion, I make it a rule never to talk to a man until he has had a drink, if I have had one." I gave in. He got a big tumbler and almost filled it with that old red whiskey of his. Well, the message never got delivered, and I was stiff when I got back to the White House and reported to Frankie.

Frankie tried again. He thought Felix Frankfurter was Machiavellian enough to go down and drink with Garner and still get the message across. I was there when Frankfurter came back. He wasn't just stiff, he couldn't stand up. He couldn't even remember what Garner said, or what he said.[28]

Looking ahead to the 1940 nominating convention, Democrats could see several qualified successors to Roosevelt. Secretary of State Cordell Hull, Postmaster General James Farley, and Garner were generally ranked as front-runners—assuming, of course, that Roosevelt bowed out. Roosevelt seemed genuinely uncertain. But most of his private signals led Democrats to believe it would be a wide-open race for the nomination. By late 1939, half a dozen Democratic hopefuls were at the starting block, awaiting a formal nod of approval from FDR. The *St. Louis Post-Dispatch* scanned the lineup and decided that Sam Rayburn was more qualified than any of them. In another article, New Deal columnist Ernest K. Lindley, reputed to be a chief conduit for information the White House wanted leaked, named Rayburn "one of three outstanding possibilities for the vice presidential nomination."[29] The Texas lawmaker, however, showed no interest. Finally, Garner announced in December that, while he would not seek the presidential nomination, he would accept if it was offered. Strongly opposed to third terms for any President, Garner said he was in the race whether or not Roosevelt stepped aside.

Rayburn's loyalty to Garner and to Texas left him no alternative but to support his friend as long as he stayed in the running, although he was more and more convinced that, when the time came, Roosevelt would be a candidate. The thought of having to oppose FDR, whom he admired and for whose programs he had fought, troubled him deeply. "Sam Rayburn is a damn good Democrat when John Garner's out of town," grumbled Maury Maverick, Texas's most liberal congressman. Rayburn dreaded having to tell the President that he would be in Garner's corner. As he recalled their meeting:

> One night at a banquet, I said to the President, "I want to come up and talk some politics with you." Roosevelt would always perk up when you mentioned politics. He said come down to the White House the next morning and come to his bedroom. When I got down there, he was still in bed. He started talking about war in Europe. I said, "Mr. President, I didn't come here to talk of war in Europe but of war brewing in Texas." I told him, "If you are a candidate, you can get the nomination," and he agreed. Then I told him Texas was going for Garner, and I was going to go along with John.
>
> He looked out the window at the Washington Monument for the longest time. Finally, he said, "That's what you ought to do. I understand your situation perfectly." Then he said, "But, Sam, John can't be nominated, and he couldn't be elected if he was nominated." Right then, I knew he was going to run for another term.[30]

After discussing his intentions with FDR, Rayburn announced his support of Garner in a typically pointed statement: "I am for that outstanding Texan and liberal Democrat, John N. Garner, for the presidential nomination in 1940, believing that if elected he will make the country a great President." His decision may have angered Roosevelt briefly, as it certainly did the New Deal loyalists around him. Most of the young intellectuals had never considered Rayburn "one of us," anyway. Even when the Texan was leading their bloodiest fights against Wall Street, New Deal zealots scorned his quiet methods and doubted his loyalty to the principles they shared.

In April 1940, Adolph Hitler launched his swift, ruthless conquest of Western Europe. Countries fell in stunning succession until finally, of the Western allies, only England remained. The valiant little nation fighting against overwhelming odds was, it seemed, all that stood between the Nazis and the United States. The war was at America's doorstep and could no longer be ignored.

Overnight, the nation's mood shifted, as a somber America followed the war in Europe. To many observers, the question was no longer whether but how long the United States could stay out of it. In the crisis, Roosevelt's popularity soared as Democrats and Republicans alike, putting aside political differences, looked to the White House for leadership. Knocked into a cocked hat was the burgeoning fight for the 1940 Democratic presidential nomination. "The situation is just about this," Rayburn wrote in April. "The President can be nominated, if he wants it, and on the first ballot, if he lets it be known that he wants it. I also think that if he goes along and says nothing, the convention will nominate him. The question is whether he will make a statement before the convention that he does not want and will not accept the nomination. I doubt if anybody in the world knows what he intends to do."[31]

In the name of national unity, Roosevelt in June appointed two prominent Republicans to serve in Cabinet-rank defense posts—Henry Stimson as secretary of war and Frank Knox as secretary of the navy. Both were proponents of broader United States participation in the defense of Europe, and their appointment, while it outraged some Democrats, effectively undercut Republican isolationists on the eve of the GOP nominating convention. Rayburn thought "we could have found two good Democrats" for the posts. "Frankly, I never had much sympathy for these so-called 'coalition Cabinets,'" he told a friend. "Senator [Joe] Bailey used to tell me that Judge [Jacob M.] Dickinson, who had always been a Democrat but did not support Bryan, went into Taft's Cabinet. The general business of the Cabinet was not embarrassing but always when something political would come up, Dickinson thought he ought to get up and leave. It was a constant source of embarrassment to him. In a political year like this, I think it may become embarrassing for Messrs. Stimson and Knox."[32]

With the Democratic National Convention in Chicago only ten days away, Roosevelt publicly was still being coy about seeking a third term, although those around him were certain that he wanted, indeed expected, to be "drafted." Garner, adamantly opposed to a third term for any President, remained in the race, as did Farley and Senator Millard Tydings of Maryland, a diehard anti–New Dealer.

Unquestionably, it would be a Roosevelt convention. The Texas delegation, committed to Garner on the first ballot, was deeply divided. Pro-FDR delegates from the Lone Star State, led by brash young Congressman Johnson of Austin, chaffed under the rules of a binding peace agreement with the state's Garner supporters, led by Rayburn. Garner backers, meanwhile, quarreled among themselves, some accusing Rayburn of secretly helping Roosevelt's nomination.

The agreement had been worked out through difficult negotiations and had been announced jointly by Rayburn and Johnson. Ickes in his entertaining but highly unreliable *Secret Diaries* speculated that the Texas compromise and publicity resulting from it upset Rayburn because he "did not want it to appear that in a Texas political matter, a kid congressman like Johnson was apparently on the same footing as himself, the majority leader."[33] Ickes may have guessed right about Rayburn's jealousy of Johnson—there is no hard evidence one way or the other—but certainly Rayburn would have discussed his feelings with no one. "Honest Harold" was not always so honest when retelling events that involved people he disliked, such as Rayburn.[34] Moreover, Johnson was a natural organizer and was widely known as FDR's most outspoken supporter in the delegation. He was the logical choice to lead the Roosevelt drive in Texas. As James Roosevelt noted years later: "Lyndon Johnson was a useful tool; father regarded Rayburn as a statesman."[35]

Texas, from almost any angle, had become a disaster for the

New Deal. Vice-President Garner was openly defying the President. Rayburn, the administration's chief advocate in the House, was backing Garner for President. Senator Connally and Congressman Sumners had ruined the President's Court reform plan. Congressman Martin Dies had worked to defeat FDR's wage and hour legislation, while others in the Texas delegation, never strong for the New Deal, battled White House social and farm programs.[36] Undoubtedly, the open support of even a junior Texas congressman such as Johnson was a breath of fresh air to Roosevelt.

Some Rayburn biographers have taken Ickes's comments as the basis for elaborate scenarios of Rayburn's burgeoning disaffection for his ambitious protégé. Robert Caro in *The Years of Lyndon Johnson: The Path to Power* claims on scant evidence that on the day the "harmony" telegram was signed Rayburn finally realized Johnson was conducting a "secret campaign to undermine Rayburn in Roosevelt's eyes" and for a year and a half barely spoke to the "kid congressman" of whom he had grown so fond.[37] A stronger case could be made that the whole idea of Rayburn's jealousy was a figment of Ickes's mischievous mind— an outgrowth of Ickes's and other New Dealers' long-nurtured disrespect for Rayburn, and Johnson's incessant bragging about his own rising importance.

In fact, a bond was growing between the two Texans. In this period, they were beginning to spend more and more time together on the job and off. Johnson and Rayburn had been acquainted since the early 1930s, when Johnson, then hardly more than a boy, first came to Washington as secretary to wealthy Texas Congressman Richard Kleberg. Young Johnson wasted no time in introducing himself to the powerful committee chairman who had once served, albeit briefly, with his father in the Texas Legislature. "I'm Sam Johnson's boy," he said with a grin, extending a bony hand. Rayburn recalled Sam Ealy Johnson "favorably," he later said, although their opposing views on the crucial "Bailey question," prohibition, and other issues kept them from feeling as warmly toward each other as Sam Johnson's son would later claim. Shortly before Lyndon's election to Congress, Sam Johnson sought to renew the acquaintance in a long, syrupy letter filled with praise for Rayburn. ("In a reminiscent mood today I looked over my picture of the Thirtieth Legislature and recalled many incidents, associations and fights over those good old days . . .") Eventually, he got to the point of his letter, a vaguely threatening appeal for Rayburn to help in finding a Washington job for Johnson's daughter Rebekah: "Many friends over the state will greatly appreciate your assisting her." Rayburn's short, friendly, but noncommittal response brought yet another bald appeal from the persevering Johnson: "I am taking the liberty of asking you to set the ball rolling in this matter and help my girl secure a better position. How deeply Lyndon and I and all our friends will appreciate your assistance I cannot tell you."[38] Rayburn did not respond, apparently ending this brief final contact between the two former colleagues.

Sent to Congress as an ardent New Dealer and unabashed Roosevelt supporter in a special election in 1937, Sam Johnson's ambitious, ingratiating son quickly attached himself to Rayburn, much as Rayburn had done with John Garner twenty-five years earlier. Rayburn was first amused, later captivated by the lanky, awkward lad who seemed to be everywhere at once, brimming with ideas, willing to tackle any job, always trying to make himself useful. Recalled Texas Congressman Bob Poage: "Mr. Rayburn became impressed with Johnson's ability and willingness to work. Mr. Rayburn helped him along since Johnson was helping Rayburn. It was a mutual thing."[39] Oklahoma Congressman Lyle Boren put it more bluntly: "Lyndon would jump when Sam said 'Frog.'"[40] In Johnson, the senior Texan saw an image not unlike himself at the same age—more polished and cunning than he had been as a new congressman but no more able, hardworking, and determined to succeed. "I think Lyndon is one of the finest young men I have seen come to Congress," Rayburn wrote in 1938. "If the District will exercise the good judgment to keep him here, he will grow in wisdom and influence as the years come and go."[41]

Johnson by 1940 had earned his spurs as a "regular" at Rayburn's after-hours Board of Education. Many evenings, after a couple of hours of drinking and gossiping in the private hideaway, Johnson would invite the Speaker to his Kalorama home—

a few blocks from Rayburn's own apartment—for a Texas-style supper that his shy, yet-to-blossom wife Claudia would have waiting on the kitchen table. Rayburn was quickly captivated by the delicate Mrs. Johnson, "Lady Bird" to her friends, who seemed in so many ways the opposite of her husband. It was her natural warmth and attentiveness, more than Lyndon's calculated flattery, that brought Rayburn back to the apartment again and again and caused him to begin inviting the pair to small dinner parties at his apartment. Mrs. Johnson remembered:

> It was our introduction, Lyndon and I, as a young congressional couple, to a pretty heady society of people that were Cabinet members, Supreme Court justices, really important folks around town. I remember Tom Corcoran and Ben Cohen were often there. Sometimes he would take us down on the waterfront and we would go to a place called Hall's. We would likely have Wright Patman with us and we would all eat lobster, seafood, and I, oddly enough, got to go. There weren't any other women along, but Lyndon just sort of carried me along and nobody said I had to stay home.[42]

Rayburn soon was treating both of the Johnsons like family, a role they readily assumed. One day shortly before World War II, AP reporter W. B. "Rags" Ragsdale entered Rayburn's office to find Lady Bird rummaging around Rayburn's desk. "Obviously, she was very much at ease there," he recalled. "It was clear that she had complete run of the place."[43] Lyndon used to infuriate Alla Clary, Rayburn's secretary, by barging past her into her boss's office unannounced. He did that once too often—the Speaker was conferring with Winston Churchill—and she never forgave him.

In the months he worked for Garner's nomination, Rayburn never hid his admiration for Roosevelt or denied that Roosevelt, if he chose to run, was the better candidate. A year before the convention, he predicted that FDR would—and should—be the party's choice. This was Garner's fight, and Rayburn was in it solely out of his loyalty and indebtedness to an old colleague.

Rayburn still had his own career to consider, and, in all likelihood, Roosevelt was going to be in the White House for another four years. In supporting a fading star such as Garner against the popular President, Rayburn was walking a fine political line. As Lyndon Johnson saw Rayburn's dilemma:

> He was very much torn, but he stood by his first loyalty to John Garner. So something had to be done to ease his problems. A bunch of us started organizing for FDR, but we couldn't have a head-on conflict in Texas, so one day several of us—Alvin Wirtz, Myron Blalock, Mr. Rayburn, myself, and others—worked out a plan and took it to FDR for approval. Both sides agreed not to clash in Texas by having the delegation to the National Convention headed by Rayburn, an open Garner supporter, as chairman, and myself, an open FDR supporter, as vice-chairman.[44]

Together with other Texas political leaders, Rayburn and Johnson persuaded state party leaders grudgingly to approve a three-point agreement whereby Roosevelt and Garner loyalists could avoid open warfare and come to the convention in relative peace.[45] Under the pact, the delegation would be instructed to vote for Garner on the first ballot, but it would acclaim the Roosevelt administration's record and would shun any "Stop Roosevelt" movement. Without the agreement, Rayburn concluded, there would surely be "a very bloody battle that would leave scars in our state that would not be healing for many years to come."[46] But the wounds cut deeper than even he imagined. The political rupture of 1940 proved to be the beginning of an irreconcilable liberal-conservative split that has kept Texas Democratic politics in turmoil for nearly half a century and even today shows no sign of healing.[47]

In Chicago, Garner received 61 first-ballot votes, Farley 72, Tydings 9, and Cordell Hull 5. Roosevelt got 946. He only needed a bare majority, the Democrats having abolished the two-thirds rule in 1936. Farley moved that the convention declare the President's renomination unanimous.

The convention then turned to the selection of a vice-presidential candidate. Garner was definitely out of the running. A bevy of contenders was available, all claiming that they had spoken to FDR in recent weeks and had personally been given a "green light" to run. Rayburn had a "green light." So did Speaker Bankhead, who marshaled all his remaining strength to deliver the convention's keynote speech.[48] So did Postmaster Farley, Jimmy Byrnes of South Carolina, Washington lawyer Louis Johnson, Senator Burton K. Wheeler of Montana, Jesse Jones of Texas, former Governor Paul V. McNutt of Indiana, and Secretary of Agriculture Henry A. Wallace. Secretary of the Interior Harold Ickes wired the President that he also was available, got no reply, and thus became one of the few aspirants, apparently, without a "green light."

Rayburn supporters pointed out that he would be a valuable asset to the ticket, a strong counterpoint to the Republicans, who had nominated for President a utility holding company executive, Wendell L. Willkie. Many remembered Rayburn's dramatic encounter with the cocky Willkie during public hearings on the Texan's bill to curb the excesses of utility holding companies.

But Rayburn's chances began to sag when he could not even win the united backing of his own delegation. Elliott Roosevelt, then living in Fort Worth, had been pushing Reconstruction Finance Chairman Jesse Jones for President against his own father. Now young Roosevelt was trying to convince fellow Texas delegates that Jones was a better choice than Rayburn for Vice-President. Delegates were still wrangling over the relative merits of the two Texans when word came that the President had selected Henry Wallace. Shortly thereafter, FDR phoned Rayburn to ask that he second the nomination of the widely unpopular secretary of agriculture. Putting aside his personal disappointment and his own dislike of Wallace, he agreed to do it. It was one of the most difficult speeches he ever had to make. "Let me say," Rayburn told the convention that evening, "that if I consulted my loyalty and my love, I would probably second the nomination of another. But under the circumstances, I cannot do otherwise than follow the wishes of my leader. I come, therefore, to second the nomination of a man of distinguished record, a distinguished statesman, a friend of the people, a friend of the farmer . . ."[49]

In Henry Wallace, Roosevelt had chosen one of the least popular candidates, a one-time Republican whose politics had shifted several degrees to the left of the New Deal. "Wallace, Roosevelt believed, would appeal to the Corn Belt and, as a trenchant antifascist, would clarify issues for the country," wrote New Deal historian William E. Leuchtenburg.[50] The convention booed lustily when Wallace's name was put into nomination. Several other nominations challenged Roosevelt's anointed candidate. Bankhead worked feverishly to build support for himself, and, for a while, it appeared that the delegates would kick over the traces and nominate the Alabama congressman. Rayburn's own delegation left him dangling alone as it voted unanimously, under the unit rule, for Bankhead. When the balloting was over, Wallace had 627 votes out of a possible 1,100.[51]

Rayburn was thankful when the ordeal was over. As Pearson and Allen put it:

> None was on as hot a spot as Rayburn and none emerged with more dignity and personal esteem. . . . Torn between two loyalties, he met each test with unflinching courage and honesty. He held the huge, seething Texas delegation in line for Garner until every obligation to him had been met. Then, just as firmly, Rayburn took the delegation to the Roosevelt column and in the fierce battle over Henry Wallace, again lined up with his chief in the White House. This must have been a secret wrench. If Speaker Bankhead were nominated it would clear the way for Rayburn to achieve the great ambition of his lifetime, to be Speaker of the House. It would have been an easy matter for Rayburn, without showing his hand, to give the nod to oppose Wallace.[52]

"I think the stew about Wallace will simmer down pretty soon," Rayburn wrote a few days later, "and the Roosevelt ticket will win the election as I do not think Mr. Willkie can keep up the glamor that he now has."[53]

The strain of the convention was too much for Bankhead. His health deteriorated through the summer; on September 15, a Sunday, his physically depleted body, weakened by years of heart trouble and stomach ailments, finally gave out. He died of a stomach hemorrhage. At the Capitol, Alla Clary, Dan Inglish, Bea Conlon, and other Rayburn staffers worked through the day, taking phone calls, advising congressmen of the funeral arrangements. With Bankhead dead, the House could conduct no further business until it chose a new Speaker.

13

Ambition Fulfilled—and War

Rayburn felt no sense of triumph as he reached his life's goal shortly after noon on September 16, 1940. As House members filed into the chamber for the ritual of electing a new Speaker, their thoughts dwelled not on the gritty Texan they were soon to honor but on the fallen Bankhead, whose funeral would immediately follow and whose flower-draped coffin already rested in the well of the House. At the marble podium, against a backdrop of lilies and palms, stood the lone figure of Clerk South Trimble who, by custom, would preside over the naming of Bankhead's successor. Rayburn's nomination without opposition had been prearranged. Rising from the Democratic side, wavy-haired, lanky John McCormack of Massachusetts placed the Texan's name before the House. Trimble glanced at Republican leader Joe Martin of Massachusetts. Martin shook his head. The minority would have no candidate. Only once before in modern times—when Bankhead succeeded Byrns—had a Speaker been elected without *pro forma* opposition.

After his election by acclamation, Rayburn was escorted to the well, where old Adolph Sabath, dean of the House, stood near Bankhead's casket to administer the oath. Sabath, short and paunchy, had been a congressman for thirty-seven years, his tenure assured by the heavy Czech population of his tiny Chicago district and his good standing with the Kelly-Nash machine. An important ally of the new leadership, he was among scores of members indebted to Rayburn. Sabath never needed reminding that, but for Rayburn, he would have been denied the chairmanship of the Committee on Rules. Other Democrats, claiming the old machine politician lacked leadership qualities, wanted to push him aside. They would have succeeded had not Rayburn, always a staunch advocate of rule by seniority, interceded in Sabath's behalf.[1]

Standing uncomfortably behind the Speaker's desk, dressed in mourning clothes, his eyes downcast and his bald dome reflecting the soft glow of the vast skylight overhead, Rayburn was introduced by Robert Lee Doughton, chairman of the Ways and Means Committee. "Muley" Doughton, who came to Congress from North Carolina in 1911, two years before Rayburn, was a trusted colleague, a key—if somewhat independent— lieutenant in Rayburn's new leadership team. The new Speaker shunned the traditional acceptance speech. "The House will be in order," he said, tapping his gavel lightly to signal the end of the election ceremony and the beginning of the funeral.

The partially empty chamber quickly filled. President Roosevelt, solemn-faced and tired, slumped into a seat directly in front of the coffin and next to the heavily veiled Mrs. Bankhead. He nearly tumbled on the floor. Close by were Bankhead's two brothers, Senator John H. Bankhead and Colonel Henry M. Bankhead, and his daughters, Mrs. Eugenia Hoyt and Tallulah Bankhead, the actress. Members of the Senate, Cabinet, Supreme Court, and diplomatic corps filled empty chairs around the already seated House members. Other invited guests peered down from the galleries. A double male quartet from St. Margaret's Episcopal Church sang. The newly elected Speaker and the minority leader offered the only eulogies, Rayburn speaking first. "I stand here in great humility and the knowledge of my poor limitation to follow in the footsteps of one as great and fine," he declared.[2]

In truth, Bankhead taught Rayburn little. Although Bankhead was popular and strong-minded, his absences, which grew more frequent and prolonged as his health declined, made him a weak leader. In the end, it was said, he died from disappointment at being passed over for the vice-presidential nomination. Roosevelt, preferring to deal with Congress in his own way, frequently chose to consult directly with chairmen whose committees held the fate of his program. Some said FDR deliberately embarrassed Bankhead to demonstrate his own dominance over Congress. Often, when asked by reporters, Bankhead would confess ignorance of specific administration legislation only to have it arrive by White House messenger minutes later.

Rayburn liked and admired Roosevelt, but his greatest loyalty was to the American system of government, which he believed was best served by a strong and independent legislature. As Speaker, he was determined that Congress not yield to the executive any more of its constitutional prerogatives. Sooner or later, he and the President would have to reach an understanding on that score.

A 63-member delegation, headed by Rayburn, accompanied Bankhead's remains to the family burial place at Jasper, Alabama. Though exhausted and deeply worried about the darkening prospect of war, Roosevelt also attended, for the third time since 1932 standing at the grave of a fallen Speaker of the House. For Rayburn, the events of that week were blurred, as in a dream. "I still can't believe I'm Speaker," he told newsman Bascom Timmons. "It's a 'fer piece' from Flag Springs."

Before going home for the elections, the House had one final chore: selecting a new majority leader. Tall, quick-tongued John McCormack of Massachusetts thirsted for the job, as did elegant, erudite Clifton A. Woodrum of Virginia. Others, including Jere Cooper of Tennessee, Patrick J. Boland of Pennsylvania, John Rankin of Mississippi, and Andrew L. Somers of New York, also were interested, but when the Democrats caucused on September 25, their names were not put in nomination.

Choosing between McCormack and Woodrum was Rayburn's first decision as Speaker—and an important one, for he would have to work closely with that person, perhaps for many years. In McCormack, he found the qualities he sought: loyalty, a desire to assume responsibility, a willingness to work long hours. McCormack fought bravely for hopeless causes, and he had an exceptional capacity for attack in debate. His quick mind, acid tongue, and Irish zest for a good fight made McCormack superbly equipped to advance his party in legislative combat. "Nobody can make a Democratic speech like John McCormack," Rayburn often remarked. He was an enthusiastic New Dealer. Last, but not least, Rayburn remembered McCormack's crucial support—the first from New England—when he himself sought the majority leadership four years before.

It was no surprise when Rayburn chose McCormack. Although some Democrats wondered how two men of such different personalities and backgrounds would get along, the caucus endorsed the Speaker's choice, McCormack getting 141 votes to Woodrum's 67. For the "Fighting Irishman of South Boston," the step was a big one. He had been a House member only twelve years and, unlike most previous Democratic majority leaders, had chaired no major committee. In time, the Bonham-Boston combination was to become one of the most effective leadership teams in House history. Rayburn provided the firm, even, overall direction that won confidence on both sides of the aisle, while McCormack, the fiery partisan, kept the opposition at bay and, when necessary, cracked the whip on his own troops. To McCormack fell the task of implementing much of the legislative strategy hashed out in Rayburn's after hours "Board of Education."

Rayburn's rise was a great source of pride in Bonham. His friends in Fannin County devoured every morsel of news about their most famous citizen. His fame was also theirs, and they gloried in it. Virtually the whole town turned out for a festive homecoming when he returned in October for the first time as Speaker—"the second most powerful job in Washington," folks were quick to add. As 15,000 spectators lined the way, a dozen north Texas college and high school bands strutted around the town square. Bunting and streamers hung from every pole. There were dignitaries waving from open cars and costumed cowboys riding high-stepping horses. Trenton sent a big stake truck bedecked with crepe paper and scrubbed-faced young girls. Ladonia contributed a "living Statue of Liberty," a pretty, torch-bearing young woman precariously posed on the deck of a decorated flatbed truck.

That evening, the celebration continued at the steps of the Athletic Field House, where, after a round of patriotic music, the honoree delivered the day's only speech—a rousing appeal for Democratic unity that dispelled any doubt that he was strong for the Roosevelt-Wallace ticket. "This was the greatest day of my life," said Rayburn later, remembering how far he had come from his days in the cotton patch. Coincidentally, it was the 100th anniversary of his father's birth.

The next day, Rayburn slipped quietly into Dallas for meetings he had arranged with a small group of wealthy Democrats, mostly independent oil producers who had struck it rich in the big east Texas find of the early 1930s. Fiercely protective of their newly acquired wealth and suspicious of most politicians, they nevertheless trusted Rayburn and had contributed to his campaigns in the past. At his urging, they also had given modestly to other selected House Democrats. Rayburn's mission this time was to ask for more money—big money—not for himself or for Roosevelt, who, he confidently predicted, would win in November. His appeal was for scores of desperate House colleagues who, without cash to keep their campaigns afloat, faced almost certain defeat in November.

Although Congress technically was still in session, many Democrats had grown increasingly worried as election day drew nearer and had returned home to campaign. Their reports filtering back to Washington in mid-October were almost universally pessimistic. Roosevelt's personal popularity seemed likely to carry him to victory, but voters apparently were looking for a change in Congress. The Republicans, capitalizing on anti-war sentiment and a rising tide of anti–New Deal feeling, had scored significant gains in special congressional elections since 1938. By the fall of 1940, they needed only forty-eight seats to capture control of the House. In one district after another, Democratic incumbents trailed GOP challengers, who not only had unlimited time to campaign but seemed, in most cases, to have bottomless war chests as well. Reported the *New York Herald Tribune* on September 15: "Republicans are confident and

Democrats fearful that the next House of Representatives will be organized and controlled by the Republican Party for the first time in 10 years." A Republican Congress would mean an abrupt end not only to the New Deal but also to Rayburn's own brief tenure in the Speakership—the job he had sought since childhood.

His own re-election behind him, Rayburn and other House Democrats from single-party states remained in Washington through September and October, keeping the House in session and alert for war developments. Meanwhile, Democrats in contested elections throughout the Northeast, Midwest, and Far West had returned home and were fighting for their political lives. "I have been around the country and a good many Democrats are going to get beat," warned former Congressman Maury Maverick in an almost frantic letter to the Speaker in early October.[3]

These men needed all the help they could get; but clearly, what they needed most was money. The problem was how to get it. The Democratic National Committee, chronically impoverished and devoting virtually all its resources to the President's re-election, offered scant hope. House Democrats' own fund-raising arm, the Democratic Congressional Campaign Committee, was scarcely a better prospect. Poorly managed, under-staffed, it had never been spectacularly successful in tapping wealthy contributors on a scale comparable to the Republicans.

For a brief moment, the situation seemed to brighten—or so Rayburn thought. "I have been getting some action here lately from both the National and Congressional Democratic Campaign Committee with reference to re-electing members of the House," he told Maverick in mid-October. "I have talked to [Democratic National Chairman] Ed Flynn and the President about it, telling the President that if this House were lost—even though he were re-elected—it would tear him to pieces just like it did President Wilson after the Republicans won the House in 1918. They are now going into action and we are getting a little money to help the boys in the bad spots."[4]

But the money, when it finally arrived, was but a fraction of that originally promised. The check that came on October 10 was for only $10,000. Flynn had led Rayburn to believe the amount would be much more. Meanwhile, the Congressional Campaign Committee, led by Congressman Pat Drewry, an amiable but inept Virginian, was sputtering along with its usual inefficiency. "Activity had become so bogged down that hard-pressed candidates had quit even asking [the Congressional Campaign Committee] for help," according to one newspaper report.

It finally began to dawn on Rayburn and others that they themselves represented the only real hope House Democrats had of getting financial help. But the hour was late—too late for reorganizing the House Congressional Campaign Committee. And internal jealousies at the DNC made it almost impossible to try to work through that organization. Rayburn already had a full calendar of speaking engagements in behalf of candidates around the country; besides, his presumably nonpartisan role as Speaker precluded his getting too openly involved in such blatantly partisan activities as fund raising.

Lyndon Johnson, unopposed for re-election himself, had been trying for weeks to get a role in the national campaign but had been rebuffed by Flynn at every turn. When Chip Roberts resigned as national party secretary, Johnson lobbied hard for that post. His intention was to use the office essentially to raise money for House Democrats. Rayburn initially was cool to the idea. He believed the post should go to a senior party member. But when Johnson persisted, Rayburn ultimately gave his blessing, as did Roosevelt. Still, Flynn—who wanted no member of Congress, particularly a junior one, meddling in National Committee affairs—refused to appoint Johnson. He reluctantly did agree, finally and at Roosevelt's insistence, to allow Johnson to serve in an informal capacity as liaison between the National Committee and the Congressional Campaign Committee. Johnson's sole responsibility would be to coordinate fund-raising efforts on behalf of candidates for the House. It was not much of an opening, but it was all the ingenious young congressman needed.

The elections were less than three weeks away when the lanky Texan set up a makeshift office in a downtown Washington office building and, joined by Rayburn and other House colleagues, began soliciting wealthy Democrats by telephone. Rayburn's self-imposed assignment was to tap the deep pockets of his rich Texas friends—the independent oil producers.

Before leaving for Texas on October 17, the Speaker telephoned several of his "wildcatter" friends in the oil industry. Most had soured on the New Deal. Independent, predominately conservative, they had supported John Garner's failed attempt to oust Roosevelt and now, by and large, were resigned to sitting out the election. Rayburn's message—that no matter how they felt about the New Deal, it was in their best interest to keep a Democratic Congress—struck home. He reminded them that many of the oil industry's coveted advantages, particularly its freedom from federal controls and its vaunted tax privileges, depended on the power of the Texas delegation in Congress. He recalled the time in 1935 when he, then a powerful committee chairman, and John Garner stood virtually alone and against all odds to block Roosevelt's plan to bring oil production under federal control.[5] "Bring in a Republican Congress, with a new Speaker and new committee chairmen, and they'll tear your depletion allowance and intangible-drilling write-offs to pieces," he warned. In private moments, he was even more blunt: "The one quirk in human nature I can't understand is that the people who were the worst broke when we came into power were the ones who recovered the fastest and got the richest, and they are the ones who hate us the most."[6]

The results of Rayburn's appeal were dramatic. Within days, checks began flowing in to Johnson. "After talking with Sam Rayburn, I have decided to send my contribution for this year's campaign to you," Charles F. Roeser of Fort Worth, president of the Independent Petroleum Association, wrote. Generous donations also arrived from oilmen J. R. Parten, long active in Democratic politics, and James Abercrombie, among others. Rayburn's two closest friends in the oil industry, crusty conservatives Clint Murchison and Sid Richardson, each sent $5,000, the legal maximum contribution.

No records have come to light on the amount of pledges Rayburn collected in Dallas and Fort Worth during the two days he spent in those cities, although two years later he told his brother-in-law, W. A. Thomas, that the Congressional Campaign Committee's 1942 war chest "had more money . . . than ever before. . . . something over $100,000," some $75,000 of which had been donated by Texans.[7] Almost certainly, the money raised in 1940 represented more than he had ever seen in politics, perhaps more than he ever dreamed of. Before 1940, he had thought of contributions in terms of his own campaign needs— a few hundred dollars from a single contributor was a lot of money. Some billboards, radio ads, bumper stickers, buttons, and maybe a little "walking around money" for volunteer workers—with a few thousand dollars for such necessities, a candidate for the House of Representatives could mount a solid race.

Now so much money flowed in that it seemed, for the times, mind boggling. A few wildcatters whose donations had already reached the $5,000 limit offered cash, which Rayburn, on behalf of the Congressional Campaign Committee, accepted, apparently without qualms. Cash—the lubricant of politics in those days, illegal yet widely condoned—would be carried by trusted couriers to Lyndon Johnson. Campaign laws then were vague and largely unenforced. Rayburn appears to have been as willing as the next public official to exploit the loopholes, although there was never the slightest hint that he gained personally from it.[8] Serious attempts to regulate campaign financing were still twenty-five years in the future.

Johnson emerged as the real hero of the fund-raising endeavor. Orchestrating the effort from Washington, he saw not only that money was raised in unprecedented amounts for Democratic candidates but that it got to those needing it the most. He also seemed to have opened Rayburn's eyes for the first time to the valuable resource that he alone controlled and could tap as needed. From then on, Rayburn would use that ability to raise money for other candidates as a source of power. According to Johnson's biographer, Robert Caro:

> Sam Rayburn had, on his trip to Texas in October, 1940, cut off the Democratic National Committee and other traditional party recipients of campaign contribu-

tions from money of the newly rich Texas independent oilmen. These men had been seeking a channel through which their money could flow to the seat of national power 2,000 miles away. . . . After Sam Rayburn's trip to Dallas, they had their channel, a brand-new channel which, ten days before, had not even existed. Sam Rayburn had cut them the channel. A new source of political money, potentially vast, had been tapped in America . . .[9]

The election was a personal triumph for Roosevelt. He would have his third term. Although Willkie ran a strong race, particularly in New York, the President had come on strong in the campaign's final two weeks and had won going away. Undoubtedly he pulled in a good many Democratic candidates with him. Still, there was no discounting the work of Johnson, Rayburn, John McCormack, and others in raising and funneling money and other assistance to Democratic congressmen, many of whom had been resigned to defeat. Not only was a Democratic debacle avoided in the House—the party actually gained seats, strengthening FDR's hand in Congress for the crucial two years ahead. "My dear Sam," wrote Johnson after the campaign,

> One of the greatest pleasures I have had since I came to Congress—and I have had a lot of them here—was working with you in the pre-election drive for our colleagues. Some of them would have been out in the bitter winter wind without any firewood if you and other veteran hands hadn't pitched in, accomplished the necessary and effected their rescue. It was inspiring to me to be in the midst of the work, and through you I learned a lot of things I needed to know. With gratitude and every good personal wish,
>
> Sincerely,
> Lyndon[10]

For young Lyndon Johnson, yet to complete two full terms, the 1940 campaign was a milestone in his political development. No longer was he the awkward "kid congressman" following Rayburn around like a hungry hound. Nor could he still be considered Rayburn's willing student, for he was beginning to teach the master a trick or two.

In December, Rayburn put McCormack in charge of the House and returned to Texas for a series of celebrations and dinners planned in his honor throughout the state. The three-week tour began in Dallas, where 1,500 people jammed the ballroom of the Adolphus Hotel for a testimonial described by the *Dallas News* as "the biggest banquet gathering" in the city's history. Among the guests were an obscure owlish senator from Missouri named Harry Truman, whose admiration for the plain-spoken Texan was beginning to grow, and Lyndon Johnson, who stuck to Rayburn like a fly to jam throughout the tour. Johnson, emerging from the recent elections with statewide stature, had been chosen to introduce the honored guest. The audience roared when the young congressman from the Texas Hill Country proposed the Bonham legislator as the Democratic presidential nominee in 1944.[11]

Rayburn's speech that night went beyond war and politics—the issues most on the minds of his audience—as he tried to describe his views on democracy and government's role in a rapidly changing society. His remarks, pointedly aimed at Dallas's well-entrenched conservative establishment, included an articulate defense of his own guiding philosophy as well as that of the New Deal and the activist government they symbolized:

> We must recognize that the rapid industrialization of our country has brought increasing inequities in wealth, economic power and economic opportunity. Whereas in the past, democracy and economic opportunity could be had by government letting people alone, today a democracy of opportunity is possible only with the active help of government. There is no opportunity for the man who wants to work and cannot find a job at a living wage. There is no opportunity for a farmer who cannot sell his crops at a fair price.[12]

Returning to the nation's capital on New Year's Day, the Speaker prepared to wind up the 76th Congress on the session's 366th day—the longest session in history—and convene the 77th. The year ahead, he could be sure, would be difficult for the nation, the House of Representatives, and himself. Important questions would have to be addressed. How far should—or could—the United States go in aiding England, Greece, and other European governments threatened by Hitler's armies? Could the isolationists of the House and Senate be won over or outmaneuvered? Should Congress delegate more power to the President, or had it already given him too much power? How could Congress best serve the nation in time of war?

Even when pressing Garner's ill-fated presidential candidacy, Rayburn's support and trust of Roosevelt never wavered. He was fully convinced—especially after FDR's latest "fireside chat"—that the President's policies at home and abroad were sound. When Roosevelt declared his determination to make America "the arsenal of democracy," the Speaker told reporters: "I'll fight in Congress to provide the President whatever he needs to forward that objective."

Still unsettled, however, was the nagging problem of Roosevelt's arrogance in dealing with Capitol Hill, expressed in his almost sneering tendency to exclude House and Senate leaders from his tight circle of advisers and confidants. Rayburn had been particularly irritated by what he perceived as a patronizing note from the President shortly before Christmas. "You, I and John McCormack are facing a very difficult session," FDR had written:

> It will not help any of the three to meet with a series of defeats in the next Congress. . . . That is especially true if any of the three accepts defeat tamely. . . . Therefore, I renew my ancient feeling that it is better to be defeated while going down fighting than it is to accept defeat without fighting. . . . What I want to get across to both of you before the new session begins is that good fellowship for the sake of good fellowship alone, an easy life to avoid criticism, and acceptance of defeat before an issue has been joined, make, all of them, less for Party success and for national safety than a few drag-down and knock-out fights and an unwillingness to accept defeat without a fight.[13]

Rayburn felt he needed no such prodding. Within recent days, he and McCormack had given the administration a significant victory by defeating the Logan-Walter bill, a conservative-backed measure that would have severely limited the authority of executive agencies.[14] If the President expected such cooperation in the future, the Texan told McCormack, he would have to show more respect for the legislative branch. When the two House leaders took their complaint to Roosevelt, they found him surprisingly agreeable. In fact, Rayburn later related, the President was so taken with the suggestion of closer cooperation that he immediately launched into a long recitation of some of the nation's most serious defense failures. "What should I tell the people about it, Sam?" he asked.

"Tell 'em the truth," replied Rayburn gruffly. "That's what the people expect from you. Don't hide the bad parts. Tell 'em just what you've told me." Roosevelt heeded that advice in his next radio talk.[15]

The President also vowed to keep the House leadership more fully informed. In return, Rayburn promised more unified support from House Democrats. "I'm depending on all of you to back us up on this," the Speaker told caucusing Democrats as the new session got under way in January. "I don't expect 100 percent support for everything the President proposes. But at the same time I don't want 50 or 60 percent support, which isn't enough to offset Republican opposition. You ought to go along at least 90 percent of the time."[16]

On January 6—Rayburn's 59th birthday—Roosevelt revealed more of his plans for national defense in his long-awaited State of the Union address. The House chamber, then undergoing massive renovation, provided a strangely appropriate setting for the grim speech. With bare steel girders and I-beams supporting the roof, the great hall resembled, as one correspondent put it, "the inside of an unfinished skyscraper or a building shored up against bombs."[17]

For the first time in Texas history and one of the few times in the nation's history, two men from the same state—Rayburn and Garner—presided over a joint session. Garner had made his peace with FDR and was preparing to leave soon for Uvalde, never to return to Washington.[18] A few days earlier, Rayburn had broken his favorite gavel, given him in 1934 by two Dallas

schoolboys in innocent anticipation of his rise to the Speakership. He selected for the President's visit a new gavel of ornately
carved mesquite. With Roosevelt at the podium, ready to speak,
Rayburn called the session to order, bringing his new gavel
down so hard that it also splintered, sending chunks of mesquite
flying. The last time he had broken a gavel, the head had whizzed
past Clerk South Trimble's ear like a bullet. The President was
not similarly endangered, but he was ruffled. At the first pause
in the cheering, without waiting to be introduced, he launched
into his speech.

Roosevelt's words, ringing clear through the hushed hall,
went to the core of the nation's darkening crisis. In solemn, short
sentences—the kind Sam Rayburn preferred—Roosevelt outlined the hard course ahead. He warned of surprise attacks on
America's shores, of secret agents ("great numbers of them are
already here"), of those "who with sounding brass and tinkling
cymbal preach the 'ism' of appeasement," and of those who seek
personal profit from a war or from "a dictator's peace."

He did not gloss over the sacrifices that victory would demand. His policy, he declared, would be: 1. commitment to an
all-inclusive national defense, 2. "full support" of Great Britain's
war effort, and 3. determination "never . . . to acquiesce in a
peace dictated by aggressors or sponsored by appeasers." America would become democracy's arsenal—furnishing besieged
friendly nations with the war materials they desperately required. What England needed, he stressed, were planes and
ships and guns, not dollars and soldiers. "The best way of dealing with the few slackers or troublemakers in our midst," he
went on, "is, first, to shame them by patriotic example, and if
that fails, to use the sovereignty of government to save government." It was a shot aimed directly at Congress's isolationist minority. The ultimate goal, he said, was a secure world "founded
on four essential human freedoms"—freedom of speech and expression, freedom of worship, freedom from want, and freedom
from fear.

Although FDR's "four-freedoms" speech would survive as
a classic example of effective presidential oratory, Congress's
immediate response gave little hint that it was well received.

Democrats interrupted with only occasional polite applause, Republicans with none at all, save for the timid clapping of a few freshmen. The *New York Times* concluded that the speech "caused deep reflection among members as to the role Congress might play" in the crisis. Even Rayburn remarked afterward that the decorum had been almost too perfect, except that he "slipped a bit" by coming down too hard with the gavel. "Sam," admonished Roosevelt afterward, "you broke a precedent today. Why didn't you introduce me?"

"You didn't give me a chance," snapped Rayburn with mock severity. "Besides, I figured everybody knew you."

On January 10, Roosevelt sent to Capitol Hill the first of a series of measures to implement his promise of military aid to England—the so-called lend-lease bill. Under the proposal, introduced by Majority Leader John McCormack and numbered HR 1776, the President would be granted wide latitude to transfer American-made weapons to friendly governments "whose defense the President deems vital to the defense of the United States." He alone would decide to whom military assistance would go, how much would be sent, and how—if at all—it would be repaid. If a needed defense article was not already being produced, he could order its manufacture. Those were extraordinary powers for a President, especially when the nation was technically at peace. "If we are to aid the democracies, Congress must enact a law giving the power to somebody to administer the law," Rayburn argued in defense of the measure. "There could certainly be no one man in this country as well qualified to administer it as the President. . . . Either we give the President the flexible powers necessary to help Britain, or by our inaction, we strengthen Hitler's power to conquer Britain and attack us."[19]

The reactionaries were skeptical. Sniffed Hamilton Fish: "It looks as if we are bringing Nazism, fascism and dictatorship to America and setting up a Führer here." Even usually enlightened Republicans and Democrats were outraged. "This is not a request for a blank check," complained Senator Robert LaFollette, Republican of Wisconsin. "It is a demand that Congress abdicate vital and important powers." The bill's passage, it was argued, would mean the abandonment of Congress's constitutional responsibility to declare war and the transference of that responsibility into the hands of one man. Besides, Wilson got no such power in World War I.

Others, concerned that lend-lease and similar measures could draw the United States into war, got little comfort from the testimony of witnesses before the House Committee on Foreign Affairs. Time was short—a European crisis could come in sixty to ninety days, warned Secretary of War Henry L. Stimson. The Nazis could be on British soil by spring, said Army Chief of Staff George C. Marshall. "Congress must weigh very seriously the question whether it wants Great Britain, Greece and China to continue to fight," added Treasury Secretary Henry Morgenthau.

Still, House sentiment remained steadfastly against the measure. When Congressman Charles Gifford, Republican of Massachusetts, asserted during a debate that Britain's navy was "the first line of defense for the U.S. Navy," jeers and hoots rocked the chamber. By late January, Rayburn could see that the bill had no chance without substantial modification.

Surprisingly, Roosevelt uttered no protest when the Speaker conveyed his assessment. Instead, he was urged to work with Chairman Sol Bloom and other Democrats on the Foreign Affairs Committee for the strongest bill they could get.[20] On January 28, Rayburn announced that the panel had agreed to amendments in response to objections raised by opponents: the program would be limited to two years, American convoys would be prohibited, and the President would have to report frequently to Congress and consult with the army and navy before disposing of any war materiel. With those changes, Rayburn was sure the bill could pass—provided he could keep it free from additional weakening amendments.

House debate on HR 1776 raged for three days. For three more days, Rayburn, McCormack, and Bloom worked the House floor, quashing threatening amendments. Jere Cooper of Tennessee presided as chairman of the Committee of the Whole, a special committee of the entire House created for the purpose of debating major legislation under strict parliamentary rules. Cooper had been well coached. "Not germane," the feisty Tennessean would snap when Republicans and dissident Democrats tried to offer amendments. "It's a slick parliamentary trick," grumbled the *New York Daily News*, "if they [Rayburn and company] can get away with it."[21] In all, the House rejected nineteen amendments before finally passing the bill, virtually without change, 260–165. The Democrats provided 236 of the winning votes. The Rayburn leadership team had come through its important first test brilliantly. "Credit for getting the bill through the House is mainly Speaker Sam Rayburn's," said columnist Paul Mallon. "In his first big job he proved himself even sterner and stronger than Garner. Even Republicans conversationally conceded his fairness."[22]

Without uttering a word in debate, Rayburn had dominated the action. "Rayburn used not only his finesse but both feet on his Democrats to keep them in line," Mallon reported. "He had them so frightened that one man declined to appear in some of the last minute voting on Republican amendments but chose refuge in the cloakroom." Etched on members' minds was a picture of the stocky Texan angrily backing Congressman Jerry Voorhis into a corner and, wielding his forefinger like a sword point, admonishing the liberal Californian for daring to offer an amendment limiting the President's powers to one year. "It was fairly well understood in the House," reported Mallon, "that any Democrat who voted for amendments was a marked man." Explained Rayburn later: "There is not time to debate endlessly the relative merits of much disputed substitute bills or amendments. Either we give the President the flexible powers necessary to help Britain, or, by our inaction, we strengthen Hitler's power to conquer Britain and attack us."[23]

The Senate passed the lend-lease bill a month later. Precious time was lost while the reactionaries, led by Senator Gerald P. Nye of North Dakota, held the floor. Finally, in a late-night session, the Senate beat down the last of the isolationist amendments and proceeded to a final vote. It was at times like these, Rayburn thought, that the Senate performed at its worst. The loose rules and tradition of unlimited debate of the "other body" were beyond his comprehension. In a time of trouble, the nation needed action not oratory, he felt.

Because the Senate bill differed slightly from the House version, a second House vote was necessary. Within hours, the Speaker had the measure back before the members and gaveled through to final passage. An hour after that, it was on Roosevelt's desk. Before nightfall, an initial shipment of weapons to Britain and Greece was on its way. The President's request for $7 billion in appropriations to "produce every gun, plane and munition of war that we possibly can" for the beleaguered democracies cleared both houses fifteen days later.

The general praise for the House that followed its quick, decisive handling of lend-lease lifted members' spirits higher than they had been in years. Rayburn felt he had struck just the tone he sought. He remembered Garner's admonition to him on the day he became Speaker: "You have the brains and industry for the job. Always do what is right for the country, remembering that while it may not be popular at the time, if it is right for the country, it will be advantageous in the end."[24] He intended to be a strong Speaker—the strongest since Tom Reed and "Uncle Joe" Cannon;[25] his handling of the debate, he believed, would help greatly to establish his dominance over the quarrelsome cliques that had for so long disrupted and manipulated the House.

The Texan brought unusual potential to the Speakership. He was personally close to the other power brokers in the House— the committee chairmen and heads of delegations. Being a leader of a big-state delegation, whose membership included five committee chairmen, accorded him additional leverage. Dozens of representatives felt beholden to him for past assistance of one kind of another. As majority leader, he had helped many land good committee assignments and others win passage of their pet bills. Older members, who had earlier been helped by Garner, now felt obligated to Garner's protégé. Younger members, such as Clinton Anderson of New Mexico and Lyndon Johnson, were devoted to him. Most of all, he was trusted by members of both parties, which gave him special entrée when dealing with various factions. Members from time to time might question his judgment but never his motives.

Though slow to respond to the rise of Nazism and fascism, Congress in 1941 finally began to accept the inevitability of war. Appropriation bills piled one upon the other until, by fall, the House had approved defense and lend-lease spending totaling more than $67 billion. Minor laws that conflicted with the President's emergency powers were suspended. A tax increase— Rayburn insisted that the defense effort be financed "by this generation"—price controls, an antistrike measure, property seizure, and lend-lease expansion were all under consideration by summer's end. All the while, the strength of the isolationists was ebbing. Their lend-lease defeat had severely damaged their House influence. Still, there was another bitter fight coming— the final showdown on extending the draft—a fight the administration seemed certain to lose.[26]

The isolationists were confident. Roosevelt had practically given his word a year earlier, when the original draft was approved, not to retain draftees more than a year. Moreover, the 1940 Democratic platform opposed extending draftees' length of service, and the Speaker himself was on record as an opponent of draft extension. The draftees had been promised a release after twelve months, the opponents argued. Now, in the summer of 1941, Roosevelt and his generals asked Congress to break that promise. The argument attracted many nonisolationist Democrats who saw the twelve-month service period as a moral contract between the government and the draftees.

Rayburn, too, was swayed by that argument. But as the world situation worsened, his view began to change. He tried to weigh the facts against what he perceived to be the public sentiment. Clearly, he decided, he would have to go along with the President, even though it meant an embarrassing turnabout from his previous position. "I do not know whether I am going to maintain completely the stand I took with reference to the draftees," he wrote. "Things are changing fast and matters are becoming more complicated and dangerous every day. The Far Eastern situation looks bad, and we have problems of transportation and shipping that might make it a good idea to keep some of the boys in for a longer period, at least temporarily."[27]

Under the Selective Service Act, Congress could extend draftees' service only after it had "declared that the national interest is imperiled . . . " "The answer is plain, as I see it," argued General George C. Marshall in testimony before the Senate Committee on Military Affairs. "Are the national interests imperiled? Does a national emergency exist? In my opinion a national emergency does decidedly exist; in the opinion of the War Department, it does; in the opinion of the President, it does." The President already had declared a limited emergency, Marshall reminded the panel.[28]

Time was running out. Without a draft extension, Marshall warned, the recently expanded army faced "disintegration." National Guard antiaircraft units serving in Alaska and Hawaii would have to be released that month, leaving those U.S. territories vulnerable to attack. Secretary of State Hull left a sickbed to testify on the "exceedingly bad effect" the proposal's defeat would have on the world situation.[29] The Nazis, he warned, would read it as a sign of American weakness and division. Their words had impact in the Senate, which hastily passed a modified resolution extending the draft eighteen months and raising the pay of draftees with more than a year's service. Still, that action fell far short of what Roosevelt wanted—authority to hold draftees in service until "such time as may be necessary in the interests of national defense."

In the House, the outlook remained bleak. Two days before debate was to begin, Rayburn advised the President that a Democratic "whip count" indicated possibly enough support for a twelve-month extension—certainly no more than that. Roosevelt at first held fast to his original request: extension for the duration of the emergency. Impossible, said Rayburn. But, he added, maybe the House could be persuaded to go along with the Senate's eighteen-month extension. Even that, he told the White House, would require at least twenty Republican votes to offset the sixty or so Democrats who had already committed to vote against any extension. Where were those Republican votes coming from, and how could further Democratic defections be prevented? Could more Democrats, the Texan wondered, be enticed back to the reservation?

The problem was still unresolved when Rayburn and Republican Congressman John J. Jennings boarded a night train that would take them to Kingston, Tennessee, twelve miles from Rayburn's birthplace in the heart of Jennings's district. A celebration in the Speaker's honor had been planned for weeks and, crisis or not, he would not disappoint the folks of Roane County.

Arriving at 6 A.M. the next morning—a Sunday—the two congressmen were met by Rayburn's cousin Mose Waller, a local stock farmer and banker, who led them on a tour of the area, including the remains of the log cabin where Rayburn was born and the farm his grandfather had carved out of the wilderness. Later, at a family reunion at the Macedonia Primitive Baptist Church, which Rayburn's father had helped to build, the Speaker chatted with kinfolk and nibbled on fried chicken as he worked the crowd around a 100-foot-long picnic table. From all over the county, people came to shake his hand. They were still coming late that day when Rayburn slipped away to catch the last train back to Washington. At 11 o'clock the next morning, he was scheduled to open debate on the crucial draft-extension resolution.

Rayburn was bone weary when he boarded the train at Lenoir City. He had worked a long day on Saturday, spent a restless eight hours on the train Saturday night, and been hauled all over Roane County since daybreak Sunday. With an anxious world awaiting the outcome of the draft-extension debate, he knew he would have to be at his best. Winning this fight would demand extraordinary effort. In a few hours the battle would be joined, and he still had compromises to sell, votes to gather, strategy to plan. As his train groaned through the east Tennessee mountains, he could not help but wonder whether he had made a serious, perhaps disastrous, mistake by indulging himself in this day of reminiscing on the eve of so important a vote.

As it had been so often, fate was on Rayburn's side. Not so lucky was Republican Congressman Albert G. Rutherford of Pennsylvania, who died over the weekend, giving the Speaker a perfect reason to postpone the showdown for another day. Seizing the opportunity, Rayburn announced that the House, out of respect for a departed colleague, would stand in recess for twenty-hour hours. Opponents of the draft remained confident. It seemed unlikely that twenty Republicans—Rayburn needed at least that many to offset Democratic defections—would support the administration, no matter what limitations ultimately were put on the draft-extension period.[30]

On Monday, Rayburn began to move. He strolled the Capitol corridors and byways, working his way slowly through the Democratic cloakroom and the House dining rooms. Sidling up to prospective supporters, he would solicit their help. His practice was not to threaten members or question their motives or patriotism. Instead, he used his most persuasive weapon: personal appeal. "I need your vote. I wish you'd stand by me because it means a lot to me," he would say, leaning in close and looking his prospect squarely in the eye. Before the final vote, several members had agreed against their own inclinations to support the resolution "for Sam." One was freshman Robert Sikes of Florida, who was agonizing over the measure when the Speaker approached him. As Sikes remembered: "Whether to support or oppose the resolution was one of the hardest decisions I had been called on to make during my brief congressional service. It was not until late in the consideration of the measure that I finally decided how I should vote, and not until after I had been 'talked to' by Mr. Sam."[31]

Some usually loyal Democrats would not budge. Some were in "mental anguish." The vote was the "most difficult I have ever cast," recalled California liberal Jerry Voorhis. In the end, Voorhis decided Congress's pledge to the draftees was inviolable and voted against extension. He later regretted his decision. "In the hindsight now permitted us," he wrote in 1947, "I would change if I could. For the roll call was one of the times when members of Congress were called upon to 'rise above principle.'" In Voorhis's opinion, the bill would have failed had it not been for Rayburn's efforts.[32]

Minority Leader Joe Martin was torn by a natural desire to reap political gain from the Democrats' predicament and an ill-defined feeling that the extension was necessary for the security of the nation. He opted for the former. "The course I followed," he said later, "was to count such popular sentiment as we could attract by opposing the bill yet, at the same time, make no great effort to defeat it."[33] While Martin was telling Republicans to "follow your own preferences on this," other isolationists were taking a more active approach. Isolationist Dewey Short of Missouri counted noses and predicted that no more than a dozen Republicans would go for even a twelve-month extension. Democratic Whip Pat Boland ordered a last-minute poll of the Democrats but told Rayburn he was unable to determine the vote "with any degree of accuracy" because "we don't know how many Republican votes we can count on."[34]

If a few wandering Democrats could be brought back into the fold and if the Republicans were free to vote as they chose, then there was a chance, Rayburn decided. At a final strategy session, the Speaker, McCormack, and Chairman Andrew J. May of the Military Affairs Committee, who would manage the bill on the floor, decided to go for broke—an eighteen-month extension. Twelve months was the safer course, but Lyndon Johnson and other Rayburn lieutenants had been bringing in encouraging reports of new support in the last few hours. Besides, the situation in Europe was worsening.

Shortly after 10 A.M. on August 12, May moved that the House resolve into a Committee of the Whole for the purpose of debating House Joint Resolution 290, providing for extension of the military draft. The routine motion carried. Rayburn left the Speaker's chair, free now to roam about the House for the next several hours and line up more support—if he could. "I've got to get more votes here," he told Texas colleague Paul Kilday. "This is too close."[35] The Speaker made a final appeal, relayed through some friendly Republicans, to Dewey Short, a pivotal isolationist, but Short sent back word that he was "adamant" and "unwilling to change." Short had a plan to gut the bill with several weakening amendments that would be included in the Republican motion to "recommit"—send the measure back to the Military Affairs Committee, in effect killing it.

During the debate, Rayburn could be found either seated in the front row, listening intently but not participating, or perched strategically on a bench in the Speaker's Lobby, from which he had a clear view of all members entering and leaving the chamber. Inside, Republicans were mercilessly attacking the draft proposal and its chief advocate, Roosevelt. "This crowning infamy," fumed Everett Dirksen of Illinois, a budding orator destined for greater fame as a senator. Carrying a large share of the administration's case was the peripatetic Lyndon Johnson, who had recently lost a bid for the Senate in a special election and was now plunging back into his House duties as a member of the Military Affairs Committee. "If we vote down this proposal," he told the House, "we will vote to send two-thirds of our present army home [when] it is just reaching a point where it is approaching adequacy."

Finally, the time allotted for debate was exhausted. Rayburn returned to the rostrum, having done—he thought—all he could do. The votes either were there or they weren't. He recognized Indiana Republican Forest Harness, an opponent of the measure, who moved routinely to recommit the resolution to the Military Affairs Committee with instructions to add Dewey Short's weakening amendments and report it back to the House. The motion was easily turned back, 215–190. Rayburn and McCormack breathed easier; perhaps all the worry had been unnecessary.

Then came the final roll call. The galleries were packed with uniformed soldiers from nearby camps. They wanted out of the service, and every House member could feel their stares. Also conspicuously seated in the galleries were solemn-faced women, members of "We, the Mothers Mobilized for America" and other draft-opposing groups. In their fists, they held small American flags.[36] Capitol policeman John Holton, later to become Rayburn's administrative assistant, had wrangled a gallery seat, from which he could see sweat glistening on the top of the Speaker's head.

Adams, Aiken, Allen—the reading clerk went down the roll. Slowly the figures on the mechanical counter in Tally Clerk Hans Jorgensen's left hand began adding up. Republican Leader Martin had a sinking feeling that the bill would fail and that he had made "a fatal miscalculation." Rayburn, listening to the meter click with each "yea," strained his eyes to see the tiny numerals. The vote seesawed—one side led for a while, then the other. Finally, the clerk had called all the names and then went back through the list a second time, repeating the names of members who had not answered the first roll call.

Jorgensen scribbled the totals on a slip of paper and handed it to Rayburn. But before the Speaker could announce the results, Andrew Somers, New York Democrat, was on his feet demanding recognition. In the press gallery, all was confusion. Some reporters' tallies showed the vote carrying, others had it losing. The House floor was in turmoil. Only this was certain: the vote was very close. Maybe the Speaker would have to cast a tie-breaking vote—a rarity in the annals of the House, where the Speaker traditionally does not vote except in cases of a tie.

Rayburn recognized Somers who, amid gasps from the floor and galleries, changed his vote from yea to nay. Rayburn's mistake; he should have ignored Somers. Others might now get the same idea. He glanced at the tally sheet; the vote still had not been announced. With Somers's switch, the vote stood at 203 for the bill, 202 against. Then New Jersey Democrat William Sutphin began waving frantically for the Speaker's attention. Sutphin had not voted in the roll call, and Rayburn was not going to be stung twice. He turned instead to Republican Dewey Short, whose intentions were predictable. Short asked for a recapitulation of the vote, a routine motion. "Does the gentleman desire that before the vote is announced?" Rayburn asked, immediately grasping the delicacy of the situation. His mastery of the House rules might pay off. Much depended on Short's answer.

"It was done, as I understand it, the other day," the Missouri congressman said, "but I shall not object." That was the answer Rayburn wanted. The Speaker then, for the first time, announced the results: "On this roll call, 203 members have voted aye, 202 members nay, and the bill is passed."

Short then reiterated his request for a recapitulation—a purely mechanical examination of the vote to determine that each member has been recorded correctly. In fairness, Rayburn could not refuse it. The clerk called the names of those who had voted in the affirmative, then the negative. Although it had not yet dawned on Short and other opponents of the measure, they had been outsmarted. By announcing the vote before recapitulation,

Rayburn had frozen the tally. Under House rules, a member failing to vote on the first or second roll call may not vote or change
a vote on recapitulation. A vote erroneously recorded or unin-
tentionally missed by the tally clerk, of course, could still reverse the outcome.

No mistakes were found in the list of affirmative votes. But at
the conclusion of the reading of the list of those voting in the
negative, Ohio Republican Albert Baumhart leaped to his feet,
claiming he had been present and had voted nay but had not
heard his name called on recapitulation. "Yes, he was here; yes,
he was," shouted his Republican colleagues. That produced one
of the evening's tensest moments. If Baumhart's vote had been
overlooked, the result would change to a tie. The clerk consulted
his roll. Yes, Baumhart had been counted. Democrats uttered a
sigh of relief. Still capitalizing on the confusion, Rayburn moved
quickly.

"There is no correction of the vote," he announced. "The
vote stands, and the bill is passed. Without objection, a motion
to reconsider is laid on the table." Suddenly, the isolationists
sensed what Rayburn had done.

"Mr. Speaker," bellowed Short, "I was on my feet . . ."

Rayburn's face grew suddenly stern, his voice icy. He replied:
"There were no changes whatsoever, and the Chair announced
the vote stood, and the bill was passed. Without objection, a
motion to reconsider was laid on the table, and there was no
objection."

"Mr. Speaker, I object and demand recognition," Short stammered. "I wanted to move to recapitulate the vote by which the
bill was passed."

"That has already been done."

"I mean to reconsider the vote by which the bill was passed."

Earl Michner, a Michigan Republican, chimed in with a parliamentary inquiry. "The gentleman will state it," said Rayburn.

"Mr. Speaker," said Michner, "there's no use getting excited
about this."

"The Chair trusts the gentleman from Michigan does not
think the Chair is excited."

"The only thing that would make me think it," Michner retorted, "was the speed with which the Speaker passed the bill and refused to recognize the gentleman from Missouri [Short] who was on the floor."

"The gentleman will state for what purpose . . ." Rayburn's reply was interrupted by Short.

"Mr. Speaker," Short blurted, "I did not have time. I wanted to move to reconsider the vote by which the bill was passed." He was still confused over the rules.

"The gentleman, in the first place, is not eligible to make that motion," Rayburn explained. A motion to reconsider can come only from a member on the winning side, and Short did not qualify. Rayburn then turned to another Republican, Francis Case of South Dakota, for a parliamentary inquiry.

"I understand the Chair to state that, at the time the Chair announced the bill had passed, he stated that without objection a motion to reconsider was laid on the table?"

"The Chair so stated," answered Rayburn.

"I am sorry," Case continued, "but I was listening and failed to hear the Chair so state. I am glad to hear the Chair make that statement." A dozen members clamored for recognition. Andrew May was recognized, but he was quickly interrupted by Minority Leader Joe Martin. Before Martin could go on, H. Carl Andersen of Minnesota jumped up angrily.

"I beg to differ with the Speaker," shouted Andersen. "He did not announce that a motion to reconsider was laid on the table."

Crimson crept up Rayburn's neck until his tight-lipped face fairly glowed with rage. "The Chair," he said slowly, "has stated *twice* that he did make that statement."

"I'm sorry to differ with you, Mr. Speaker . . ." Andersen responded.

"The Chair," snapped the short-fused Texan, "does not intend to have his word questioned by the gentleman from Minnesota—or anybody else. The gentleman from Kentucky [Andrew May] is recognized."

The fight was over. Some isolationists grumbled as they left the chamber, but even they recognized Rayburn's clear victory. The next day's newspaper headlines told the story: "Rayburn Wields

an Iron Fist on House to Jam through Draft Extension Bill,"
bannered the *Cleveland Press*. As *Time* correspondent Frank
McNaughton assessed it, "Sam Rayburn for a moment literally
played the role of dictator within the framework of representative government, for the safety and good of the government
itself."[37] He had pushed the Speaker's powers to the limit—
which he would do only rarely again—and had triumphed, not
only for himself but, as later events proved, for the nation as well.

A century earlier, Henry Clay had dominated the House
through the force of his own magnetic personality. Speaker Tom
Reed at the end of the 1800s relied on his superior intelligence,
while Joe Cannon cowed his colleagues with restrictive rules and
swift punishment for all who opposed him. Sam Rayburn's
unique leadership style—friendly persuasion backed by his own
rockbound integrity and insistence on fairness—was already
clear.

Hampered by its size and diversity, the House tends to rise to
its responsibilities on great national issues only under strong
leadership. In Sam Rayburn, it now had that leadership. Passage
of the draft-extension resolution prevented the dismantling of
the armed forces a scant four months before the Japanese attack
on Pearl Harbor. It also firmly established the determined Texan
as master of the House, the strongest Speaker since Reed and
Cannon. He proved that he knew the Speaker's powers and that,
when aroused, he would use them. It was a lesson his opponents
would long remember.

In the closing weeks of 1941, the Texan helped rescue still
another administration bill critical to the nation's defense—a
measure to repeal parts of the Neutrality Act and allow armed
American merchant ships to enter combat zones or belligerent
ports. The isolationists, their earlier defeats notwithstanding,
believed they still could block further U.S. involvement in the
war when the Neutrality Act amendments came before the
House.

Bolstering the isolationists' cause was mounting malaise and
frustration across the land. Congress itself was increasingly on
edge. The unrest seemed to grow worse by the day. In one state

after another, labor had embarked on a rampage of strikes, seriously threatening the defense effort. Workers had walked off their jobs at Ford and General Motors. Roosevelt had been forced practically to beg mining czar John L. Lewis to allow his 53,000 coal miners to return to work. The "Big Five" rail unions had announced a walkout of their 350,000 members to begin December 7; and in shipyards on both coasts, welders, building trades craftsmen, and other vital workers were locked in bitter and prolonged dispute over wages, working conditions, and benefits. The administration hoped to ride out the crisis, fearing the political and social impact of punitive antistrike legislation, but the issue was ready to explode on Capitol Hill. The House Labor Committee already had approved one drastic antistrike measure. It had sailed through the conservative-dominated Committee on Rules, and now only Sam Rayburn stood in the way of the bill's final passage. The Speaker, determined to keep what he considered unfair legislation from reaching the House floor, refused to schedule it for debate.

Debate on the neutrality amendments took a predictable course, with the same characters on both sides of the issue reciting their now-familiar lines. Republican leaders and the press forecast defeat of the proposal by at least twenty votes. Again it became Rayburn's task to rescue the bill for the administration, if he could. McCormack had just finished a rousing speech in defense of the amendments when the Texan signaled that he wanted to address the House. Eleven minutes remained of debate time allotted to the bill's proponents, and Rayburn, who had not spoken in debate since becoming Speaker, requested the entire eleven minutes. Silence fell over the chamber, and every eye turned to the stumpy, bald figure in the well. *Washington Post* correspondent Robert C. Albright was there. "None doubted as Rayburn stood before rebellious Democrats on the late afternoon of November 13 that he now faced the supreme test of his career," Albright later recounted.[38]

Holding his audience in rapt attention, the Speaker slowly took from his pocket a letter. In a last, desperate effort to save the bill, he and McCormack had persuaded Roosevelt to make his own personal appeal for the amendments and to say something—anything—that would defuse the House's mounting anger over the strikes. The President responded with a lengthy note reiterating his well-known arguments against the restrictions of the Neutrality Act. About the strikers he said little, beyond restating his vow never to yield to their demands.

Rayburn could sense that the letter, which took ten precious minutes to read, had missed the mark. Members expected more. They wanted assurance that defense commitments would not be undermined by a collapse of production; they wanted the antistrike bill that Rayburn refused to send to the floor. He knew what he had to do. Leaning over the podium so all could hear, he said: "If it is of any interest to anyone to know my position on both capital and labor in this titanic, this fateful struggle for democracy, it is that I am ready to follow or to lead in any movement by legislation, or sanely otherwise, that will keep defense production going." With that sentence, Rayburn reversed his position on the antistrike bill and, by conservative estimate, brought a score of votes back to the administration. The President got his neutrality amendments by a vote of 212–194.

If Rayburn deserved credit for winning repeal of the neutrality restrictions, he also shared blame for allowing a harsh antistrike measure to pass the House a few days later. The bill, sponsored by conservative Democrat Howard W. Smith of Virginia, required thirty days' notice of a strike or lockout in a defense plant and set strict guidelines for unions. Labor leaders, hoping to tone down the measure when it reached the Senate, frantically gathered in Washington the following Sunday, December 7, to confer with key senators.[39]

A cold wind swept the nation's capital on Sunday, December 7, breaking several weeks of unseasonably warm weather. United States relations with Japan had deteriorated through the fall, but negotiations with the belligerent Asian nation were continuing, and official Washington was taking the day off. Sam Rayburn, trying to help a Texas youth who was in a jam with the Virginia police, had scheduled a meeting with the governor in Richmond. George Donovan wheeled the Speaker's Cadillac around to the Anchorage early that morning, and, with Rayburn in the back seat, they headed south across the 14th Street bridge to the Virginia capital, a three-hour trip away.[40]

Washington's top event that day was a season-climaxing match between the Washington Redskins and the Philadelphia Eagles. Despite the freezing temperature, the sun beat warmly on the east grandstands at Griffith Stadium, so 27,000 hardy football fans, including a sprinkling of congressmen, military officers, reporters, and bureaucrats, turned out for the game. Many lawmakers from nearby districts had gone home for the weekend. Vice-President Wallace was in New York to make a speech. President Roosevelt was at the White House, enjoying a casual afternoon with Harry Hopkins.

In the early afternoon, teleprinter circuits in the War Department and State Department suddenly came to life with a furious clatter. The news they brought was shattering: "Pearl Harbor attacked by enemy air and naval fire. . . . This is no drill . . ." Reports were spotty, but soon the press services were flashing throughout the country what little information they could confirm. Roosevelt and Hopkins had just finished lunch when the call came from Secretary of War Knox. "Mr. President," he said, "it looks as if the Japanese have attacked Pearl Harbor." At Griffith Stadium, there was no general announcement, but the crowd quickly sensed something amiss when the stadium announcer began calling out names of reporters and high-ranking military officers, advising them to call their offices. By the start of the game's last quarter, many seats were empty. At 3:07, Roosevelt put in a call to Rayburn at his apartment. The Speaker had not yet returned, so the switchboard operator took the message: "President Roosevelt requests you call him at once."

Meanwhile, Rayburn had finished his business in Richmond. After stopping for lunch at a Broad Street cafe, he and Donovan were headed back to Washington on what was then Route 2, a narrow highway west of U.S. 1. Donovan noticed an unusual number of army trucks and a few convoys and mentioned it to Rayburn. Inexplicably, neither thought to turn on the car radio. Rayburn first learned of the attack from the Anchorage's desk clerk, who ran out to meet his arriving car. The President, she said breathlessly, wanted congressional leaders at the White

House at 9:30 that evening.

Weaving through a silent crowd that had gathered along the black iron fence surrounding the presidential mansion came Rayburn, Senator Connally, and a score of other key House and Senate leaders and top military brass. Their briefing lasted an hour and a half. "The effect on the congressmen was tremendous," recalled Secretary Stimson. "They sat in dead silence, and even after the recital was over they had very few words."[41] Connally was first to emerge from the session. He announced that the President would address a Joint Session of Congress at noon the next day. Reporters spotted Rayburn, his collar turned up against the wind and his black hat pulled tight on his head. "Mr. Speaker, will the President ask for a declaration of war?"

"He didn't say," replied Rayburn, barely pausing.

"Would Congress support a declaration of war?"

"I think," said the Speaker, his words coming out slowly and distinctly, "that is one thing on which there would be unity."[42]

In fact, Roosevelt already had drafted his war message and informed his Cabinet that he intended to ask for war. But he did not disclose his plans to the congressional leaders. For maximum impact, he wanted his message to be a surprise when he delivered it and, according to Harry Hopkins, doubted Congress's ability to keep its contents a secret. "It would be all over town in five minutes," wrote Hopkins in a personal memorandum before going to bed Sunday night.[43]

On Monday, hours before the President's scheduled address, the Capitol bristled with guards. At the east entrance stood solemn-faced Marines, their rifles tipped with bayonets. Behind them, forming a secondary line, were the less-fearsome Capitol police, a motley force made up largely of patronage employees. Rayburn a few months earlier had voiced concern about the inadequacy of the Capitol police, but Congress had not gotten around to beefing up the force. Steel cables, strung overnight on posts along the curbs, held back the hundreds of spectators who came to witness the historic occasion. Few doubted that the President would ask for a declaration of war.

Roosevelt, accompanied by a phalanx of aides, arrived early. He waited in the Speaker's private office, a few feet from the

House Chamber, until members of Congress, the Cabinet, the Supreme Court, and the foreign diplomatic corps were all seated. Then, braced on the arm of his son James, the President mounted the steps of the rostrum. Applause rose in great swells and gave way to cheers. Except for the bright sun streaming through the glass ceiling, the scene matched that of the night of April 2, 1917, when President Wilson requested a declaration of war against Germany. Mrs. Wilson, in a red dress, watched from the gallery with Mrs. Roosevelt as history was repeated.

Rayburn let the cheers continue for an unusually long time, then with a single hard rap of his gavel commanded the crowd to be silent. Remembering FDR's last appearance before a joint session, he made the proper introduction. Then slowly, sternly, the President began to speak. Those present instinctively knew they were witnessing a great moment in history as Roosevelt's immortal phrases rolled forth:

> Yesterday, December 7, 1941—a day that will live in infamy—the United States of America was suddenly and deliberately attacked by naval and air forces of the Empire of Japan. . . . The people of the United States have already formed their opinion and well understand the implications to the very life and safety of our nation. . . . Always will we remember the character of the onslaught against us. . . . I believe I interpret the will of the Congress and of the people when I assert that we will not only defend ourselves to the uttermost but will make very certain that this form of treachery shall never endanger us again. . . . I ask that Congress declare that since the unprovoked and dastardly attack by Japan on Sunday, December seventh, a state of war has existed between the United States and the Japanese Empire.

Short, straight-from-the-shoulder, the speech articulated the national mood. Roosevelt's request for a war declaration took only twelve minutes, compared with Wilson's thirty-eight minutes. Congress debated Wilson's war request for four days; Roosevelt wanted his approved in minutes. At 12:40 P.M., the Joint Session was dissolved. At 1 o'clock, the Senate returned to its session and nine minutes later, without a word of debate, voted for war, 82–0.

Barely had the House floor been cleared of visitors when Rayburn gaveled for order. He recognized John McCormack, who would offer the war resolution. From the corner of his eye, the Speaker spotted the gray head of Jeannette Rankin, the Montana pacifist, as she rose from her seat on the front row of the Republican side. "Mr. Speaker, I object," she blurted. Along with Rayburn and fourteen others in Congress in 1941, Rankin had been a House member when the nation went to war twenty-four years earlier. Tearfully, she had voted against war in 1917. It had cost her defeat. She was back in Congress after an absence of twenty-two years; obviously, she intended to vote once more against going to war.

With a cold stare, Rayburn cut her short. "There can be no objection," he said, signaling McCormack to continue. McCormack's resolution was identical to that passed in 1917, except for the substitution of the words "Imperial Government of Japan" for "Germany." The majority leader requested twenty seconds to speak in behalf of the resolution. "This," he said, "is the time for action."

"Vote! Vote!" shouted House members on both sides of the aisle, amid wild applause and cheers. Gaveling for order, the Speaker recognized the minority leader, who asked for the resolution's "unanimous approval." Hamilton Fish, Jr., of New York appealed to fellow isolationists: "The time for debate is past. The time for action has come. Noninterventionists and interventionists must present a united front. There is only one answer to the treacherous attack by Japan—war to victory." Fish thereupon offered his services as a reserve officer and said that he would like to lead black troops, as he had done heroically in the previous war.

"Mr. Speaker! Mr. Speaker!" Jeannette Rankin was on her feet again.

"Sit down, sister," yelled a Democrat. Others demanded to be heard. America had been "stabbed in the back" by the treacherous Japanese, noted Edith Nourse Rogers of Massachusetts. The country has only two choices—"fight or surrender," added

Luther Johnson of Texas.

Once more, Rankin sought the Speaker's attention. "I rise to a point of order," she shouted at the top of her voice. Rayburn, fixing his eyes on McCormack, ignored her. The majority leader asked for a roll-call vote. While Rankin continued to shout for recognition, the clerk began calling members' names. Rayburn halted him briefly to inform the distraught congresswoman that "nothing is in order" once the roll call has begun.

The vote was 388–1. Rayburn signed the resolution at 3:15, Wallace, as president of the Senate, at 3:25, and Roosevelt at 4:10 in a hastily arranged White House ceremony. The United States was officially at war. Three days later, the House and Senate declared war on Germany and Italy, this time with Congresswoman Rankin voting "present."

Rayburn in the eventful year of 1941 firmly established his leadership and won important concessions from the President. If Roosevelt still did not accept Congress as an equal, at least he was beginning to see the value in closer cooperation and compromise. In Rayburn, at last, he had found a dependable ally. That the modest but determined Texan had stepped in— sometimes against heavy odds—to salvage essential defense bills did not go unnoticed at the White House. However belatedly, a bond of mutual trust and respect was growing between the wartime President and the new Speaker.

14

Wartime Speaker

"There is only one thing that can defeat us," Rayburn warned in early 1942, "and that would be our own disunity." In one speech after another, the gruff Texan damned with feeling the wartime profiteers, faultfinders, and those he labeled "Grumlins"—chronic complainers who refused to accept the rationing, travel restrictions, price and wage controls, and other wartime inconveniences. Noting that the only real sacrifices were those of the men and women in uniform and their families, Rayburn told his friends, "I have no son to give my country, and I can't think of a single sacrifice I've made that hurts."

United, at least, in their desire to win the war, Democrats and Republicans temporarily put aside their differences to give Franklin Roosevelt the basic laws he needed to strengthen the war effort. Victories came deceptively easy for the House leadership as Congress handed the President vast wartime powers, appropriated staggering sums for the military, found new revenue to finance the war by adding some 25 million Americans to the tax rolls, and expanded the draft to include 18-year-olds. "No administration in time of war ever had greater cooperation than we have given the present administration," said House Republican Leader Joe Martin.

Congress can be grand; it can also be foolish. Even while asking the nation to tighten its belt, the lawmakers were voting themselves a liberal pension—the first congressional retirement plan. The measure, attached to a routine civil service bill, sailed through both houses unnoticed by the press and public until after it had become law. In the uproar that followed, the House and Senate were inundated with what Rayburn termed "insulting" letters. The episode evolved into a national farce when lawmakers began receiving "Bundles for Congress"—mainly old clothes and food—from constituents. No other issue, remarked Senator Scott Lucas of Illinois, "is so dividing the American people." The law was quickly repealed.

Congress soon was in trouble again when gasoline rationing went into effect and almost half the members applied for a coveted "X" card allowing them to buy unlimited gas. Technically, they were eligible for the card, but what the average American saw was another example of Congress refusing to accept for itself the sacrifices it asked of others. Again, public reaction was swift. Most lawmakers turned in their X cards. Rayburn was— as always, when Congress came under attack—extremely defensive of his colleagues. He saw in the criticism "a studied effort to destroy the faith and confidence of the American people in their elected representatives." At Muhlenberg College in Pennsylvania, where he had gone to accept an honorary degree, he declared: "There has never been a dictatorship built up in any land until the faith and confidence of the people have been destroyed in the legislative branch, and the legislative branch itself has been destroyed."[1] The speech seemed to make him feel better, and won praise from fellow members of Congress, but did little to change public attitudes.

With the outbreak of war, many members of Congress and their staffs rushed to enlist in the armed forces. Among them was Lyndon Johnson, a freshly commissioned lieutenant commander in the naval reserve, who was placed on active duty four days after the attack on Pearl Harbor. Five members of Rayburn's staff donned uniforms and headed overseas, overwhelming Rayburn with a mixture of pride and concern. Those who worked for him through the years were his children—surrogates for the family he never had. In forty-eight years, he hired fewer than forty people, and he loved them all. He never fired anyone. Almost never did anyone quit. It was as if his own sons were going off to war when the bulky Texan bid farewell to John Holton, Ray Roberts, Dan Inglish, Ted Wright, and William Cantrell. He did nothing to stop them. When Cantrell, the last to go, announced that he was heading overseas, the Speaker swallowed hard, then said, almost roughly, "Well, damn it, good-bye Bill, and good luck."[2]

Johnson's departure was even more emotionally wrenching for the Speaker. The two had become almost inseparable in the past two years. Their friendship had survived some particularly bumpy times during Johnson's unsuccessful senatorial campaign the previous summer, but those misunderstandings were quickly healed when the young congressman returned to Washington and plunged back into his work with no loss of enthusiasm. Rayburn was proud of Johnson's role in the draft-extension fight. The junior congressman loved the politics of a legislative battle— the strategy sessions and maneuvering for votes—and was becoming masterful at the game. He had little use, however, for the study and preparation needed for effective participation in debate. For the first time, Johnson had followed Rayburn's advice and done his homework. Although he was no orator, his well-rehearsed speech supporting the draft had been a highlight of the historic legislative battle.

A combination of misinterpreted motives, beginning with Rayburn's reluctance openly to endorse Johnson for the Senate, had led to the brief period of tension between the two friends. The Austin congressman had decided to join twenty-eight other Democrats in competing for a Senate vacancy that materialized suddenly when 65-year-old Morris Sheppard dropped dead of a stroke on April 9, 1941. Johnson saw the race as a rare chance to fulfill a long-held dream—a small-town boy's seemingly unattainable ambition to hold statewide office. As Texas director of the National Youth Administratin in the mid-1930s, he carefully built a network of personal and financial support across the state, a network he hoped one day would be the nucleus of a campaign organization. Rayburn had long known of Johnson's dream, and although he accepted it, he often counseled his talented but impetuous friend not to abandon a promising House career for what he viewed as the less satisfying life of a senator.

Sheppard's death opened a path to advancement much sooner than Johnson expected. Texas voters, then as now, tended to reelect their senators as long as they provided adequate service, protected a few sacred interests such as tax breaks for the oil industry, and remained reasonably free from scandal. Sheppard was first elected to the Senate to fill the vacancy created by the resignation of Joseph W. Bailey in 1913—the same year that Rayburn went to the House. The state's junior senator, Tom Connally, had served since 1928 and was still going strong.[3] Johnson believed that such an opportunity might not come again for years. Within hours, he had checked with his financial backers, won their approval, and set his campaign in motion.

The competition—led by Governor W. Lee "Pass the Biscuits, Pappy" O'Daniel, young Attorney General Gerald Mann, and Red-baiting Congressman Martin Dies—would be fierce.[4] But the young congressman had much in his favor. His long-nurtured ties to the huge Houston construction firm of Brown and Root and to Sid Richardson and other millionaire oilmen assured him virtually unlimited money. His old NYA network provided him a wealth of young, eager campaign volunteers. His widely publicized friendships with Roosevelt and Rayburn—his political "daddies"—gave him prestige and the aura of being destiny's candidate, advantages that money could not buy.

Running as an unabashed FDR supporter, as he had in three House campaigns, the Austin congressman had no trouble lining up ample financial backing and firing up his cadre of young supporters. A third leg of his campaign strategy—winning the President's open endorsement—proved more difficult. After his disastrous attempt to "purge" errant Democrats in 1938, Roosevelt vowed never again to intervene in intraparty elections. But he liked the young congressman who seemed so committed to the New Deal and who brought such fascinating Capitol Hill and Texas gossip to the Oval Office. Against the advice of some of his top aides, FDR offered his support. On April 22, the lanky Texan visited the President, then stood on the White

House steps to announce to an audience of reporters his Senate candidacy.

The final—potentially crucial—element of Johnson's strategy proved the most elusive. Getting Sam Rayburn to help in the campaign was important because of what he could do for Johnson in a critical section of Texas. Rayburn, so Johnson thought, held the key to skeptical, populist, rural inhabitants of northeast Texas. The area, which could be pivotal in a close race, was a part of Texas the Hill Country congressman never understood and felt he could never win on his own.

Northeast Texas was O'Daniel territory. The popular radio huckster prospered there in the late 1930s. His daily broadcasts of hillbilly music and folksy philosophy attracted a wide following—wide enough to send him to the statehouse as governor. And now, in all likelihood, it would propel him to the Senate as well. Also popular in Rayburn's area was Attorney General Mann. A young, sincere idealist with strong religious convictions, Mann was a local boy from nearby Sulphur Springs who had first brought glory to northeast Texas as a football star at Southern Methodist University. The fourth serious contender, Martin Dies, represented the First Congressional District, adjoining Rayburn's district on the east. Many Texas conservatives saw the demogogic rabble-rouser as their only shield from the menace of communism.

With Rayburn's open backing, Johnson and his advisers believed, Johnson could win the critical clump of counties lying between Dallas and the Oklahoma border. But for weeks Rayburn resisted. It was no lack of enthusiasm for Johnson that caused the Speaker to balk. He very much wanted his young, ambitious friend to succeed and had said as much—in private. But Rayburn had survived politically for nearly forty years by adhering to the basics, one of which was never to mix in other Democrats' campaigns, particularly if the candidate you favor is out of tune with your own constituents. "I find that people usually resent a man who has been nominated by them mixing up in other races," he said.[5] Only rarely had he stretched the point to help—discreetly—a particular candidate. He was ready to provide Johnson the same quiet assistance. Already, he had paved the way for Johnson to run as *the* New Deal candidate by pressuring Wright Patman out of the race. Patman, Rayburn's closest friend in Congress until Johnson came along, had long yearned to be in the Senate, where he might find a wider forum for his populist ideas. But Rayburn convinced him that if both he and Johnson ran, neither would have a chance. Patman himself admitted, "Lyndon can be financed, and it takes a lot of money to run for the Senate."[6] He swallowed his disappointment and stood aside. Had he run, splitting the vote of New Deal supporters, Johnson's cause would have been hopeless.

What Rayburn resisted—at least as long as possible—was publicly endorsing Johnson. His own instincts, backed by reports from his campaign sources in every Fourth District county, told him to stay out of the fight. He knew his people—he knew his involvement would gain Johnson few votes while alienating thousands of supporters of O'Daniel, Dies, Mann, and other candidates. Rayburn personally was tired of having to fight for re-election every two years and wanted nothing more than respite from the chronic opposition at home that dogged him even in the lofty position he now held. He had gone through a nasty campaign fight just the year before and did not want to stir up more trouble. But Johnson persisted. On May 29, with the election only a month away, he telegraphed campaign manager John Connally: "Call Rayburn today and ask him if he will release or permit you to release statement . . . to the effect that he is going to vote for and support me for senator. . . . Tell him this ought to be done today in order to help us get organized in North Texas."[7] There is no evidence that Connally followed through. In any case, Rayburn issued no such statement. Finally, with the election a week away, one of Johnson's chief benefactors, Austin publisher Charles E. Marsh, someone powerful enough in his own right not to be intimidated by the Speaker, fired off his own angry wire: "IF YOU DON'T SPEAK OR SEND MESSAGE BY SATURDAY NIGHT AT DENISON PLEASE DO NOT SPEAK AT ALL, AS I BELIEVE IT WILL BE POLITICALLY HARMFUL THE LAST WEEK. IT WILL BE INTERPRETED AS RELUCTANT, TARDY, AND POOR STATEMENT. YOUR POSITION, WHATEVER IT IS, ALREADY BECOMING UNIMPORTANT, BECAUSE TIMING COMING TOO SLOW TO BE EFFECTIVE."[8]

Few people—in or out of government—would have dared address Rayburn with such arrogance. But Marsh, partly in ignorance, partly in desperation, pulled it off. Two days later, the Speaker disclosed at his daily press conference that, "with malice toward none," he had cast his absentee ballot for Lyndon Johnson. Said the Speaker: "It appears to me we need another senator who will stand without fear, four-square with our program of total defense and victory; one who is in accord with our great Chief Executive and with the leadership in the Senate and in the House on issues, both foreign and domestic; one who is in step with our splendid delegation from Texas and not unfriendly to it. For these and other considerations . . . I have today cast my vote for Lyndon Johnson."[9] He still hoped he could help Johnson without alienating his own supporters, most of whom were strong for O'Daniel or Mann. He had delayed his public endorsement for two months—too long, in the opinion of many Johnson advisers, who viewed the Speaker's contribution as too little and too late to be of much help.

Hoping to squeeze all the benefit possible from the Speaker's press conference, the resourceful Johnson, his manager John Connally, or someone else in the candidate's Austin headquarters had Rayburn's remarks copied to a Western Union Telegraph blank to appear as if they had been received as a formal endorsement. The next day copies of the bogus wire addressed "to the people of Texas" flooded north Texas. Rayburn first learned of the deception when voters in his district began complaining about his intervention in the election. He was furious. All his efforts to stay in the background went down the drain. "You are correct in stating that someone in the [Johnson] headquarters was responsible," he testily told one of his constituents.[10] He was even more angry when friends informed him that strangers purporting to be on Rayburn's staff had swept through the district urging people to vote for Lyndon Johnson. Rayburn vowed to get to the bottom of the matter, but he never did. Apparently, he blamed overzealous Johnson workers, not the candidate.

The counting of election returns went on for days as the lead shifted back and forth between Johnson and O'Daniel amid charges of vote stealing on both sides. Johnson had run a strong race and established his future claim on statewide office. But he lost this election—by a scant 1,300 votes—to an opponent more experienced in ballot-box manipulation. As one Johnson supporter put it, "He [O'Daniel] stole more votes than we did, that's all." [11]

It took Rayburn a few days more to assess his own damage. Johnson was beaten badly in the Fourth Congressional District, winning less than a third of the total vote. In Fannin County, O'Daniel won over Johnson by a two-to-one margin. Rayburn's endorsement caused widespread resentment among voters—as Rayburn had feared—although the problem probably never was as serious as it seemed. "You are at this time in bad condition politically in Hunt County and other sections of your district on account of your subscription of $500 to the Johnson campaign fund, and for the oral and circulatory declarations coming from you for Johnson," wrote one key Rayburn supporter. "Your congressional district is composed of pure de American citizens, very little foreign element, who resent very much any dictation or influence from anyone elected by them, how and for whom they should vote for other offices, especially from Washington. . . . At this time sentiment is strong against you, and you should get busy from now on, and seek to overcome this." [12]

The issue, however, soon faded, although Rayburn's opponent in the 1942 Democratic primary, backwoods preacher George T. Balch, did his best to keep it alive. "When did he get to be your politician guardian? Why does he think he can tell you how to vote? Why did he join up with that bunch who came to Texas and spent millions of dollars trying to elect Lyndon Johnson over O'Daniel?" asked one scurrilous anti-Rayburn flyer. "In late years Sammy has outgrown his congressional pantaloons—or in other words, he has gotten TOO BIG FOR HIS BREECHES." The flyer continued:

One of his Dallas friends told us *very confidentially* that he was recently in Sam's bachelor apartment at Washington, and the guests all being hale fellows, well met, they threw a big party and after a while, when they were all "pretty well lit up," Sam drained his glass, fell over on the bed, rattled the ice in his glass and said, "Listen, fellows, did you know that I represent the driest district in Texas and here I am drunk as a fiddler's wench—I wonder what those old boys back home would think if they could see me?"[13]

Balch's outrageous attacks had little impact. Ignoring them, Rayburn disposed of the pesky preacher with ease in the July primary. Elsewhere, however, House Democrats were not so fortunate. Many faced an increasingly hostile electorate as the November elections approached. Most voters clearly were unhappy with Congress and with the Democratic management of the war. Everywhere were heard objections to price, wage, and rent controls, rationing, and the newly imposed 48-hour work week. The result: thirty-nine House Democrats were defeated in 1942, leaving a bare, five-seat majority for Rayburn's party. Bravely, if inaccurately, the Speaker labeled it "a victory." At least, he rationalized, the Democrats were still in control.

The Democrats could organize Congress, but they could not set national policy. Rayburn had lost his effective working majority. For the next two years, he would have to appeal for bipartisan cooperation, knowing full well that he would seldom get it. Even his vaunted patience, persuasiveness, and willingness to compromise could not sway members who felt that they had a mandate to oppose the administration. In the 78th Congress, the Republicans won more roll-call victories than did the Democrats and were able to amend noncontroversial legislation almost at will. Before the next elections, deaths reduced the Democratic majority in the House to two, causing some to wonder whether the party would maintain its majority for the remainder of the session and avoid a mid-term GOP takeover.

Compounding the problem, the proliferation of unpopular wartime agencies resulted in the election of a number of antibureaucracy Republicans and Democrats in 1942. Congressional investigations flourished, with frequent barrages directed at such unpopular targets as the Office of Price Administration and the War Production Board. Under constant fire from Capitol Hill, OPA Administrator Leon Henderson resigned in 1943; his harried replacement walked out a few months later. With the realignment of party strength, the facade of cooperation between the parties quickly crumbled, and domestic squabbling reminiscent of the prewar years reappeared. Republican Charles L. Gifford of Massachusetts spoke for many when he told the House that it was now necessary to "win the war from the New Deal."

For the Democratic majority to function under these circumstances, Rayburn believed, the relationship between the congressional leadership and the White House must be especially close and trusting. No tricks, no fancy dealing. On this score, he was personally satisfied that Roosevelt would live up to his promises. The weekly leadership meetings were helpful. "These are not blow-pulling sessions," the Texan told the House.[14] But he was not sure the cooperative spirit had filtered down to the departments and agencies. "Before determinations are reached or proposals are announced," he said, "those in positions of responsibility upon the Hill must be consulted. I trust and believe this will be done."

Rayburn had virtually no room to maneuver. The Republicans blocked him on one side, the increasingly hostile conservative southerners on the other. The troublesome Republican–southern Democratic coalition grew in strength, constituting, for all practical purposes, the real House majority in 1943 and 1944. It dealt House leaders one defeat after another. Significantly, it controlled the Committee on Rules, where two southern Democrats consistently voted with the four Republican members to keep administration bills from reaching the House floor. Still, under Rayburn's leadership, the House managed to function reasonably, if not spectacularly, well. Congress, the Speaker felt, met its major war obligations, including passage of such sensitive measures as wage and price controls and a law to include fathers in the draft. Its greatest failure, he believed, was its slowness to act on war appropriations and its constant harassment of the OPA and other unpopular war agencies.

Rayburn's own reputation grew as a result of his handling of the fractious House during this period. Noting his hard-won legislative successes, *Time* featured him on its September 27, 1943, cover. The quiet-talking Texan was hailed as "the great compromiser"—the best since Henry Clay—a notion he indignantly rejected. "I am not a compromiser," he bristled. "I'd rather be known as a persuader. I try to compromise by getting people to think my way."

In February 1944, Secretary of War Stimson asked to meet with Rayburn in his office on a matter of highest urgency.[15] With Stimson came Army Chief of Staff George Marshall and Vannevarr Bush, director of U.S. scientific research and development. Thus, Rayburn became the first member of Congress to be told of the government's highly secret, crash effort to build a new superweapon—an atomic bomb. German scientists had been experimenting with atomic energy for years and were believed on the verge of producing such an explosive device. Without informing Congress, in clear violation of the Constitution, the U.S. government since 1941 had secretly funded its own research—the Manhattan Project—by hiding the necessary funds in the budgets of other wartime programs. Now members of the House Committee on Appropriations were close to uncovering the deception. It was imperative, the secretary explained, that the secret be maintained.

Scientifically, it was all beyond Rayburn's comprehension. He could not visualize a weapon powerful enough to obliterate an entire city. But he grasped the bomb's importance to the war effort. And if the President wanted secrecy, that was good enough for him. Secrecy he would get. He was reasonably sure he could persuade the Appropriations chairman, cantankerous Clarence Cannon, to go along. He was less confident about the Republican leaders, who would have to be brought into the conspiracy. What about suspicious old John Tabor, the committee's ranking Republican? Rayburn summoned his friend House Minority Leader Joe Martin to the meeting. As Martin later told it:

> When I arrived I found that Rayburn was waiting with Stimson, Marshall, Bush and Representative McCormack. Marshall described the design of the bomb in some technical detail. Stimson said that if the Germans got this weapon first, they might win the war overnight. They told us that they would need an additional 1.6 billion dollars to manufacture the bomb. Because of the overriding necessity

for secrecy, they made the unique request that the money be provided without a trace of evidence as to how it would be spent. No more extraordinary request was ever made to leaders of the House of Representatives, the trustees of the people's money. . . . Like Rayburn and McCormack, I agreed to use my influence to obtain an inscrutable appropriation. . . . While Rayburn and McCormack went to work on Representative Cannon, I won the assent of John Tabor. Together we all slid the appropriation through the House without any breach of secrecy.[16]

Congress's role in the atomic project was pivotal and delicate. Leaders of both houses—the Senate leadership was informed in 1944—performed superbly in that they provided the money requested by the scientists while maintaining total secrecy. Whether they reneged on a higher responsibility to question the long-range implications of such a weapon is debatable. For a year and a half, eight House members, and later four senators, shared information so secret that not even the Vice-President was included. Ultimately, the conspiracy was joined by the press. One morning, Rayburn was stopped by a reporter who said he was puzzled by a large unexplained sum in the current defense appropriations bill. Did the Speaker know anything about it? "Son," replied Rayburn, "if you love your country, you'll forget whatever you've heard about that $800 million." Nothing about the project appeared in the press until after the bombs fell on Hiroshima and Nagasaki in August 1945.

Despite the cost and moral significance of the project, Rayburn and most others who shared the secret showed amazing lack of curiosity about it. Only Clarence Cannon balked when spending reached $2 billion. Cannon later said he had "great doubt as to the eventual success of the experiment. The news that the bomb had fallen was a great relief."[17] The charge, made forty years later, that Truman based his decision to drop the bomb in part on a need to show Congress results for the project's extraordinary secrecy and cost may be well founded. In Rayburn's case, he trusted the scientists and was awed by their expertise. He was uninterested in the weapon's scientific implications, but he seemed fully aware of its fearsome potential and of the government's intention to use it in the war. The scientists, to their credit, tried to keep the lawmakers informed. About fifteen months into the project, Dr. Bush invited the Speaker to a demonstration at the Oak Ridge, Tennessee, atomic laboratories. He declined. Recalled Rayburn: "I said, 'No, I wouldn't know anything about it. I would see a lot of buildings and pots and pans and jars that nobody could explain to me, but if you say you got it, it is all right.'"[18]

The year 1944 held much promise. Rayburn's power and prestige were soaring. He was highly regarded by Democrats and Republicans alike; and since his widely acclaimed "unity" speech, his public popularity was higher than ever. The war, at last, was going well—eventual victory seemed certain—and Congress, on the whole, had met its obligations. Roosevelt's political plans were still shrouded in secrecy, but whether or not FDR decided to seek a fourth term in 1944, Rayburn was a contender for the Vice- Presidency. With FDR's health in question and many insiders predicting he would not survive another term, the Vice-Presidency was the year's great prize. Deciding he would never have a better chance, Rayburn joined a crowded field of contenders that included Justice William O. Douglas and Senators James Byrnes, Alben Barkley, and Harry Truman.

The Texan already had been tagged as a favorite to replace the unpopular Henry Wallace, if FDR ran again, which seemed more and more likely. Wallace's views had shifted so far to the left of his party that only the most diehard New Dealers were still behind him. When Rayburn was named principal speaker at the party's Jackson Day dinner—a selection that implied Roosevelt's approval—Washington reporters nodded knowingly. The intent, they wrote, was to give Democratic leaders a close look at a top vice-presidential prospect. The Speaker, observed Texas newsman Bascom Timmons, "will be paraded before party wheel horses from every state." Rayburn's appeal to party leaders, added Frank R. Kent of the *Baltimore Sun*, was largely on his reputation for being "balanced and sensible" and "more of a Democrat and more of a conservative than other New Deal prospects." Such qualities appealed strongly to southern Democratic leaders searching for a candidate to pit against Wallace. They decided in February to support the Texan, although some loudly questioned his "southern" credentials.

Rayburn, despite later denials, was more than casually interested in the nomination—as his private correspondence proves. "Sam would like it very, very much," observed Joe Martin, "and his friends would like it."[19] But, always a realist, Rayburn was not misled by gossip. His age, his politically unstable home state, and his indispensability to Roosevelt as Speaker all were against him. "It is extremely doubtful that I will be nominated," he wrote, "and frankly, I do not think I will be."[20] Still, he decided it was worth a try.

With state and local Democratic organizations clamoring for a look at him, he agreed to speak in four major cities—Los Angeles, San Francisco, Chicago, and Detroit. Southern Californians turned out in record numbers to hear his familiar, plainspoken call for national unity in the war effort. At a Los Angeles press conference, he coyly dodged questions about his political intentions: "You do not seek that nomination. It is handed to you on a platter." In Chicago, Rayburn unveiled his proposal for postwar conversion of the national economy and announced his intention to create a select House committee to examine postwar problems. Again, he was on the front pages, this time not as the apostle of unity but as a forward-looking statesman, warning that America could win the war but lose the peace. His appearance before the austere Detroit Economic Club was a test of sorts. Businesspeople were concerned about his reputation—a legacy from his days as crusading chairman of the House Interstate and Foreign Commerce Committee—as an enemy of business. "I have come over here," he said, "to ask you not to be afraid of us . . ."

On February 2, Marshall McNeil of Scripps-Howard made his Groundhog Day prediction: FDR and Rayburn would lead the Democratic ticket in 1944. Correspondent Raymond P. Brandt of the *St. Louis Post-Dispatch* took a long look at the vice-presidential picture in March and found three serious contenders—Wallace, Rayburn, and Senator Harry Truman of Missouri. "Cold political calculations, the balancing of assets and liabilities, give Rayburn the edge," Brandt concluded. "If a second place man can attract voters, Rayburn would influence those who think Wallace is 'too far to the left,' those who want a Southerner on the ticket and those who think a 'persuader' like former Vice-President Garner would be a handy man to have in the Senate now and during the post-war years."

Rayburn faced a major obstacle: his southern background. As a states' rights, rural Texas congressman, he was automatically tainted among party liberals, who, despite his moderate-to-liberal voting record over the past thirty years, still doubted his commitment to what was then the Democratic mainstream. Many thought of him only as part of the southern power structure of very senior members that controlled the House.[21] To be taken seriously for the Vice-Presidency, he had to prove he was more than that. He had to dramatize his national outlook to impress the skeptics.

The opportunity came in early June, and from a most unlikely source. Crusty Howard W. Smith of Virginia picked that time to challenge the Speaker's leadership with a breathtakingly bold maneuver that could not be ignored or glossed over. Rayburn had to fight. Lean, tough, and smart, "Judge" Smith, one year younger than Rayburn, was ranking Democrat behind Chairman Adolph Sabath on the Rules Committee and leader of a coalition of conservative Democrats and Republicans that controlled the committee. He and Rayburn had generally gotten along, but it was understood that important legislation reached the House floor only at Smith's sufferance. Legislation about which the Judge felt strongly—civil rights and social-spending bills, for example—often died in his committee. He was especially feared and despised by liberals, who believed the Rules Committee dominated the House and that Smith, in certain areas, had become more powerful than the Speaker himself.

Smith also was chairman of a special committee to "investigate acts of executive agencies beyond the scope of their authority," which had been proposed by the Rules Committee and approved by the House over Rayburn's objection. Clearly anti-Roosevelt in tone, the panel had wide jurisdiction to "ride herd" over the bureaucrats. It became especially zealous in attacking the Office of Price Administration and the Works Progress Administration.

When the committee made a series of legislative recommendations involving wage and price controls, Rayburn quietly had them referred to the Committee on Banking and Currency, which had authority to propose legislation, while the Smith committee did not. Soon thereafter, Banking and Currency reported out a price-control bill that was primarily an extension of existing law. Missing were Smith's proposals for wage and rent controls.

When the bill came to the Rules Committee for a routine rule setting procedure for debate by the full House, the Judge was waiting. At his insistence, the committee promptly adopted a rule that permitted the Smith bill to be offered as an amendment to the Banking and Currency Committee's bill. The House, in other words, was being asked by the Rules Committee to consider a bill previously rejected by a legislative committee. The implications were far reaching: if the Rules Committee could change the content of this bill, it could similarly alter any future legislation. Never before had the Rules Committee gone so far.[22]

Smith knew that, by challenging their powers and prerogatives, he would be fighting all committee chairmen as well as the Speaker. Undeterred, he was willing to match his own prestige among southern conservatives against the Speaker's. He counted on strong Republican backing. When the rule came before the House for approval, prior to consideration of the bill itself, the Judge spoke briefly in its defense. His aim, he said, was not to challenge other committees but to bring before the members legislation he and others considered important. Then, grim-faced and determined, the Speaker left the rostrum to close the debate:

> The Committee on Rules was never set up to be a legislative committee. It is a committee on procedure. . . . I do not want to take away any of the rights of the Committee on Rules, and I do not want the Committee on Rules to take away the rights, prerogatives and privileges of other standing committees. . . . If we settle it like it should be

settled today, I think there will be an end to this trespassing of one committee in the House on the rights, prerogatives and privileges of other committees.[23]

Resoundingly, the House rejected Smith's rule. With a few softly spoken words, Rayburn crushed the wily Virginian's scheme. But Smith was not finished. There would be other encounters. It was just a skirmish in the mounting conflict between the two legislative giants—a battle ended only by Rayburn's death seventeen years later.

Liberals were deeply impressed. Rayburn "shattered a myth—the myth of invincibility which has hung over the Rules Committee for these many years," said the editors of *Progressive* magazine, who confessed that before the Rules fight they "knew little about this man Rayburn." The liberal *New Republic* asked Congressman Jerry Voorhis to tell its readers where Rayburn really stood in the political spectrum—no easy task. Wrote Voorhis: "Some of his views are conservative ones, but to call him a 'conservative' would not be accurate. He has supported the basic New Deal reforms, but he does not fit into the glib catch-phrases loosely used to catalogue men in public life."[24]

Meanwhile, Rayburn's bid for the Vice-Presidency was being undermined at home. Serious rifts in the Texas Democratic party, which first appeared in 1940, had grown steadily worse. By 1944, division between pro–and anti–New Dealers had hardened into definite alignments—two warring factions whose differing social and economic philosophies had driven them bitterly, irreconcilably apart.

Guided by a pervasive hatred for Roosevelt and his policies, wealthy Texas conservatives set out early in 1944 to buy control of the Texas Democratic party, the state's only major party. The financial backers were never all identified, but included oil independents such as Hugh Roy Cullen, Arch Rowan, and E. B. Germany as well as powerful representatives of the majors such as Hiram King of Sinclair Oil, Clint Smith of Humble Oil, R. A. Weinert of Socony-Vacuum, and, from faraway Philadelphia, Joseph Pew of Sun Oil. Gas and sulphur interests also were deeply involved.

United under the banner of the American Democratic National Committee, a national anti–New Deal group led by
FDR's former Secretary of War Harry Woodring, they dominated the Texas Democratic Convention, handpicked National
Convention delegates opposed to Roosevelt's renomination, and
approved a platform that, among other things, condemned the
"Communist-controlled New Deal" and called for "restoration
of the supremacy of the white race." The liberal minority, representing perhaps a third of the delegates, marched out of the convention, singing "The Eyes of Texas Are upon You." Reconven-
ing a rump session, they voted to send a competing delegation
to the National Convention in Chicago.

The "regular" State Convention adjourned without endorsing Rayburn for Vice-President. Sam "had been deliberately
murdered by the anti-Roosevelt leaders in Texas," said W. A.
Thomas.[25] The convention bolters, questioning Rayburn's liberal
purity, treated him only slightly better—voting after a short,
sharp fight to support him for Vice-President for one ballot as a
"courtesy." His hopes, dependent on strong support within his
home state, were dashed. The state party's failure, for the first
time since he entered Congress, even to name him a delegate to
the Chicago convention only added to the humiliation. "I had
no chance after the Texas convention did as they did," said a dejected Rayburn.[26] Wrote one Texas friend: "Every enemy you
have made I think was made in supporting the administration.
A small reward indeed you are getting."[27]

The prize that seemed within his grasp a few weeks earlier
was suddenly gone. As late as two days before the National
Convention, Rayburn claimed he was still on party chairman
Robert E. Hannegan's "list of men acceptable to President
Roosevelt." John McCormack wired that the Massachusetts
delegation had pledged its support to Rayburn. He urged the
Speaker to fight for the nomination in Chicago. Harry Truman,
whose speeches endorsing the Texan for Vice-President had
helped in the spring, said he went to Chicago to advance Rayburn's cause, not his own. Tom Clark, at Truman's urging, called
Rayburn from Chicago, insisting that he come. "You have to

be on the ground to get any support," Clark advised.[28] But Rayburn, in his heart, knew he had no chance. Even the timing of the National Convention seemed calculated against him. It opened July 19, three days before the Texas primary. The vice-presidential nominee would be picked the very day voters went to the polls in the Fourth Congressional District. Facing one of his toughest re-election challenges, Rayburn dared not leave his district in the crucial final hours of the campaign. Disappointed but philosophical, he stayed behind, after urging other Democratic leaders from his area to go to Chicago and help swing the nomination to Harry Truman.

Two candidates filed against Rayburn in the July primary. One was George Balch, the lightweight preacher trounced by Rayburn two years earlier. The other was 32-year-old State Senator Grover Cleveland Morris of Greenville. As a legislator, Morris had gained statewide attention by successfully blocking Pappy O'Daniel's proposed sales tax. He was popular, attractive, brilliant, well connected—a worthy challenger indeed. Rayburn sized up Morris's lavishly financed campaign and decided that somebody must really want a new congressman for the Fourth District. "I doubt if there is another district in the United States where they could find a man who would run against the Speaker of the House of Representatives in a primary, whether he be Republican or Democrat," he wrote. "These interests outside of the district hate Roosevelt and are saying that if they could defeat me as a leader in the Democratic primary in an overwhelmingly Democratic district that would assure them the defeat of Roosevelt in November by showing that he is unpopular even in Democratic strongholds."[29]

Buoyed by their success in capturing the State Convention in May, the anti-Roosevelt faction—the so-called Texas Regulars—focused on a new goal: defeating the handful of Texas congressmen they considered too liberal, too cozy with the President. Their main targets were Wright Patman of Texarkana, Lyndon Johnson of Austin, and the big prize—the Speaker of the House. Defeating Rayburn would send a warning to other members of Congress who would support and cooperate with the New Deal. Cash to fuel the campaign of Rayburn's opponent poured in from the conservative strongholds of Dallas and Houston. A group calling itself the Committee for Constitutional Action paid for radio time, special mailings, and other campaign expenditures aimed against the three congressmen.[30] Exact amounts were never known, but Rayburn later learned that $56,000—a huge sum in those days—had been raised in Dallas alone. "More money was spent in that election," he later asserted, "than in the past 30 years combined."[31]

Encouraged by the *Dallas News*—"Rayburn is trailing," read one headline—and other anti-Rayburn newspapers, Morris waged a tireless campaign. He ridiculed the Speaker's effectiveness as a national leader and belittled his ability to win federal projects for the district. In rebuttal, Rayburn dedicated the $54-million Denison Dam a few days before the election. The challenger snidely referred to Rayburn's "haughty voice and personal appearance" and to his lifelong single status "with a brief interlude of a few weeks."[32] He reminded voters of the incumbent's age—62—and his extraordinarily long tenure in office. "Does it not seem," Morris asked, "that in thirty-two years, the congressman from the Fourth District has become tired of representing his people? . . . How long has it been since the present congressman has contacted you?"[33] Rayburn, after years of mingling with the rich and powerful, had lost touch with the simple folk of north Texas, Morris and his supporters argued. Otherwise, why did he not fight harder to protect north Texas values? Why did he remain silent in the Speaker's chair and not use his vaunted influence to block creation of the Fair Employment Practices Commission, which was designed to remove racial discrimination in hiring in essential industry? "You probably do not know that the FEPC is 60 percent Negro controlled, or. . . . that in many cases throughout the nation, Negro executives are working white girls as their secretaries," one pro-Morris newspaper added.[34]

Through all this, Rayburn remained in Washington, partly because Congress was still in session, partly because he was getting bad advice from his well-meaning but politically naive brother-in-law, W. A. Thomas. "The failure of your opponent to arouse enthusiasm anywhere seems to make it advisable to delay aggressive action on our part," Thomas wrote in May.[35] Thomas misread the situation. In fact, Morris was gaining steadily. By early June, Rayburn was getting disturbing reports from other, more astute observers throughout the district. One was from Lee Simmons, his top organizer in Sherman:

> The most damaging thing we have is on the negro preju-
> dice caused by the FEPC. Morris keeps bearing down on
> that, and there is not much defense we can make when the
> fellow says that if Rayburn was not a "rubber stamp" for
> the President he would have had something to say against
> it. . . . I know and you know there are bigger things with
> which you are concerned but you would be surprised at the
> little things that cause the prejudice of many folks in times
> like these. I am not criticizing you, but feel that I should
> give you this information in order that you may know the
> situation before you get home.[36]

The election was less than two weeks away when Rayburn did come home. Blitzing the district, with handshaking stops at every country crossroads and speeches at every town square, he never mentioned his opponents. He talked mainly about the war, holding out the prospect that the recent invasion of Europe put victory in sight, and stuck to tried and true campaign themes. He recited his record, recalling life in north Texas before the New Deal—"Don't Go Back to 5-Cent Cotton"—and allaying fears that Washington favored labor over farmers. His efforts to keep the campaign on a high level were not always successful. Occasionally, Rayburn's supporters, acting against his wishes, responded to Morris's bitter, slurring attacks—one group bought newspaper ads to question why this strapping young specimen of a man was not in uniform.[37] That tactic was quickly dropped when Morris fired back a reminder that Rayburn had been single and healthy in World War I but had not served.

Though aging and seemingly losing touch with the district's younger voters, Rayburn's organization—led by G. C. Harris in Hunt County, Lee Simmons in Grayson County, and the faithful Judge H. A. Cunningham in Fannin County—rallied for one more campaign. Many of Rayburn's friends, who had kept his fences up at home while he fought the battles in Washington, were either dead or too tired to fight again. "Last night we had a meeting in my office with several of your friends in attendance," G. C. Harris wrote in June. "The attendance was not as good as I had hoped for, but several were here."[38]

Working with what volunteer assistance they could round up, the Rayburn organization did what it had been doing in campaigns for thirty years: it sent word into the small towns and crossroads communities throughout the district that Sam needed help. Newspaper and radio advertising was purchased in Rayburn's behalf by local supporters. "As far as I know, we never spent a cent in Rains County," said one key Rayburn worker. "We never raised any money and never spent any money. We just by telephone and by word of mouth and by other means got people to vote."[39] Large families of known Rayburn supporters were asked to lobby their friends and be sure everybody voted. Special appeals went out to country editors, judges, ministers, bankers, and other community leaders. Farmers were reminded of the grim days of 5-cent cotton and of life before REA, farm-to-market roads, soil conservation, and other programs that bore Rayburn's imprint. Politically appointed rural postmasters and mail carriers pointedly were reminded to whom they owed their jobs. Merchants heard repeated references to Rayburn's role in bringing to the area the Denison Dam, a series of outstanding recreational lakes, four military air bases, and a scattering of National Guard armories, hospitals, and veterans' facilities. It was stressed over and over that the Fourth District always got its share of federal programs—and more. Just recently, when wartime labor shortages threatened local farm production, Rayburn had seen to it that a German prisoner-of-war camp was located in Kaufman County. The prisoners were put to work, saving 2,000 acres of cotton.[40]

Going into the election, Rayburn and his friends thought defeat was a distinct possibility. The final outcome was not really close. Rayburn polled 24,507 votes to Morris's 18,736 and Balch's 933. Of the district's seven counties, Rayburn carried four, Morris three. It may not have been Rayburn's closest race, remarked the *Commerce Journal*, "but it was the dirtiest."

In Chicago, the Democrats nominated FDR again. Roosevelt told the delegates he would accept either William O. Douglas or Harry Truman as a replacement for Vice-President Wallace. He never seriously considered Rayburn. "I don't want Sam Rayburn," he remarked to Treasury Secretary Henry Morganthau, Jr. He told Lyndon Johnson that Rayburn lacked a world viewpoint, having never traveled outside of North America, and that labor would never accept him.[41] Besides, as Speaker, his leadership would be needed in the House when the administration presented its postwar legislative program for enactment. Shortly before the convention, Rayburn was told he was out of the running. He learned on the day of the Texas primary that the nomination had gone instead to his old friend Harry Truman.

Roosevelt, tired and ailing, won his fourth term in November in the closest presidential race—in terms of the popular vote—since 1916. In Texas, Roosevelt crushed Republican Thomas E. Dewey by a four-to-one margin. Earlier doubts that the state's presidential electors would support the popular winner dissolved when loyal Democrats, led by Alvin Wirtz, recaptured party control in September. In Congress, the Democrats retained a slim Senate majority, while gaining thirty-six House seats. Rayburn was delighted and relieved. "The majority of more than 50 in the House will make my work easier," he said, "and I think we will move along without any halts."[42]

Renewed optimism gripped Washington as 1945 began. It promised to be an eventful year. The Democrats firmly controlled Congress. Political appointees could see four more years of job security ahead. In Europe, the allies were drawing a tight ring around Hitler's Germany; in the Pacific, U.S. Marines were advancing rapidly toward a final showdown with Japan. The war would be over in a year, according to most predictions. Rayburn, after thirty-three years in Washington, celebrated by hosting his first large party—a gala at the Hotel Carleton for four hundred of his closest friends and colleagues.

One cloud marred the horizon. Roosevelt's failing health had been a whispered conversational topic for months. Age and the heavy strains of the past dozen years had sapped the powerful man's strength until, some thought, he was living from day to day on little more than an indomitable will to see the war to a successful end. He had less heart for a good fight, less time for friends and staff. In 1945, he declined to deliver his State of the Union message personally. Many in Washington, doubting whether the President would serve out his term, found their thoughts turning more and more to the new Vice-President— the owlish little man from Missouri about whom little was known. On April 11, Rayburn vowed to "have a little talk with Harry." He remarked to friends, "I've got a feeling Roosevelt's not going to be with us much longer . . . and Harry's got to be ready for it."

15

Gains and Losses

Almost daily, after the formal work of the House was done, Rayburn would wind his way down to his private hideaway on the Capitol's ground floor, beneath the Speaker's Lobby. There, with a few trusted friends and occasional outside visitors, he would spend a relaxing hour or two, talking politics, reminiscing, philosophizing, mapping strategy, and sipping whiskey. From key lieutenants, mostly young men as eager and ambitious as he had been thirty years earlier, he would glean all the latest news and gossip. This was Rayburn's "Board of Education," as it was widely known, an important part of his life and a vital tool of his leadership.

Rayburn never called it that. It was always "the little room," or simply "downstairs." "You coming downstairs tonight?" he would say. The sessions were modeled after the old "Bureau of Education" presided over by political opposites Jack Garner and Nicholas Longworth in the 1920s. But while the "Bureau" stressed bipartisan fellowship, the "Board" was more attuned to the needs and interests of the Democratic leadership. Inside Rayburn's little room, strategy could be discussed, information exchanged, politics analyzed, Texas news traded. Occasionally, he would invite promising freshmen as a compliment—a flattering gesture to promote his support in the House. Nearly everyone in the federal establishment knew of the Board of Education, and many craved an invitation to "strike a blow for liberty" with the Speaker and his intimates. Lyndon Johnson was obsessed with getting an invitation when he first arrived in 1937. But the harder the young lawmaker hinted, the more he was ignored by the majority leader. Finally, he turned to Texas newsman Cecil Dickson to find out why he could not get through the door of the little room. "What about this guy Johnson?" Dickson asked Rayburn one day.

"He hasn't shown me anything," Rayburn replied. Not until later, after Johnson began taking a more active role in floor debate, was he was finally invited. "Your boy did pretty good today," Rayburn told Dickson. "Bring him around sometime."[1]

"Regular" attendees were few; guests came only if invited by Rayburn or someone of the stature of Wright Patman or—later—Lyndon Johnson. Patman, a master at wrangling special treatment, got his own key in the late 1930s. Not to be outdone, Johnson also persuaded Rayburn give him a key when he eventually became a regular. A typical gathering in the mid-1940s might include Patman, Johnson, and Eugene Worley of Texas, Lyle Boren of Oklahoma, Eugene Cox of Georgia, newsman Dickson, and House Parliamentarian Lewis Deschler.

Deschler, so painfully shy that he blushed when he talked, first served under Speaker Longworth. He was a Republican, but his knowledge of the House's complex procedural rules was so extensive and his loyalty so unquestioned that he was kept on as parliamentarian by succeeding Speakers until his retirement in 1975.[2] Garner, as Speaker, had to fight off dissidents in his own party who wanted Deschler replaced by a Democrat. When Rayburn became Speaker, Garner's first advice was to retain Deschler and keep him by his side at all times. "He'll be your good right arm," said Garner.[3] It was perhaps the best advice Rayburn ever got from the old warrior. Proving his competence and loyalty many times over, Deschler was there to back Rayburn up whenever he ruled on a controversial issue. His unsurpassed knowledge of the House's 11,000 rules and precedents, including many not formally recorded, was a great source of the Speaker's power. From Longworth to Carl Albert, no Speaker served by

Deschler was ever overruled by action of the House. As one of Rayburn's most trusted advisers, he came to the little room almost every evening. He, too, was proud of having his own key.

Gene Cox was a particularly unusual member of the clan. Others could not fathom why Rayburn tolerated him and seemed to like having him around. Cox was uncouth, foul-mouthed, belligerent. He opposed every piece of progressive Democratic legislation and suffered mightily through the New Deal. He was forever losing his temper, and once he got into a fistfight on the House floor with doddering Adolph Sabath. Rayburn frequently would call him up to the Speaker's rostrum and talk him out of making some outrageous speech. Cox was, at best, a pain to have around. But, from the Texan's standpoint, he was valuable for two reasons: 1. totally loyal, he seemed almost to worship Rayburn; 2. he was a ranking member of the Rules Committee, and anytime Rayburn needed help in getting a bill out of that balky panel, Cox provided it, no matter how distasteful it was to him. "Mr. Speaker, I can't vote for that bill. That's a terrible bill. Don't make me do it," he would plead. But, in the end, he did whatever Rayburn wanted until his death in 1952.

John McCormack, who had taken an oath of abstinence as a youth and had never tasted liquor, would sometimes drop by briefly to trade political notes. Another floating member, junior Congressman Clinton Anderson of New Mexico, once described a typical session:

> We rarely discussed business. There was a lot of laughing and fooling around. Cox and I often played bridge and sometimes a few of us would go into an inner room for a few hands of poker. Rayburn himself never played cards, but he liked to drink—bourbon and branch water usually—and after two or three drinks or more, we'd often go downtown to a Chinese restaurant to eat. Rayburn loved Chinese food. But whatever we did, he was acknowledged to be the boss, to whom we all deferred.[4]

Rayburn made the rules, dominated the conversation. Whiskey loosened tongues and kept conversation flowing, but excessive drinking was unacceptable, as were off-color stories and those ridiculing human frailties. Always conscientious of how these conversations might sound if they became public, the Speaker would quickly set straight any newcomer who got out of line. "We don't talk about that down here," he might say icily. Yet, on rare occasions, Rayburn unpredictably would repeat a vulgar story that seemed especially humorous to him. Another cardinal rule: anything discussed in the room was strictly grave-yard. All knew that to violate this rule was to incur the great risk of being forever unwelcome. Like Garner, Rayburn frequently invited trusted reporters to the little room. He had no qualms about discussing the most intimate House business in their presence, and if any reporter ever violated his rule of secrecy, he never learned of it.

The hideaway, small by Capitol standards, measured twelve by twenty feet. A high, ornately decorated ceiling was the sole remaining evidence of its impressive beginning as a House committee room. For many decades, it had been assigned to the Speaker for whatever use he wanted. John and Ettie Garner practically lived in it in the early 1930s. It proved ideal for Garner's afternoon naps and his taste for Mrs. Garner's home cooking. He often went there for lunch that she prepared on a stove installed especially for him.[5] Custody of the room eventually fell to Speaker Bankhead, who found no need for it. When Rayburn, then majority leader, mentioned his desire to use it as a hideaway, Bankhead readily handed over the keys.

Rayburn immediately sought to make the room homey. He added a few pictures, a frayed Oriental carpet, and some well-worn furniture he had brought up from the Capitol storeroom. At the room's west end, he placed two flags on stanchions—Old Glory and the Lone Star banner carried by the Texas delegation in the 1932 Democratic National Convention. A massive glass cabinet on the opposite wall he filled with perhaps fifty photos, most of them autographed. Later he hung in a recess on the east wall the official Speaker's portrait of himself by Douglas Chan-dor.[6] Scattered about on other walls were framed political cartoons by Rayburn's favorite cartoonist, Cliff Berryman of the *Washington Evening Star*. A large refrigerator, concealed in a veneer box, was installed at the room's east end. In a corner, behind and to the left of Rayburn's desk, a small sink served as a semipublic urinal for some of America's most famous political figures.[7]

The Speaker sat at a long mahogany desk whose drawers were crammed with bottles of Scotch and bourbon—usually Haig and Haig and Virginia Gentleman. Lyndon Johnson, as his tastes and pretensions grew more refined, scornfully brought his own Cutty Sark and stashed it in a bottom drawer. Waiters from the House restaurant each day would provide fresh supplies of seltzer and ice water for mixes. At the end of a long day, tired bodies found comfort on the long leather couch or in big, well-worn "Turkish" leather chairs around Rayburn's desk. There were eight chairs in all, including several straight-backed ones. Leaning forward in an oversized swivel chair, elbows on the desk, Rayburn talked, listened, traded news, and reminisced about Texas or Tennessee or great historic figures or dramatic events in congressional history. Here, surrounded by men he trusted and enjoyed, he was as happy as a man could be in a home away from home.

Rayburn presided, more or less, but mostly he listened. Gathering bits and pieces of information, he gauged the mood of the House and learned what really was on members' minds. Casually, and without making a major point of conveying information, friends brought him the cream of the day's news, conversations, and rumor. He tucked all of it away in his retentive mind. "I always keep him informed, usually without asking him to say yes or no," explained Congressman Olin Teague in 1957. "But he likes to know what's going on, and often I refrain from asking his opinion so as not to put him on the spot."[8] Congressman Frank Ikard, a "regular" in the 1950s, thought Rayburn and later Lyndon Johnson "had the two best intelligence systems ever devised by the human mind." Noted Ikard: "If somebody was having trouble, of whatever kind, Rayburn knew about it."[9] (Dr. George W. Calver, the House physician, also helped Rayburn keep abreast of members' health through regular private briefings.) Realism and the art of the possible reigned in the little room. Compromises were struck and opposing factions brought together. Nose counts were analyzed and plans made

for dealing with Democrats who were not "right" on a particular issue.

Typically, the sessions broke up around 7 o'clock. Married
men wandered home to their families, leaving Rayburn and perhaps a straggler or two to close up. Occasionally the stragglers
piled into the Speaker's limousine, and they all went to dinner,
often at Billy Martin's Carriage House in Georgetown. "Let me
know if you hear anything," Rayburn would call out as they
broke up for the evening.

About 3 o'clock on the afternoon of April 12, 1945, Rayburn
telephoned Harry Truman. "Come over," he said, "and let's have
a visit." The Vice-President, not burdened with excessive responsibility under Roosevelt, was presiding over the Senate that
day. He savored the prospect of joining Rayburn and the boys
later for "a libation." Shortly before 5 P.M., he adjourned the
Senate and, eluding his Secret Service guards, strolled through
the Rotunda and down the stairs to Rayburn's little room on the
other side of the Capitol. The Speaker was already there.[10]
"Steve Early wants you to call him right away," Rayburn said.
Truman mixed a drink, put it down, and dialed the President's
press secretary at the White House. "This is the V.P.," he said.[11]

Early spoke in a strained voice, "Please come right down, and
come through the main Pennsylvania Avenue entrance." It struck
him as a strange request, Truman later said. He normally entered
through the east gate. His face suddenly went pale. "Jesus Christ
and General Jackson," he muttered, hanging up the phone and
reaching for his broad-brimmed white hat. He didn't know why,
but he was wanted at the White House right away, the Vice-
President told Rayburn. As Truman later explained:

> What I really thought was this: Bishop Atwood, the for-
> mer Episcopal bishop of Arizona, had died and was to be
> buried in Washington. I knew Roosevelt was an honorary
> pallbearer. I thought he probably had come back up here
> for the funeral and wanted to see me before he went back to
> Warm Springs. I walked back through the basement of the
> Capitol to get my car. It was the only time while I was

Vice-President that I needed the Secret Service men and they weren't there.[12]

Lyndon Johnson arrived as Truman was leaving. The telephone rang again. Rayburn answered. "Uh-huh, uh-huh, uh-huh," he nodded, then hung up. "The President is dead," he said to no one in particular, and went limp in the chair.

William S. White, a reporter for the *New York Times*, also had been invited to the little room that afternoon. As he strolled idly through the unlit House corridor, he noticed a slim, white-hatted figure hurrying briskly in the opposite direction. Turning the corner, he saw the tall frame of Lyndon Johnson standing in the darkness outside the hideaway. Johnson's black hair was mussed, his necktie was askew, and, as the reporter later described the young congressman, "he looked, in fact, very much like a man who had had far too much to drink, though this was not the case at all."[13]

"He's dead, he's dead," Johnson sobbed, holding out both hands to White and stepping out of the gloom. "He was always like a daddy to me." In the little room, Rayburn sat alone, crying softly in the dark. "His heavy and nearly immobile face was still in the shadows and the only movement upon it were the small and barely visible tears," White observed. No one had thought to turn on the lights.

Rayburn spoke slowly in short phrases as though talking to himself: "Now the sons of bitches will start trying to dance all over his grave. Well, by God, let them try." Someone flicked a light switch, bringing him back to the present. The press would want a statement. He wheeled over an old typewriter and, using one stubby finger, tried to peck out words that expressed his feelings. He soon gave up on the typewriter. Eventually, he dictated these words to one of John McCormack's secretaries: "We know not how to interpret God—in the way he performs. The world has lost one of the great men of all time. President Roosevelt's passing will shock and sadden good people everywhere. The American nation has been well led in every crisis. In Harry Truman we have a leader in whom I have complete confidence."[14]

Rayburn's love for Roosevelt did not come easy. Roosevelt had

an intellectual vanity—a belief that he was smarter than any of
his associates—that made it hard for anyone, especially someone as lacking in arrogance and notions of self-importance as
Rayburn, to feel really close to him. He treated Cabinet members like children. He was devious. As Tommy Corcoran observed: "Frankie grew up in New York politics. His was a slick
city world, an aristocratic world—not the kind of world Rayburn knew. Frankie would change his mind every fifteen minutes. He would lie. He just wasn't as honest as Sam was accustomed to, and Sam couldn't get used to it."[15]

But Roosevelt had other qualities that evoked Rayburn's great
admiration. He was a genius at politics. He was courageous. He
loved his country. He had imagination. "When he talked of the
little man, his eye really sparkled," Rayburn noted many times.
Though far from perfect, FDR was a figure bigger than life who
took America from the brink of ruin to renewed vigor; when he
died, Rayburn knew America had lost something—a towering
leader with qualities rare in the nation's history. His sorrow was
more for the country than for the man, a loss for America rather
than a loss for Rayburn.

The telephone rang again. It was Truman, apparently unaware
that the news had already reached the little room. "Sam," he
said, "you better finish that libation I left. I am President of the
United States. You better come on down here."[16]

Rayburn anticipated Roosevelt's death, but when it came, he
was unprepared. The death of a member of his family or an associate always hit him hard. Indeed, few Americans knew how
to accept FDR's passing. Along with other Democratic leaders,
Rayburn had toiled for twelve years in the great man's shadow.
Perhaps they had all leaned on him too much, demanded too
much, shared with him the exhilarating victories but left him
lonely in defeat. Who now would replace him? "It is terrible to
lose President Roosevelt," Rayburn wrote shortly after the funeral, "but sometime people are fortunate to die at the height of
their career."[17] A year later, in House ceremonies commemorating the first anniversary of FDR's death, Rayburn summarized
his assessment of the President who had had the greatest impact
on his own life:

Franklin D. Roosevelt will go down in impartial history standing along side of Washington, Jefferson, Jackson, Lincoln, Theodore Roosevelt, Cleveland and Wilson. There are mountain peaks, there are valleys, and there are hills in the history of every country and every age. Franklin D. Roosevelt will be known as one of the mountain peaks of the United States of America and of the civilized world as long as history is recorded.[18]

Truman, unprepared for the task of running the country, candidly sought the advice and counsel of leading Democrats. He leaned heavily on Rayburn at first. To him, it seemed natural to turn to the Speaker—his friend from congressional days, a humble, self-made, honest man who viewed problems from much the same perspective as himself. "Harry—Mr. President—we are going to stand by you," Rayburn had told the shaken chief executive after the brief swearing-in ceremony at the White House. Rayburn's early confidence in Truman, when others were doubting his leadership capacity, is noteworthy. "It is my belief that Mr. Truman is going to make good," he wrote a constituent. "I am going to help him every way I can to make the best President possible. He is a good, sound, honest man."[19]

The new President and his burdens weighed heavily on Rayburn as he left the White House on the Thursday evening of the swearing-in. All day Friday and through the weekend, his mind dwelled on his lonely friend and how unprepared he was for such high responsibilities. "I wanted to help the fellow," he later recalled. Monday morning, Rayburn telephoned the White House and asked to see the President. It seemed unnatural to address his old friend as "Mr. President," but Rayburn said, "You are not 'Harry' to me any more. I am not going to call any President by his first name."[20] Then he got to the point:

I haven't got a thing in the world to ask of you. I have come down here to talk to you about you. You have got many great hazards, and one of them is in this White House. I have been watching this thing a long time. I have seen people in the White House try to build a fence around the White House and keep the very people away from the President that he should see. That is one of your hazards. The special interests and the sycophants will stand in the rain a week to see you and will treat you like a king. They'll come sliding in and tell you're the greatest man alive—but you know and I know you ain't.[21]

Despite Rayburn's best intentions, he soon became the first person in history to address a President by his first name over nationwide radio. It happened at Truman's first appearance before a Joint Session. The President was understandably nervous as he stood before the wildly cheering assemblage. Rayburn was nervous, too, as he had been the first time he introduced Roosevelt in 1941. When the applause died, Truman did precisely what FDR had done—he launched into his speech before being introduced. This time, the Speaker would have none of it. Leaning within range of the microphones, he whispered, "Just a moment, let me present you, Harry, will you?"

"Sure," a surprised Truman replied, to the amusement of millions of radio listeners.

"Frankly, I did not just exactly intend to say 'Harry,'" Rayburn later explained. "But I have been so used to calling him that over the years that it just came out anyway."[22]

Reaching out for all the help he could get, the new President was drawn closer to the plain-talking Texan. He could depend on Rayburn to give him the facts with the bark off. As Truman later recalled: "We'd get together on what had to be done, then try to do it. When we made an agreement he would stand pat on it and so would I. We never tried to put each other in the hole. When we had a meeting neither of us would give out statements that might put the other on the spot. We both had the same thing in mind—to make the government proceed. . . . Sam and Fred Vinson and Alben Barkley and myself and some of the others would get together and compare notes on people, and it wouldn't take us long to figure out who the real shitasses were."[23] Eventually, as Truman's interest in domestic affairs waned and he turned more and more to demanding foreign problems—matters outside Rayburn's range of interest and knowledge—the President leaned less on the Texan for advice. But Rayburn remained the totally loyal soldier, supporting the President, often even when they disagreed, which was not infrequent as time went on.

At a White House reception for the regent of Iraq, Truman introduced the Speaker as "probably the most influential man in the United States, next to the President." Rayburn's great influence in the new administration was freely accepted by Washington officials and the press. Few were surprised by the President's casual, unorthodox invitation to Rayburn and the Senate president *pro tempore*, Kenneth McKellar of Tennessee, to attend Cabinet meetings. Both declined. "Even if the changing balances of power in the government raise the Speakership to a prestige it hasn't enjoyed in years," wrote newspaper correspondent Jack Stinnett, "it won't change Sam Rayburn."

On June 19, Truman left Washington for the first time as President to attend the final session of the United Nations conference in San Francisco. Before going, he asked Congress to revise the 60-year-old presidential succession law. His own succession had left the Vice-Presidency vacant, and he was concerned about the uncertainties that could result in the event of his own death or disability. Next in the succession order, under existing law, was Secretary of State Edward R. Stettinius, who commanded little respect on Capitol Hill and who might have found resistance in assuming the reins of power. Truman also believed that the Presidency should be held only by elected officials. His proposal: put the Speaker next behind the Vice-President in the succession order, followed by the president *pro tempore* of the Senate. He argued: "The Speaker of the House of Representatives, who is elected in his own district, is also elected to be the presiding office of the House by a vote of all the representatives of all the people of the country. As a result, I believe that the Speaker is the officer in the federal government whose selection next to that of the President and the Vice President can be most accurately said to stem from the people themselves."[24]

Truman wanted a new succession law before he departed on his first trip abroad—a "Big Three" conference in Berlin. He underestimated the opposition. On June 29, the measure passed the House by a resounding voice vote, the members adding cheers for Rayburn at the end of a short debate. But upon reaching the Senate, the bill stopped dead. Some senators had constitutional qualms; others simply wanted no part of legislation that would boost House prestige. Although Rayburn refused to lift a finger to expedite the measure, he watched it closely. "How much pressure President Truman is going to put on the Senate, I do not know," he confided to a friend. "But it is going to take every bit he has and then he may fail. They [senators] have all sort of objections, especially some of the fellows who were sent over to the Senate from the House. They seem to have more jealousy toward the House than some who never served in the House."[25] The Senate was still sitting on the bill when the 79th Congress adjourned *sine die* in 1946.

The allied victory in Europe on May 8, 1945, followed by Japan's surrender on August 15, brought new problems and challenges. "Now that the war is over," the Speaker said in a speech in Texas, "we must be willing to exert force to the limit to keep the peace. And if it takes an international army to do it, I'm in favor of my country contributing its share of the manpower."[26] For the first time, Rayburn talked of retirement. He told a Denison audience that he hoped to remain in Congress until he had "completed the task of peace," then return to Bonham to live. "I expect to lay aside my responsibilities voluntarily, and not involuntarily," he added.

More than ever, Rayburn delighted in the days spent at his modest ranch near Ivanhoe. There he could escape the pressures of his office and the incessant clamor of people he did not know. "These water tanks, pastures and ponies make mighty good recreation," he told his county agent, Valton Young. "I always keep my body in condition through moderate exercise, and no type of exercise such as cutting wood, riding a horse or working the hay makes my muscles the least bit sore."[27] He liked to sit outside and chat in the cool of an evening with his foreman and others who dropped by. Occasionally, he joined in a game of dominoes or "42," a game his brother-in-law, W. A. Thomas, claimed to have invented; but Rayburn played badly and was an ungraceful loser.

He sometimes spent weekends at the nearby ranches and camps of friends. Accompanied by a Rayburn brother or two, and once by county agent Young, he would drive down dusty Texas roads "at a rate of speed," Young later noted, "at which he can observe everything as he travels." (Not a good driver, Rayburn never learned to back up a car skillfully or to park parallel.) He especially enjoyed the hospitality of Major B. S. Graham, whose Lazy Eight Ranch spread across the foothills of the Arbuckle Mountains near Sulphur, Oklahoma. After a big country meal, the men would sit in rustic yard chairs under a full moon, their discussions ranging from ranching to world affairs. "He is never more buoyant than when among people who look upon any kind of useful work as elevating and not degrading," Young observed.[28]

It was smart politics for a congressman whose constituents were largely rural to promote the interests of farmers and agriculture, but Rayburn got more out of it than just political advantage. His passions and sympathies for rural life ran deep. "The teachings of the farm and the farmers' understanding of the wonders of the soil, the goodness of people and the great power of prayer and humility—those things have been my guiding principles in all that I have done on down through life," he declared in a speech in 1948. On the House floor or in the legislative drafting rooms, he was always quick to defend those who, like himself, felt a closeness to the soil.

An example was a bill providing federal aid for highways, which came before Congress in 1944. One afternoon William Robinson of Utah, chairman of the committee overseeing roads and highways, stopped by the Speaker's office to discuss scheduling the measure for debate. Wright Patman was present:

At once, Rayburn asked what was contained in the bill for country roads. Robinson replied that at present nothing had been definitely designated, but it was expected that a part of the authorized funds would be spent on secondary roads. Mr. Sam replied without hesitation and with firm conviction in his voice that the bill should be returned to the committee. "I want you to take that bill back and bring it out with at least 30 percent of that money to go to farm-to-market roads," he said. "I feel very strongly about that."[29]

Robinson complied; the bill was scheduled and quickly passed. "I think that these secondary highways are very important to our folks," Rayburn told John S. Redditt of the Texas State Highway Commission. "I feared, in the future, that if young men were not given the comforts and conveniences of rural electrification and all-weather roads then it was going to be pretty hard to keep them down on the farm." To another friend, he wrote: "When we can get all the farm houses on all-weather roads and give them the conveniences and comfort of rural electrification, we will really have people who will stay on the farm. It is a so much better place to live if the housewives and men on the farm can have conveniences."[30]

Rayburn's expertise on soil conservation was widely accepted in Congress, and when he spoke on the subject, his colleagues listened. For more than two decades, he fought attempts by eastern liberals to reduce federal spending for such purposes. "If our soil is not fertile enough, if the 30 million people who live upon the farms of the country today do not have dirt on which they can raise a crop and a price to sell it at to give them a buying power, your city people will be walking the streets, because your factories will be closed," he often warned. His own farm was his best argument for conservation, Rayburn believed. When he bought the old Steger ranch shortly before his election as Speaker, it was a worn-out parcel, economically worthless. The deep, sandy loam had been overgrazed for years and was sadly in need, as Rayburn described it, of being "re-established." None of the land cost him more than $12 an acre.

Soil conservation was in those days still viewed skeptically by many local farmers. But Rayburn set about sowing native grasses and legumes and eradicating brush and weeds. He dug water tanks and installed good fences. He introduced to the area terraced ridges and contoured rows as a way to save water and reduce soil erosion. When the old farmers argued that straight rows were much easier to plow than curved, terraced rows, Rayburn chuckled and said, "Yes, keep running your straight rows up and down the hill and your harvest will be much lighter and easier, too."[31] His ranch became a model for the area as other ranchers and farmers adopted his advanced techniques.

Even from Washington, he watched over every detail of his farm. He wrote brother Will one April:

> With as many cattle as are in now I think it would be a good idea to build the fence bull tight on the North side. I would use all of the old wire that I could but enough new to make it a goat or sheep fence while I was at it. Of course, you will have to hire one extra hand for that work, but only one to help Dewey do the heavy work will be enough. Let me know when you start and we can arrange to buy wire, good wire, where you can get it cheapest. . . . I want the little mare Queen bred to a saddle horse if you can find one. . . . Write me often how things go,
>
> your devoted brother,
Sam
>
> P.S. Have all land disced possible. It will not hurt the grass but help it.[32]

When a group of urban congressmen, led by New York Republican Jacob Javits, sought in 1952 to cut $50 million out of a soil conservation bill, Rayburn responded with one of the longest and most impassioned floor speeches. He described how he and his brothers had "re-established" the 600-acre Steger farm and 300 adjoining acres that he later purchased. "We feel that we are only tenants for a short time on that dirt," he said, "that we owe it to this generation and those who come after us to leave that soil as fertile as we found it, not to deny the people of the next generation or generations for a hundred years in the future the right to have soil that will feed and clothe the millions of people that will inhabit this country in those years to come. . . . You better think of that."[33] The amendment, a foretaste of environmental and pollution control debates a generation later, was defeated.

Swamped with postwar legislation, Congress in 1945 worked until Christmas. At session's end, members scattered for home, generally satisfied and looking forward to 1946—which promised to be the first full year of world peace in a decade. Rayburn, however, was apprehensive. He remembered the years following World War I and the clamor for change. He advised his colleagues to be prepared to explain their actions but to apologize for nothing. "I have never been the type or the character of man who did things, then went out and apologized for them," he said. "I am just not built that way." [34]

Rayburn arrived in Bonham on Christmas Eve and—after changing into his Texas uniform: old khaki pants, boots, an open shirt—immediately set to work decorating a huge tree that filled one corner of the living room. The clan took childlike delight in the Yule season. The house was always gaily decorated. Logs crackled in the fireplace and gifts were exchanged among family members. Torn paper, ribbon, and empty gift boxes remained on the living room floor for days. Always there were visitors filing in through the rear screen door to see the Speaker. He would greet them all and lead them to a spot in front of the fireplace, where he kept his favorite rocking chair.

The 1946 session saw Rayburn beginning his sixth year as Speaker. By year's end, he would have held the job longer than any predecessor except Henry Clay, Andrew Stevenson, Joseph G. Cannon, and Champ Clark. Quietly but with determination, he had transformed the House's highest post from the relatively weak, largely internal office it had been for the previous three decades to a position whose great power and prestige extended well beyond the confines of Capitol Hill. His self-appointed mission to reclaim the full authority that had been stripped from the Speakership by a rebellious House in 1910 was nearly complete. But preserving that authority, he believed, required constant vigilance on his part. As he wrote in 1946: "I am exercising all the leadership that I know to straighten one thing out after another but practically every day somebody comes in to me and says, 'This is the greatest problem in the world,' and in an hour someone else will come in and say that another problem is twice as great. There are a dozen or more outstanding problems that we must solve before we level off and get back to anything normal." [35]

In June, the Senate passed a sweeping bill to reorganize the legislative branch. The measure would sharply reduce the number of House and Senate committees and redefine their jurisdiction. It also gave members bigger staffs, more money to run their offices, and more facilities. Other provisions dealt mainly with strengthening party responsibility and improving the flow of legislation and ideas between the two houses, and between Congress and the executive. When the bill reached the House, Rayburn gave it a skeptical glance and let it sit on his desk for six weeks. He refused to send it to committee or discuss further movement until its supporters agreed to certain changes.

His main objection was a provision creating majority and minority policy committees. These panels were designed to strengthen party responsibility and accountability, but Rayburn saw them as unnecessary and perhaps even damaging to the strong Democratic leadership he exercised. The Democratic policy committee would have responsibility for scheduling legislation and for disciplining recalcitrant members—two important functions of the Speaker that Rayburn would not willingly relinquish. "I don't want any debating societies around me," he grumbled. Neither was he pleased with a provision calling for a Legislative-Executive Council intended to improve relations with the executive branch through periodic meetings with the President. If such meetings were needed, he wanted the Speaker, not some faceless "council," in charge. Only when he had been assured that these, and a few minor irritants, were stricken from the bill did he send it on its way. The measure passed the House, 229–61.[36]

The House adjourned on August 2—the earliest since 1938—ending one of the least constructive, most acrimonious sessions in years. It had been a year marked by constant controversy and bitter quarreling between the parties as members jockeyed for advantage in the November elections. The Democratic leadership, unable to control many of its own party members, was on the defensive almost constantly as it battled for orderly reconversion legislation. Rayburn had to intervene personally to stave off a popular effort to lift all price controls. In a moving speech, he defended a bill giving postwar financial aid to Great Britain

("I do not want Western Europe, England and all the rest pushed further into and toward an ideology that I despise") and fought unsuccessfully to limit military demobilization until a more secure peace was assured.

He also clashed again with an old enemy—the utility companies—this time in defense of one of his pet parochial interests, the Southwestern Power Administration, which managed rural electric service over a large area that included north Texas and which Rayburn had helped create. Seldom had he fought with such ferocity as he did to overturn a House appropriations subcommittee's recommendation to cut the agency's funding in half. His indignation rising, juices boiling, he was back to his glory days as a New Deal warrior standing bravely and alone against the Philistines of big business. "This town for the past six months has been seething with utility lobbyists" bent on "killing off" the SPA, he told the House. "I had a brush with these people in 1935," he continued, to the cheers of his colleagues. "If they are spoiling for another fight with me, as far as I am concerned, they can get it, because I am just the one who is not afraid of them." Rarely does the House overturn an Appropriations Committee recommendation, but this was an exception—a matter of personal importance to the Speaker. The Southwestern Power Administration got its full funding.[37]

With adjournment, members returned to their districts to prepare for the crucial fall campaigns. Rayburn—who somehow escaped opposition in the July primary—cut short his vacation in order to help his colleagues. He was worried. "This is going to be a damned 'beefsteak election,'" he told a friend. He feared a voter rebellion, brought on by a severe shortage of meat—a symbol of disillusionment with the slow pace of reconversion.[38] To John McCormack he wrote: "We have to take care of our boys this year with twice as much money and in many instances more than twice as much than ever before."[39] Rayburn did what he could, making numerous speeches, recording more than sixty endorsements for radio broadcast, and writing "a great many" letters to be used in individual races. To a friend, he confided his deepest dread:

I will leave here for Washington around October 11 with one speech in Missouri, then arrive in Washington about the fourteenth. I will make some speeches around there and try to help some boys out. This I am very anxious to do for I think it would be just too bad for the next two years if Truman had a Republican House or Senate. . . . I am not a radical but I would fear for a reactionary administration and its doings. I just do not think that farmers, laborers, etc. are going to be willing to give up the gains they have made.[40]

His fear of a Democratic debacle proved well founded.

16

Minority Leader

In November, the Republicans swept both houses of Congress by substantial margins, ending the long, productive Democratic reign. As abruptly as it had begun, the New Deal was over. All evidence of its existence would be erased, the victors vowed. Predicting a bitterly partisan session ahead, Rayburn told reporters: "We'll see whether they have courage enough to repeal the so-called New Deal laws they have criticized so much; I doubt it."[1]

Losing the House was, for Rayburn, a severe personal blow. It meant relinquishing the Speakership, the job he cherished, to resume the role of an ordinary congressman. For the first time, he weighed the idea of retirement. Perhaps, he mused, this would be his last term.[2] The long, grueling sessions of the war years had left him exhausted, mentally and physically. Intrigued by the notion of having less responsibility, thus more time for family and friends, he announced soon after the election that he would not serve as minority leader "under any circumstances." "I do not feel like stepping down and replying to every little yapping Republican who bounces up," he wrote.[3] Nor would he accept a committee assignment. Instead, he offered to work as a mediator for both parties—an "elder statesman" bridging the gap between a Republican Congress and a Democratic Presi-

dent. "If World War II should be followed by a two-year legislative stalemate and political struggle," he said, "our nation
would be throwing away the fruits of victory at a time when we
have a real chance to achieve prosperity and happiness for all our
citizens." He rejected all appeals to reconsider. "Before I made
my decision, I thought the thing through thoroughly," he said.
"My decision was final."[4] Bewildered and dismayed by the election results—now leaderless as well—House Democrats saw no
place to turn.

John McCormack was Rayburn's logical successor. But the
fiery Boston liberal had weak support among southerners.
Moreover, he had a host of enemies who objected to his rough-
and-tumble political style. Among the southerners, no natural
leader of wide appeal, other than Rayburn, could be found.
Moderate John Sparkman of Alabama might have made an attractive alternative had he not just been elected to the Senate.
Outside the South, Pennsylvania's Francis E. "Tad" Walter was
capable and interested, but no ground swell developed for him.
The decision of ill-tempered, bigoted John Rankin of Missis-
sippi to offer his services only underscored the sad shortage of
Democratic talent.[5] Without Rayburn at the helm, predicted
Percy Priest of Tennessee, the party "will be torn apart inter-
nally." Observed Edward Hébert of Louisiana: "Sam Rayburn is
to us what Winston Churchill is to his party in Parliament.
When the Conservative Party was defeated last year, Churchill
continued to be the spokesman of his party in Parliament.
Rayburn should do the same."[6] Democrats finally concluded: if
Rayburn won't volunteer, he'll have to be drafted.

But Rayburn, remaining in Bonham through December, doggedly held firm. Not until he headed back to Washington on January 1 did he begin to waver. During the two-day train ride, members of the Texas delegation stung his pride by comparing his
decision to John Garner's sour departure from public life in 1941.
Truman weighed in a few days later, arguing that McCormack
could not win and that Rayburn's refusal to serve would allow a
reactionary southerner to step into a House leadership vacuum.
Finally, he could resist no longer. "I couldn't help it," the Texan
said afterward. "Twenty minutes before the Democratic caucus

convened, McCormack came to me and said they were going to elect me in spite of myself. When I was voted for unanimously, I yielded like I figured a good soldier should."[7]

Thus Rayburn, shortly before his 65th birthday, handed the Speaker's gavel to Republican Joe Martin of Massachusetts and stepped into the new and unfamiliar role: leader of the minority. No longer did he have the mantle of powerful office and no longer did he preside over the House. Otherwise, he lost little. His personal prestige remained high. President Truman persisted in calling him "Mr. Speaker," much to Speaker Martin's displeasure.

He had to give up the stately Speaker's Rooms and the choice personal office suite overlooking the Capitol's West Terrace and the Mall. He also had to relinquish the Speaker's limousine, a loss soon replaced by a sleek new Cadillac, a gift from House Democrats. Some Republicans kicked in to help buy the car, but their checks were returned with Rayburn's thanks; even the slightest suspicion of a conflict of interest must be avoided. Rayburn dug into his own pocket to buy gasoline and hire a new driver, Nick Nicastro. His old chauffeur and fishing companion, George Donovan, a House employee, was assigned to Speaker Martin.

Traditional good humor and light partisanship marked the transfer of power from one Speaker to another, as it had since 1791. For the first time, the ceremony was broadcast over the new medium of television. "Viewers," noted the *New York Times*, "could even see the bandage on the tally clerk's finger as the voting for Speaker progressed." Even Rayburn was impressed, as he admitted in his first TV interview. He congratulated those "who brought television in and those who are conducting the proceedings under it now. It is an occasion for me and also for the people out there who will hear and see." His infatuation with the electronic eye would prove short-lived.

Throughout the next two difficult, anger-filled years, the warm friendship between Rayburn and Martin never faltered, even when they differed intensely over political issues.[8] That could not be said of Republicans and Democrats generally, as pressures and emotions of postwar readjustment soared to almost intolerable levels.

Rayburn had ample reason to worry about the coming session. The history of divided government offered little promise of cooperation between the parties. Since the Civil War, the anti-administration party had controlled both houses of Congress eight times. Each time, the nation's legislature ground to a virtual standstill or became locked in internecine conflict with the President. Rayburn had personal memories of the Republican 66th Congress, which thwarted Wilson after World War I, and the Democratic 72nd, which battled Hoover in the early 1930s.

In an effort to reduce areas of potential conflict, Truman terminated some fifty wartime laws, thus defusing a major GOP issue—the inflated power of the Presidency. He also accepted Rayburn's suggestion to continue his regular meetings with congressional leaders. On January 27, the President met for the first time with House Speaker Martin and Senate Majority Leader Robert A. Taft, joined by House Minority Leader Rayburn and Senate Minority Leader Barkley. In yet another peace gesture, Truman resubmitted his presidential succession bill, which, to everyone's surprise, was identical to the 1945 bill. It put the Speaker, a Republican, ahead of the secretary of state, a Democrat, in the succession order. Two years earlier, the Republicans had fought the measure. Now Martin and his colleagues enthusiastically applauded the President's "commendable lack of partisanship." The bill, originally conceived with Rayburn in mind, breezed through the GOP-controlled House, 365–11, and Senate, 50–35.

Rayburn believed it was bad government and poor politics for the minority to oppose "every ticky little bill that comes along." Save your energy and ammunition for important issues, he argued. "If measures are presented by the Republicans for the welfare of the country and the good of the people," he promised, "we're going along with them—just as if they were Democratic measures."[9] He might have to call on Republicans to support the President on crucial national issues; in return, he was ready to stand aside occasionally for a bill he personally believed unwise.

As minority leader, he participated actively in floor debate. When he rose to speak, a hush fell over the House, just as it had on those rare occasions when he had addressed the House as

Speaker. Gallery attendants called to reporters in the press rooms—"Rayburn is up"—and the galleries rapidly filled. Scurrying pages paused; members halted their noisy conversations behind the rail and drifted back to their seats. Sometimes the squat Texan stood at the Democratic table, draping an arm lightly over the microphone stand; other times, he slowly ambled down to the well. Bracing his arms against the oak lectern, he would gaze about the chamber for a moment, his inscrutable dark eyes darting right and left, his mind registering who was present and who was not. "Before you go on here," he might say to the opposition with conversational calmness, "I want to tell you this: You are about to make a mistake here, a very big mistake . . ."[10]

The Republicans believed they had a mandate to redirect the nation's entire domestic course. As Speaker Martin put it: "This government's control over the private affairs of the citizens must be ended, and the people's control over their government must be fully restored as soon as practical."[11] GOP leaders, by and large, cared less about reshaping America's foreign policy. The presidential election of 1948 would be won, many were convinced, on issues close to home—tax reduction, control of labor unions, and a balanced budget—not by events in Eastern Europe or China. Noted Senate Majority Leader Taft: "It would be ironical if this Congress which really has its heart set on straightening out domestic affairs would end up in being besieged by foreign problems."

In handling an array of pressing foreign issues, the 80th Congress proved surprisingly nonpartisan. It accepted Truman's bold new approaches and implemented his call for massive economic aid for the re-emerging European nations. Rayburn helped fashion winning coalitions in the House, but the bulk of the credit belonged to GOP leaders of both houses, especially Michigan's Arthur Vandenberg, chairman of the Senate Foreign Relations Committee, who risked his own considerable prestige to support a Democratic administration's foreign policy.

There was doubt at first that Truman's bold initiatives could be sold on Capitol Hill. The first test came early in the European Recovery Act—the beginning of the Marshall Plan—hastily drafted in the spring of 1947 after Britain decided to cut off further economic aid to Greece. With no support, Greece almost certainly would fall to the Communist guerrillas then challenging the government. If Greece joined the Soviet orbit, Turkey was likely to follow, along with other east Mediterranean nations. Truman, convinced by Secretary of State Marshall that only a substantial infusion of U.S. assistance could turn back the tide of communism in Eastern Europe, sought Rayburn's advice:

Sam said, "I don't know whether we can do it or not. How much is this going to cost?"

I said, "It's going to cost about a billion dollars, but I have another one coming up that is going to cost 17 billion." I was referring to the Marshall Plan.

Sam said, "You are asking for a hell of a lot."

I told him: "I want all I can get and maybe more." Actually, we got by in Greece and Turkey for 350 million and the Marshall Plan cost us 13 and a half billion. They were the greatest things that ever happened to Europe.[12]

Truman, accepting Vandenberg's challenge to go before Congress and "scare the hell out of the country," later described to the nation how Communist activities throughout Europe were undercutting American security, and he outlined a tough new policy of support to nations "resisting attempted subjugation by armed minorities or by outside pressures." In the widely quoted speech, Americans got their first hard look at the new President as a forceful, confident leader. Support for his policy—the "Truman Doctrine"—grew rapidly.

On May 7, as a final vote neared on Truman's aid package, word spread through the House: "Rayburn is up!" The hour was late and, typically, his words brief. "I trust that, in our consideration, this thing called isolation may not crawl out of the shadows and defeat the hopes of men and again break the hearts of the world," he said, recalling the dark period after World War I. The nation "again has leaders asking for certain action, and whether we like that leadership or not, we have it. It is the voice of America and whether that leadership is followed or spurned will have tremendous effect upon our position and influence in the world." Nations "who do not want to be smothered by Communism" are appealing for help. "If we do not assure peace, God help us. God help the world." The bill passed easily— a historic moment in American foreign policy.[13]

The Marshall Plan was the 80th Congress at its best. Labor-bashing, climaxing in the passage of the Taft-Hartley Labor Act, showed Congress at its vindictive worst. Antilabor sentiment had festered on Capitol Hill for years. Union irresponsibility surfaced as a key issue of the 1946 congressional races, and many House Republicans owed their election to a pledge to curb organized labor. Truman, hoping to head off punitive measures, in early 1947 proposed limited legislation that would outlaw some strikes and boycotts and require unions and management to submit to compulsory arbitration. Even as he spoke, strike threats crackled in the coal, steel, and other major industries. His bill, judged inadequate, was largely ignored. With labor-management problems mounting daily, labor committees of the House and Senate opened hearings on some sixty bills, all aimed at controlling labor. As Fred Hartley, chairman of the House Education and Labor Committee, later noted: "Most of us among the leaders of the Republican congressional delegation were convinced that the future of our party—and, more than that, the future of the country—lay in the speedy enactment of legislation designed to equalize the positions of management and labor."[14]

The Hartley committee finally approved a bill so hysterically antilabor that it shocked even the most pessimistic labor supporters. Freshman John F. Kennedy of Massachusetts, elected despite the Republican sweep in 1946, and another young Democrat on the Education and Labor Committee, Adam Clayton Powell of New York, protested that the bill had been drawn up exclusively by Republican members meeting in "secret session." Among the bill's sweeping provisions were strict rules for the formation of union shops as well as prohibitions against closed shops, industrywide bargaining with competing employers, employer contributions to union-administered welfare funds, jurisdictional strikes, secondary boycotts, and sympathy strikes.

The legislation tested Rayburn's own feelings about organized labor. Over the years, he had vacillated on the question of "curbing labor." Basically, a "pro-working man" legislator, he nevertheless thought unions often made excessive demands and were too quick to strike. On issues pitting labor against farmers, he consistently sided with the farmers—an easy course for him, since his district had little organized labor. From 1920, when the railroad brotherhoods sought his defeat, until that time, he had never won labor's backing. As Speaker, he took no strong steps to block antilabor legislation from the time of the so-called Smith Act in 1940 through the strongly antilabor Case bill that came before the House in 1946. But the Hartley bill left him heartsick and angry. This was an unfair bill, designed for revenge, he concluded. He knew it would pass by a wide margin. Most southern Democrats would vote with the Republicans. In Texas, including his own district, the bill was highly popular. Even so, Rayburn saw but one choice for himself.

The House, bitterly divided, debated the measure for three days. Intemperate words flew. Only in the closing minutes did Rayburn speak. "I do not know all that is in this bill," he told a hushed House. "Few do or can. But, from what I know of it, I know that what you are doing here is not fair. The bill is not fair. I'm not going to vote for it."[15] Only three Texans joined him. Lyndon Johnson, in the midst of his second bid for the Senate, seized the issue as his opportunity to show his conservative bent.[16] Together with sixteen other Texans, and most southern Democrats, he voted for the bill. It passed 308–107. A milder version later cleared the Senate, under Taft's leadership. Ultimately, the Taft-Hartley Act, a compromise close to the original Hartley bill, was sent to the White House and was promptly vetoed. The veto was easily overridden. In the Texas delegation, only Ewing Thomason and Albert Thomas joined Rayburn in voting to sustain the veto.[17]

Rayburn saw the Republican control of Congress as a freakish accident that the voters would soon correct. "Viewing the actions of the Republicans in the House and Senate up to now, I think the country has more disgust than admiration for them," he wrote in 1947. "They do not know where they want to go, and if they did, they would hardly know the course to take."[18] Later that spring, he wrote: "We Democrats are not doing any too badly now. The Republicans could probably have won the House and Senate without making a single promise, but they did get out and made some that they cannot live up to. There is a great deal of difference in being on the sidelines and jeering at what other people are trying to do and being in the middle and trying to carry some of the load."[19] Still later: "If our Republican brethren had not won control of the Senate and the House in 1946, they would not have had these tremendous responsibilities, which I assure they are not enjoying one bit. I doubt if they can get up a man that can beat Truman in 1948."[20] Rayburn never doubted that Truman would run or that he would be elected. "I think . . . he will be our unanimous choice for leader in 1948," he predicted. "He can be sold, I think, as just a plain, good American with a head full of good, sound common sense, and with a burning desire to serve the people here and elsewhere. He is fast becoming what he should be—a world leader."[21]

But as winter turned to spring, Truman's popularity dwindled further. "Truman is really at a low ebb right now," Rayburn noted in March. He remained confident of Truman's ultimate victory, however, despite the disquieting noises from the South. The problem there—and in Rayburn's own district—was a burgeoning new issue: civil rights.

Personally and politically, Truman long had been committed to black equality. He spoke up for blacks in his campaigns for the Senate. As President, he considered it a duty to champion justice for American blacks. Rayburn, on the other hand, remained a product of his southern, rural heritage. He supported racial segregation as then practiced in his district and throughout the state. When Truman in 1948 sent Congress a bill calling for the strongest civil rights program since Reconstruction—including a ban on segregation in interstate transportation, elimination of the poll tax, and protection of voting rights—Rayburn knew he could not support the measure and still survive politically.[22] He made no issue of it, but when Truman handed him the bill to introduce in the House, he simply put it in a back drawer of his desk, where it remained for the rest of the session. "Sam did that," Truman later recalled, "but I understood. I had to have it put in in the Senate. Sam knew I had to do that."[23]

At home, Rayburn confronted the mounting furor over civil rights with no more bravery than most other southern politicians. Facing stiff challenge in the 1948 primary and under fire for his close ties with Truman, he declared his unyielding determination to preserve racial segregation:

> In my announcements in the papers of the district it was stated that I was opposed to the whole civil-rights program. . . . That is and has been my position. . . . I voted against everything that looked like an attack on our segregation laws. We have been able to hold down any vote on the [civil rights bill] this year because we feared that the Republicans unanimously and many Northern Democrats would support it. I voted against the antilynching bill in the 67th Congress under Republican administration; I voted against it in the 75th Congress under Democratic administration, and I voted against it in the 76th Congress under a Democratic administration. If the opposition desires to go on saying that I am for the civil-rights program in the face of this record then the people will know that they are deliberately distorting and falsifying my record.[24]

The pressures of a heated campaign probably led Rayburn to defend southern racial practices beyond his true convictions. "Undoubtedly, he shared the reservations of his peers regarding Negro equality," observed Rayburn biographer Dwayne Little. "He believed as a race Negroes were inferior to the white race, especially to old-line Anglo-Saxon stock. Complete social equality, which he felt was the aim of integration, would lead to intermarriage—and that was unthinkable."[25] Yet Rayburn's long association with highly educated, well-to-do, socially astute blacks in Washington had accorded him insights into black potential not generally known to his constituents. For the first time in a campaign, he was uncomfortable, vaguely embarrassed with his position on a great moral issue, particularly the continued denial of *political* equality to blacks. He vowed to oppose "any bill that has any tendency towards crippling our segregation laws . . . I have been too long voting on these matters to change."[26] But imperceptibly, perhaps even to him, his lifelong public position on the most crucial domestic issue of the age was beginning to shift.

After 1948, he continued resisting federal intervention in racial matters, but he began in small ways prodding the South to lead in solving its own problems. In Texas, he urged Attorney General Price Daniel and members of the Legislature to abolish the state poll tax, which had effectively disfranchised blacks and other minorities for generations. Only seven states still retained the much-despised tax. "If these seven states will do away with the question of poll tax, we will not have that problem to cope with here," he wrote from Washington in 1949. "I am opposed to a poll tax as a prerequisite to voting, but I cannot vote for the abolition of the poll tax here as I think it is a matter pertaining to the states and localities and should be handled by them."[27] He warned other southerners that federal intervention was inevitable if blacks continued to be denied basic rights. "You can't filibuster forever," he told them.[28]

Rayburn's differences with Truman extended to other issues, most notably, federal aid to education and state ownership of the oil-rich submerged coastal lands—the so-called tidelands. Although a strong proponent of an improved educational system, he saw danger, for the South, particularly, in federal aid of any kind. "I am very fearful that we would run into all kinds of segregation problems if we ever enact federal aid to education," he wrote. "Our curriculum, I am sure, would be affected as I do not know of anything the federal government has gone into that it does not control."[29]

The southern civil rights revolt worried Democratic leaders. If the South defected—as it increasingly threatened to do if Truman remained firm on civil rights—the party faced almost certain defeat in the 1948 presidential election. A few Democrats, eager to dump Truman, chased popular, Texas-born General Dwight Eisenhower, who had not yet declared his Republican leaning. Most, however, endorsed Rayburn's view that "we have to nominate Truman or be repudiating three and one-half years of the Democratic administration."[30] He predicted, ignoring overwhelming evidence to the contrary, that the South would "cool off." Meanwhile, party prospects grew dimmer as Henry Wallace led a liberal splinter movement out of the Democratic fold to form a new party—the Progressives.

As a sop to the South, party chiefs decided to feature two border-state southerners at the National Convention in Philadelphia: Senator Alben Barkley of Kentucky, old and tired but still popular and eloquent, was selected for the keynote address, and Sam Rayburn, the party's most respected member, was chosen to be permanent chairman—the highest honor the National Convention can bestow. It meant Rayburn would have to interrupt his own primary campaign to attend the party's ritual gathering.

Philadelphia had been simmering for days in oppressive July heat when Rayburn arrived for what was almost certain to be, as Bernard Baruch put it, the "dullest, dreariest, most dispirited gathering ever assembled . . . to pick a President." Hotels, restaurants, and bars already were jammed with other early-arriving delegates, their long faces and subdued conversations giving clear signal that they were facing the business ahead more with resolute determination than with enthusiasm. Truman would be nominated; that much was clear. But he could not win the election; everyone seemed to know that, too. Feigning exuberance, Missouri delegates distributed "victory kits"—a Truman badge, cigarette lighter, pencil, and tin whistle—to other arriving delegates. One perspiring Iowan pocketed the lighter and pencil, but handed back the whistle. "You blow it," he said. James Hagerty of the *New York Times* found among party leaders "an atmosphere of despondency" and "a spirit of defeatism" amounting to "a confession that President Truman seemed to have little chance of election."

As usual, trouble brewed in the Texas delegation. Most delegates were pledged to hold the line for Truman and his as yet unnamed running mate. But the support was thin. Nearly a fourth of the state's fifty delegates backed a resolution asserting

that Texas would not support Truman "in any circumstances."
On convention eve, the delegation met in a noisy, all-night caucus. The best show in town, it drew swarms of reporters, nearly
all of whom saw turmoil in the Lone Star State as sure evidence
of the hopelessness of Truman's cause. At the height of the furor,
a disgusted Rayburn grabbed his hat and stalked out, ostensibly
to lobby the platform committee for a softer civil rights plank.
Actually, he took the elevator to his room and went to bed.

On opening night, 70-year-old Barkley, a sentimental Democratic favorite, delivered a spirited, perfectly timed keynote
speech that galvanized the delegates into a whooping, stomping
party of purpose. He strode onto the platform a leading vice-
presidential contender. Blinded by the lights, he could not see
well enough to read a prepared text. His 68-minute extempo-
raneous address thrilled the crowd and assured him the No. 2
role. Delegates were so taken with the warm, tale-spinning Kentuckian that they forgot he was too old for the job and from the
wrong state for that year's ticket.

Rayburn's address the following night was, in its way, even
better. He began by admonishing dispirited delegates, "The
Democratic Party has been the majority party for 16 years—for
God's sake let's act like it." [31] Lashing the Republicans with eager
ferocity, he labeled GOP nominees Thomas E. Dewey and Earl
Warren "false fronts" for "a party of privilege." Third-party
candidate Henry Wallace he dismissed as the "Pied Piper of the
Politburo"—an allusion to Wallace's leftish connections. He
ridiculed Dewey's promise of "administrative efficiency" in a
Republican government. "There is nothing so dangerous as energetic, efficient people administering wrong ideas," the fired-
up Texan contended. "That's why we have never wanted the administrative efficiency of a dictator."

Still under the spell of Barkley's rouser of the night before, the
convention picked up Rayburn's theme, punctuating his phrases
with deafening roars. Under the hot lights—it was 94 degrees in
the stifling hall—Rayburn dripped with perspiration. Occasionally pausing to mop his bald head, he continued his unrelenting
verbal assault. "Without a Democratic President and Democratic Congress would we expect adequate appropriations for

the Marshall Plan?" he asked rhetorically.

The delegates thundered: "No!"

"Could we expect from a Republican Congress any legislation to curb the rising cost of living?"

"No!"

"Could we expect from a Republican Congress adequate or even decent housing legislation?"

"No!"

"Could we expect fair extension of our Social Security laws?"

"No!" roared the delegates, some of whom were now standing on their chairs to get a better look at this fiery, stocky, old man, whose bald dome glistened like a dew-drenched melon in the sun.

"Who opened the banks in 1933?"

"The Democrats!"

"Who brought the farmer out of his bankruptcy courts of 1933 and into his prosperity of 1948?"

"The Democrats!"

"Who safeguarded the investments of the plain people of the United States and brought Wall Street under regulation and insured the bank deposits of the country?"

"The Democrats!"

"Who has reclaimed the arid lands of the West? You know the answer. Not the Pennsylvania Association of Manufacturers."

Two old war-horses had brought the convention to life. These delegates were Democrats again, and Harry Truman, most certainly, was their man. As Rayburn concluded, hundreds of delegates fished from their pockets the tin whistles they had earlier scorned. The noise was deafening. It was not Rayburn but the Democratic party that they celebrated.

There was still the problem of adopting the party platform. Several southern delegations planned to walk out if it carried a strong civil rights plank. Delegates' wrangling over the issue stretched late into the night. By accepting a civil rights plank, said the southerners, the party would be writing off the South in November. Civil rights supporters, led by youthful Mayor Hubert H. Humphrey of Minneapolis, brushed such threats aside. "It is time for the Democratic Party to get out of the shadow of states' rights and walk in the sunshine of human rights," he declared, seeming to speak for a majority of delegates. Rayburn and other party leaders were convinced that a southern walkout not only would ruin Truman's chances in November but would devastate the party, perhaps forever. As permanent chairman, the Texan felt a heavy responsibility to avoid such a calamity. But how? He would have to find a way.

The situation was not without hope. He knew through experience that a presiding officer must, at times, take extraordinary action to maintain order and thus allow the majority to work its will. Delegates, he believed, understood the difficulties of managing a large convention and accepted occasional arbitrary rulings. They would, in short, permit infrequent minor abuses of the rules, if handled fairly.

Alabama, Rayburn learned, would lead the walkout when its name was called on the vote to adopt the platform. When that time came, he was ready. Instead of going directly to a roll call, he ordered a voice vote. The convention shouted its overwhelming approval of the platform. Expecting a roll call to follow—for the record—Alabama delegates stirred restlessly. But Rayburn was not following the script. Without pausing, as the voice vote concluded, he slammed the gavel and announced the platform's adoption. The chair, he said, would entertain no more motions, except a motion to recess. Southern delegates were furious. With no roll call, there would be no opportunity for a dramatic walkout. Waving his state's banner frantically, his face glowing purple, Alabama's Eugene "Bull" Connor screamed for recognition.[32] He was ignored. Amid lusty boos, Rayburn recessed the convention. "It was rotten, the adjournment," shouted Connor.

Alabama finally staged its walkout the next evening during the presidential nominations. About half the Mississippi delegation followed, along with a few delegates from other states. Some 35 of the South's 278 delegates walked out, far fewer than had been ready to quit the convention the night before. Meanwhile, most southern delegates had found a more constructive means of demonstrating their unhappiness—by supporting the nomination of Georgia's Senator Richard B. Russell for the

Presidency. Truman was easily nominated, but Russell got the South, including Texas's 50 votes.

While the proceedings droned on, the President sat alone in a doorway of the Convention Hall's lower level, his chair facing the cool evening air. He had arrived unexpectedly in the late afternoon, determined to stay through the nomination of both President and Vice-President so that he could deliver his acceptance speech that night. Barred by tradition from entering the hall during the balloting, he waited in a wooden, straight-backed chair overlooking a service alley until well past 2 A.M. Finally, with the nomination of 71-year-old Alben Barkley for Vice-President—Rayburn refused to enter the contest—the ticket was complete. Amid wild applause, a smiling President, still immaculate in his white-linen suit, strode onto the platform.

At the precise moment of Truman's entry, a squadron of pigeons caged near the platform was released. Bewildered and tired from their long imprisonment, they flew wildly around the great hall, perching on rafters, on protective covers of the giant electric fans, and even—according to Truman's account— on top of Rayburn's head. "Sam was disgusted," he later recalled. "Funniest thing at the convention."[33] Truman's pigeon story was later related to Rayburn, who hotly denied it. "Harry Truman's a Goddamn liar," he snorted. "No pigeon ever lit on my head."

Later that month, Rayburn defeated his two Democratic rivals, G. C. Morris and David Brown, without a runoff. Morris, who ran a strong race against Rayburn four years earlier, seemed formidable for a while with his attacks on Rayburn's segregation record and with his platform of "Freedom of Opportunity"— the right of every Fourth District Texan to hope for a seat in Congress and not have that right preempted. "I was born in the month the present congressman was first elected," Morris complained. "Isn't it time to let someone else have a crack at the job?" The voters decided otherwise. By mid-July, Rayburn had pulled well ahead. He continued, however, to pour it on his opponents. His intent, Rayburn's lieutenants later admitted, was to "bury" Morris and show, once and for all, the futility of opposing Sam Rayburn.[34] The tactic paid off. The old veteran garnered 63 percent of the vote—his greatest victory and his last hard race.

Rayburn then turned to the task of salvaging Texas for the Democratic ticket, if he could. He had no statewide power, little experience in state politics, and pitifully meager help. But with a firmness he had not shown in years, he began herding stray Democrats back into the fold. In September, at the State Convention in Fort Worth, an intraparty squabble allowed Rayburn-led loyal Democrats to seize control of the party machinery—temporarily. At the convention, he implored the 1,500 delegates, many of whom threatened to join Strom Thurmond's Dixiecrat party: "Stay with the party that stayed with you. Remember when the Democrats came to power in 1933—14 million people were out of work, cotton was 5 cents a pound, corn was 15 cents, wheat brought 20 cents and beef 3½ cents?" The delegates remembered, and they responded with deafening cheers.[35]

The Dixiecrats, nevertheless, did bolt the convention, their leader shouting, "You can't put me in bed with Truman and his Commiecrats." Among them was the man who had paid the rent for the convention's furniture and equipment. He immediately ordered everything hauled away. The movers carried away Rayburn's table. When he got up to protest, they took his chair.[36] Rayburn hoped to keep party control through the November elections, but he knew that when he returned to Washington, the power would have to pass to other hands.

His last hope of keeping Texas in the Democratic column rested with Truman himself. Democratic leaders happily had discovered earlier in the year that Truman had tremendous impact when—wrapped in the mantle of the Presidency—he could stand before voters to denounce, in his folksy manner, the Republican party and "that do-nothing, Republican 80th Congress." A short campaign swing by train in May proved so successful that Truman's strategists—Clark Clifford, Charlie Ross, Howard McGrath, Les Biffle, Jack Redding, and others—persuaded him to expand that technique in the fall. "He certainly woke the people up and scared the Republicans nearly to death on his western trip," Rayburn wrote in June. "He is good on the back end of a train because he is one of the folks. He smiles with them and not at them, laughs with them and not at them."[37] Traveling in a specially fitted coach, the President crisscrossed the nation, speaking in every hamlet and town that could be scheduled between September and election day. He logged more than 31,000 rail miles and delivered more than 500 speeches in eight weeks—twice as many miles and more than twice as many speeches as Dewey. One of the President's important early swings took him through Texas and, of course, to Bonham.

The train pulled into the Bonham station on a perfect Monday evening. More than 25,000 north Texans and Oklahomans had driven from nearby farms and small towns to glimpse the President. Excitement rippled through the throng as Rayburn, who had traveled with Truman through parts of the state, emerged first from the rear coach, followed by the smartly dressed President. Behind them came Mrs. Truman in a blue suit and black hat and daughter Margaret, wearing a navy blue suit to which was pinned a huge bronze chrysanthemum. A motorcade led them through the town to the high school stadium, where Rayburn proudly introduced his "dear, personal friend" who "has wanted to come to Bonham for a long time."[38] Truman took aim at his usual targets in a 20-minute, nationally broadcast address. "The Democratic Party will give you," he said, "the kind of government that Sam Rayburn stands for— government in the interest of the farmer, the working man and all the people." He urged Texans to vote for Lyndon Johnson and Oklahomans to vote for Robert S. Kerr, running for the Senate in their respective states. "If Lyndon Johnson and Robert Kerr get to the Senate," he said, "we'll certainly make the Republicans dance in the next Congress."

Afterward, Rayburn led the President and his family to the white frame house on Highway 82, where hundreds of well-wishers had gathered for a reception. The dining table, spread with a lace cloth and silver serving pieces, was piled high with fried chicken. In the center was a big round cake, decorated with American and Texas flags and inscribed "Mr. President." Guests waited in a line that stretched out the front door and across the lawn. The Secret Service, claiming the President's safety could be not assured in such a setting, refused at first to let Truman participate in a receiving line. When the agents demanded the names of all the guests, Rayburn exploded. "I know every man, woman, and child here," he snapped. "They're all my friends, and I'll vouch for them personally."[39] The line was formed. Rayburn sent Rene Kimbrough, his secretary, to fetch a pint of whiskey from his closet. "Don't let Lou catch you," he admonished. "She'll raid that closet and throw it out."[40] Throughout the evening, he and Truman stood at the door, surreptitiously sipping weak drinks, while Rayburn called out names of arriving guests.

Truman's upset victory coupled with a Democratic sweep of the House and Senate confounded political pundits and stunned all but the voters. Rayburn, too, was surprised by the magnitude of voter support, although late in the campaign he sensed a Democratic surge. "I found great interest everywhere," he wrote. "If labor does what it says it is going to do, and we can have a reasonable split among the farm population, there are going to be a lot of upsets in senatorial and House seats."[41]

Rayburn stumped for the ticket in the South and Midwest. In the campaign's closing days, he traveled to South Carolina, stronghold of Dixiecrat candidate Strom Thurmond, to urge Democrats not to bolt the party. His address, broadcast throughout the region, constituted the party's major effort to hold the South. It failed in South Carolina, Alabama, Mississippi, and Louisiana. But the Democrats held Texas, Arkansas, Florida, North Carolina, and Virginia. Texas gave Truman his largest majority of any state. Lyndon Johnson's bitterly contested win over Coke Stevenson in the Senate runoff a few weeks earlier rounded out the victory—a triumph that Johnson, despite his inevitable complaints about inadequate help from friends, owed in no small measure to Rayburn.[42] Johnson's critics claimed he owed even more to south Texas political boss George Parr, whose flagrant ballot-box stuffing gave Johnson his 87-vote margin of victory and the derisive nickname "Landslide Lyndon."

Political analysts scrambled to explain the Truman upset.

Some cited Dewey's lackluster campaign. Others said voters were nervous over rising Soviet belligerence and reluctant to change leaders in a crisis. Many pointed out Truman's firm leadership in ordering the Berlin airlift after the Soviets blockaded the city in midsummer. Rayburn had his own explanation: the Republicans simply miscalculated the life and vigor left in the New Deal. "The people got really to thinking before they voted," he told Texas publisher Houston Harte. "They realized their universally prosperous condition and began wondering why they should vote for a change. When they got through with that wondering, they just went and voted the ticket that they thought would continue the various programs that they believe will bring them continued prosperity. The grass roots really came out this time, and us 'wool hats' from the farm voted the ticket." [43] Basically, he concluded, it was Truman's victory. "I think 90 percent or more of the credit belongs to Harry S. Truman—the fighter who wouldn't give up or be discouraged in the face of dire predictions from every source," he wrote in November. [44]

The postelection euphoria was followed, as always, by the sobering reality of organizing a new Congress. "If Dewey had been elected, I would have had no desire to return to the Speakership," Rayburn said. [45] But with a Democrat in the White House for four more years, he was eager to reclaim his old job. In mid-November, he visited the President at his Key West retreat to plan the coming session. Influenced by Truman's casual attire, he donned a colorful sport shirt printed with waving palms and flapping cranes. He was buoyant. Commented the *New York Times*: "If Mr. Rayburn is in harmony with the administration, we can take his cranes and palm trees as good omens."

17

Mr. Sam

Backed by strong majorities in both houses, the Democrats euphorically reclaimed control of Congress in 1949. Now the Truman administration could really spread its wings, or so everybody thought. There were new Democratic policies to shape, a task Rayburn, frisky as a young colt, approached with noticeable enthusiasm. Returning to the Speakership, he was serenely confident—comfortable with power, tougher than ever, less willing to bend to the minor emotional currents that constantly sweep the House.

Strengthening the Speaker's hand was the House's adoption of a procedural change effectively stripping the Rules Committee of much of its vaunted power. For years, the conservative-dominated committee had been a graveyard for liberal legislation. Scores of key bills sent to Rules for final clearance simply were ignored because the controlling coalition found them objectionable.[1] Now, if the Rules Committee failed to act on any bill within three weeks, the bill could be brought directly to the floor by the legislative committee in whose jurisdiction it fell. Rayburn supported the change—"The rules of a legislative body should be such at all times as to allow the majority to work its will"—despite southern warnings that it inevitably would lead to votes on civil rights and other dreaded liberal legislation.[2]

More important, he felt, was the need to crush the coalition that long had plagued the Democratic leadership. Now *he* would control the flow of legislation. Only after being recognized by the Speaker could a committee chairman bypass Rules and bring a bill directly before the House. The power of recognition—one of the few great powers of the Speaker to survive the 1910 Cannon revolt—became more potent than ever. Rayburn made his intentions clear: he would recognize no chairman whose bill "has not been cleared with me in advance." He soon proved the point, snubbing Labor Committee Chairman John Lesinski when the Michigan Democrat sought to pry Truman's long-delayed FEPC bill out of the Rules Committee.

Although the so-called 21-day rule proved short-lived— Rayburn eventually decided it could lead to irresponsible legislation and supported a successful southern-led effort to repeal it two years later—it awakened many to the fact that the taciturn Texan held a firmer grip on the House than any Speaker in decades. Said the *New York Times*: "Mr. Rayburn has received a power and a responsibility not given in generations to a Speaker of the House."[3]

Rayburn relied heavily on his prestige and knowledge of the House's intricate rules and precedents. He always had wielded a firm gavel, but now his decisions came faster and with even less room for challenge than ever before. On the first day of the 1949 session, he reached for an obscure technicality to shut off debate on the 21-day rule, leaving Mississippi's John Rankin red-faced and sputtering. "Mr. Speaker, we have a right to be heard," stammered the hot-tempered congressman. But by then Rayburn had moved on to other matters. Later his patience was tested by an attempted southern filibuster on an anti–poll tax bill. After sitting through seven quorum calls before debate on the bill even began, Rayburn warned that he had had enough. When still another quorum call was demanded, he simply ignored the motion, noting that a quorum was "obviously" present.

The Congressional Reorganization Act of 1946 required Congress to adjourn by July 31 each year, except when the country was at war or in a state of emergency. It was an appealing but totally unrealistic idea that soon had Rayburn searching for a loophole. In 1949, he declared that, because World War II technically had not ended, a state of emergency still existed and, therefore, the session should continue until the House had completed its business for the year. Many members objected; some threatened to go home after July 31, whether or not Congress had adjourned, and one—irascible Noah Mason of Illinois—did just that every year thereafter. John Rankin complained that the Supreme Court probably would invalidate all laws enacted after July 31. "The Chair," snapped Rayburn, "would think that the Supreme Court of the United States reads the *Congressional Record.*"[4]

Restoration of the House Chamber, long delayed because of the war, finally resumed in 1949. It was the first of what were to be many controversial Rayburn-led changes in the Capitol. The House was forced to meet in the large, marble-columned hearing room of the Committee on Ways and Means in the Longworth House Office Building. Clare Hoffman of Michigan argued one hot August day that, by convening in a different chamber, the House was no longer "a competent legal tribunal." In no mood for another of the eccentric congressman's complaints, Rayburn cut him off sharply: "The Chair overrules the point of order."

"May I not cite the provision of the Constitution . . . ?" Hoffman said, trying to finish.

"The Chair does not desire to hear the gentleman on the point of order," Rayburn interrupted again, ending the matter with a declaration House members were to hear him repeat time and again in the years to come.[5]

Few Rayburn rulings stirred more anger and resentment among his colleagues and the press than his 1952 decision to ban radio and television broadcasts of House committee hearings. His reasoning: the House rules did not permit broadcasts of proceedings of the House; therefore, by implication, the same policy applied to House committees. Jealous of the publicity bonanza befalling their counterparts in the Senate, where hearings were freely televised, House members screamed, hurling charges of "one-man edict," "discriminatory edict," and "raw censorship." But Rayburn stood firm, determined to keep out of his House of Representatives the circus atmosphere that he felt had consumed and ruined the Senate.[6] The House, he reminded, could change its rules at any time, but until then he would be the final interpreter of the existing rules. Though challenged again and again, the ban on TV and radio remained in force as long he was Speaker.[7] Concluded *U.S. News & World Report*: "Sam Rayburn quietly and discreetly wields more cold power than any other congressional figure in decades. He is a man all factions consult sooner or later in the process of turning a bill into a law."[8]

Part of Rayburn's power stemmed from the fact that he held all the cards. Unlike most of his predecessors, he refused to convene Democratic caucuses where members might discuss and choose a party position on major issues. As a result, Democratic discipline was a sometime thing. Members were free to vote largely as they wished, subject only to their own interests and Rayburn's personal appeal. John Garner once chided his old friend, "Why don't you take those fellows into caucus and bind 'em? That's what I did. I'd bind 'em, and by God, if they didn't stay bound, I'd put 'em down in my book and they'd never get through paying for it." Dismissing Garner's advice, Rayburn huffed: "John, you haven't been around the House in twenty years. You don't know what the hell you're talking about. You can't do that any more. This is a different group of men. You get in that caucus and a wild man from the North will get up and make a wild speech. Then someone from another section will answer him with a wilder speech. First thing you know, you've got the Democratic party so divided that you can't pass anything."[9]

Rayburn understood, better than anyone, the limits of his power. "The old days of pounding on the desk and giving people hell are gone," he said. "We've all grown up now. A man's got to lead by persuasion and kindness and the best reason— that's the only way he can lead people. And a Speaker should be personally popular. He can't crack down on people." He once told an interviewer that two principles guided him:

> First, I believe in people and the soundness of their judgment when they have the facts. I know that 98 percent of

the people have more good than bad in them and can be trusted to do the right thing. My experience with the Speakership is that you cannot lead people by trying to drive them. Persuasion and reason are the only ways to lead them. In that way the Speaker has influence and power in the House.

Second, I have seen a lot of politicians and officeholders in my day, and there is no job so big that it should change a man's outlook and manners. When you see a man get stuffy or arrogant because he holds a big job, it means he was not big enough for the job when he got it. There is no reason why a man should not be able to look you square in the eye and tell you what he will or will not do. I've found that people respect you if you tell them where you stand. If you shilly-shally and are afraid to say, "No," you'll get into trouble, and there's no reason for any man to get "uppity" in a government job.[10]

In May 1949, Rayburn and Republican Senator Arthur Vandenberg of Michigan were named recipients of the annual *Collier's* awards for distinguished service to the nation. The magazine's editors picked Vandenberg for his role in creating the North Atlantic Treaty and other postwar regional pacts. Rayburn was cited not for his wartime performance as Speaker but for his two-year stint as minority leader—the job he didn't want—and his party loyalty, described as "a fundamental quality if our two-party system is to survive." Silver plaques and $10,000 cash prizes were presented by the President in a White House ceremony.[11]

The money worried Rayburn. He never considered keeping it. "This," he said, "goes home." It would be used, he decided, as seed money for a library in Bonham—a library that would be a lasting monument to Sam Rayburn as well as a depository for his papers, books, and mementos. He envisioned scholars from all over America coming there to do research on the Speaker's life and times. He was nearly 70. There was vanity in his decision; there was generosity and smart politics, too. The way Rayburn described it, the facility would belong to the people of Fannin County. It would be a "public library," a symbol of their

achievement, not his, and a source of pride for future generations.[12] "The library will be a monument to him, and to the
wisdom his constituents have shown in keeping him on the job
in Washington," noted the *Dallas Times Herald*.

A building fund was set up to accept contributions. Money
flowed in, much of it from special interests seeking attention and
favor. Rayburn returned checks when he suspected the donor's
motives. But he did accept several large amounts, some in cash,
from Texas oil and other interests. Myron Blalock sent $50,000
in cash. The money came from friends, Blalock said, but he
died without providing a list of contributors. A $10,000 check
from millionaire conservative William Blakley in May 1958
raised even more serious questions of propriety. The Blakley
money, accompanied by a note imploring Rayburn, "please—
no publicity," came at an inappropriate time—just as Blakley
was seeking Rayburn's support for the U.S. Senate. Even so,
Rayburn took the money, apparently without pause, and endorsed Blakley's opponent, Ralph Yarborough.[13] The Speaker's
dream was fulfilled in 1957, when scores of state and national
dignitaries joined him and his north Texas friends for the dedication of the Sam Rayburn Library, an imposing marble shrine built
to dominate Bonham's busiest street for generations to come.

More honors were bestowed on the aging congressman as the
1950s opened. On January 30, 1951, Miss Lou and brother Dick
joined the President, Vice-President, Chief Justice, and congressional leaders at a White House ceremony commemorating
Rayburn's completion of 3,057 days as Speaker, topping by half
a day the record established by Henry Clay between 1811 and
1825. Congratulations streamed in from all over the world. The
House met early the following day to pass a resolution praising
him for the manner in which he "has steadfastly maintained and
added new luster to the great office of Speaker." His dark eyes
swelling with tears, the Texan's voice cracked as he noted: "I am
one man in public life who has achieved every ambition he
ever had."[14]

Initially, despite the large Democratic majority, Truman's "Fair
Deal" agenda faltered in the House. Throughout 1949, the

administration delivered on practically none of its campaign promises. Repeal of the Taft-Hartley Act, a key Democratic pledge to labor, was lost from the beginning; even Rayburn opposed the effort, although he tried to find an acceptable compromise. Truman's courageous if premature civil rights proposals also were rejected; again, partly because of the Speaker's opposition. The President and the Speaker also parted company on other issues, including farm control and oil and gas policies. There was irony in *U.S. News & World Report*'s observation that "to rescue the administration program, President Truman is putting his main hope in one man, the quiet Speaker of the House." "In the present situation," the magazine noted, "there can be little legislation without compromise. Mr. Rayburn used his prestige to tone down Fair Deal bills and make them more to the liking of conservatives, and to soften coalition measures."[15]

Rayburn was uniquely qualified for the mediator's role. Only he, among all House members, could move easily among the three opposing forces—the administration, southern Democrats, and Republicans. It was largely through his efforts that the House revived and passed modified versions of a few Fair Deal initiatives in the second session. With the outbreak of the Korean War in June 1950, Rayburn was thrust into a familiar role: helping the President win approval, with as little delay and scrutiny of the request as possible, of whatever appropriations were needed to expand the military.

Rayburn during this period was particularly active in behalf of the Texas oil and gas industry, a role that brought him little but embarrassment, ingratitude, and grief. Although a powerful behind-the-scenes guardian of petroleum interests—oil and Texas were inseparable, he believed—he was never the industry's pawn, as critics often alleged. No oil or gas was produced in his district until near the end of his career. He had no financial stake in the industry and, except for a brief period, never owned a share of oil stock. It was true that he was friendly—perhaps too friendly—with a few wealthy independent producers, notably James Abercrombie, J. R. Parten, and Sid Richardson, with whom he had worked in 1935 to defeat Harold Ickes's plan for federal controls over oil production and pricing. By defying the

President himself on the Ickes bill, Rayburn had won the wildcatters' lasting trust and admiration. They would gladly have
made him a wealthy man and, undoubtedly, conspired to do so
on many occasions. But, as Parten ultimately concluded, "he
was impervious to money."[16] They gave up trying to ply him
with expensive gifts after seeing that their presents were always
returned in one form or another. When one of them sent him a
fine horse, he sent back one of his champion Herefords. He accepted their political contributions, sometimes in large amounts,
for distribution to other Democratic candidates, but his own
campaign needs were modest, and he was winning elections
long before oil money came along. Only late in life, when the
endowment of his library became his consuming passion, did he
bend his principles to accept large contributions from oil and
other interests to the Sam Rayburn Foundation. Rayburn's oil
friends eventually realized that his support of the industry, often
in the face of harsh criticism, was rooted in nothing more complicated than this: he favored a prosperous Texas, and oil and gas
made Texas prosperous.

For years, he helped block legislation that would have reduced
the industry's favorable resource-depletion allowance that sharply
reduced the federal tax on oil revenues. "If I or Frank Ikard
[Rayburn's man on the Ways and Means Committee] said 'we
don't care,' the Ways and Means Committee would report a bill
cutting the depletion allowance within three hours," he said in
an unguarded moment in 1960. "We have held the line and we
have never let it get out on the floor."[17] He told other Texans:
"For twenty years, I've saved that 27½ percent depletion allowance. If it ever gets to the House floor, the members will eat it
up."[18] It never did, while he lived.

Democrats seeking appointment to Ways and Means, where
all tax laws originate, were invariably screened by Rayburn. Few
were allowed on the committee until he decided they were
"right" on depletion. For years, he kept Texas conservative
O. C. Fisher off the committee because "the party leadership is
entitled to have its own men on Ways and Means and Rules, and
Fisher is a consistent party bolter."[19] For some appointees, such
as Texan Frank Ikard, he knew without asking how they stood

on oil.[20] As one Ways and Means member explained: "Rayburn knew that I would not be a radical on depletion. . . . He knew I wouldn't go off half-cocked."[21] Others recalled similar scrutiny before they passed Rayburn's muster.

But it was not enough. "With the oil industry, like any industry, you never give them enough," observed former Congressman J. T. Rutherford, whose district covered some of Texas's richest oil land. "He helped them, he helped them, he helped them, he helped them, but he could never do enough for the oil industry, never."[22]

The oil and gas industry after the war had three priorities on Capitol Hill: retention of the 27½ percent resource-depletion allowance, federal deregulation of natural gas pricing, and affirmation of state ownership of the mineral-rich coastal tidelands. Rayburn supported the industry on all three issues. Ultimately, his crucial involvement in battles over the last of these objectives—the explosive tidelands question—would bring him more personal anguish than any controversy since he had tangled with Wall Street in the 1930s.

"Tidelands!" It was just a word—a misnomer for a seabed that was never exposed by the tide—but in Texas in the late 1940s, it was a call to arms, a rallying cry for all loyal Texans to defend their state's rights, honor, and wealth against the encroaching federal Goliath. The controversy began with the discovery of vast pools of oil off the California, Texas, and Louisiana coasts in the late 1930s. Between 1939 and 1948, all three states recognized the submerged lands as a potentially rich source of revenue and began selling leases to oil producers. Although Interior Secretary Ickes was first to acknowledge the lands belonged to the states, not the federal government, doubts lingered about their ownership. In 1945, Truman ordered Attorney General Tom Clark to file a test suit against California. Lobbied intensely by oil producers, Congress responded by passing quitclaim legislation ceding the submerged lands to the states. Truman vetoed the bill, and there the matter rested until 1947, when the Supreme Court ruled against California. The federal government, it declared, had "paramount rights" in and full domination and power over the California coastal lands "extending seaward three nautical miles."

The decision left Texas's claim unresolved. Texas contended that the resolution under which it was annexed to the Union in 1845 ceded no undersea land to the federal government. On the contrary, Texas could trace its claim to submerged lands extending to "three leagues"—10.35 miles—seaward into the Gulf of Mexico back to 1836. Because of the peculiar circumstances under which Texas joined the Union, state lawyers believed their dispute with the federal government rested on a sounder foundation than California's.[23]

Soon after the 1947 decision, Texas Attorney General Price Daniel began urging Rayburn to lead the Texas tidelands battle. He proposed quick passage of another quitclaim bill. Rayburn hesitated. For one thing, he had listened to his friend Tom Clark's explanation of the issue and was no longer convinced that individual states should own these lands. He felt a deep responsibility to Texas, but, as Speaker, he also felt a broader obligation to the nation. Many of his friends, including Lyndon Johnson, privately shared his misgivings. Moreover, he was busy running the House and had no heart to lead another bitter, drawn-out crusade. He told Daniel: "Sometimes it is better to let sleeping dogs lie as it is doubtful whether we could pass a bill through the Senate and the House here declaring what we think would be Texas rights."[24]

Still, Daniel persisted. His letters implored the Speaker to use his influence with President Truman to protect Texas interests. "When you demonstrate your personal interest and the political implications," he wrote, "I am sure [the President] will agree for you to sit in on further consideration of matters pertaining to this issue."[25] That fall, the Justice Department filed suit against Louisiana and Texas. Rayburn arranged for Daniel to meet with Truman, which pacified the Texas attorney general temporarily but solved nothing. Spurred by the latest court filings, the House overwhelmingly passed another quitclaim bill. It died, as Rayburn predicted, in the Senate.

By 1950, the Speaker was under almost unbearable pressure from Daniel and others representing Texas interests. Many argued that he could push a quitclaim bill through Congress if he tried. The fact that no bill was moving, they said, proved that Rayburn secretly sympathized with the federal government against his own state.[26] Rayburn decided it was time to seek a compromise. In collusion with Truman and Attorney General Tom Clark, the Speaker proposed a plan that would allow Texas, Louisiana, and California the rights to two-thirds of the oil and gas within a 10.35-mile limit, and one-third from there out to the continental shelf, some 125 miles. The federal government would keep one-third of the rights within the 10.35-mile limit, and two-thirds of the rest.[27] It seemed like a good deal for the state, since there was considerable doubt that any oil of consequence existed within the 10-mile area, while huge reserves were known to be present at distances 17 miles out and beyond. The compromise, therefore, would allow the three states to share in potentially vast proceeds derived from oil and gas beyond the 10-mile limit—proceeds that otherwise would revert entirely to the federal government. Even so, the "Rayburn Plan," as it became known, sparked angry debate in Texas.

Three Texas officials held the key to its approval—Governor Allan Shivers, Attorney General Daniel, and Land Commissioner Bascom Giles. Giles thought it was the best deal Texas could hope for. Shivers seemed undecided. Daniel unhesitatingly rejected it as "half a loaf." Eventually, public opinion—fanned by Daniel—turned against it as well. Daniel told reporters: "The few Texans who are publicly advocating a tidelands compromise and doubting our chances to win either in the Court or Congress are not expressing the opinion of the elected officials who bear the legal responsibility for the lands." Years later, Rayburn recalled: "Shivers and Giles were inclined to accept the plan as a good deal for Texas. But after watching Daniel a few times, I realized that he didn't want a settlement—he wanted the issue to run for office on. He wanted to demagogue it. So it couldn't be settled."[28]

His compromise snubbed, Rayburn grew pessimistic. "I am still very fearful that the Supreme Court will hold in other instances as they held in the California case," he wrote in 1950.[29] His fears proved well founded. On June 5, 1950, the Supreme Court by a vote of 4–3 (two members not voting) decreed that the federal government owned submerged lands off Texas all the way to the continental shelf. Instead of half a loaf, Texas would get nothing. In January, Texas Congressman Ed Gossett introduced yet another bill giving coastal states undisputed title to the tidelands. Rayburn by now realized that the tidelands had become a transcendent public issue in Texas, one he could no longer ignore. He threw his weight behind the Gossett bill. In the Senate, Lyndon Johnson did likewise. "This is the psychological time for the House to move," Rayburn declared.

Now Rayburn, the national leader, began feeling pressure from the other side. He was under fire, first from the press, then from political associates in Washington, who almost universally saw the bill as the attempt of a few states to steal rich assets belonging to all Americans. In a sharp letter, dripping contempt, the blunt Ickes, whose views had shifted 180 degrees since he first said the tidelands belonged to the states, spoke for many:

> Speaker Rayburn long ago ceased to be the property of Texas. He belongs to the United States. . . . I would be unhappy if in the great days—who knows, perhaps in the closing years—of his leadership, the weight of Speaker Rayburn should be cast for the narrow view of Texas and against the United States as a nation. Sam Rayburn is beyond the verdict of the ballot box, the headlines of high office or the satisfaction of favorable publicity. There is only one judgment on him yet to be made—that of history. I hope, at this late day, that he will not impair what I, and many more besides, confidently believe that judgment should be . . .[30]

The letter was condescending, insulting, typically Ickes. Rayburn brushed it aside. "It is always painful to me when I cannot agree fully with you," he replied.

Gossett's quitclaim bill passed both houses in 1952. Truman, denouncing the measure as "robbery in broad daylight," vetoed it. The Senate made no attempt to override. Governor Shivers, Attorney General Daniel, and other Texans were outraged. The tidelands, they felt, had been within their grasp, then lost. They blamed Truman, whose popularity in the state dropped to an all-time low. Some asked, "Wasn't Rayburn a close personal friend of that SOB in the White House? Why couldn't he influence Truman?" The issue that had brought Rayburn nothing but grief still festered under Texas skins as another presidential election approached. The last word on the tidelands was yet to be heard.

18

Rayburn for President

The 1952 Democratic National Convention was barely four months away when Harry Truman announced his decision not to seek re-election. A historic turning point in Democratic politics, his surprise withdrawal meant that, for the first time in twenty years, the party would have to look outside the White House for its presidential candidate. A wild scramble for the nomination resulted.

Senator Estes Kefauver of Tennessee, a dauntless challenger, led the early field after his stunning upset victory over a non-campaigning Truman in the New Hampshire presidential primary. Kefauver's decisive victory, in all likelihood, hastened Truman's decision to retire. Others eager for the nomination included Vice-President Alben Barkley, Senator Robert Kerr of Oklahoma, and Senator Richard Russell of Georgia. The press, meanwhile, gave extensive publicity to erudite Governor Adlai Stevenson of Illinois, who denied any interest in the Presidency. Quietly making himself available as a dark-horse contender was Sam Rayburn.

Rayburn's interest in the nomination was unexpected. Careful not to seek the office openly, he listened attentively to his promoters, led by Senators Mike Monroney of Oklahoma and John Sparkman of Alabama. Well before Truman's announcement,

Monroney declared himself to be Rayburn's "manager" and without Rayburn's approval began touting his candidacy, contingent on Truman's decision not to run. Energetically extolling the reluctant Speaker, Monroney circulated an endorsement petition among members of the House and Senate. The petition quickly attracted seventy-three signatures before Rayburn got wind of it and ordered it withdrawn. Reporters, nabbing Rayburn after a White House meeting one January morning, peppered him about published rumors that he was secretly mounting a bid for the Presidency. "I don't accept it," he shot back grumpily.

"The story?" asked UP's Merriman Smith.

"No, the office," Rayburn replied, chuckling at his little joke. He was not amused, however, when his snappy comment appeared in print. He quickly called White House Press Secretary Joe Short, asking him to lodge a protest with White House reporters. "That comment about declining the presidential nomination was off the record," he complained. "It wasn't supposed to get in the papers."[1]

When Truman bowed out, Rayburn's resistance evaporated, although he fought to suppress his desire for the office that had always seemed beyond his reach. "I was born in the wrong place at the wrong time" was his standard response to queries about his presidential aspirations. But, like many another politician, he found the dream irresistible. He soon was slyly but definitely cooperating with his boosters and confiding to friends that, while he would not seek the nomination, he would accept an honest draft "like a good soldier."[2]

At 70, he was too old to mount a successful open campaign. Yet a look at other Democratic contenders was encouraging. The "Veep"—Alben Barkley—was 75; Kerr had made bitter, powerful enemies with his slashing, selfish tactics; Russell bore the stigma of an ultraconservative segregationist from the deep South. Adlai Stevenson had, again and again, denied any interest in the nomination. The most aggressive, highly publicized contender, Estes Kefauver, was unacceptable to the party's power structure. In their view, Kefauver had befouled his own nest with his headline-grabbing subcommittee investigations into alleged links between Democratic big-city bosses and organized crime. So, given the alternatives, Rayburn's compromise candidacy had a ray of hope.

The Texan was Truman's "logical replacement," argued Monroney.[3] His "liberal" voting record would appeal to northern Democrats, more than offsetting his conservative views on civil rights. "Economic issues will weigh heavily," Monroney declared. "Considering all the progress we have had since 1932, I think northern Democrats would rather take someone with Rayburn's liberal record." In the senator's rosy scenario, organized labor also would find the Speaker acceptable because the Republicans would nominate Senator Taft, co-author of the Taft-Hartley Act, and "with the choice between Taft and Rayburn, labor has only one place to go."

A Rayburn boomlet, orchestrated by Monroney and Sparkman, blossomed simultaneously with the Texan's appearance at the spring meeting of the Southern Governors Conference in Hot Springs, Arkansas. There he issued a tough warning that the South would suffer catastrophic losses in committee chairmanships and power if the GOP gained control of Congress. Unimpressed with Rayburn's call for southern Democratic unity was one attentive listener, Governor Allan Shivers of Texas. "Me thinks thou protests thy virtue too loudly," the handsome governor sniffed, adding that he had always supported the Democratic ticket, and "I hope I always can." Shivers repeatedly praised another Texas native, General Eisenhower, whose name had climbed prominently in Republican speculation.

On January 9, retired mail carrier J. W. Cummings of Ivanhoe had joined with 150 other Texans to form a Rayburn for President Club. Cummings, a lifelong Rayburn friend, wisely noted that it would take the efforts of a united Texas to put the Speaker across to the rest of the country. If Texas Democrats remained divided—as they had been since 1940—Rayburn could forget the Presidency. Added Cummings naively: "I feel that every Texas Democrat will back Mr. Rayburn."

The Rayburn bandwagon picked up speed. Congressman Lloyd Bentsen of Texas announced that he would go to the Democratic National Convention in Chicago to work for

Rayburn's nomination. House Majority Leader John McCormack said he would support the Speaker. Some who were committed to other candidates privately said Rayburn was their second choice. Democratic observers began predicting a Kefauver-Russell deadlock—more good news for Rayburn. "Speaker Sam," wrote Allen S. Otten of the *Wall Street Journal*, "is one of the better bets to cop the Democratic nomination."[4] The winning strategy, as outlined by Monroney: "Ours is a tenth-ballot proposition. When a few ballots have gone by and it becomes obvious that none of the candidates is going to get past first base, the delegates will be ready to switch to someone who can hit a home run."[5]

Rayburn again would preside as the convention's permanent chairman. He would stand before the delegates throughout the proceeding, a constant reminder of his availability for the nomination. Moreover, this would be the first Democratic convention televised from coast to coast—a new dimension in politics. Millions of Americans would be sizing up "the good soldier" for the first time. "He'll be standing there with klieg lights bouncing off that bald dome, looking as solid and substantial and trustworthy as the rock of ages," one supporter explained. Also noted by his backers was that among the state delegations would be scores of past and present House members who had served with the Speaker. Rayburn partisans feared only two other contenders: Barkley and Stevenson. They, too, had the makings of attractive compromise candidates.

By summer, Rayburn backers could only sit and wait. No effort was made to line up convention votes; his only avowed delegate support was half a vote in Maine. The Texan remained noncommittal in public, skirting the inevitable questions from reporters but making himself available for speeches and interviews. In May, his delivery of a 30-minute prepared speech on U.S. foreign policy fanned speculation that he was moving toward an open candidacy. "The Texas legislator seldom addresses the House," observed the AP, "never from a prepared text."[6] Noted the *Louisville Courier-Journal* on June 1: "His is the newest and longest lightning rod to appear in the campaign. You never saw a man run so hard as Sam without admitting it." Two weeks before the Chicago convention, Rayburn received a letter from Houston lawyer Charles I. Francis offering to assist in his quest for the nomination and alleging that such an effort would have Shivers's blessing.[7] The governor, said Francis, had informed him that "he had every intention of supporting the ticket and on no condition would he bolt the ticket regardless of the candidate. . . . He assured me that if conditions should develop whereby you would be a compromise candidate such would be acceptable to him, and you would have his support." Rayburn knew better. He ignored the Shivers question in his reply to Francis:

> I do not know whether the time will come when you could serve me personally at Chicago or not. Many think that a deadlock will come sometime at the convention and friends of various states are suggesting that my name be sent in at some moment in a dramatic way. Whether this will develop, we must wait and see, although I think it is more or less doubtful. If it should come, however, I think you might be helpful with some members of the Texas delegation.[8]

Arriving in Chicago on Sunday, July 20, Rayburn temporarily put aside his own thoughts of the Presidency to concentrate on the more crucial problem of holding the party together. Every effort must be made, he believed, to avoid another southern walkout like that in 1948. There were serious questions of party loyalty to settle among southern delegates. Once again, Texas had come to the convention with two bitterly competing delegations battling for recognition. The Texas Democratic organization was backing Georgia's Richard Russell, while the challenging delegation, led by former Congressman and San Antonio Mayor Maury Maverick, supported Rayburn. Lacking proper credentials, the liberal Maverick group eventually lost its bid for recognition as the state's official delegation and had to watch the proceedings from the gallery. Meanwhile, Kefauver's backers, convinced that the Tennessean was the people's choice, threatened to disrupt the convention if he was denied the party's nomination.

In his dark suit and broad-brimmed white hat, the stocky
Rayburn looked more like a well-to-do Texas rancher than a national statesman as he paused in the summer sun outside the
Blackstone Hotel to greet friends and chat with reporters. "Will
you allow your name to be put in nomination?" he was asked.

"Not today."

"Will you set up a headquarters like the other candidates?"

"My hotel suite will be my headquarters—no ribbons, no
buttons, no noise."

"Would you accept the nomination?"

"I am only a candidate for re-election to Congress. If there is
a prolonged deadlock, then and only then, would I allow my
name to be put before the convention." The convention, in the
International Amphitheater, opened the following day.

In 1948, the Democratic and Republican gatherings were seen
by television viewers only in New York, Philadelphia, and Baltimore. By 1952, the whole nation could tune in. The political
impact of the new medium was immediate and profound as the
flickering small screen brought the drama, passions, and in-
trigue of the convention into millions of living rooms and transformed the participants into nationally recognized personalities.
Viewers were at once baffled and endlessly fascinated by the
mass confusion, parliamentary maneuvering, and verbal brawls.
And on camera, hour after hour, day after day, was Rayburn—
short, totally bald, now smiling, now snarling, banging his
gavel with visible confidence, resembling a veteran ringmaster at
a three-ring circus. He was an unlikely TV figure. The hot,
bright lights bothered him: they dimmed his vision and caused
him to perspire profusely. Technicians worried that the glare off
his shiny dome might annoy viewers, but he stubbornly refused
to allow makeup on his baldpate. Through it all, what came
across most vividly to most Americans was Rayburn's sincerity,
his powerful demeanor, and his poise under pressure.

Television wrought a dramatic change in Rayburn's status,
personally and politically. For years, his legislative skill, his
judgment, and his unwavering loyalty to friends and party were
legend among political professionals. But to average Ameri-

cans—including many in his own district—he was essentially unknown. Television, beginning with the 1952 convention, changed that. Overnight, his bald head, his mobile face, his deep voice, his paternalistic toughness as chairman became immediately recognizable to millions. He was, for the first time, a national figure to the average American. For the remaining nine years of his life, he and the Democratic party would become inseparable in the public's mind. He became "Mr. Democrat," a title he cherished.[9] He owed much to television.

Rayburn's performance at the 1952 convention captivated the press. Reporters were quick to credit the feisty chairman when things went smoothly and blame him when decorum slipped. "The bald eagle from Bonham has choked off more potential free-for-alls than a bouncer in a Chicago saloon," reported INS. His skill and finesse were tested repeatedly. Kefauver supporters, believing that Rayburn favored Stevenson, challenged his rulings at every opportunity. In one instance, the Tennessee senator invited TV viewers to wire Rayburn in protest of his "arbitrary" handling of debate on the party platform; many did. Meanwhile, southern delegations, craving an excuse to stage a dramatic walkout for the benefit of TV viewers back home, were poised for any hint of unfairness toward them. All the explosive emotions of a political convention ultimately converged in a bitter floor fight that forced Rayburn to dig deeply into his bag of parliamentary tricks to keep the fragile party from splintering.

The catalyst for potential chaos was a convention rule requiring all state delegations to pledge support of the party's nominees. Rayburn personally obtained Shivers's promise that Texas would back the ticket, whoever the nominee. On that condition, he supported seating the Shivers-led conservative delegation over Maury Maverick's liberal insurgents.[10] Three states— Virginia, South Carolina, and Louisiana—balked at the loyalty oath. Their credentials denied, they stood aside awaiting the chair's ruling on whether they had forfeited the right to participate in the party's main business—the nominations.

The three states begged for eviction. As Virginia's Harry Byrd explained, "Our strategy is not to communicate with the credentials committee, just remain in our seats and let them be the aggressors and let them read us out of the convention or throw us out bodily if they will." [11] Rayburn, whose duty was to decide the issue, faced this dilemma: 1. having refused the loyalty oath, the three delegations clearly were ineligible to vote in the convention; 2. if they were evicted and other southern states left with them, Kefauver might be nominated; and 3. party hopes of beating the Republicans in November dictated that some way be found to keep the South from bolting. Rayburn, searching for some method of keeping the party intact, delayed his ruling until, finally, it was time to choose the ticket.

Tempers were overheating as the chairman slammed his gavel to start the nominating ritual. The roll call of the states brought nominations in quick succession: Russell, Kefauver, Kerr, finally Stevenson, the enigmatic, brooding dark horse. At 7 P.M., the clerk called "Louisiana"—the crucial moment had arrived. Tension rose. What would Louisiana do? Would delegates, after all their bombast, submit to the oath and be seated? Louisiana yielded to Virginia. How, some wondered, could Louisiana, not legally in the convention, yield to another state that was itself ineligible to participate?

"Follow the rules," shouted Minnesota's Hubert Humphrey as he and other angry delegates surged toward the platform, their state standards waving defiantly in Rayburn's face.

"Get those things away," the Texan thundered, with a broad sweep of his arm. "There'll be no recognition of anyone until there is order. The Chair treats everyone with respect and expects to be so treated."

"Follow the rules!" yelled a crimson-faced Humphrey.

"That's exactly what I am doing," snapped Rayburn, his own anger showing. "Furthermore, the Chair knows the rules." He gaveled until the noise receded, then he recognized Virginia Governor John S. Battle to speak for the three challenged states.

Thus began a series of partly preplanned, partly spontaneous maneuvers of great complexity, with Rayburn at the vortex. At stake was party unity in a crucial election year, perhaps even the future of the Democratic party itself. Politicians still debate whether Rayburn interpreted the rules correctly—he always insisted that he did—or whether the wily old parliamentarian improvised as he went along to prevent a convention breakup. This much is certain: in a volatile situation, he displayed cool mastery. It was, for delegates and TV viewers alike, an evening of high drama, starting with Governor Battle's request for Rayburn's "specific ruling as to whether we are, or are not, members of the convention, entitled to full participation in its deliberations and votes."

In no hurry to get to that unhappy business, Rayburn first asked if any state desired to be polled. Was any delegate unrecorded? Did any delegate want to change his or her vote? His questions had the cutting edge of a command.[12] Senator Russell Long and another Louisianan accepted his offer to administer the pledge to any delegate who had not yet taken it. They were recognized as members of the convention.

Finally, after Governors Battle and Kennon were allowed to address the assembly, both speaking emotionally of their obligation to uphold the laws and the wishes of their states, Rayburn was ready. The convention floor was chaotic. He waited for delegates to settle down. "The Chair," he said, "holds that the delegations from South Carolina, Virginia, and Louisiana have not complied with the rules adopted in this convention." Clearly, then, they could not participate. The issue apparently settled, all eyes focused on the three rebuffed delegations, who remained seated, waiting, as Harry Byrd phrased it, "to be thrown out bodily."

But Rayburn was playing out a scenario that was not yet ended. He recognized Lansdale Sasscer of Maryland, who stunned the convention by moving not to oust the three holdouts but to seat them, starting with Virginia, which he argued with dubious logic was "in substantial compliance with the spirit of the rule." The half-empty hall buzzed with angry voices. What was going on? many asked. The surprise resolution, prearranged by Rayburn and other party leaders, was a long shot—a last desperate attempt to keep the party from coming unglued. Maybe, they thought, enough delegates could be convinced to support it. Holding out scant hope for such an outcome, Rayburn quickly ordered the yeas and nays. Even he was unprepared for the overwhelming rejection that seemed inevitable after the first roll call:

35½ votes in favor of seating Virginia, 462½ against, 416 not voting. There would be one more fast run through the roll to allow for changes and additions of votes, and the fight would be over.

Then, as many delegates drifted back from nearby bars and restaurants, the hall stirred with new excitement. Leaders of the draft-Stevenson movement, seeing an opportunity to curry southern support, decided to jump into the fight. While Kefauver rooted for a walkout—from which he would benefit—Stevenson supporters blanketed the hall, arguing for Virginia's seating. They desperately needed more time. Rayburn proved coopera-tive, delaying the proceedings while Stevenson operatives moved frantically among the states. At one point, Rayburn himself left the platform and, for nearly an hour, went from one delegation to another appealing for Virginia's seating. Votes were being added and changed so fast that even the tally clerks lost track. Still, after all the pleading and politicking, the result was a dis-appointing 475½ for seating, 650 against. Although the maneu-ver seemed doomed, Rayburn continued to stall, ignoring the shouts of a growing army of irate Kefauver backers clustered at the foot of the platform.

Finally, the break Rayburn had been waiting for: the skilled "old pros," absent until now, took charge. Returning from a lei-surely dinner, the three Illinois political kingpins—Joseph Gill, Jacob Arvey, and Scott Lucas—grasped the situation and made the whole exercise seem easy. For the next hour, as the trio worked the hall, one state after another reversed its vote. Swept up in the frenzy, Russell Long waved Louisiana's banner wildly. Earlier, Long had tried to cast the vote of the state's two "loyal" delegates. Rayburn had rebuffed him, ruling that Louisiana was ineligible to vote. Now Long cast his state's 20 votes for Vir-ginia, and Rayburn unhesitatingly allowed them to be counted. When all the dust had settled, the final tally stood: 650½ in favor of seating Virginia, 529 against, 86 not voting.

With each new pro-Virginia vote, Kefauver supporters grew more and more furious. The standard of South Dakota bobbed frantically. "South Dakota," shouted delegation Chairman George A. Bangs, a Kefauver supporter, "is leaving the floor in protest against the grossly unfair rulings of the Chair." With that, Bangs grabbed the standard and disappeared in the smoke and haze at the rear door. Rayburn was visibly upset by the incident. "This is the first time anyone has ever questioned my fairness," he told the convention. Minutes later, the banner reappeared, as did a subdued Bangs, who denied reports that he had been punched in a scuffle with another delegate over the standard. Later Rayburn defended his rulings: "Any convention can do anything it wants to about seating and unseating delegates. So my ruling in this was according to parliamentary law. I did give time for anybody who wanted to change their vote to do so. . . . I did not want to give anybody the right to go out and say they had been thrown out of the convention or that they were not allowed to make the proper motions in order to get seated if the convention desired to seat them."[13]

The next day, delegates turned to the business of picking a party candidate. Stevenson's star was definitely on the ascent. Despite the governor's renewed plea to the convention "that you will abide by my wishes not to nominate me," it was now clear that, if nominated, he would accept.

Kefauver, as expected, led on the first ballot, with Stevenson and Russell trailing. After the second ballot, which also proved inconclusive, the draft-Stevenson scenario began to unfold. "He will be nominated on the third ballot," Stevenson strategist James A. Finnegan whispered to a colleague. Several states, having fulfilled pledges to Kefauver and Russell on the first two ballots, now could switch to Stevenson. Arkansas led the parade; others followed. It was soon clear that Stevenson was the convention's choice. There would be no deadlock, no frantic search for a consensus candidate, no last-minute rush to Sam Rayburn. His last hope ever for the Presidency died without even a whimper.

But the theatrics were not over. Thirteen minutes after the roll call started, the hall began to buzz. At the rear of a long aisle leading to the platform, clutching the arm of Paul Douglas, stood Estes Kefauver. More than a surprise, it was unprecedented for a candidate to appear on the convention floor during balloting. As the pair slowly made their way toward the plat-

form, delegates began to roar. On the platform, Parliamentarian
Clarence Cannon hopped up and down angrily. "You can't interrupt a roll call," he exclaimed to Rayburn. "You can't interrupt a
roll call for any reason."

"Dammit, Clarence, I know that," Rayburn snapped.[14] Glowering, he met the two men at the top of the stairs. "What the
hell do you want?" he demanded.

"I'm going to withdraw in favor of Paul [Douglas, though
not a contender, also had been nominated] and then Paul is
going to withdraw in favor of Adlai," Kefauver said.

"What the hell does that get you?" Rayburn scoffed. "Besides,
you can't interrupt a roll call." Kefauver argued that, in 1932,
William Gibbs McAdoo had been permitted to interrupt a
roll call with a speech that ensured the nomination of FDR.
Rayburn, who had lost a footrace to the platform with the devious McAdoo, remembered that incident all too well. This was
different. "Such things aren't done," he said with finality. "Sit
down, and when the roll is finished, I'll recognize you." He had
no intention of letting Kefauver with a grand gesture stampede
the convention into putting him on the ticket with Stevenson.
Only after Stevenson had won was Kefauver allowed to announce his concession. A potentially brilliant political maneuver
had failed.

The convention had far less trouble choosing a vice-
presidential candidate. As Rayburn told it:

> The boys were determined to settle the vice-presidential
> nomination that night. So we—Harry Truman, Adlai,
> [Democratic National Chairman] Frank McKinney, Les
> Biffle, and myself—found a little room back of the plat-
> form. Adlai told us, "The man I really would like most to
> have is Alben Barkley. He's able, he has served the party for
> so long, and we are distant kinsmen. But labor at this con-
> vention refuses to support him because he is too old. And,
> if we are to make anything of Eisenhower's age in this cam-
> paign, Barkley on the ticket won't help. [It effectively ruled
> out Rayburn as well.] Kefauver has a large and very loyal
> following, but I suppose what I want most in a Vice-

President is a man who could help me get my program through the Senate."

I remember Truman saying, "Then you damn sure don't want Kefauver! He doesn't have a single friend in the whole damn Senate unless it's Paul Douglas."

We narrowed it to two men—John Sparkman and Mike Monroney—and talked about their pros and cons. Both were "my boys" in the House; both had fine records in the Senate. Mike was a former newspaperman and popular with the press boys. John had worked his way up from a tenant farmer's family. I think it was the tenant farmer thing that made the difference, so we agreed on Sparkman.[15]

Mail and telegrams swamped Rayburn after his return to Bonham. If he had any doubts about television's great influence, they quickly disappeared as he pored over stack after stack of comments from people who had followed the Chicago proceedings from their living rooms. Some condemned his "arbitrary, ruthless and totally high-handed methods." But, overall, the mail was favorable. Before going to Chicago, the Texan had told a small gathering of his close friends: "I'll promise you one thing. I'm not going to come home and apologize and say I got run over at any convention. I'm going up there and run that thing like it ought to be run."[16] A Roper poll showed 46 percent of the TV audience thought Rayburn "handled himself well," by far the highest favorable rating given anyone at either of the major national conventions. When TV transformed his life, Rayburn was 70 and had been in public office for nearly half a century. He had been content to work in semiobscurity. Now, for the rest of his years, he would grow as a national figure, an elder statesman greatly admired and much beloved by millions who, before they tuned in to the Democratic National Convention in 1952, had never heard his name.

He was pleased with the convention outcome but did not underestimate the difficulties ahead for the Democratic party. The Republicans at their own fiery convention had nominated General Eisenhower, one of the most popular figures of the century. Truman, his administration in shambles amid charges of corruption and of harboring Communists in government, was scraping bottom in the public opinion polls. The Democrats would be on the defensive throughout the campaign. But Rayburn believed that, in Adlai Stevenson, the party had an attractive, able, clean, idealistic nominee with a great gift of expression. In the years ahead, as many party leaders turned their backs on the brilliant but aloof former governor, Rayburn always felt real warmth for him. Stevenson, with all his political faults, had a conception of duty and selflessness that touched the Texan deeply.

Rayburn showed no lasting disappointment that his own fragile aspirations for President never got off the ground. Although he talked about benefiting from convention deadlocks all his political life, he never really expected it to happen and in his final years would vehemently deny—presumably with fingers crossed—that he ever wanted to be President in this or any year.

After Stevenson's nomination, Allan Shivers and his Texas followers slammed the door on the national Democratic party. The governor, taking most of the able young Texas conservatives with him, marched into the Republican camp, a defection not surprising to those who had watched his maneuverings over the preceding year. With "Shivercrats for Eisenhower" controlling the state Democratic organization, the Democratic National Committee turned to Rayburn as the party's last hope for keeping Texas's twenty-four electoral votes in the Democratic column.

Rayburn could see that he was leading a lost cause. But he was still the loyal Democrat, the "good soldier." So, with State Representative Jim Sewell of Corsicana, former State Representative D. B. Hardeman, and a handful of party diehards, he opened a Stevenson-Sparkman headquarters in the Adolphus Hotel in Dallas. He had no idea how to run a state campaign and no money, save for the few thousand dollars scraped up from old sources, including friends such as Dallas millionaire Stanley Marcus, and the meager sums that trickled in through the mail each day.[17] To get the operation off the ground, he turned to his most trusted and loyal friends—the Texas delegation in Congress—asking them to speak out publicly for Stevenson. Several, including Lyndon Johnson, ran for cover. "We couldn't find him [Johnson] when the fighting got rough," complained the Bexar County Democratic finance chairman.[18] Most Democrats refused to get deeply involved. "This is one of the worst organizational setups I have ever been in," complained a Rayburn field manager.[19] Liberals chafed under Rayburn's leadership, complaining that he was being too soft on the hated Allan Shivers. Still, working fourteen-hour days, the old fighter and his small staff gave their all. In letters, speeches, and personal visits, they blanketed the state, urging farmers and other traditional Democrats to "heed the counsel of an old friend" and stay with the party.

Democratic chances in Texas vanished when Stevenson, goaded by Shivers, declared his support for federal ownership of the disputed tidelands. Texas patriotism flared to an angry peak. "They're trying to rob us" became the cry across the state. Eisenhower, seizing the opportunity, quickly announced that as President he would favor giving Texas full rights to the tidelands. Democratic politicians scattered like doves in hunting season. Shivers and Senate nominee Price Daniel endorsed Eisenhower; so did the Democratic State Convention and the Democratic State Committee. Some state officials hid out, incommunicado, in the New Mexico mountains or in hospitals. Only young Agriculture Commissioner John White openly supported Stevenson. Although Rayburn tried hard to cool down the inflamed tidelands issue, it was a political debacle. "Granting that Stevenson is wrong on this question, does that make Eisenhower and the reactionary-isolationist Republicans right on every other issue?" he argued, repeating a line of dubious political value that he stole from Lyndon Johnson. No one was impressed.

Before the string ran out on the 1952 Texas campaign, Rayburn himself was an issue. Furious at Shivers for breaking his commitment to support the Democratic candidate, Rayburn lashed out at the governor at every opportunity. Publicly, he condemned Shivers's duplicity. Privately, his language was more pungent. Shivers, denying any promises to Rayburn, retaliated viciously.[20] He and his followers denounced and ridiculed Rayburn from the podium, assailing the Speaker as a "pinhead," a "peanut brain," and, in the ultimate Texas insult, a modern-day Santa Anna— the Mexican general in command at the Alamo. Said Claude Gilmer, chairman of the newly organized Texas Democrats for Eisenhower: "It was too much to hope that Sam Rayburn would put loyalty to Texas above the political obligations he has to the Truman crowd in Washington."[21] Recalled former Senator Ralph Yarborough: "None of Mr. Rayburn's friends from Texas then in high office who professed such great love for him would take the stump against Allan Shivers to answer his attacks on Sam Rayburn. It wasn't popular then to answer Shivers on Rayburn. But I did."[22] Yarborough, running for governor in 1952, billed himself as a "Sam Rayburn Democrat." He lost.

Eisenhower's seemingly inexorable march to victory in November was bitter medicine for Rayburn. Even Fannin County went for Ike, wounding the Speaker deeply. But, as he told a friend: "I was working in the cause to which I am loyal, and it matters not what anyone may say or do or think of me, I am going down the line always for the party that has been so good to me and so helpful to our common country."[23] To another, he wrote:

> We lost the election for several reasons. First was the Republicans had a national advertised product which was easy to sell. The next was they talked of change, change, change until a great many people got to thinking it was necessary for the life of the country to have a change. Another big thing was the treachery of our people right here in Texas. Little men in big places who do not have much regard, if any, for their word or promises. They promised everything and now we will have the opportunity to see if they produce or want to.[24]

Though they lost the election, Rayburn was more convinced than ever that the Democrats had found in Adlai Stevenson one of the nation's great leaders. "He made one of the grandest campaigns and some of the most thoughtful speeches I have ever listened to," he told colleagues. "He seems to be a Woodrow Wilson and a Franklin Roosevelt all in one. We must keep him

26. *Showing rural admirers that he can still plow a straight furrow*

27. *Rayburn, at his ranch, with County Agent V. J. Young*

28. Impromptu press conference, 1947

29. *Rayburn is swarmed by children at his birthday party, an annual event attended
by the offspring of his younger friends and hosted by the doting Lyndon and Lady
Bird Johnson, parents of Lynda Bird Johnson (on left).*

30. *President Truman enjoys a laugh with the congressional "Big Four" at the White House, 1952.* Left to right: *Alben Barkley, Truman, Rayburn, Ernest McFarland and John McCormack.*

31. *Rayburn homeplace on Highway 82 in Bonham, Texas*

32. With Miss Lou. "I like her because she thinks like a man," said Rayburn.

33. A surprise birthday gift from the President, 1950

34. *Rayburn surveys his domain at the 1952 Democratic National Convention.*

35. *Enjoying a cool piece of watermelon at the Rayburn farm north of Bonham*

36. Breaking ground for the Sam Rayburn Library in Bonham, December 10, 1955

37. *Rayburn's determination to restore the Capitol made him a host of enemies.*

38. *Sidewalk supervisor Rayburn inspects work on Capitol East Front, 1960.*

39. With Lyndon Johnson and Adlai Stevenson at LBJ Ranch, 1955

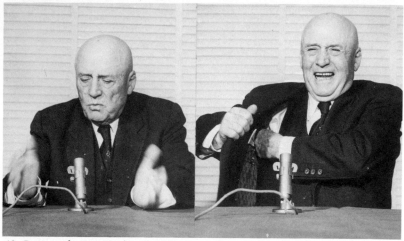

40. *Press conference. Rayburn's expressions often told more than his words.*

41. *Rayburn arriving at a testimonial dinner for Congressman Francis Walter in 1961*

42. *President Eisenhower signs the Alaska statehood bill.*

43. *Sam Rayburn Library*

44. *Rayburn being interviewed from the floor of the Democratic Convention*

45. *Talking turkey with Democratic standard bearers Kennedy and Johnson*

The fish haven't got a chance!
Affectionately — Jacqueline Kennedy
And neither has the
House of Representatives
John Kennedy

46. *Memorable snapshot by Jacqueline Kennedy catches Rayburn indulging in his favorite pastime at Kennedy compound in Palm Beach, 1961.*

47. *Rayburn at 78, holding a birthday cake from his staff*

48. *Rayburn and Lyndon Johnson*

49. Rayburn at his desk in the Speaker's office

for the future." [25]

The Eisenhower landslide gave the GOP control of the House and Senate, making the defeat complete. Rayburn, approaching 71, again would be giving up the Speakership. His thoughts fell fleetingly on Bonham, the homestead, and the ranch. There would never be a better time to retire. But on November 21, he wired John McCormack that he had decided to accept the minority leadership come January, "if the position is offered to me."

19

The Peak of Power

"You expect a lot of fun this session?" reporters asked Rayburn shortly before the House convened in January 1953. "Gruesome fun," the Texan growled as he strode briskly into the chamber for the traditional balloting for Speaker, a strictly partisan vote that the Republican candidate, Joe Martin, would win. The loser, Rayburn, would become leader of the minority. With customary grace, the Massachusetts Republican reclaimed the Speaker's chair he had relinquished to his Texas friend four years earlier. "We assume the leadership mindful that only a few months ago we ourselves were the minority party," Martin said, accepting the gavel. "Yet you treated us with respect and dignity, and we shall do the same."

Not all Republicans shared Martin's spirit of generosity. Partisan friction was still the rule. Holding a 221–211 majority, with one independent and two vacancies, the GOP had one overriding obsession: to weather the 1954 off-year elections with their House and Senate majorities intact. Democrats, meanwhile, sought to exploit deep rifts within Republican ranks. Politics crackled from the opening gavel, and, as Rayburn predicted, it was "gruesome fun."

Rayburn, though no longer Speaker, was by now an institution unto himself. "Mr. Democrat," Adlai Stevenson had la-

beled him, and the title stuck. With the death of Adolph Sabath
and the retirement of Muley Doughton, he was now, at 71, dean
of the House. Making his age an asset, he began reminding colleagues of his senior status. When he began a speech with the
phrase "As I said forty years ago on the floor of this House . . . ,"
colleagues stopped and listened: a man of history and vast experience was giving them his candid judgment.

Across the Capitol, Rayburn's irrepressible protégé, Lyndon
Johnson, was elected Senate minority leader. For the next two
years, the pair would lead the Democrats in Congress. At 44,
Johnson was the youngest party leader in fifty-two years. The
father-son relationship between the two Texans was already a
Washington legend. Everyone one knew they would make a
strong team. Remarked one observer: "Lyndon is going to be
the idea man, and Sam will tell him when it's all right to go
ahead."

As leaders of the minority, Rayburn and Johnson found easy
agreement on basic philosophy and strategy: they rejected former Senate Minority Leader Taft's doctrine—summed up in
Taft's phrase "the business of the opposition is to oppose"—and
pledged not to "criticize for criticism's sake only," particularly
in matters of national security and foreign policy.[1] "It is not the
duty of the opposition to oppose," Johnson said. "It's a new era
and a new Congress."[2]

Rayburn added one caveat. He would fight the administration
if it tried to undo "the good things we Democrats did" in the
previous twenty years. "Any jackass can kick a barn down,"
Rayburn noted, "but it takes a good carpenter to build one."
He and the new President began on friendly terms. When
Eisenhower was elected, Rayburn told him: "I'll help you on
international affairs and defense, if you can get a majority of
your own party to go along." Moreover, he would help provide
the House votes any time the President sought to extend existing Democratic programs. On other domestic matters, however, especially if there were attempts to reverse Democratic
policies on public power, reclamation, public housing, taxes,
and farm assistance, he reserved the right to oppose. "It is pretty
hard for the minority to have a program because they don't get

them considered by the committees," he wrote. "I have always thought it better for the minority to simply pick to pieces bad legislation proposed by the majority and try, if possible, to take the bad parts out and put good parts in."[3]

For many Republicans, the new administration represented a long-awaited opportunity to test the application of business techniques to modern government—something the GOP had preached for twenty years. Eisenhower, rankling at the "business administration" label slapped on his regime, had his own priorities. He warned his party not to let the Democrats claim interest in the "little fellow," while Republicans represent "big business." His biggest headaches were to come not from Democrats, but from quarreling, disgruntled members of his own party. Rayburn predicted that unity would prosper among Democrats because, with Roosevelt and Truman gone, "the haters" in both parties would now direct their venom at Eisenhower. "They hated Roosevelt and Truman because of civil rights," he remarked. "Now they will start hating Eisenhower for the same reason."

Rayburn and the new President were, by and large, cut from the same cloth: Eisenhower, eight years younger, was born in Denison, a small city in Rayburn's district. "He was a wonderful baby," Rayburn often said with a grin. They had easy rapport. In private, Rayburn would call the President "Cap'n" and joke about being his "vicarious congressman."[4] Both had middle-of-the-road political philosophies and a strict sense of national duty. Both understood the necessity of compromise. Both were men of goodwill, abhorring venomous personal attacks. They stood poles apart, however, in their attitude toward politics. Rayburn thrived on politics; Eisenhower viewed it all as "clackety-clack." As events developed, they disagreed on other crucial matters as well.

Rayburn's disillusionment with Eisenhower began with an incident shortly after the new President took office. The House minority leader, anxious to continue a bipartisan approach to foreign policy and national security, told Ike at a White House meeting: "just let me know what you want" in defense appropriations—the Democrats would support it. Eisenhower looked puzzled. Mistrustful, fearing a trap, he ignored the offer and changed the subject, leaving Rayburn nonplussed.[5] He confided to a friend:

> I told President Eisenhower the other day that he should know more about what it took to defend this county than practically anyone and that if he would send up a budget for the amount he thought was necessary to put the country in a position to defend ourselves against attack, I would promise him to deliver 95 percent of the Democratic votes in the House. What he is going to do about these things I do not know, but I know one thing and that is, he must assert some leadership soon or we may wind up before long having a leaderless country.[6]

Eisenhower's program foundered in the Republican Congress. Conservatives rejected his innovations as vigorously as they had fought Democratic ideas in earlier administrations. The narrow GOP majority—one vote in the Senate and ten votes in the House—seldom produced administration victories. "If I were the Republican leadership, in either the House or Senate with the thin majority they have and as thin ice as they are skating on at this time," Rayburn remarked in April, "I would try to get things done in just as nonpartisan manner as I possibly could, because there comes a time when partisanship can be practiced on both sides of this House. I know how to cause trouble if I want to. I know something about the rules of the House and the rights of the minority, and I want to see this administration one of these days spread its wings and get off the ground . . . "[7]

Several times in the spring of 1953, Eisenhower appealed to Rayburn for Democratic votes to save important administration programs. When Ike asked for Democratic help in defeating a conservative-backed effort to kill the excess profits tax on corporations, the Texan finally exploded. He rounded up the votes but then sent word to Eisenhower that it was the last time Democrats would "bail him out" when Republican factions refused to follow him.[8] "It seems that they have been out of power so long that they have lost all ability to lead and be constructive," he told a constituent.[9] Later he told a friend, shaking his head: "I'm sorry for President Eisenhower. If there ever was a man since General Grant who needed help, it's my friend, General Eisenhower. He's not getting any help from Congress or his Cabinet." [10]

By December, Rayburn's disenchantment with Eisenhower was complete. "He can't find his ass with both hands," he grumbled privately. [11] To a constituent, he wrote: "He is a good man and wants to do the right thing, but he is in an entirely new field for him. He needs more help than any man who has been President for many years, but he called around him men who never had any political or government experience, not any of them but one has ever held public office or run for a public office that I know anything about." [12]

Rayburn had little respect for most Eisenhower advisers. "They're very poor, especially Secretary of Agriculture Ezra Benson. . . . He scares the living daylights out of all the farmers, every time he opens his mouth," he commented. [13] He mistrusted White House Chief of Staff Sherman Adams, who, the Texan insisted, was deliberately trying to destroy New Deal regulatory laws by packing independent agencies with conservatives. He had special contempt for one Bernard M. Shanley, the President's secretary. "He's made some of the meanest speeches ever made by anybody in the United States," Rayburn wrote in 1953. "My estimation of him is that he is a 'pipsqueak.' I sent word to him one day that if he made any more speeches like he was making around here, that I would take the floor and take his pants off." [14]

The Eisenhower administration, Rayburn ultimately concluded, was simply "the most inept and blundering administration I have ever served with." [15] To him, the Republicans had defaulted on virtually every campaign promise. The national debt, unemployment, and taxes on individuals had all increased under the GOP. As for the Republican 83rd Congress, he said, "it is as dynamic as the dodo and as forward looking as yesterday." [16] Ultimately, as Rayburn should have anticipated, some of his more personal comments about Eisenhower's ineptitude found their way into the press. When Republicans complained, he denied ever having spoken ill of any President and, ducking behind the politician's traditional cover, claimed he had been misquoted. By the fall of 1953, Minority Whip John McCormack was sniffing Republican blood. Writing from Boston, he urged Rayburn to press the attack: "There is no question but that a determined drive is on for a national sales tax, either manufacturers or consumers, which I think we should oppose as a party policy. . . . I think it would be a good idea for me to poll our members now because the sentiment among our boys will be overwhelmingly against it—and to make public the results of the poll. . . . I would like your reaction."

Rayburn, with typical caution, alerted McCormack to the risks but allowed him to make the final decision. His response illuminated their casual, friendly relationship:

> As to making a poll of our members now, I would think it is probably a little early to do it, but it may be best to let some Republicans kick over the traces before we show too much of our hand. On the other hand, it may be wise to follow the course that you have suggested and get our boys on the line, and then if they do not bring up [a national sales tax], it might be we can claim the credit for scaring them away from bringing it up on the theory that we were going to overwhelmingly defeat the proposition. I will leave the decision in this matter to your own good judgment.[17]

When the Republicans lost important local elections in November, Rayburn sensed a rising Democratic tide. Still, he resisted partisan attack. "With this scare thrown into individual Republicans," he said, "poor Eisenhower is going to have a tough time in the next session because these Republican members are going to be looking out for their own skins and have found out they just can't be elected by saying they are supporting Eisenhower. . . . I think we can sit back awhile and watch them try to do something because we will have plenty of time to criticize."[18]

Rayburn again warned McCormack against jumping too quickly: "With all the Republicans getting scared about the elections last fall, I think they will be ready to sit and do little or nothing and be looking after themselves as individuals and not

Eisenhower and his administration. I think that we are going to have a good deal of rowing between the Republicans, right on the floor of the House, if we do not drive them together by premature criticism and statements."[19]

In Rayburn's opinion, the 83rd Congress had only five notable achievements. He placed at the top passage of the Tidelands Act, which fulfilled Eisenhower's promise to Texas to relinquish all federal claims to the disputed offshore oil properties. ("Where's Texas?" Eisenhower called out jovially as he signed the measure on May 22, 1953; Rayburn, no big factor in the legislation's passage, sheepishly stepped forward to accept a ceremonial pen.) Also on Rayburn's list: laws to assist refugees from the Hungarian revolt, build the St. Lawrence Seaway, revise the tax code, and deal with Communist subversion. Overall, "a dismal record," he said, "a solemn and tragic spectacle" in which Republicans "brazenly hail defeats as victories and embarrassing compromises as achievements."

Rayburn at first withheld criticism of Republican Senator Joseph McCarthy, chairman of the Senate Permanent Investigations subcommittee and gifted demagogue, whose angry, fear-provoking charges of Communist subversion at home raged across the nation in the early 1950s.[20] People would soon tire of "McCarthyism," Rayburn predicted. McCarthy was a Republican embarrassment—best for Democrats to stay on the sidelines and watch the show, he said. "I have thought all along," the Texan wrote in 1954, "that McCarthy was the problem of the Republican Party and that they would finally have to come to grips with him if they did not allow him to take over the party entirely."[21]

But when, in 1954, the junior Wisconsin senator charged previous Democratic administrations with "20 years of treason," when Attorney General Herbert Brownell declared that Truman had knowingly promoted a Communist,[22] and when Vice-President Richard M. Nixon embraced the notion that Democrats were "soft on communism," Rayburn decided he had heard enough. "I can stand charges of crime and corruption," he told the House. "But charges implying treason are unfor-

givable, and my back is getting pretty sore." Attacks on Democratic patriotism are "mean, untrue and dastardly," he added.
"They should be stopped by somebody, and there is one man in
the United States that can stop that kind of talk."[23] Privately, he
blamed Nixon most of all. "When the Republicans say they
want a bipartisan foreign policy and then allow Nixon to go out
and insult Democrats, it is a pretty poor way to make people on
the other side enthusiastic about bipartisan foreign policy," he
told friends. "Nixon is the next thing to McCarthy in the United
States."[24] Lyndon Johnson added that "irresponsible statements"
by high administration officials endangered any hope of a bipartisan approach to legislative problems. Eisenhower got the message. The next day, for the first time, he appealed publicly to
Republicans to "tone down" their criticisms of Democrats, although he refused to condemn the Wisconsin senator by name.

Rayburn advised all Democrats not to answer McCarthy,
Nixon, and other GOP critics in kind: "We are not going to in-
dict people *en masse*, call them Communists or subversives because we don't like their views. . . . and no Democrat in a position of responsibility is going to do it without being frowned on
and repudiated by me."[25] He never forgot that seemingly responsible Republicans had joined in hurling charges of "treason"
and "soft on communism" at his party. And he never forgave,
especially Richard Nixon—"The meanest face I've ever seen in
the House." He said in 1958: "There's a lot of talk about how I
hate Nixon. I have hated some things he's said and all that, but as
far as Mr. Nixon and I personally are concerned, we are on very
friendly terms when we meet. I just don't like cruel people, and I
thought in 1954 that Mr. Nixon was very cruel."[26]

McCarthyism's abrupt slide into oblivion began with the Senate's decision to investigate a relatively minor dispute involving
charges by the army that preferential treatment was demanded
for a drafted member of McCarthy's subcommittee staff. The
hearings soon drifted far beyond their original pretext. Before
a spellbound national television audience, the hollowness of
McCarthy's investigations and the repugnance of his methods
were laid bare under the relentless questioning of army Special
Counsel Joseph Welsh. Timidly at first, increasingly more bold

as the vastness of the abuses by McCarthy and his staff came to light, the Senate moved to bell the cat. A special committee recommended censure, but not until after the 1954 elections—and after McCarthy had lost his chairmanship—did the Senate act, voting even then not to "censure" but to "condemn" him for relatively minor transgressions. It was action enough. His days of power were ended.

When McCarthy died in 1957, at age 48, Rayburn discussed his inner feelings with *Time* correspondent Neil MacNeil: "When the press boys called me, I just said that I had no comment because I did not know him well. I don't like to speak ill of the dead in public. If I had said what I really felt, I would have said, 'The world gained nothing by his having lived, and it lost nothing when he died.'"[27]

The Korean War was finally settled inconclusively in June 1953. Only Secretary of State John Foster Dulles seemed satisfied with the peace agreement. "Truman and Dean Acheson could have gotten this kind of truce 18 months ago," Rayburn complained.[28] But Americans were tired of war and eager to turn to other matters. Lasting peace and expanding prosperity were elusive dreams as the United States began to move out of the bedeviled post–World War II period.

Eisenhower still fought constantly with his Republican Congress. Protectionists rebelled at his bill extending reciprocal-trade agreements with other nations. Once again, Ike looked to Rayburn's Democrats for help and got it. "Reciprocal-trade arrangements will save our country," the minority leader told the House. Rayburn criticized Ike's "more-bang-for-a-buck" defense policy but agreed nevertheless to help push it through the House. "I'd rather be alive with an empty pocket than dead with a full one," he told colleagues worried about the high cost of defense. He balked, however, when Eisenhower first proposed Hawaiian and Alaskan statehood. He believed that, for security and other reasons, the United States should remain a nation of contiguous states—a position he would later abandon to become an advocate of statehood for both territories.

According to *Congressional Quarterly*, Rayburn in 1953 supported the President on 74 percent of "Eisenhower issue" roll calls; only eight House members backed the President more often. In the first session, Democrats "saved" White House bills fifty-eight times when Republicans defected, providing the winning margin for such legislation as aid for drought-stricken farmers, foreign aid, reciprocal-trade extension, and renewal of the excess profits tax.[29] Meanwhile, the Americans for Democratic Action declared Rayburn to be Congress's most liberal southern Democrat, with an ADA approval rating of 86.[30]

Trauma followed trauma in 1954.

A few seconds after 2:30 P.M. on March 1, as the House debated a routine immigration bill, gunfire erupted from the visitors' gallery, producing the wildest scene in the history of Congress. Members—Rayburn and Martin were among the 243 on the floor—scattered as the first shot rang out at the extreme left of the Speaker's chair where Martin sat. Martin thought it was a firecracker. Then came a second and a third shot. From where he stood in the far right aisle, Rayburn could see all the action. Four men—later identified as Puerto Rican nationalists—stood in the gallery, firing randomly at the figures below, some of whom remained frozen in their seats. The Capitol police, many unarmed, had scrambled for cover, as had other spectators. Rayburn's initial concern, he said later, was for Martin, a conspicuous target. After wheeling to get a better view of the rostrum, he began slowly walking backward toward a rear exit, motioning all the while for Martin to get down. Temporarily stunned, Martin finally reacted, blurting out in a classic understatement, as he ducked behind a marble pillar, "The House stands recessed."[31] Before the assailants were finally subdued, five congressmen had been wounded.[32] Afterward, House security was tightened slightly, but Martin and Rayburn vetoed the FBI's recommendations for stringent restrictions, including limited admission to the Capitol and bulletproof partitions around the visitors' galleries. Both men agreed that Americans did not want to seal off their legislative chambers.

In May, the nation's capital was jolted by an even bigger shock: the Supreme Court's decision outlawing racial segregation in public schools. It meant Congress, after nearly a century of evasion, could no longer duck the most crucial moral and legal issue confronting the nation. For many in Congress, it meant painful reassessment of old alliances and beliefs. For Sam Rayburn, reared in a segregated rural southern community, the landmark ruling demanded great adjustment, which he accepted reluctantly but with philosophical resignation: "I have always been for segregation in the schools and still am, but the Supreme Court has spoken, and it is the last word. However, I think it will take a long time to work out in the schools in the South, which I hope the Supreme Court will give us. I don't see how they can put this decision into operation soon."[33]

After his own easy victory in the 1954 Texas primary, Rayburn turned to the task of building a Democratic majority in the House. He missed the Speakership and its great power. "The situation," he said, "is such between the President, who has much of the Democratic legislative program, and the Republicans in Congress, who have resisted it, that the country will be better off if it returns a Democratic Senate and House in the November election."[34] As GOP hopes of holding Congress dwindled by the day, Eisenhower warned voters that a Democratic-controlled House and Senate would mean the return of divided government, the end of progress, and the start of "a cold war of partisan politics." The jab, which Ike immediately regretted, was too tempting for Rayburn and Johnson to ignore. They fired back a stinging telegram, reminding the President of past Democratic help and advising that any future "cold war" would be of his making, not theirs.[35] Later Eisenhower sought to make amends by inviting the two Texans to the White House for a private discussion of foreign policy—a move widely interpreted as a tacit apology.[36]

The party of the administration normally loses congressional seats at mid-term, and 1954 was no exception: Democrats came away with a solid majority in the House and razor-thin control in the Senate. Lyndon Johnson's re-election for another six-year term meant that, come January, he and Rayburn again would team up to lead the two houses. Although disappointed, Eisenhower found comfort in the fact that Democratic control would submerge the Republican right wing, which had badgered him for two years. Importantly, the dangerous Joe McCarthy would lose his chairmanship of the Senate Permanent Investigations subcommittee.

For Joe Martin, aged and failing, the loss was catastrophic. This term as Speaker was to be his last hurrah. Republicans had complained for years about his loose leadership. "Not tough enough," said some. "He's too chummy with Rayburn," said others. Sadly, he prepared to vacate the "front office" near the House Chamber and the choice "back office" with its breathtaking panoramic view of the Mall and the Washington Monument, the suite traditionally occupied by the Speaker. Sensing Martin's disappointment, Rayburn stopped him in the hall one day and said, "Joe, I'm tired of all this moving around. Why don't we just stay where we are?" Martin was delighted. From then on, Rayburn kept the minority leader's side office, while Martin and his Republican successors occupied the more appealing office traditionally set aside for the Speaker. The simple gesture, typical of Rayburn, cemented a friendship that was to last and produce tangible dividends as long as they both lived.

The two old men—Martin and Rayburn—stood side by side on many issues over the years. Rayburn was incensed when he learned of a quiet White House effort to replace Martin. "I don't want amateurs messing in House politics," he told presidential aide Sherman Adams.[37] The White House backed off temporarily, but the message was clear: Martin's days as Republican leader were numbered.

Ahead lay new challenges. In 1947 and 1948, Rayburn had known the effects of divided government—with Democrats controlling the White House and Republicans the legislature. Now the tables were turned, and the nation wondered whether the Democrats could do better. Would Eisenhower's prediction prove prophetic? Would there be a "cold war" between the two branches? Wrote James Reston: "If Sam Rayburn and President Eisenhower, both middle-of-the-roaders, can agree, the chances are that an effective bipartisan coalition can overcome the existence of politics. If they cannot, then the stalemate foreshadowed by the President in the closing days of the campaign last week will become a serious reality."[38]

A few days after the election Johnson flew up to Bonham from his Hill Country ranch. The peripatetic Senate leader brimmed with ideas to discuss with the Speaker-to-be. Rayburn often wondered why Johnson could never relax, why he was always in a hurry. The press already was speculating on how the two Texas leaders would operate in the new Congress. Johnson, said the *Washington Evening Star*, "lacks the firm grasp, finesse and actual power of Sam Rayburn" but can "complement" Rayburn "without acting as foil or stooge." Added *Business Week*: Johnson will be the "idea man," but if Rayburn says no, "that's the end of it."

"LBJ is one of Rayburn's proteges," wrote James Reston of the *New York Times*, "and while he and the senator have had their differences in the last year or so, Johnson is not likely to take a hostile attitude toward any project backed by 'Mister Sam.'"[39] "In other words," concluded John O'Donnell of New York's *Daily News*, "Sam Rayburn is running the Capitol Hill show."[40]

Rayburn was beginning his sixth full term as Speaker. He had already held the office a total of ten years, a formidably long time in the constantly evolving world of politics. He approached the future with optimism and vigor. He intended to prove that a Democratic Congress could work with a Republican administration. But he had seen enough of divided government to know that the task would never be easy.

20

Rayburn and Johnson

While Sam Rayburn ran the House, Lyndon Johnson made his own mark in the Senate. The older man followed with unconcealed pride his protégé's burgeoning as a legislative leader. He marveled at Johnson's mastery of his job and his relentless passion to succeed. He was convinced that within that restless, sometimes tormented body was the raw stuff of a good President, if the opportunity ever came, which in the mid-1950s seemed highly improbable. Rayburn ranked Johnson as one of the greatest legislative and political geniuses this country has produced. His success, the Speaker believed, was based not on brilliance but on hard work. He worked harder than any politician Rayburn had ever seen. He was smart, he was a fine strategist, and he was indefatigable. While recognizing his friend's obvious weaknesses, Rayburn admired him and saw him early for what he was—a man of enormous ability.

In private conversation, Rayburn often spoke critically of Johnson's "vaulting ambition." He told his nervous friend to relax, slow down, "wait a minute." At first, when Johnson was a young, eager congressman, he would listen. Now when he visited the Board of Education, he talked incessantly about his own accomplishments and plans for the future—and "discussed" matters with Rayburn hardly at all. He ridiculed the

Speaker's staff, his old-fashioned ways, and his loose organization. Johnson, addicted to multiple-line telephones and other
electronic gadgets, could never understand Rayburn's preference
for simplicity.[1] When Johnson bragged at the Board of Education about the new mobile telephone he had installed in his car,
Rayburn told him: "I never get a call so important that it can't
wait until I get to my apartment." Occasionally, Rayburn would
get fed up and, interrupting a Johnson monologue, snap: "Listen, boy, you handle your end of the Capitol, and I'll handle
mine."[2] Johnson would bolt down his Cutty Sark, grab his hat,
and stalk out. Next day he'd be back. Neither man could stay
angry at the other for long. But they argued frequently, often
over trivialities, such as whether the ground beef that Johnson
shipped up from Texas for his locally acclaimed hamburgers
was fit for human consumption. Rayburn, who deplored hamburgers, insisted that it was not. Recalled Rayburn aide H. G.
Dulaney: "Mr. Johnson had more desire for power than anybody I have known and wasn't too particular about how he got
it. . . . Mr. Rayburn undoubtedly loved him. Lyndon Johnson
would listen to Sam Rayburn more than anybody."[3] Another
Rayburn staffer observed: "I think they both would have liked to
have been more like the other one."[4]

At times, Johnson could barely conceal his jealousy of the
older man. He began noticing in the 1950s that Rayburn was
gravitating more and more to younger members and seemed to
prefer their company over the brooding Johnson's.[5] He constantly sulked about the new competition for Rayburn's attention. "I'm getting too old for him," he complained. "He doesn't
like to be around older men." The Senate leader also admitted in
a moment of candor:

> Sam Rayburn has one quality that I envy but sometimes
> find irritating. He and I can do the exact same thing. His
> action will be applauded; mine will be criticized. We both
> put out the same statement, for example declining to serve
> on the Democratic Advisory Council. But all the criticism
> was directed at me, not at Rayburn. The average man some-
> how believes that if Sam Rayburn does something, he must

have a good reason. But if Lyndon Johnson does the same thing, well . . .[6]

Johnson's sensitivity to criticism, particularly from the press, puzzled Rayburn. "I just don't understand it," he would say. "Lyndon reads something that has 99 nice things to say about him and one uncomplimentary thing, and he'll raise hell about that one thing." On the other hand, criticism seldom bothered Rayburn. He wanted to know what was being said about him, good and bad. He once asked an aide to read him a current magazine article concerning the House leadership. The piece was highly critical, accusing Rayburn and others of being old, tired, and ossified. "That's a pretty good article," he said afterward. "It's a little more favorable than unfavorable." He would play for 51 percent any time; Johnson wanted it all his way. "Those newspaper boys admire Lyndon," Rayburn once observed. "They want to help him. But he always goes in with his guard up against them."[7] The Speaker sympathized with reporters who came to him seeking advice on how to deal with the abrasive Senate majority leader.[8]

The two congressional leaders kept their promise of "constructive opposition," mainly by muting their criticism of administration foreign policy. Rayburn single-handedly persuaded Democrats to reverse a defeat of the reciprocal-trade bill, a key component of Eisenhower's 1955 agenda. "Mr. Rayburn stilled the tumult, came down from his Speaker's rostrum and, in a spine-tingling speech that few will forget, appealed for the Eisenhower–Cordell Hull program," wrote the *Christian Science Monitor*.[9] Allowing no debate, the Speaker also delivered the votes of all but one House Democrat for Eisenhower's Formosan resolution. "We are not going to play politics—the country comes first," he told a group of rebellious House Democrats chafing under his edict of no foreign policy criticism. "I remember how the Republicans patted Truman on the back when he first went into Korea, then kicked him in the pants afterward. We are not going to do that."[10] Rayburn stretched the limits of his authority to stifle dissent on Eisenhower's aggressive policy in the Middle East. On one occasion in 1958, while presiding, he publicly rebuked Democrat Henry Reuss of Wisconsin for a speech criticizing Ike's decision to land troops in Lebanon. "In times like these," he told the congressman, "we had better allow matters to develop rather than make remarks about them." The next day, the Speaker announced that he would no longer recognize members "to talk about foreign affairs in this critical situation."[11]

Eisenhower, realizing that the two Texans were crucial to his success, courted them assiduously at first, less fervently later as both made clear the limits of their support. The President frequently praised the pair in public and brought them into the inner councils of the White House. Some afternoons, after the House and Senate had adjourned for the day, Rayburn and Johnson would pile into the Speaker's black limousine and ride up Pennsylvania Avenue to the White House. Unnoticed by the press, they would arrive at the secluded southwest entrance and be taken swiftly to the President's family quarters on the second floor. There, over drinks, the two Democratic leaders, the Republican President, and, occasionally, a White House aide or two would discuss current issues and hash out informal bipartisan compromises to make the government work.[12] In private moments, Eisenhower often wondered why he seemed to get along better with Democrats in Congress than with his own Republicans. "I think it's pretty obvious," he told aide Emmet John Hughes, with no visible sorrow, "that when it comes to domestic affairs, the people would rather have the Democrats running things."[13]

Some Democrats complained that the two Texans worked too closely with the administration. National Chairman Paul Butler, for one, demanded more partisan fire in Congress. Rayburn and Johnson, it was said, spent too much time in worrying about unity and not enough in probing the opposition's weaknesses. But none of it seemed really to rub off on the Speaker. Said the *New York Times*: "The payoff has been this: If the Democrats have not achieved a spectacular record of positive partisan accomplishment, neither have they let their chronic regional hostilities break out into the open. This will at least allow the

Democrats to go into the next election campaign with a convincing united front."[14] Added the *Christian Science Monitor's* Richard L. Strout: "Mr. Rayburn may well be the strongest cohesive force in the majority party, which is split about as widely as the Republicans."[15] The Speaker and the President often collided on domestic issues. On such occasions, Rayburn went his own way —as in his support of a $20 per person tax cut that Ike vehemently opposed. Eisenhower thought Rayburn was trying to embarrass him personally. "I think it's about time that I personally went after Rayburn," he told GOP legislative leaders. "I wouldn't mind if some of you fellows would pass the word to him that he better think more than twice and stop his nonsense if he wants me to sign those natural-gas bills" that "he wants very badly."[16] The tax legislation appealed to Rayburn because, he said, "it would give the 'little fella' a break." He was personally offended when Eisenhower labeled the election-year bill "irresponsible." The result was a definite cooling of their relationship. Their hard feelings became public gossip when, shortly after the tax measure passed the House, the President pointedly snubbed the Speaker, sitting only three seats away at the White House Correspondents Dinner.[17]

Rayburn and Johnson had their sharpest break with Eisenhower when, under intense pressure from Texas oil and gas interests, they teamed up in 1955 behind Congressman Oren Harris's highly controversial bill to exempt independent gas producers from federal price regulation. Although Truman had vetoed similar legislation in 1950, the Texans had reason to hope that Eisenhower, a friend of the industry, would be more sympathetic. The industry did its part, opening its coffers wide for a carefully orchestrated campaign of propaganda and political pressure.

To most Americans, especially those in the fuel-dependent urban Northeast, the gas bill meant one thing: higher consumer prices. For their role in pressing the legislation, Rayburn and Johnson were widely condemned. But, as Rayburn saw it, Texas interests were at stake; besides, he had somehow convinced himself that prices would not rise and that the independents' demand for relief was well founded.[18] (Whether Johnson was similarly convinced, only he knew.) Finally, when Rayburn scheduled a crucial vote on the bill on a Friday, knowing that most eastern big-city liberals had already gone home for the weekend, the protests reached a crescendo. Even with Rayburn calling in all his IOUs, the Harris bill barely squeaked through the House by six votes.

In the Senate, the gas lobby pulled out all the stops—and, typically, went too far. Before Johnson could bring the bill to a vote, charges of attempted bribery were flying. Republican Senator Francis H. Case of South Dakota stunned colleagues with his announcement that a Texas gas lobbyist had attempted to sway his vote by offering him a $2,500 "campaign contribution." Case said he had planned to support the measure but would now vote against it. Amid the furor, Johnson hurriedly rushed the bill through the Senate. But the damage had been done. Eisenhower, even if he favored the measure, could not now sign it. In his veto message, the President referred to efforts by the bill's proponents "so arrogant" as to "risk creating doubt among the American people concerning the integrity of governmental processes." [19] Rayburn suffered no lasting stigma from his role in the whole affair. His roughshod tactics in pushing the legislation were soon forgotten, except in Texas, where he emerged a hero, particularly to his new admirers in the oil and gas industry. Though embarrassed at having been on the wrong side of a "people" issue, he was philosophical: "I told some of those fellows Ike would never sign it. He thought he would, but I knew that when the bill actually got on his desk and he started hearing from all those cookstove women, he'd change his mind." [20]

As the 84th Congress's first session drew toward a close, Lyndon Johnson looked forward to a relaxing July 4 weekend at the Virginia country estate of his longtime Texas friend and benefactor George Brown. The Senate majority leader was exhausted from working eighteen-hour days for the past six months, but he felt the results were worth it. Congress, he bragged, had hung some important "coonskins" on the wall: the Formosan resolution, reciprocal-trade extension, a highway-construction bill, an increase in the minimum wage to $1 an hour, and a boost in foreign aid above the President's request.

For weeks Johnson had ignored the warnings of Rayburn and others to slow down. At the Texas delegation lunch the previous Wednesday, he had been unusually agitated. He spent most of the hour either on the telephone or sitting grumpily with his chin on his chest while he shoved food with his fork from one side of his plate to the other. Finally, when he got up to leave, Rayburn yelled out: "Lyndon, where the devil do you think you're going? Get yourself back over here and finish your lunch." Johnson, like a typical little boy, returned to the table and again began making a show out of playing with his food. "Johnson," said Rayburn with annoyance, "get the devil out of here. You are not going to eat. Your butt is here but your heart and head are over there on that damn Senate floor." As the Senate majority leader donned his hat and headed out the door, Rayburn called to him once again: "Johnson, let me tell you something. This Congress was operating long before you were born and this Congress is going to be operating long after you're dead, which, if you don't settle down, is exactly where you are going to be."[21]

By Friday, the Senate leader was in a state of high excitement. With Rayburn's blessing, he had decided to test the water for a possible run for the Presidency in 1956, and the first "leaks" of his availability were set to appear over the weekend in the *Washington Post* and other papers.[22] Martin Anderson, publisher of the *Orlando Sentinel* and an LBJ friend, had just sent over the wire an advance copy of his July 3 editorial calling for Johnson's nomination. After bolting down a lunch of frankfurters and beans, Johnson called for his car and, with driver Norman Edwards, began the one-hour trip to the Brown estate near Middleburg. He was nauseous all the way to Middleburg. Other guests at the estate, quickly recognizing his symptoms as those of a heart attack, wanted to rush him to a hospital, but he resisted. Senator Clinton Anderson, one of the guests, said later: "Characteristically, Johnson's first concern was not whether he would live or die but how the heart attack would affect his ambitions to become President."[23] Finally, over his objections, a doctor was called.

Johnson had been rushed back to the Bethesda Naval Medical Center before Rayburn learned of the seizure. The Speaker later said his first thoughts, after determining that Johnson would recover, also were of how the new situation would affect his friend's presidential aspirations. Rayburn thought it improbable that Johnson would be well enough to participate fully even in the state Democratic party fight in Texas—which had become routine every four years—much less stick to his own presidential timetable. But he underestimated the determined Texan and the power of his "vaulting ambition."

By late September, Johnson was at his Hill Country ranch, on the road to full recovery. Congress adjourned, Rayburn was in Bonham. The "Big Two" of Texas politics, as the Texas press called them, talked almost daily by phone, exchanging political gossip and plotting to recapture the Texas Democratic party from Allan Shivers and his forces—a fight they knew would not be clean and easy. Johnson, with more to lose than Rayburn, was reluctant to challenge the popular governor. "You'll have to make a strong statement," insisted Rayburn.

"But I don't want to see Allan kicked around," Johnson replied.

"I'll kick him around every chance I get," shot back Rayburn.

On September 28, the Speaker flew to the LBJ ranch near Austin to join Johnson in welcoming Adlai Stevenson, who was visiting Texas for the first time since the disastrous 1952 campaign. Their private meeting under the massive shade trees in Johnson's backyard was relaxed and friendly. But afterward, Johnson still shied from endorsing the former Illinois governor for another run at the Presidency in 1956. Even then, thoughts of his own candidacy still burned, however dimly, in Johnson's mind. "The nomination," he said, "is a matter for the Democratic National Convention to decide, and not for an individual."

For Johnson even to think of the Presidency so soon after a major heart attack was unrealistic and foolish. By year's end, he could no longer contain his ambition. "Lyndon doesn't expect to be President, but he does want to be Vice-President," the Speaker told a friend in December. "I'm going to tell him to stay out in '56. We've got to wait and see about his heart condition. People don't want a sick man. There's still plenty of time

for him. He will still be young enough in 1960 and 1964."
Johnson, he added, had indicated an interest in going to the National Convention as Texas's favorite son candidate for President, and "I told him that would be all right."[24]

Throughout the winter, Johnson continued to shy from a
slugfest with Shivers. When Rayburn tried to push him out
front, he would find an excuse to wait a little longer. Finally,
Rayburn decided to push harder. At home during a recess
in March 1956, he telephoned Robert Cantrell, editor of the
Bonham Daily Favorite. "Bob, why don't you come out to the
house?" he said. "I've got a little squib for the paper." The written statement that Rayburn handed Cantrell was a bombshell
that jolted Texas politics to the core: his endorsement of Johnson
not only to be the state's favorite son candidate for President but
also to head the Texas delegation to the National Convention.[25]
"Under Lyndon Johnson's leadership we can begin to put our
house in order," Rayburn declared. "He is the man best equipped
to restore order and prevent a repetition of the chaos." It was, at
bottom, a thinly disguised declaration of war against Governor
Shivers for control of the Texas Democratic party. Shivers earlier had agreed on Johnson as the favorite son candidate, but he
expected—and had every reason to expect—that as governor, *he*
would head the Texas delegation.[26]

With that one gesture, Rayburn had pushed Johnson to the
summit of Texas politics, where the reluctant warrior now stood
toe-to-toe with the infidel Shivers and his party-bolting conservative followers. Rayburn had consulted no one, especially
Johnson.[27] Although they had been close friends for more than
fifteen years, he didn't know Johnson well enough to predict his
reaction. Would he fight Shivers for control of the party, or
would he back away? Rayburn thought Johnson would fight but
decided it was high time to find out for sure what stuff his friend
was made of.

Forcing Johnson into a bare-knuckles confrontation with
Shivers was the only way party loyalists could hope to regain
control of the state machinery. It was a fight that neither of the
principals wanted. Both saw advantage in coexistence. But now
there was no way out. When the governor, rejecting Johnson's

desperate attempts to strike an accommodation, criticized the senator so sharply that even mutual friends were shocked, the battle was on. "I had either to run or fight," Johnson later recalled. "I chose to fight."[28]

The fight was not without risk to Rayburn. Shivers earlier had threatened to have the Legislature redraw the state's congressional districts with the aim of redistricting the Speaker of the House right out of Congress. Now he almost certainly would try to follow through. In the abstract, it seemed logical and fair to shift part of the district representing Dallas's bulging 615,000 population into Rayburn's tiny adjoining district, whose 227,000 residents made it the nation's smallest.[29] Twenty years earlier, Rayburn might have trembled at the prospect of having Dallas's conservative suburbs spill over into his rural populist area. But now he felt safe from such threats. If nothing more, his position as protector of the oil-depletion allowance and other vital Texas interests made him too valuable an asset to be ground into the dust of state politics.[30] He was right. Shivers, as expected, did raise the redistricting issue again, but the idea died quickly in the Legislature after leaders of the oil and gas industry, heavily beholden to Rayburn since the battle over gas decontrol, sent word to the statehouse that Rayburn's district was to be left alone.

Rayburn's motives in challenging Shivers were complex: he loathed the slick-talking governor for his duplicity in the 1952 Democratic campaign and wanted him destroyed politically. He wished to send a loyal Texas delegation to the National Convention to erase the 1952 embarrassment. He also had faith in the leadership potential of Lyndon Johnson. He had watched closely in the months following Johnson's heart attack and had marveled at his friend's rapid recovery. He was not, however, playing national politics with his endorsement of Johnson for favorite son. This was Texas politics. There was time enough in the future to present Johnson seriously for the Presidency.

Rayburn was obsessed with the notion of sending a loyal Texas delegation to the National Convention. It was, he told friends in Washington, his "greatest remaining ambition."[31] The Democratic split in Texas had nagged him for years. He could

never forget—or forgive—the senseless hatred that had ruined
his own best chances for national office in the 1940s. He often
wondered whether there was any hope for orderly politics in his
home state. Sometimes, in a melancholy mood, he complained
of the changes—economic and political—that had transformed
his beloved Texas in the past quarter century. Some parts of the
state, he would say, had become "too rich—too much Yankee
infiltrated and a good deal too Republican." Other times, he
would ruefully declare that "big money is running Texas today."

Rayburn and Johnson had tried earlier at least to establish a
truce between the loyalists and the Shivers faction. Johnson, particularly, recognized Shivers's hold over the state party and was
reconciled to it. The two sides managed to compromise in filling a temporary vacancy on the National Committee. But when
time came to fill the position permanently, their irreconcilable
differences reappeared—worse than ever. A loyalist would trust
a Shivercrat, remarked Judge Jim Sewell, "no more than a rattle-
snake in a paper sack."

In such an atmosphere, Rayburn released his statement to the
Bonham Daily Favorite. Shivers, his party control under open
challenge by the state's most respected political figure, fought
back viciously. "Cynical and calculated," said the governor of
Rayburn's proposal to back Johnson as both delegation chairman
and favorite son.[32] "Rayburn still insists, as he has always insisted throughout his career," the governor added, "on being a
Democrat first and an American second." Replied Rayburn:
"That's cruel and untrue, and Allan Shivers knows it."

Rayburn planned to win back the party by appealing to the
people he knew best—farmers, factory workers, and small businesspeople, whose roots in the Democratic party ran deep. With
the help of organized labor and newly emerging minority blocs,
plus the organizational genius of such party newcomers as
John B. Connally, he and Johnson would turn out sufficient
party loyalists to sweep the May 5 precinct conventions and gain
control of the machinery that chooses delegates for the State
Convention. The State Convention, scheduled May 22, picked
delegates to the National Convention.

Warming up to the fight but still hesitant to take Shivers on directly, Johnson opened his attack in a statewide broadcast on April 10. "I will have no part of any move that can create tensions and turmoil in the party," he declared. "I am appealing to all Democrats without prefixes and suffixes . . ." The words were vintage Rayburn. While Connally organized the state, precinct by precinct, Rayburn and Johnson appealed to their network of influential friends, notably the oilmen, who constituted an important segment of conservative power in Texas. Labor-liberals, who had no love for Johnson but who hated Shivers more, worked their side of the street. Texans by the tens of thousands received union-produced "Dear Friends" letters, signed by Johnson, urging them to "telephone your neighbors" and "ask them to join you at the precinct convention." Meanwhile, Johnson toured the state, urging Democrats to trust the wisdom of Sam Rayburn, whom he praised as one of the great leaders in Texas history. "From Sam Houston to Sam Rayburn . . . ," his perorations invariably began.

"Santa Anna to Sam Rayburn" was closer to the truth, shot back Shivers. Protested Rayburn: "This is rat-alley politics. This statement was made by a man who must feel that the Democrats of Texas are through with him, as I believe they are. I do not believe that the decent people of Texas will endorse this kind of personal attacks on me and my patriotism."[33]

When the results were in from the May 5 precinct conventions, the combined liberal-loyalist forces led by Rayburn and Johnson had beaten the Shivercrats by a three-to-one margin. "A victory for moderation over the rash extremists and hot heads of passion," proclaimed Johnson. "Next time we'll knock down the extreme left wing; we won't allow either the right or the left to carry our buggy off the road." Rayburn was enormously satisfied. "We put Texas where it belongs—a Democratic state in a Democratic column," he said. The May 22 State Convention in Dallas was anticlimactic. Johnson held all the cards. His only problem was in controlling the liberals. Having tasted Shivers's blood, they wanted to drive all of the governor's followers from the party hierarchy. But Johnson was not interested in revenge. He preferred to make peace, if possible, with the defeated enemy.

Although Johnson emerged as undisputed leader of the 1956 delegation to the National Convention as well as a possible dark-horse candidate for President, he prudently foresaw a difficult political year for Texas Democrats. Party unity was still a worthwhile goal then and in the future. Besides, as Rayburn had learned a decade earlier, no contender for the Presidency from a state with an irreconcilable party split has a chance. With that in mind, Johnson sought a few months later to strike his own separate peace with the Shivers faction, over the bitter protests of the labor-liberal faction, which envisioned purging the state organization of all such impurities. The effort, climaxed at a raucous State Convention in the fall, was to cost Johnson dearly. For liberals, who never trusted him anyway, it was the last straw. They would hound him for that and other transgressions, real and imagined, through his remaining years in politics.[34]

The score settled in Texas, at least temporarily, Rayburn turned to the Democratic National Convention in Chicago, over which he would again preside as permanent chairman. Lyndon Johnson's favorite son candidacy was but a minor concern for the Speaker as the August 13 opening day approached. For the next week, the spotlight would be on presidential front-runners Adlai Stevenson and W. Averell Harriman, the former New York governor being pushed by Harry Truman. Estes Kefauver, his campaign out of gas, had withdrawn from the race and was sitting back in confident anticipation of the vice-presidential nomination.

A Gallup poll placed Rayburn himself among the five "most-wanted" Democratic presidential nominees. But the Speaker knew he was out of it. He told Congressman Francis E. "Tad" Walter of Pennsylvania: "My doctor says my heart is good to age 95 or 100, but men of 40 think that 70 is too old. If the convention is deadlocked, somebody will mention my name and nominate me on the next ballot. I don't want that to happen."[35] The possibility of a deadlock also occurred to Lyndon Johnson. He mentioned to Rayburn and Dick Russell that a Johnson candidacy might have hope. Rayburn disagreed but said nothing. Instead, he listened with bemusement as Johnson's fertile imagination soared in outlining his scenario of what might happen in the week ahead.

Stevenson deserved the nomination, Rayburn believed. He had been convinced of Stevenson's claim for some time, particularly since their long, warm meeting under the live oaks at the Johnson ranch. At that meeting, the two Texans urged Stevenson to help put the party on a moderate course. The South, particularly Texas, would be lost, they argued, if the Democratic ticket strayed too far left in 1956. Stevenson promised his cooperation. "I agree that it is time for catching our breath," he said. "I agree that moderation is the spirit of the times." The most important political development of 1955, concluded the *Texas Observer*, "was the conversion of Adlai Stevenson to the Johnson-Rayburn concept." [36]

While Rayburn presided over the convention, Johnson followed the proceedings from his suite at the Conrad Hilton, headquarters hotel for the Texas delegation, and waited for the front-runners to falter. On Tuesday, his hopes climbed when it appeared that the contest might go beyond the first ballot. If Stevenson and Harriman deadlocked—neither able to muster a majority—a dark horse might slip through as an acceptable compromise. Johnson, who had promised his own delegation not to present himself as a serious contender, could not openly solicit votes. But he saw no harm in letting everyone know that Lyndon Johnson was in Chicago—and available. After all, he already had the endorsement of half a dozen senators. He put his staff to work. Overnight, the Hilton blossomed with garish "Love That Lyndon" signs. Before breakfast, Texas and other southern delegates had been pinned with bilious-yellow "Love That Lyndon" ribbons. For three days, he conducted quite a serious campaign.

But then, as suddenly as it had appeared, Johnson's bubble burst. At the International Amphitheater, the Stevenson forces were in command. The nominations went smoothly, and the balloting ensued without serious mishap or confusion. "I feel the Democrats were in the best humor with each other—North, South, East and West—than at any convention I have attended in many years," Rayburn said later. "There were no brawls, no fist fights; there was no pulling and hauling at state standards, and everyone looked to be their best."[37] Stevenson was easily nominated on the first ballot.

Shortly before the balloting, Stevenson telephoned Rayburn on the platform. He had an important matter to discuss, the candidate said. Would the Speaker mind walking over to the Stockyards Inn, a nearby restaurant, to meet with him, Paul Butler, and some others? Rayburn hesitated to leave the hall at such a crucial time but, when Stevenson insisted, finally agreed to come. About 9:30, he turned the proceedings over to the clerk for the roll call of the states and, joined by Johnson, made his way out a side door and across the parking area to the busy restaurant where Stevenson, Butler, Chicago Mayor Richard Daley, Jake Arvey, Bill Blair, and James A. Finnegan waited in a private room.

Going directly to the point, Stevenson told Rayburn that he had decided not to select his own running mate but instead to throw the selection open to the convention. He had tested the plan on a number of his friends, and most liked the idea. An open nomination, he added, would be a "fresh breeze" for the convention. Rayburn's face clouded over, then reddened with anger. He found no merit in the idea, he told the nominee. It would ruin the convention. The leading vice-presidential contenders—Kefauver, Hubert Humphrey, and Senator Jack Kennedy of Massachusetts—would cut each other up. Besides, people already were talking about indecisiveness in Stevenson's character, and this would only seem to confirm the Hamlet-like quality of the party's nominee. Butler agreed with Rayburn. Stevenson, with a shrug, dismissed their arguments. As he later recalled: "Mr. Sam was really unhappy. He thought the open convention would cause friction, prolong the convention and a lot of other things. Lyndon was startled, but he tried to compromise things. . . . I remember Lyndon saying, 'Mr. Sam, it's the governor's decision. After all, he has to live with it, not us.'"[38]

Finally, Rayburn subsided. "All right," he said, "if your mind's made up, give me your arm and I'll take you out there and introduce you to the convention." Democratic Deputy Chairman Hy

Raskin bumped into Rayburn as the group left. "Stay out of the old man's way—He's madder'n hell," Raskin warned a friend. Rayburn was still visibly angry when he went before the convention to introduce Stevenson, whose nomination had just been declared. The candidate spoke briefly, then the convention was recessed until the following day, when the vice-presidential nominee would be chosen.

Deciding to try once more to change Stevenson's mind, Rayburn and Johnson attended the nominee's victory party at the Blackstone. For more than an hour, the two Texans and the urbane party standard bearer could be heard arguing behind a closed bedroom door. Stevenson would not be dissuaded. Reporters cornered the Speaker as he left. How did he feel about an open convention? they asked. "That's it," he snapped. "It doesn't matter what I think." Muttered Stevenson to his young campaign aide John Sharon, who conceived the idea: "I have either done the smartest thing in my life—or the dumbest."[39]

The candidate's prospective running mates were not happy either; all felt they were victims of a political sellout. At the Hilton, Kefauver packed his bags, preparing to return home. He believed the dice were loaded in Kennedy's favor. Kennedy and Humphrey both thought the odds favored Kefauver, who had campaigned for the Presidency and still had a substantial following among the delegates. Elmo Roper, an old Kefauver friend, ultimately persuaded the tall Tennessean to stick around. Johnson, after the fizzle of his presidential boomlet, was not among the contenders.

All the candidates courted Rayburn. Former Rhode Island Governor Dennis Roberts urged him to swing the Texas delegation to Kennedy. "Nothing doing," the Speaker answered. "You fellows are too young to remember the Al Smith thing. . . . I've been through it."[40] Moreover, although he found Kennedy likable, his impression of the young man's performance as a legislator was not at all favorable. He had observed the handsome war hero when he first came to Congress as a House member and pegged him as a wealthy dilettante. If Kennedy's Catholicism troubled Rayburn, Kefauver's maverick tendencies bothered him more. Humphrey was more acceptable to the Speaker than either of the other leading contenders, but the engaging Minnesotan had no chance. As Rayburn surveyed the field, Kennedy began to look better—anybody but Kefauver. Ultimately, he yielded to the arguments of Hale Boggs and others who contended the nationally popular Kennedy would be an asset to the ticket. It is unclear whether Rayburn or Johnson was persuaded first. At the next Texas caucus, Johnson announced that he was for Kennedy. Rayburn followed: "I don't know about the rest of you, but Sam Rayburn is voting for Kennedy."[41]

Finally, after a night of frantic politicking, the convention reconvened. Seven candidates were nominated. Late in the second ballot, neck and neck between Kefauver and Kennedy, Texas's Deputy Chairman John Connally sent the convention into a wild frenzy with his announcement: "Texas proudly casts its fifty-six votes for the fighting senator who wears the scars of battle . . ." Kennedy jumped ahead. As the end of the roll call neared, he was leading by forty votes and pulling away. Several states were ready to switch their votes. Rayburn, who had turned over the gavel to Senator Warren G. Magnuson, watched from a passageway at the rear of the platform as state banners bobbed for recognition. Magnuson recognized Kentucky, which, its chairman boomed over the microphone, "joins the majority and changes its vote for John Kennedy." The delegates' roar was deafening. Kennedy was well ahead.

What followed will be debated as long as Democrats discuss the 1956 convention, arguably the most exciting in the party's history. Magnuson was surveying the waving standards, trying to decide which state to recognize next—a crucial consideration—when Rayburn stepped forward to reclaim the gavel. Another switch for Kennedy and the momentum would be irresistible. Rayburn and Clarence Cannon studied the tumultuous scene below, all aware of the chairman's power in such situations. Which state to recognize? "As far as I can see," Rayburn said to Hale Boggs, who had joined him on the platform, "it's a fielder's choice."

"Tennessee! Tennessee! Tennessee is going for Kennedy!" someone shouted from the floor directly in front of the platform. "Tennessee! Tennessee!" Cannon yelled to Rayburn.

Rayburn signaled for order. "Does the state of Tennessee desire recognition?" he asked. Delegation Chairman Herbert S. Walters asked that Albert Gore, one of the lesser nominees, be allowed to make a brief announcment. "The Chair," said Rayburn, "recognizes the senator from Tennessee by unanimous consent only."

Gore, perspiring profusely from the heat and excitement, grabbed the microphone. "Mr. Chairman," he began, "I respectfully withdraw my name and support my distinguished colleague, Estes Kefauver." Estes Kefauver? Rayburn blanched.

"I'll never forget the look on Rayburn's face as long as I live," remembered Kefauver worker Bill Haddad, who was standing at the base of the platform. "He was so shocked, he really lost his composure for a moment."[42] Tennessee's thirty-two votes cut deeply into the Kennedy lead. Next Rayburn recognized Oklahoma, which had been committed to Gore, but now felt free to switch also—to Kefauver. Minnesota was recognized, giving thirty more votes to Kefauver. Then came Missouri with thirty-seven votes for Kefauver, and Michigan with forty-four. It was all over in a few minutes. Kefauver had the nomination.

Was Rayburn tricked into recognizing Tennessee? Was he secretly for Kefauver? He had to know that Tennessee almost certainly would go for Kefauver, its senior senator, after Gore released his delegates. And why did he follow the recognition of Tennessee with three more successive Kefauver switches? Rayburn never fully explained, although he later privately blamed the fiasco on poor eyesight brought on by old age—a surprise to close associates, who did not learn that his eyes were failing until 1958.[43] The Tennessee delegation, seated directly in front of the platform, was the easiest to see, but, as Boggs noted, Rayburn had decided it made no difference which state he recognized first. Still, some Kennedy workers contend that if Rayburn had pointed to North Carolina, Indiana, or any of several other pro-Kennedy states seeking recognition at the time, the bandwagon might have rolled another way—and history taken a different course.

The loss of the Democratic ticket in November was no surprise. Stevenson did not even bother to campaign in Texas, so certain was an Eisenhower victory there. But the Republicans could not transfer Ike's popularity to the House and Senate elections. There the Democrats won handily, assuring at least two more years of divided government.

Soul-searching and bitter recrimination flowed from open Democratic wounds in the wake of the presidential defeat. "By hindsight," said former Senator Herbert Lehman of New York, "the election of 1956 was lost before the campaign began. . . . The mistakes that really hurt were mistakes made in Congress during the three-and-a-half-year period from the beginning of 1953 until the summer of 1956. The Democrats in Congress failed to make the issues during the 18 months we were in control. On the contrary, almost everything the leadership did during that time was designed to prevent any controversial issue from being seriously joined or vigorously debated. On the two main issues of our time—civil rights and foreign policy—there was a virtual blackout."[44]

National Chairman Butler—chosen in 1954 over Rayburn's objections—proposed a "Democratic Advisory Council" to help set party policy and shape a legislative program. It was, Butler said, in a slap at the Democratic congressional leadership, "quite generally considered that the party had not filled the true role of an opposition party from 1952 up to the presidential campaign. It will be different from now on, if the advisory group has its say."[45] On December 5, Butler named his council— eleven members of Congress and nine outside Democrats. Angry that Stevenson's defeat was being laid at their doorstep, Rayburn and Johnson were not about to give Butler and the National Committee a toehold in congressional business.[46] Rayburn said he would not participate. Johnson sent a similar message, noting that such a body "would only cause delays and confusion."

The Texas duo proceeded as they had in the past. If their methods displeased some Democrats, that was too bad. Only Rayburn, among all of Congress and the executive, had lived through the final Wilson years and seen the results of divided government at its worst. He looked on that period as one of the darkest in America's history. He was determined not to repeat it.

21

The Golden Years

On most afternoons as he grew older, and particularly when he was under pressure, Rayburn would slip quietly away from his office to stroll the Capitol grounds alone. He would savor the fresh air, nod to passersby, and pause frequently to inspect trees and shrubs. He had gauged the distance around the Capitol Plaza and the circle of sidewalk between the Supreme Court and the Library of Congress. Six laps equaled two miles—his normal daily walking goal. From his window, Associate Justice Tom Clark sometimes watched the rotund, dark-suited figure making his rounds. The Speaker would be drawn to a smallish white oak tree at the grounds' southeast corner. He had planted the tree in 1949 and thereafter traced its growth with parental pride. He regularly pulled at the tree's boughs to test their strength and, with a piece of string that he always carried, measured changes in its girth.

He found a new interest in 1959 with the beginning of work to replace the deteriorating East Front of the Capitol, a project he had promoted and defended for years against a chorus of critics in architecture, historical preservation, and the press. "Vandalism and desecration," said the American Institute of Architects scornfully. "Absolutely profane," added architect Frank Lloyd Wright. "They should leave it alone. I'm sure they can't improve it."[1] But Rayburn, supported by Senate Majority Leader Johnson, could not be deterred. He was in full accord with a special commission, which he chaired, that first recommended rebuilding and enlarging the entire east section, even though it meant destroying the historic facade.

The problem of the decaying wall had nagged Congress for years. The original east wall, built of soft Virginia sandstone, was deteriorating even before the first coat of paint was applied in 1819; 140 years and thirty-five coats of paint later, it was riddled with huge scars. Moldings and carved ornaments had literally washed away, and chunks of rock had popped out, leaving fist-sized craters.[2] There was concern, probably overstated, that the whole wall might collapse, sending the Capitol's 5,000-ton cast-iron dome thundering down.[3] Importantly, in Rayburn's view, the plan called for extending the wall forward 32½ feet to provide needed office space. The Capitol, he believed, was "not a shrine but a workshop" that "must continue to grow as the country grows."[4] He finally prevailed, turning the first spade of earth to start the project in February 1959. The East Front, mocked the *Milwaukee Journal*, "will be a magnificent tribute to Rayburn's persistence, stubbornness and determined use of the power position which he holds."[5] At least once a week, the old man ended his daily walk by donning a hard hat and inspecting the rising Capitol addition, of which he was inordinately proud.

His health remained excellent. "Physically, you're a man of 55," his physician said after an examination in 1955. He slept well, had a good appetite, and was rarely sick. He was proud of still having a full set of teeth. His weight held at 176 pounds, unchanged in thirty years. He remained active, walking his daily quota and, on quiet weekends, fishing with friends in nearby lakes or at the Jefferson Island Club, a Democratic retreat on the Potomac. John Garner once advised him to find an outside interest, a release from the tensions of his office. Fishing, especially with his companion George Donovan, gave Rayburn that release. "The Speakership is the hardest job in Washington," Garner said. "By going to the Vice-Presidency, I prolonged my life."[6] Rayburn, perhaps to deny that he was a very old man, would brag that he thrived on hard work and ridicule others who complained of being tired. He once said: "It's a funny thing, when I was young, I used to get awfully tired. I would be so tired when I got home, I would have to lie down on the couch. Probably it was because I was so tense. I just knew I had to succeed. If I didn't succeed, I was a ruined man, and I was going to do whatever it took to succeed. I would rather have died than have failed. I never get tired any more. A man feels tired only if he thinks he's tired."[7]

Although Rayburn still seemed as solid as the Rock of Gibraltar, time was taking its relentless toll among his friends and loved ones. One by one, those closest to him—those with whom he had shared the satisfactions and sorrows of a long life—were dying. "There's one thing about it," he said philosophically, "if you have loved ones, and if you live long enough, you're going to lose them." Chief Justice Fred Vinson, Rayburn's "best friend in Washington," died in 1953. Their friendship had blossomed when they met in Congress in 1924 and continued after the soft-spoken Kentuckian joined the Supreme Court. Rayburn visited the Vinson home at least twice a month, and he grieved for weeks when Vinson died. "I left here," he wrote John Garner from Bonham, "and flew to Washington and then to Charleston, W. Va., and drove 90 miles to help bury our old friend, Fred Vinson. I do not know how I am going to get along without him."[8] He described Vinson as "one of those men you never tire of. . . . He had the most unfailing judgment of any man I have ever known."[9]

Death continued to strike hard at the Rayburn clan. In 1956, it came to the one closest to him: Miss Lou. Lucinda Rayburn— tall, regal, handsome, stern—ruled the Bonham household almost like a duchess. Rayburn worshipped her. He respected her judgment and often sought her counsel. He liked a woman who "thought like a man," and Miss Lou had inherited from their mother a strong, orderly mind. She read, she thought, she analyzed. She enjoyed discussing public issues. Rayburn used to say, half jokingly, that she was the only person he was afraid of and that one reason he never remarried was that "two women can't run the same household."

Miss Lou, struck by cancer in the spring, declined rapidly.

For weeks, the family attended her as she grew ever weaker. To
be with her as much as possible, the Speaker reluctantly took to
flying. He had traveled by air occasionally after the war but, like
his brother Will, whose fear of flying kept him from a lucrative
airline job in the 1930s, he had never been comfortable aloft.
Now, forced to shuttle frequently between Texas and Washington, he learned to enjoy air travel, ultimately to prefer it.

He skipped the important Texas Democratic Convention that
spring to be with his sister and was at her bedside on Saturday,
May 26, as the convention nominated Lyndon Johnson as Texas's
favorite son candidate for President. That same day, Miss Lou
died. While Rayburn comforted his dying sister, an ill nephew,
Charles Rayburn, died in surgery. Upon learning of her son's
death, Rayburn's sister-in-law, Mrs. James L. Rayburn, suffered a
fatal heart seizure.

Miss Lou's death forced Rayburn for the first time to confront
his own mortality. In August, remembering the little church his
father attended, he asked his friend Lee Simmons to help him
find a Primitive Baptist Church to join. Simmons knew of such
a church in Grayson County and promised to speak to the pastor. "Those old men in my father's church," Rayburn would say,
"were the finest men I've ever known. They had higher moral
standards than any other men I've ever met." While fundamen-
tally religious, Sam had never been a consistent churchgoer, although he occasionally attended the First Baptist Church in
Bonham and, for a time, had been a Sunday school superinten-
dent. He conformed as much as he felt that he must, politically,
but organized religion of his day gave him no solace, no inspiration. Church meant more to his sisters, particularly Miss Lou,
who insisted on religious conformity. The sisters' church activities also had political value. One of Rayburn's gauges for political evaluation was their weekly report, which invariably began,
"The women at church are saying . . ." Now, perhaps seeing
eternity's shadow closing in, the aging son was returning to his
father's simple church. "Yes, the foot-washing kind," he used to
say proudly.

Grady Ball, a grocer and a leading citizen of the town of
Tioga, had been elected in accordance with church practice as

unpaid pastor of the small Primitive Baptist congregation every year for forty years. Ball told Simmons that he "couldn't say yes or no" to Rayburn's request for baptism until the two had talked privately. A few days later, the Speaker passed Ball's scrutiny and, on September 2, was received into the church. The total-immersion service, witnessed by the forty-member congregation, was short and simple. Rayburn never went back to the little church, nor did he mention his baptism to anyone. It remained unreported until discovered by a local newspaper two years later.

In 1956, *Look* magazine asked fifty top lobbyists to name Washington's most powerful men. Rayburn came in second, surpassed only by the President. "As Speaker of the House, with a Democratic majority behind him," said *Look*, "he is more valuable to have on your side than any other man in Washington, if it's pending legislation you have in mind." Lyndon Johnson finished seventh and Vice-President Nixon ninth in the survey.[10]

For all his power, Rayburn remained outwardly unchanged, except that after Miss Lou's death he began to accept more social invitations and to spend more time in the Board of Education. He also began expanding friendships with younger people and seeking new friends, mostly younger members of Congress. It was a conscious effort on his part. "As I have advanced in years I have stepped back in my associations, boys, young people, ten, twenty years younger than I—their bodies are not only more resilient, but their minds are, too. They can learn faster than fellows advanced in years," he told an interviewer in 1961.[11]

His office was still directed more toward the Fourth Congressional District of Texas than toward the nation as a whole. The casual air of the "back office," where most of the staff worked, and the "front office," near the House Chamber, rankled some members. He should organize his staff better and extend more services to the rank and file, they grumbled. "The Speaker runs a horse and buggy shop," observed Texas Congressman George Mahon, not without affection. "He doesn't have an efficient staff like other congressmen."[12] Added Texas colleague Olin Teague: "The greatest test of a human being is to give him power and watch him use it. Sam has possessed great power for many years, but I have never seen him use it for selfish or personal purposes. He never comes close to using the money allotted him for running his office. Few congressmen would do that."[13]

Rayburn instructed his staff never to ask "Who's calling?" when answering the telephone and insisted on placing most of his own calls. He would see almost anyone in his office, provided they waited their turn. "My office is my place of business, and if people think they have business with me, I'll see them as soon as I can," he explained. He shunned appointments. "Come by tomorrow afternoon," he might say. There were exceptions for ranking officials, but most callers—lobbyists, constituents, reporters—usually had to cool their heels in the outer office until their turn came. A man who did not waste words, he had the capacity to see many callers in a day. His open-door policy had two notable exceptions in the 1950s: Teamster lobbyist Sidney Zagri, who, Rayburn believed, had physically and verbally abused some congressmen during the fight over the Landrum-Griffin labor bill, and Louisiana parish boss Leander Perez, the segregationist mastermind, whose violent race-baiting repulsed the Speaker. When Perez came to Washington as Louisiana's representative at a tidelands conference, Rayburn flatly refused to allow him in his office. "Perez is not coming to any meeting in my office," he snapped. "Just tell the son of a bitch that I won't sit in the same room with him."

Rayburn could be equally blunt in answering obnoxious letters. To a Texas editor who wired him a long diatribe on the menace of communism, the Speaker replied: "Some crackpot sent me a telegram and signed your name to it. I think you should look into it."[14] To a Dallas businessman who accused him of a litany of sins, he wrote: "I seldom answer an insulting or silly letter—both of which yours is. The only reason I am answering it at all is to say that by your letter you prove the perfect ass that you must be."[15] His earthiest retort in response to a particularly insulting letter: "I have your letter before me. Now it's behind me, and I'm about to pull the chain." These were exceptions, however. Rayburn generally answered his mail, even from strangers, with care and courtesy. Handwritten letters got special attention. "If I get a letter written in longhand on a lined tablet, I want to see it," he said. "It is the first and only letter that feller ever wrote his congressman, and he wouldn't have written unless this was mighty important to him."[16]

Just before the House convened at noon each day, the Speaker held a two-to-five minute press conference in his front office. Questions focused largely on the day's business but, occasionally, ranged far afield. He knew most of the reporters and spoke to them candidly—too candidly at times. He trusted the "regular" House correspondents to protect him, and they did, routinely omitting from their files any comment that might have embarrassed him. "The reason the newspaper people loved him so well," recalled former Rayburn aide H. G. Dulaney, was "because he would tell them exactly what the story was. They couldn't print it, though." As far as Rayburn was aware, no regular member of the press ever seriously violated his confidence.[17] Explained William Arbogast, the AP's chief House correspondent: "He used to say many a thing that would have got him in hot water. If we noticed a strange reporter at one of the sessions, we'd tell him that everything was off the record."[18]

Rayburn gave special access to reporters for Texas newspapers, including the *Dallas Morning News*, which he loathed for its far-right views and its unrelenting criticism of him throughout his career. The paper's editorial writers dogged him, and he, in turn, gave as well as he got. He could always win easy applause in north Texas by ridiculing Dallas conservatives and the newspaper he saw as their mouthpiece. "A great man in this state forty or fifty years ago said that the *Dallas News* editorial page reads like it was written by children," he wrote in 1952. "It hasn't improved in fifty years, but their editorials are now written by meaner children."[19] When the Dallas Press Club invited him to its annual Gridiron Dinner in 1957, Rayburn told an aide: "Wire them, 'Kiss my ass,' and sign my name." The order was not carried out.

As much as he was respected and loved by Washington's pencil press, he was hated by those of the electronic and photographic press. His ban on broadcasts of committee hearings made life miserable for radio and television reporters, and his unrelenting

restrictions on still photographers sent them scurrying to the
Senate, where there was freedom of movement and respect for
their trade. Rarely, Rayburn would allow the press to photograph him, but only under strict conditions that the ordeal
would last no more than sixty seconds and that there would be
no pictures taken from the back. Generations of photographers
thought Rayburn's ban on rear angles stemmed from his baldness. It was true that he bristled at any mention of his hair, or
lack of it.[20] But even more, he was sensitive over his right ear,
the top of which grew flat against his head. The ear is visible in
few photographs.

Reporters could gauge whether Rayburn had any news by the
number of minutes he allowed for his daily press briefing. If he
summoned them into his office at two minutes to noon, they
knew he had little to say. John Holton, who ran the front office,
watched the clock. At one minute to noon, he would yell: "Time,
Mr. Speaker"—the signal for Rayburn, invariably trailed by reporters, to start his short trek. Without pausing, he would
march across the hall to the Speaker's Lobby and through the
swinging doors into the House Chamber. Just as the sergeant-
at-arms placed the silver mace—symbol of the Speaker's authority—on its pedestal, he would ascend the rostrum and gavel
the House to order. Rayburn's perfectly timed entrance was
thwarted briefly in the late 1950s by one Randall S. "Front
Porch" Harmon, an Indiana Democrat, whose day was incomplete until he had cornered the Speaker and shaken his hand.
Harmon would station himself squarely in the doorway, blocking the Speaker's path until the ritual was performed. "Front
Porch," who acquired his nickname when the press disclosed
that he had rented his own front porch as a taxpayer-provided
district office, was among a number of odd fish swept into the
House by the 1958 Democratic landslide. The voters mercifully
retired him after one term.

When the House was in recess, Rayburn would spend the
morning answering mail. Afternoons were times for relaxing,
beginning with a long lunch in the House dining room. He especially looked forward to the Texas delegation's regular Wednesday
lunch in the Speaker's private dining room. The state's senators

would come over, and often a prominent Texas visitor would be invited. Talk almost invariably centered on Texas political gossip or on congressional business. When Dallas voters sent Republican right-winger Bruce Alger to Congress in 1955, the sessions became the Texas *Democratic* luncheons in order to exclude the brash ideologue, whom Rayburn found totally obnoxious. The Speaker severed all dealings with Alger after their initial meeting. He felt that his friendly gesture of inviting the freshman to his office had been thrown back in his face when, after the meeting, Alger told reporters: "Rayburn is all right, but as I expected, he always puts his party ahead of his country."[21] The two never exchanged another word.

After lunch on quiet days, Rayburn would wander to the back office, where, until about 3:30, he signed mail and conferred with staff. The atmosphere was easy and informal. Occasionally, he napped on a long black leather sofa in his private office. He might ask Bernice Frazier, a staff secretary, to clip his fingernails. He would lie on the couch, while Bernice worked away at his short, plump fingers. "My 'manurist,'" he called her. Kidding the office women about his masculine irresistibility was a favorite pastime. "See, the women just can't leave me alone," he would say. "They just love to touch me." Later, after a final check of the front office, he would put on his hat, pause in the doorway, and invariably say: "I'm leaving now. But please don't take the skin off my heels getting out behind me."

Unless he had arranged to go fishing, he would come to the office on Saturday, joining his male staff members, who were expected to work a six-day week. The women were given the day off, although Rene Kimbrough often came in, just in case he wanted to dictate letters. But there is little for a Speaker of the House to do on Saturday. There is no legislative business to transact. Few members seek advice. Lobbyists are home with their families. The day drags. Typically, he would pace from office to office, looking for something—anything—to occupy him. To pass the time, he would open the big center drawer of his desk and carefully examine its contents. Pens, cuff links, long-forgotten trinkets and souvenirs, old letters and notes all became items of unusual interest. One by one, he would pull them from the drawer, hold them up to the light, and examine them as if he had discovered a hoard of precious jewels and documents. Saturday lunch, usually with a few Texas colleagues, was a relief from the boredom. He would sit for hours swapping political gossip around a big round table in the members' dining room. Finally, he would head home, allowing just enough time to catch a golf match or baseball game on TV. Weekdays, he seldom missed *The Lone Ranger*, his favorite show. The Lone Ranger "always does the right thing and it comes out like it ought to," he said. Dusk on Saturday would find him in his apartment, often alone, sometimes with a friend, hunched up to the TV, perhaps with a half-consumed drink in his hand. For Rayburn, as for many another single person, televised sports were a welcome antidote for weekend loneliness.

In January 1956, Congressman Richard Bolling of Missouri approached Rayburn about supporting a voting-rights bill, aimed primarily at disfranchised southern blacks. The need for such legislation had been discussed among liberals in and out of Congress for years, and now the time seemed ripe. The Eisenhower administration, through the office of Attorney General Herbert Brownell, was examining growing complaints of civil rights denial and trying to decide whether to propose its own rights bill in 1956—a presidential election year.

Bolling, one of Rayburn's young lieutenants and self-appointed liaison between the House leadership and the liberal House Democratic Study Group, decided that, if any civil rights legislation was to get through Congress, the Speaker's full support was essential. He was needed, Bolling noted later, "not so much because of his influence in the House itself but because of his prestige and influence among Southerners in both the House and Senate."[22] Through Rayburn, the bill's chief proponents hoped to win the support of Senate Majority Leader Johnson, who could be crucial in avoiding a Senate filibuster—the ultimate weapon against all civil rights legislation since 1875. An abrasive, shrewd legislator who enjoyed Rayburn's full confidence, Bolling outlined to the Speaker the need for such a bill. Candidly, he described the pressures for its enactment and the political implications.

The old man said little as he turned over in his mind the proposal—and the personal challenge—Bolling was laying out. Rayburn was trying to be sympathetic, and he wanted to be in step with the times; Congress and the nation must pay its debt to blacks, and the time for payment was coming, he believed. Finally, he interrupted the young congressman. "I'm not against the right to vote," he said. "Every citizen should have that." He thanked Bolling for coming but offered no aid. Bolling, like many another congressman who sought Rayburn's support on specific legislation, left the meeting unsure of the depth of the Speaker's commitment. Bolling later recalled:

> Nevertheless, I walked from his office in relief and delight. I was certain that if certain preliminary tasks could be performed, the Speaker would step in at the critical time in order to give the bill the push that only he could effectively give. My hunch that the Speaker would ultimately play a crucial favorable role could not be mentioned. As in the past, to involve him too soon in a legislative matter would probably be to lose him or to reduce his effectiveness.[23]

The bill seemed ill-fated. Eisenhower, never enthusiastic over civil rights legislation, vacillated. The Justice Department dragged its heels in drafting a proposed administration bill. House liberals had their usual problems in working together. Bolling and his colleagues even had trouble convincing organized labor and civil rights groups that this was the best bill possible. Finally, it was clear that no bill could be passed and sent to the Senate before July—which meant that Senate opponents could easily stall it until final adjournment. A southern-led filibuster on the eve of a presidential campaign would do the Democratic party no good.

Bolling, as the liberals' chief strategist, decided that the best course was deliberately to impede the bill's progress even more, so that it reached the House floor before adjournment but too late to be taken up by the Senate. House liberals would have a civil rights vote on which to campaign in the fall. He discussed the tactic with Rayburn, advising the Speaker to inform Johnson

that the Senate was getting only temporary relief. The House
would certainly pass and send to the Senate a new civil rights
bill early in 1957. "I understand what you are saying," Rayburn
replied impatiently.

Although he tried, Rules Committee Chairman Howard
Smith this time could not block a civil rights bill. The momentum was too strong, even for the much-feared conservative
coalition. On July 16, the measure reached the House floor. Opponents sought to expedite the debate. With a quick vote, they
hoped to catch the liberals—notorious for their absences—
unprepared. Rayburn saw through this strategy at once. He
found Bolling in the corridor and told him sharply: "You'd
better get your boys here quickly." Rayburn never explained
how he could sense trouble brewing on the House floor, but he
had that ability, as scores of members have testified over the
years. Harry R. Sheppard, Democrat of California, said in 1956:
"Speaker Rayburn senses the mood of the House better than any
living man. He often goes to committee chairmen handling a
bill and says, 'The boys are upset today. They're getting unhappy. I think you better put this off a day or two until they
settle down.' He does that on bills he wants and those he doesn't
want. He saves many a chairman."[24]

Bolling took Rayburn's warning as a good sign. "I knew then
for the first time," he said later, "that I had been correct in believing that Rayburn would be a supporter of the civil-rights
bill."[25] What Bolling did not know was that even before his first
meeting with Rayburn early in 1956, the Texan had been re-
appraising his views on civil rights. He supported a voting-
rights bill, not only because it made sense politically, but, more
important, because he felt it was right for the nation. He had
agonized over the whole question of racial equality and segregation for years—especially since the Supreme Court put the issue
squarely before the nation with its landmark school desegregation decision, *Brown* vs. *The Board of Education of Topeka, Kansas*. "If you had been on that Court," Rayburn said shortly after
the 1954 ruling, "you'd have voted exactly as they voted—if you
were an honest man."[26]

On the record, he was no champion of civil rights before

1956. He had helped block Truman's FEPC bill, had consistently opposed federal anti–poll tax and antilynch legislation (although he supported state action on these issues), and, in the heat of his own campaigns, had stood firmly for preserving racial segregation. But times were changing, and he sensed the need for a new outlook, in himself and the nation. "Men are not angels," he told the graduating class at Syracuse University in June. "It is not, therefore, criminal that inequities should exist among us. But it would be criminal if we should ignore them. This we will not do." [27]

Politically, Rayburn was walking a fine line—his national responsibilities and his conscience on one side, his role as representative of a strongly prosegregation constituency on the other. But he always believed that if he was thinking straight, he could fly in the face of public opinion at home, that he could go home and convince his people that he was right. He despised colleagues who were, as he put it, "afraid of their districts." [28] Carl Albert, whose conservative "Little Dixie" district in Oklahoma was just over the state line from Rayburn's, faced a similarly painful decision: whether to go along with the overwhelming sentiment of his constituents or to risk trying to lead them on this explosive issue. He asked the Speaker for advice. "Carl, under the Constitution, every man has a right to vote," said Rayburn. "You can defend that position before any audience in this country."

"That cleared it up for me immediately," Albert later said. "For the first time, I saw the issue in moral terms." [29]

The civil rights bill was back before the House early in 1957, this time with the full backing of the administration and the House Democratic leadership. Rayburn, less hesitant now to have his name associated with the legislation, met with key backers to plan swift House passage. He lobbied wavering members, especially those from prosegregation districts. "You can weather it," he told Jim Wright of Fort Worth. "I believe in two or three years, you will be very proud that you voted for it." [30] He offered to meet with Rules Committee Chairman Smith and to convince Senate Majority Leader Johnson of the bill's importance—although Johnson, undergoing his own metamorphosis on civil rights and anxious to bolster his credentials among northern moderates, needed no convincing. The House had little difficulty with the bill the second time around. Smith made one feeble effort to kill it on a technicality but was overruled by the Speaker. On June 18, the measure cleared the House virtually intact and was sent to the Senate.[31]

The Senate, as predicted, was the crucial battleground for the Civil Rights Act of 1957. Johnson, in one of the most agile parliamentary performances ever witnessed in the Senate, kept debate moving. Cajoling colleagues, assuaging reluctant southerners, he salvaged most of the bill. A provision empowering the President to use troops to enforce existing civil rights laws was dropped, and an amendment guaranteeing jury trials in criminal contempt cases arising from the voting-rights measure was added. The compromises Johnson had to strike with southern opponents diluted the bill's enforcement provisions—a price many thought too high for southern acquiescence. But the heart of the legislation remained. After twenty-four days of debate and the fizzling of a southern filibuster, the measure cleared the Senate on August 7.

The jury-trial provision so angered House liberals that they refused at first to go to conference with the Senate. "The country took an awful beating," said Eisenhower. It fell to Rayburn, acting as intermediary between House civil rights supporters and the Senate leadership, to get the negotiations going. Ultimately, he, Johnson, and the House and Senate Republican leaders worked out a compromise that softened the disputed provision while satisfying the liberals, the administration, and the southerners. On August 29, the two bodies gave final approval to the first civil rights legislation in eighty years—a milestone that proved to be only the beginning of the fight for racial integration. Four days later, Governor Orval Faubus of Arkansas launched a bloody new chapter in the burgeoning civil rights battle by ordering units of the National Guard to prevent blacks from entering all-white Central High School in Little Rock.

In March 1957, Eisenhower invited Rayburn, Johnson, and other congressional leaders to the White House to discuss a matter that had troubled him for a long time: potential problems of governing that might arise when a President is incapacitated. It was an issue that Eisenhower had wanted to discuss publicly since his own heart attack in 1955 but had postponed, at the urging of his advisers, until after the presidential elections.[32]

Before the assembled lawmakers, Eisenhower and Attorney General Brownell spelled out their plan for a constitutional amendment that would provide for the Vice-President temporarily to assume the duties of an ill or otherwise incapacitated President. The transfer could take place at the instigation of the President or, with the concurrence of a majority of the Cabinet, the Vice-President. A frown clouded Rayburn's face as he listened. "This plan is nonsense," he finally said. "Suppose the President steps aside and puts in the Vice-President as President, and the Vice-President likes the job. Then when the first man wants it back, the second man doesn't want to give it up. What are you going to do then? You say the Cabinet will decide. But this new man has gotten a new Cabinet that wants him to stay on. What then?"[33] Rayburn, always trying to ferret out hidden dangers in legislation, said he could envision a "civil war," with half the nation lining up behind the President and the rest behind the Vice-President. "Mr. President," he told Eisenhower, "if you send that message, the American people will never understand it. They elected you, not Mr. Nixon. They don't expect you to abdicate."[34] Eisenhower seemed to agree, but just to be sure that the proposal was dead, Rayburn later instructed Judiciary Committee Chairman Emanuel Celler to "just let that thing lie. I don't know who thought up such nonsense."[35]

In 1958, after he had suffered three serious illnesses, Eisenhower entered into an unusual personal agreement with Nixon authorizing the Vice-President temporarily to assume the President's duties should the latter became too ill to serve. The letter agreement, not binding on future Presidents, seemed prudent in light of Ike's medical history and the Constitution's silence on this important contingency.[36] But Rayburn remained skeptical. The memo was "illegal," he complained, although he did not try to fight it. In private, he admitted that his distrust of Nixon might have influenced his thinking.[37] He eventually gave a re-

luctant go-ahead to a bill allowing Congress to participate in
the replacement of any disabled President. The bill was never
enacted.[38]

Rayburn again wielded his power in June 1957, when the
House Committee on Un-American Activities opened a series
of hearings in San Francisco and, in direct violation of the
Speaker's specific rulings in 1952 and 1955, permitted a local station to televise the proceedings. The hearings became a front-
page sensation across the nation when a prospective witness,
fearful of appearing on TV, jumped to his death from a hotel
window. The incident infuriated Rayburn. Not only had the
committee embarrassed the House with its roughshod treatment
of witnesses, but, with its televised hearings, it had flouted the
authority of the Speaker himself. Rayburn's ban on televised
House committee hearings, wherever held, had always been
very clear—often disputed but never in doubt.

His challenger was formidable—Francis E. "Tad" Walter of
Pennsylvania. The two men had long been friends and political
allies. But now Walter had become a powerful figure in his own
right—head of the Democratic Patronage Committee, chairman
of the Judiciary subcommittee on immigration, and chairman of
the Un-American Activities Committee, then the most controversial and feared committee in Congress. Viewed by many as a
possible Rayburn successor, he had in weeks preceding the San
Francisco incident begun staking out his independence from the
House leadership. His speech favoring the jury-trial amendment
to the civil rights bill was a blatant appeal to the South, the heart
of Rayburn's support. Now he was challenging the Speaker
again. Rayburn's response was unequivocal. "There will not be
any more House committee or subcommittee hearings in Washington or anywhere else televised or broadcast by radio. Period," he declared.

"Outside Washington," answered HUAC Staff Director Richard Arens smugly, "we use the facilities of the federal courts. We
take the point of view that we are guests of the local federal
judge. We follow whatever rules he applies in the courtrooms we
use."[39] Standing before the cameras in San Francisco, Walter

supported his staff director. Rayburn's rules "apply only in Washington and are no longer in force anyway," he said. "There is no such rule."

Rayburn's face reddened and his lips curled in an angry snarl as he read Walter's defiant comments coming over the UP ticker in the Speaker's Lobby. To reporters gathered in anticipation of an explosion, he growled, "No comment." Word of the Speaker's fury spread through the cloakrooms. Turning to Wilbur Mills, the first to reach him, he said, "Tad Walter's investigative methods have gone too far." Assured of solid backing from other members, Rayburn wired Walter to halt all broadcast coverage of his hearings and to meet with him as soon as he got back to Washington. Walter returned immediately. He later emerged from Rayburn's office a thoroughly beaten man. As a Rayburn aide told it: "I don't know what Mr. Rayburn said, but when Mr. Walter emerged to the outer office, he was as white and shaken as I never saw him before or since. The old man obviously had pulled no punches."

Afterward, the Speaker told reporters, "Tad Walter is not going to televise any meetings any more. I have said all I am going to say. When I get what I want, I am satisfied."[40] But Walter's defiance had been a warning. Although the 75-year-old Rayburn left no doubt that he was still firmly in command, his critics were growing louder and his challengers bolder. He was too old, out of touch, soft on the opposition, they argued. The sharks were circling, and he knew that a defeat, no matter how trivial, would bring them rushing in for the kill. He could not afford to drop his defenses for a minute.

22

Johnson for President

As he approached a half century in Congress, Sam Rayburn had gained acceptance by his colleagues and Americans everywhere as the final arbiter of congressional conduct, the embodiment of Congress itself. He was "Mr. Speaker," "Mr. Democrat," "Mr. Sam," and, to the *New York Times*, "Mr. Everything." His philosophical truisms—"Rayburnisms"—were sought and repeated until they became as fixed as the House rules in the minds of members with whom he served in the 1950s. Many remembered, and years later could recite, the nuggets of wisdom that he invariably offered freshmen at the opening of each new session:

A man doesn't have to be brilliant to make a success here. All you need is a reasonable amount of intelligence and the will power to tend to your own business.

Young men ought to come to Congress. It is a school.

No two people anywhere, anytime agree on everything. If they do, that's proof that one of them is doing all the thinking for the two.

When a man has common sense, he has all the sense there is.

There are no degrees of honesty. A man is either honest, or he isn't.

It's the easiest thing in the world to be honest, the hardest thing in the world to be dishonest.

If you tell the truth the first time, you don't have to remember what you said.

Legislation should never be designed to punish anyone. Ordinarily, it's a question of regulating the minority—the pistol totin' minority.

The greatest ambition a man can have is to be known as a just man.

Damn the man who is always looking for credit. I have always noticed that if a man does his job, and does it well, he will get more credit than he is really entitled to.

The fellow who jabbers all the time gets no attention. If he gives the House some meat when he speaks, they will quiet down and listen.

Like Cal Coolidge, I found out early in life that I never have to explain anything I haven't said.

You really can't say how you lead. You feel your way, receptive to those rolling waves of sentiment. If a man in politics can't feel, as well as see and hear, he is lost.

A man doesn't learn his job in the House until he has had his head bloodied a couple of times, but a leader may as well quit if his head is bloodied too often.

In this House, the people who get along the best, go along the most.

One of the wisest things ever said was, "Wait a minute."

A politician has got to have publicity to live, but he can damn well get too much of it.

I've never had time to hate people. I've found that the world will meet you halfways, if you will let it.

A little applied Christianity never hurt anybody.

A man who is not willing to get out and defend what he has done will ultimately find himself in poor shape politically.

Politics is the most honorable profession in the world. A man could have no higher ambition than to get in a position to serve other people. Service is the greatest word in the language.

A man must be a politician before he can be a statesman.

The 1958 Democratic landslide transformed Congress dramatically. Swarming through the House, upsetting comfortable old patterns of behavior, was a new generation of Democratic representatives—liberal in political outlook, well-informed, impatient, bold. While their respect for Rayburn was high—their initiation was incomplete until they had met the Speaker and received a bit of fatherly advice—the restless Democrats were more interested in action than in preserving institutions.

When disgruntled House Republicans, self-critical and frustrated after a devastating defeat at the polls, overthrew kindly, aging Joe Martin as minority leader and replaced him with a tough partisan, Charlie Halleck of Indiana, Rayburn knew the old ways of doing business were dying.[1] Martin, who had held the job for twenty years, was ousted partly because of his senility, partly because Republicans decided he had been too friendly and accommodating to the opposition. Rayburn, too, was an old man, starting his forty-seventh year in Congress. It was conceivable to him that the day might come when he would share Martin's humiliating fate.

Rayburn responded quickly and enthusiastically to the new climate. He asserted himself more in public discussion of leading issues; he took a commanding role in handling major legislation. Importantly, he listened more to dissenting voices within his party. Through Chet Holifield and James Roosevelt of California, Richard Bolling of Missouri, and others, he communicated with the increasingly militant liberals, although he rejected their demand that he lead a movement to enlarge the conservative-dominated Committee on Rules.[2] Attempting to pack the committee with more liberals would trigger a bloody fight the likes of which the Democratic party had not seen in years. And that, on the eve of a presidential election, he sought to avoid.

He did, however, promise to do everything possible to see that essential Democratic bills reached the House floor.[3] In the past, Rules Chairman Howard Smith usually released bills in which Rayburn expressed special interest, and the Speaker had every reason to think his gentleman's agreement would continue. He also was counting on Joe Martin for one Republican vote, or at least a timely absence, on the committee. But he had not figured on Martin's ouster as GOP leader. The new Republican leadership filled two GOP vacancies on the committee with reactionaries who would be present and voting whenever Smith needed them.[4]

Democratic Chairman Paul Butler and his toothless Advisory Council still nipped at Rayburn and Johnson from outside. Butler criticized their "attitude and policies," labeled them "soft on Eisenhower," and insisted they "exert more progressive leadership," so that Democratic candidates would have "a record of legislative accomplishment on which to run in 1960." His sniping subsided only after influential Democrats told him to shut up or resign.[5]

The 86th Congress thus was launched in January 1959 in an atmosphere of contention from which it never emerged. The cooperative years of divided government were over. Eisenhower, weary of the Presidency and obsessed with balancing the budget, virtually ignored Congress, except when legislation was put before him to sign. In his final two White House years, he vetoed forty-four bills, only two of which the Democratic majority overrode. Ike chortled at press conferences about this power—"my veto pistol," he called it. While Halleck enforced strict discipline over his depleted GOP forces, southern Democrats joined them in sufficient numbers to make the President's vetoes virtually invincible. Democratic initiatives in education, medical care for the aged, interstate highway funding, housing, urban renewal, farm price supports, and water pollution control all met defeat. Some key Democratic bills died in the Rules Committee, where Smith now turned a deaf ear to Rayburn's appeals for cooperation; some were shot down by Eisenhower's veto pistol.

Frequently intervening to break committee deadlocks, Rayburn embroiled himself more deeply in drafting and enacting specific bills than he had in years. In 1960, he went to bat for a new civil rights bill, a Democratic priority, lending his support to a discharge petition that would force its release by the Rules Committee. He supported the Forand bill—a radical new idea to provide medical care for the elderly under Social Security. It was leadership the times demanded, but it was risky. When legislation failed to pass, Rayburn took a larger share of the blame. Rumors of a Democratic revolt surfaced periodically. "Well covered up for the present," said *U.S. News & World Report*, "are murmurings of an effort to displace Mr. Rayburn as Speaker when the 87th Congress convenes in January, 1961." But most House observers quickly dismissed such talk. "There is a little grumbling by members who don't know what's going on," Rhode Island Democrat Aime Forand told reporters. "And there is legitimate criticism that Democrats don't hold caucuses often enough in which the grumblers could blow off steam and find out what's going on."

Senate investigations of organized labor racketeering, particularly within the International Brotherhood of Teamsters, run by James R. Hoffa, generated irresistible public pressure for labor reform legislation in 1959. The AFL-CIO supported a weak bill amounting to little more than a slap on the wrist. The administration backed a sweeping reform measure that would sharply alter practices throughout organized labor, not merely in the racket-infested unions. The administration bill, which carried the name of its bipartisan House sponsors, Georgia Democrat Phil M. Landrum and Michigan Republican Robert P. Griffin, quickly attracted congressional support. The Landrum-Griffin bill, Rayburn felt, violated his lifelong belief that "legislation should never be written to punish someone." He endorsed a moderate measure, reported but later largely abandoned by the House Committee on Education and Labor. A proposal that organized labor could live with, this bill would weed out the crooks without imposing "crippling legal restraints on the honest, legitimate interests of the working man," the Speaker said.[6]

The controversy aroused more vicious animosity than the House had known since the public utility holding company fight of the 1930s. While outraged voters demanded punitive legislative medicine against labor corruption, union lobbyists roamed the Capitol corridors, threatening Democrats in coming elections. With scant help, Rayburn fought for the committee bill and against the harsh Landrum-Griffin substitute. In a nationwide radio broadcast, he pleaded for "fair play" for labor.[7] The aging Speaker, beginning to hear the footsteps of a few restive Democrats who felt he might be losing his grip, believed as seldom before that his own prestige and perhaps his leadership could be on the line. But antilabor sentiment in the House was too overpowering; Landrum-Griffin was approved, 229–201. Rayburn felt humiliated.

He believed, but could not prove, that Lyndon Johnson secretly had a hand in the Texas delegation's almost solid support for Landrum-Griffin.[8] He was so furious that his closest Texas friends had deserted him that he refused to join them in the Board of Education that evening. He took the defeat very personally and was particularly hurt that two Texans whose careers he had promoted, Homer Thornberry and Frank Ikard, had voted the other way. Never had anything in his life hurt him the way they did, he told an aide. "They're all down there waiting for me, wondering what I'm going to say," he said. "Well, I don't want to see the sons of bitches. I'd rather drink up here with my friends." He offered the aide a whiskey, poured one for himself, and gazed out a window at the gathering darkness.[9] Not for weeks did his fury subside to allow Johnson and the other errant members of the Texas delegation back in his good graces.

Sometime in 1959, Rayburn concluded that the nation sorely needed new leadership—Democratic leadership—and that it was time for Lyndon Johnson to make his move.[10] Johnson had reached the same conclusion years earlier and had been feeding Rayburn his notions of how the country should be run. With

Eisenhower leaving office, the Texan would never have a better opportunity to see his dream a reality. But as the 1960 presidential campaign approached, Johnson vacillated, much to the irritation of his supporters. He seemed uncertain how or when to jump into the race. "He's acting just like John Garner did in 1932," Rayburn complained privately. "I knew damn well that Garner was anxious to be the nominee but he kept refusing to talk about it because he thought it would jeopardize his leadership in the House. If anyone brought it up, he'd change the subject, or get up and leave the table."[11]

Johnson was no Garner. But he baffled Rayburn and others urging him to begin laying the necessary foundation for a serious campaign. The man of legendary skill as a political organizer lagged far behind other contenders in every category from raising money to courting convention delegates. He often waxed eloquent about his soaring prospects, as when he told the Speaker that Tammany boss Carmine DeSapio had promised him the votes of at least ninety New York delegates. Rayburn went away thinking that his protégé really might put together a winning combination. At other times, the mercurial Texan complained angrily: "All this talk about my candidacy is destroying my leadership. I'm trying to build a legislative record over there. The Senate already is full of presidential candidates. If I really get into this thing, they'll gang up on me and chop me up as leader so that I'll be disqualified for the nomination."[12]

When friends argued that Johnson would never reach the White House because he carried too much baggage—southerner, heart attack, lack of charisma, stigma of the oil and gas industry—Rayburn would flare up. "You don't know what you're talking about," he would respond testily. "In my opinion there are a hell of a lot of Republicans that don't want to vote for Richard Nixon. They're not going to vote for Jack Kennedy, not for Adlai Stevenson, not for Hubert Humphrey. But they'll cross the line to vote for Lyndon, if he gets the nomination, because they don't want Nixon."[13]

Rayburn had another reason for pushing Johnson: he wanted an alternative to the hard-driving, well-organized front-runner, John F. Kennedy. As a House member and as a senator, the Massachusetts millionaire's son left the Speaker unimpressed. "He's a good boy," was about the best Rayburn could say of him. A likable, amiable fellow, yes; presidential material, no. "Jack is one of the laziest men I ever talked to," he told friends. He had supported Kennedy for Vice-President in 1956 as an alternative to Estes Kefauver. But the young man was not serious enough, nor seasoned enough, to be reaching for the nation's highest office, Rayburn thought.

Kennedy also had, in Rayburn's opinion, a politically fatal handicap: his Roman Catholic faith. Rayburn was devoid of religious prejudice—"It is a terrible thing to hold a man's religion against him in a country whose very existence is based on freedom of religion"—but the Al Smith campaign in 1928 had convinced him that millions of Americans were anti-Catholic and that they carried their biases into the voting booth.[14] An enthusiastic Smith supporter, who worked hard in a losing cause, Rayburn retained in 1960 the firm belief that a Catholic candidate would lead the Democratic party to defeat. And, above all, in the twilight of his career, he longed for another Democrat in the White House. The alternative—four or eight years under a President Nixon—was so repugnant to him that he dreaded thinking about it.

He firmly believed that Johnson, if he could win the nomination, would be the Democrats' strongest candidate. Of one thing he was sure: Johnson was the only Democrat who could carry Texas. He had a high, almost extravagant, opinion of his friend's qualifications. Rayburn often said that Johnson was the ablest legislator with whom he had ever worked. Even Kennedy agreed that Johnson was the most qualified Democrat, in terms of government experience. Beyond his unrivaled ability as Senate leader, Rayburn saw in him the vision, patriotism, and idealism that promised greatness. Respected, sometimes feared, he was "a senator's senator."[15] Yet, while Kennedy piled up delegates and popular support across the country, Johnson remained largely unknown outside of Washington. "Go around the country more, make more speeches," Rayburn urged. But Johnson put him off, preferring the familiar Senate surroundings and a passive, subtle campaign.

A sort of strategy evolved out of Johnson's hesitant approach: while Kennedy and Humphrey battled each other in the state primaries, he would remain on the job in the Senate—"tending the store"—enhancing his reputation as a master legislator. They would cut each other up in the primaries; he would emerge unsullied, everybody's second choice, a perfect compromise candidate. Faced with the more liberal alternatives, the solid South would be his for the asking. All he needed, then, were the border states, a strong showing in a couple of big northern industrial states, and the Far West. Johnson would not be hurt by avoiding the primaries, Rayburn told reporters. "I've never thought much of the primaries as a way to decide these matters."[16]

In fashioning a presidential bid, the two Texans proved incredibly naive. They were experts in analyzing congressional races but out of their element in a national campaign. They had an entirely erroneous notion of where political power resided in most states. Both thought they could reach the state power centers through friendly members of Congress. And while they courted senators and House members, many of whom proved grossly out of touch with political realities in their states, the Kennedy people astutely circulated in state capitals, city halls, and local precincts. In contrast to Johnson's hip-pocket campaign, Kennedy's was organized in depth, lavishly financed, practical in outlook. Johnson and his political advisers, including Rayburn, bathed in self-deception. Any sign of friendliness by a political power broker, even one of such depleted coinage as Tammany's Carmine DeSapio, was interpreted as a commitment to deliver delegates. As the convention neared, Johnson's hopes were built on such fragile underpinnings.

In the House, Rayburn corralled all the Johnson support he could find. Some members, such as Philadelphia's William Green, Sr., he cornered in the Board of Education. Appealing for Green's help, Rayburn cited all the reasons why he ought to back Johnson, including the recently detected—highly overrated, as it turned out—"friendliness" of Pennsylvania Governor David Lawrence. "You know, Bill," confided Rayburn, "If you pitch in on this thing, we can get Pennsylvania." Green squirmed uncomfortably, glanced at his watch. "I got to get," he said, moving toward the door. Pausing, he said he was reminded of the story of the weak-willed fruit peddler who was constantly being enticed by women customers into trading his fruit for their amorous favors. Finally, with no money to show for the day, he rang one last doorbell. When a voluptuous female appeared, the peddler started to weep. What's the matter, she asked? "Oh, hell," the peddler bawled, "I've already been fucked out of my apples and oranges, and now you're about to get my peaches." Amid the laughter, Green escaped, completely uncommitted to Rayburn.[17]

Cautiously, the Johnson presidential campaign expanded. The reluctant, still unannounced, candidate finally yielded to the pleadings of his top advisers, Rayburn and John Connally, to open a Washington headquarters.[18] Speaking tours were booked—one through Ohio and West Virginia, another in California and several western states. Although the candidate complained constantly about arrangements and press coverage, he left a favorable overall impression on local politicians and voters. Finally, on July 5, he made the leap. Before a gathering of reporters and supporters in the Senate Auditorium, he formally proclaimed his candidacy. Avoiding direct assault on the front-running Kennedy, whose campaigning had kept him away from his Senate duties for most of the past two years, Johnson justified his own delay: "Someone had to tend the store."

It was too little, too late. Kennedy had already swept seven primaries, including even West Virginia, which Johnson strategists had expected him to lose in a tide of anti-Catholicism. Instead of a Humphrey-Kennedy standoff in the primaries, the wealthy Irish liberal emerged as the clear primary winner, the party's most appealing vote-getter since Roosevelt. For Johnson, the situation in the nonprimary states was equally dismal. In one state after another where he had secured the support of the senators and leading House members, Kennedy operatives had come in the back door and locked up the convention delegates. States that Johnson and Rayburn confidently listed as theirs—Arizona and Wyoming, for example—went to Kennedy.

Congress recessed in early July, a week before the Democratic

National Convention in Los Angeles. Rayburn and Johnson had planned to adjourn for the year, but with half a dozen important bills still on the agenda, they decided that the session would reconvene after the two national conventions. Both denied Republican accusations that the decision was a last-minute maneuver "to hold certain bills over the heads of key Democrats who can deliver convention delegates." [19] Rayburn, accompanied by aides John Holton and D. B. Hardeman, flew to Los Angeles two days early. For the first time in twenty years, "Mr. Democrat" would not be a platform official, merely a Texas delegate. He had declined, after considerable agonizing, to preside over the convention on the grounds that he wanted to devote his energies to securing Johnson's nomination. As a declared partisan, he thought Democratic Chairman Butler might try to keep him from serving again. He did not want to give Butler that opportunity.

There was another, equally compelling reason for giving up the convention chairmanship, which he loved and which contributed so much to his national fame. Rayburn was nearly blind: his left eye had been growing dim for several years, and in late 1958, while in Bonham, he suffered a hemorrhage in his other eye. That eye now was completely blind. He could still read, but it was a strain. He gave up wearing the pince-nez glasses that he had carried for years and began reading with a magnifying glass. Doctors said he would never go totally blind. But in 1960 he could see only shadows and vague outlines of people. Vain, perhaps more afraid that his House leadership would be jeopardized, Rayburn sought to keep his disability a secret. Inside the Capitol, he had little trouble because he knew its every room and corridor. His staff and close associates protected him. They read him the daily mail and helped him identify people. When he presided over the House, Parliamentarian Lew Deschler whispered the names of members seeking recognition and helped him count votes. He developed a keen sense of hearing and learned to distinguish most of his acquaintances by their voices. Few outside of the Speaker's close inner circle knew his secret. "I've presided three times as permanent chairman without a bobble," he told his staff. "I've got a perfect record.

But the way my eyes are, I might make a mistake if I was presiding."

Kennedy was close to victory. Johnson's last hope—a slim one—was to prevent the popular Yankee from winning on the first or second ballot. That would require all secondary candidates and favorite sons to hang in the race. Frantically, Johnson's supporters sought to keep Humphrey from releasing his forty pledged delegates. Behind the scenes, they aided the burgeoning candidacy of Adlai Stevenson. If Humphrey, dark horse Stuart Symington, and the favorite sons held fast, if Stevenson could pick up support in Illinois and elsewhere, if Johnson could retain his own support—then, possibly, Kennedy could be denied an early victory. After two ballots, Kennedy's support might begin to fade. It might become a brokered convention. As Kennedy told top aide Theodore Sorensen: "We'll either win by the second ballot, or never." [20]

Rayburn had never participated in a "stop" movement against a candidate and did not relish this one. He disdained the personal assaults that overzealous Johnson partisans John Connally and India Edwards leveled against Kennedy and his father in those last desperate hours. It was not Rayburn's style to attack a candidate on the basis of health, or to question his—or his father's—patriotism. Although Johnson called Rayburn "my campaign manager," the Speaker's role was, in fact, that of a senior adviser. Connally and other Johnson friends directed the hour-to-hour quest for votes, while Rayburn greeted the steady stream of important visitors who came by his seventh-floor suite at the Biltmore. When he managed John Garner's campaigns in 1932 and 1940, Rayburn insisted on strict control over all convention activities conducted in the candidate's name. He demanded a fair campaign and shunned collusion with other trailing candidates. The Johnson campaign, however, was not in his hands but in those of a younger, pragmatic, sometimes cynical group of political professionals.

Johnson's last hope all but collapsed on the convention's first day when caucusing Pennsylvania delegates broke overwhelmingly for Kennedy. Led by Congressman Green, an enthusiastically pro-Kennedy contingent apparently changed the mind of Governor Lawrence, the delegation's leader and erstwhile Johnson supporter. Lawrence's support tipped the Keystone State to Kennedy.

Two days later, Rayburn sat with the Texas delegation on the convention floor as the presidential balloting began. In shunning the rostrum, the Speaker said he wanted to "to see what a convention looks like from the other side." Like an old fire horse at the sound of a bell, his pulse quickened at the noise, the heat of the hall, and the repeated crack of the chairman's gavel. From his seat below, he bellowed a constant stream of advice to his successor on the platform, Governor LeRoy Collins of Florida. "Bang the gavel! Bang the gavel!" he shouted. "Rule! Rule!" Collins, of course, could neither see nor hear him, but it made an amusing show for those in the old man's vicinity and the millions watching on television.

Johnson took an early lead but was soon overtaken by Kennedy. As the roll call neared the midpoint, Kennedy had jumped well ahead. New York gave Kennedy 104½ of its 114 votes. Where was DeSapio, Johnson partisans wondered? Finally, Wyoming's Senator Gale McGee, a key Johnson backer, stood on a chair and shouted joyfully that Wyoming was giving its 15 votes to Kennedy, putting him over the top. With 761 votes needed for the nomination, Kennedy polled 806 to Johnson's 409.[21]

Seated in the dejected and emotionally drained Texas delegation, Rayburn took a phone call from the defeated candidate. "Mr. Speaker, I've been talking to Price and Will [former Texas Governor Price Daniel and former State Attorney General Will Wilson]," Johnson said. "They think Kennedy will offer me the Vice-Presidency, and they say that if he does, I ought to take it. I told them that will never happen. We've said too many harsh things about each other. But if he asks me, what should I say?"[22]

"Lyndon, you know what I think," snapped Rayburn. "So don't you be going off here and doing something foolish before we talk it over. Don't you do it." Everyone knew the old man was opposed. Although it was inconsistent with his own earlier quest for the nomination, he had often stated his belief that the Vice-Presidency was a less important office than either Speaker or Senate majority leader. The night before he left for Los Angeles, he told his good friends Gene and Ann Worley: "The first thing I'm going to do when I get off that airplane tomorrow is to announce to the world that Lyndon Johnson ain't interested in second spot on a ticket with Kennedy."[23] The matter was still highly speculative, but Johnson agreed not to accept any offer from Kennedy, in the unlikely event an offer was made, without first consulting the Speaker.

Exhausted, Johnson went to bed. In Rayburn's suite nearby, several of the Speaker's friends and aides gathered to drink some of the boss's whiskey and conduct the inevitable postmortem. Rayburn listened gloomily for a while, took a few phone calls, then retired to his bedroom. There was no mention of a Johnson vice-presidential nomination. Speculation focused primarily on Symington. Nobody, Rayburn included, thought Kennedy would offer it to Johnson, or that Johnson would accept any such offer.

Meanwhile, Kennedy was getting conflicting advice. According to Ted Sorensen, the candidate had refused to think about the Vice-Presidency until his own nomination was secured. Now he turned to the lists of prospective running mates compiled earlier by Sorensen and other trusted advisers. Johnson's name led nearly all the lists.[24] No one disputed Johnson's qualifications, or the strength he, a southerner and a Protestant, would bring to the Democratic ticket. Kennedy liked and admired Johnson personally. He was indebted to Johnson for helping him get ahead in the Senate—in 1957, Johnson supported Kennedy over Estes Kefauver for a vacancy on the Foreign Relations Committee—and for delivering the Texas delegation to Kennedy in the losing fight for the vice-presidential nomination in 1956.

But several Kennedy advisers, particularly Robert Kennedy, still fumed over the last-minute personal attacks against the candidate and his father leveled by some Johnson partisans. Aside from his own feelings, Bobby Kennedy wondered if the Texan would accept the offer—the consensus was that he would refuse to go on the ticket—and whether he would fight for the nomination, if necessary, in the face of opposition from liberals and organized labor. They decided to sound him out first thing in the morning. Johnson later recapped the sequence of events:

The next morning the phone rang, and Lady Bird answered it. It was Kennedy. He said he wanted to come down and talk. I told him, "No, Jack, I'll come up and see you." But he insisted. When he got to my room, he said he wanted to discuss the Vice-Presidency.

I told him, "Now, Jack, let me say something before you say anything more. There are two thoughts I want to give you. First, what I think you need most is someone who can help your program in the Senate. Second, you should insist that the convention nominate whoever you want. Don't do what Adlai did in 1956 when he let you and Estes cut each other up needlessly. That was very foolish. Make your choice and make the convention agree with you."

Kennedy said, "I agree with you, and that's why I want to ask you to be on the ticket."

Then I told him: "Before I can say yes or no to that, there are a couple of problems that have got to be worked out. Sam Rayburn is dead set against this. You'll have to get him to withdraw his objection. Second, a lot of your own people are going to be madder than hell. You're going to have a lot of static out of your own people, and you'll have to straighten them out." [25]

Rumors of a Kennedy-Johnson ticket swept the convention. By mid-morning, Johnson was in a lather; clearly, he wanted the nomination, but many of his closest political allies, men and women whose views he respected, were urging him to decline. In the Johnson suite, a distraught Lady Bird tearfully told visitors, "I don't want him to take it. I don't want him to take it. I don't want Lyndon to be the number two man." [26] A few friends, such as Hale Boggs of Louisiana, took the opposite position. In any case, Johnson said he was committed not to accept without Rayburn's approval. He had been trying frantically all morning to call the Speaker. Oblivious to the whole flap, Rayburn had kept a breakfast date with some north Texans at another hotel. When Johnson finally reached him about 11 o'clock, Rayburn had not changed his view. He said he agreed with Lady Bird but that he would talk with Kennedy. "I think

Jack will be calling you soon," Johnson replied.

Rayburn could have been playing a game with Johnson and Kennedy at this point. It is hard to understand why he remained so vehemently against his friend's taking the Vice-Presidency, a job he himself coveted in the 1940s. There was no real reason for Johnson not to take it. He had proved an unsalable product for the Presidency on his own. The only way he was likely ever to reach the White House was the hard way—by first serving as Vice-President. Rayburn certainly recognized that. He also knew that John Garner, whose judgment he deeply respected, strongly favored it. He had received Garner's message, delivered through Lawrence "Chip" Roberts, a former Democratic official, urging him to seek the No. 2 post for Johnson. "I want you to say to Sam that I strongly recommend that he fight to hold the delegates together, but be prepared to have Lyndon accept the vice-presidential spot with the boy as soon as he offers it to him" was the message relayed.[27] It is conceivable that the Speaker had determined that the young presidential nominee needed Johnson more than vice versa and had decided to withhold his approval until the last minute in order to strike the best deal possible. If he was playing such a game, he did it masterfully—confiding in no one, including Johnson.

Wright Patman, on a Johnson-inspired mission to soften the old man's opposition, found Rayburn "blistering mad" when he burst into the Speaker's suite. "It will ruin Lyndon for the future," Rayburn shouted from the bathroom. Later, Boggs, acting as a self-appointed intermediary between Kennedy and Johnson, found Rayburn nervously pacing the floor. Tommy Corcoran was there, giving all the wrong arguments, Boggs thought. Easing Corcoran aside, the congressman went directly to the point: "The Democratic ticket needs Johnson for the unity of the country. You don't want to give this country eight years of Richard Nixon, do you?" He repeated the Nixon line several times. Rayburn frowned, said nothing for a long while. Finally, he said, "Lyndon's got to do it." He agreed to call Kennedy. The young candidate, rejecting Rayburn's offer to come up, said he would be right down—a gesture of courtesy that pleased the Speaker very much. But when he did not appear, Rayburn grew restless. To Boggs he snapped: "Get up there and see if that boy's coming down here."[28]

Boggs soon returned with Kennedy and aide Kenny O'Donnell in tow. Two flights up, in the Kennedy suite, there was pandemonium. Important Kennedy supporters, Walter Reuther of the United Auto Workers among them, were threatening to desert the campaign if Johnson came on the ticket. But in Rayburn's quarters, all was serene. "Shall we talk?" asked the smiling, relaxed candidate. Boggs pointed them toward Rayburn's bedroom and closed the door after them. Rayburn later reconstructed their conversation:

> I told him, "I'm dead set against this, but I've thought it over, and I'm going to tell you several things: if you tell me that you have to have Lyndon on the ticket in order to win the election, and if you tell me that you'll go before the world and tell the world that Lyndon is your choice and that you insist on his being the nominee, and if you'll make every possible use of him in the National Security Council and every other way to keep him busy and keep him happy, then the objections that I have had I'm willing to withdraw."
> Kennedy said to me, "I tell you all those things."[29]

Rayburn, believing the matter settled, stepped down the hall to Johnson's suite. There, amid the noise and confusion that now engulfed the place, he found Bobby Kennedy. "Oh, Mr. Speaker," said Kennedy, "the liberals are just tearing Jack to pieces—labor is raising Cain about Johnson. It's awfully confusing up there. Is Lyndon sure he wants to go through with this? There might be a terrible floor fight if he does."[30] The two moved into the empty bedroom of Mary Margaret Wiley, Johnson's personal secretary, and shut the door. Rayburn later recalled:

> Bobby came to see me, his hair all hanging down in his face, and told me that there'd be a fight over Lyndon and that he wanted to be sure Lyndon knew that. I said, "Now, Bobby, we're not talking to but one man, and that's your brother. I'll tell you what I told him: we don't want any-

thing, we aren't asking for anything, we aren't seeking anything. I've been dead set against this, but if Jack tells me he
needs Lyndon to win . . . will insist on his nomination . . . will use Lyndon every way he can, I'll withdraw
my objections, and we'll take our chances on the convention floor."

Bobby slapped his knee and said: "It's got to be Lyndon.
I'm going up to tell Jack."[31]

Some have speculated that Bobby Kennedy sought out
Rayburn on his own initiative, that he was privately seeking re-
inforcement of his own objections to a Kennedy-Johnson ticket.
The late Philip Graham, publisher of the *Washington Post*, who
was close to Kennedy throughout the convention, alleged in a
personal memorandum that Bobby Kennedy's mission was to
dissuade Johnson from accepting the nomination and that,
among other inducements, he offered Johnson the chairmanship
of the Democratic National Committee.[32] No such offer was
made through Rayburn—he would have considered it absurd
and would have laughed at young Kennedy or, more likely,
thrown him out. Sorensen later said the candidate sent his
brother simply to inform Johnson of the hostility upstairs and to
confirm that Johnson wanted the nomination enough to fight
for it. Even Sorensen, however, was under the mistaken notion
that Johnson was offered, through Rayburn, the party chairmanship as an alternative to the vice-presidential nomination.

After John Kennedy announced his choice, the anti-Johnson
uproar—never as widespread as it seemed from the perspective
of the Kennedy suite—subsided. A few northern and mid-
western delegates continued to fume, but no alternative candidate appeared. Johnson was nominated by acclamation. For the
first time, the Democrats had picked two incumbent senators to
head the ticket.

In the campaign that followed, Rayburn's attitude toward
the young presidential nominee shifted dramatically. As he
observed Kennedy closer in the short, disastrous postconven-
tion session of Congress and on the political stump, his ad-

miration for the candidate soared. He watched the televised Kennedy-Nixon debates with keen fascination and was amazed at the depth of Kennedy's knowledge. "My God, the things that boy knows!" he exclaimed during the second debate. He personally campaigned for the ticket in several states. When Kennedy confronted the religious issue head-on before the Houston Ministerial Association, Rayburn knew he had misjudged Kennedy—and hoped that he had also miscalculated the impact of Kennedy's religion. The New Frontier had no more enthusiastic supporter than Rayburn when the Kennedy-Johnson ticket, aided by Texas's twenty-five electoral votes, emerged victorious in November.

23

"The Worst Fight of My Life"

On New Year's Eve in 1960, Sam Rayburn cut short his holiday in Bonham and flew back to Washington for what he knew would be a tumultuous year. Although in a few days he would be 79, the Speaker showed few signs of old age. He walked briskly with a springy step and held his square shoulders far back like those of a young infantryman. His mind was alert and active, his hunger for information as voracious as ever. Poor eyesight was the only outward sign of his advancing age.[1]

Rayburn looked to his eightieth year with both eagerness and dread—eagerness, because a new Democratic administration was coming to power, led by young Jack Kennedy, the brash Bostonian for whom Rayburn had developed an extravagant admiration; dread, because he knew he must launch a bitter, merciless fight against some fellow Democrats, a fight he had postponed for years but could avoid no longer. Rayburn strongly felt that young Kennedy's program had to be enacted to carry out Democratic campaign pledges to the nation. The new President's most threatening obstacle lay in the House, where the Republican–conservative Democratic coalition had stymied progressive legislation for more than twenty years. To break the coalition's power, Rayburn knew that he had to strike at its heart—the Committee on Rules. If Kennedy's program could not get past the Rules Committee, his administration would be a failure from the start. The old man had made his decision. He would join the battle with the conservatives. He would try to break their stranglehold over legislation. The battle would be excruciating, the outcome uncertain. Flying to Washington that bright December Saturday, Rayburn was heading, at age 79, into what he would later describe as "the worst fight of my life."

Control of the Committee on Rules, the principal scheduling and policy committee of the House, was the most powerful weapon in the hands of the coalition. The committee was created in the late 1800s as an instrument of the House leadership to ensure the orderly flow of legislation to the floor. When the "leadership"—consisting of the Speaker, majority leader, majority whip, and chairmen of major committees, with the Speaker having the final decisive voice—decided to put a certain bill before the House, the committee determined the length of debate, type of amendments to be permitted, and other procedural questions. The committee was designed to help, not obstruct, the leadership.[2]

Sometimes the leadership used the committee to bottle up bills on which it did not want a vote.[3] This important function served largely to protect the House against pressures from the executive and from politically potent lobbying groups. The committee's refusal to "grant a rule" on a bill usually was its death sentence. There were other procedural devices, such as discharge petitions and Calendar Wednesday, that could force a House vote on a bill, but they were complicated and seldom successful. The Rules Committee had, in effect, life-or-death power over most important legislation.

When the coalition was born in the late 1930s, the committee's role began to change. Conservatives sought and won places on the committee. Two southern Democrats, re-elected by their constituencies term after term, moved steadily up the committee's seniority ladder and minimized the Democratic leadership's opportunities to fill vacancies. The Republicans routinely appointed conservatives to the committee as a matter of party policy. Insidiously, the conservatives took control of the committee and dominated its actions. Instead of confining itself to procedural matters, the committee began to exercise its judgment on the contents of bills before it. Bills disliked by the coalition were simply pigeonholed. In other cases, the committee, before allowing the bill to go to the House floor for a vote, forced revision to reflect the extremely conservative views of the coalition.

Although Rayburn viewed the coalition as an outrageous usurpation of power, he lived with it because, to that point, he had usually been able to get essential bills to the floor through personal persuasion. But in August 1960, Smith and his supporters served notice that the days of gentlemanly personal cooperation with Rayburn were over. The coalition grew increasingly confident of its power and ignored the wishes of the Democratic leadership, which had the responsibility for directing the work of the House.

An impasse had been building for more than a year—ever since Charlie Halleck overthrew Joe Martin as Republican leader and the party's extreme conservative wing began exercising strict control over minority affairs. Two moderate Republicans left the committee; Halleck filled the vacancies with conservatives Homer H. Budge of Idaho and B. Carroll Reece of Tennessee. Chairman Smith and his alter ego on the committee, William Colmer, Democrat of Mississippi, now had four extreme right-wing Republicans with whom they voted on nearly every issue. The twelve-member committee was deadlocked: six Democrats would stand with Rayburn, two Democrats and four Republicans were sure to oppose him. To get a controversial bill through the committee required seven votes. The coalition now had virtually complete power to say what bills the House could consider and under what terms such bills could be debated. Rayburn's hands were tied.

In 1960, the situation became intolerable. Congress recessed for the national conventions, then reconvened in August. The session was important to Senators Kennedy and Johnson, the Democratic nominees, who hoped to push through a program on which to take their candidacies to the country. An increase in the minimum wage, federal aid to education, and an expanded housing program were the heart of their proposals. All three measures were chloroformed by the Committee on Rules. The session had been a fiasco for the Democrats. Smith, Colmer, and four Republican committee members had scuttled the Kennedy-Johnson program. Rayburn and the House Democratic leadership were humiliated; Kennedy and Johnson were embarrassed; moderate and liberal Democrats were furious; Republicans were jubilant. During the 1960 campaign, Smith, Senator Harry Byrd, and the Democratic Byrd machine sat glumly silent while Richard Nixon carried their state of Virginia; Bill Colmer bolted the Democratic party to vote for the independent "States' Rights" ticket.

Rayburn was elated by the election of Kennedy and Johnson, but he knew their victory spelled personal trouble for him. The coalition would do its best to wreck the Kennedy program, and he was determined not to let that happen. He had to break the coalition, although, as he told friends, it would mean "a devil of a fight"—one that he had long dreaded. But after years of waiting for the problem to resolve itself, he knew he could no longer avoid the challenge. Even he underestimated his opponents' strength and tenacity. By winning the struggle, one of the historic confrontations in the history of Congress, Rayburn elevated the Speakership to heights of power and prestige it had not known for fifty years.

The Democratic party's future was involved. Kennedy and Johnson had promised the voters a progressive program, most of which was anathema to the coalition. If the coalition was not checked, Rayburn knew much of that program would die in the committee without the House itself ever having a chance to vote on it. Kennedy would be labeled a "do-nothing" President. Remembering the razor-thin margin by which the young President had been elected, Rayburn decided Kennedy's re-election chances would be slim indeed.

Moreover, Rayburn deeply felt that American security demanded that the nation once more get moving. There had been too much drifting during the eight Republican years, he felt, and a nation retains leadership not by drifting but by action. A Kennedy administration incapable of action would be dangerous to the national welfare.

Rayburn's own prestige was deeply involved. Continued success of the Rules Committee in obstructing his leadership in the House had led to a rising tide of complaint by some representatives and political writers that he was too old for the job, that he was losing his grip. The Speaker snorted at such criticism, but he knew it was increasing.[4] Basically, however, Rayburn saw the fight as a matter of political principle. "The issue is very simple," he said. "Shall the elected leadership of the House run its affairs, or shall the chairman of one committee run them?" In the back of his mind, he nurtured another compelling reason for wanting to break the committee's power. He was approaching the inevitable day when his tenure as Speaker would end. His fierce pride in the institution of the Speakership instilled in him a burning determination to turn over to his successor a more powerful, more prestigious office than he had inherited. Once he said: "When the House revolted against Speaker Cannon in 1910, they cut the Speaker's powers too much. Ever since I have been Speaker, I have been trying to get some of that power back for the office."[5]

Coalition members knew they were in trouble. Judge Smith, opposing any change in his committee, asserted he was "ready for a fight." Soon after the 1960 elections, Smith and Colmer met with House GOP Leader Charlie Halleck of Indiana to chart a strategy. Halleck promised full support; he would oppose any tampering with the committee. During November and December, attention focused on Rayburn, who was relaxing in Bonham and keeping his silence. But he was doing plenty of thinking. It was one of the trickiest problems of his long career. He must not only break the committee's power, but must do it as painlessly as possible to avoid permanently alienating southern Democrats, whose votes Kennedy—and Rayburn—would need later on.

President-Elect Kennedy, meeting with Rayburn and other congressional leaders in Palm Beach, agreed with his conclusions. Still furious over the embarrassment Smith and company had handed him the previous August, Kennedy concluded that unless the Rules Committee bottleneck was broken, "our whole program would be emasculated."[6] Rayburn urged the new President to stay out of the fight. It was a House affair, and Kennedy's active involvement could do more harm than good, he argued. Besides, the Speaker explained, it was his prestige on the line. Kennedy agreed to remain in the background, providing moral support—and maybe a post office or judgeship here and there— to help Rayburn's cause. Ultimately, however, the President could not remain aloof from a battle upon whose outcome so much rested. Kennedy telephoned several members, although, according to Rayburn's later assessment, "he didn't change a vote."[7]

Rayburn had a plan. Reaching Washington on New Year's Eve afternoon, he drove straight to the Capitol. There, after explaining his intentions to his closest Democratic allies, he telephoned Howard Smith and asked him to drop by the Speaker's Rooms for a chat. A few minutes later, Smith shuffled in and dropped his lanky frame into one of the huge black chairs that flanked the Speaker's desk. Quietly Rayburn told his adversary that the Kennedy program had a right to be considered by the House and that he intended to see that the members got that opportunity. The Rules Committee had to be reshuffled, Rayburn said, adding his hope that the change could be made without hard feelings. The easiest way was for Smith himself to propose that the committee be enlarged from twelve to fifteen members. If Smith made the proposal, a fight would be avoided. The addition of three members—two Democrats and one Republican—would let Rayburn name two Democrats friendly to the Kennedy program and the House leadership. The Kennedy-Rayburn forces would have an eight-to-seven margin on the committee.

Smith flatly rejected the offer, which was no surprise. But that was part of Rayburn's strategy—he wanted to be able to say that Smith had been given a chance to avoid open confrontation and had refused it. They shook hands and Smith departed. The die was cast. The fiercest battle for control in the House since the revolt against Speaker Joe Cannon fifty-one years before was now a certainty. The two opponents were dramatic figures. Between them Sam Rayburn and Howard Smith had seventy-eight years of congressional service. The Speaker had served with eight of the nation's thirty-four Presidents; the Judge with five.

"The two wily old congressional giants have much in common," noted *Time*:

> Sam Rayburn and Howard Smith both have the patina of age—Rayburn is 79, Smith 78—and the special dignity that accrues to old men who have long exercised power in causes greater than their own ambitions. Both are gruff on the surface, kind underneath. They were country boys, raised on farms, and they still, whenever they can get out of Washington, instinctively head for rustic serenity—the Rayburn cattle ranch near Bonham, Texas, or the Smith dairy farm near Broad Run, Va. They grew up, pinched by poverty, in a South still seething with Civil War hatreds and sunk in economic misery.[8]

But, *Time* observed,

> the most striking difference, the Great Divide of personality, is a matter of the temperature of the heart. Smith is a bit frosty; displays of emotion make him visibly uncomfortable. Sam Rayburn, in contrast, is a sentimentalist, a man of strong and easily stirred feelings, who unashamedly weeps in public when moved. Men who were there still choke up when they recall Rayburn's anguished speech in the House on the death of his old friend Alben Barkley, the speech that ended, "God comfort his loved ones. God comfort me."

On January 2, Rayburn played his first ace. He told a group of liberal Democratic congressmen of Smith's refusal to sponsor enlargement of the Rules Committee. Now there was only one real choice left, Rayburn declared. He would drop the idea of enlarging the committee and, instead, seek the removal of Colmer on the grounds that he had bolted the Democratic party in November.[9] A moderate Democrat could then be appointed to the panel. When Rayburn's plan became known, tempers flared among southern Democrats. John Bell Williams of Mississippi threatened that if the Speaker persisted in trying to purge Colmer, southern Democrats might vote with Republicans to elect a Republican Speaker instead of Rayburn. Moderate Democrats from southern and border states heard the news with anguish. They recoiled from the prospect of having to oppose the Speaker as well as the new Democratic President at the outset of his administration. On the other hand, many knew they would be subjected to excruciating pressure from powerful political and economic forces back home to resist any change in the committee. For many, it was the most painful dilemma of their political careers. "If I cross the Speaker, I'm ruined here," one said ruefully, "and if I vote with him, I can't get re-elected." [10]

Rayburn and his lieutenants went to work, talking, pleading, cajoling members to support them. Smith and his supporters applied pressure from the other side. Tension mounted. Many members were emotionally upset, some visibly angry, others frightened. Some hedged their bets—pledging support to both Rayburn and Smith. Alabama Democrat Frank ("Everything is made for love") Boykin, an affable character who had difficulty saying no to anybody, switched sides at least six times. Whoever got to him last, got his pledge of support. Finally, Rayburn told his lieutenants to leave the anguished Alabamian alone. He ultimately voted with most other southerners—against Rayburn.

Meanwhile, Kennedy announced five key bills in his program—an expanded housing program, increased minimum wage, medical care for the aged under the Social Security system, relief for depressed areas, and federal aid to education. Dreading a showdown, Smith went to see the Speaker. He offered a guarantee that all five bills would be cleared by his committee if Rayburn would drop the plan to purge Colmer. "Shit, Howard, Kennedy may have forty bills in his program before he's through," Rayburn snorted.[11] There would be no deal.

The purge plan, theoretically, would involve only Democrats. House rules specify that the entire House must approve all committee assignments, but by unbroken custom neither party ever interfered with the other's assignments. Rumors circulated that Halleck was planning to let Republicans vote with southern Democrats to keep Colmer on the Rules Committee. Rayburn bristled with anger: "Two can play at that game. If they start messing in our party affairs, we can do the same on Republican nominations to committees—and we have a majority." Halleck backed off.

Would-be peacemakers appeared. Moderate southerners pleaded for a compromise "so we won't have to choose between Howard and Sam." Crafty 77-year-old Carl Vinson of Georgia, hard-fisted chairman of the Committee on Armed Services, who had served longer in the House than anyone except Rayburn, was a Rayburn supporter. Vinson, who held the confidence of southern Democrats, teamed up with Francis E. "Tad" Walter, veteran Pennsylvania conservative and chairman of the Committee on Un-American Activities, a man popular with conservative southerners. Together they sought to avert a bitter confrontation.

Vinson and Walter shuttled back and forth between factions, conferring with Rayburn, with Smith, with Democrats from southern and border states. They found strong sentiment for compromise among moderate southerners, who saw the purging of Colmer as a threat to the seniority system that had served southern interests for so long. And they believed Rayburn was being unreasonable—or at least inconsistent. He had not sought to purge Harlem Congressman Adam Clayton Powell when he supported Eisenhower for President in 1956. He had not sought the removal of others who were convicted of crimes. The removal of Colmer from the seniority ranks would so anger the South, the moderates warned, that all southerners would turn against the new administration and its legislative program. Vinson and Walter sought a compromise formula. On January 10, they informed the Speaker that if he would drop his plan to purge Colmer, they could round up enough southern Democrats to put over the original plan to enlarge the committee by three members—but they warned that Smith would fight this to the finish.

Rayburn from the beginning had been aware of the arguments against purging Colmer. He had used Colmer as bait to attract what moderate southern support he could for the committee enlargement plan. The tactical maneuver had worked—many representatives had decided that enlargement was the lesser of two evils, and the one they could more easily justify to their home constituencies. Acting on the recommendation of Vinson, Walter, and John McCormack, who despite the vast ideological gulf between them was a close friend of Colmer's, the Speaker announced he was dropping the purge plan. Instead, he would throw his full weight behind the proposal to enlarge the committee by adding two Democrats and one Republican. The House, he predicted hopefully, would accept this as a "painless way to solve the problem. . . . the way to embarrass nobody if they don't want to be embarrassed."

Rayburn was in more trouble than he had foreseen. Some southern members who had promised to support enlargement of the committee if he abandoned his plan to purge Colmer now reversed themselves. Also, the decision to try to enlarge the committee broadened the battlefield. Only Democrats would have voted on purging Colmer, and Rayburn had a clear majority in his own party. But enlargement required a change in House rules, meaning that Republicans as well as Democrats would have to vote.

Republicans were certain to support Smith overwhelmingly in resisting any change in the committee. To win, Rayburn had to have some Republican votes, perhaps as many as thirty. They would be hard to come by. No Republicans relished the prospect of antagonizing their leader, Charlie Halleck, and the senior Republicans, led by Clarence Brown of Ohio, who were all fiercely opposed to tampering with the committee. A few progressive Republicans favored the change. Ex-Speaker Joe Martin wanted to help, but his influence among House Republicans had waned almost to insignificance.

Rayburn knew he would have to throw in his whole stack. Through many years, House Democrats had incurred IOUs to him. He had helped dozens of them enact their pet bills. Scores had gotten choice committee assignments because he helped them. Others had received his invaluable political help when they faced re-election troubles. He had raised campaign funds and made speeches for them in their districts, throwing his enormous prestige behind their candidacies. Now he needed their help. In the Speaker's Lobby, on the House floor, he stopped one member after another to ask: "Are you going with me?" Others he called to his office to ask the same question. He worked tirelessly, constantly. Rayburn lieutenant Frank Thompson of New Jersey kept a master list of supporters, which he updated daily with fresh reports brought to him by other Rayburn supporters and by liberal lobbyists active in the fight. When lieutenants reported that a member was "shimmying," as Rayburn put it, the Speaker phoned him "to stiffen his backbone." Newly elected members, still lacking committee assignments, were summoned; defiance of Rayburn was not a wise way to start a House career.

Northern and western Democrats were solid in support of the Speaker. His trouble lay with the southern and border state members. He used every stratagem he could think of. Organized labor turned the heat on congressmen obligated to it. The National Education Association, pushing federal aid to education, mobilized teachers and school officials to back Rayburn. Civil rights organizations were active, except for the National Association for the Advancement of Colored People, which feared that the fight would become a race issue. But such organizations, unfortunately for Rayburn, packed little political punch in the South.

At his first press conference as President, Kennedy made it clear where he stood. "It is no secret that I would strongly believe that the members of the House should have an opportunity to vote . . . on the programs which we will present, not merely members of the Rules Committee. But the responsibility rests with members. I merely give my view as an interested citizen." [12] Privately, Kennedy ordered Vice-President Johnson and his Cabinet to bring as much behind-the-scenes pressure for the enlargement as they could.

Smith had his own powerful allies. The southern press, with a few exceptions, conducted a noisy campaign against the Rayburn plan, insisting it was a scheme to force new civil rights legislation on the South. That was a phony issue. The coalition had dissolved in both 1957 and 1959 when the only two civil rights bills passed since Reconstruction days came before the committee. Republicans dared not oppose such legislation, coalition or no coalition. Other influential groups supporting

Smith included the National Association of Manufacturers, U.S. Chamber of Commerce, American Farm Bureau Federation, and American Medical Association. House members were inundated with letters, telegrams, and phone calls generated by those groups angrily demanding their support of Smith.

On January 17, the House Democratic Caucus by voice vote formally endorsed Rayburn's proposal. Smith agreed at the meeting to bring the resolution to the floor. On January 19, the House Republican Policy Committee unanimously rejected the enlargement plan. Four days later, the Republican Conference voted overwhelmingly in caucus to oppose the plan. A few maverick Republicans were kicking over the traces, but they were under heavy pressure to stay with their party. "Charlie Halleck says he's not putting any pressure on the Republicans," said Rayburn. "I have to believe him—but somebody sure as hell is."

In fact, Halleck was making life miserable for Republicans who were not firmly committed to Smith. Angrily, Halleck stalked members of his party thought to be wavering. *Time* correspondent Neil MacNeil recalled Halleck's encounter with one such member—Glen Cunningham of Nebraska: "Halleck grabbed him on the House floor, both hands on Cunningham's coat, and literally shook him as he spat out arguments against 'packing' the Rules Committee. Cunningham wrenched himself free of Halleck's grasp and staggered away from him. 'That bastard!' Cunningham muttered." [13]

On January 24, the day before the vote was scheduled before the House, the *New York Times* reported: "Opponents of the plan apparently have been gaining strength. . . . Speaker Rayburn appeared less confident today." Inevitably, rumors began to fly—Rayburn is in trouble . . . he's too old . . . he's losing control. Columnist Doris Fleeson wrote that Rayburn's only hope was for Kennedy to throw the full weight of the White House behind the embattled Speaker.

As the day of reckoning neared, the old Speaker grew increasingly nervous. He checked and rechecked his lists of supporters and began pondering ways he might later punish Democrats who deserted him. "Have you decided to go with me?" he would ask of those whose names were listed as doubtful. When he learned that one of his supporters, Tom Steed of Oklahoma, had scheduled a speaking engagement at home on the day of the vote, Rayburn was furious. "If you'll cancel it and stay here, I'll come to your district and make two of the damnedest speeches for you that you ever heard." [14] Steed agreed to stay. He phoned former Governor and U.S. Senator Earle Clements of Kentucky. Could Clements help line up support in the Kentucky delegation? Clements said he would try. Despite his earlier determination to keep the White House on the sidelines, he decided to pay a call on Larry O'Brien, the President's chief lobbyist. "Do you know what to do?" he asked O'Brien. "I do," O'Brien replied. Before the fight ended, presidential assistant Ted Sorensen later recalled, the White House had "used all the influence a new administration could muster—patronage, sentiment, campaign commitments and federal actions of all kinds." [15]

Lyndon Johnson, meanwhile, cruised the Capitol corridors like a one-man enforcer. More than one hapless congressman found himself pinned against a wall, staring into the accusing eyes of the Vice-President. "If Sam Rayburn is hurt, his blood will be on your hands," he told Texas Congressman Joe Kilgore. [16] When a delegation of supporters appealed to the Speaker to seek a compromise with Smith, the old man exploded:

> "Hell, no. We're going to vote. I've met with Howard three times and he won't give an inch. The only way to avoid a vote is for me to abdicate and I won't do it. If they lick me, that's that. For the next three months, I'll have those who vote against me come to my office, and there'll be more ass-kicking than they ever dreamed possible. We'll use discharge petitions and Calendar Wednesday and whatever else we can find to get bills to the floor, and we'll just stay here until we get a vote on Kennedy's program." [17]

Rayburn knew that the vote would be extremely close. One count showed him winning by two or three votes—if nobody reneged on a promise of support. But much could go wrong. The risk of losing was too great. He wanted more time. With a few days' delay, his lieutenants could continue their quest for a sure majority. Also, the House would be given an opportunity to hear the new President deliver his State of the Union address. A mind or two might be changed. With the showdown just hours away, Rayburn abruptly announced a five-day postponement. Smith forces, sensing mounting uncertainty in the Rayburn camp, were gleeful.

On January 27, Carl Vinson and Tad Walter approached Rayburn with a new plan. With Rayburn's concurrence, they would offer Smith a deal: if Smith would agree to report out any bill that Kennedy wanted, the fight to enlarge the committee would be dropped. Rayburn, now more uncertain than ever about his chances, agreed. But when they took the deal to Smith, they found him sullen and unbending. "I've got the votes," he said. That evening, the Speaker told his staff: "We don't have the votes. I'm not as worried about my prestige taking a licking as you and some of my friends are. I'm one politician who cannot be hurt—I've already had mine. But Kennedy is going to remember this. He is that kind of Irishman." With a shrug of his shoulders, he added: "We're going to vote next Tuesday. If we lose, we lose." [18]

On January 30, the eve of the vote, Bill Arbogast of the Associated Press checked with the Republicans, Judge Smith, and the Rayburn forces. His tally: for, 216; against, 218. Rayburn lieutenant Dick Bolling did his own count and came up with an identical 216 votes for Rayburn. A sure majority of the 435 House members would be 218, but there would be absentees. "When eagles are flying, it's time for us sparrows to take cover," John Holton, Rayburn's administrative assistant, joked to the staff. The "eagles" indeed were flying—Speaker Rayburn, Judge Smith, Charlie Halleck, Majority Leader John McCormack, Carl Vinson, Clarence Brown, labor lobbyists, and reporters scurried back and forth to last-minute conferences. Hundreds of phone calls were made. Little huddles of nervous men and women filled Capitol hallways. The tension was painful. Shortly after noon the issue would be decided. The outcome was still in the balance.

At 11:55 A.M., reporters crowded into Rayburn's front office for his daily presession press conference. The Speaker, his face showing the last month's strain, was in rare good humor. He felt a sense of relief in knowing that, whatever the outcome, the fight would soon be over. Leaning back in his tall chair, his hands clasped, he predicted, "We have the votes if all of them honor their promises."

The demand for gallery tickets had been frantic. One of the largest crowds, perhaps the largest, in the history of the House filled the Chamber. Spectators jammed all gallery steps and stood against the walls. Hundreds of others, unable to get in, thronged the corridors, struggling to press through the double swinging doors. On the floor, every seat was occupied; standing room along the sides of the Chamber was filled. The press galleries were likewise packed.

Exactly at noon, Rayburn briskly walked up the steps of the Speaker's rostrum as he had hundreds of times before. At the sight of the embattled old man, with his deep-lined face, his gleaming bald head, his square shoulders held far back, the House exploded in a roar of applause. This was a violation of custom for which longtime congressional observers could recall no precedent. Rayburn gaveled for order. H. R. Gross of Iowa, the tiny Republican gadfly, demanded a quorum call. Of 435 members, 427 were present. Among the 8 absentees was Republican ex-Speaker Joe Martin, out of the country. Rayburn sorely needed Republican votes and could have used Martin's support, which he had been promised early.[19]

When Smith rose to speak, the House rustled. A wave of applause from Republicans and southern Democrats greeted the old Judge as he ambled, stoop-shouldered, down the aisle. Bob Donovan of the *New York Herald Tribune* was struck by Smith's drab appearance. "Wraithlike and gray—gray, bushy eyebrows, thin gray hair combed back, gray complexion, gray suit, blue-gray necktie," Donovan wrote. "He is stooped. Whatever spark he has he conceals under a drab exterior. His whole appearance is misleadingly meek."[20]

Quietly complaining that he had only eight minutes to speak, Smith made his thrust. "A lot of people around here these days talk about this being a matter of a quarrel between the Speaker and myself. . . . I have no quarrel with the Speaker. . . . If there is any quarrel between the Speaker and myself it is all on his side."[21] There was a roar of laughter from the tense, harried representatives. Rayburn threw his head back with a laugh.

Smith pledged, "I'll cooperate with the Democratic leadership of the House of Representatives just as long and just as far as my conscience will permit me to do." Another roar of laughter went up from Rayburn supporters. Clearly, Judge Smith's cooperation with Kennedy's New Frontier would not last long, nor go very far. Sharply stung, Smith lashed back: "Some of these gentlemen who are laughing maybe do not understand what a conscience is." Quietly, earnestly, Smith pleaded with the House to postpone action. "If this matter were left dormant on the calendar, it would remain there for two years and if this committee did something that the House thought it should not do, then you would have cause to complain and could call it up any day," he said, concluding his appeal. Republicans and southern Democrats cheered as the old battler slowly walked back to his seat.

Republican leader Halleck, labeled by the press a "gut-fighter," was the final speaker against the resolution. He came out swinging. "I have an avalanche of mail, most of it handwritten, from people opposed to this resolution. . . . They are concerned about rash and reckless platform promises repeated in the campaign. . . . They are afraid the floodgates will be let down and we will be overwhelmed with bad legislation," he shouted.[22] Republicans clapped lustily. When Halleck finished, the House stirred uneasily. The great clock showed nine minutes of debate remaining.

Democrats and Republicans alike burst into a roar of cheers and applause—short, compact Sam Rayburn was slowly descending the steps of his rostrum to speak. Some Smith supporters were silent; the Virginian leaned far back in his chair, his expressionless face turned toward the ceiling. Rayburn had a sheet of paper in his hand.

"Whether you vote with me today or not," Rayburn began gently, "I want to say that I appreciate your uniform kindness and courtesy that has been displayed toward me."[23] Then he got down to business. "This issue, in my mind, is a simple one," he said. "We have elected to the Presidency a new leader. He is going to have a program that he thinks will be in the interest of and for the benefit of the American people. We are neither in good shape domestically or in the foreign field. . . . He wants to do something about that. . . . I think this House should be allowed on great measures to work its will, and it cannot work its will if the Committee on Rules is so constituted as not to allow the House to pass on those things."

Rayburn's deep voice took on an angry tone as he went on the attack. Holding a paper up, he rumbled, "I have a letter here, that if I were easily insulted, it would rather do so to me." Judge Smith cocked his head. "The gentleman from Virginia sent out a letter and in that letter he used the words 'stack' and 'pack' four times," Rayburn went on. He angrily slammed his fist on the lectern; it rang through the House like a pistol shot. "The gentleman from Virginia nor any other member can accuse me of packing any committee for or against anything," he shouted. Smith's eyebrows arched in curiosity. "Back in 1933," Rayburn recalled, "'our side' packed the Committee on Rules with the gentleman from Virginia.[24] Then in 1939 the gentleman from Mississippi [Colmer] came to me and said he very much desired to be on the Committee on Rules. I told him I thought it would be a mistake . . . for various reasons. But he insisted, and then we packed the committee with Mr. Colmer." House members and spectators roared with laughter. The wily Speaker had drawn blood.

Gravely, Rayburn dropped his voice. "Let us move this program. Let us be sure we can move it. And the only way that we can be sure . . . in my opinion, my beloved colleagues, is to adopt this resolution today." Finished, he turned abruptly from the lectern. Again the House chamber rang with cheers and applause as the old man slowly mounted the rostrum. Smith and his supporters sat glumly silent. Rayburn rapped his gavel. "The Clerk will call the roll."

An eerie silence settled over the House. The moment of truth had arrived. Weeks of anguish, worry, pressure were at an end.

Members scrambled for tally sheets, spreading them awkwardly on their laps to record the tense vote. "Abbitt, Abernethy, Adair, Addabbo, Addonizio . . ." the reading clerk's voice split the silence. The first three answered "no," the next two, "aye"; the roll call seesawed. Rayburn three votes ahead, now two, now one. The score was tied. Judge Smith ahead one, two, four. Each shift increased the unbearable tension. Some congressmen used their fingers to signal to gallery spectators the course of the battle. Two fingers up, now three, back to two, down to one, now all even, now one finger turned down—"We're behind by one . . ."

Only the reading clerk's call and that of the answering representatives broke the church-like silence. "Members, who generally gossip and roam about during roll calls, were fixed in their seats," wrote the *Herald Tribune*'s Bob Donovan. "The galleries were frozen." When the clerk reached Wright of Texas—with only twelve more names to be called—Rayburn was ahead by one vote, 212–211. There was a late spurt of pro-Rayburn votes as the clerk neared the bottom of the list. When the first roll call ended, Rayburn led by five votes, 214–209. The names of the eleven members who had failed to answer the first time would be called again. They could change the result. The chamber rumbled into conversation. Rayburn gaveled for order. The reading clerk called the names of the eleven. Only six answered: three for Rayburn, three for Smith.

The tally clerk handed his card to Rayburn. "On this vote, there being 217 ayes and 212 noes, the resolution is adopted," he announced serenely. Pandemonium swept the House. Members on the winning side slapped each other on the back, shook hands, shouted to friends in the gallery. Some losers looked glum. Judge Smith, expressionless, shuffled out of the Chamber, where reporters waited to ask why he had lost. "We didn't have enough votes," he said. He took out an unlighted cigar, chewed on it, looked tired. "It's all baloney," he said, walking away.

Rayburn left the Chamber smiling, brushing past members and reporters who trailed behind, offering congratulations. A television reporter wanted him to tell the American people about his victory. The Speaker waved him aside. "They'll know about it," he said. As he disappeared into his office, someone asked: "How do you feel?" Rayburn's eyes twinkled. "I feel all right. That's about as good as a man can feel. I always feel good when I win."

24

Willow Wild

The torch, as President Kennedy said in his spirited inaugural address, had passed to a new generation "born in this century, tempered by war, disciplined by a hard and bitter peace, proud of our ancient heritage—and unwilling to witness or permit the slow undoing of those human rights to which this nation has always been committed." There remained only Rayburn and a few others to bridge America's past and promising future. Still the "vital cement" between North and South, young and old, liberal and conservative, rural and urban, the old Texan enthusiastically embraced the lofty goals of the youthful new leader. He who had grown up on the "old frontier" felt equally at home on John Kennedy's New Frontier. "I'm running the House more nearly now than I ever have before," he confided to Time's Neil MacNeil.[1]

Enlarging the Committee on Rules helped the aging Speaker bring Kennedy's legislative program to the House floor, but it could not solve the fundamental problem: the determined resistance of conservatives of both parties to the administration's aggressive, innovative ideas. "With all we had going for us," Kennedy said after the Rules Committee fight, "with Rayburn's own reputation at stake, with all of the pressures and appeals a new President could make, we won by five votes. That shows you what we're up against."[2] On the Rules issue, sixty-four Democrats crossed party lines, compared with only seventeen Republicans. Similar wholesale Democratic defections would turn every controversial bill into an uphill fight, Kennedy rightly concluded. Antirecession, farm subsidy, area redevelopment, minimum wage, aid to education, and foreign aid bills all were decided in 1961 by a handful of votes.

Rayburn was working hard but feeling good. "He has a new enthusiasm," the *Wall Street Journal* noted. Wrote *Time*'s MacNeil: "Mr. Sam is older than he was—and stronger."[3] Playing on the team of an activist Democratic administration invigorated him. "I feel like a two-year-old colt," the Texan told friends on his 79th birthday.[4] He continued to get his walking exercise—six laps around the Capitol Plaza every morning—which he now supplemented with daily isometric routines. In June, columnist George Dixon found the Speaker alone on the stone balcony near the House Lobby. Rayburn was raising and lowering himself on his toes. "Takes the kinks out of the old legs," he told Dixon, adding that he was in training for "a big celebration coming up on Monday. At high noon on June 12, I will have been Speaker twice as long as anybody else."[5] A warm, affectionate House ceremony marked his completion of 16 years and 273 days as Speaker—double Henry Clay's tenure. Afterward, the stumpy old man, now clearly showing the ravages of age, shuffled down from the rostrum. Tears welling in his dimming eyes, he thanked his colleagues for their praise and added:

> If I have been able to live up to the things you have said about me . . . then my life is rich enough. I am satisfied. My political career has climaxed everything I ever hoped or trusted it might be. So that when I leave here, I will leave without any regrets, but being thankful and grateful to the people of a great congressional district for their trust and faith in me, and equal to if not above that, my gratitude for your faith and confidence in me.[6]

Sam Rayburn's decline from exceptionally robust health in old age to death was, as humans measure time, swift and unforeseen. He flew home for a July 4 vacation. He returned tired, pained, and worried. "The damnedest thing hit me while I was home," he said. "My back hurt like the devil. I went to my doctor, and he gave me some shots. They didn't help. I went back and told him, 'You've got to do better.'"[7] Vice-President Johnson urged him to visit President Kennedy's personal physician, Dr. Janet Travell, an orthopedic specialist. Her examination failed to reveal the cause. She did not dispute Rayburn's self-diagnosis of a bad case of "lumbago," but she did suggest X-rays and further tests at the National Institutes of Health. She gave the Speaker novocaine to ease his discomfort and taught him a new way to put on his pants. "I'm 79 years old," Rayburn grumbled, "and no woman is going to tell me how to put on my pants." But he relented when she explained that back disorders can result from balancing the body on one leg while stepping into trousers. Henceforth, he put on his pants from a sitting position.[8]

For perhaps the first time in his life, Rayburn was deeply troubled by the malfunctioning of his body. He had enjoyed—reveled in—exuberant good health during his long, productive years. Now, in addition to constant back pain, he began to lose his appetite. As his weight dropped, he worried more and more about his appearance. His eyesight was so poor that he could not know how he looked. His face was emaciated more than he knew. "Do I look bad?" he asked George Donovan, his friend and driver. "No, Mr. Speaker, you look fine," Donovan replied. Disbelieving, Rayburn said, "George, I think I ought to get away from here so the boys won't see me until I lick this thing." He told his nephew, Robert Bartley, "Thank God, I don't have a malignancy. The X-ray man said there was nothing organically wrong with me." But in his solitude, Rayburn pondered long and often on the possibility of cancer. Miss Lou had died of the disease; so had other Rayburns. "My brother thinks I have cancer of the gut, but the X-rays don't show it," he said. "If I can just get home for some sunshine, I'll be all right."

Rayburn worried about leaving the House at the height of the session. Great issues were at stake. With the program of the new administration hanging in the balance, his leadership was des-

perately needed by his party and his President. Even a sick
Rayburn was better for the administration than the inevitably
weak successor who would take his place. The aid to education
bill was coming up, and the Texan would not, could not, miss
the fight. "My boys are going to get beat, and I got to be here to
get beat with them," he said.

By late August, it was clear that he could not go on. Weak, in
constant pain, he twice suffered dizziness while presiding. Finally, he called Dr. Joe Risser in Bonham. "Let me bring you
home," said the Speaker's longtime friend and physician. He
proposed rest in Bonham and more exploratory examinations at
the Baylor University Medical Center in Dallas. On August 31,
after an emotional final evening at his apartment with a few
members of his staff, Rayburn slipped quietly out of Washington for the last time.

"I'm going to get over this thing," he told reporters who
phoned him in Bonham in mid-September. Rumors that he
might retire were started by a "lot of damned idiots," he barked.
"Nobody dies of lumbago." Through the month, Rayburn's
body steadily deteriorated. The suspicion of a malignancy—
probably of the pancreas, where cancer can grow undetected by
X-rays—was almost universal among doctors who watched his
case. But no scintilla of evidence supported their suspicion.
Meanwhile, Dr. Risser, finding red amoebas in his patient's system, diagnosed his ailment as amebiasis, a disease usually associated with the tropics whose symptoms Rayburn displayed. He
prescribed treatment but warned that if the patient did not respond, "another lesion must be sought." With an indomitable
will to live, Rayburn fought to rid himself of the "poisoning"
that infested him. He never mentioned cancer or malignancy.
Some who were close to him in the final days believe he never
realized the gravity of his illness. Almost certainly, he did, although his doctors later said he never asked, and they never volunteered to tell him.

To the end, he insisted on seeing visitors who dropped by the
house. They sat silently in the living room, waiting to be ush-
ered, in turn, into the back room where Rayburn lay stretched
out, fully clothed, on his favorite daybed. He allowed his friend

W. B. "Rags" Ragsdale of *U.S. News & World Report* to bring his recording equipment down from Washington for a long, forward-looking interview.[9] Among the last to see him at home was a small delegation from the National Conference of State Parks. "I'm sorry I couldn't get up to greet you," he told them weakly. "You know, I don't understand it. I've never been sick before in my life, and my doctor keeps telling me I'm getting better. I told him today he must be talking about himself, because I don't feel any better."

Wracked with pain, his mind refusing to dwell at length on earthly matters, on September 30 Rayburn dictated his last letter. It was addressed to students at Grace College in Winona Lake, Indiana, who had asked his advice on "How young people can best accomplish their desires and ambitions for success." His advice was the same as it would have been sixty years earlier:

> At an early date in life, a young man should make up his mind on the profession or vocation he intends to follow, and then bend every energy to that point. Energy must go along with ability. There is not so much difference in the native ability of people because most of them have good common sense. It is what they do with it. Ability without energy and purpose amounts to little. . . . Every American boy and girl should study United States history and government. I say this because I know the more you know about the United States history and government, the more loyal you will be to it, because there is no other government in the world where people have the freedoms that they have in the United States of America.[10]

Two days later, he entered Baylor University Medical Center. On October 5, a biopsy of the lymph gland in his right groin revealed a metastatic malignancy, indicating the pancreas as the most likely primary site.[11] The cancer had entered the lymph system and was spreading rapidly throughout his body, making surgery impossible. Doctors gave him a week, perhaps two, to live.

He lived six more weeks. For a full month, the doctors sought frantically to prolong his life and, in the process, undermined the thing Rayburn most cherished: his dignity. He clung tenaciously to life, but he objected during periods of lucidity to artificial or heroic medical efforts that caused him discomfort and, ultimately, could not help him. "I want to die with my boots on, and a gavel in my hand," he told House colleagues when he left Washington. Instead he found himself with all the indignities that can befall a terminally ill patient in a lavishly equipped modern hospital. His doctors did what they are taught to do: as if personally affronted, they fought with all their skill and resources to keep the body alive, to cheat death, even for a few hours. When chemotherapy failed, radiation treatments were tried. When Rayburn developed pneumonia, devoted medical effort saved him but left him extremely weak and semi-delirious with intermittent periods of lucidity. Tubes were inserted in his air passages to help him breathe and, when he refused to eat, into his stomach to give him nourishment. The possibility of temporary improvement, said one attending physician, "while not good, is sufficiently good that it is felt eminently worth striving for." [12]

A parade of important visitors came to pay respects—President Kennedy, former President Truman, Vice-President Johnson (four times), and scores of others. Their visits cheered him greatly. "He told me where to get off, just like he did when I was in the White House," quipped a bouncy Truman as he left the room. Finally, the family decided that he had had enough. On October 31, Sam Rayburn went home to die. He rode ninety miles to Bonham in an ambulance, his wasted body wrapped in a blanket, his head covered with a towel. He went to the Risser Clinic and was placed in a room in an old two-story house adjoining the modern one-story clinic. The return to Bonham, John Holton told reporters, recognized "the Speaker's often expressed desire to end his days among, in his words, 'those friends and neighbors who for so long have given me a love and a loyalty unsurpassed in any annals.'"

For two more weeks, he clung to life. "This man is not easy to give to Him who has sent for him," Dr. Risser wrote on his medical chart. [13] On November 16, at 6:20 A.M., the patient ceased breathing. "He died quietly," said Dr. Risser. "His respi-

ration stopped. His heart continued to beat for four minutes. . . .
He seemed as one in sleep. . . . It was a very easy death."[14] For
twenty-five hours Rayburn's body lay in state in the marble foyer
of the Sam Rayburn Library. The family kept the library open
into the evening to allow additional thousands of mourners to
pay their final respects. The simple open coffin, blanketed with
gold, white, and bronze chrysanthemums, rested near a bust of
Rayburn by Felix de Weldon.

On a cold, bleak November afternoon, he was buried. The
short, simple funeral produced perhaps the biggest gathering of
the nation's leaders outside of Washington in history. Among
them: President Kennedy, former Presidents Truman and Eisenhower, Vice-President Johnson, Associate Justice Tom Clark,
and 128 members of the House and Senate. Enough other dignitaries and members of the national press showed up to overflow
Bonham's First Baptist Church. Members of the church relinquished their pews and joined 20,000 others listening over loud-
speakers set up on the church lawn. Across the nation, Americans by the millions followed the entire service on network
television. Elder Grady Ball of the Primitive Baptist Church at
Tioga offered an inspired sermon. The 74-year-old grocer-
preacher chose not to eulogize Rayburn. "Everybody knows his
accomplishments," he said. Instead, in a comparison with the
Apostle Paul, he probed the meaning of Rayburn's life:

> Paul was able to meet the great of the earth or the poor,
> the noble or the agnostic, and he was able to bring himself
> in harmony with them and their life so that they might be
> of service to the classes of men in the world. And so, our
> good friend made himself a servant, not of the classes but
> of all the men and women and the boys and the girls and the
> children who have fought and loved the freedom that our
> great country affords us. He maintained this out of his en-
> ergy. Now, he can say, in the language of Apostle Paul in his
> letter, "I have fought the good fight." In the liberties and
> freedom of our country, he has fought a good fight. For the
> friends in this community and all those he represented, he

has fought a good fight. He has been a fair and loyal man. He has kept faith, not only with the people of Fannin County, but the adjoining counties. He has kept faith with the democracy of our country. I think it could be truthfully and nobly said, "He has finished his course."

Rayburn was buried in Willow Wild Cemetery, near the graves of those who had meant most to him in life—his parents, Miss Lou, Abner, and the other relatives and neighbors who for half a century had supported his highest ambitions. "Willow Wild—what a beautiful name," he once said.

A long acquaintance, H. W. Stevenson, dug his grave. "This is my last chance to do anything for Mr. Rayburn," Stevenson said, as he turned the waxy black earth. "Did he do me any favors? Lots of 'em. I guess the best thing he did was—what I like the most—was just being recognized by the man when he'd see me. And when I used to drive a truck on the Red River project, and they owed me $600, he saw to it I got it. A poor man don't forget a thing like that."

The words of the world's mighty, whose tributes flowed in from around the globe, had been topped by the simple eloquence of an old country preacher, whose congregation never exceeded forty-five members, and a lonely gravedigger. Rayburn would have been pleased.

Sources and Notes

Researching the biography of a man whose active years spanned so many generations was a daunting task that Hardeman approached with trepidation. He began with no formal plan. He simply scooped up any material—official and otherwise—that touched the main currents of the Speaker's life. He read, asked questions, and slowly developed a framework for this book. He wanted the result to be factual, balanced, and, wherever possible, told in the words of the participants. In finishing the work that Hardeman began, the co-author has followed those same guidelines.

Rayburn, for all his cooperation in the early preparation of this book, remained an essentially private man, who revealed even to his closest friends and relatives—much less his biographer—as little as possible about himself. He harbored sensitivities that simply were not matters for discussion. His friends were well aware of those sensitivities and steered around them in order to remain his friends. In hundreds of interviews and conversations with Rayburn over a five-year period, Hardeman sought to penetrate the Speaker's shell. He believed there had to be more to Rayburn's life than a series of disjointed, often-told anecdotes. It became a sort of game—the wise old man guarding his innermost thoughts from the seductive biographer.

Hardeman enticed his subject to talk about himself more than
he ever had before. Often, however, Rayburn stiffened, abruptly
ending conversations that cut too close to his psyche. It was
soon clear that whatever secrets lay behind the Rayburn mys-
tique would have to be learned, if at all, from others.

Fortunately, when this project was begun, not only Rayburn
but also many of his lifelong friends, relatives, and associates
were still living. Hardeman set out to interview as many of
them as he could find. Some of those reputedly closest to the
Speaker knew surprisingly little about him beyond the familiar
public image. Others described events and incidents in Rayburn's past that almost certainly never happened or told them in
such a distorted, self-serving way as to render them virtually
useless to a biographer. Occasionally, a fact or point of view cast
new light on the elusive subject until, gradually, one could begin
to see the whole man. Most interviews were conducted before
the widespread use of portable tape-recording devices. A former
newspaper reporter, Hardeman relied on handwritten notes and
his amazingly retentive memory, which allowed him to recon-
struct lengthy passages of conversation without missing a word.
It is lamentable that most of those interviews were not recorded,
but if the absence of a microphone encouraged candor (Rayburn
was still a powerful influence on those around him), then the
product of this endeavor has been strengthened.

Some interviews stood out for their usefulness—John Garner, still enjoying good conversation and good whiskey in his
90s, was generous with his time and insights. His mind crystal
clear, he recalled incidents in Rayburn's early years in Congress
and, with typical bluntness, verified numerous anecdotes—
some unflattering to himself—relating to the Rayburn-Garner
relationship.

Lyndon Johnson, setting aside an afternoon from his busy life
as Senate majority leader, laid bare his mixed feelings of love,
frustration, and envy in discussing Rayburn. Johnson furnished
leads for others to be interviewed and through the 1960s kept an
interest in seeing this book finished.

In retirement, a jovial Harry Truman proudly led a visitor
through his presidential library and described the origins of his

long, warm association with Rayburn. He gave us, among other
things, previously undisclosed details of Rayburn's role in helping an untested new President to govern effectively in the crucial
period after World War II. True to form, Truman agreed to be
interviewed only after he had "cleared it with Sam."

New Dealer Tommy Corcoran in a series of interviews provided a behind-the-scenes account of Rayburn's largely forgotten battles to enact Roosevelt's depression-era programs and
helped us put Rayburn's often stormy relationship with FDR in
perspective. Corcoran and Benjamin Cohen, partners in drafting much of the New Deal's most innovative legislation, agreed
to be interviewed jointly on one occasion. It proved a painful
experience for the unassuming Cohen, who spent much of the
time admonishing his irrepressible former colleague to refrain
from overdramatizing events. Interviews with other leading figures from the Roosevelt years, especially former SEC Chairman
James M. Landis and Associate Justice William O. Douglas, also
were invaluable to our understanding of a pivotal period in
Rayburn's life.

Tracing the Waller-Rayburn family history, partly for this
book, partly to satisfy Rayburn's own curiosity about his roots,
took Hardeman in the late 1950s through western Virginia and
into eastern Tennessee, where he sought out then-living Rayburn
relatives. Rayburn's cousin, Mose Waller, Sr., showed Hardeman
the remains of Rayburn's birthplace and furnished enlivening details about the family. Tax and property records buried deep in
the Roane County courthouse, Confederate Army files, family
correspondence, and some long-forgotten contemporary accounts by local writers helped round out a picture of life in rural
east Tennessee in the last century.

In the 1950s, there still were people in north Texas who remembered Rayburn as a boy. Some had campaigned for him and with
him for half a century. One was Judge Henry Cunningham,
Rayburn's closest political "lieutenant" in Fannin County for
forty years. Cunningham, along with key Rayburn allies A. P.
Bolling, Buster Cole, and others, helped us define the Speaker's
cross-generational appeal in his district. Two Rayburn sisters,

Medibel Rayburn Bartley and Katherine Rayburn Thomas, graciously added important family insights about their brother.
Gladys Mayo remembered Rayburn's impressionable years at her
father's little country college and her own lifelong close relationship with him. R. Bonna Ridgway and J. Lee Aston shared rec-
ollections of their years with Rayburn in the State Legislature
during a tumultuous period of Texas history. Hal Horton, Rayburn's first secretary, described the excitement and chaos of a
freshman congressman's entry into the arena of Washington
politics at the beginning of the Wilson administration.

A listing of all House and Senate members who shared their
views with us at various times and settings would read like a
Congressional Directory of the 1930s, 1940s, 1950s, and 1960s.
Among those whose insights proved particularly helpful, some
now deceased, were Hale Boggs, George Mahon, Richard Bolling, John McCormack, Marvin Jones, Fritz Lanham, Luther
Johnson, Carl Albert, Homer Thornberry, Hatton Sumners,
John Dempsey, Carter Manasco, Robert Sikes, Ralph Yarborough, Olin Teague, Francis E. "Tad" Walter, Harry R. Sheppard, Frank Thompson, Jim Wright and Frank Ikard.

In addition, the authors reviewed transcripts of hundreds of
interviews available through so-called oral history projects now
popular among historians. Such collections, practically unknown when this biography was launched, are growing at most
of the presidential libraries. Among the most fruitful in terms of
research on Rayburn's years in Congress are collections at the
Lyndon B. Johnson Library in Austin, the John F. Kennedy
Library in Cambridge, and the Dwight D. Eisenhower Library
in Abilene. With the addition of important new interviews in
the 1980s, the Sam Rayburn Library in Bonham also has become a significant repository for oral history transcripts.

Neither of the authors approached this book with academic
pretensions. Our sole objective was to portray, as honestly as
possible, one man's achievements, his times, his methods, and
his impact on history. That, as implied at the top of this section,
required a lot of research into old records, correspondence,
newspaper and magazine morgues, scholarly manuscripts (published and unpublished), and the personal papers of Rayburn

and his contemporaries, including those of all the Presidents with whom he served. We examined every Rayburn reference indexed in the *Congressional Record* from 1913 through 1961. For accounts of major national events involving Rayburn, we studied six newspapers whose Capitol Hill reporting in the first half of this century we judged to be consistently outstanding: *New York Times, St. Louis Post-Dispatch, Washington Post, Washington Evening Star, Wall Street Journal,* and *Christian Science Monitor.* We examined five Texas newspapers: *Bonham Daily Favorite, Houston Post, Dallas Morning News, Dallas Times Herald* and *Austin American-Statesman.* We reviewed the extensive clip files of Bascom Timmons, whose Washington news bureau served several Texas and other southwestern newspapers for forty years, and the personal notes of Texas newsman and Rayburn intimate George Stimpson, which were graciously made available to us by his widow. Scrapbooks compiled over the years by Rayburn's staff and constituents were helpful, although they tended to exclude articles critical of the Speaker. (Rayburn was not above censoring clippings before allowing them to be pasted in.)

Some avenues for research opened unexpectedly. After the Speaker died, Hardeman wrote major publications across the country asking for any no-longer-needed Rayburn material from their morgues. Some newspapers sent their entire Rayburn files. It was not until a decade later, however, that we struck gold. Sometime in the 1970s, the Washington editors of *Time* decided to clean out their old files; in the process, we acquired copies of every reporting file and internal memo pertaining to Rayburn written by the magazine's reporters and editors from 1940 to 1961. Much of the material had never been published. Some of it, typical of any news operation, was never meant to be published. Like kids at Christmas, growing more excited with each new discovery, we dug through the thick stack of papers. We found accounts of background interviews with the Speaker and other leading House figures, detailed reporting for cover and other stories on Rayburn, candid analyses of Rayburn's leadership, and more. What we found required us to re-examine some of our original conclusions, including our assessment of the early years of the Rayburn-Johnson relationship. "Our pumpkin papers," Hardeman playfully called them.

The thrill of discovery was repeated in the early 1980s when
W. B. Ragsdale, Sr., congressional correspondent for the Associated Press in the 1920s, 1930s, and 1940s and for *U.S. News &
World Report* in the 1950s, telephoned out of the blue to offer
us his personal files on Garner and Rayburn. "Rags" had been
a friend of both men, and his files brimmed with unpublished
anecdotes, quotes, and observations. Importantly, they also included unedited transcripts of his extended, perceptive interviews with Garner in 1957 and Rayburn in October 1961. For
both Garner and Rayburn, the interviews, only a small portion
of which were ever published, were to be their last.

As a Texas politician and later member of Rayburn's staff,
Hardeman witnessed many of the events of the 1950s and 1960s
described in this volume. In some cases—the Adlai Stevenson
campaigns, the fight over the Landrum-Griffin labor bill, the
1960 presidential race, Rayburn's last days—he kept personal
notes and diaries. Here, a small confession: the most extensive
interviewing for this book, aside from those with Rayburn himself, was the co-author's on-going questioning of Hardeman,
much of it recorded on tape, in the 1960s and 1970s. By then,
Rayburn was dead and, although Hardeman clearly was the best
living source on the Speaker's life, the responsibility for completing this biography had devolved largely to the co-author.

A full bibliography for this book necessarily would cover
many of the leading players and events that shaped the history of
this country in the nineteenth and twentieth centuries. It would
be a book in itself. Doubtless the authors, working separately
and together, were influenced by hundreds of books, reports,
and articles read in whole or part during the course of this research. These include scores of full-length biographical studies
of Rayburn and his contemporaries in books, magazines, and
newspapers. Listing them all, we believe, would serve little purpose. We have chosen, therefore, to cite—in the Notes—only
those books and articles that are quoted or otherwise mentioned
in the text. Also, in the interest of saving space, the following
abbreviations are used:

DBH (D. B. Hardeman)
DCB (Donald Conrad Bacon)
DDE (Dwight David Eisenhower)
FDR (Franklin Delano Roosevelt)
HST (Harry S. Truman)
JFK (John Fitzgerald Kennedy)
JNG (John Nance Garner)
LBJ (Lyndon Baines Johnson)
LC (Library of Congress)
SR (Sam Rayburn)
SRL (Sam Rayburn Library)

1. Growing Up

1. Much of this chapter is based on D. B. Hardeman's interviews with Sam Rayburn and other immediate Rayburn family members between late 1956 and mid-1961. Also interviewed were various Rayburn relatives and friends in east Tennessee and north Texas. Dates and other details regarding early family history of the Rayburns and Wallers were, for the most part, taken from official records on file in Roane County, Tennessee, and Fannin County, Texas. For scholars wishing to pursue further the Rayburn and Waller genealogies or the Civil War record of William Marion Rayburn, Hardeman's extensive research in these areas will be made available to the Sam Rayburn Library in Bonham.

2. Frederick J. Turner, *The Frontier in American History* (N.Y.: Henry Holt, 1920), p. 192. See also James Hastings, *Encyclopedia of Religion and Ethics, Vol. IV* (N.Y.: Scribner's Sons, 1925), pp. 210–224.

3. George F. Black, *Surnames of Scotland* (N.Y.: New York Public Library, 1946), p. 706.

4. John Fiske, *Old Virginia and Her Neighbors* (Cambridge, Mass.: Riverside Press, 1902), pp. 371–376.

5. See Thomas W. Humes, *The Loyal Mountaineers of Tennessee* (Knoxville, 1888; rpt. Spartanburg, S.C.: Reprint Co., 1974), pp. 77–119; also James W. Festy, *Secession and Reconstruction of Tennessee* (Chicago: U. of Chicago Press, 1898); and James W. Patton, *Unionism and Reconstruction in Tennessee* (Chapel Hill: U. of North Carolina Press, 1934).

6. William Rayburn file, Co. B, 2d (Ashby's) Regiment, Tennessee Cavalry, Confederate Army Records, National Archives, Washington, D.C.

7. Humes, *The Loyal Mountaineers of Tennessee*, pp. 77–119.

8. Emma M. Wells, *The History of Roane County, Tennessee, 1801–70* (Chattanooga: Lookout Publishing, 1927), pp. 297–298.

9. "All the children were Rayburns but Sam—he was a Waller." Mose Waller, Sr., interview with DBH, Dec. 9, 1956.

10. See Mitford M. Mathews, *A Dictionary of Americanisms on Historical Principles* (Chicago: U. of Chicago Press, 1956), vol. 1, p. 752.

11. Mrs. W. P. Jennings letter to DBH, Lubbock, Texas, March 9, 1957.

12. See Greene article, *Sherman Daily Democrat*, Sherman, Texas, Dec. 12, 1954.

13. Lorraine Kimbrough interview with Anthony Champagne, Dec. 23, 1980, SRL.

14. Moreland interview, unidentified newspaper clipping, October, 1941 (Sam Rayburn scrapbooks), SRL.

15. Medibel Rayburn interview with DBH, Washington, Feb. 28, 1957.

2. Ambition Kindled

1. Much has been written about Joe Bailey. For years, the standard biography has been Sam Hanna Acheson's *Joe Bailey, The Last Democrat* (N.Y.: Macmillan, 1932). See also David Graham Phillips article, "Treason of the Senate," *Cosmopolitan*, July 1906, 267–276; Samuel G. Blythe, "The Great Bailey Myth," *Saturday Evening Post*, May 27, 1911, 3–4, 34–36, and Alfred Henry Lewis, "The Hon.(?) J. W. Bailey," *Cosmopolitan*, April 1913, 601–605.

2. Blythe, "The Great Bailey Myth," *Saturday Evening Post*, May 27, 1911, 34.

3. There are many slightly varying versions of this story, which Rayburn told and retold through the years.

4. SR interview with DBH, Jan. 14, 1960.

5. See James M. Bledsoe, *A History of Mayo and His College* (Dallas: Harben-Spotts, 1946). Although Gladys Mayo, daughter of Professor Mayo, disputes its accuracy, the book gives a thorough and moving account of a most unusual man and the institution he founded. See also the *East Texan*, student newspaper of East Texas Normal College, March 22, 1917.

6. Mrs. Bartley interview with DBH, Washington, Feb. 28, 1957.

7. Denney letter to DBH, March 16, 1957.

8. Claude C. Crawford, later a professor at the University of South Carolina, quoted in Bledsoe, *A History of Mayo and His College*, pp. 242–243.

9. SR press conference, Jan. 29, 1958.

10. Gladys Mayo letter to DBH, May 16, 1962. Rayburn had a special attachment to Gladys Mayo. She was 7 and he was 19 when they first met. Bright, curious, interested in politics, she peppered Rayburn with thoughtful questions as a child and was unawed by him as an adult. Their "pitch-battles" over political differences became well known among the Rayburns. "I suppose one reason that Sam and I were forever good friends was that he could so reasonably 'forgive my trespasses,'" Gladys Mayo explained in 1962. "Even as a child I had 'needled' him with questions I had not the courage to ask others. If he flared up, he would soon follow with a lovely smile of forgiveness."

11. Quoted in Bledsoe, *A History of Mayo and His College*, p. 105.

3. State Legislator

1. Henry A. Cunningham interview with DBH, Dec. 12, 1956.

2. C. Dwight Dorough, *Mr. Sam* (N.Y.: Random House, 1962).

3. It was the start of a lifelong friendship. Gardner became one of Rayburn's staunchest political supporters. Later Rayburn had his first political opponent appointed as postmaster of Honey Grove.

4. SR interview with DBH, undated, 1957.

5. R. Bonna Ridgway letter to DBH, Jan. 5, 1957.

6. Cunningham interview with DBH, Dec. 12, 1956.

7. Texas State Representative E. Pharr of Sulphur Springs.

8. R. Bonna Ridgway interview with DBH, Dec. 31, 1956.

9. Seth S. McKay, *Texas Politics, 1906–1944* (Lubbock: Texas Tech Press, 1952), pp. 20–54.

10. *House Record*, Reg. Sess., State of Texas, Jan. 22, 1907.

11. Johnson was in his second and final term when Rayburn arrived. Although much alike in their rural upbringing and populist outlook, the two Sams never hit it off as close friends, perhaps because of their deeply felt differing views on prohibition and the Bailey question, perhaps because their ambitions clashed. Still, they remained on good terms. Years later, responding to a letter from Sam Johnson, Rayburn wrote: "You are one man that I served with in the Legislature of Texas that I have always remembered with interest and kindly feeling" (SR letter to Sam Ealy Johnson, Johnson City, Texas, Feb. 22, 1937, Papers of John Holton, LBJ Library).

12. *Washington Post*, Jan. 24, 1907.

13. *Galveston News*, Feb. 27, 1907; also Acheson, *Joe Bailey, The Last Democrat*, pp. 237–238.

14. Bailey was defiant, arrogant, unrepentant to the end. Edmonds Travis, Bailey's publicity man in 1920, interview with DBH, Dec. 30, 1956. Also, Rayburn told of an exchange he had with Bailey long after the senator had returned to private life. "Senator," said Rayburn, "if I had been one of your good friends that night you made the 'Rogue's gallery' speech, I would have broken your leg or put you in jail or done anything to you to keep you from making it."

"No, Sam," Bailey replied, "I had to make that speech." SR interview with DBH, undated.

15. Judge A. P. Bolling interview with DBH, Bonham, Texas, Dec. 12, 1956.

16. Ibid.

17. However, the budding politician kept his standing in the legal profession. In March 1915, after his election to Congress, he was admitted to practice before the U.S. Supreme Court. Presenting him to Chief Justice Edward D. White, Associate Justices Oliver Wendell Holmes, Charles Evans Hughes, and the others was none other than Joe Bailey, who earlier had declined President William Howard Taft's offer to name him to the High Court.

18. *Fort Worth Record*, Feb. 25, 1909.

19. An early indication of Rayburn's feelings about racial equality may be found in his vote on an amendment that would have exempted blacks from the compulsory school attendance bill. The amendment offered by State Representative Homer A. Dotson was voted down, 86–24, Rayburn joining the majority. Another significant vote came on Sept. 2, 1910, on a resolution memorializing Congress to submit a constitutional amendment revising the 14th Amendment and repealing the 15th Amendment to disfranchise blacks. The House voted, 52–33, to approve the resolution, Rayburn voting no.

20. Legislative secretaries in those days worked from 8 to 6, six days a week, for $4–$5 a day.

21. *House Journal*, 31st Legislature, Reg. Sess., State of Texas, March 12, 1909, p. 1224.

22. R. Bonna Ridgway letter to DBH, Jan. 5, 1957.

23. The article first appeared in the *Fort Worth Record*, which was partly owned by Joe Bailey, on Feb. 25, 1909. It was embarrassingly complimentary. "He hasn't any mission in life except to make others happy and do his full part in shaping good legislation," it said. "Rayburn is one of the most popular members, not only of the House but of the entire legislature. Strong in mind, in body, in fidelity and devotion, it is perfectly natural that popularity should be his."

24. J. Lee Aston interview, *Houston Post*, March 16, 1949.

25. The press later estimated his true margin of victory was 68–65 and that, on the second ballot, two members switched to Rayburn in the belief his election was assured.

26. *House Journal*, 32nd Legislature, Reg. Sess., State of Texas, Jan. 10, 1911, pp. 7–8.

27. Teenager Gladys Mayo, sent by her father, Professor Mayo, to Austin to represent the family at Rayburn's inaugural as Speaker, was infuriated at her first sight of the motley assemblage. In a letter to DBH, dated May 16, 1962, she wrote: "I had observed our representatives, in both House and Senate, sprawling in their chairs, coatless and with suspenders glaringly soiled, their 'hooves' on their desks, spitting cuds of tobacco toward the cuspidors, missing the target, of course. I asked Sam why we couldn't get some gentlemen—some folks with half-way educated minds—to make our laws. 'Well,' drawled Sam, 'first we must educate the voters.'"

28. SR to DBH, March 6, 1961.

29. Bailey's response to Randell's announcement: "Ha, ha. Just say that I laughed." Bailey subsequently resigned from the Senate as a symbol of protest against proposed policies of incoming President Woodrow Wilson.

30. "Open Letter to Democrats," signed by SR, *Dallas Morning News*, Oct. 29, 1911.

31. From Perkins's handwritten copy, sent to Rayburn in the 1950s by Tom Perkins, Jr.: Rayburn 4,983; Perkins 4,493; Jones 4,365; Erwin 656.

4. Young Congressman

1. Hal Horton letter to DBH, Sept. 10, 1956.
2. SR interview with DBH, undated, 1959. See also Bailey letter to W. M. Rayburn, Bonham, Texas, Aug. 4, 1916.
3. Sam Rayburn, "The Speaker Speaks of Presidents," *New York Times Magazine*, June 6, 1961, 32.
4. One of the most admired men in Congress, Kitchin was tall and handsome, with a kindly face and a pleasant, often radiant personality. He was widely regarded as the House's leading authority on questions of finance. In debate, he could be devastating, particularly when quoting statistics, which he memorized by the hour. His only rival as a debater, Republican James Mann, once said that a verbal blow from Kitchin was like being hit by "a brick in a towel." On one occasion, a brash, young Republican rose to challenge Kitchin only to be yanked back to his seat by then Speaker Joe Cannon of Illinois. "Sit down, Lenroot!" ordered Cannon. "Don't you know better than to interrupt that man. He's loaded with grape and canister." See Alex M. Arnett, *Claude Kitchin and the Wilson Era Policies* (Boston: Little, Brown, 1937).
5. Both houses of Congress were firmly in the grasp of southerners, who themselves were split into two factions—the organization or administration faction and the "Southern Agrarians." See Arthur S. Link, "The South and the New Freedom: An Interpretation," *American Scholar*, Summer 1951, 314–324: "The Southern Agrarians of the Wilson period were the direct inheritors and now the prime articulators in the Democratic party of the philosophy underlying the Agrarian crusade—namely, that it was government's duty to intervene directly in economic affairs in order to benefit submerged or politically impotent economic interests. . . . Whereas the administration usually followed the regular party line, the Southern Agrarians were often far to the left of it; and in the end, they helped to make Wilson an advanced progressive and helped to commit his administration to a broad program of welfare legislation. . . . Southern progressives were more concerned with strengthening the political and economic position of the farmers, through regulation of railroads and corporations, a low tariff, the direct primary and the like, than with tenement reforms, minimum wage legislation or workmen's compensation legislation."
6. See Arthur S. Link, *Wilson: The New Freedom* (Princeton: Princeton U. Press, 1956), pp. 57–60; also Josephus Daniels, *The Wilson Era* (Chapel Hill: U. of North Carolina Press, 1944), pp. 104–106.
7. Edouard V. Izac, "Former Member Recalls Wilson's Inauguration," *Roll Call*, Washington, D.C., date unknown, 1957. Former Congressman Izac was then a midshipman, standing in a brigade a few feet away from the inauguaral platform.
8. Soon after they were assigned to the Maltby Building, fellow Texan Garner invited them to share his office, which he seldom used, in the House

Office Building. Hal Horton recalled that they moved in with Garner, becoming a part of the crusty congressman's daily afternoon ritual: the opening of his well-stocked liquor cabinet. "Mr. Garner had a large closet in his office and he kept his refreshments stored here. He had many bottles in it—some in little crock jars with funny little stoppers, some green liquids and some amber. Mr. Garner would come to the office late in the afternoon with some of his many cronies, and with much bantering and jesting, just like school boys, they would 'Strike a blow for liberty' (Garner's phrase). I got to believe that liberty was safe as long as there was anything in the closet and it was never empty. Liberty evidently was an elusive thing and must constantly be guarded." Horton letter to DBH, Sept. 19, 1956.

9. Cochran was later a U.S. representative from Mississippi and a close Rayburn ally in the 1940s.

10. Raw transcripts of John Garner interviews with W. B. Ragsdale, Sr., *U.S. News & World Report.* Ragsdale's remarkable series of interviews, conducted in Uvalde, Texas, April 8–12, 1957, was never published. Although the former Vice-President was then in his nineties, his mind was clear and his memory precise.

11. Texas did institute the two-primary system, but not until after Rayburn had been elected to Congress with 23 percent of the vote cast.

12. Senator Tom Connally, as told to Alfred Steinberg, *My Name Is Tom Connally* (N.Y.: Thomas Y. Crowell, 1954), pp. 108–109.

13. Willis Davis interview with DBH, Atlanta, Ga., undated. In 1913, Davis was clerk of the House Committee on Interstate and Foreign Commerce.

14. Adamson, then 57, physically striking and popular, advised new members that the only habits worth forming were to work, pray, save money, and respect your fellow man. See the *Independent*, May 1, 1913, 980.

15. SR interview with Elizabeth Carpenter, *Houston Post*, March 3, 1955.

16. Both the House Speaker and majority leader had opposed Wilson for the Democratic presidential nomination the year before. Wilson never forgave them. See JNG interview with Ragsdale of *U.S. News & World Report*: "I used to go up there once a week and talk with President Wilson as long as he wanted to. . . . He knew I took a little something and he did. We'd take one drink. Joe Tumulty was his secretary. I'd go into Tumulty's office and get another."

17. SR interview with DBH, Feb. 17, 1957.

18. Connally, *My Name Is Tom Connally*, pp. 77–78.

19. JNG interview with DBH, Uvalde, Texas, Nov. 30, 1959.

20. Marvin Jones, former congressman, later chief justice, U.S. Court of Claims, interview with DBH, Washington, April 16, 1957.

21. SR interview with DBH, Dec. 14, 1957.

22. SR interview with Ed Jamieson, *Amarillo News*, Sept. 27, 1940.

23. Garner made the comment to Lindsay Warren, then a freshman representative from North Carolina. See Bascom Timmons, *Garner of Texas* (N.Y.: Harper and Brothers, 1948), p. 112.

24. Paul Healy, *Saturday Evening Post*, Nov. 24, 1951. Reprinted in the *Con-

gressional Record, Jan. 9, 1952, p. A57.

25. Greenville, Texas, July 19, 1932.

26. Marvin Jones interview with DBH, April 16, 1957. Jones, who came to Congress in 1917, met Rayburn while both were students at the University of Texas Law School. He roomed with Rayburn in Washington for several years and introduced Rayburn to his sister, whom Rayburn subsequently married. Jones later was appointed chief justice of the U.S. Court of Claims in Washington.

27. See Connally, *My Name Is Tom Connally*, pp. 89–91.

28. He spoke of Washington as "a city of disillusionment" and predicted that Texas would soon be furnishing Presidents, Vice-Presidents, Cabinet members, and ambassadors. The speech was "a happy hit," noted the *Sherman Daily Democrat*, April 21, 1913.

29. *Congressional Record*, May 6, 1913, pp. 1247–1248.

30. Raymond Moley, *27 Masters of Politics* (N.Y.: Funk and Wagnalls, 1949), p. 246.

31. Ray Stannard Baker, *Woodrow Wilson—Life & Letters* (N.Y.: Doubleday, Page, 1927), vol. 4, pp. 373–374.

32. See Link, *Wilson: The New Freedom*, pp. 421–448.

33. *Congressional Record*, June 2, 1914, pp. 9684–9689.

34. See Ed Jamieson article, *Amarillo News*, Sept. 27, 1940.

35. See *New York Times*, June 12, 1914.

36. See Alfred Lief, *Brandeis* (N.Y.: Stackpole Sons, 1936).

37. Sam Rayburn campaign card, 1914 (DBH-DCB files).

38. SR letter to Katharine Rayburn Thomas, Aug. 26, 1914.

39. See letter signed "Thos. P. Steger," *Greenville Banner*, July 22, 1914.

40. SR statement, July 23, 1914.

41. In one such mood, Rayburn penned a long, revealing letter to an old friend from the days before he entered politics: "This is a lonesome, dark day here. You wouldn't think it but a fellow gets lonesomer here I think than any place almost. Everybody is busy and one does not find that congeniality for which a fellow so thirsts when he is away from home and loved ones. . . . It is a selfish, sour-bellied place, every fellow trying for fame, perhaps I should say *notoriety* . . . and are ready at all times to use the other fellow as a prize-poll for it." SR to Dr. H. B. Savage, Bonham, Texas, April 26, 1916.

42. The imposing new home was costing more than Rayburn could afford. Shortly after Abner's death, he confided in sister Kate that he was strapped for cash and trying to save money by doing without a secretary. With building costs, campaign expenditures of between $1,500 and $2,000, improvements to the old family farm, and "expenses incident to the sad bereavement last summer, which will necessarily fall on me, you will realize how long it takes to pay them out." SR letter to Katharine Thomas, Bonham, Texas, undated.

43. SR letter to Martha and Will Rayburn, Sunday, undated, 1914.

44. SR handwritten letter on House Interstate and Foreign Commerce Committee stationery, Aug. 25, 1914 (DBH/DCB files).

45. Link, *Wilson: The New Freedom*, pp. 421–448.

46. *Nation*, 99, July 16, 1914, 61–62.

47. Baker, *Woodrow Wilson—Life & Letters*, pp. 373–374.

48. See *Railway Age Gazette*, Jan. 28, 1916, 154; also *New York Times*, July 16, 1916.

49. Papers of Woodrow Wilson, Executive Offices Diary, May 1, 1916, p. 122, LC.

50. See Link, *Wilson: The New Freedom*, pp. 61–70.

51. Lorraine Kimbrough interview with DBH, July 18, 1956.

52. SR letter to W. A. Warden, McKinney, Texas, March 21, 1916.

53. Thomas letter to SR, May 16, 1916. This was the beginning of a lifetime of questionable political advice from Thomas, who later was appointed regional administrator of the Internal Revenue Service in Dallas and who fancied himself a man of astute political insight. Rayburn generally brushed aside the advice but often could not ignore Thomas's tendency to get himself and Rayburn into potentially damaging entanglements at home. In 1920, Rayburn complained to his sister Kate Thomas that he was "very much grieved" because her husband had signed on as Dallas chairman of an attempted political comeback by discredited former Senator Bailey. "Everyone knows our relationship and can never be convinced that it has not at least my passive sanction." What's worse, Bailey's opponent "is a constituent of mine and his friends in Hunt County are my friends. . . . I hope they will not settle any wrath on me but I fear they will." See SR letter to Kate Thomas, March 13, 1920.

54. SR letter to N. A. Burton, Feb. 23, 1916. Quoted in Anthony Champagne, *Congressman Sam Rayburn* (New Brunswick, N.J.: Rutgers U. Press, 1984), p. 98.

55. It was true that he voted against child-labor restrictions. For years, that vote hurt him politically in Denison, the district's only town with a sizable union force. He believed such laws were a state responsibility. He also was afraid the laws would be used to prevent farmers from having their young sons work in the fields. Wrote Rayburn: "I am, and have always been, an earnest advocate of child-labor laws but when 44 states have child-labor laws that are enforced by local authorities, I can see no reason for the Federal government to force its hand into our local affairs." Letter to H. E. Ellis, Denison, Texas, April 24, 1916.

56. Wilson letter to Andrew L. Randell, Sherman, Texas, July 11, 1916.

57. SR conversation with DBH, Dec. 20, 1957.

58. SR letter to H. E. Ellis, Denison, Texas, April 24, 1916.

59. Quoted in Dorough, *Mr. Sam*, p. 147.

5. Wilson Days

1. See Alex M. Arnett, *Claude Kitchin and the Wilson War Policies* (Boston: Little, Brown, 1937), p. 228.

2. *St. Louis Globe-Democrat*, April 7, 1917.

3. Marvin Jones interview with DBH, April 16, 1957.

4. *Congressional Record*, June 30, 1939. p. 8509.

5. SR interview with DBH, Oct. 1, 1956.

6. See Ray Stannard Baker, *Woodrow Wilson: Life and Letters* (N.Y.: Doubleday, Page, 1939), vol. 7, p. 11.

7. See James A. Lofty, "The Soldiers and Sailors Insurance Act" (Ph.D. dissertation, Catholic U., 1921); also *The World War Veterans and the Federal Treasury* (N.Y.: National Industrial Conference Board, 1932).

8. William Gibbs McAdoo, *Crowded Years* (Boston and N.Y.: Houghton, Mifflin, 1931) pp. 428–435.

9. Adamson resigned from the House in 1917 to accept appointment to the Board of U.S. General Appraisers, later known as the U.S Customs Court.

10. See *Congressional Record*, Sept. 7–13, 1917, pp. 5752, 6750–6773.

11. Jones interview with DBH, April 16, 1957.

12. See Louis M. Hacker, *The U.S. in the 20th Century* (N.Y.: Appleton-Century-Crofts, 1952), p. 203; also McAdoo, *Crowded Years*, pp. 455–509.

13. See McAdoo, *Crowded Years*, p. 458.

14. *Congressional Record*, Feb. 22, 1918, p. 2543, and Jan. 30, 1919, p. 2393.

15. *Congressional Record*, Jan. 30, 1919, p. 2393.

16. *The Return of Railroads to Private Ownership*, Public hearings of the House Committee on Interstate and Foreign Commerce, July 15–Oct. 4, 1919, p. 669.

17. See *Extension of Tenure of Government Control of Railroads*, Hearings of the Senate Committee on Interstate Commerce, Nov. 20–Dec. 19, 1918, 65th Congress, 3rd Session, vol. 2, pp. 1884, 1918–1919.

18. See Harold Faulkner, *From Versailles to the New Deal* (New Haven: Yale U. Press, 1950).

19. See *Dallas Morning News*, Nov. 13, 1919.

20. *Congressional Record*, Feb. 20, 1920, p. 3209.

21. See *Dallas Morning News*, Feb. 21, 1920. But some Texans praised Rayburn's political courage. The *News*, Feb. 23, 1920, commented: "Mr. Rayburn . . . has opened his mind frankly and unafraid to the facts of the situation."

22. Rayburn said in 1919 that he had voted for his last socialistic program. Occasionally in the past, he confided, he had followed the mob "when it seemed there was nothing else to do, when one's action would have been misunderstood and branded him with the mark of Cain. Conditions and times have changed. I am done. I shall not vote again for any measure that smacks of socialism, it matters not what the mob may seem to want at the moment." SR letter to W. A. Thomas, Jan. 10, 1919.

23. See Link, *Wilson: The New Freedom*, pp. 274–275.

24. Woodrow Wilson, *Congressional Government* (15th ed., 1900; repr. N.Y.: Meridian Books, 1956), p. 22.

25. See *Congressional Record*, Feb. 22, 1918. p. 2540.

26. SR interview with DBH, undated.

27. See Sam Rayburn, "The Speaker Speaks of Presidents," *New York Times Magazine*, June 4, 1961, 32.

28. See SR letter from Ancon, Canal Zone, to "Homefolks," Bonham, Texas, May 25, 1913.

6. Republican Years

1. SR interview with DBH, Oct. 1, 1956.

2. Johnson interview with DBH, Fort Worth, Texas, Dec. 19, 1956.

3. SR interview with DBH, Oct. 1, 1956.

4. SR interview with DBH, Dec. 14, 1956.

5. See JNG interview with W. B. Ragsdale of *U.S. News & World Report*, April 9, 1959, unpublished.

6. SR letter to Katharine Thomas, Feb. 2, 1922.

7. SR letter to W. A. Thomas, Feb. 19, 1922.

8. Ibid.

9. Ibid.

10. See Harold Faulkner, *From Versailles to the New Deal* (New Haven: Yale U. Press, 1950), p. 139.

11. See John Moffett Mecklin, *The Ku Klux Klan* (N.Y.: Harcourt Brace, 1924), p. 31; also R. L. Duffus article, *World's Work*, June 1923, 178–182.

12. See Brent Tarter interview with Deward Brown, Oct. 3, 1970, SRL.

13. SR letter to W. A. Thomas, Feb. 19, 1922.

14. Cecil Dickson interview with Anthony Champagne, June 29, 1980, SRL.

15. Ibid.

16. SR interview with DBH, Bonham, Texas, Dec. 14, 1956.

17. *Bonham Daily Favorite*, June 6, 1922.

18. In the same election, a Klan-backed candidate, Earle B. Mayfield, was elected to the U.S. Senate in Texas. It proved to be high-water mark for the hooded order in Texas. Membership declined steadily over the next several years until, by 1926, the group was no longer a significant factor in state politics.

19. Jones interview with DBH, April 16, 1957.

20. See House Parliamentarian Lewis Deschler interview with DBH, Aug. 17, 1957.

21. See former Congressman John E. Lyle interview with Anthony Champagne, undated, SRL.

22. Cecil Dickson, longtime Rayburn friend and former Capitol Hill reporter for AP, INS, and other news organizations, interview with DBH, Washington, May 21, 1957. See also Marquis James, *Mr. Garner of Texas* (Indianapolis: Bobbs-Merrill, 1939), pp. 111–113.

23. See James, *Mr. Garner of Texas*, p. 112.

24. Deschler interview with DBH, Aug. 17, 1957; Dickson interview with DBH, May 21, 1957.

25. Deschler interview with DBH, Aug. 17, 1957.

26. SR interview with DBH, undated.

27. Marvin Jones interview with DBH, April 16, 1957.

28. SR interview with DBH, Dec. 14, 1956.

29. Jones interview with DBH, Washington, April 16, 1957.

30. See Kenneth L. Roberts, "The Troubles of the House," *Saturday Evening Post*, June 3, 1922, 7, 65–68.

31. Vituperative attacks upon a President always angered him. "It matters not to me to what party a President belongs; I have a respect for that office that almost awes me," he once told the House. "I know that the American people in electing a man for the Presidency out of their wisdom or unwisdom do so actuated by patriotic motives, and as long as I live, I will never admit that there has been a dishonest man or an unintelligent man in the White House," *Congressional Record*, Feb. 9, 1939, p. 1729.

Rayburn's faith in the fundamental goodness and honesty of Presidents seems particularly naive in light of more recent history, especially the events of the 1970s known collectively as Watergate. Even with his firm belief in the symbolic Presidency, it is at least questionable whether Rayburn could have remained silent in the attack on President Richard Nixon, whom he openly loathed and mistrusted almost from the day of Nixon's arrival in Washington. In any case, Watergate and Nixon's subsequent resignation would have shaken the Texan deeply and caused him sorrow and anguish.

32. SR press conference, Speaker's Rooms, July 8, 1957.

33. SR interview with DBH, undated, 1956.

34. SR interview with DBH, Dec. 14, 1956.

7. Metze

1. This chapter is based largely on interviews with Rayburn's social friends from the mid-1920s through the 1950s. Interviews were conducted in the late 1950s. In many cases, interviews were granted reluctantly and with the understanding that quotations would not be attributed.

2. SR conversation with DBH, June 11, 1961.

3. Rayburn was not above censorship. He once asserted in a conversation with Hardeman that he would not have a book in his library "that had Allan Shivers's name in it." Hardeman replied: "You're like the Russians, you go through your books and cut out the names of all the people you don't like." Rayburn chuckled but did not recant.

4. DBH interview with Alla Clary, undated.

5. SR letter to Will and Martha Rayburn, undated, 1914.

6. *Dallas Morning News*, Oct. 16, 1927.

7. Mose Waller, Sr., interview with DBH, Dec. 9, 1956.

8. "Driest Christmas I ever spent," Rayburn later recalled. Alla Clary interview with DBH, July 12, 1956.

9. Mrs. Schuyler Otis Bland interview with DBH, 1962.

10. After Rayburn's death in 1961, Marvin Jones volunteered to ask his sister whether she would talk to Hardeman. She told her brother firmly: "Through all these years I have never discussed this with a soul and I see no reason to change. Anything I might say, somebody might be upset about it. There's no need for it. I think I'll just go on as I have."

11. Kate Reed Estes interview with Anthony Champagne, Trenton, Texas, undated, 1980, SRL.

12. Marvin Jones interview with DBH, April 16, 1957.

13. Samuel Fenner Leslie interview with Wayne Little, July 26, 1965, SRL.

14. Buster Cole interview with Anthony Champagne, Aug. 21, 1980, SRL.

15. Associate Justice Tom C. Clark interview with DBH, undated, probably 1958.

16. Waller interview with DBH, Dec. 9, 1956.

8. Kingmaker

1. Hearst served two terms in the House, the last starting in 1907. Typically, Garner had been unawed by the California newspaper czar's wealth and had been one of the few House members to befriend him. The Texan on several occasions rescued Hearst, an inept politician, when the Californian got into embarrassing rows on the House floor. In an interview with W. B. Ragsdale of *U.S. News & World Report* on April 10, 1957, Garner vividly recalled Hearst's editorial in 1932, advocating him for President. "It almost stopped me from breathing for a while," he said.

2. SR letter to Thurman Barrett, Jan. 2, 1932.

3. See Earland Irving Carlson, *Franklin D. Roosevelt's Fight for the Presidential Nomination, 1928–1932* (Champaign: U. of Illinois Press, 1955), pp. 237–241.

4. Hoover later vetoed the bill.

5. JNG interview with DBH, Nov. 23, 1959.

6. SR letter to Oscar Callaway, Jan. 11, 1932.

7. SR interview with DBH, undated.

8. Ibid.

9. Ibid.

10. See SR letter to T. W. Davidson, Dallas, Texas, Jan. 26, 1932.

11. Congress voted to submit a prohibition repeal amendment to the states the following year. Rayburn joined the wets in voting for submission, although he continued giving lip service to prohibition in deference to his district, which to this day remains substantially opposed to the sale of alcoholic beverages. As he explained at the time: "I shall always oppose the repeal of the 18th amendment but believe that the best way to stop clamor on this question and turn to other very pressing questions was to submit the matter to the states." SR letter to E. M. Taylor of Greenville, Texas, Feb. 21, 1933.

12. SR interview with DBH, Dec. 14, 1956.

13. Jim Farley, *Jim Farley's Story* (N.Y.: McGraw-Hill, 1948), p. 18; see also Jim Farley, *Behind the Ballots: The Personal History of a Politician* (N.Y.: Har-

court, Brace, 1938), p. 75.

14. Relations between Rayburn and McAdoo were cool from that point on. Rayburn was convinced the Californian tried to steal the vice-presidential nomination for himself by claiming responsibility for putting FDR over the top. Wrote Texas delegate Karl A. Crowley: "By the time we wrested control from the anti-Roosevelt crowd in charge of Texas and got out to the convention in time to hear Mr. McAdoo's speech, he was engaged in taking from Texas all of the full credit and glory that should have been hers, but our appearance ended the speech." In "The Party and Roosevelt Record of Karl A. Crowley," submitted to "Jim" (Farley), April 8, 1938, President's Personal Files, 2871, FDR Library.

McAdoo later had a different recollection of the events leading to FDR's nomination. In an exchange of letters with Rayburn in 1938, McAdoo claimed that he informed Rayburn before the Texas caucus that California was switching to FDR and that McAdoo was first to suggest that Rayburn ask Garner if he was interested in the Vice-Presidency. Rayburn, in response, stuck to his own version of the events.

15. SR interview with DBH, Dec. 14, 1956; also SR conversation with DBH, March 1959.

9. "The Fight for Economic Justice"

1. *Dallas Times Herald*, Jan. 23, 1949.

2. See Lionel V. Patenaude, "The New Deal in Texas" (Ph.D. dissertation, U. of Texas, 1953).

3. See SR letter to W. B. Bankhead, Jasper, Ala., July 25, 1932; and SR letter to J. L. "Tuck" Milligan, Richmond, Mo., July 25, 1932.

4. *Inaugural Addresses of the American Presidents*, annotated by David Newton Lott (N.Y.: Holt, Rinehart and Winston, 1961), p. 232.

5. See Margaret L. Coit, *Mr. Baruch* (Boston: Houghton, Mifflin, 1957), p. 412: "No one who does not remember can understand the feeling in the United States on that fourth of March. It was a journey into the unknown, a shock from a giant electric battery, revitalizing the nerve cells of a nation . . ."

6. *Inaugural Addresses of the American Presidents*, p. 233.

7. See Edward F. Willett, "The Securities Act of 1933" (Ph.D. dissertation, Princeton U., 1939).

8. Thomas Corcoran interview with DBH, May 23, 1957.

9. Mitchell Broadus, *Depression Decade* (N.Y.: Rinehart, 1947), p. 155; also Ferdinand Pecora, *Wall Street under Oath: The Story of Modern Money Changers* (N.Y.: Simon and Schuster, 1939).

10. See C. A. Miller, *The Interstate Commerce Commission and the Commission's Secretaries* (Washington, D.C.: Government Printing Office, 1946), pp. 145–147.

11. Walter Splawn interview with DBH, San Antonio, Texas, Jan. 2, 1957.

12. When FDR passed over Splawn to fill an opening at the ICC, Rayburn

refused to speak to the President during his next White House visit. "Sam, Sam, what's the matter?" Roosevelt asked, tossing his large head back and smiling broadly.

"You didn't give Dr. Splawn that job on the ICC," Rayburn responded with a frown.

"Sam, my friend, I'll make it up to you," FDR shot back. "He'll have the next opening, I promise." This time the President kept his word, nominating Splawn to the ICC in January 1934.

13. See *Railroad Holding Companies*, Hearings before the House Committee on Interstate and Foreign Commerce on HR 9059, 72nd Congress, 2nd Session, Feb. 17–March 24, 1932; also John E. Tracy, "The Emergency Railroad Transportation Act, 1933," *Michigan Law Review*, 31, 1932–1933, 1118–1124. For more on Dr. Walter Splawn, see Miller, *The Interstate Commerce Commission and the Commission's Secretaries*, pp. 145–147.

14. For the most authoritative account of the Securities Act of 1933, see James M. Landis, "The Legislative History of the Securities Act of 1933," *George Washington Law Review*, 28, Oct. 1959, 29–49.

15. See *The Federal Securities Act*, Hearings before the House Committee on Interstate and Foreign Commerce on HR 4314, 73rd Congress, 1st Session, March 31–April 5, 1933; also Willett, "The Securities Act of 1933," p. 119.

16. See *The Federal Securities Act*, Hearings before the House Committee on Interstate and Foreign Commerce on HR 4314, pp. 135–136.

17. See "The Legend of Landis," *Fortune Magazine*, August 1934, 118–120.

18. Benjamin Victor Cohen interview with DBH, May 16, 1957.

19. SR interview with DBH, June 20, 1956.

20. James M. Landis interview with DBH, New York, April 7, 1958.

21. In perfecting a final draft, the trio had the able assistance of Middleton Beaman, chief legislative draftsman of the House of Representatives. Wrote Landis in 1959: "Middleton Beaman is a difficult man to describe. I thought I knew something of legislative draftsmanship until I met him. . . . For days Beaman would not allow us to draft a line. He insisted instead on exploring the implications of the bill to find exactly what we had or did not have in mind. . . . It was exasperating to both Cohen and myself." See Landis, "The Legislative History of the Securities Act of 1933."

22. Cohen interview with DBH, May 16, 1957.

23. Joining others in congratulating the Texas lawmaker was Professor Frankfurter: "I do indeed believe that you have turned out not only a 'pretty good' piece of legislation in the Securities Bill but, if I may say so, a first-rate bill. But for your leadership, it would not have been such a bill." Felix Frankfurter letter to SR, May 11, 1933.

In a letter to Roosevelt, the Harvard scholar again singled out Rayburn: "He worked indefatigably for a law that should be fair to the legitimate interests of finance, while at the same time protecting the exploitation of the credulity and limited knowledge of investors, and the qualities of courage that he showed were no less striking." Felix Frankfurter letter to FDR, May 24, 1933.

24. See Bernard Flexner, "The Fight on the Securities Act," *Atlantic Monthly*, February 1934, 232–250; also Sam Rayburn, "Is the Securities Act Sound," *Today*, Dec. 30, 1933.

25. See *Securities Exchange Act of 1934*, Report 1383, U.S. House of Representatives, April 27, 1934.

26. See Joseph Alsop and Robert Kintner, "Battle of the Market Place: Richard Whitney Leads the Fight," *Saturday Evening Post*, June 11, 1938; also *Time Magazine*, Feb. 26, 1934, pp. 53–56.

27. See *Fortune Magazine*, June 1940, 92–126; also Alsop and Kintner, "Battle of the Market Place," *Saturday Evening Post*, June 11, 1938.

28. Roosevelt advised Rayburn on March 26: "It has come to my attention that a more definite and more highly organized drive is being made against effective legislation to this end than against any similar recommendation made by me during the past year. . . . The bill seems to meet the minimum requirements. I do not see how any of us could afford to have it weakened in any shape, manner, or form," reprinted in Securities Exchange Act of 1934, Report 1383, U.S. House of Representatives, April 27, 1934.

29. Karl Schriftgiesser, *The Lobbyists* (Boston: Little, Brown, 1951), pp. 64–65.

30. Ibid., p. 65.

31. See *Congressional Record*, April 30, 1934, p. 7693.

32. Rayburn had 5,000 signatures on letters, cards, and petitions analyzed. A large portion proved to be false. Other signatures were those of brokerage-house employees and customers. SR interview with DBH, undated.

33. *Congressional Record*, May 3, 1934, p. 8012.

34. Ibid., p. 7943.

35. Ibid., p. 8013.

36. Cohen interview with DBH, May 16, 1957.

37. See *Federal Communications Act of 1934*, Report 1850, U.S. House of Representatives, 73rd Congress, 2nd Session, June 1, 1934.

38. FDR rewarded the Texan by accepting his recommendation for a high-level job with the new commission. For the post of director of the Telegraph Division, Rayburn suggested his nephew, Robert T. Bartley. President Truman later named Bartley an FCC commissioner.

39. SR interview with DBH, undated.

40. SR conversation with DBH, Jan. 26, 1961.

41. Ray Tucker, "A Master for the House," *Collier's*, Jan. 5, 1935, 22–49.

42. The incident left Ickes with lingering contempt for Congress and a strong dislike for Rayburn that would be vented time and again in the interior secretary's *Secret Diary*. "Rayburn has pretty much opposed everything I have ever wanted on the Hill," Ickes complained in December 1935. See Harold Ickes, *The Secret Diary of Harold L. Ickes: The First Thousand Days* (N.Y.: Simon and Schuster, 1954), p. 491.

43. FDR, "Memorandum for Congressman Rayburn," May 23, 1935, FDR Library.

44. *New York Times*, June 6, 1934; also *Dallas Morning News*, April 17, 1935.

45. Cecil Dickson interview with DBH, May 21, 1957.

46. SR interview with DBH, undated.

47. Dickson interview with DBH, July 20, 1956.

10. "The Greatest Congressional Battle in History"

1. Contemporary accounts of the battle are found in *Time*, *Newsweek*, *New Republic*, *Literary Digest*, and other magazines. The newspaper accounts add more obscure details, particularly the *New York Times* and the *St. Louis Post-Dispatch*, whose correspondent Paul Y. Anderson worked actively with Senator Black in developing his investigation of lobbying. Valuable, too, are the dispatches of Ruth Finney in the Scripps-Howard newspapers, such as the *New York World-Telegram*. Finney also collaborated actively with Black in the investigation.

2. See Stewart H. Holbrook, *The Age of the Moguls* (N.Y.: Doubleday, 1953), pp. 230–244.

3. See James C. Bonbright and Gardiner C. Means, *The Holding Company: Its Significance and Its Regulation* (N.Y.: McGraw-Hill, 1932); also Norman S. Buchannan, "The Origin and Development of the Public Utility Holding Company," *Journal of Political Economy*, Feb. 1936, 31–53; and N. R. Danielian, "Power and the Public," *Harper's*, June 1935, 26–47.

4. See SR speeches in the House of Representatives, *Congressional Record*, June 27 and Aug. 1, 1935, pp. 10315–10326, 12271–12273.

5. *Congressional Record*, Jan. 4, 1935, pp. 116–118.

6. See letter from Attorney General Homer Cummings to President Roosevelt, Feb. 26, 1935, FDR Library: "Whether this measure should provide only for orderly liquidation and salvage by enumerating certain specific prohibitions, or should provide for comprehensive regulation and control under wide administrative discretion is the question of policy which I called to your attention at the conference yesterday."

7. Ben Cohen interview with DBH, May 16, 1957.

8. Burton K. Wheeler, with Paul F. Healy, *Yankee from the West* (N.Y.: Doubleday, 1962), pp. 307–308.

9. *Congressional Record*, Jan. 11, 1935, pp. 374–378.

10. Years later, Wendell L. Willkie, president of Commonwealth and Southern Corporation, claimed without verification that he invented the phrase. See Joseph Barnes, *Willkie* (N.Y.: Simon and Schuster, 1952), pp. 82–83.

11. SR interview with DBH, undated.

12. Cohen interview with DBH, May 16, 1957.

13. Reprinted in the *Congressional Record*, Feb. 20, 1935, pp. 2432–2435.

14. See Rayburn's speech, Harvard Law School, Feb. 27, 1937.

15. Reporter Theodore C. Wallen of the *New York Herald Tribune*, quoted in Barnes, *Willkie*, pp. 86–87.

16. Burton K. Wheeler interview with DBH, May, 1957.

17. Drew Pearson and Robert S. Allen, "Washington Merry Go-Round," *St. Louis Post-Dispatch*, June 14, 1935.

18. DBH interview with Alla Clary, undated; also Paul Mallon column, *Washington Evening Star*, July 16, 1935.

19. Marion L. Ramsey, *Pyramids of Power* (Indianapolis: Bobbs-Merrill, 1937), pp. 256–257.

20. Ibid., p. 257.

21. See *Congressional Record*, June 27, 1935, pp. 10315–10326.

22. *Congressional Record*, June 28, 1935, p. 10353.

23. Twenty-five years later, Democratic Congressman Clarence Cannon of Ohio, eulogizing the Alabamian, recalled that his speech had been "classed by older members as one of the greatest ever delivered on the floor of the House."

24. *Congressional Record*, July 1, 1935, pp. 10500–10520.

25. See *Business Week*, July 6, 1935, 5: "The President had suffered a tremendous defeat, his most significant one so far. The flood of letters from millions of stockholders turned the tide and showed many a surprised rural congressman that he represented a great many investors in his district."

Said "T.R.B." in the *New Republic*, July 9, 1935, 244: "It seems doubtful whether Mr. Roosevelt can regain the mastery over Congress he once had. He flung his full strength into his fight against the death-sentence clause, and was publicly beaten. His reputation as a political wizard, with mysterious power, has vanished."

26. One notable exception was Rayburn's arch rival, Speaker Joe Byrns, who complained to members privately that the bill had been "miserably handled in committee." Rayburn, in turn, blamed Byrns's personal animosity toward him for some of the bill's difficulty in the House. The bitterness between the two congressmen grew out of their opposing candidacies for Speaker and never subsided.

27. *St. Louis Post-Dispatch*, July 2, 1935.

28. *New York World-Telegram*, July 3, 1935.

29. See *Newsweek*, July 13, 1935, 5–6.

30. See *Investigation of Lobbying Activities*, Hearings of the Senate Special Committee to Investigate Lobbying Activities, 74th Congress, 1st Session, 1935.

31. See *Investigation of Lobbying on Utility Holding Company Bills*, Hearings of the House Committee on Rules, 74th Congress, 1st Session, 1935.

32. See *Time*, July 22, 1935, 15.

33. See *Time*, July 29, 1935, 9–10.

34. Wrote Walter Lippmann: "The question was not whether the House bill or the Senate bill was the better. That was the pretext for a test of strength between the President and his progressive allies on the one hand, and the utilities and their conservative allies on the other. What they were really fighting about was whether the one side or the other could deliver a knockout blow." See Lippmann, *Interpretations, 1933–35* (N.Y.: Macmillan, 1936), pp. 283–285.

35. *Congressional Record*, Aug. 1, 1935, pp. 12265–12267.

36. See *St. Louis Post-Dispatch*, Aug. 2, 1935; also *Congressional Record*, Aug. 1, 1935, p. 12267.

37. The most complete and accurate reporting of this phase of the utility holding company fight appeared in the *St. Louis Post-Dispatch*.

38. See the *Washington Evening Star*, Aug. 14, 1935.

39. *Congressional Record*, Aug. 22, 1935, pp. 14162–14171.

40. Pete Brandt wrote of the compromise in the *St. Louis Post-Dispatch*, Aug. 24, 1935: "If it means what it seems to say, it is almost as severe as the Senate section which caused all the trouble."

41. *St. Louis Post-Dispatch*, Aug. 26, 1935.

42. *St. Louis Post-Dispatch*, Aug. 31, 1935.

43. William O. Douglas interview with DBH, June 18, 1956.

44. John Dempsey interview with DBH, July 17, 1956.

11. Up the Ladder

1. Dickson interview with DBH, May 21, 1957.

2. See Deward Brown, "Rural Electrification in the South 1920–1955" (Ph.D. dissertation, U. of California, Los Angeles, 1970), pp. 119–165; also M. W. Childs, *The Farmer Takes a Hand* (N.Y.: Doubleday, 1953).

3. *Congressional Record*, March 11, 1946, p. 2115.

4. SR speech at Princeton, Texas, Aug. 29, 1941.

5. One report had the utilities prepared to spend $15,000—a tremendous sum in those days—in Grayson County alone. See letter to SR from Will H. Evans, a Rayburn leader in Sherman, March 16, 1935.

6. See Frank C. Walker, *Request for Allocation of Funds for the Comprehensive Plan for Improvement of Red River Valley*, Division of Application and Information, National Emergency Council, Washington, D.C., May 24, 1935.

7. SR to Harold L. Ickes, Western Union night letter, Nov. 25, 1935.

8. See exchange of telegrams between SR and Ickes, Nov. 12–30, 1935, and Ickes letter to SR, Nov. 30, 1935; also Harold Ickes, *The Secret Diary of Harold L. Ickes: The First Thousand Days* (N.Y.: Simon and Schuster, 1954), p. 474.

9. Dick Rayburn to SR, May 1, 1935.

10. SR interview with George B. Tindall, associate professor of history, U. of N.C., July 2, 1959.

11. The one exception in the twentieth century came in 1919 when the Republicans passed over their leader, James R. Mann of Illinois, to elect Frederick H. Gillett of Massachusetts.

12. Cecil Dickson interview with DBH, May 21, 1957.

13. SR speech reported in the *Denison Herald*, Aug. 25, 1943.

14. Ibid.

15. This huge majority was, in Rayburn's opinion, a mixed blessing. Garner had long argued—and Rayburn concurred—that the most workable House majority was from fifty to sixty seats. With larger numbers, it was harder to convince members their votes were needed and to keep them on the floor, even for important votes. The apparent abundance of votes also led many members to vote as they wished, ignoring appeals for party unity on key issues.

16. Interestingly, in the final balloting, Rayburn's southern colleagues—who should have constituted his most dependable bloc—split, largely due to efforts of the utility companies. In Virginia, Rayburn got only one vote out of nine. Among Virginians voting against him was Rules Committee member Howard W. Smith, with whom Rayburn would cross swords many times in years to come. In Tennessee, Mississippi, and Oklahoma, votes divided almost equally between the two candidates.

17. Vinson, one of the ablest political figures of the century, who later would be named Chief Justice of the Supreme Court, and Rayburn served together for more than a decade. Quiet, honest, plainspoken, the pair were alike in many ways, and between them developed perhaps the closest friendship of Rayburn's life.

18. JNG interview with DBH, Uvalde, Texas, Nov. 23, 1959; see also contemporary notes of *Houston Post* reporter George Stimpson. Said Rayburn to DBH years later: "I'll tell you one thing about John Garner. When the time came for him to throw his feet out for you, he threw them all the way out."

19. See *New York Times*, Dec. 1, 1936.

20. The delegation's preference for Rayburn was only part of a broader scheme. Huey Long, implacable foe of FDR, was dead from an assassin's bullet. Members of his machine read the 1936 returns and decided they had better try to get back on the Roosevelt team. They were fully aware that before Long's assassination, Internal Revenue agents had been scrutinizing the financial affairs of Long and his lieutenants with great interest. Later Governor Leche and several other Long leaders were to go to prison for income tax evasion.

21. One member, Charles I. Faddis, refused to abide by the unit rule.

22. Thomas Corcoran interview with DBH, May 23, 1957.

23. Joe Bailey would have frowned on Rayburn's generosity toward opponents. Congressman John J. Dempsey cited this instance in an interview with DBH on July 17, 1956: "On Byrns's funeral train to Tennessee, O'Connor started talking to me about the new majority leader, telling me it was normal for the Rules Committee chairman to move up and asking me if I'd support him. I promised I would. When Rayburn was finally elected, I told him I thought he would make a fine leader.

" 'I didn't know you supported me,' he said.

" 'Don't get me wrong,' I replied, 'I supported O'Connor.'

" 'I'm glad you told me that,' Rayburn said. 'O'Connor got a lot of votes, but you're the first to tell me you voted for him.'

"From that day on, he treated me wonderfully."

12. Majority Leader

1. George Dixon column, *Washington Post*, Nov. 23, 1961.
2. William O. Douglas interview with DBH, June 18, 1956.
3. If Rayburn ever chewed tobacco in Washington, nobody ever saw it.
4. Medibel Bartley interview with DBH, Feb. 28, 1957.
5. SR conversation with DBH, June 12, 1959.
6. Cecil Dickson interview with DBH, May 21, 1957.
7. Paul Mallon, "Presenting Sam Rayburn—Man in the Shadows," in *Today*, Feb. 3, 1934. Mallon labeled Rayburn "one of the Secret Six who make the wheels go round, a power in government."
8. SR interview with DBH, undated.
9. Ibid.
10. SR letter to Judge John McDuffie, U.S. District Court, Mobile, Ala., April 30, 1937.
11. JNG interview with DBH, Nov. 23, 1959.
12. SR letter to R. L. Mullins, Wolfe City, Texas, March 29, 1937.
13. Lionel V. Patenaude, "The New Deal in Texas" (Ph.D. dissertation, U. of Texas, 1953), pp. 178–179.
14. Hatton Sumners interview with DBH, Dallas, Texas, Dec. 18, 1956.
15. Rayburn never forgave Sumners for refusing to help work out a compromise that would avoid a damaging party split. See former Congressman W. R. "Bob" Poage interview with Anthony Champagne, Nov. 8, 1979, SRL.
16. See William E. Leuchtenburg, *Franklin Roosevelt and the New Deal* (N.Y.: Harper and Row, 1963), pp. 271–273.
17. SR letter to R. L. Mullins, Wolfe City, Texas, March 29, 1937.
18. See *Newsweek*, April 18, 1938, p. 13.
19. FDR letter to Felix Frankfurter, Aug. 12, 1937.
20. SR letter to Hal C. Horton, Greenville, Texas, Nov. 26, 1937.
21. Rayburn sometimes shared the duty of presiding over the House with Edward Taylor of Colorado, which left him free to work the floor. See Carter Manasco, former administrative assistant to William Bankhead, interview with DBH, Jan. 24, 1957.
22. SR interview with DBH, Dec. 9, 1959; see also syndicated columnists Joseph Alsop and Robert Kintner, "The Capitol Parade," unidentified newspaper clipping, Feb. 1, 1938 (SR scrapbooks), SRL.
23. SR letter to the Reverend John A. Ellis, First Baptist Church, Sherman, Texas, Feb. 18, 1939.
24. Emil Hurja letter to SR, Sept. 7, 1937; SR letter to Hurja, Sept. 13, 1937; Ettie Garner letter to SR, Sept. 11, 1937.
25. Harold L. Ickes, *The Secret Diary of Harold L. Ickes* (N.Y.: Simon and Schuster, 1954), vol. 2, p. 699.
26. Ibid., p. 699.
27. JNG interview with DBH, Nov. 23, 1959.
28. Thomas Corcoran interview with DBH, May 25, 1957. Years later,

when Rayburn presided over his own "Board of Education," Frankfurter, then an associate justice of the Supreme Court, paid a return visit. Rayburn took great delight in retelling Corcoran's story to the assembled friends while Frankfurter, blushing furiously, silently nodded his head.

29. The other two: Attorney General Frank Murphy of Michigan and Governor Lloyd C. Stark of Missouri. Rayburn's nomination, Lindley argued, would subdue the threat of a serious bolt by conservatives in 1940 and would compel Garner himself to support the ticket. Ernest K. Lindley column, publication not identified, June 2, 1939 (SR scrapbooks), SRL; see also Lindley column, "Rayburn Held Hero," *Washington Post*, Aug. 18, 1939.

30. SR interview with DBH, undated, 1956.

31. SR letter to Alvin M. Owsley, Indianapolis, Ind., April 22, 1940.

32. SR letter to U.S. District Judge John McDuffie, Mobile, Ala., July 4, 1940.

33. Ickes, *The Secret Diary of Harold L. Ickes*, vol. 3, pp. 167–168.

34. Clinton Anderson, a young congressman in the early 1940s, was one of Ickes's many victims. See Anderson's *Outsider in the Senate* (N.Y.: World Publishing, 1970), p. 41.

35. James Roosevelt interview with Anthony Champagne, May 17, 1984, SRL.

36. See Lionel V. Patenaude, "The New Deal in Texas," (Ph.D. dissertation, U. of Texas, 1953), p. 131.

37. Robert A. Caro, *The Years of Lyndon Johnson: The Path to Power* (N.Y.: Knopf, 1982), p. 618.

38. See exchange of correspondence between SR and Sam Ealy Johnson, Feb. 12–27, 1937. In papers of John Holton, LBJ Library.

39. W. R. "Bob" Poage interview with Anthony Champagne, Nov. 8, 1979, SRL.

40. Lyle Boren interview with Anthony Champagne, May 28, 1985, SRL.

41. SR letter to Alvin J. Wirtz, Austin, March 9, 1938, Papers of Alvin J. Wirtz, LBJ Library.

42. Lady Bird Johnson interview with Anthony Champagne, Nov. 13, 1979, SRL.

43. W. B. Ragsdale interview with DCB, July 2, 1984.

44. LBJ interview with DBH, Jan. 11, 1957.

45. See series of letters and telegrams among SR, Myron Blalock, Alvin J. Wirtz, Austin Mayor Roy Miller, and others regarding the Texas political situation, April 10–30, 1940; also SR's handwritten revisions of the proposed compromise agreement drafted by Johnson (DBH-DCB files).

46. SR letter to W. A. Thomas, Dallas, Texas, March 8, 1940.

47. See George Norris Green, *The Establishment in Texas Politics: The Primitive Years, 1938–1957* (Westport, Conn: Greenwood Press, 1979; repr. Norman: U. of Oklahoma Press, 1984), p. 30.

48. Bankhead told Cecil Dickson: "If I make that speech it will kill me, but I think I would like to be Vice-President." Two months later, Bankhead was

dead. Dickson interview with DBH, May 21, 1957.

49. See *Dallas Morning News*, July 19, 1940.

50. William E. Leuchtenburg, *Franklin D. Roosevelt and the New Deal* (N.Y.: Harper Torchbooks, Harper and Row, 1963), p. 317.

51. See James A. Farley, *Jim Farley's Story* (N.Y.: McGraw-Hill, 1948), pp. 299–302.

52. Drew Pearson and Robert S. Allen, "Washington Merry-Go-Round," United Features Syndicate, *Odessa News-Times* and other papers, July 28, 1940.

53. SR letter to E. B. Germany, Dallas, Texas, July 31, 1940.

13. Ambition Fulfilled—and War

1. Sabath repaid Rayburn many times over by helping pry bills out of the Rules Committee after it was taken over by a coalition of Republicans and southern Democrats opposed to civil rights and other social legislation, although he was often philosophically opposed to such bills himself. Sometimes he would pretend to faint, the committee proceedings would stop, and he would be carried to a couch in a small side office. "While I'm fainted," he would say, "get the bill out." See former Congressman John E. Lyle interview with Anthony Champagne, undated, SRL.

2. See *Time*, Sept. 30, 1940, 15; also *Congressional Record*, Sept. 16, 1940, p. 12233.

3. Maury Maverick, then mayor of San Antonio, Texas, letter to SR, Oct. 5, 1940.

4. SR letter to Mayor Maury Maverick, San Antonio, Texas, Oct. 16, 1940. For more details on the Democratic congressional fund-raising effort, see Robert A. Caro, *The Years of Lyndon Johnson: The Path to Power* (N.Y.: Alfred A. Knopf, 1982), pp. 607–664.

5. See Patrick J. Nicholson, *Mr. Jim: The Biography of James Smither Abercrombie* (Houston: Gulf Publishing, n.d.), pp. 274–275; also J. R. Parten interview with Anthony Champagne, Jan. 19, 1980, SRL.

6. *The Leadership of Sam Rayburn, Collected Tributes of His Congressional Colleagues* (Washington, D.C: Government Printing Office, 1961), p. 26; also Booth Mooney, *Roosevelt and Rayburn* (Philadelphia: J. B. Lippincott, 1971), p. 142.

7. SR letter to W. A. Thomas, Oct. 19, 1942.

8. As Ray Peeler, who performed numerous political chores for Rayburn, described it: "Someone like [oilman Arch Rowan] could come up and visit him and say, 'Now, Sam, you are going to need money to get somebody elected in Idaho. Here is $2,000 in cash.' Of course, that is not a bribe in any sense of the word. Mr. Rayburn put it in his pocket and when the time came he got to Washington he would give it to somebody to go help the guy in Idaho get elected." Ray Peeler interview with Anthony Champagne, Feb. 25, 1981, SRL.

9. Caro, *The Years of Lyndon Johnson: The Path to Power*, p. 636.

10. LBJ letter to SR, Washington, Nov. 14, 1940.

11. "Bonham Man Boomed for Presidency," proclaimed a headline in the next day's *Austin American*. The *Dallas Morning News* was less enthusiastic in its headline: "Speaker Rayburn Termed of Presidential Timber." Rayburn did nothing to discourage such speculation. On the contrary, he seemed to encourage it by making himself available for more speeches, testimonials, and other appearances in the state.

12. *Dallas News*, Dec. 10, 1940.

13. FDR confidential letter to SR, Dec. 23, 1940.

14. Leading the fight for the bill was Rayburn's old friend and colleague, now an embittered anti–New Dealer, Hatton Sumners. See David Porter, "The Battle of the Texas Giants: Hatton Sumners, Sam Rayburn and the Logan-Walter Bill of 1939," *Texana*, 12, no. 4, 349–361.

15. See Bruce Catton column for NEA, Jan. 13, 1941 (SR scrapbooks), SRL.

16. See Marquis Childs article, *St. Louis Post-Dispatch*, Jan. 5, 1941.

17. Richard L. Strout in the *Christian Science Monitor*, Jan. 7, 1941.

18. See JNG letter to FDR, Dec. 26, 1940, FDR Library. "Dear 'Boss,'" Garner wrote, "I am certain you realize that I have a *real* affection for you, and I hope to have your good opinions to the end of my days. By the way! I am going to live to be ninety-three which gives me twenty-one years to go." (He lived to be ninety-nine.) FDR attached a note to Garner's letter, telling his secretary: ". . . as soon as Garner gets in . . . arrange to have him come around and see me some time that day."

19. SR letter to R. A. Clifton, McKinney, Texas, Feb. 1, 1941; also SR speech, NBC Blue Network, Feb. 9, 1941.

20. See column by Joseph Alsop and Robert Kintner, *Washington Post*, Jan. 30, 1941.

21. See *New York Daily News*, Feb. 7, 1941.

22. *Washington Evening Star*, Feb. 11, 1941.

23. SR speech, NBC Blue Network, Feb. 9, 1941.

24. JNG letter to SR, Sept. 16, 1940.

25. Of Speakers Reed and Cannon, Rayburn said in 1939: "I think [Reed] was one of the most fearless, one of the boldest and one of the ablest statesmen America ever produced. . . . I have always admired Mr. Reed and Mr. Cannon for one thing especially, and that is that they had the ability, they had the confidence in themselves to believe that they could exercise, well, all the power that went with the great office of Speaker under the rules of the House of Representatives. When I used to look upon Mr. Cannon in this House, I always thought that I looked upon a man with iron in his backbone and brains in his head." *Congressional Record*, Special Session, 1939, p. 570.

26. See George S. Wills, "Mr. Speaker and the Call to Arms: The Role of Sam Rayburn in the 1941 Extension of the Selective Service Act" (M.A. thesis, U. of Virginia, 1961), pp. 6–11.

27. SR letter to R. Morrison, San Antonio, Texas, July 26, 1941.

28. See *New York Times*, Aug. 11, 1941.

29. Ibid.

30. *New York Times*, Aug. 12, 1941.

31. Robert Sikes interview with DBH, July 12, 1956.

32. Jerry Voorhis, *Confessions of a Congressman* (N.Y.: Doubleday, 1947), p. 239.

33. Joe Martin, as told to Robert J. Donovan, *My First Fifty Years in Politics* (N.Y.: McGraw-Hill, 1960), pp. 96–99.

34. *New York Times*, Aug. 11, 1941.

35. Paul Kilday interview with DBH, 1957.

36. See Ned Brooks account, *Cleveland Press*, Aug. 12, 1941.

37. *Time* correspondent Frank McNaughton memorandum to his editors, Sept. 2, 1943 (DBH-DCB files).

38. See Robert Albright article, *Washington Post*, Nov. 25, 1941. "For 11 short minutes the future of the foreign policy of this government rested in the hand of one man. The hand was not the President's. The man was Sam Rayburn . . . "

39. The following March, the bill was passed by the Senate and sent to the President, who promptly vetoed it. Within five minutes, the Senate overrode the veto, the House following suit an hour later.

40. George Donovan interview with DCB, Feb. 1, 1967.

41. Stimson diary, Dec. 7, 1941, quoted in Gordon W. Prange, *At Dawn We Slept* (N.Y.: McGraw-Hill, 1981), p. 558.

42. *New York Times*, Dec. 8, 1941.

43. Robert E. Sherwood, *Roosevelt and Hopkins: An Intimate History* (N.Y.: Harper and Brothers, 1948), p. 433.

14. Wartime Speaker

1. Speech on accepting an honorary doctorate of law from Muhlenberg College, May 30, 1942. See *Congressional Record*, June 1, 1942, pp. A2157–A2158.

2. Internal memorandum of *Time* correspondent Frank McNaughton to his editors, Sept. 7, 1943, p. 37 (DBH-DCB files).

3. Connally retired from the Senate in 1952.

4. George Norris Green, *The Establishment in Texas Politics: The Primitive Years, 1938–1957* (Westport, Conn.: Greenwood Press, 1979; repr. Norman: U. of Oklahoma Press, 1984), pp. 32–38; see also Robert A. Caro, *The Years of Lyndon Johnson: The Path to Power* (N.Y.: Alfred A. Knopf, 1982), pp. 676–753.

5. SR letter to P. M. Jenkins, Austin, Texas, Aug. 6, 1954.

6. Wright Patman interview with Joe B. Frantz, Aug. 11, 1972, LBJ Library, Oral History Project.

7. See Caro, *The Years of Lyndon Johnson: The Path to Power*, p. 755.

8. Charles Marsh telegram to SR, June 15, 1941, LBJ House Papers, LBJ Library. This is a carbon copy of Marsh's original. It is possible—but un-

likely—that the wire was never sent.

9. Memorandum of *Time* correspondent David Bulburd to his editors, June 20, 1941 (DBH-DCB files).

10. SR letter to Joseph F. Nichols, Greenville, Texas, July 29, 1941.

11. A Texas State Senate committee later investigated the campaign finances of O'Daniel and Johnson. Apparent irregularities were found on both sides. Brown and Root Construction Company, Johnson's leading financial backer, later paid a scaled-down tax assessment and fraud penalty of $372,000, allegedly in connection with its election expenses. See Green, *The Establishment in Texas Politics: The Primitive Years, 1938–1957*, pp. 37–38; also Caro, *The Years of Lyndon Johnson: The Path to Power*, pp. 741–753.

12. Joseph F. Nichols, Greenville, Texas, July 2, 1941.

13. Unsigned leaflet sent to Ira C. Turner, Bonham, Texas, July 21, 1942.

14. *Congressional Record*, Jan. 6, 1943, p. 7.

15. John McCormack contended that the meeting took place earlier, perhaps as early as April 1943. See McCormack correspondence, SRL.

16. Joe Martin, *My First Fifty Years in Politics* (N.Y.: McGraw-Hill, 1960), pp. 100–101.

17. Clarence Cannon letter to author Roland Young, undated. See Roland Young, *Congressional Politics in the Second World War* (N.Y.: Columbia U. Press, 1956), p. 45.

18. SR interview with David Brinkley, "Biographies in Sound: George C. Marshall," NBC radio network, July 3, 1958.

19. Memorandum of Joe Martin interview with *Time* correspondent Eleanor Welch, Sept. 18, 1943 (DBH-DCB files).

20. SR letter to Charles R. Jones, Bonham, Texas, April 25, 1944.

21. See James Roosevelt interview with Anthony Champagne, May 17, 1984, SRL.

22. See Roland Young, *The American Congress* (N.Y.: Harper and Brothers, 1958), pp. 121–123.

23. *Congressional Record*, June 7, 1944, p. 5471.

24. *New Republic*, July 10, 1944, pp. 44–46.

25. W. A. Thomas letter to G. C. Harris, Greenville, Texas, July 19, 1944.

26. SR letter to Lt. Dan Inglish, Pacific Theater, Aug. 7, 1944.

27. Karl A. Crowley letter to SR, May 24, 1944. In their resolution of dissolution, filed in late 1945, the Texas Regulars admitted by implication that they purposely blocked Rayburn's vice-presidential ambitions and took credit for the "accomplishment of bringing about the selection of Harry S. Truman," who was then President. See Paul Bolton column, *Marshall News Messenger*, Marshall, Texas, Aug. 6, 1945.

28. Tom C. Clark interview with Joe B. Frantz, Oct. 7, 1969, LBJ Library, Oral History Project.

29. SR letter to Lem Tittsworth, Bonham, Texas, Feb. 29, 1944.

30. See Green, *The Establishment in Texas Politics: The Primitive Years, 1938–1957*, pp. 52–54; also Anthony Champagne, *Congressman Sam Rayburn* (New

Brunswick, N.J.: Rutgers U. Press, 1984), pp. 104–105; and Clinton Anderson, with Milton Viorst, *Outsider in the Senate* (N.Y.: World Publishing, 1970), pp. 49–50.

31. SR letter to John and Ettie Garner, Uvalde, Texas, July 28, 1944.

32. Quoted in Champagne, *Congressman Sam Rayburn*, p. 107.

33, *Whitewright Sun*, Grayson County, Texas, July 13, 1944.

34. *Greenville Morning Herald*, July 13, 1944.

35. W. A. Thomas letter to SR, May 1, 1944.

36. Lee Simmons letter to SR, June 13, 1944.

37. Morris, who was married, with two children, was eligible for exemption as a state legislator.

38. G. C. Harris letter to SR, June 9, 1944.

39. W. M. "Pete" Rodes interview with Anthony Champagne, Emory, Texas, May 9, 1980, SRL.

40. For more on the Rayburn network and Rayburn's political style at home, see Champagne, *Congressman Sam Rayburn*.

41. See Booth Mooney, *Roosevelt and Rayburn* (Philadelphia: J. B. Lippincott, 1971), p. 197.

42. SR letter to William C. Mathes, Los Angeles, California, Nov. 24, 1944.

15. Gains and Losses

1. Cecil Dickson interview with Anthony Champagne, June 29, 1980, SRL.

2. See Lewis Deschler interview with DBH, Aug. 17, 1957.

3. See O. C. Fisher, *Cactus Jack* (Waco: Texian Press, 1982), p. 78; and Bascom N. Timmons, *Garner of Texas* (N.Y.: Harper and Brothers, 1948).

4. Clinton Anderson, with Milton Viorst, *Outsider in the Senate* (N.Y.: World Publishing, 1970), p. 40.

5. See Wright Patman interview with Joe B. Frantz, Aug. 11, 1972, LBJ Library, Oral History Project.

6. Douglas Chandor was commissioned by the House to paint Rayburn's official portrait, which was to hang, after Rayburn's death, in the Speaker's Lobby. Rayburn kept it meanwhile in the Board of Education. Another Chandor portrait of Rayburn was presented to East Texas State Teachers College in 1943. Said Chandor: "A more recalcitrant, a more rebellious subject I never had. . . . I'd get him placed and turn around to the flesh tints, and before I knew, I'd hear a swish and the slam of a door, and my subject would be gone." Unidentified newspaper clipping, Aug. 6, 1943 (SR scrapbooks), SRL.

7. DBH memorandum, "Experience with Sam Rayburn," Aug. 17, 1957.

8. Olin Teague interview with DBH, July 16, 1956.

9. Frank Ikard interview with Anthony Champagne, June 24, 1980, SRL.

10. See William S. White, *Majesty & Mischief* (N.Y.: McGraw-Hill, 1961), pp. 11–17; Harry S. Truman, *Year of Decisions* (N.Y.: Doubleday, 1955), pp. 4–5; Bernard Asbell, *When F.D.R. Died* (N.Y.: Holt, Rinehart and Winston, 1961), pp. 62–67; Booth Mooney, *Roosevelt and Rayburn* (Philadelphia:

J. B. Lippincott, 1971), p. 213.

11. HST interview with DBH, Independence, Mo., Oct. 5, 1961.

12. Ibid.

13. White, *Majesty & Mischief*, p. 12.

14. See Paul Bolton article, *Marshall News Messenger*, Marshall, Texas, April 24, 1945; also White, *Majesty & Mischief*, pp. 14–16.

15. Thomas G. Corcoran interview with DBH, May 23, 1957.

16. HST interview with DBH, Oct. 5, 1961.

17. SR letter to Roy Scott, Cleveland, Ohio, May 28, 1945.

18. *Congressional Record*, April 12, 1946, p. 3582.

19. SR letter to Sam N. Mays, Greenville, Texas, May 4, 1945.

20. Rayburn was adamant. "I told him to go on calling me Harry," Truman recalled later. "He said, 'No, I won't do it. After you are out of the White House, I go back to calling you Harry.' Sam was right about that. It's not because it was me, but is a mark of respect for the greatest office in the world." HST interview with DBH, Oct. 5, 1961.

21. SR conversation with DBH, 1959; see also SR interview with Paul Niven, "Washington Conversation," CBS radio network, Feb. 26, 1961.

22. SR letter to Alston Cockrell, Jacksonville, Fla., April 20, 1945.

23. HST interview with DBH, Oct. 5, 1961.

24. HST message to Congress, June 19, 1945.

25. SR letter to U.S. District Judge John McDuffie, Mobile, Ala., July 18, 1945.

26. *Denison Herald*, undated article, sometime before Sept. 1, 1945 (SR scrapbooks), SRL.

27. Valton J. Young, *The Speaker's Agent* (N.Y.: Vantage Press, 1956), p. 30.

28. Ibid., pp. 70–71.

29. *Sam Rayburn, Memorial Services Together with Remarks Presented in Eulogy*, 87th Congress, 2nd Session (Washington, D.C.: Government Printing Office, 1962), pp. 20–21; see also Wright Patman interview, 1972, LBJ Library, Oral History Project; SR letter to Mrs. F. H. Stalcup, Denison, Texas, April 12, 1945; and SR conversation with DBH, 1957: "I told the committee that unless they set aside a considerable sum for farm-to-market roads I would not approve it."

30. SR letter to R. Bonna Ridgway, Austin, Texas, April 17, 1945.

31. Young, *Speaker's Agent*, pp. 27–30.

32. SR letter to Will Rayburn, Bonham, Texas, April 27, 1939.

33. *Congressional Record*, May 1, 1952, p. 4730; also Sarah McClenden article, *Sherman Daily Democrat*, Sherman, Texas, May 4, 1952.

34. *Congressional Record*, Dec. 21, 1945, p. 12544.

35. SR letter to Pat Wilson, Leonard, Texas, Feb. 23, 1946.

36. See Peter Edson column for NEA Syndicate, July 30, 1946.

37. *Congressional Record*, May 16, 1946, pp. 5131–5132; also Nathan Robertson, "Rayburn Warns Capital 'Seethes with Lobbyists,'" *PM*, New York, March 12, 1946.

38. See William S. White, *The Taft Story* (N.Y.: Harper and Row, 1954), p. 56; also Dwayne L. Little, "The Political Leadership of Speaker Sam Rayburn, 1940–1961" (Ph.D. dissertation, U. of Cincinnati, 1970), p. 132.

39. SR letter to John McCormack, Oct. 23, 1946.

40. SR letter to U.S. District Judge John McDuffie, Mobile, Ala., Oct. 3, 1946.

16. Minority Leader

1. SR letter to J. N. Russell, Hico, Texas, Dec. 17, 1946.

2. Years later, Rayburn denied that he seriously considered retiring in 1948. "I never intended to retire unless I thought the Republicans would be in for a long time," he said. SR conversation with DBH, June 11, 1961.

3. SR letter to Ganson Purcell, Washington, Nov. 13, 1946.

4. SR letter to Don D. Dyer, Brownwood, Texas, Nov. 15, 1946.

5. See "Tex" Easley dispatch, AP, November 16, 1946 (SR scrapbooks), SRL.

6. "Rayburn Draft Growing," unidentified newspaper clipping, Nov. 12, 1947.

7. AP dispatch, Jan. 2, 1948; Les Carpenter article, *Dallas Times-Herald*, Jan. 4, 1947 (SR scrapbooks), SRL; Elizabeth Carpenter article, *Anniston Star*, Anniston, Ala., undated, 1947; also John McCormack interview with Anthony Champagne, March 11, 1980, SRL.

8. Said Rayburn: "There has never been an unpleasant moment between us. We have always had a definite understanding each with the other. When you have an understanding with Joe Martin, you can go on and forget it, because there is not any element in his makeup that makes for deception or for deceit." *Congressional Record*, Aug. 23, 1958, p. 17987.

9. AP story, unidentified newspaper clipping, Jan. 4, 1947 (SR scrapbooks), SRL.

10. William S. White, "The Untalkative Speaker," *New York Times Magazine*, Feb. 27, 1949, 10.

11. *Congressional Record*, Jan. 3, 1947, pp. 35–36.

12. HST interview with DBH, Oct. 5, 1961.

13. *Congressional Record*, May 7, 1947. p. 4741; see also "House Set to Vote on Greek Relief: Debate Closes in Blaze of Oratory," *Washington Post*, May 8, 1947; and *Dallas News*, May 8, 1947.

14. Fred A. Hartley, Jr., *Our National Labor Policy* (N.Y.: Funk and Wagnalls, 1948).

15. See Raymond Moley, *27 Masters of Politics* (N.Y.: Funk and Wagnalls, 1949), p. 248.

16. See Claude Wild interview with David G. McComb, Oct. 3, 1968, LBJ Library, Oral History Project.

17. *Congressional Record*, April 17, 1947. p. 3664; and *Congressional Record*, June 17, 1947, p. 7144; see also *Congressional Quarterly Almanac* (Washington, D.C.: Congressional Quarterly Service, 1947), pp. 279–307.

18. SR letter to Stephen M. Young, Cleveland, Ohio, Feb. 22, 1947.

19. SR letter to Roy Scott, Cleveland, Ohio, March 14, 1947.

20. SR letter to R. Ewing Thomason, El Paso, Texas, Oct. 13, 1947.

21. SR letter to Stephen M. Young, Cleveland, Ohio, Feb. 22, 1947.

22. *Congress and the Nation: 1945–64* (Washington, D.C.: Congressional Quarterly Service, 1965), pp. 1615–1616.

23. HST interview with DBH, Oct. 5, 1961.

24. SR typewritten statement, May 31, 1948.

25. Dwayne L. Little, "The Political Leadership of Speaker Sam Rayburn, 1940–1961 (Ph.D. dissertation, U. of Cincinnati, 1970), pp. 150–151.

26. SR letter to Lewis West, Hugo, Okla., March 30, 1948.

27. SR letter to Fagan Dickson, first assistant district attorney general of Texas, Austin, Texas, Jan. 25, 1949.

28. Quoted in C. Dwight Dorough, *Mr. Sam* (N.Y.: Random House, 1962), p. 435; also Little, "The Political Leadership of Speaker Sam Rayburn," pp. 214–215.

29. From SR form letter to constituents, June 9, 1948.

30. SR letter to J. L. "Tuck" Milligan, Kansas City, Mo., April 17, 1948.

31. SR speech text as released by the Democratic National Committee, Convention Headquarters, Philadelphia, Pa., July 14, 1948; also "Rayburn Hits Party 'Apathy' in Blunt Talk," *Washington Post*, July 14, 1948.

32. AP dispatch, Democratic National Convention, July 15, 1948. Connor would later attract national attention as Birmingham's black-bashing segregationist sheriff during the southern civil rights movement.

33. Jack Redding, *Inside the Democratic Party* (Indianapolis: Bobbs-Merrill, 1958), p. 169; also J. Leonard Reinsch interview with J. R. Fuchs, undated, HST Library.

34. See Buster Cole interview with Dwayne L. Little, Bonham, Texas, Aug. 12, 1965, SRL.

35. See *Dallas Morning News*, Sept. 15, 1948, 1.

36. See Frank Chappell in *Dallas Times Herald*, Sept. 22, 1948; see also Green, *The Establishment in Texas Politics: The Primitive Years, 1938–1957*, p. 111.

37. SR letter to Robert L. Holliday, El Paso, Texas, June 19, 1948; see also Truman memoirs, *Years of Trial and Hope, 1946–1952* (N.Y.: Doubleday, 1956), p. 179; and Redding, *Inside the Democratic Party*, pp. 175–184.

38. See various newspaper clippings, September–October 1938 (SR scrapbooks), SRL.

39. Ibid.

40. Lorraine Kimbrough interview with Anthony Champagne, Dec. 23, 1980, SRL; see also HST interview with DBH, Oct. 5, 1961.

41. SR letter to Garrett S. Claypool, Chillicothe, Ohio, Oct. 23, 1948.

42. An Austin intimate of Johnson's wrote Rayburn: "I told Lyndon that you made the best speech that I had heard and that he should be glad to give you either of his two arms if you ever needed one. Seriously, you did Lyndon more

good than any other person—and I am sure he does appreciate it." Colonel
Edwin R. York letter to SR, Oct. 11, 1948.

43. SR letter to Houston Harte, San Angelo, Texas, Nov. 16, 1948.

44. SR letter to U.S. District Judge Minor Moore, Los Angeles, California,
Nov. 30, 1948.

45. SR letter to Houston Harte, San Angelo, Texas, Nov. 16, 1948.

17. Mr. Sam

1. The coalition simply trampled over aging Chairman Adolph J. Sabath of
Illinois. The 21-day rule was, in part, Sabath's revenge. He insisted on personally proposing the new proviso to the House and supported Rayburn's controversial decision not to allow any debate or record vote on the motion. See
memo of *Time* correspondent Frank McNaughton to his editors, Jan. 3, 1949
(DBH-DCB files).

2. See *Congressional Record*, Jan. 20, 1950, p. 708.

3. See William S. White article, *New York Times*, Jan. 1, 1949; also James A.
Robinson, *The House Rules Committee* (Indianapolis: Bobbs-Merrill, 1963),
p. 71.

4. *Congressional Record*, July 27, 1949, p. 10291, and July 28, 1949, p. 10486.

5. *Congressional Record*, Aug. 17, 1949, p. 11683.

6. Correspondents of the House Radio and Television Gallery once peti-
tioned the Speaker to relax his TV ban. After laboring long for just the proper
wording of their remonstration, a delegation took the petition to his office and
presented it with great formality. Warily, Rayburn began reading it aloud: "We,
the correspondents of the House Radio and Television Gallery, remons . . .
remonstr . . . remonstr . . . Sheee-itttt." He held the petition over a waste
can, released it, watched it flutter down, and left the room. Issue closed.

7. See AP and UP dispatches, *Washington Evening Star* and other newspapers, Feb. 26–28, 1952, SRL.

8. *U.S. News & World Report*, April 7, 1950, 39.

9. DBH memorandum of SR visit, accompanied by Dolph Briscoe, H. G.
Dulaney, and DBH, to Garner's home in Uvalde, 1956.

10. SR interview with Raymond P. Brandt, *St. Louis Post-Dispatch*, Feb. 11,
1951.

11. See *Congressional Record*, May 16, 1949, pp. 6282–6283; also *New York
Times*, May 6, 1949.

12. See *Bonham Daily Favorite*, May 8, 1949, and Nov. 3, 1949 (SR scrapbooks), SRL.

13. "I received your letter of May 28, 1958, with reference to our friend and
his magnificent contribution," Rayburn wrote Buster Cole, treasurer of the
Sam Rayburn Foundation, on June 6. "I am sure you have written him something, therefore, I will not write him." See Dwayne L. Little, "The Political
Leadership of Speaker Sam Rayburn, 1940–1961" (Ph.D. dissertation, U. of

Cincinnati, 1970), pp. 375–378; also Anthony Champagne, *Congressman Sam Rayburn* (New Brunswick, N.J.: Rutgers U. Press, 1984), pp. 30–31.

14. *Mr. Speaker*, excerpts from the *Congressional Record*, Jan. 31, 1951, "not printed at government expense," no publisher identified, pp. 85–86.

15. *U.S. News & World Report*, April 7, 1950, 39.

16. J. R. Parten interview with DBH, undated.

17. SR speech to Texas oil executives and other Democratic contributors in Abilene, reported by Richard L. Lyons, *Washington Post*, Sept. 10, 1960.

18. SR conversation with DBH and others, June 20, 1956.

19. Olin Teague interview with DBH, July 16, 1956.

20. See Frank Ikard interview with Anthony Champagne, June 24, 1980, SRL.

21. Quoted in John Manley, "Recruitment to Ways and Means and Its Effect on Committee Behavior," Research Paper for the American Political Science Association, Study of Congress Project, 1964.

22. J. T. Rutherford interview with Anthony Champagne, June 18, 1980, SRL.

23. See *United States* vs. *Texas*, 339 U.S. 707 (1950); also "Symposium on the Texas 'Tidelands' Case," *Baylor Law Review*, Winter 1951, 201–240.

24. SR letter to Price Daniel, Austin, Texas, July 12, 1947; also Green, *The Establishment in Texas Politics: The Primitive Years, 1938–1957*, p. 143.

25. Price Daniel letter to SR, Jan. 19, 1948.

26. See Harry C. Withers column, *Dallas Morning News* June 23, 1949.

27. See "Offshore Oil Pact Asked by Rayburn," *New York Times*, May 31, 1949; also *Dallas Morning News*, June 23, 1919; and Price Daniel interview with Anthony Champagne, 1980, SRL. Daniel contended the compromise was initiated by oil lobbyists Clayton Iron of Ohio Oil Company and Elmer Patman of Superior Oil Company, who, in turn, sold it to Rayburn.

28. SR interview with DBH, undated.

29. SR letter to Howard D. Dodgen, executive secretary, Texas Game, Fish and Oyster Commission, Austin, Texas, March 3, 1950.

30. Harold L. Ickes letter to SR, June 8, 1951.

18. Rayburn for President

1. Internal memo, Washington Bureau, *Time* magazine, Jan. 21, 1952 (DBH-DCB files).

2. See SR letter to John D. Mitchell, Odessa, Texas, April 3, 1952; also SR letter to M. M. William, Houston, Texas, May 10, 1952.

3. See Allen S. Otten, "House Leader Rayburn Gets a Quiet Build-Up for Presidential Post," *Wall Street Journal*, June 10, 1952.

4. Ibid.

5. Ibid.

6. William Arbogast article, AP, May 24, 1952.

7. Charles I. Francis letter to SR, June 30, 1952.

8. SR letter to Charles I. Francis, Houston, Texas, July 6, 1952.

9. Democratic National Chairman Stephen A. Mitchell apparently was first to give Rayburn the title of "Mr. Democrat." See *Sherman Daily Democrat*, Nov. 1, 1953.

10. See Green, *The Establishment in Texas Politics: The Primitive Years, 1938–1957*, p. 145.

11. *New York Times*, July 22, 1952.

12. See Lyle Wilson's dispatch for UPI, "Rayburn's Firm Hand Averted Split by Demos in 1952 Meet," *Austin Statesman-American*, Jan. 15, 1960.

13. SR letter to Silliman Evans, Nashville, Tenn., Aug. 21, 1952. Rayburn told Evans, a disgruntled Kefauver backer: "You can't be King-Maker unless you have the right material to make a King of, and in my opinion, you did not have it in this instance."

14. Rayburn and Cannon cordially detested one another. See the *Progressive*, June 1959. Denying published reports that the two did not get along, Cannon told the House: "Simply because no one else likes Speaker Rayburn is no reason why I should not like him. . . . Speaker Rayburn told me he was for me and would always be for me, even if I went to the penitentiary, which, he added reflectively, was quite likely."

15. SR interview with DBH, undated.

16. Robert Slagle interview with Anthony Champagne, Oct. 17, 1980, SRL.

17. See SR letter to Alf Morris, Winnsboro, Texas, Nov. 10, 1952; also Ray Peeler interview with Anthony Champagne, Feb. 25, 1981, SRL.

18. Sturge Steinert letter to SR, March 8, 1956. Rayburn's response: "I think you will find Lyndon has been a good Democrat all the time. . . . He was in the Dallas office many times and was very helpful all the way through." SR letter to Steinert, San Antonio, Texas, March 15, 1956, LBJ A files, LBJ Library.

19. Pat Mayse letter to SR, Nov. 15, 1952. See Green, *The Establishment in Texas Politics: The Primitive Years, 1938–1957*, pp. 146–147.

20. See Allan Shivers interview with Joe B. Frantz, May 29, 1970, LBJ Library, Oral History Project: "I talked to Mr. Rayburn on several occasions about it, before and after we got to Chicago, and told him that we could not pledge that we would vote for whoever the nominee was. . . . Events which caused us not to support Stevenson occurred after the convention, not during the convention."

21. INS dispatch, Sept. 23, 1952.

22. Ralph Yarborough letter to Random House, Inc., Aug. 13, 1962.

23. SR letter to Judge Ewing Thomason, U.S. District Court, El Paso, Texas, Nov. 30, 1952.

24. SR letter to Paul Bolton, KTBC, Austin, Texas, Nov. 15, 1952.

25. SR letter to Judge Thomason, El Paso, Texas, Nov. 30, 1952; also SR letter to Cecil B. Dickson, Paeonian Springs, Va., Nov. 10, 1952.

19. The Peak of Power

1. See SR interview, AP, Jan. 6, 1953; also *Dallas Morning News*, Nov. 21, 1952.

2. *Time*, Jan. 12, 1953, 21.

3. SR letter to Mrs. Samuel Wolff, Reading, Pa., March 13, 1954; also *U.S. News & World Report*, Jan. 8, 1954, pp. 51–53.

4. DDE interview with Raymond Henle, July 13, 1967, Herbert Hoover Presidential Library.

5. *U.S. News & World Report*, Jan. 8, 1954, pp. 52–53.

6. SR letter to James O. Hall, El Paso, Texas, April 2, 1953.

7. *Congressional Record*, April 21, 1953, p. 3492.

8. *U.S. News & World Report*, Jan. 8, 1954, p. 53.

9. SR letter to E. J. Lilley, Denison, Texas, March 13, 1953.

10. See *Dallas Morning News*, undated clipping, November 1953.

11. SR conversation with DBH, Dec. 18, 1955.

12. SR letter to G. E. Hutcheson, Anne, Texas, Dec. 14, 1953.

13. SR letter to James S. Alderman, Bellaire, Texas, Oct. 30, 1953.

14. SR letter to John W. Carpenter, Dallas, Texas, March 25, 1955.

15. SR letter to Raymond Wilson, McKinney, Texas, Aug. 18, 1954.

16. SR speech, nationally telecast over NBC from Fort Worth, Sept. 10, 1954. See *New York Times*, Sept. 11, 1954.

17. SR letter to John W. McCormack, Dorchester, Mass., Sept. 22, 1953.

18. SR letter to John J. Dempsey, Santa Fe, N.M., Nov. 11, 1953.

19. SR letter to John W. McCormack, Dorchester, Mass., Dec. 28, 1953.

20. *Congress and the Nation* (Washington, D.C.: Congressional Quarterly Service, 1965), pp. 1718–1727; also Richard H. Rovere, *Senator Joe McCarthy* (N.Y.: Harcourt, Brace, 1959); and William F. Buckley, Jr., and L. Brent Bozell, *McCarthy and His Enemies* (Chicago: Henry Regnery, 1954).

21. SR letter to Mrs. Samuel Wolff, Reading, Pa., March 13, 1954.

22. Harry Dexter White.

23. See James Reston column, *New York Times*, Nov. 5, 1954.

24. SR letters to Eugene G. Bizzell, Austin, Texas, July 10, 1954, and Joseph S. Myers, Houston, Texas, Oct. 25, 1954.

25. *Congressional Record*, Jan. 5, 1955, p. 10.

26. SR speech, National Press Club, May 27, 1958.

27. Neil MacNeil conversation with DBH, undated.

28. SR speech, San Antonio, Texas, Oct. 15, 1953.

29. *1953 Congressional Quarterly Almanac, 1953* (Washington, D.C.: Congressional Quarterly Service, 1954), p. 77.

30. See the *Progressive*, June 1959, 25–28.

31. See *New York Times*, March 2, 1954; see also Joe Martin, as told to Robert J. Donovan, *My First Fifty Years in Politics* (N.Y.: McGraw-Hill, 1960), pp. 216–220.

32. Kenneth Roberts (D-Ala.), George H. Fallon (D-Md.), Clifford Davis (D-Tenn.), Alvin M. Bentley (R-Mich.), and Ben F. Jensen (R-Iowa).

33. SR letter to Mr. and Mrs. M. L. Crowell, Royse City, Texas, May 21, 1954.

34. SR statement in the *Dallas Morning News*, Aug. 23, 1954.

35. SR-LBJ telegram to President Eisenhower, Nov. 4, 1954. "It takes two belligerents to make a war, and therefore, there will be none unless it is initiated by the Executive Branch. We believe that you will not let that occur . . . " See also AP story from Washington, various newspapers, Oct. 10, 1954.

36. See Robert Donovan, *Eisenhower: The Inside Story* (N.Y.: Harper and Brothers, 1956), p. 311; and Rowland Evans and Robert Novak, *Lyndon B. Johnson: The Exercise of Power* (N.Y.: New American Library, 1966), pp. 86–87.

37. John O'Donnell in the *New York Daily News*, Nov. 18, 1954.

38. *New York Times*, Nov. 5, 1954.

39. Ibid.

40. *New York Daily News*, Nov. 19, 1954.

20. Rayburn and Johnson

1. When dial telephones were installed in the Capitol, Rayburn refused to use them. He insisted on keeping one direct line to the Capitol operator and continued to place all his calls through the operator. When the Sam Rayburn Library opened in Bonham in 1957, he ordered the telephone company to remove a second line that had been installed. The library still had only one line in 1986.

2. William Arbogast interview with DBH, Dec. 11, 1957.

3. H. G. Dulaney interview with Anthony Champagne, Aug. 15, 1980, SRL.

4. Lorraine Kimbrough interview with Anthony Champagne, Dec. 23, 1980, SRL.

5. In a commencement speech in 1955, Rayburn said: "I have lived quite a while but I know that I shall be old only when some day I find myself sitting around with others bewailing the younger generation and talking about how much better we did things in our day."

6. LBJ interview with DBH, Jan. 11, 1957.

7. SR conversations with DBH, various dates.

8. John W. Mashek, chief national correspondent, *U.S. News & World Report*, interview with DCB, July 28, 1980.

9. Richard L. Strout's article, *Christian Science Monitor*, Feb. 18, 1955.

10. Quoted in Drew Pearson column, *Washington Post*, and other newspapers, March 15, 1955.

11. See *Congressional Record*, July 16, 1958, p. 13978; also UPI story, *Bonham Daily Favorite* and other newspapers, July 16, 1958; and Robert K. Walsh article, *Washington Evening Star*, July 17, 1958.

12. See Bryce Harlow interviews, Feb. 27–March 27, 1967, DDE Library,

vol. 1, p. 29, and vol. 2, p. 64.

13. Emmet John Hughes, *The Ordeal of Power* (N.Y.: Atheneum, 1963), p. 232.

14. *New York Times*, June 12, 1955.

15. *Christian Science Monitor*, Dec. 12, 1954.

16. James C. Hagerty diaries, Feb. 22, 1955, DDE Library.

17. *New York Times*, March 1, 1955; also Drew Pearson column, *Washington Post*, March 15, 1955; and Doris Fleeson column, *Washington Evening Star*, Feb. 27, 1955.

18. See SR statement, *Congressional Record*, June 23, 1955, p. A4615.

19. *Congress and the Nation* (Washington, D.C.: Congressional Quarterly Service, 1965), pp. 980–984.

20. SR interview with DBH, May 1, 1957.

21. Former Texas Congressman J. T. Rutherford interview with Anthony Champagne, June 18, 1980, SRL.

22. See Rowland Evans and Robert Novak, *Lyndon B. Johnson: The Exercise of Power* (N.Y.: New American Library, 1966), pp. 88–92.

23. Clinton Anderson, with Milton Viorst, *Outsider in the Senate* (N.Y.: World Publishing, 1970), p. 140.

24. SR conversation with DBH, Dec. 18, 1955.

25. Rayburn's "little squib" later was selected as story of the year by Texas newspaper editors.

26. See Allan Shivers interview with Joe B. Frantz, May 29, 1970, LBJ Library, Oral History Project.

27. Shivers claimed Byron Skelton, chairman of the loyalist Texas Democratic Advisory Council, originated the idea and "used Rayburn as his voice." It is true that Skelton and Houston attorney Marlin Sandlin flew to Washington to persuade Rayburn to endorse LBJ for favorite son. Their aim was to block Shivers from either seeking the honor for himself or embracing Johnson for the role, thus ensuring Shivers's own selection as party chairman. There was no mention of endorsing LBJ for both roles. See Byron Skelton interview with Anthony Champagne, Aug. 13, 1980, SRL. Skelton told the press in 1956: "No one tells Sam Rayburn what to do and no one uses him as a voice for anything." Rayburn also denied Skelton had influenced his action. SR press conference, March 26, 1956; also *Texas Observer*, March 28, 1956; and Elizabeth Carpenter's article, *Houston Post*, May 28, 1956.

28. LBJ interview with DBH, Jan. 11, 1957. See also Elizabeth Carpenter's article, *Houston Post*, May 28, 1956; and Green, *The Establishment in Texas Politics: The Primitive Years, 1938–1957*, pp. 171–172.

29. The population in the district, 215,000 when Rayburn was elected in 1912, had grown only slightly in half a century. Rayburn was redistricted only once, after the 1930 census, receiving two relatively small counties that shared the characteristics of the other counties.

30. See Anthony Champagne, *Congressman Sam Rayburn* (New Brunswick, N.J.: Rutgers U. Press, 1984), pp. 16–18; also C. Dwight Dorough, *Mr. Sam*

(N.Y.: Random House, 1962), p. 453; and Texas State Senator A. M. Aikin, speech transcript, Sam Rayburn Memorial Day ceremonies, Bonham, Texas, Jan. 6, 1978, SRL.

31. Congressman Hale Boggs of Louisiana, conversation with DBH, June 20, 1956.

32. Speech by Allan Shivers, Houston, Texas, March 28, 1956.

33. SR press release, April 28, 1956.

34. See Green, *The Establishment in Texas Politics: The Primitive Years, 1938–1957*, pp. 174–178; also J. R. Parten interview with Anthony Champagne, Jan. 19, 1980, SRL.

35. Francis E. "Tad" Walter interview with DBH, undated.

36. Creekmore Fath article, *Texas Observer*, April 15, 1960.

37. SR letter to Mrs. R. D. Randolph, Aug. 24, 1956.

38. Ralph G. Martin, *Ballots and Bandwagons* (Chicago: Rand McNally, 1964), p. 400. Martin, a member of Stevenson's campaign staff, has provided the most detailed account of maneuvering for the vice-presidential nomination. Soon after the Convention, he interviewed most of the principals. Several quotations in this section are from his book.

39. Ibid., p. 402.

40. Ibid., p. 413.

41. See Evans and Novak, *Lyndon B. Johnson: The Exercise of Power*, p. 238; also Martin, *Ballots and Bandwagons*, p. 437.

42. Martin, *Ballots and Bandwagons*, p. 442.

43. Rayburn's admission that he had been "unable to preside effectively in 1956" was made in casual conversation with a stranger seated next to him on an American Airlines flight to Dallas, April 22, 1959. Nearly blind, he had asked the stranger, John A. Fahey, an associate professor at Old Dominion University, Norfolk, Va., to read to him a magazine article. Fahey later described their fascinating two-hour conversation, which included verifiable personal observations by the Texan that he seems never to have discussed with close friends.

44. Lehman statement, Jan. 18, 1957, reprinted in the *Texas Observer*, April 15, 1960.

45. See Evans and Novak, *Lyndon B. Johnson: The Exercise of Power*, p. 161; Butler's 1956 comment quoted in the *Texas Observer*, April 15, 1960.

46. See *New York Times*, Dec. 13, 1956.

21. The Golden Years

1. See "Capital Face-Lift Battle Flaring into Bitterness," AP, *Temple Telegram*, Temple, Texas, and other newspapers, March 13, 1958.

2. Memorandum to the Speaker from the Architect of the Capitol, May 26, 1958.

3. SR speech, National Press Club, Washington, May 27, 1959.

4. Ibid.

5. Editorial, *Milwaukee Journal*, Feb. 27, 1959.

6. JNG interview with DBH, Nov. 23, 1957.

7. SR interview with DBH, March 4, 1959.

8. SR letter to JNG, Sept. 22, 1953.

9. *Congressional Record*, Jan. 6, 1954, p. 10.

10. See *Look*, June 16, 1956.

11. SR interview with Paul Niven, "Washington Conversation," CBS television network, Feb. 26, 1961.

12. George Mahon interview with DBH, July 16, 1956.

13. Olin Teague interview with DBH, July 16, 1957.

14. SR letter to J. C. Phillips, editor *Borger News Herald*, Borger, Texas, April 10, 1961.

15. SR letter to Charles R. Campbell, Dallas, Texas, May 7, 1957.

16. SR interview with *Time* correspondents Neil MacNeil and Loye Miller, Jan. 19, 1961.

17. H. G. Dulaney interview with Anthony Champagne, Aug. 15, 1980, SRL; also various SR conversations with DBH. One Texas newspaperwoman in the 1950s did break Rayburn's rule to report a private conversation in which the Speaker confided to a colleague that he had just cast his absentee ballot for Ralph Yarborough for governor in the Democratic primary. But Rayburn never counted that incident as a breach of trust because he intentionally allowed the reporter to eavesdrop. It was his way of helping Yarborough without openly getting involved in a state race.

18. William Arbogast interview with DBH, Dec. 11, 1957.

19. SR letter to Mrs. Pearl L. Wincom, Dallas, Texas, Oct. 14, 1952.

20. See J. T. Rutherford interview with Anthony Champagne, June 18, 1980, SRL.

21. See H. G. Dulaney, Edward Hake Phillips, and MacPhelan Reese, *Speak, Mr. Speaker* (Bonham, Texas: Sam Rayburn Foundation, 1978), p. 259.

22. Richard Bolling, *House Out of Order* (N.Y.: E. P. Dutton, 1965), p. 177.

23. Ibid., p. 177.

24. Harry R. Sheppard interview with DBH, July 16, 1956.

25. Bolling, *House Out of Order*, p. 181.

26. SR interview with DBH, undated.

27. *Congressional Record*, June 8, 1956, pp. 8914–8916.

28. See Jim Wright interview with Anthony Champagne, June 23, 1980, SRL.

29. Carl Albert interview with DBH, undated, 1956.

30. Jim Wright interview with Anthony Champagne, June 23, 1980, SRL.

31. See *Congressional Quarterly Almanac* (Washington, D.C.: Congressional Quarterly Service, 1957), p. 553.

32. See Richard Hansen, *The Year We Had No President* (Lincoln: U. of Nebraska Press, 1962), pp. 69–87.

33. SR interview with DBH, May 1, 1957.

34. See Drew Pearson column, *Washington Post*, and other newspapers, April 8, 1957; also Dwight D. Eisenhower diaries, March 29, 1957, Box 13, DDE Library.

35. SR interview with DBH, May 1, 1957; see also Sherman Adams, *First-hand Report* (N.Y.: Harper and Brothers, 1961), pp. 200–201. Eisenhower, who believed the Presidency should be handed down to members of the same political party, favored removing the Speaker from the order of succession. Because of Brownell's opposition, no such recommendation was made.

36. The defect was remedied with the ratification of the 25th Amendment in 1967.

37. See Donald Young, *American Roulette* (N.Y.: Holt, Rinehart and Winston, 1965), pp. 273–274.

38. See UP article "Rayburn Reluctantly Agrees on Bill to Let Ailing President Step Aside," various newspapers, Jan. 30, 1958; also Marshall McNeil article, *Pittsburgh Press*, and other Scripps-Howard newspapers, Feb. 3, 1958.

39. See Warren Unna analysis, *Washington Post*, June 21, 1957; also Frank Eleazer article, UPI, *Washington Post,* June 20, 1957.

40. Speaker's staff memorandum, June 27, 1957.

22. Johnson for President

1. Martin's defeat came on Rayburn's birthday. That evening, tired and shaken, the old GOP war-horse attended a party for Rayburn at the National Democratic Club. "Have you got some little cubbyhole down in the basement that you can put me in?" he asked the Speaker. "It's the first defeat I have suffered. It may put five years on my life." Martin, two years younger than Rayburn, died in 1968.

2. See *New York Times*, Jan. 3, 1959.

3. See *Texas Observer*, April 15, 1960.

4. See David C. Williams, "Mr. Sam's House," *Progressive*, June 1959, 23–25.

5. See *New York Times*, July 7, 1959.

6. See AP dispatch, "House Speaker Backs Disputed Labor Curb Bill," *Sacramento Bee*, Sacramento, California, and other newspapers, Aug. 3, 1959.

7. SR speech over Mutual Broadcasting System, Aug. 10, 1959. See also *New York Times*, Aug. 11, 1959.

8. SR conversation with DBH, undated, 1959.

9. See DBH letter to his mother, Aug. 16, 1959; also Phil M. Landrum interview with Ronald J. Grele, Oct. 20, 1965, JFK Library. Landrum, noting that Rayburn remained silent during debate and made little last-minute effort to change votes, speculated that the Speaker had secret misgivings about the measure. Landrum never knew just how furious Rayburn was when the bill passed.

10. See HST letter to SR, June 30, 1960. "You and I had a conversation once

when we decided on two men that were capable of being President of the United States under present conditions; one was Lyndon Johnson and the other was Stuart Symington."

11. SR conversation with DBH, undated, 1959.

12. LBJ remarks to SR at the Board of Education, spring 1960, overheard by DBH and others.

13. SR conversation with DBH, undated, 1960.

14. See SR letter to the Reverend Billy Graham, Aug. 18, 1960; also SR conversation with John W. Mashek, then a reporter for the *Dallas Morning News*, June 1960.

15. In a *Newsweek* poll of fifty Washington correspondents (June 20, 1960), Johnson and Rayburn were chosen "the ablest men in Congress." Johnson got forty-one votes, Rayburn thirty-six.

16. *Washington Evening Star*, March 27, 1960.

17. DBH personal memorandum, undated.

18. See *Congressional Record*, June 2, 1960, p. 10925.

19. AP dispatch, *Washington Evening Star*, July 1, 1960.

20. Theodore C. Sorensen, *Kennedy* (N.Y.: Harper and Row, 1965), p. 155.

21. Rayburn predicted in March that Johnson would get 400 votes on the first ballot. See *Washington Evening Star*, March 27, 1960.

22. SR conversation with DBH, summer 1960.

23. Former Congressman, later U.S. Customs Court Judge, Eugene Worley interview with T. Harrison Baker, Oct. 16, 1968, LBJ Library.

24. Sorensen, *Kennedy*, p. 163.

25. LBJ conversation with DBH and others, July 1960.

26. Robert Notti, personal aide to H. L. Hunt, interview with William McHugh, April 10, 1967, LBJ Library. Notti and Hunt were in the Johnson suite.

27. See *U.S. News & World Report*, Jan. 16, 1967, 44–45.

28. Hale Boggs interview with DBH, 1962; see also Boggs interview with Charles T. Morrissey, May 10, 1964, JFK Library; and Arthur Krock's chronology, *New York Times*, Aug. 30, 1965.

29. SR conversation with DBH, summer 1960.

30. Ibid.

31. Ibid.

32. See *Washington Post*, June 20, 1965.

23. "The Worst Fight of My Life"

1. Most of the descriptions and conversations in this chapter are based on D. B. Hardeman's account as Rayburn's staff assistant and confidant. Hardeman's personal diary, which he kept daily during this period, has been used extensively in piecing together Rayburn's actions and view of the Rules fight. Interviews with other principals and examination of documents, press accounts,

and other contemporary studies, particularly those of Professor Robert L. Peabody of Johns Hopkins University and *Time* congressional correspondent Neil MacNeil, also have been useful in rounding out the picture of the complex events.

2. Roland Young, *The American Congress* (N.Y.: Harper and Brothers, 1958), pp. 120–123.

3. Smith always suspected that Rayburn used him as a "buffer." In 1966, he told Robert C. Albright of the *Washington Post*: "When any civil rights legislation came along, I fought it from the beginning to the end. Sam knew that. He wasn't too enthusiastic about some of the bills either." *Washington Post*, Aug. 29, 1966.

4. For the best description of the Rules fight as viewed by a leading House liberal, see Richard Bolling, *Power in the House* (N.Y.: E. P. Dutton, 1968), pp. 195–220.

5. SR conversation with DBH, undated. For more on the Cannon episode, see Kenneth W. Heckler, *Insurgency* (N.Y.: Columbia U. Press, 1940), pp. 27–82; also Milton C. Cummings, Jr., and Robert L. Peabody, *New Perpectives on the House of Representatives*, edited by Robert L. Peabody and Nelson W. Polsby (N.Y.: Rand McNally, 1963), p. 169.

6. SR conversation with DBH, undated.

7. SR conversation with DBH and others at the Board of Education, Feb. 4, 1961.

8. *Time*, Feb. 10, 1961, 11–12.

9. Three other Mississippi Democrats—John Bell Williams, Jamie Whitten, and Arthur Winstead—also bolted the party in 1960. All held senior positions on key committees. Southerners believed the House would have been hard pressed to punish Colmer and not the other party defectors. Conservatives, therefore, viewed Rayburn's threat to purge Colmer as a broader threat to the seniority system itself.

10. DBH diary.

11. Ibid.; see also Neil MacNeil, *Forge of Democracy* (N.Y.: David McKay, 1963), p. 440.

12. *New York Times*, Jan. 25, 1961.

13. MacNeil, *The Forge of Democracy*, p. 440.

14. DBH diary.

15. Theodore C. Sorensen, *Kennedy* (N.Y.: Harper and Row, 1965), p. 341.

16. DBH diary.

17. Ibid.

18. Ibid.

19. On the day of the vote, Jim Milne, Martin's assistant, frantically tried to get a Republican to "pair" with the ex-Speaker—that is, abstain from having his vote counted by making a pair with Martin as a courtesy. One Republican after another turned him down. "I just have to be on record on this vote," they would say. Only at the last moment was the pair arranged. DBH diary.

20. *New York Herald Tribune*, Feb. 1, 1961.

21. *Congressional Record*, Jan. 31, 1961, p. 1504.

22. Ibid., p. 1507; also DBH diary.

23. Ibid., p. 1508; also DBH diary.

24. Majority Leader John McCormack interrupted Rayburn to say that, during McCormack's thirty-three years as a House member, Smith was the only person elected to the Rules Committee who had not been recommended by the Speaker and majority leader.

24. Willow Wild

1. SR conversation with Neil MacNeil, May 2, 1961.

2. Theodore C. Sorensen, *Kennedy* (N.Y.: Harper and Row, 1965), p. 341.

3. Neil MacNeil, congressional correspondent, *Time*, internal file to his editors in New York, June 16, 1961. Queried by his editors about rumors that Rayburn was "over the hill," MacNeil fired back a testy response: "Washington reporters for years have been writing that Rayburn is losing his grip, will soon retire. This magazine, in a recent issue, fell into the same blunder. The truth is that Rayburn is not as alert and vigorous as he was 20 years ago—who is? But he rules the House now with more force than he ever has." (DBH-DCB files).

4. See Lady Bird Johnson interview with Anthony Champagne, Nov. 13, 1979, SRL: "The Speaker was remarkably young in spirit all his life and didn't seem to know that he was old. He would say something about that old man, so and so, and as a matter of fact, *he* was the same age."

5. *Washington Post*, June 10, 1961.

6. *The Leadership of Sam Rayburn*, House Doc. 247, 87th Congress, 1st Session (Washington, D.C.: Government Printing Office), p. 118.

7. SR conversation with DBH, July 1961.

8. See Jack Anderson article, "Washington Merry-Go-Round," *Washington Post*, Aug. 14, 1961.

9. See SR interview with W. B. Ragsdale, *U.S. News & World Report*, Oct. 9, 1961, 58–61; also Ragsdale article, "An Old Friend Writes of Sam Rayburn," *U.S. News & World Report*, Oct. 23, 1961, 69–72.

10. SR letter to Knute Larson, student body president, Grace College.

11. News release, Baylor University Medical Center.

12. News release, Baylor University Medical Center, Oct. 24, 1961.

13. DBH unfinished letter to William C. Gibbons, Washington, Nov. 13, 1961.

14. AP article, "Speaker 'Just Quit Breathing,'" *Washington Post*, Nov. 16, 1961. Rayburn left the bulk of his modest estate—valued at less than $300,000 and consisting almost entirely of the family home in Bonham and three parcels of local farm land—to a surviving brother, two widowed sisters, and a host of nieces, nephews, grandnieces, and grandnephews. His treasure of personal papers, books, and historical mementos went to the Sam Rayburn Library in

Bonham. Medibel Rayburn Bartley was willed the Bonham home for her life-time, after which it was to pass to the library. See SR Last Will and Testament, Dec. 16, 1960, SRL; also "Sam Rayburn Will Filed for Probate," *McKinney Daily Courier*, Dec. 4, 1961.

Index

Abercrombie, James, 250, 349
Acheson, Dean, 383
ADA. *See* Americans for Democratic Action
Adams, John, 72
Adams, Sherman, 379, 386
Adamson, William C., 67–69, 75–77, 84, 88, 90, 486n.14
AFL, 98
AFL-CIO, 431
Agrarians, 485n.5
Agriculture, 111, 315–18, 507n.29
Agriculture Committee. *See* House Agriculture Committee
Alaska, 383
Albert, Carl, 304, 421
Albright, Robert C., 184
Aldrich, Winthrop, 177
Alexander, Joshua W., 93
Alger, Bruce, 417
Allen, Robert S., 175, 197, 241
American Democratic National Committee, 296
American Farm Bureau Federation, 162, 458
American Federation of Labor, 98, 431
American Institute of Architects, 409
American Medical Association, 162, 458
Americans for Democratic Action, 384

Amos, Lucinda. *See* Rayburn, Lucinda Amos
Amos, William, 12
Andersen, H. Carl, 269
Anderson, Clinton, 260, 305, 395, 501n.34
Anderson, Martin, 395
Anderson, Paul Y., 195, 496n.1
Appropriations Committee. *See* House Appropriations Committee
Arbogast, William, 415, 460
Arens, Richard, 424
Arkwright, Preston, 174
Arvey, Jacob, 366, 403
Ashby, Henry M., 13
Ashurst, Henry F., 222, 223
Aston, J. Lee, 53, 478
Atomic bomb, 289–91

Bagby, W. T., 56
Bailey, Joseph Weldon: assessment of SR, 3, 60, 484n.23; attempted political comeback, 488n.53; campaigns, 55, 109–10; career, 25–28; coalition Cabinets, 234–35; expensive tastes, 39; involvement with Waters-Pierce Oil Company, 39–42; resignation from Senate, 282, 484n.29; "Rogue's gallery" speech, 44–45, 483n.14; SR admitted to practice before Supreme Court, 483n.17; SR's view of as teenager, 27–28; Texas House investigation of, 43–45; treatment of opponents, 499n.23; U.S. senator, 39, 42–43
Baker, Ray Stannard, 75, 84
Balch, George T., 286–87, 297
Ball, Grady, 412–13, 473
Bangs, George A., 366–67
Bankhead, Henry M., 244
Bankhead, John H., 244
Bankhead, Mrs. William, 244
Bankhead, Tallulah, 244
Bankhead, William B., 164–65, 207, 222, 226, 227, 240–45, 306, 501–502n.48
Banking, 49, 148–49
Banking and Currency Committee. *See* House Banking and Currency Committee; Senate Banking and Currency Committee
Barkley, Alben: appointment to House Interstate and Foreign Commerce Committee, 67, 116; committee hearings, 69; death, 453;

Democratic National Convention keynote address, 334, 335; election to Senate, 116; presidential bid, 357, 358, 360; Senate leadership, 227, 312, 326; utility holding companies bill, 196; vice-presidential bid, 291, 338, 368
Barkley, Mrs. Alben, 128
Barryman, Cliff, 61
Bartley, Medibel Rayburn, 1, 6–7, 14, 21, 29, 36, 82, 218, 478, 521–22n.14
Bartley, Robert T., 469, 495n.38
Baruch, Bernard, 334
Battle, John S., 364, 365
Baumhart, Albert, 268
Beaman, Middleton, 494n.21
Benson, Ezra, 379
Benton, Thomas Hart, 107
Bentsen, Lloyd, 359–60
Berryman, Cliff, 306
Biffle, Les, 339, 368
Black, Hugo, 188–91, 193–95
Blacks: Civil Rights Act of 1957, 421–22; during 1920s, 111, 113; Fair Employment Practices Commission, 298; legislation pertaining to, 484n.19; Supreme Court school desegregation decision, 384–85; Truman civil rights program, 331–33; voting-rights bill, 418–20. *See also* Civil rights
Blair, Bill, 403
Blakley, William, 348
Blalock, Myron, 239, 348
Bland, Mrs. Schuyler Otis, 126
Blanton, Thomas L., 163, 164
Bloom, Sol, 258
Board of Education, 303–308, 389–90, 413, 500–501n.28. *See also* Bureau of Education
Boggs, Hale, 127–28, 405, 406, 441–43
Boggs, Lindy, 127–28
Boland, Patrick J., 212, 245, 265
Bolling, A. P., 48, 477
Bolling, Richard, 418–20, 460
Bonds. *See* Securities
Boren, Lyle, 237, 304
Boykin, Frank, 454
Brandeis, Louis Dembitz, 78–79

Brandt, Pete, 498n.40
Brandt, Raymond P., 292
Brewster, Owen, 187–88
Britten, Fred, 159
Broadcast legislation, 160–61. *See also* Television
Broun, Heywood, 187
Brown, Clarence, 456, 460
Brown, David, 338
Brown, George, 394
Brown and Root, 282, 505n.11
Brown vs. *The Board of Education of Topeka, Kansas*, 384–85, 420
Brownell, Herbert, 381, 418, 423, 518n.35
Bryan, William Jennings, 25, 26, 49
Buchanan, James P., 164
Budge, Homer H., 449
Bureau of Education, 114–15, 136–37, 231–32, 303. *See also* Board
    of Education
Bush, Vannevarr, 289, 291
Butler, Ollie, 150–51
Butler, Paul, 392, 403, 407, 430, 437
Byrd, Harry, 363–65, 450
Byrnes, James, 240, 291
Byrns, Joe, 147, 163–65, 178, 184, 206, 497n.26

California, 351–53
Callaway, Oscar, 135
Calver, George W., 307
Cannon, Clarence, 289, 290, 368, 405, 497n.23, 512n.14
Cannon, Joe, 27, 108, 260, 270, 318, 344, 451, 452, 485n.4, 503n.25
Cantrell, Robert, 397
Cantrell, William, 281
Capitol renovation, 345, 409–10
Caro, Robert, 251
Carpenter, John W., 179–80
Carter, Amon, 139, 141–43
Case, Francis H., 269, 330, 394
Celler, Emanuel, 423
Chamber of Commerce, 161–62, 458
Chandor, Douglas, 306, 506n.6
Child labor legislation, 488n.55

Churchill, Winston, 238

Cigarette smoking, 47

Civil rights: Democratic platform in 1948, 336–37; Eisenhower program, 418–22, 431; House Rules Committee blockage, 457, 520n.3; Supreme Court decisions, 384–85; Truman administration, 331–33, 349

Civil Rights Act of 1957, 421–22

Civil War, 13–14, 94

Claflin (H. B.) Company, 82

Clapper, Raymond, 185–86

Clark, George, 23

Clark, James Beauchamp "Champ," 27, 62, 65, 107, 318

Clark, Tom, 130, 296–97, 352, 353, 409, 473

Clary, Alla, 8, 122, 213, 238, 242

Clay, Henry, 270, 318, 348, 468

Clayton Antitrust Act, 75, 99

Clements, Earle, 459

Cleveland, Grover, 7, 62

Clifford, Clark, 339

Cochran, Jack, 64

Cohen, Ben: interview for SR biography, 477; Securities Act of 1933, 151–54, 494n.21; SR loyalty to, 217; stock exchange regulation bill, 157, 159, 160; utility holding companies bill, 169–70, 172, 175, 182, 190, 192, 196; Washington society, 238

Cohn, David, 17

Cole, Buster, 128, 477, 510n.13

Collins, LeRoy, 439

Colmer, William, 449–51, 453, 454, 463, 520n.9

Colquitt, O. B., 46

Commerce Committee. *See* Senate Commerce Committee

Committee for Constitutional Action, 298

Committee of Public Utility Executives, 189, 193

Committees. *See* headings beginning with House; Senate

Common Carriers Committee. *See* Texas Legislature

Communications legislation, 160–61

Communism: charges of by Sumners, 223; McCarthy's attack on, 381–83; U.S. assistance to Europe, 328–29

Congress. *See* House of Representatives; Senate

Congressional Reorganization Act of 1946, 344–45

Conlon, Bea, 242

Connally, John B., 284, 285, 399–400, 405, 436, 438

Connally, Tom, 67, 69, 72, 136, 223, 236, 274, 282
Connor, Eugene, 337, 509n.32
Constitution: Fifteenth Amendment, 73; presidential incapacitation, 422–24, 518nn.35, 36; Twenty-fifth Amendment, 518n.36
Cooke, William A., 43
Coolidge, Calvin, 117–18, 428
Cooper, Jere, 245, 258–59
Cooper, John G., 191, 196
Corcoran, Tommy: assessment of FDR, 310; communication between Congress and FDR, 227; interviews for SR biography, 477; LBJ as vice-presidential candidate, 442; meeting with Garner, 231–32; Securities Act of 1933, 151–54; SR's loyalty to, 217; SR's majority leadership bid, 212–13; stock exchange regulation bill, 157, 159, 160; utility holding companies bill, 169–70, 175, 176, 182, 187–88, 196; Washington society, 238
Cox, Eugene, 304, 305
Cox, S. S., 107
Cramer, E. P., 191
Crowley, Karl A., 493n.14
Culberson, Charles A., 25, 108
Culberson, David, 25
Cullen, Hugh Roy, 295
Cullen, Tom, 212, 213
Cummings, Homer S., 221–22, 496n.6
Cummings, J. W., 359
Cunningham, Glen, 458
Cunningham, Henry A., 36, 37, 299, 477

Daley, Richard, 403
Dallas Press Club, 415
Daniel, Price, 333, 352–54, 371, 439, 511n.27
Danielson, Paul Elmer, 190
Dean, Arthur, 153
Democratic Advisory Council, 407, 430
Democratic Congressional Campaign Committee, 163–65, 248–49, 251
Democratic National Campaign Speakers Bureau, 206
Democratic National Committee, 248–49, 252, 370, 407, 444
Democratic National Convention: in 1932, 138–43; in 1940, 235, 239–42; in 1944, 301; in 1948, 334–38; in 1952, 367–69; in 1956,

401–406; in 1960, 437–44; southern confrontations, 336–37, 361, 363–67; SR as presiding officer, 334, 363–67; television coverage, 360, 362–63; Texas delegation, 361, 363

Democratic Patronage Committee, 424

Democrats: accused as soft on Communism, 381–82; anti-New Deal sentiment, 295–97; campaign funds, 247–52, 502n.8; Congressional control 119, 209, 301, 343, 385–86, 407, 429; defeats in 1942, 287; during 86th Congress, 430–432; Eisenhower administration, 392–94; federal jobs, 71–72; in House of Representatives, 65, 134–35, 167; optimum majority in Congress, 499n.15; platform, 148; Texas party, 295–96, 339, 396–401. *See also* names of specific party leaders

Dempsey, John J., 198, 499n.23

Denison Dam, 204–206, 298, 300

Denney, D. E., 31

Depression, 147

DeSapio, Carmine, 433, 435

Deschler, Lewis, 115, 304–305, 437

Devane, Dozier, 190

Devanter, Willis Van, 223

Dewey, Thomas E., 301, 335, 339, 342

Dickey, Abner, 16

Dickey, Elizabeth Rayburn, 16

Dickinson, Jacob M., 234–35

Dickson, Cecil, 111–12, 164, 165, 201–202, 208, 219, 304

Dies, Martin, 163, 236, 282, 283

Dill, Clarence, 160

Dirksen, Everett, 266

Dixiecrat party, 339, 341

Dixon, George, 216, 468

DNC. *See* Democratic National Committee

Donovan, Bob, 461, 464

Donovan, George, 3, 272–73, 325, 410, 469

Dotson, Homer A., 484n.19

Doughton, Robert Lee, 244, 376

Douglas, Paul, 367–69

Douglas, William O., 198, 217, 291, 301

Draft extension bill, 261–70

Drewry, Pat, 249

Dulaney, H. G., 390, 415

Dulles, John Foster, 153, 383

Duncan, A. J., 174

Earle, George, 212
Early, Steve, 308
East Texas Normal, 28–34, 48
East Texas Oil Field, 162
Education, 50, 333, 457
Education and Labor Committee. *See* House Education and Labor
    Committee
Edwards, India, 438
Edwards, Norman, 395
Eisenhower, Dwight: civil rights legislation, 418–22, 431; defense
    policy, 383; Democratic support, 370–72, 512n.20; end of Korean
    War, 383; foreign policy, 391–92; health, 423; legislative program,
    377–81, 383–84; oil and gas legislation, 393–94; presidential can-
    didate, 333, 359, 368, 369; presidential incapacitation bill, 422–24;
    presidential succession, 518n.35; presidential victory, 372–73, 406–
    407; priorities for administration, 377; reciprocal-trade agreements,
    383, 391; relationship with Congressional Democrats, 392–94; re-
    lationship with SR, 385, 514n.35; response to Republican criticism
    of Democrats, 382; SR's funeral, 473; SR's opinion of, 376–80;
    statehood for Alaska and Hawaii, 383; tax legislation, 393; tide-
    lands issue, 381; vetoes during 86th Congress, 430–431
Election laws, 35
Electric power industry. *See* Utility holding companies
Emergency Railroad Transportation Act, 149–50, 201
Emergency Relief Act of 1935, 202
English Companies Act, 151–52
Erwin, Ivan B., 57
Esch, John J., 89, 97
Esch-Cummins Transportation Act, 89, 97–98
European Recovery Act, 327
Evans, Silliman, 140–42, 512n.13
Executive Reorganization Act, 225

Faddis, Charles, 499n.21
Fahey, John A., 516n.43
Fair Deal, 348–49
Fair Employment Practices Commission, 298, 299, 344, 421
Farley, James, 140, 142, 206, 209, 212, 232, 235, 240
Farm Labor Union, 111, 113
Farmers. *See* Agriculture

Faubus, Orval, 422
FBI. *See* Federal Bureau of Investigation
FCC. *See* Federal Communications Commission, 495n.38
Federal Bureau of Investigation, 384
Federal Communications Act, 201
Federal Communications Commission, 160, 495n.38
Federal Deposit Insurance program, 49
Federal Power Commission, 190
Federal Reserve System, 75, 99
Federal Trade Commission, 75, 99, 150, 152, 156–57, 160, 168, 182
FEPC. *See* Fair Employment Practices Commission
Finance. *See* Securities; Stock exchanges; Utility holding companies
Finance Committee. *See* Senate Finance Committee
Finnegan, James A., 367, 403
Finney, Ruth, 185, 496n.1
Fish, Hamilton, 257, 276
Fisher, O. C., 350
Fleeson, Doris, 458
Fletcher, Duncan U., 155, 159
Flexner, Bernard, 155
Flynn, Ed, 212, 248–49
Forand, Aime, 431
Forand bill, 431
Foreign Affairs Committee. *See* House Foreign Affairs Committee
Foreign Relations Committee. *See* Senate Foreign Relations
    Committee
Formosan resolution, 391
Francis, Charles I., 361
Frankfurter, Felix, 151, 159, 232, 494n.23, 500–501n.28
Frazier, Bernice, 417
Frieze, E. K., 34
FTC. *See* Federal Trade Commission

Gadsden, Philip H., 189
Gardner, Sam H., 36, 483n.3
Garner, Ettie, 71, 137, 306
Garner, John Nance: advice to FDR, 231; advice to new members
    of Congress, 70–71, 77; advice to SR, 260, 410; appointment to
    House Ways and Means Committee, 65; Bureau of Education, 114–
    15, 136–37, 231–32, 303; communication between Congress and

FDR, 227; Democratic caucuses of House members, 346; departure from public life, 324; disillusionment with New Deal, 225; dislike of Byrns, 165; federal control of oil production, 250; gambling, 107–108; head of Texas delegation, 115–16; House Democratic whip, 68; interviews for SR biography, 476; office, 306, 485–86n.8; opposition to Esch-Cummins Transportation Act, 98; opposition to railway stock and bond bill, 78; optimum Democratic majority, 499n.15; personality, 136; petition of support for, 229–30; popularity, 69–70, 229, 230; presidential bid, 133–43, 232–42, 433, 438, 492n.1; relationship with FDR, 503n.18; relationship with Hearst, 492n.1; Speaker of the House, 116, 119, 134–35; SR's mentor, 3, 67, 69–71, 90, 136–37, 165, 211, 219; SR's view of, 499n.18; support for Deschler, 304; support for LBJ as vice-presidential candidate, 442; Supreme Court expansion plan, 221–24, 231; vice-presidential bid, 135, 137, 138, 140–41, 143; Vice-Presidency, 146, 209, 493n.14; World War I, 92
Garner, Tully, 92
Garrett, Finis, 136
Gas power industry. See Utility holding companies
Germany, E. B., 295
Gifford, Charles L., 258, 288
Giles, Bascom, 353
Gill, Joseph, 366
Gillett, Frederick H., 498n.11
Gilmer, Claude, 372
Gilmore, Clarence, 52–53
Glass, Carter, 92–93, 160, 223
Gompers, Samuel, 98
Gore, Albert, 406
Gossett, Ed, 354
Gould, Jay, 45
Graham, B. S., 315
Graham, Billy, 519n.14
Graham, Philip, 444
Granberry, Read, 38
Great Britain 257–60, 319–20
Great Depression. See Depression
Green, William, Sr., 435–36, 438–39
Greene, Roger D., 17
Griffin, Robert P., 431
Gross, H. R., 461

Gruett, J. P., Sr., 41, 43
Guffey, Joseph F., 212

Haddad, Bill, 406
Hagerty, James, 334
Halleck, Charlie, 429, 430, 449, 451, 454–56, 458, 460, 462
Hannegan, Robert E., 296
Hardeman, D. B., 7–9, 370, 437, 475–80
Harding, Warren, 117
Harmon, Randall S., 416
Harness, Forest, 266
Harriman, W. Averell, 401, 402
Harris, G. C., 299–300
Harris, Oren, 393–394
Harrison, Pat, 142–43
Harte, Houston, 342
Hartley, Fred, 329
Hawaii, 383
Healy, Robert E., 168, 169
Hearst, William Randolph, 133, 141, 492n.1
Hebert, Edward, 324
Henderson, Alexander, 153
Henderson, Leon, 287
Heslep, Charter, 185
Hickman, Tom, 112
Highways, 315–16, 507n.29
Hitler, Adolph, 228, 234
Hobby, H. P., 161
Hoffa, James R., 431
Hoffman, Clare, 345
Hogg, James Stephen, 23, 24
Holifield, Chet, 429
Holmes, Oliver Wendell, 483n.17
Holton, John, 8, 266, 281, 416, 437, 472
Hoover, Herbert, 118–19, 134, 138, 188, 492n.4
Hopkins, Harry, 273, 274
Hopson, Howard C., 193–95
Horton, Hal, 59–60, 80, 478, 485–86n.8
House Agriculture Committee, 164
House Appropriations Committee, 25, 163, 289

House Banking and Currency Committee, 294
House Education and Labor Committee, 329
House Foreign Affairs Committee, 258
House Interstate and Foreign Commerce Committee: antitrust leg-
    islation, 75–77; Esch as chairman, 97; Hoover as witness, 118;
    Plumb Plan, 96–97; railroad holding companies, 149–50; Securi-
    ties Act of 1933, 148; SR appointment, 65–68; SR as chair, 119,
    292; SR as member, 90, 116; SR resignation from, 220; stock ex-
    change legislation, 156–58; utility holding companies, 173–75;
    War Risk Insurance Act, 93–94
House Judiciary Committee, 25, 223
House Labor Committee, 271, 344
House Military Affairs Committee, 265, 266
House of Representatives: accomplishments of 84th Congress, 394–
    95; antistrike bill, 271–72; atomic bomb, 289–91; bipartisan con-
    servative coalition, 224; civil rights legislation, 418–22; committee
    to investigate executive agencies, 293–94; Democratic control,
    119, 134–35, 167, 209, 301, 385–86, 407; Democratic liberals, 429;
    draft extension bill, 262–70; Eisenhower legislative program, 377–
    81, 383–85; Fair Deal program, 348–49; Formosan resolution,
    391; gasoline rationing, 280; importance of committee work, 64;
    isolationism, 256, 261, 265, 276; legislative program in 86th Con-
    gress, 431–32; lend-lease bill, 257–61; majority leader in 1940,
    245–46; need for bipartisan cooperation, 287–89; Neutrality Act
    amendments, 270–72; oil and gas legislation, 393–94; optimum
    Democratic majority, 499n.15; pension for members, 280; presi-
    dential succession law revision, 313–14; Rayburn bill, 77–79,
    84–85; reciprocal-trade bill, 391; reorganization of legislative
    branch, 319; Republican control, 97, 119, 323, 375; Republican
    gains in 1938 and 1940, 247–48; restoration of House chamber,
    345; Securities Act of 1933, 150–55; Speakership election in 1934,
    163–66; stock exchange legislation, 155–60; Supreme Court ex-
    pansion bill, 223; tax legislation, 393; television ban, 345–46,
    510n.6; Texas influence, 146; tidelands issue, 352, 354–55; utility
    holding companies, 171, 173–97; violence of Puerto Rican nation-
    alists, 384; wage and hour legislation, 225; World War I legislation,
    91–94; World War II declaration, 274–77; World War II legislation,
    288. See also names of specific members of Congress
House Rules Committee: Bankhead as chairman, 164; civil rights
    legislation, 420, 421, 520n.3; conservative control of, 6, 288, 293,
    448–50; Cox's membership, 305; enlargement of, 467; investiga-

tion of influence during utility holding companies bill, 187–89, 194–95; Kennedy program, 447–48; O'Connor as chairman, 209; power of, 448–49; Rayburn bill, 84; role of, 294–95, 448–49; Sabath's assistance in getting bills out, 502n.1; Smith's control of, 430–31; Smith's election to, 521n.24; SR's confrontation with, 396–401, 447–65; twenty-one day rule, 343–44, 510n.1; utility holding companies bill, 176, 185, 207–208; wage and price control legislation, 294–295

House Un-American Activities Committee, 424–25, 455

House Ways and Means Committee, 25, 64–65, 72, 350–51

Houston, Sam, 127, 133

Hoyt, Eugenia, 244

HUAC. *See* House Un-American Activities Committee

Huddleston, George, 180–83, 190, 191–92, 196–97

Hughes, Charles Evan, 483n.17

Hughes, Emmet John, 392

Hull, Cordell, 73, 74, 77, 141, 232, 239, 262

Humphrey, Hubert, 336, 364, 403–405, 435, 438

Hunt, H. L., 519n.26

Hunt, J. C., 54

Hurja, Emil, 229

Hurley, Patrick J., 194

ICC. *See* Interstate Commerce Commission

Ickes, Harold, 163, 205, 229, 230, 235, 240, 349, 351, 354, 495n.42

Igoe, William L., 64

Ikard, Frank, 5, 307, 350, 432

Immigration legislation, 100

Inch, S. R., 174

Income tax, 73

Inglish, Dan, 242, 281

International Brotherhood of Teamsters, 431

Interstate and Foreign Commerce Committee. *See* House Interstate and Foreign Commerce Committee

Interstate Commerce Commission, 24–25, 76–79, 149, 150, 493–94n.12

Interstate Commerce Committee. *See* Senate Interstate Commerce Committee

Investment securities. *See* Securities

Iron, Clayton, 511n.27

Izac, Edouard V., 485n.7

James, Marquis, 127

Javits, Jacob, 317

Jennings, John J., 263

Jennings, Mary McFarland, 17

Johnson, Lady Bird, 223, 238, 441, 521n.3, 4

Johnson, Louis, 240

Johnson, Luther, 106

Johnson, Lyndon: ambition, 389–90; Board of Education, 237–38, 304, 389–90; campaign finances investigation, 505n.11; campaign fund raising, 249–52; Capitol renovation, 410; civil rights legislation, 418, 421–22; draft extension bill, 265, 266; drinking habits, 307; Eisenhower program, 391–94; endorsement of Stevenson for president, 396; enlistment in World War II, 280–81; FDR's death, 309; heart attack, 394–96, 398; intelligence system, 307; interviews for SR biography, 476; lack of support for Stevenson, 371; Landrum-Griffin bill, 432; oil and gas legislation, 393–94; opposition to, 297; personality, 118, 391, 395; petition of support for Garner, 230; presidential aspirations in 1956, 395–96, 401–402; presidential bid in 1960, 432–39, 518–19n.10, 519n.21; pro-FDR, 235–36; recognition, 413, 519n.15; relationship with SR, 4–5, 236–38, 252, 260, 387, 389–94; response to Republican criticism of Democrats, 382; Rules Committee confrontation, 457, 459; Senate leadership, 376, 387, 389–94; Senatorial bid in 1941, 281–86; Senatorial election, 340, 341, 385, 509–10n.42; Shivers confrontation, 396–401; SR's assessment of, 389–91, 512n.18; SR's funeral, 473; support for JFK, 440; Taft-Hartley Act, 330; tidelands issue, 352, 354; vice-presidential bid, 403–404, 439–44

Johnson, Rebekah, 237

Johnson, Sam Early, 42, 236–37, 483n.11

Jones, B. L., 55

Jones, Frank, 124

Jones, Jesse, 240

Jones, Marvin: assessment of SR, 72, 94, 117; career, 487.26; friendship with SR, 113, 122, 130, 487n.26; House Speakership race, 164; SR's divorce, 127; SR's marriage, 124, 492n.10; World War I declaration, 92

Jones, Metze, 122–27, 130, 131, 492n.10

Jorgensen, Hans, 266

Jouett, Edward S., 78

Judiciary Committee. See House Judiciary Committee

Justice Department, 352

Kefauver, Estes: position on Foreign Relations Committee, 440; presidential bid, 357–61, 364, 366–68, 512n.13; vice-presidential candidate, 369, 401, 403, 404–406, 434
Kelly, Ed, 212
Kennedy, A. M., 49–51, 54, 55, 57
Kennedy, John F.: choice of vice-presidential running-mate, 439–44; inaugural address, 467; legislative program, 454; member of Congress, 329; presidential candidate, 433–39; Rules Committee confrontation, 450–52, 457; SR's admiration of, 444–45, 447; SR's funeral, 473; support from LBJ, 440; televised debate, 445; vice-presidential bid, 403–405, 434; visit to dying SR, 472
Kennedy, Robert, 440, 443–44
Kennon, Governor, 365
Kent, Frank R., 291
Kerr, Robert S., 340, 357, 358
Kilday, J. E., 142, 265
Kilgore, Joe, 459
Kimbrough, Rene, 341, 417
King, Hiram, 295
Kirby, John Henry, 39
Kitchin, Claude, 61, 91, 485n.4
Kleberg, Richard, 236
Knox, Frank, 234–35
Korean War, 349, 383
Ku Klux Klan, 111–13, 490n.18
Kuhn, Otto H., 149

Labor: antistrike bill, 271–72; Landrum-Griffin bill, 431–32; opposition to Esch-Cummins Transportation Act, 97–98; reaction to LBJ as vice-presidential candidate, 443; Rules Committee battle, 457; Senate investigations of, 431; strikes, 111–13, 271–72, 329–30; support for SR, 359; Taft-Hartley Act, 329–30, 349
LaFollette, Robert, 220, 257–58
LaGuardia, Fiorello H., 135
Landis, James M., 151–54, 156–57, 160, 494n.21
Landrum, Phil M., 431, 518n.9
Landrum-Griffin bill, 431–32
Lawrence, David, 435
League of Nations, 101, 106
Leche, Richard, 211, 499n.20

Lehman, Herbert, 407
Lend-lease bill, 257–61
Lesinski, John, 344
Leslie, Fenner, 127
Leuchtenburg, William E., 241
Lewis, John L., 229, 271
Lincoln, Abraham, 72
Lindley, Ernest K., 232
Link, Arthur S., 85
Lippmann, Walter, 497n.34
Little, Dwayne, 332
Logan-Walter bill, 255, 503n.14
Long, Huey, 499n.20
Long, Russell, 365, 366
Longworth, Alice Roosevelt, 115
Longworth, Nicholas, 114–15, 303, 304
Louisiana, 352, 353
Louisville and Nashville Railroad, 78
Louisville Courier-Journal, 18, 21
Love, Thomas B., 51
Lovett, Robert S., 78
Lucas, Scott, 280, 366

McAdoo, William Gibbs, 93–94, 95, 142–43, 368, 493n.14
McCarthy, Joseph, 381–83, 386
McCormack, John: atomic bomb, 289–90, 505n.15; draft extension
    bill, 265; House leadership, 245–46, 252–54, 324, 380; lend-lease
    bill, 257, 258; member of Board of Education, 305; Neutrality Act
    amendments, 271; Rules Committee battle, 456, 460; Smith's elec-
    tion to Rules Committee, 521n.24; SR's comments on 1946 elec-
    tion, 320; support of SR, 212, 296, 360; war declaration, 276–77
McDuffie, John, 114, 146, 221
McGee, Gale, 439
McGrath, Howard, 339
McGugin, Harold, 159
McKellar, Kenneth, 313
McKinney, Frank, 368
McNatt, John, 12
McNaughton, Frank, 270
McNeil, Marshall, 292

MacNeil, Neil, 383, 458, 467, 468, 521n.3
McNutt, Paul V., 240
Magnuson, Warren G., 405
Mahon, George, 413
Mallon, Paul, 219, 259
Manhattan Project, 289–91
Mann, Gerald, 282, 283
Mann, James, 485n.4, 498n.11
Mapes, Carl, 159
Marcantonio, Vito, 223
Marcus, Stanley, 370
Marsh, Charles E., 284–85
Marshall, George C., 258, 262, 289, 328
Marshall Plan, 327–29
Martin, Joe: atomic bomb, 289–90; death, 518n.1; draft extension
    bill, 264–66, 269; friendship with SR, 386, 508n.8; House Rules
    battle, 461; loss of Speakership, 386; ousted as minority leader,
    429, 430, 449, 518n.1; Rules Committee battle, 456; Speakership,
    325–27, 375; SR's presidential bid, 292; World War II, 279
Mashek, John W., 519n.14
Mason, Noah, 345
Maverick, Maury, 233, 248, 361, 363
May, Andrew J., 265, 269
Mayfield, Earle B., 490n.18
Mayo, Gladys, 32, 482n.5, 482n.10, 484n.27
Mayo, William Leonidas, 28–33, 37, 48
Merritt, Schuyler, 158
Mexico, 4, 101, 164
Michner, Earl, 268–69
Middle East, 392
Military Affairs Committee. *See* House Military Affairs Committee
Milligan, Tuck, 114
Mills, Roger Q., 25
Mills, Wilbur, 425
Milne, Jim, 520n.19
Mitchell, Charles E., 149
Moley, Raymond S., 74, 151, 153
Monroney, Mike, 357–60, 369
Moreland, Ivan, 20
Morgan, J. P., 76, 149
Morgenthau, Henry, 258, 301

Morris, Grover Cleveland, 297–99, 338, 505n.27
Morris, Jess, 204
Mullen, Arthur, 141
Murchison, Clint, 250
Murphy, Frank, 501n.29

NAACP, 457
NAM. *See* National Association of Manufacturers
Nash, Ed, 212
National Association for the Advancement of Colored People, 457
National Association of Manufacturers, 162, 458
National Education Association, 457
Neely, Jeff, 127
Negroes. *See* Blacks
Neutrality Act, 228
New Deal, 147, 201–202, 235–36, 295–96. *See also* names of specific
    pieces of legislation
New Frontier, 445
New Haven and Hartford Railroad, 76
Newlands Committee, 88–89
Nicastro, Nick, 325
Nixon, Richard, 381–82, 413, 423, 433, 434, 442, 450, 491n.31
Norris, George, 203
North Atlantic Treaty, 347
Notti, Robert, 519n.26

O'Brien, Larry, 459
O'Brien, Tom, 212
O'Connor, Basil, 194, 208
O'Connor, John J., 176, 188, 194–95, 207–13, 226, 499n.23
O'Daniel, W. Lee, 282, 283, 285–86, 297, 505n.11
O'Donnell, John, 387
O'Donnell, Kenny, 443
Office of Price Administration, 287, 288, 294
Oil and gas industry: campaign contributions, 250–52, 350; exemp-
    tion from federal price regulation, 393–94; federal control of pro-
    duction, 162–63; resource-depletion allowance, 350–351; SR's sup-
    port for, 349–55; tidelands, 351–55
OPA. *See* Office of Price Administration
Otten, Allen S., 360

Panama Canal, 4, 101
Parker, James, 149
Parr, George, 341
Parten, J. R., 250, 349–50
Patman, Elmer, 511n.27
Patman, Wright, 217, 284, 297, 304, 315, 442
Payne, Sam, 20
Pearl Harbor, 272–75
Pearson, Drew, 175, 197, 241
Pecora, Ferdinand, 148–49
Peeler, Ray, 502n.8
Pennsylvania Railroad, 79, 95
Perez, Leander, 414
Perkins, Tom, 55, 58, 79, 80–81
Petroleum industry. *See* Oil and gas industry
Pew, Joseph, 295
Pharr, E., 38
Philippines, 101–102
Pierce, Henry Clay, 40–41
Plumb, Glenn E., 96–97
Plumb Plan, 96–97
Poage, Bob, 237
Polk, James K., 22, 62
Poll tax, 333, 344, 421
Populist movement, 24
Pou, Edward W., 114, 135
Powell, Adam Clayton, 329, 455
Presidential incapacitation, 422–24, 518n.35, 518n.36
Presidential succession, 313–14, 326, 518n.35
Priest, Percy, 324
Progressives, 334
Prohibition, 42, 46–47, 52, 57, 99, 125–26, 138–39, 492n.11
Public utility holding companies. *See* Utility holding companies
Public Utility Holding Company Act. *See* Utility holding companies
Public Works Administration, 205
PWA. *See* Public Works Administration

Racial segregation. *See* Segregation
Radio Act of 1927, 160
Ragsdale, W. B., 238, 471, 480, 492n.1
Railroads: bankruptcy, 83; deterioration of, 95; financing of, 75–76;

government control during World War I, 89, 95–96; government
ownership in Alaska, 100; investigation of holding companies,
149–50; legislation, 75, 97–98, 149; Newlands Committee, 88–89;
opposition to antitrust legislation, 76, 78; Plumb Plan, 96–97;
Rayburn bill, 77–79, 84–85; regulation of rates, 24–25; return to
private control after World War I, 95–97; scandals, 75–77, 94–95;
Texas legislation, 45–46, 78

Railway Labor Board, 111

Rainey, Henry T., 134, 146–47, 163

Ramsey, Marion L., 178

Randell, Andrew, 86–88

Randell, Choice B., 55, 86, 484n.29

Rankin, Jeannette, 91–92, 276–77

Rankin, John, 245, 324, 344, 345

Raskin, Hy, 403–404

Rayburn, Abner, 15, 17, 80–82

Rayburn, Charles, 14, 412

Rayburn, Dick, 15, 205–206, 348

Rayburn, Elizabeth. See Dickey, Elizabeth Rayburn

Rayburn, Jim, 14, 17, 19

Rayburn, John, 12

Rayburn, John Franklin, 14

Rayburn, Katherine. See Thomas, Katherine Rayburn

Rayburn, Lucinda, 14, 82, 145–46, 218, 348, 411–12

Rayburn, Lucinda Amos, 12

Rayburn, Martha Waller: 14–15, 17–22, 123–24

Rayburn, Medibel. See Bartley, Medibel Rayburn

Rayburn, Metze Jones. See Jones, Metze

Rayburn, Mrs. James L., 412

Rayburn: religion, 18–19

Rayburn, Sam

—Democratic Party: campaign funds, 247, 250–52, 502n.8; 350;
chairman of National Campaign Speakers Bureau, 206; Garner's
presidential bid, 133–43, 229–30, 232–42, 438; Kennedy's presidential bid, 433–34; LBJ's presidential bid, 432–39; LBJ's Senatorial bid in 1941, 281–86; LBJ's vice-presidential nomination,
439–44; National Convention of 1932, 138–43; National Convention of 1948, 335–36; National Convention of 1952, 362–67, 369;
National Convention of 1956, 401–406, 516n.43; National Convention of 1960, 437–44; 1946 elections, 320–21; presidential bid,
357–62, 367, 370, 503n.11; presiding officer of National Conventions, 334, 369; Senatorial interests, 108–11; televised coverage of

National Conventions, 362–63, 369; Texas party split, 398–99; Truman's presidential campaign, 339–41; vice-presidential bid, 232, 240–42, 291–93, 295–97, 301, 501n.29, 505n.27
—honors and awards: Bonham's pride in, 246–47; bust, 473; celebrations in Texas, 253; honorary degree, 280; honors, 347–48, 384, 413, 468, 519n.15; "Mr. Democrat," 375–76, 427; national prestige, 362–63, 369; official portrait, 306, 506n.6; popularity of, 219, 484n.23; prestige within Congress, 146; recognition, 117, 197–99, 219, 226–27, 288–89, 427; symbol of House, 3, 6, 375–76, 427; Tennessee celebrations, 263
—House of Representatives: ambition for Speakership, 37–38, 72, 116–17, 133, 146; antistrike bill, 271–72; antitrust legislation, 75–79; atomic bomb, 289–91; attendance record, 69; Board of Education, 303–308, 413, 500–501n.28; Bureau of Education, 114–15, 136–37; campaigns, 55–58, 80–81, 85–88, 102, 105, 111–13, 187, 198–99, 204–206, 226, 286–87, 297–300, 338–39, 385; Capitol renovation, 345, 409–10; child labor legislation, 488n.55; choice of McCormack as majority leader, 245–46; civil rights legislation, 331–33, 338, 418–22, 431, 484n.19, 520n.3; Committee on Interstate and Foreign Commerce, 65–68, 119, 220; committee work, 113; conservative views, 98, 161, 295; Denison Dam, 204–206, 298, 300; draft extension bill, 261–70; early accomplishments, 5, 88–90; Eisenhower legislative program, 377–81, 383–84, 391–94; Esch-Cummins Transportation Act, 97–98; FDR's State of the Union address in 1941, 255–57; federal aid to education, 333; first months in Congress, 59–61, 64, 71–74, 485–86n.8; foreign affairs, 101–102, 228; grants to states, 99; immigration legislation, 100; labor legislation, 330, 431–32, 518n.9; leadership style, 4–6, 54–55, 260–61, 270, 288–89, 346–47, 503n.25; lend-lease bill, 257–60; loyalty to presidents, 100–101, 311, 491n.31, 507n.20; McCarthyism, 381–83; majority leader, 207–13, 221, 224–25; Marshall Plan, 328–29; minority leadership, 323–25, 326–27, 373, 375–77, 514n.35; Neutrality Act amendments, 270–72; New Deal support, 147, 201, 204, 206, 253, 295; New Frontier, 445; Newlands Committee, 88–89; office routines, 413–18; oil and gas legislation, 162–63, 250, 349–55, 393–94; optimum Democratic majority, 499n.15; patronage system, 71–72; poll tax, 333, 344, 421; post–World War II legislation, 319–20; presidential incapacitation bill, 422–24; press briefings, 415–16; prohibition, 52, 57, 99, 492n.11; railroads, 77–79, 84–85, 94–98, 149–50; refusal to convene party caucuses, 346; relations with press, 415–16; relations with staff, 8, 280–81, 413–14; reorganization of legislative branch,

319; Republican control, 105–106, 330–31; Rules Committee confrontation, 396–401, 447–65; Rural Electrification Act, 201–203; rural legislation, 315–18, 507n.29; Securities Act, 148, 150–55, 494n.23, 495n.28; segregation, 112–13, 385, 420–21; socialist programs, 489n.22; Speaker pro tempore, 226, 500n.21; Speakership, 243, 245, 342, 343, 386–88, 467–68, 499n.16, 521n.3, 521n.4; Speakership bid, 163–66; Speakership relinquished, 323–25, 373; speeches, 219–20, 326–27; stock exchange legislation, 155–60; Supreme Court expansion plan, 222–24; Taft-Hartley Act, 329–30; tariff legislation, 73–74; television ban on committee hearings, 345–46, 415–16, 424–25, 510n.6; tidelands battle, 352–55, 381; use of power, 3–4, 344–47, 414, 450–51; utility holding companies legislation, 169–97, 497n.26; view of Republican presidents, 117–19, 376–80; wage and hour legislation, 225; Wilson legislative program, 98–100; wiretapping legislation, 161; woman suffrage amendment, 99; World War I, 92–94; World War II, 272–77, 279
—personal life: adolescent personality, 29; Bonham home and farm, 2, 217–18, 314–15, 317–18; brothers and sisters, 14–15, 17–18, 20–22; cancer, 468–73; childhood, 1–3, 15–22; college education, 28–34; death and funeral, 472–74; deaths of family members, 80–82, 105, 411–12, 487n.42; divorce, 126–28, 130–31; drinking habits, 126, 305, 307; early education, 20–21; eating habits, 19, 305; estate, 521–22n.14; eulogy, 497n.23; family closeness, 4, 18, 81–82, 145–46, 218; financial situation, 487n.42; frugality, 38; gambling, 108; health, 145, 215–16, 410–11, 468; law practice, 47–48, 483n.17; lifestyle, 107–108, 215–16; loneliness, 3, 4, 17–18, 209, 418, 487n.41; marriage, 105, 121–28, 130–31; move to New York City, 208–209; parents, 11–22, 81–82, 123–24; personality, 3–4, 20, 51–52, 68, 118, 217–18, 391, 475–76; philosophy, 6–7, 201–202, 253, 471; physical appearance, 3; political ambitions as young man, 28, 34; poor eyesight, 406, 437–38, 447; Primitive Baptist Church membership, 412–13; reading, 106–107; relations with women, 128–30; religion, 18–19, 412–13; retirement, 314, 323, 373, 508n.2; rural values, 3, 315; study of law, 47; teaching jobs, 33–34; television viewing, 418; Texas politics during 1890s, 23–28; travel outside of U.S., 4, 101–102, 164; view of old age, 514n.5
—relationships and friendships: Bailey, 27–38; Byrns, 165, 497n.26; Eisenhower, 376–80; FDR, 206, 207, 227, 234–35, 254, 277, 288, 309–11; friendships, 3, 38–39, 90, 113–15, 411, 413, 499n.14; Garner, 70, 71, 136–37, 229–30, 238–39, 499n.18; Ickes, 495n.42; JFK, 444–45, 447; LBJ, 236–38, 281, 389–91; loyalty, 39, 50–51,

217, 230, 238–39; McAdoo, 493n.14; McCormack, 380; Martin, 325, 386, 508n.8; Nixon, 434; opponents, 499n.23; Splawn, 168, 493–94n.12; Stevenson, 370; Truman, 311–13, 331–33, 507n.20; Wilson, 79, 86–87
—Texas State Legislature: awareness of conflict of interest issues, 48; bid for Speakership, 49, 51; campaign for, 35–37; committee responsibilities, 45–46, 49; defense of Bailey, 42–45; defense of Speaker Kennedy, 50–51; legislative record, 46–47; prohibition, 42, 46–47; railroad legislation, 45–46; second term, 49–52; Speakership, 52–54, 484n.25, 484n.27; swearing in, 37; third term, 52–55
Rayburn, Tom, 15
Rayburn, Will, 11–22, 30
Rayburn, William, 14, 124, 125, 317, 412
Rayburn Foundation, 350, 510n.13
Rayburn Library 347–48, 350, 473, 514n.1, 521–22n.14
Rayburnisms, 427–29
REA. *See* Rural Electrification Act of 1936
Reagan, John, 24–25
Reconstruction Finance Corporation, 151
Redding, Jack, 339
Redditt, John S., 316
Reece, B. Carroll, 449
Reed, Tom, 260, 270, 503n.25
Republicans: antilabor legislation, 329–30; control of Congress, 97, 119, 323, 327, 330–31; denounced by Truman, 339; interest in business techniques in government, 377; majority in House in 1953, 375; power of, 247–48, 287–88; SR's view of 83rd Congress, 379–81; tariff policy, 73–74. *See also* names of specific party leaders
Reston, James, 386–87
Reuss, Henry, 392
Reuther, Walter, 443
Richardson, Sid, 250, 282, 349
Ridgway, R. Bonna, 37–38, 50, 51, 478
Risser, Joe, 470, 472
Roberts, Chip, 249
Roberts, Dennis, 404
Roberts, Lawrence, 442
Roberts, Ray, 281
Robinson, Joseph T., 222–24
Robinson, William, 315–16

Rockefeller, John D., 40

Roeser, Charles F., 250

Rogers, Edith Nourse, 276

Roosevelt, Alice. *See* Longworth, Alice Roosevelt

Roosevelt, Elliott, 240

Roosevelt, Franklin D.: advice from Garner, 231; appointment of Robert T. Bartley, 495n.38; Bankhead's funeral, 244–45; charges of seeking dictatorial power, 225; communication with Congress, 227, 245, 254–55, 288; death, 308–309; declaration of war, 272–75; Denison Dam, 205–206; draft extension bill, 261–70; Executive Reorganization Act, 225; failing health, 301–302; federal control of oil production, 250; fourth term, 291, 292, 301; hatred of Texas conservatives, 295; hostility toward O'Connor, 208; inauguration, 147–48; isolationist early in World War II, 227–28; lend-lease bill, 257–61; Neutrality Act amendments, 271–72; oil production legislation, 163; personal qualities, 310; presidential nominations and elections, 133, 135, 204, 209, 228–29, 232–42, 252, 493n.14; problems with Congress, 224–26; rejection of SR as vice-president, 301; relationship with Garner, 503n.18; relationship with SR as Speaker, 277; Securities Act of 1933, 495n.28; Splawn appointment to ICC, 155, 493–94n.12; SR's assessment of, 309–11; State of the Union address in 1941, 255–57; stock exchange legislation, 158, 160; support for LBJ, 235–36, 282–83; support for SR, 163–65, 211; Supreme Court expansion plan, 221–24, 236; utility holding companies, 169–70, 173, 175, 183, 196, 497n.25; view of SR, 207, 217, 235; wage and hour legislation, 236; wartime powers, 279

Roosevelt, James, 235, 275, 429

Roosevelt, Theodore, 41

Roper, Elmo, 404

Ross, Charlie, 339

Rowan, Arch, 295, 502n.8

Rules Committee. *See* House Rules Committee

Rural electrification, 201–203, 320

Rural Electrification Act of 1936, 201–203

Rural Electrification Administration, 202

Russell, Richard, 337–38, 357, 358, 360, 361, 364, 367, 401

Russia, 231

Rutherford, Albert G., 263

Rutherford, J. T., 351

Sabath, Adolph, 243–44, 305, 376, 502n.1, 510n.1
St. Lawrence Seaway, 381
Sales tax, 380
Sam Rayburn Foundation. *See* Rayburn Foundation
Sam Rayburn Library. *See* Rayburn Library
Sandlin, Marlin, 515n.27
Santa Fe Railroad, 48
Sasscer, Lansdale, 365
Sayers, Joseph D., 25
Scripps-Howard newspapers, 185, 496n.1
SEC. *See* Securities and Exchange Commission
Secession movement, 13
Securities, 148–55. *See also* Stock exchanges
Securities Act of 1933, 148, 150–56, 201, 494n.23, 495n.28
Securities and Exchange Commission, 160, 196, 198
Segregation, 47, 384–85, 420–21. *See also* Civil rights
Selective Service Act, 92, 262
Senate: atomic bomb, 289–91; civil rights legislation, 418–22; Demo-
   cratic control, 301, 407; gasoline rationing, 280; investigation on
   lobbying on utility holding companies bill, 188–95; investigation
   of organized labor, 431; lend-lease bill, 259–60; oil and gas legislation, 394; pension for members, 280; presidential succession law
   revision, 314; reorganization of legislative branch, 319; Republican
   control, 97, 119; Securities Act of 1933, 155; stock exchange legislation, 159–60; Supreme Court expansion bill, 223–24; television
   coverage of committee hearings, 345; tidelands issue, 352, 354–55;
   utility holding companies bill, 175, 197. *See also* names of specific
   members of Congress
Senate Banking and Currency Committee, 148–49, 155
Senate Commerce Committee, 170
Senate Finance Committee, 72
Senate Foreign Relations Committee, 228, 327, 440
Senate Interstate Commerce Committee, 78, 79, 84
Senate Investigations subcommittee, 381–83
Senate Judiciary Committee, 223, 224
Senate Military Affairs Committee, 262
Senate Permanent Investigations subcommittee, 386
Sewell, Jim, 370, 399
Sexton, Harry, 137
Shanley, Bernard M., 379

Sharon, John, 404
Sheppard, Harry R., 420
Sheppard, Morris, 86, 281–82
Sherman Antitrust Act, 75
Shivers, Allan: confrontation with LBJ and SR, 396–401, 515n.27;
    party loyalty, 363; SR's opinion of, 491n.3; SR's presidential bid,
    361; support for Eisenhower, 359; support for Republican Party,
    370–72, 512n.20; tidelands battle, 353, 354
Short, Dewey, 265, 265–69
Short, Joe, 358
Sikes, Robert, 264
Simmons, Lee, 299, 412–13
Sims, Thetus W., 94
Skelton, Byron, 515n.27
Slavery, 13
Smith, Al, 139–40, 143, 404, 434
Smith, Clint, 295
Smith, Howard: antistrike legislation, 272; blocking of legislation
    by Rules Committee, 449–50; civil rights legislation, 420, 421,
    520n.3; confrontation with SR over power of Rules Committee, 6,
    451–65; conservative leader of House Rules Committee, 293–95;
    control of Rules Committee, 430–31; election to Rules Commit-
    tee, 521n.24; investigation of executive agencies, 293–94; opposi-
    tion to SR's Speakership bid, 499n.16; wage and price control leg-
    islation, 294–95
Smith, Merriman, 358
Smith, William R., 66
Smith Act of 1940, 330
Snell, Bert, 114
Social Security, 431, 454
Socialism, 489n.22
Soil conservation, 316–17
Somers, Andrew L., 245, 267
Sorensen, Theodore, 438, 440, 444, 459
Southern Agrarians, 485n.5
Southern Railway, 88
Southwestern Power Administration, 320
Sparkman, John, 324, 357, 359, 369
Splawn, W. M., 149–50, 168–69, 171, 493–94n.12
Standard Oil Company, 40–41
Stark, Lloyd C., 501n.29

Steed, Tom, 459

Steffens, Lincoln, 41

Steger, Tom P., 47–48

Steinert, Sturge, 512n.18

Stettinius, Edward R., 313

Stevenson, Adlai: campaign, 370–72; divorce, 128; presidential bid in
     1960, 438; presidential nomination in 1952, 357, 358, 360, 364,
     366–68; presidential nomination in 1956, 401–403; Texas visit,
     396; vice-presidential running mate, 403–406; view of SR, 375–76;

Stevenson, Andrew, 318

Stevenson, Coke, 341

Stevenson, H. W., 474

Stimpson, George, 9

Stimson, Henry, 234–35, 258, 274, 289

Stinnett, Jack, 313

Stock Exchange Act, 155–60

Stokes, Isaac Newton Phelps II, 155

Strikes, 111–13, 271–72, 329–30

Strout, Richard L., 393

Sumners, Harold, 236

Sumners, Hatton, 59–61, 63, 64, 106, 131, 222–23, 500n.15, 503n.14

Supreme Court: Congressional Reorganization Act of 1946, 345; ex-
     pansion plan, 221–24, 231, 236; school desegretation decision,
     384–85, 420; tidelands decision, 351, 353–54

Sutphin, William, 267

Symington, Stuart, 438, 440, 518–19n.10

Tabor, John, 289

Taft, Robert A., 326, 327, 359, 376

Taft, William Howard, 63

Taft-Hartley Act, 329–30, 349, 359

Taliaferro, Eliza Waller, 14–15

Taliaferro, Samuel, 14–15

Tarbell, Ida, 41

Tariff legislation, 72–75, 106

Tax legislation, 106, 393

Taylor, Telford, 155

Teague, Olin, 307, 413–14

Teamsters, 431

Teapot Dome scandals, 117

Television: ban on House committee broadcasting, 345–46, 415–16, 424–25, 510n.6; broadcasting of House Committee on Un-American Activities hearings, 424–25; coverage of McCarthy committee hearings, 382; Democratic National Convention coverage, 360, 362–63, 369; House Speakership transfer broadcast, 325; relations with SR, 415–16; SR's first interview, 325; SR's viewing habits, 418

Tennessee, 12, 13

Tennessee Valley Authority, 203

Terrell Election Law, 35

Texas: politics during 1890s, 23–28; power in federal government during

1890s, 24–25; tidelands decision, 351–54, 381

Texas and Pacific Railroad, 45

Texas Democratic Party, 295–96, 339, 396–401

Texas Legislature: banking legislation during 31st Legislature, 49; Common Carriers Committee, 45–46, 49, 66; education legislation during 31st Legislature, 50; ethical conduct of Speaker A. M. Kennedy, 50–51; investigation of Joe Bailey, 43–45; progressivism of 30th Legislature, 46–47; prohibition question, 42, 46–47, 52; re-election of Joe Bailey to U.S. Senate, 42–43; view outside of state, 43

Texas Rangers, 112

Texas Regulars, 296–97, 505n.27

Texas Society of Washington, 72

Texas State Democratic Convention, 339, 399–401

Thom, Alfred P., 76, 84

Thomas, Albert, 330

Thomas, Katherine Rayburn, 1, 14, 80, 108–109, 478, 487n.42, 488n.53

Thomas, W. A., 86, 109, 110, 251, 298–99, 314, 488n.53

Thomason, Ewing, 330

Thompson, Frank, 457

Thompson, Huston, 150

Thornberry, Homer, 432

Thurmond, Preston C., 47–48

Thurmond, Strom, 339, 341

Tidelands, 333, 351–55, 381

Tidelands Act, 381

Tilson, John, 114

Timmons, Bascom, 245, 291

Townsend, Secretary of State, 53

Transportation. *See* Railroads

Transportation Act of 1920, 89

Travell, Janet, 469

Trimble, South, 243, 256

Truman, Harry: accused as soft on Communism, 381; addressed as Harry by SR, 311, 312, 507n.20; appointments to FCC, 495n.38; atomic bomb, 290; civil rights program, 331–33, 349; decision not to seek re-election, 357; Democratic National Convention of 1952, 368; Fair Deal program, 348–49; Fair Employment Practices Commission, 421; FDR's death, 308–10; interviews for SR biography, 476–77; Korean War, 349, 383; labor legislation, 329–30; Marshall Plan, 327–29; oil and gas legislation, 393; popularity dwindling, 331, 369–70; preparation for duties of President, 302; presidential nomination and campaign, 334–42; presidential succession bill, 313–14, 326; relationship with SR, 253, 296, 309, 311–13; SR as minority leader, 324; SR as "Mr. Speaker," 325; SR's funeral, 473; termination of wartime laws, 326; tidelands issue, 352–55; vice-presidential candidate, 291, 292, 297, 301, 505n.27; visit to dying SR, 472

Truman, Margaret, 340

Truman, Mrs. Harry, 340

Truman Doctrine, 328

Truth-in-Securities Act. *See* Securities Act of 1933

Tucker, Ray, 162

Tumulty, Joe, 177, 486n.16

TVA. *See* Tennessee Valley Authority

Tydings, Millard, 235, 239

U.S. Chamber of Commerce, 161–62, 458

U.S. House of Representatives. *See* headings beginning with House

U.S. Senate. *See* headings beginning with Senate

Underwood tariff, 72–75, 99

Union Pacific Railroad, 78

Unions, 97–98, 330, 431. *See also* Labor

United Nations, 313

University of Texas, 47

Utility holding companies: abuses, 167–69, 174, 179–80; compromise position, 196–97, 498n.40; forgery, 177; House Committee on Rules, 207–208; House investigation of improper influence in regard to bill, 187–89; House vote on legislation, 184–87; opposition to SR, 204, 498n.5; plight of investors, 181–82; reaction to proposed legislation, 171–78; regulation versus abolition, 169–76, 180–83; rural electrification, 320; Senate action, 175; Senate investigation on propaganda, 188–95; stocks and bonds market value, 168

Vandenberg, Arthur, 327–28, 347
Veterans' benefits, 93
Vinson, Carl, 455–56, 460
Vinson, Fred, 210, 312, 411, 499n.17
Voorhis, Jerry, 259, 264, 295

Wage and price legislation, 225, 236, 288, 294–95
Wall Street. *See* Securities
Wallace, Henry, 240–41, 273, 291, 292, 334, 335
Waller, Eliza. *See* Taliaferro, Eliza Waller
Waller, John Barksdale, 14, 15–16
Waller, Martha. *See* Rayburn, Martha Waller
Waller, Monroe, 2, 16, 17
Waller, Mose, 125, 131, 263, 477
Waller, William, 15
Walter, Francis E., 324, 401, 424–25, 455–56, 460
Walters, Herbert S., 406
War Production Board, 287
War Risk Insurance Act, 93–94
Warren, Earl, 335
Washington, George, 229
Waters-Pierce Oil Company, 39–42
Watterson, Henry, 18
Ways and Means Committee. *See* House Ways and Means Committee
Weinert, R. A., 295
Weldon, Felix de, 473
Welsh, Joseph, 382
Westbrook, Ed, 111, 113
Wheeler, Burton K., 141, 170–71, 175, 189–90, 196, 223, 240
Wheeler, Joe, 13, 18
White, Edward D., 483n.17
White, John, 371

White, William S., 309
Whitney, Richard, 156–57, 173
Whitten, Jamie, 520n.9
Wigley, George, 20
Wiley, Mary Margaret, 443
Wiley, T. W., 86
Wilkie, Wendell L., 173–74, 240, 241, 252, 496n.10
Willard, Daniel, 79
Williams, John Bell, 453, 520n.9
Wilson, Will, 439
Wilson, Woodrow: antitrust program, 75; *Congressional Government*, 100; courting of big business, 82–83; *History of the American People*, 60; impact of, 62–63; inauguration, 63; League of Nations, 101; New Freedom program, 62, 63; opposition to, 486n.16; personal note to SR, 79; railroad legislation, 84–87, 95, 97; request that Congressmen not enlist, 93; special congressional session in 1913, 72; visits with congressional members, 68; War Risk Insurance Act, 94; withdrawal of support from SR, 84–87; World War I, 258, 275
Winstead, Arthur, 520n.9
Wiretapping, 161
Wirtz, Alvin, 239, 301
Woman suffrage amendment, 99
Woodring, Harry, 296
Woodrum, Clifton A., 245
Works Progress Administration, 294
World War I, 83, 89, 91–94, 258, 299
World War II: atomic bomb, 289–91; congressional members deciding to enlist, 280–81; draft extension, 261–70; end of, 314; gasoline rationing, 280; German prisoner-of-war camp in Texas, 300; isolationism, 256, 259, 261, 265, 270–71, 276; Japanese attack on Pearl Harbor, 272–75; legislation affecting, 288; lend-lease legislation, 257–61; need for unity during, 279; Neutrality Act amendments, 270–72; status in 1945, 301; U.S. declaration of war, 274–77; U.S. reaction to, 227–28, 234; U.S. support for Great Britain, 256–72
Worley, Ann, 440
Worley, Eugene, 304, 440
WPA. *See* Works Progress Administration
Wright, Frank Lloyd, 409
Wright, Jim, 171
Wright, Ted, 281

Yarborough, Ralph, 348, 372, 517n.17
Young, Valton, 314–15

Zagri, Sidney, 414

Photography Credits

All photographs within this book were graciously provided by the Sam Rayburn Library, Bonham, Texas.

Individual credit lines are as follows:
Photo 14: *Greenville Daily Register* (undated)
Photo 21: U.S. Office of War Information, Photo #306–NT–339T–2 in the National Archives
Photo 23: Robertson Studio, Greenville, Texas
Photo 28: U.S. Information Agency, Photo #306–NT–17158V in the National Archives
Photo 32: Reni Photos, Reni Newsphoto Service
Photo 39: J. A. Dodd, Kingsville, Texas
Photo 42: Abbie Rowe, Courtesy National Park Service, White House

Cover photograph courtesy of Senator Lloyd Bentsen